Export Practice and Management

Fourth Edition

Professor Alan E. Branch
FCIT, FIEx, FILT

International Business/Shipping Consultant

Examiner in Export Practice/Shipping/International Marketing;
Visiting Lecturer Cardiff University /Reading University/Plymouth
University/Leicester University/ London City College/Rennes
International School of Business France

Fellow Chartered Institute of Transport and Fellow Institute of Export

THOMSON
LEARNING

Australia • Canada • Mexico • Singapore • Spain • United Kingdom • United States

THOMSON LEARNING

Export Practice and Management

Copyright © 2000 Thomson Learning

The Thomson Learning logo is a registered trademark used herein under license.

For more information, contact Thomson Learning, Berkshire House, 168-173 High Holborn, London, WC1V 7AA or visit us on the world wide web at: http://www.thomsonlearning.co.uk

British Library Cataloguing-in-Publication Data
A catalogue record for this book is available from the British Library

ISBN 1–86152–473–0

First published in 1979 as Elements of Export Practice by Chapman & Hall
Second edition 1985
Third edition 1994
Reprinted by Chapman & Hall 1984 and 1985
Reprinted by Thomson Learning 1999
This edition by Thomson Learning 2000
Reprinted 2001 by Thomson Learning

Typeset by LaserScript, Mitcham, Surrey
Printed in Singapore by Markono Print Media Pte Ltd

Contents

Preface to the fourth edition

It is appropriate that the fourth edition of this book, which today is firmly established as the standard work on the subject and market leader in its field, should be published on its 21st anniversary. The title is read in over 200 countries by both the student and undergraduates studying the subject and international entrepreneurs, who use it as an aide memoire. Many readers across the world have been introduced to the techniques of professional exporting by and owe their continuing livelihood to, this publication.

The fourth edition has been completely up-dated and reflects the many changes that have emerged in the past six years in this fast changing global market. Moreover, it takes full account of the likely future trends in the conduct of international trade, its environment and its undoubtedly increasing complexity. Some 60 per cent of the material is new for the fourth edition. Overall, it places more emphasis on management techniques and strategy in the computer literate, logistically focused globalization of todays international trade.

The opportunity has been taken to introduce a new chapter on logistics and globalization. Many existing chapters have been expanded including Export finance, Export documentation, Processing the export consignment including Incoterms 2000, Electronic data interchange, Dangerous cargo, Containerization, advantages of exporting, freight rates, and the European Union. Additional material is featured on major trading areas of the world, particularly economic blocs, the World Trade Organisation, the range of market entry options and the criteria of market selection. Particular emphasis is placed on the international environment in which the exporter, and ultimately the global entrepreneur, strives to operate on a profitable basis. Many additional case studies feature in the fourth edition together with diagrams and specimen documents.

Such enrichment to the fourth edition will further its popularity in colleges of higher education and universities throughout the world. This includes degree level undergraduates studying International Business and International Marketing, International Physical Distribution, Maritime Transport and International Logistics and students taking professional examinations sponsored by one of the numerous institutes such as the Chartered Institute of Marketing, the Chartered Institute of Purchasing and Supply, the Institute of Export, the Institute of Chartered Shipbrokers, the Chartered Institute of Logistics and Transport, the British Institute of Management and the British International Freight Association and Chartered Institute of Bankers. It is also a popular title for Chambers of Commerce, Trade Associations and Training Agencies conducting short courses and seminars on International Trade. This book is currently used at over 210 higher education colleges and universities in 45 countries.

The latest edition continues to focus strongly on management techniques and strategy, albeit on a pragmatic but thoroughly professional basis. It will also prove increasingly popular among universities which continue to expand their International Trade degree portfolios and require publications written in a lucid style and providing a pragmatic yet professional approach to the subject. This includes Diploma in Management Studies and BTEC Higher National Certificate and Diploma courses.

The fourth edition contains a much enlarged input from organizations and practices around the world. This not only enriches the book but also enables the reader to have a better understanding of world cultures and strategies as emphasized in the numerous examples and case studies found in this publication. The extent and breadth of such input is exemplified in the increasing number of organizations who have helped me so enthusiastically with each new edition, as recorded in the Acknowledgements, and for whose assistance I am most grateful. Also the interest shown by many colleges and universities including the University of Leicester International Management Studies faculty, with whom I work closely in the International Trade and Maritime areas.

Finally, I would particularly like to acknowledge with grateful thanks the generous secretarial help from Mr and Mrs Splarn and as always my dear wife Kathleen in proofreading. This trio has provided encouragement, forbearance and above all complete professionalism in enabling this much enriched fourth edition to be completed, for which I am greatly indebted.

Professor Alan Branch Academic Advisor on Shipping/International Trade
19 The Ridings Management Centre
Emmer Green University of Leicester
Reading University Road
Berkshire Leicester LE1 7RH
England RG4 8XL England
Tele/Fax (0044) 0118 9476291 Tele (0044) 0116 252 5520
 Fax (0044) 0116 252 3949
 Internet: http://www.le.ac.uk/lumc/

January 2000

Acknowledgements

Alex Lawrie Factors Ltd
Altrom
AT&T Istel
Atlantic Container Line Agencies Ltd
Baltic Exchange
Baltic International Freight Futures Market
Belo-o-Pak (UK) Ltd
Bowring Credit
British Airways
British International Freight Association
British Standards Institution
Chamber of Shipping (UK)
Chartered Institute of Marketing
Confederation of British Industry
Cotechna International Ltd
Credit Insurance Association
Danzas UK
Department of Trade and Industry
European Central Bank
Export Credit Guarantee Department
Export Master Systems Ltd
Felixstowe Dock and Railway Company
Foreign and Commonwealth Office
Formecon Services Ltd
Freight Network Ltd
Freight Transport Association
HM Customs and Excise
HSBC Trade Services (Midland Bank)
Institute of Export
International Air Transport Association
International Chamber of Commerce

International Maritime Organisation
International Software Marketing Ltd
Kay O'Neill
KPMG Peat Marwick
London Chamber of Commerce and Industry
London Fox
Lloyd's Bank (International)
Lufthansa Airline
Norman Shipping
Maersk Line
MAT Transport Ltd
P&O Nedlloyd
Pira International
Port Klang
Port of Rotterdam
Port of Singapore Authority
Price Waterhouse
Royal Mail International
Sea Containers Ltd
Sea-Land
Simpler Trade Procedures Board
Staple Inn Actuarial Society
Syn quest
Thai Cargo
Trade Indemnity
World Customs Organisation
World Trade Organisation

1

International trade

1.1 Scope of book

Since this book was first published some 21 years ago the pattern and complexity of world trade has changed enormously. Today, it is a very high profile international business which is driven by many elements including technology, logistics, marketing politics, finance, innovative strategies, social/economic well-being, wealth creation and the economic development of markets/regions. Overall, trade means wealth and political power and influence worldwide.

Moreover, it is becoming increasingly complex and is likely to continue to do so as we progress through the first decade of the twenty-first century. This is best exemplified by citing the exporter who hitherto designed, manufactured and assembled the product in the exporter's country. Today more and more exporters are out-sourcing some of their components to take advantage of high tech and lower cost, and assembling the product in the importer's or third country.

Hence, there is a paramount need for all involved in the conduct of international trade to be completely professional. This book aims to realize this objective and is written primarily for the student or business person (export/import/ shipping executive) who has limited knowledge of export practice involving the processing of the export sales contract. With this in mind it deals with the salient aspects of the subject including transportation, documentation, rates, customs, export/shipping office, computerization/electronic data interchange, international trade organizations, contracts of sale/affreightment/insurance, export planning, logistics, export packing, credit insurance, international distribution management and strategy and shipping/international trade terms and abbreviations. The fourth edition also features an in depth overview of major trading areas of the world and information technology, numerous case studies and additional chapters on logistics/ globalization and market entry options, and enlarged chapters on export finance, cargo insurance and containerization.

Overall, the book is written in a simple but lucid style and reflects the author's experience in the export industry spanning 40 years embracing not only work and consultancy on a worldwide scale in the industry itself, but also as a lecturer/chief examiner at home and overseas. This has involved overseas governments and multi-national industries. This book treats the subject on the basis that international trade must be developed on a profitable basis and this is only realized through complete professionalism at all levels.

Basically, there are three major trading areas of the world: Europe, incorporating the expanding European Union and single market (p. 428); North America, incorporating long-term NAFTA (p. 10) and the Far East which incorporates ASEAN, China and Japan (p. 10).

An analysis of the growth in world merchandise trade by selected region in 1990–98 (Table 1.1) and growth in the value of world merchandise trade by region 1990–98 (Table 1.2) is given below and merits close study. The main driving force in the world economy remains trade and investment. Service trade will continue to grow faster than goods trade, and goods trade and investment will continue to grow faster than trade.

Exporters worldwide are now focusing their attention on developing a global strategy in their search for new markets and lower production cost. This embraces in particular the physical distribution strategy and is one which requires constant review in a changing market and infrastructure situation. Overall, it requires complete professionalism at all levels – a feature extolled in this book.

1.2 Function of international trade

International trade is the process of exchanging goods or services between two or more countries, involving the use of two or more currencies. Overall, it produces a

TABLE 1.1 Growth in volume of world merchandise trade by selected region 1990–98. (Annual percentage change)

Exports					Imports			
Ave. 1990–95	1996	1997	1998		Ave. 1990–95	1996	1997	1998
6.0	5.5	10.5	3.5	World	6.5	6.0	9.5	4.0
7.0	6.0	11.0	3.0	North America (a)	7.0	5.5	13.0	10.5
8.0	11.0	11.0	6.5	Latin America	12.0	8.5	22.0	9.5
5.5	5.5	9.5	4.5	Western Europe	4.5	5.5	7.5	7.5
5.5	5.5	9.5	5.0	Europ. Union (15)	4.5	5.0	7.0	7.5
5.0	6.5	12.5	10.0	Transition econom.	2.5	16.0	17.0	10.0
7.5	5.0	13.0	1.0	Asia	10.5	6.0	6.0	−8.5
1.5	1.0	12.0	−1.5	Japan	6.5	5.5	1.5	−5.5
11.5	7.5	11.5	2.0	(b) E. Asian traders	12.0	4.5	6.5	−16.0

Reproduced by kind permission of the World Trade Organisation.
(a) Canada and the United States. (b) Chinese Taipei, Hong Kong, China, Malaysia; Korea; Singapore and Thailand. Note: Separate volume data are not available for Africa and the Middle East, although estimates for these regions have been made in order to calculate the world total.

TABLE 1.2 Growth in value of world merchandise trade by region 1990–98

Exports (f.o.b.)						Imports (c.i.f.)				
Value $ Billions	Annual percentage change					Value $ Billions	Annual percentage change			
1998	1990–95	1996	1997	1998		1998	1990–95	1996	1997	1998
5225	7.5	4.5	3.5	−2.0	World	5410	7.5	5.0	3.0	−1.0
898	8.5	6.5	9.5	−1.0	North America	1151	8.0	6.0	10.5	4.5
274	9.0	12.5	10.0	−2.0	Latin America	339	14.5	9.5	19.0	5.0
118	14.0	20.5	15.0	6.5	Mexico	129	12.5	25.5	23.5	14.0
157	7.0	8.0	7.0	−7.0	Other Latin America	211	15.5	2.5	16.5	0.5
2338	6.0	3.5	−0.5	2.5	Western Europe	2359	5.5	3.5	−1.5	5.0
2171	6.5	3.5	−0.5	3.0	European Union (15)	2163	5.5	3.0	−2.0	5.5
178	7.0	6.5	5.0	−1.0	Transition economies	207	5.0	17.0	9.5	3.0
99	7.5	6.0	8.0	9.0	Central/Eastern Europe	133	11.5	17.0	7.0	11.5
106	0.5	16.5	2.0	−16.0	Africa	129	5.5	−1.0	6.0	−1.5
26	3.5	5.5	6.0	−15.0	South Africa	29	10.5	−1.5	9.5	−11.0
138	1.5	17.0	4.0	−21.0	Middle East	139	5.5	7.0	6.5	−6.0
1294	12.0	0.5	5.5	−6.0	Asia	1090	12.0	4.5	0.5	−17.5
388	9.0	−7.5	2.5	−8.0	Japan	281	7.5	4.5	−3.0	−17.0
184	19.0	1.5	21.0	0.5	China	140	20.0	5.0	2.5	−1.5
504	14.0	3.0	2.5	−7.5	Six East Asian traders*	438	15.0	3.0	0.5	−25.0

* Chinese Taipei; Hong Kong, China; Malaysia; Korea; Singapore; and Thailand.
Reproduced by kind permission of the World Trade Organisation.

more efficient employment of the productive forces of the world. Hence it embraces two basic elements. First, it is carried out between two or more nations. Thus when trade is executed beyond national frontiers, it is invariably subject to political, social, economic and environmental policies introduced by nations from time to time. To a large extent, such policies (though desirable from a national point of view) have either somewhat encouraged or hampered the free flow of merchandise in international trade. The second factor is the use of different currencies with their inherent exchange rate differentials: the terms of trade (p. 5), or alternatively the balance of trade. This produces a favourable result in some countries but is unfavourable to others.

There are numerous reasons why nations trade with one another; and there are differences in taste, preferences and consumption patterns to be satisfied. This applies to consumer goods, clothing and foodstuffs. It manifests itself through culture, and it is stimulated by travel and education. Production costs differ by country and this is influenced by labour costs, technology, volume of production, transportation and product costs. Lack of mobility is a major factor. Products/resources can only be utilized where they are located or found (tourist attractions or minerals for example). Economies of scale vary by product/service both internally and externally within an economy. Finally, differences arise in factor endowments, which extend to differences both in qualities and quantities and variations in climatic conditions.

The benefits derived from the development of international trade are numerous, including a wider range of goods/services becoming available. This permits a wider consumer choice and higher levels of consumer satisfaction. Lower production costs, through economies of scale, result in lower prices to the consumer. A good example is the Volkswagen car plant in Germany which has a high-volume production base serving markets worldwide and relying on specialized 18-deck car carriers for transportation. Enlargement of the market is achieved through increased production, lower production costs, increased investment and expansion of the economy. The electronics market is an example of an area where research and development is continuous and high cost. Moreover, such investment is worldwide; likewise, production plants and consumers which become ubiquitous through competitive pricing.

International trade increases competition and prevents the monopolistic control of the home market by local exporters. It also provides a stimulus to economic growth, developing technology and raising living standards. Overall, it provides wealth to the economy and extends opportunities to exchange ideas and develop the infrastructure of a country or region and its resources. Trade develops beneficial links between countries and encourages tourism and education. This brings both political and economic stability to a country or region.

The rapid growth in international trade and specialization raises the question of the economic reasons for trade. Why does Japan export mainly manufactured goods and import principally raw materials? Why is the agricultural sector in the USA so different to that of the Netherlands? But most important of all, do countries gain or lose from opening up their boundaries to international trade?

The key to such questions lies in the theory of comparative advantage. This principle holds that a nation can raise its standard of living and real income by specializing in the production of those commodities or services in which it has the highest productivity or comparative advantage. The benefits of specialization may also be affected by transport costs: goods and raw materials have to be transported around the world and the cost of the transport will narrow the limits between which it will prove profitable to trade.

Extending the principle of comparative advantages a little further, where a country has 'absolute advantage' in the production of two or more products, it is still beneficial to trade. For example, the USA may have a higher output per worker (or per unit output) than the rest of the world both in steel and computers. However, it might still benefit the USA to engage in trade – exporting computers (in which it is relatively more productive) and importing steel (in which it is relatively less productive). Similarly, a country will gain by trading with the USA, even if it is absolutely less efficient in the production of a range of goods. It is unrealistic to believe a country has no comparative advantage in anything. It may be the least efficient at everything, but it will still have a comparative advantage in the industry in which it is relatively least bad. Even if a country were the most efficient in every industry, giving it an absolute advantage in everything, it could not have a comparative advantage in everything. In some industries, its margin would be more impressive than in others.

To conclude our review of absolute advantage, a country with no absolute advantage should concentrate on the products and/or services which bring the greatest comparative advantage; and for a country having an absolute advantage in all lines of production, then it would still be worthwhile to enter into trade provided there are comparative advantages in certain commodities. In such circumstances, the country should concentrate on the products which bring the greatest comparative advantage. Trade will not take place, however, if there is no comparative advantage.

In examining the theory of comparative advantage it should be remembered that it assumes free trade which limits the benefits from specialization. Additionally, the theory ignores foreign exchange difficulties; fails to take account of transportation and logistics costs, where increasing costs can wipe out gains from trade; assumes constant cost of production and free mobility of factors of production; and finally, it assumes full employment and flexibility in the economy. A rigid state-controlled economy allows partial specialization. Such constraints must be considered when examining the theory of comparative advantage in any trade strategy.

International trade can disadvantage some countries. For example, it lowers the standard of living in a poor country as the specialized industries, such as those with high technology, may not generate enough jobs, and unemployment results. Countries specializing in agriculture may face persistent adverse terms of trade which will result in an adverse balance-of-payments situation. Moreover, backward countries may become dumping grounds for obsolete products. International trade increases monopoly and this can be abused. Finally, international trade transmits slumps and booms between countries, and this is particularly serious in economic terms when a slump hits a poor country with limited resources. The strategies of WTO and ILO have endeavoured to lessen such disadvantages and practices.

Finally, it is appropriate to examine the relationship between the balance of trade and terms of trade. It will be recalled that the balance of trade is the relationship between the total volume of exports and imports of a country for a certain period of time. Examples are given below.

Balance of trade
  Country A exports 1000 units of x at $3.00 each
  Country A imports 700 units of y at $4.00 each
  The value of exports is $1000 \times \$3.00 = \$3000$
  The value of imports is $700 \times \$4.00 = \$2800$
  The Balance of Trade = Total exports – Total imports
                       $= \$3000 - \$2800$
                       $= \$200$ surplus

Hence the balance of trade is favourable.

The terms of trade (TOT) are defined as the quantity of domestic goods that must be given up to get a unit of imported goods. They refer to the opportunity cost of obtaining goods through international trade rather than producing them directly.

Measurement of terms of trade

$$\text{TOT index} = \frac{\text{Index of export prices}}{\text{Index of import prices}} \times 100$$

Base year = 1996 (100)

Year	Export price index	Import price index	TOT
1997	100	110	$\frac{100}{110} \times 100\% = 91\%$
1998	80	100	$\frac{80}{100} \times 100\% = 80\%$
1999	120	100	$\frac{120}{100} \times 100\% = 120\%$

Comparing 1997 and 1998 TOT worsened by 11 per cent for the year 1998; in 1999 TOT improved by 40 per cent.

Favourable terms of trade do not necessarily lead to a favourable balance of trade. This is because as the prices of exports rise, importers will substitute with cheaper goods. This results in the loss of foreign exchange earnings. Hence the balance of trade will be less favourable or even adverse.

Unfavourable terms of trade do not lead to unfavourable balance of trade. As the prices of exports fall, demand for them rises. With an increase in the volume of exports, foreign exchange earnings will also increase, resulting in a favourable balance of trade.

In regard to the relationship between the terms of trade and balance of trade, an improvement in the former will lead to a favourable result of the latter only if the demand for imports and exports is relatively inelastic. If the demand is elastic, then the balance of trade will be less favourable or even worse.

A decline in the terms of trade does not imply an unfavourable balance of trade. If the demand for imports and exports is relatively elastic, then a decline in the terms of trade will cause demand to rise. Hence foreign exchange earnings will be increased, resulting in a favourable balance of trade.

To sum up, the terms of trade and balance of trade are not directly connected. The relationship between these two depends on the elasticity of the demand for imports and exports. The foregoing analysis does not take account of any government intervention policy to stimulate favourable results.

1.3 Survey of international trade

In our brief examination of a survey of international trade we will focus on the international agencies of the International Chamber of Commerce (ICC), the Organisation for Economic Co-operation and Development (OECD) and the World Trade Organisation (WTO); a number of the regional trading areas of the world (the EU is examined separately in Chapter 18) and a selection of countries which provide both short- and long-term favourable opportunities to the exporter. In 1998 the determination to strengthen regional trading agreements continued. Regional arrangements include Customs Unions, free trade agreements and a range of other trade related initiatives such as APEC. This has become the norm of international trading relations accelerated particularly by political impetus. By mid 1998 over 100 regional trade agreements were in force.

As a first stage in our evaluation and to ensure the exporter has a correct perspective of individual countries market share two tables are reproduced. Table 1.3 features leading exporters and importers in world merchandise trade in 1998 and Table 1.4 features leading exporters and importers in world trade in commercial services in 1998. It is significant that the G-7 group of countries feature in the top thirteen in both tables and constitute over 40 per cent of the world trade. Moreover, the top five countries in both tables are the same. This data must be reconciled with the earlier Tables 1.1 and 1.2 (pp. 2–3).

International Chamber of Commerce (ICC)

The International Chamber of Commerce (ICC) was founded in 1919 with the objective to serve world business by promoting trade and investment, open markets for goods and services and the free flow of capital. Today, it has become a world business organization with thousands of member companies and associations representing every major industrial and service sector in over 130 countries. It is based in Paris and in 1945 was granted consultative status with the UN and its specialized agencies.

The ICC has fourteen specialized committees/commissions representing experts from the private sector which drive the ICC in formulating new strategies. Subjects include banking techniques, financial services, taxation, competition law, intellectual property rights, telecommunications, information technology, international investment, trade policy and transport modes. Overall, the ICC has national committees in 63 countries.

The ICC International Court of Arbitration is the world's leading body for resolving international commercial disputes by arbitration. Other areas of ICC participation include Incoterms 2000 (see p. 233) and the Uniform Customs and Practice for Documentary Credits 1993 – UCP500 (see pp. 246–53). Additionally the ICC has developed a number of initiatives to combat commercial crime especially corruption, fraud and crimes in electronic communications. This includes the International Maritime Bureau (IMB), the Counterfeiting Intelligence Bureau (CIB) and the Commercial Crime Bureau (CCB) (see p. 31).

Overall, the ICC continues to take a leading role in the development of world trade facilitating a sound business infrastructure of confidence, essential for the exchange of goods in a competitive global market.

Organisation for Economic Co-operation and Development (OECD)

The Organisation for Economic Co-operation and Development (OECD) is based in Paris, France. It has 25 member countries plus 33 countries classified as partners in a transition programme – a forum permitting the governments of the industrialized

TABLE 1.3 Leading exporters and importers in world merchandise trade, 1998 (Billion dollars and percentage)

Rank	Exporters	Value (f.o.b.)	Share	Change	Rank	Importers	Value (c.i.f.)	Share	Change
1	United States	683.0	12.7	−1	1	United States	944.6	17.0	5
2	Germany	539.7	10.0	5	2	Germany	466.6	8.4	5
3	Japan	388.0	7.2	−8	3	United Kingdom	316.1	5.7	3
4	France	307.0	5.7	6	4	France	287.2	5.2	7
5	United Kingdom	272.7	5.1	−3	5	Japan	280.5	5.0	−17
6	Italy	240.9	4.5	1	6	Italy	214.0	3.8	3
7	Canada	214.3	4.0	−1	7	Canada	205.0	3.7	2
8	Netherlands	198.2	3.7	2	8	Hong Kong, China	188.7	3.4	−12
						retained imports[a]	38.9	0.7	−26
9	China	183.8	3.4	1	9	Netherlands	184.1	3.3	4
10	Hong Kong, China	174.1	3.2	−7	10	Belgium-Luxembourg	158.8	2.9	2
	domestic exports	24.3	0.5	−11					
11	Belgium-Luxembourg	171.1	3.2	2	11	China	140.2	2.5	−2
12	Korea, Rep. of	133.2	2.5	−2	12	Spain	132.8	2.4	8
13	Mexico	117.5	2.2	6	13	Mexico	128.9	2.3	14
14	Chinese Taipei	109.9	2.0	−9	14	Chinese Taipei	104.2	1.9	−9
15	Singapore	109.8	2.0	−12	15	Singapore	101.5	1.6	−23
	domestic exports	63.3	1.2	−13		retained imports[a]	54.9	1.8	−31
16	Spain	109.0	2.0	5	16	Korea. Rep. of	93.3	1.7	−35
17	Sweden	84.5	1.6	2	17	Switzerland	80.0	1.4	5
18	Switzerland	78.7	1.5	3	18	Austria	68.3	1.2	5
19	Malaysia	73.3	1.4	−7	19	Sweden	67.6	1.2	3
20	Ireland	63.3	1.2	19	20	Australia	64.7	1.2	−2
21	Austria	61.7	1.1	5	21	Brazil	61.0	1.1	−6
22	Russian Fed.[b]	56.2	1.0	−16	22	Malaysia	58.5	1.1	−26
23	Australia	55.9	1.0	−11	23	Poland	48.0	0.9	13
24	Thailand	53.6	0.9	−7	24	Turkey	46.4	0.8	−4
25	Brazil	51.0	0.9	−3	25	Denmark	45.8	0.8	3
26	Indonesia	48.8	0.9	−9	26	Russian Fed.[b]	44.7	0.8	−18
27	Denmark	47.0	0.9	−4	27	Ireland	43.7	0.8	11
28	Finland	42.4	0.8	4	28	India	42.9	0.8	4
29	Norway	39.6	0.7	−18	29	Thailand	41.8	0.8	−33
30	Saudi Arabia	38.8	0.7	−35	30	Norway	36.2	0.7	1
	Total of above[c]	4748.8	88.3	−1		Total of above[c]	4696.0	84.4	−2
	World[c]	5375.0	100.0	−2		World[c]	5560.0	100.0	−1

[a] Retained imports are defined as imports less re-exports.
[b] Data exclude trade with the Baltic States and the CIS. Including trade with these States would lift Russian exports and imports to $73.9 billion and $59.5 billion, respectively.
[c] Includes significant re-exports or imports for re-exports.

Reproduced by kind permission of World Trade Organisation

TABLE 1.4 Leading exporters and importers in world trade in commercial services, 1998 (Billion dollars and percentage)

Rank	Exporters	Value	Share	Change	Rank	Importers	Value	Share	Change
1	United States	233.6	18.1	1	1	United States	161.5	12.5	6
2	United Kingdom	99.5	7.7	8	2	Germany	121.8	9.4	3
3	France	78.6	6.1	−2	3	Japan	109.5	8.5	−10
4	Germany	75.7	5.9	1	4	United Kingdom	76.1	5.9	7
5	Italy	70.1	5.4	−2	5	Italy	69.3	5.4	−1
6	Japan	60.8	4.7	−11	6	France	62.8	4.9	1
7	Netherlands	48.3	3.7	−1	7	Netherlands	44.8	3.5	2
8	Spain	48.0	3.7	10	8	Canada	34.8	2.7	−3
9	Belgium-Luxembourg	34.7	2.7	4	9	Belgium-Luxembourg	33.6	2.6	6
10	Hong Kong, China	34.2	2.6	−11	10	Austria	28.7	2.2	1
11	Austria	31.0	2.4	6	11	China	28.6	2.2	−5
12	Canada	28.8	2.2	−2	12	Spain	27.3	2.1	12
13	Switzerland	26.3	2.0	3	13	Chinese Taipei	23.4	1.8	−3
14	Korea, Rep. of	23.6	1.8	−7	14	Korea, Rep. of	23.0	1.8	−21
15	China	23.0	1.8	−6	15	Hong Kong, China	22.7	1.8	−2
16	Turkey	22.4	1.7	17	16	Sweden	20.6	1.6	6
17	Singapore	18.2	1.4	−40	17	Brazil	18.9	1.5	7
18	Sweden	17.4	1.4	−1	18	Ireland	18.0	1.4	20
19	Chinese Taipei	16.6	1.3	−2	19	Singapore	18.0	1.4	−7
20	Australia	15.8	1.2	−14	20	Russian Fed.	17.8	1.4	−7
21	Denmark	15.7	1.2	4	21	Austria	16.7	1.3	−9
22	Norway	13.9	1.1	−2	22	Switzerland	15.0	1.2	6
23	Russian Fed.	12.9	1.0	−7	23	Denmark	14.9	1.2	−1
24	Thailand	12.8	1.0	−18	24	Norway	14.8	1.1	2
25	Mexico	11.9	0.9	6	25	Saudi Arabia	13.9	1.1	0
26	Malaysia	10.9	0.8	−27	26	India	13.7	1.1	12
27	India	10.5	0.8	22	27	Mexico	12.5	1.0	6
28	Greece	9.9	0.8	8	28	Thailand	12.2	0.9	−29
29	Poland	8.9	0.7	−1	29	Indonesia	11.9	0.9	−26
30	Israel	8.7	0.7	4	30	Malaysia	11.9	0.9	−32
	Total of above	1123	87.0	−1		Total of above	1100	85.2	−1
	World	1290	100.0	−2		World	1290	100.0	−1

Note: Secretariat estimates based on incomplete or preliminary data.

Reproduced by kind permission of World Trade Organisation

democracies to study and formulate the best possible policies in all economic and social spheres.

Areas examined by the OECD in recent years include the creation of employment, economic growth and raising living standards through fiscal, monetary and structural economic policies, managing competition among nations in an era of globalization of production and of the continuing opening of borders to trade and investment; trade facilitation such as thorough certification of agricultural seeds; consolidating and advancing reform in agricultural policies; and improving the efficiency of government and quality of public sector spending and taxation.

The OECD has neither supranational legal powers nor financial resources for loans or subsidies; its sole function is to direct co-operation among the governments of its member countries, the principal industrialized countries of the world. It focuses on specific issues through the expertise of the various OECD Directorates. Additionally, it encourages co-operation among nations in domestic policies where these interact with other countries – in particular trade and investment. The reports produced by the OECD are useful to the exporter in the market evaluation and selection process.

European Free Trade Agreement (EFTA)

The European Free Trade Agreement is a trading and economic bloc involving seven countries: Austria, Finland, Iceland, Liechtenstein, Norway, Sweden and Switzerland. The Agreement covers the free movement of goods, services, capital and people. In 1991 political agreement was reached in the creation of the European Economic Area (EEA) by the European Community (EC) and EFTA. The aim is to extend most of the single market principles to the EFTA countries.

North American Free Trade Agreement (NAFTA)

In August 1992, 14 months of negotiations involving Mexico, Canada and the USA were completed to establish the world's largest and richest trading bloc. It ratified the North American Free Trade Agreement (NAFTA) which over a period of 15 years will abolish almost all tariffs and trade barriers. This involves 360 million consumers with a $6000 billion gross domestic product.

Association of South East Asian Nations (ASEAN)

The Association of South East Asian Nations (ASEAN) was formed in 1967. Today it has ten members including Brunei, Cambodia, Indonesia, Lao PDR, Malaysia, Myanmar, Philippines, Singapore, Thailand and Vietnam. As a trading group it is very active and has certain economic and free trading links designed to develop the resources in the region and increase wealth. An area of significance is the recent formation of the ASEAN Investment Area (AIA). Its objective is the promotion of inter-ASEAN investment and investment from countries outside the group. This involves the provision of three segments which will become fully operational by 2010 and include investment facilitation and co-operation; investment promotion and investment liberalization. The facilitation segment involves the free flow of capital, technology and skilled labour within the region.

Operative from 1993, the ASEAN nations agreed to accelerate tariff cutting of key product sectors from 15 to 10 years. The 10-year timeframe provides for the reduction of tariffs over 20 per cent. For products with a tariff of less than 20 per cent there is a timeframe of seven years. Overall, the objective is to have a tariff level below 5 per cent within the ASEAN group by the year 2008. ASEAN identified 15 product sectors comprising 4000 items for tariff cutting, including chemicals, pharmaceuticals, plastics, ceramics and vegetable oils. Emerging from the currency crisis ASEAN decided in 1998 to accelerate tariff liberalization and further open up foreign direct investment. The ASEAN region is attracting much inward investment, technology transfer, indigenous capital and is developing a low-cost fast-improving technical workforce with assiduous and very competitive attitudes. Emerging from the Far East currency crisis in 1997, the ASEAN nations continue to refocus their economic and fiscal strategies with a view to the development of a more stable economic region to attract, as hitherto, global trade and investment.

MERCOSUR

Mercosur currently unites Brazil, Argentina, Uruguay and Paraguay with Chile and Bolivia as associate members. It was formed in 1995. It is the world's largest integrated market and has a population of 200 million and represents half the gross domestic product (GDP) of Latin America as a whole. Mercosur is a free trading region which became operative from 1995 with the aim of removing internal tariffs in all but 25 products – a policy which accelerated in 1998.

The customs union was introduced in 1995. Work continues to reduce bureaucracy, streamline customs procedures and encourage regional trade – but the Mercosur message of low inflation, strong and sustainable economic growth and stable democratic structures is clear.

In 1995, the EU signed a co-operation agreement with Mercosur, and has now completed the first stage of a process which will lead towards a trade liberalization agreement. The EU is already the second largest source of foreign investment; exports total over $23 billion a year.

As Brazil, Argentina, Uruguay and Paraguay liberalize their domestic economies, they are becoming increasingly attractive markets. As regional trade barriers come down, the potential of Mercosur as a whole is huge – having a GDP equal to Russia, Norway, Saudi Arabia, Poland, Hong Kong and the Czech Republic combined. Enormous investment, both financial and technical, is going into gas distribution, oil and petrochemicals. The motor giants have announced plans for $14 billion worth of investment in Brazil and Argentina, in turn stimulating demand in the motor components sector. Agri-business, consumer goods and electronics have seen rapid growth – and with this expansion has come the need to improve all aspects of infrastructure, from ports and airports to roads and telecommunications.

Mercosur has proved to be successful. The original forecast for regional trade in 2000 was achieved in 1997. Chile and Bolivia have joined as associate members, and negotiations are underway with Mexico, Canada and the Andean Community (Peru, Venezuela, Colombia, Ecuador). A free trade area covering the whole of South America, with Mercosur at its heart, is now a real long-term possibility.

Asia Pacific Economic Co-operation (APEC)

The Asia Pacific Economic Co-operation forum objective is to create a grand goal of free trade in the Pacific by 2020, but no trade agreement exists at the moment. It was formed in 1993 and has a membership of 12 countries including USA, Japan, Malaysia, Australia, Thailand, etc.

CARICOM

The Caribbean Community and Common Market is the Caribbean trade bloc and a regional community whose principal objective is economic integration. It has 14 members and in 1998 it reached an agreement with the Dominican Republic to help prepare their economies for a hemisphere free trade area to be created in 2005. The pact took effect from January 1999 and covers trade in goods and services, the reciprocal promotion, and protection of investment, government procurement, sanitary measures and standards, and technical barriers to trade.

Free Trade Area of the Americas (FTAA)

In 1998 an agreement was signed between 34 countries to create the Free Trade Area of the Americas by 2005.

Africa

In 1998 the new Economic and Monetary Union embracing Francophone countries, based in West Africa, including the Ivory Coast, Guinea, Senegal, Central African Republic, Gabon, etc. laid plans, among other objectives, to bring into effect a common external tariff. In Southern Africa negotiations to create a free trade area among the members of the Southern Development Community (SADC) continue. This includes the South Africa Customs Union embracing Botswana, Lesotho, Namibia, South Africa and Swaziland who are also renegotiating their customs unions relations.

1.3.1 Asia–Pacific Region

During the 20 year period up to 1996 the Asia–Pacific share of world imports had doubled to about 17 per cent. Meanwhile, the developed countries' share had been static. The region's share of GDP had risen from 20 to 30 per cent in this period, overtaking both Western Europe and North America. In late 1997 a recession commenced. By 1998 the recession had emerged in Japan and the deeper and more widespread repercussions of the financial crisis in East Asian countries manifested itself. It particularly focused on the decline of intra-Asian trade. The former tigers of the region, Indonesia, Korea, Malaysia, the Philippines and Thailand saw imports decline by 33 per cent whilst their exports decreased by 3 per cent. This demonstrated their strategy to export their way out of the financial currency crisis. Japan experienced a decline of 17 per cent in imports and 7 per cent in exports.

The region offers a diversified industrial and commercial base with massive natural resources and large areas still to be developed, together with substantial populations. To the exporter it offers good prospects with growth as the region recovers from its currency crisis. In the longer term the fiscal measures and economic strategies adopted will strengthen the economic vibrancy of the region, but progress may be slow as the International Monetary Fund (IMF) loans are extinguished. Ultimately, the sustained economic recovery will be determined largely by the speed with which the authorities are able to push through a range of policy reforms in restructuring the banking and corporate sectors. It will be influenced by recapitalizing the banks, and clearing the bad loans as well as satisfying the basic needs of the unemployed. This will impose a considerable strain on government finances across the region. With government revenues also falling steeply, in line with the magnitude of the contraction of the economy, Asian governments almost without exception will experience large fiscal deficits at the start of the next millennium.

Being far less homogeneous than the other two large regional markets of Western Europe and North America, the Asia–Pacific markets have quite distinct characteristics. They are at widely different states of development, diverse in their trade and investment demand profiles, and with differing industrial, commercial and social priorities. Prior to the financial crisis the region had been fuelled in the main from Japan. The Chinese economy has been less affected by the Far East currency crisis and remains an excellent market for a large range of goods and services. In particular major projects are continuously available for infrastructure development.

Overall, the region has a full spectrum of goods and services including high technology, industrialization, basic infrastructure (water, transport and power) and consumer goods, and a range of services including health care, education, technical and professional training. By 1999 the region had become more relaxed in developing their import led strategies as the financial position continued to improve and market confidence was restored.

The Asia–Pacific region remains an excellent cost effective import source of finished and intermediate goods and an internationally competitive manufacturing base for labour-intensive to high tech finished products and services. It is an ideal area for out-sourcing component manufacture (see p. 32). It is important that the exporter develops a viable market entry strategy as fully explained in Chapter 17.

A brief commentary on each of the countries in the Asia–Pacific region is given below:

Brunei – area 5765 km^2, population 260 000, per capita GNP US$17 000. A rich small nation anxious to diversify away from the oil and gas sector which currently dominates the economy, together with petrochemicals. Brunei plans investment in infrastructure to support its aim of becoming a trade and tourism hub for the region.

Opportunities lie in hotel and medical projects, infrastructure development and defence. One of the countries less affected by the currency crisis.

Cambodia – area 181 035 km², population 10.2 million, per capita US$287. An underdeveloped market with limited economic growth.

China – area 9 579 000 km², population 1250 million. China is an important export market and provides good opportunities for services and investment. The later 1990s have seen the opening up of the economy as an essential part of Chinese economic policy. Current export growth is slower than in earlier years and to compensate there has been a relaxing of monetary controls to increase domestic demand – a move made more possible by China's very low inflation rate as well as an acceleration of government spending on infrastructure projects. Export opportunities include aerospace, power, automotive, airports, telecommunications, financial services, insurance and chemicals.

The opening up of China as a trading destination has been accompanied by an increase in distribution services from major shipping lines, airlines, express carriers and freight forwarders. Additionally, the country is investing in its transport infrastructure. With so many major destinations along China's seaboard, many of the shipping services call at ports such as Shanghai or Hong Kong. Feeder services are then used to reach other smaller ports around China. Air transport has developed similarly. Hong Kong, which already acts as a major air freight hub for onward delivery to China has been further developed by the new Chek Lap Kok airport. This airport, built on reclaimed land, houses two freight terminals and a specialist facility for express freight. Inside China there are several choices when it comes to moving goods. As well as road transport, more than 40 per cent of freight moves by rail, with waterways and internal air freight services also taking a significant share of the market. Internal movements are being improved by US$96 billion (£56.5 billion) investment in the transport network as part of the Government's Ninth Five Year Plan (1996–2000).

Hong Kong – area 1067 km², population 5.0 million, per capita GNP US$12 000. Hong Kong was absorbed into China in 1997. China, however, has undertaken to maintain a 'one country' 'two systems' policy for the first 50 years. It is now a special administrative region of China. Overall, it remains a regional trade centre. It is a new industrialized economy. Hong Kong offers good opportunities for the discerning exporter.

Indonesia – area 1 904 559 km², population 205 million, per capita GNP US$620. Indonesia is a country addressing significant currency depreciation, private sector debt and a range of austerity measures. It is a country with opportunities for joint ventures, consulting and investment.

Japan – area 370 000 km², population 127 million, per capita GNP US$32 000. Japan has the third largest economy in the world, and has recovered dramatically from the Second World War to achieve a GNP third only to the USA. Despite being heavily dependent on oil imports and raw materials, it still maintains a higher GNP growth rate than most OECD countries. Imports have increased rapidly during the period

1985–97 due to a stronger yen, an expansion in domestic demand and active promotion by the Japanese government, especially in relaxing many trade controls. Currently, however, Japan is going through its most serious economic crisis since the Second World War, but it still remains a strong market for exporters. This applies to both consumer and industrial goods. Japanese manufacturers have been less badly affected than the country's financial sector and still need components and machinery. The prospects of an economic recovery look very favourable.

It has a homogeneous population which is highly nationalistic concerning its own manufactured products. Japan remains a very stable market and main imports include speciality chemicals, aerospace, computer software, scientific instruments, automative components, opto-electronics, third-country business, medical equipment, agricultural machinery and livestock, pharmaceuticals, fire safety and security equipment, textiles, furniture and interiors, marine leisure, food and drink, body products (clothing, jewellery, cosmetics), sport and leisure goods, and personal and corporate giftware.

Distribution networks are based on very tight relationships between customers and suppliers. The common pattern in any product distribution system in Japan is for there to be a middleman – the wholesaler – who stands between the manufacturer and retailer or industrial end-user. There may well be two wholesalers – primary and secondary wholesalers – and sometimes even more. This pattern is the same for imported goods as for domestic products, the primary wholesaler often acting as agent for the foreign supplier. The number of layers is nearly always greater for consumer products than for industrial goods, although for some of the latter (e.g. building materials), there are also many layers. The exact structure will depend on the nature of the products and on the number of final outlets or customers. Japan continues to relax its tariff barriers and become more of an open market, but its populace remains very nationalistic.

Laos – area 236 800 km^2, population 5.2 million, per capita GNP US$180. An underdeveloped country, but one rich in resources. In 1997 its currency was devalued by 90 per cent.

Malaysia – area 329 293 km^2, population 21.0 million, per capita GNP US$2475. This politically stable country has come to terms with problems experienced through the 1997 currency crisis in the region. Some capital projects have been cancelled or deferred and a series of austerity measures introduced. It has a large foreign-owned export manufacturing base and a well-educated committed low labour cost workforce. In the early 1970s, more than 80 per cent of exports were commodities – mainly rubber, tin and petroleum products, whilst by 1998 some 75 per cent of its exports were manufactured goods. Ideal export targets are education, training, information technology, tourism, hotel, oil, gas, power, telecommunications and, in the longer term, major capital infrastructure projects.

North Korea – area 121 200 km^2, population 24.8 million, per capita GNP US$1050. An underdeveloped market, but one rich in resources. Ultimately, North Korea could merge with South Korea.

The Philippines – area 300 000 km^2, population 70 million, per capita GNP US$725. Generally a low growth market, but there is an opportunistic market for particular types of investment, goods and services. The Philippine economy suffered less from the financial crisis and export opportunities include agri-business, infrastructure developments including power, ports, marine transport, water, oil, gas, environmental technology and consumer goods featuring retail and health care.

Singapore – area 620.2 km^2, population 3 million, per capita GNP US$13 600. A wealthy city state moving into the higher-value industrial and commercial sectors for trade and investment. Singapore is also a regional centre for trade and investment with many multi-national businesses; it is a newly industrialized economy. Overall, Singapore economic strength has helped to insulate it against the region's economic problems. Export opportunities include aerospace, financial services, environmental technology, ports and marine, education and training, energy, information technology, telecommunications and railway infrastructure.

South Korea – area 99 091 km^2, population 45.9 million, per capita GNP US$5550. A newly industrialized economy and high-tech market – a regional power in both trade and investment (see Table 1.3, p. 8). The economy is currently in recession following the financial crisis in the region and recovery will be slow as South Korea repays its large IMF loan. It has poor industrial and economic resources but offers long-term good export opportunities in domestic markets for all types of goods and services.

Taiwan – area 35 981 km^2, population 22 million, per capita GNP US$8685. A newly industrialized economy – a regional power in both trade and investment; resources are poor, but industrially and economically it is wealthy and with significant domestic markets for all types of goods and services.

Thailand – area 514 000 km^2, population 60 million, per capita GNP US$1605. Thailand has experienced an economic downturn, currency depreciation and other problems in its financial sector, in common with South Korea. An IMF recovery package has been formulated. Export opportunities include education, environment, food processing, health care, power, transportation and consultancy. It is a major location for foreign investors and has a large industrial base.

Vietnam – area 331 688 km^2, population 74 million, per capita GNP US$200. An underdeveloped market. The country faces serious economic problems but has been largely insulated from the worse effects of the crisis. Direct foreign investment and aid are driving the economy forward. Export opportunities include agriculture, airports, construction, oil, gas, power and road transport. Participation in joint ventures also exists.

1.3.2 Central and Eastern Europe

Albania – population 3.18 million, per capita GNP US$900. A country endeavouring to become Westernized in its economic international strategies and encouraging inwards investment, business and joint ventures. The privatization programme of small, and medium sized companies is scheduled for completion in the next two years together with the larger strategic sector state companies featuring banks, tele-communications, ports, mines and utilities.

Bulgaria – population 8.95 million, per capita GNP US$4827. A country eager to pursue market-related reforms and development of an enterprise economy. An attractive country for inward investors with a well-developed industrial base, a highly skilled and educated workforce and a work ethic which has survived the communist rule. Ideal for inwards investment and joint ventures.

Hungary – population 10.15 million, per capita GNP US$4450. A country which is developing a market-led structure encouraging joint ventures, business ventures and inwards investment. It is following through a privatization programme of its major industries embracing manufacturing, hotels and tourism, transport and commerce. Today over 80 per cent of the economy is in private hands.

Poland – population 38.7 million, per capita GNP US$3485. Poland is an attractive market with a determined strategy to develop Westernized policies in its recent economic and political reforms. It is a very resilient nation, attracting much inwards investment, joint ventures and developing privatization programmes. Poland remains one of the strongest performing economies in Central and Eastern Europe benefiting from its proximity to export markets, relatively low labour costs and a large domestic market. It may become a member of the European Union in *circa* 2005.

Romania – population 23.1 million, per capita GNP US$4073. Romania has a fragile economy and experiences a relatively slow pace of economic reform. Its political future is rather uncertain. It has a serious foreign debt repayments situation.

Russia – population 147.74 million, reliable GNP data are not currently available. Russia's economic and political problems are unlikely to go away overnight, but neither will its fantastic potential for future economic prosperity and as a possible market for just about every conceivable type of product or service.

Russia had achieved a great deal in the period following the dissolution of the USSR in 1991 when it adopted policies to become a market economy, up until the sudden dismissal of the Kiriyenko Government in 1998. There followed an initial period of economic and financial turmoil. The devaluation of the rouble and consequent effect on the banking system have created demands for a change in reformist policy. There has been a massive disruption to production brought about by the collapse of central planning, the break-up of traditional trade and payments systems and increasing economic imbalances. As a consequence, since the beginning of the 1990s there has been a substantial decline in real GNP. Many observers believe that fundamental reforms are needed – particularly of the tax collection system which leaves government short of revenue – before the economy can truly prosper again.

Russia remains a market of great potential for companies willing to take a long-term view, research the market thoroughly and proceed with caution. Much has already been achieved and exports and investments have grown steadily, even in the face of earlier crises. Prior to the recent economic problems there were good opportunities to sell both industrial and consumer goods and once the economy is put back on a stable footing, these are soon likely to re-emerge – in fact many companies are adopting a policy of maintaining their Russian contacts so that they will be in the best possible position when the upturn comes. Demand for equipment to modernize the economy and to exploit Russia's vast reserves of oil, gas and minerals are likely to be just one area where sales and investment could be made. Others include telecommunications, health care, pharmaceuticals and chemicals, not to mention branded consumer goods, for which the Russian population has already proved it has an unquenchable thirst.

1.3.3 Other trade associations

Gulf Markets

The Gulf market of Saudi Arabia, United Arab Emirates, Kuwait, Oman, Bahrain, Qatar and Yemen are developed markets with generally sophisticated and well-off consumers who seek good quality and well designed products. It is a market which is steady within the local cultural bounds becoming increasingly westernized and therefore broadening the range of products which can be marketed.

There is a wide range of potential sectors including oil and gas, construction, leisure and tourism, education (the large youth population generates a large demand for education services and equipment), health care and the youth market. Most people are under 30 and Western influence such as computers, video games and the Internet are all contributing to broadening the buying habits of these young people.

An analysis of export opportunities in each market in the Gulf region is given below.

Saudi Arabia – The key opportunities for exporters include: food products, consumer goods, electrical equipment and machinery, building materials, medical equipment and supplies, computer hardware and software and telecommunications equipment, oil, gas and petrochemical equipment and supplies, and desalination equipment. Emerging sectors include leisure, home entertainment, education and training and electronic publishing.

United Arab Emirates (UAE) – Abu Dhabi holds vast oil reserves and accounts for two-thirds of the UAE's GDP, with Dubai claiming a quarter. Abu Dhabi offers opportunities in the oil, gas and petrochemical sectors, water and power, construction and sport, tourism and leisure. It is considering privatization in the power sector.

Dubai's oil resources are running out and over recent years it has developed a strong base as the commercial and tourism centre of the UAE. It has very good transport infrastructure in roads, seaports and airports, as well as hotels and leisure facilities. Opportunities are in sport and leisure, power generation, medical supplies and construction including building materials.

The northern emirates are in various states of development. Sharjah is bidding to become the manufacturing base, concentrating on light and medium industry.

Bahrain – The first centre in the Gulf to develop oil, Bahrain is now striving to develop various niches which other parts of the Gulf are not undertaking. Education, training and human resources are areas of specialization. Opportunities exist in oil and gas, water and sewerage, telecommunications, financial services, construction, health care and tourism.

Kuwait – In Kuwait the main emphasis is on developing the oil and gas resources further. These, along with consumer goods and other sections, provide scope for companies to do business.

Oman – Oil resources are declining but gas is being developed in Oman. Tourism is another area to explore because of the country's natural beauty. Other growth sectors include power generation, water, agriculture, ports and fisheries.

Qatar – Development of what is believed to be the largest gas field in the world will bring Qatar huge wealth in the future. The main opportunities for exporters are in food products, consumer goods, building materials, oil, gas and petrochemical equipment and supplies.

Yemen – The Yemeni economy is now in good shape following some IMF treatment and it is the one country in the region which does not have large oil or gas reserves. It is developing a manufacturing base centred on light industrial products to complement its expanding oil sector and the agricultural and fisheries industries.

Commonwealth of Independent States (CIS)

In December 1991 the Commonwealth of Independent States (CIS) was formed as a successor to the Soviet Union. This involves the states of Armenia, Turkmenistan, Tajikistan, Kyrgystan, Georgia, Russian Federation, Uzbekistan, Azerbaijan, Ukraine, Belarus, Moldova and Kazakhstan.

Listed below are other major international organizations concerned with economies and trade development:

Asociación Latinoamericana de Integración (ALADI)

(Latin American Integration Association, LAIA). Members: Argentina, Bolivia, Brazil, Chile, Colombia, Ecuador, Mexico, Paraguay, Peru, Uruguay, Venezuela.

Central American Common Market (CACM)

Members: Costa Rica, Guatemala, El Salvador, Honduras, Nicaragua.

Colombo Plan for Co-operative Economic and Social Development in Asia and the Pacific

Members: Afghanistan, Australia, Bangladesh, Bhutan, Burma, Canada, Fiji, India, Indonesia, Iran, Japan, Kampuchea, Korean Republic, Laos, Malaysia, Maldives,

Nepal, New Zealand, Pakistan, Papua New Guinea, Philippines, Singapore, Sri Lanka, Thailand, UK and USA.

The Commonwealth

Members: Antigua and Barbuda, Australia, Bahamas, Bangladesh, Barbados, Belize, Botswana, Brunei, Canada, Cyprus, Dominica, Gambia, Ghana, Grenada, Guyana, India, Jamaica, Kenya, Kiribati, Lesotho, Malawi, Malaysia, Maldives, Malta, Mauritius, Naura, New Zealand, Nigeria, Pakistan, Papua New Guinea, St Kitts and Nevis, St Lucia, St Vincent and Grenadines, Seychelles, Sierra Leone, Singapore, Solomon Islands, South Africa, Sri Lanka, Swaziland, Tanzania, Tonga, Trinidad and Tobago, Tuvalu, Uganda, United Kingdom, Vanuatu, Western Samoa, Zambia and Zimbabwe.

South Africa – population 37.9 million, per capita GNP US$3340. South Africa is the most recent re-entry to the Commonwealth. International confidence in the country's economic management and in its policy implementation had been growing in the mid-1990s. The government's medium term economic strategy stresses the importance of privatization, fiscal prudence and the overall direction of economic policy is acknowledged. By mid-1999 the tentative first steps in the privatization process, action reducing the remaining exchange controls has been phased in and trade policy formulated within the WTO guidelines. Major exports to South Africa include machinery and transport equipment, chemicals, food and a wide range of consumer and manufactured goods. Inward investment, particularly in joint ventures, is strong.

Communauté Française Africaine (CFA) (The Franc Zone)

Members: Benin, Burkina Faso, Cameroon, Central African Republic, Chad, Comoro Islands, Congo, Côte d'Ivoire, Equatorial Guinea, Gabon, Mali, Niger, Togo and Senegal.

Co-operation Council for the Arab States of the Gulf

Members: Bahrain, Kuwait, Oman, Qatar, Saudi Arabia and United Arab Emirates.

Council of Arab Economic Unity

Members: Egypt, Iraq, Jordan, Kuwait, Libya, Mauritania, Palestine Liberation Organization, Somalia, Sudan, Syria, United Arab Emirates, Yemen Arab Republic and Yemen People's Democratic Republic.

Economic Community of West African States (ECOWAS)

Members: Benin, Burkina Faso, Cape Verde, Gambia, Ghana, Guinea, Guinea-Bissau, Côte d'Ivoire, Liberia, Mali, Mauritania, Niger, Nigeria, Senegal, Sierra Leone and Togo.

League of Arab States

Members: Algeria, Bahrain, Djibouti, Egypt, Iraq, Jordan, Kuwait, Lebanon, Libya, Mauritania, Morocco, Oman, Palestine, Qatar, Saudi Arabia, Somalia, Sudan, Syria, Tunisia, United Arab Emirates, Yemen Arab Republic and Yemen People's Democratic Republic.

Nordic Council

Members: Denmark (with the autonomous territories of the Faroe Islands and Greenland), Finland (with the autonomous territory of the Aland Islands), Iceland, Norway and Sweden.

Organization of African Unity (OAU)

Members: Algeria, Angola, Benin, Botswana, Burkina Faso, Burundi, Cameroon, Cape Verde, Central African Republic, Chad, Comoro Islands, Congo, Côte d'Ivoire, Djibouti, Egypt, Equatorial Guinea, Ethiopia, Gabon, The Gambia, Ghana, Guinea, Guinea-Bissau, Kenya, Lesotho, Liberia, Libya, Madagascar, Malawi, Mali, Mauritania, Mauritius, Mozambique, Niger, Nigeria, Rwanda, São Tomé and Príncipe, Seychelles, Sierra Leone, Somalia, Sudan, Swaziland, Tanzania, Togo, Tunisia, Uganda, Zaire, Zambia and Zimbabwe.

Organization of American States (OAS)

Members: Antigua and Barbuda, Argentina, Bahamas, Barbados, Bolivia, Brazil, Chile, Colombia, Costa Rica, Dominica (Commonwealth of), Dominican Republic, Ecuador, El Salvador, Grenada, Guatemala, Haiti, Honduras, Jamaica, Mexico, Nicaragua, Panama, Paraguay, Peru, St Kitts and Nevis, St Lucia, St Vincent and the Grenadines, Suriname, Trinidad and Tobago, USA, Uruguay and Venezuela.

To focus on world trade prospects is a difficult exercise with so many uncertainties. Tables 1.3 and 1.4 feature trends and possible short-term developments. Table 1.3 identifies the volume of world merchandise trade by selected region in 1990–98 (p. 8) and Table 1.4 features the growth in the value of world merchandise trade in 1990–98 (p. 9).

With regard to the future, the North American economy continues to be strong and the USA remains the leading global player. Europe, embracing the European Union (see pp. 428–44) is likely to continue to record strong trade growth especially the United Kingdom, Germany, France and Italy.

The Middle East region is an oil/gas based export economy, with oil and gas representing 70 per cent of their GDP. The stagnation of the dollar value of oil has contributed to the depressed trade performance of this region in recent years, but this may change in the event of a rise in oil prices.

In Africa the agricultural economy evident in many countries remains very sensitive to the fluctuation of price developments for these commodities throughout the world.

Asia's growth future is very much influenced by the financial crisis in the economies of the Republic of Korea, Malaysia, Thailand, Indonesia and Philippines, and the economic and fiscal remedies adopted. China and Japan remain dominant players in international trade.

In 1997 Latin America, featuring Argentina, Brazil, Chile, Colombia, Mexico, Peru and Venezuela, recorded its highest annual growth rate in the 1990s of 5.2 per cent. Future trends are less certain particularly with the Brazilian devaluation in January 1999. Overall, the region is experiencing a large increase in its current account deficit.

The benefits to be derived from free trade areas, economic blocs and customs union are now very manifest and by 1999 over 100 such areas existed. Overall, some 70 per cent of world trade today is conducted between such groups. The benefits emerging from such areas include: wealth creation within the regions; stimulation of trade development, more political power as a trading group rather than an individual country; the potential development of indigenous resources; higher living standards; expansion of the service sector; infrastructure development; raised standards and the generation of a more competitive culture/outlook.

The activities of the various trading groups have to conform to the principles laid down in the General Agreement on Tariffs and Trade (GATT), which requires its signatories to conform to the following:

(1) To concert together, to achieve a mutual reduction of tariff barriers and preferences.
(2) To avoid discrimination by means of tariffs against foreign products which compete with home products.
(3) To abolish quantitative controls.
(4) To remove existing restrictions imposed by exchange control.

Although several of these objectives have been given practical application as trade has been liberalized, it is unlikely that the general requirements of GATT, and now WTO, will be implemented in the present state of world trade.

It is important that the exporter takes a close look at the foregoing preferential trading groups and identifies those which best suit his/her needs, having regard to product quality, competitive pricing, on-going commitment and relationships between buyer/seller, market profile, political situation and so on. Full use should be made of the National Chambers of Commerce (Appendix A) commercial attachés to obtain more data. At the same time, advice should be sought from the trade associations and Department of Trade and Industry (DTI).

1.4 World Trade Organisation

The World Trade Organisation (WTO) is the legal and institutional foundation of the multilateral trading system. It provides the principal contractual obligations determining how governments frame and implement domestic trade legislation and regulations. And it is the platform on which trade relations between countries evolve through collective debate, negotiation and adjudication. The WTO was established on 1 January 1995. Governments had concluded the Uruguay Round of negotiations on 15 December 1993 and ministers had given their political backing to the results by signing the Final Act at a meeting in Marrakesh, Morocco, in April 1994. The 'Marrakesh Declaration' of 15 April 1994 affirmed that the results of the Uruguay Round would 'strengthen the world economy and lead to more trade, investment, employment and income growth throughout the World'. The WTO is the embodiment of the Uruguay Round results and the successor to the General Agreement on Tariffs and Trade (GATT).

Out of a potential membership of 152 countries and territories, 76 governments became members of the WTO on its first day, with some 50 other governments at various stages of completing their domestic ratification procedures, and the remainder engaged in negotiating their terms of entry.

Not only does the WTO have a potentially larger membership than GATT (132 by the end of 2000), it also has a much broader scope in terms of the commercial activity and trade policies to which it applies. The GATT applied only to trade in merchandise goods; the WTO covers trade in goods, services and 'trade in ideas' or intellectual property. In 1998 it started to focus attention on potential international trade gains from electronic commerce.

The WTO is based in Geneva, Switzerland. Its essential functions are: administering and implementing the multilateral and plurilateral trade agreements which together make up the WTO; acting as a forum for multilateral trade negotiations; seeking to resolve trade disputes; overseeing national trade policies; and cooperating with other international institutions involved in global economic policy making.

1.4.1 The principles of the trading system

The WTO Agreement contains some 29 individual legal texts – covering everything from agriculture to textiles and clothing, and from services to government procurement, rules of origin and intellectual property. Added to these are more than 25 additional ministerial declarations, decisions and understandings which spell out further obligations and commitments for WTO members. However, a number of simple and fundamental principles run throughout all of these instruments which, together, make up the multilateral trading system.

1.4.2 Trade without discrimination

For almost 50 years, key provisions of GATT outlawed discrimination among members and between imported and domestically produced merchandise. According to Article 1, the famous 'most-favoured-nation' (MFN) clause, members are bound to grant to the products of other members treatment no less favourable than that accorded to the products of any other country. Thus, no country is to give special trading advantages to another or to discriminate against it: all are on an equal basis and all share the benefits of any moves towards lower trade barriers.

There are a number of exceptions to Article 1 – notably that covering customs unions and free trade areas. However, most-favoured-nation treatment generally ensures that developing countries and others with little economic leverage are able to benefit freely from the best trading conditions wherever and whenever they are negotiated. A second form of non-discrimination, known as 'national treatment', requires that once goods have entered a market, they must be treated no less favourably than the equivalent domestically produced goods. This is Article III of the GATT.

Apart from the revised GATT (known as 'GATT 1994'), there are several other WTO agreements which contain important provisions relating to MFN and national treatment. That on Trade-Related Aspects of Intellectual Property Rights (TRIPS) contains, with some exceptions, MFN and national treatment requirements relating to the provision of intellectual property protection by WTO members. The General Agreement on Trade in Services (GATS) requires members to offer MFN treatment to services and service suppliers of other members. However, it permits listed exemptions to the MFN obligation, covering specific measures for which WTO members are unable to offer such treatment initially. Where such exemptions are taken, they are to be reviewed after 5 years and should not be maintained for more than 10 years. On the other hand, national treatment is only an obligation in GATS where members explicitly undertake to accord it for particular services or service activities. This means that national treatment is often the result of negotiations among members.

Other WTO agreements with non-discrimination provisions include those on rules of origin; pre-shipment inspection; trade-related investment measures and the application of sanitary and phytosanitary measures.

1.4.3 Predictable and growing access to markets

The multilateral trading system is an attempt by governments to provide investors, employers, employees and consumers with a business environment which encourages trade, investment and job creation as well as choice and low prices in the market place. Such an environment needs to be stable and predictable, particularly if businesses are to invest and thrive.

The existence of secure and predictable market access is largely determined by the use of tariffs or customs duties. While quotas are generally outlawed, tariffs are legal in the WTO and are commonly used by governments to protect domestic industries and to raise revenues. However, they are subject to disciplines – for instance, that they are not discriminatory among imports – and are largely 'bound'. Binding means that a tariff level for a particular product becomes a commitment by a WTO member and cannot be increased without compensation negotiations with its main trading partners (Article XXVIII of GATT 1994). Thus it can be the case that the extension of a customs union can lead to higher tariffs in some areas for which compensation negotiations are necessary.

Following the establishment of the GATT in 1948, average tariff levels fell progressively and dramatically (see below) through a series of seven trade rounds. The Uruguay Round added to that success, cutting tariffs substantially, sometimes to zero,while raising the overall level of bound tariffs significantly. The commitments on market access through tariff reductions made by over 120 countries in the Uruguay Round are contained in some 22 500 pages of national tariff schedules.

Tariff reductions, for the most part phased in over 5 years, will result in a 40 per cent cut in developed countries' tariffs on industrial products, from an average of 6.3 per cent to 3.8 per cent, and a jump from 20 to 44 per cent in the value of imported industrial products that receive duty-free treatment in developed countries. At the higher end of the tariff structure, the proportion of imports into developed countries from all sources that encounter tariffs above 15 per cent will decline from 7 to 5 per cent and from 9 to 15 per cent for imports from developing countries.

The Uruguay Round increased the percentage of bound product lines from 78 to 99 per cent for developed countries, 21 to 73 per cent for developing economies and from 73 to 98 per cent for economies in transition – results which are providing a substantially higher degree of market security for traders and investors.

The 'tariffication' of all non-tariff import restrictions for agricultural products provided a substantial increase in the level of market predictability for agricultural products. More than 30 per cent of agricultural produce had been subject to quotas or import restrictions. Virtually all such measures have now been converted to tariffs which, while initially providing substantially the same level of protection as previous non-tariff measures, are being reduced during the 6 years of implementation of the Uruguay Round agricultural agreement. The market access commitments on agriculture will also eliminate previous import bans on certain products.

While tariffs at the border do not exist for trade in services, there is no less of a need for predictable conditions. To meet that need, governments undertook an initial set of commitments covering national regulations affecting various service activities. These commitments are, like those for tariffs, contained in binding national schedules and will be extended through further rounds of services negotiations in the future.

Many other WTO agreements seek to ensure conditions of investment and trade are more predictable by making it very difficult for member governments to change the rules of the game at whim. In almost every policy area which impinges on trading conditions, the scope of members to pursue capricious, discriminatory and protectionist policies is constrained by WTO commitments.

The key to predictable trading conditions is often the transparency of domestic laws, regulations and practices. Many WTO agreements contain transparency provisions which require disclosure at the national level – for instance, through publication in official journals or through enquiry points – or at the multilateral level through formal notifications to the WTO. Much of the work of WTO bodies is concerned with reviewing such notifications. The regular surveillance of national trade policies through the Trade Policy Review Mechanism provides a further means of encouraging transparency both domestically and at the multilateral level.

1.4.4 Promoting fair competition

The WTO is not the 'free trade' institution it is sometimes described as – if only because it permits tariffs and, in limited circumstances, other forms of protection. It is more accurate to say it is a system of rules dedicated to open, fair and undistorted competition.

Rules on non-discrimination are designed to secure fair conditions of trade and so too are those on dumping and subsidies. Previous GATT rules, which laid down the basis on which governments could impose compensating duties on these forms of 'unfair' competition, were extended and clarified in WTO agreements.

The WTO agreement on agriculture is designed to provide increased fairness in farm trade. That on intellectual property will improve conditions of competition where ideas and inventions are involved, and the GATS will do the same thing for trade in services. The plurilateral agreement on government procurement will extend competition rules to purchases by thousands of 'government' entities in many countries. There are plenty of other examples of WTO provisions which are designed to promote fair and undistorted competition.

1.4.5 Encouraging development and economic reform

Over three-quarters of WTO members are developing countries and countries in the process of economic reform from non-market systems. During the 7-year course of the Uruguay Round – between 1986 and 1993 – over 60 such countries implemented trade liberalization programmes. Some did so as part of their accession negotiations to GATT, while others acted on an autonomous basis. At the same time, developing countries and transition economies took a much more active and influential role in the Uruguay Round negotiations than in any previous round.

This trend effectively killed the notion that the trading system existed only for industrialized countries. It also changed the previous emphasis on exempting developing countries from certain GATT provisions and agreements. With the end of the Uruguay Round, developing countries showed themselves prepared to take on most of the obligations that are required of developed countries. They were, however, given transition periods to adjust to the more unfamiliar and, perhaps, difficult WTO provisions – particularly so for the poorest, 'least-developed' countries. In addition, a ministerial decision on measures in favour of least-developed countries gives extra flexibility to those countries in implementing WTO agreements; calls for an acceleration in the implementation of market access concessions affecting goods of export interest to those countries; and seeks increased technical assistance for them. Thus, the value to development of pursuing, as far as is reasonable, open market-orientated policies based on WTO principles is widely recognized. But so is the need for some flexibility with respect to the speed at which those policies are pursued.

Nevertheless, the provisions of the GATT which were intended to favour developing countries remain in place in the WTO. In particular, Part IV of GATT 1994 contains three articles, introduced in 1965, encouraging industrial countries to assist developing nation members 'as a matter of conscious and purposeful effort' in their trading conditions and not to expect reciprocity for concessions made to developing countries in negotiations. A second measure, agreed at the end of the Tokyo Round in 1979 and normally referred to as the 'enabling clause', provides a permanent legal basis for the market access concessions made by developed to developing countries under the generalized system of preferences (GSP).

1.4.6 A brief history of GATT

The WTO's predecessor, the GATT, was established on a provisional basis after the Second World War in the wake of other new multilateral institutions dedicated to international economic cooperation – notably the 'Bretton Woods' institutions now known as the World Bank and the International Monetary Fund (IMF). The original 23 GATT countries were among over 50 which agreed a draft Charter for an International Trade Organisation (ITO) – a new specialized agency of the United Nations. The Charter was intended to provide not only world trade disciplines but also contained rules relating to employment, commodity agreements, restrictive business practices, international investment and services.

In an effort to give an early boost to trade liberalization after the Second World War – and to begin to correct the large overhang of protectionist measures which remained in place from the early 1930s – tariff negotiations were opened among the 23 founding GATT 'contracting parties' in 1946. This first round of negotiations resulted in 45 000 tariff concessions affecting $10 billion – or about one-fifth – of world trade. It was also agreed that the value of these concessions should be protected by early – and largely 'provisional' – acceptance of some of the trade rules in the draft ITO Charter. The tariff concessions and rules together became known as the General Agreement on Tariffs and Trade and entered into force in January 1948.

Although the ITO Charter was finally agreed at a UN Conference on Trade and Employment in Havana in March 1948, ratification in national legislatures proved impossible in some cases. When the US government announced, in 1950, that it would not seek Congressional ratification of the Havana Charter, the ITO was effectively dead. Despite its provisional nature, the GATT remained the only multilateral instrument governing international trade from 1948 until the establishment of the WTO.

1.4.7 International trade and shipping scene

Although, throughout its 47 years the basic legal text of the GATT remained much as it was in 1948, there were additions in the form of 'plurilateral' – voluntary membership – agreements and continual efforts to reduce tariffs. Much of this was achieved through a series of 'trade rounds' as detailed in Table 1.5.

The final round – number eight, the Uruguay Round, signed in 1995 – predicts it will add some US$755 billion to world exports and raise incomes by some $235 billion annually, excluding China and the CIS. By 2002, it is predicted world income gains will be US$235 billion annually and that trade gains will be $755 billion annually.

TABLE 1.5 GATT trade rounds

No.	Year	Subjects covered	Participating countries
1	1947	Geneva Tariffs	23
2	1949	Annecy Tariffs	13
3	1951	Torquay Tariffs	38
4	1956	Geneva Tariffs	26
5	1960–61	Geneva (Dillon Road) Tariffs	26
6	1964–67	Geneva (Kennedy Round) Tariffs and anti-measures	62
7	1973–79	Geneva (Tokyo Round) Tariffs, non-tariff measures, 'framework' agreements	102
8	1986–93	Geneva (Uruguay Round) Tariffs, non-tariff measures rules, service, intellectual property rights, dispute settlement, textiles and clothing, agriculture, establishment of the WTO, etc.	123

As we progress through the early years of the millennium the influence of the WTO in trade development and facilitation will grow immensely. It has already become the driving force of trade development and business confidence on a global scale.

1.4.8 Lomé Conventions

The fourth Lomé Convention, signed in 1989 between the EC and the 69-strong ACP (African–Caribbean–Pacific) group of countries provides for an increase in EC aid, duty and quota-free access for almost all ACP exports, guaranteed sugar purchases and funds for trade promotion and development. Moreover, they will receive aid in both absolute and per capita terms.

Recommended reading

WTO Focus – latest issues available from the Media Division of the WTO.

Advantages of trading overseas and the role of the export and shipping office

2.1 Export benefits and risk

The responsibility of moving from a domestic market to an export market and ultimately to a global market (see p. 116) is a management task at Director level. It involves new management culture internationally focused; multi-lingually equipped at all management levels; computer and logistical equipment; empathy with the buyer; a good knowledge of international regulations and the international environment; and complete commitment to developing and serving the export market. Two key factors emerge, namely innovation and adaptation to the needs of the importer coupled with continuing commitment to the buyer. Moreover, one must, at all times, be professional.

Successful exporting emerges from the following strategies:

(1) The development of ideas and techniques should be seen as being as important as physical goods and services.
(2) A belief that growing world competition drives companies growth strategies.
(3) Recognizing the importance of technology.
(4) An increasing blurring of the distinction between low tech and high tech.
(5) Developing long-term strategies on a growth market basis – this encourages a proactive rather than a reactive strategy.
(6) Striving to find new markets opening up new sales opportunities.
(7) Continuously reviewing and implementing internal company changes such as new manufacturing and disciplines dedicated to improving product specification.
(8) Exploiting new technology and new technological processes such as E-Commerce, the Internet and Websites.
(9) Developing a strong service philosophy.
(10) Developing empathy with the buyer.
(11) Undertaking continuous market research.

We will now briefly consider the benefits and risks involved in the export business.

2.1.1 Export benefits

(1) There is the potential for greatly increased company turnover.

(2) Higher calibre staff of a professional managerial status can be attracted to the business due to the potential for greater challenges, improved confidence/self-esteem and more job satisfaction. Personnel working in an export environment must be culturally focused at all times which develops more *esprit de corps*.

(3) The company becomes more competitive in all areas of the business: product specification, management skills, and value added benefit transmitted to the buyer in both price and non-price areas – the latter featuring servicing warranty.

(4) Economies of scale are achieved through a larger order book and better utilization of company resources, especially in the areas of production, design, administration and procurement.

(5) Company exposure is greatly increased on an international scale through publicity and product/service analysis and market penetration.

(6) The product or service offered is more competitive. It reflects overseas market needs and conforms to a wider legal environment.

(7) Company risk and business is not confined to one market as is found at the domestic level, but is spread throughout ten or more markets depending on the nature of the business. The number of markets served, their location, and the culture presented in each market is closely related to company resources, level of profitability, degree of risk and market forecast. An analysis of market entry options is found in Chapter 17. Hence, by operating in a range of markets the company should experience peaks and troughs at differing times in each market, thereby spreading the risk and opportunities.

(8) Companies become more integrated with the market they serve and this encourages higher standards and the use of more high technology, which would not obtain when serving only the domestic market, an environment which may be shielded through high import tariffs imposed to protect local manufacturers.

(9) Potential levels of profitability are much increased. This provides more income for investment and research and development – ingredients which all work to ensure a company remains competitive.

It is stressed that the benefits outlined will vary by company and product/service and it is unlikely that all the benefits will apply to any one individual company or product/service. Similar remarks apply to the risks inherent in exporting.

2.1.2 Export risks

(1) The export market involves a longer time scale of payment. This may be 90 or 180 days or several years. In the domestic market it is usually 30 days. This may pose a serious cash flow problem for a smaller company. Possible solutions include factoring (see p. 259); cash in advance; or operating an open account.

(2) Problems are inherent in the increased range of interest rates, exchange rates and economic and trade cycles. Forward planning can counter such problems, particularly in the short-term with strategies such as hedging the market on exchange rate variation, keeping in contact with the International Bank and focusing continuously on the political, legal and economic environment in the buyer's market.

(3) Export risk can be divided into economic/political risk involving a country (see item (2)); financial risk such as foreign exchange, interest rates and working capital (see item (1)); or commercial risk such as buyer default or contractual dispute. Such risks can be reduced by having a buyer status audit conducted by a bank, and employing a solicitor to formulate an agency–distributor agreement or an export sales contract featuring an arbitration mechanism. Debt defaults can be difficult to resolve, particularly those with a political content.

(4) Trade barriers (see p. 412) are politically and economically manipulated. This includes both customs tariff and non-tariff barriers.

(5) Corruption, crime, expropriation and fraud are regretfully on the increase despite government's and international agencies' efforts to counter them. Such bodies include the London based International Maritime Bureau, the Counterfeiting Intelligence Bureau and the Commercial Crime Bureau all under the auspices of the International Chamber of Commerce (see p. 7).

(6) New skills are required which emerge from the foregoing items including methods of financing and how to cope with cash management; and issues such as the collection of receivables, repatriation of funds and foreign exchange, and interest rate exposure and Forex risk. Adding value to enhance competitive advantage can make a difference: exporters should make it easy for customers to buy; credit should be part of the product proposition; and foreign exchange risk should be managed and not passed on. Exporters should develop a strategy to ensure they receive payment where the key risks are identified and then managed. Realistic financial plans should be identified and much of the aforementioned risk can be minimized by consulting the company's bank.

(7) A product launch in an overseas market is more costly and complex in comparison with a domestic launch. The product specification must comply with all the overseas market legislation and the legal environment of the market in which it is to be sold. Good research and visits to the intended market can serve to reduce such risk.

The way to reduce the risks outlined above is to employ experienced, professionally qualified and internationally focused personnel. The export company must have a company business plan with an international focus and put the necessary resources into finance, production, technology and personnel to ensure the plan's execution. Comprehensive control systems are essential to monitor performance and to adapt it when necessary as a remedial measure. Empathy with the buyer is vital on an ongoing basis. Distribution, logistics and the outsourcing of components and assembly in a third country play a decisive role in competitive exporting today. Overall, the exporter must have complete commitment to the buyer, the market and the product they are selling overseas.

2.2 The export office role

Exporting today is exceptionally complex and functions in a rapidly changing market. It is highly competitive and manufacturers now frequently outsource their products to keep up with technology and competitiveness in the market. It is driven by logistics (see p. 101) and high technology, making it essential for the company to employ computer literate, multi-lingual, professionally trained personnel. An example of a product which embodies these attributes is NIKE footwear: it is designed in the USA; prototypes are adopted in Taiwan; the soles are manufactured in South Korea; the leather is bought from Spain; the cloth is produced in Bangladesh; the footwear is assembled in the Peoples Republic of China using Chinese labour; and the distribution is logistically handled from Hong Kong to serve a global market.

A key factor is to manufacture the consumer or industrial product to the required standard. Such standards vary by market with the USA and Japanese markets out of step with those found in the European Union (see p. 430).

With a growing level of privatization in many countries bringing about a move away from state owned enterprises, export manufacturers are having to adapt to the changing needs of their customers. The increasing emphasis is on reduced product lifecycle costs, improved efficiency and greater equipment availability. There has been an enormous change in the customer–supplier relationship. The traditional concept of carrying out corrective maintenance and unscheduled repairs has been expanded to include preventive inspections, maintenance partnerships, plant upgrading, training and joint production.

A further factor is the globalization of markets with the buyers sourcing a range of products from different markets and conducting the assembly and distribution in a third country. This is possible through an increasingly sophisticated, logistically-driven global container network offering combined transport services with complete reliability and cost efficiency. An increasing number of the mega-container operators now have logistic organizations dedicated to their shippers, offering a transparent transport system in a high tech communication network. (see Chapter 6).

It is in the light of the foregoing factors that the role of the export/shipping office must be considered. Many companies call it the logistics office. One other vital factor is the structure of the organization itself, which must be capable of achieving its objectives as found in the business plan.

Exporting today is a highly skilled and professional operation. To be successful in this field requires an adequate and cost effective organization designed to enlarge the company product market share overseas. Above all, the results of exporting must be profitable and, accordingly, it is most desirable that the export personnel are of a high calibre, with language proficiency, adequately qualified and rewarded, to attain this objective.

To be successful the Company must have an export culture management strategy with all personnel totally focused to an international business entrepreneur environment. This requires continuous training, and total commitment to work with the global markets they serve and their buyers. It must embrace the total product. This includes not only the product delivered on time in accordance with the export sales contract, but also involves continuous communication with the buyer to sustain and develop existing business opportunities. Moreover, the exporter must be fully informed of the environment in which the product will be used and identify how best to reduce the product lifecycle cost (see p. 102).

The size of the company, its products, and scale of export business will largely influence the form of export organization. Moreover, cognizance must be taken of company structure and organization, and how the export role can best be injected into it. In broad terms, the industrial company has three functions – production, finance and sales. Additionally, there are various other subsidiary activities which significantly contribute to the running of the company, which include personnel, administration, research/development, training, purchasing, etc.

If the company is rather small with only an element of export business, it is likely that an export manager with a secretary and a clerk would be adequate but, as the export trade grows, it will soon become necessary to have a properly structured export organization with qualified specialist staff designed to exploit the export trade potential. One can no longer rely on inexperienced unqualified personnel in the export field (whether it be marketing, sales, or shipping), as standards will tend to be low, overseas product reputation poor and the overall financial results probably very indifferent. Exporting is a highly professional activity which is increasing annually in terms of its overseas market competition.

The export department has two main functions: marketing and shipping/logistics. The former is responsible for sales, pricing enquiries, quotations, recording and checking orders, and other marketing functions such as promotion, research, after sales service, product servicing and development, etc., whilst the latter is responsible for transportation/distribution and the relevant documents involved, packaging, costings for distribution, etc. There must be at all times close liaison with the accounts department particularly on credit audit and control, costings and financial documentation/information. Overall, the export department objective is to ensure that the export order proceeds smoothly from start to finish to obtain complete customer satisfaction and produce a modest profit for the company. Unless the profit motive is present throughout the export activities of the company, it will produce indifferent results with little discipline or technique. Hence, all the aspects of an export operation are interlinked with clearly defined functions and responsibilities. The export office may be horizontally or vertically organized, but it must have efficient and well-trained specialist and professional staff. Finally, the export organization must have a strong interface and be fully integrated with other departments, nowadays the computer facilitates this communication.

2.3 The export office organization and structure

The smallest export department may consist of an export manager, shipping clerk, typist and accounts clerk. At first, the department may be engaged merely in shipping orders secured by the sales organization, but as the export trade develops the department will enlarge and have its own sales organization, attend to their shipment and collect payment. Hence, it will become a self-contained export-focused unit fully integrated within the company structure.

In such circumstances, the overall aim of the export department is to collect sufficient data to enable them to quote promptly and accurately a competitive CIF (cost insurance freight), or other delivery term price for any consignment to the important centres of the world. This involves an evaluation of the most suitable method of despatch and requires knowledge of rates, services, routes, terminal charges, insurance, packaging, documentation and so on. It is likely the exporter will be responding to a logistically driven order and be in contact with the logistics division of a mega-container operator such as P&O Nedlloyd.

The department must study the needs of different markets, their trends and likely future developments together with possible methods of increasing overseas sales. A full understanding of the global logistic mechanism is essential (see p. 101). This extends to keeping up-to-date with the changing infrastructure and opportunities to speed up transit times. It involves the scrutiny of overseas agents and branch reports and the provision of adequate publicity by overseas journals/ publications. Additionally, close liaison must be maintained with trade associations and relevant government departments on overseas market development opportunities. Moreover, a continuing dialogue must be maintained with overseas representatives on all developments at home. This involves manufacturing and technical aspects of the commodity, distribution methods and future developments (e.g. a new product range). Such an exchange of information is vital to the future well-being of the company, and any reports indicating shortcomings in product, distribution, inadequate packing, faulty products, etc. should be acted on quickly and remedial measures taken.

The export department has the task not only of obtaining and executing the export orders, but also of ensuring payment is received without undue delay in accord with the terms of sale as prescribed in the export contract. Enforcement of rights in foreign courts of law is often a troublesome business and tends to create a bad public image for the company. It is prudent to liaise closely with and/or use the export services provided by banks and the credit insurance companies on financial matters.

In the larger export-oriented company a greater degree of specialization is essential which usually involves the appointment of an export marketing manager, an export sales manager, and a shipping manager, each with defined responsibilities (Figures 2.1 and 2.2). In the small to medium-sized firm an export manager is usually found dealing alone with all sections of his company's export business. In the larger firm, on the other hand, the work is split between the three appointments in the following manner:

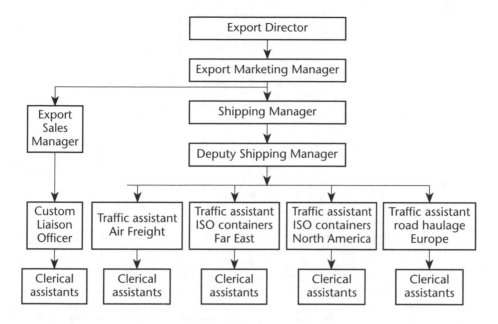

FIGURE 2.1 Structure of shipping manager organization

(1) The export marketing manager has overall executive control usually under an export marketing director. He controls and coordinates the activities of the other two functions, deals with policy, and usually represents the export department at internal sales conferences.

(2) An export sales manager is generally responsible to the export marketing manager and in a limited way is involved with sales inasmuch as he controls the agents and representatives and promotes actual sales to customers everywhere. His job is done when the export order is obtained and passed on to the export office for issuing to the factory or, in the case of a merchant, to the manufacturer. This involves the following stages:

    (a) receiving the enquiry, ascertaining its feasibility, ensuring that the price is calculated and preparing the quotation;

    (b) ascertaining the despatch date by the specified mode of transport;

    (c) obtaining the sanction of the credit controller and approval of a quotation before it is sent to the customer;

    (d) ensuring the quotation is sent to the customer and following it up, initiating investigations into orders presumed to be lost;

    (e) receiving the order from the customer and checking it against the quotation (where the order is received without earlier quotation much of (a)–(c) has to be done at this time);

    (f) obtaining production controller's sanction, priority rating and credit controller's permission (if applicable);

```
┌─────────────────────────────┐
│ Export director             │
├─────────────────────────────┤
│ Overall policy-strategy     │
│ and export development       │
└─────────────────────────────┘
```

Export marketing manager

Advertising (sales promotion)
Agency appointments
Brochure production
Budget formulation/monitoring
Economic statistics and analysis
Electronic data interchange
Export planning/strategy formulation
Liaison with trade associations/chambers of commerce etc.
Marketing and sales plan
Market analysis and development/selection
Market research
Product research/development
Trade exhibitions, trade weeks, store promotions.

Shipping manager

Accounting
Claims
Conditions of carriage and
  customs/transport regulations
Costing/computerization of order/transit
  analysis and execution
Credit control – audit and liaison
Documentation – completion and control
Electronic data interchange
Filing and order analysis
Insurance finance and invoicing
Management data on freight rates,
  schedules, transit times, currency rates
  etc. in computerized form
Market research on transport distribution
  strategy
Liaison with airlines, shipowners, port,
  airports, customs, freight forwarders,
  underwriters, liner conferences
Liaison with production and technical
  departments
Regarding execution of the order
Liaison with consuls, embassies,
  commercial attaches, diplomatic corps
  relative documentation attestation
Order processing
Packing
Planning – resources/distribution
Production/assembly
Strategy formulation on distribution policy
Supervision, appointment of personnel –
  traffic assistant, clerical personnel
Training
Transportation to airport/Seaport/ICD

Export marketing manager

After-sales
Agents' reports
Budgets – execution/accountability
Claims
Costing – all elements in quotation
Customer audit/monitoring with credit
  control
Export sales contract
Liaison with Production Department etc.
Licensing – overseas/monitoring
Management information
Market intelligence
Market trends
Monitoring of sales records
Quotations
Sales conferences/seminars
Sales reports
Selling – direct or via agents
Supervision of overseas sales personnel
Training

FIGURE 2.2 Export office job description of senior managerial personnel

(g) acknowledging the order and informing the local agent (if necessary) of the order;

(h) arranging for the preparation and issue of the works order;

(i) informing records or statistics department of the details of the order;

(j) confirming date of despatch to clients, agents or distributors and notifying any unavoidable changes;

(k) progress chasing;

(l) handing over the order to the shipping department to arrange the delivery procedure (overall one can conclude by saying the export sales office function is to deal with enquiries and orders up to the point of despatch).

(3) The export shipping manager is informed of any orders booked, usually by a copy order and later receives definite notice from works/manufacturer when the goods are nearing completion. This involves the following stages:

(a) linking with export sales, checking that the order complies with import/ export controls and establishing from letters of credit relevant details of items which have to be reconciled with the ultimate forwarding arrangements (see also Chapter 15);

(b) deciding on the method of transportation (if not already specified);

(c) issuing instructions for packing and marking (if not already given);

(d) chartering or booking shipping (or air) space;

(e) pre-entering at customs (if necessary);

(f) issuing instructions to works, transport office, and freight forwarders;

(g) drawing up all the necessary documents and later collecting, collating and cross-checking all documents after shipment;

(h) passing documents to accounts department for collection of payment.

The export shipping function normally commences when the works order is issued and takes over fully when the goods ordered have been produced and are ready for despatch. It is a section where a sense of urgency is essential. The Shipping Manager is responsible for obtaining shipping or air freight space, arranging despatch, documentation, insurance, possibly packing and customs clearance (Figure 2.2).

The export salesman involved in direct selling overseas in the field has a very demanding job requiring many aptitudes. He must be multi-lingual, ideally have good product knowledge, with good managerial potential and knowledge of export practice. Moreover, the person must be tenacious, have good judgement and be sufficiently diplomatic to secure the most favourable export sales contract.

Today most companies engaged in exports use computers to improve their cost efficiency relative to the processing of an export order. This involves all aspects of the order processing task and enables the exporter to reduce costs and improve efficiency throughout (see Figure 15.3, p. 368).

It cannot be stressed too strongly that the ultimate organization structure will depend on the size of the company and the nature/volume of export business. Likewise, the precise relationship and division of responsibilities between the foregoing three functions will vary from firm to firm.

Basically, there are two main forms of shipping office organization structure: the vertical and horizontal, as detailed in Figure 2.3.

The vertical organization structure streamlines the documentation activities and thereby assists simplified documentation. Personnel are selected on the basis of their expertise, that is, transportation, insurance, packing, etc. and efficiency in all the stages through which the export order must be processed is high. Hence the overall knowledge of export techniques becomes limited to a specific area of activity, with the result that there can be a tendency for personnel to become disinterested in the total operation and frustration can set in.

The horizontal structure, however, produces total involvement and expertise in a group of markets and thus identification with the progress of the markets. The personnel will probably handle several aspects of the subgroup's activity thus avoiding boredom. Overall this type of system could produce unnecessary rivalry and overlap (Figure 2.3).

An increasing number of export companies now tend to adopt both the vertical and horizontal structures within a particular export office. In so doing the company may prefer to use the vertical organization for one group of overseas markets – particularly those with a common code of practice such as in a Free Trade Area – but adopt the horizontal organization in markets where the situations tend to differ rather widely, thereby benefiting from the expertise in market development on a country/

1. Vertical organization

Export marketing manager controlling departments
dealing with individual aspects as under:

a) Credit control
b) Order processing
c) Product/Assembly
d) Packing
e) Transportation and Insurance   for ALL MARKETS
f) Invoicing
g) Documentation
h) Filing
i) Finance/Accounting/Costing

2. Horizontal organization

Export marketing manager controlling sections, each
dealing with all aspects for one market, as under:

Group market 1	Group market 2	Group market 3	Group market 4	Group market 5	Group market 6
USA	EC	South	Middle	Central and	South
Canada	EFTA	East	East	Eastern	America
Mexico	EEA	Asia		Europe	

FIGURE 2.3 Organization of export and shipping office

countries basis. The choice of the vertical or horizontal organization can also be influenced by the degree to which – if any – the export company relies on a freight forwarder to process the export documentation and international transportation arrangements. Many exporters adopt the policy of using the freight forwarder where the export volume for a market is small or rather irregular in terms of overseas market demand. This works to keep down the export shipping department cost.

Basically there are three types of sales office as detailed below and in Figure 2.4.

(1) Products orientated. This type tends to be warranted where the products are technically complex, or the number of products in the range is vast, or where the products are completely unrelated. It is ideal for the company which feels that product knowledge is paramount in the interests of giving good customer service. For example, it is suitable for a company selling overseas medical equipment, cycles, bathroom fittings, etc. Conversely, it can inflate cost as various representatives will call on the same customer which could cause customer irritation.

(2) Customer orientated. Under this system each representative specializes in a class of customer thereby gaining expert knowledge of the industry concerned, its

FIGURE 2.4 Sales office organization

technology, its decision patterns and so on. Thus the salesman will get to know the specific customer needs and will be able to satisfy them more efficiently. Conversely, it does encourage duplication of journeys involving increased costs of the export product when more than one representative visits the same area to see different types of companies. It tends to be used by the larger companies.

(3) Market group or area-based organization. This involves allocating the salesman a specific world area to service – as found in the horizontal system in the shipping office. It results in a clear definition of responsibility and interest in that area which will tend to lead to the cultivation of local business and personal ties. Travelling expenses will be kept to a reasonable level. This system works satisfactorily when the area is not too large, where the products and customers are homogeneous, but once the situation arises where the company's products become diversified to the extent that the representative is physically incapable of learning everything about the products, then this method becomes less effective.

For the export department to function efficiently, close cooperation with other sections of the business is imperative. The export manager should have powers to ensure prompt delivery of his or her orders from the factory, and compliance with his or her instructions as regards packing and despatch. Moreover, he or she should be able to secure exactly the right type of goods. The dangers from lack of cooperation between all departments arise when the factory is asked to expedite urgent orders for both the home and export markets. An understanding between the department heads will obviate a lack of attention to overseas needs in this respect.

For the whole business to work satisfactorily, someone must make it his or her business to coordinate the work of all the departments and to adjust differences that may arise. If the export department complains that it is not being well served by the traffic department, the matter is best settled by a conference between the heads of both departments, supervised by a senior official of the business. The traffic/transport manager is usually able to advise the export department as to the quantities most convenient for packing and transportation. In an increasingly competitive overseas market the need to ensure delivery dates are maintained is paramount, otherwise orders will be lost and goodwill impaired.

Finally it must be recognized (see p. 423) that in many multinational companies the technical division is internationally focused with a very large part of their order book being overseas. This embraces not only supplying the product as specified, but also providing technical commitment in terms of servicing, technical training, contractual maintenance and product development. It may be a turnkey project and could apply to power stations, railway rolling stock, a mass transit system, hydro-electric power plant, etc.

2.4 Export policy and records

As we progress through the millennium, manufacturing based companies which rely on international markets will be the norm and companies relying almost exclusively on their domestic market the exception. The latter usually will be very vulnerable to home market recession as they cannot rely on the multi-country, broadly based overseas markets inherent in the export focused company.

The chief concern of a company will be to combine stability with the highest financial return obtainable. In many industries this is achieved by a balance or mixture between home and overseas markets, but much depends on the product. This is important where:

(1) exports may rely on the continued existence of one or two foreign markets, which may be cut off by changes in import licensing laws, etc. in the countries concerned;
(2) demand abroad may be seasonal for goods which require a constant market to make them pay;
(3) overseas enthusiasm for a product may depend on the fact that it is in use in the home market.

Some businesses virtually exist solely for export with no significant home market. In such a situation, it is prudent, where possible, to have the export markets broadly based and extending to several countries, thereby lessening the impact of a change of export demand in any one of the countries.

Export marketing research is an important function and involves fact-finding enquiry on which marketing policy is then based. Overall there are four basic areas to focus on continuously.

(1) *Statistical*. This involves the determination of the total existing market insofar as the quantity bought, the price range and their locations. Additionally, it should indicate, where relevant, a comparison with the company's own sales in the area, and whether the total market is expanding or otherwise.
(2) *Economic*. This involves evaluation of the product market potential and its acceptable market price bearing in mind competition.
(3) *Social*. This indicates the public attitude towards the products and their adequacy in terms of design, durability, and so on.
(4) *Psychological*. This involves what motivates the consumer to buy the product; an evaluation of measures which could be devised to further its market growth; and in what ways it is adversely influenced by competition/substitutes.

The results of research in the export market can be correlated with parallel activities on (a) the home market and (b) the international marketing plan projections so that an overall marketing policy may be formulated. However, the divergence of treatment called for by home and overseas markets makes a fusion of the export department with the home marketing organization under a general marketing manager most unwise.

Today much statistical and economic data is available as countries worldwide develop their information resources. Moreover, market research database companies are available providing 'online access' to export orientated company subscribers. Such companies specialize in commodities, products or markets and provide up-to-date information to help the export strategist's decision-making process.

With regard to accounting, there is no fundamental difference between the accounting methods adopted in an export company and those in any other concern. In a manufacturing or wholesaling business which maintains an export department certain accounts will be subdivided with the export department having separate sales, cash, etc. returns budgets.

There does arise however, the need to have a strategic focus on how to deal with funds generated from the overseas markets. The multinational enterprise could form an overseas subsidiary which may generate tax advantages in transfer pricing and display total commitment to the market. Also all the sales revenue would not be repatriated to the parent company but would remain *in situ*. The smaller company may decide to set up an offshore account in the buyer's country to which all monies on overseas sales in that territory would be remitted and thereby avoid bank transfer charges. The account could also be used for local expenses and monies could be transferred to the parent company when exchange rates are most favourable. Advice from an international bank should be sought (see also pp. 264–73).

A trading firm engaged solely in the export business does so either (a) as an export merchant on its own account exporting its own goods to buyers overseas; (b) as a commission agent for foreign importers; or (c) as export agents undertaking the export business of manufacturers in a variety of industries. Freight forwarders do not engage in a trade of goods, but undertake the transportation arrangements, sometimes including a packaging service.

In the case of a manufacturer, it is usual for the export department to keep separate accounts. Hence, when an order is received from an overseas buyer, the goods will be subsequently invoiced giving details of the sale price. Where appropriate, further records will be maintained of such other charges as insurance, freight, packaging, etc. The usual method of charging export orders is to use serially numbered invoice sets. These give instructions to finished stores department, and advise and charge the customer. An alternative method is to issue warehouse instructions and process it through the various offices. The former is the most modern and is often computerized.

If the exporter does not manufacture his or her own products, he or she either buys the goods for export on his or her own account or exports on behalf of a manufacturer. An exporter on his or her own account may concentrate solely on the overseas trade or he or she may be a general wholesaler maintaining an export department. In the latter case, the accountancy of the export department will be similar to that in a manufacturing concern, the sole difference being that instead of producing merchandise for home and overseas markets, the business merely purchases the goods, bulking or breaking bulk as the case may be. The organization of the export department is thus much the same in either type of concern.

There is no doubt today that the export and shipping office structure should be well thought-out and adequate to exploit the company products overseas. It should be able to market successfully and to develop the export market profitably, particularly in terms of identifying, processing and executing the export order. Full use should be made of computers to improve cost efficiency. Ideally the organization should be reviewed every two or three years to reflect and take advantage of new market opportunities and changes in market structure, including threats. Moreover, close liaison should be maintained with all the various organizations, particularly trade associations and government departments, available to facilitate overseas market development. These additionally include identifying new markets and taking up opportunities to exhibit at overseas trade fairs and exhibitions.

Today, more and more small companies are entering the export business. Usually this involves the appointment of an export manager with a small staff. Transportation arrangements are normally undertaken by the freight forwarder, leaving the export management department to concentrate on sales, pricing enquiries, quotations, receiving the checking orders, together with other marketing functions. As the business prospers, the export department expands and the shipping office emerges. In some cases, the exporter actually provides his own transport to undertake the distribution task. This applies particularly within Europe.

One must stress in conclusion that export companies today are usually fully computerized in all activities of their business and thereby rely on Internet and E-commerce for communication, including research. The processing of the export order is fully computerized with very limited manual input. Moreover, the distribution is logistically driven with a high tech communication and an international documentation transmission network.

3

Characteristics of international transport modes: 1

3.1 The role and essentials of a transport system

Transport is an essential facility for the exploitation or development of economic resources on a national or international scale. It allows articles or materials to be conveyed from areas of low utility to areas of high utility and thereby adds value to the product.

Transport's provision arises for economic, social or political reasons. In a society where transport costs are relatively high, the need for a balanced social policy is paramount, otherwise isolated communities may cease to exist.

The political influence on transport is often considerable, to the extent that many large transport operators are state-owned. Moreover, such policies extend to the provision of uneconomical services for political reasons, such as an international air service retained for reasons of national prestige in the face of competition from other national airlines. Another example of the political influence on transport is flag discrimination practised in shipping whereby countries insist on certain imported cargoes being moved in ships of their own flag, so sustaining their fleet.

Transport permits the development of economic resources to the full. It makes possible specialization in economic development whether it be mining, car manufacturing or farming. Without a low-cost reliable and well-managed transport system, goods or services would not be exchanged, to the serious detriment of living standards worldwide. Today we have an efficient professionally managed global transport network which is the prime stimulant to the continuous expansion of world trade. Goods will not be moved unless a good transport infrastructure exists. Moreover, the global transport network must keep ahead of market needs through continuous investment and strive to reduce transit times and offer realistic rates. Overall, it is driven by logistics (see Chapter 6) in a high tech environment.

Transport is a product which is consumed immediately it is produced. Hence it cannot be stored. Its intensive economic deployment is, therefore, paramount to help ensure its viability.

The essentials of a transport system embrace three elements: the way route, the vehicle (including motive power unit), and the terminal. The way route may be naturally occurring such as the seas or river, or artificially made by man such as the railway, canal or motorway. One can have a combination of these two circumstances embracing the inland waterway system where new canals have been built into an established river or lake network such as the St Lawrence Seaway thereby offering a through inland waterway network. The way route may be for general public use administered in user terms by the state as, for example, the vehicle registration licensing system in the UK and most other countries. Alternatively, the exclusive use system is found in the railway network. The latter has the distinct advantage of operating under a disciplined timetable to obtain maximum use of the network but conversely, unlike the road operator, is responsible for financing all the initial, maintenance and replacement cost of the railway system. Moreover, the railway company provides a policing system through a signalling complex, but the road user relies on traffic control which is financed by the state.

The transport unit may either be of the integral type embracing the carrying and motive power unit, such as an aircraft or ship, or have an independent motive power unit, such as a railway locomotive. Examples of the carrying unit are found in the road trailer and barge. A further refinement exists whereby the integral or separate motive power unit either carries its own energy fuel, such as cars, ships or aircraft, or relies on remotely situated generated energy such as electric rail traction. The advantage of separate carrying and motive power units is their independence and flexibility in operation. Moreover, whilst the carrying unit contents are being transshipped, the motive power unit can be operational elsewhere. A further factor is that the failure of the motive power unit does not immobilize the carrying unit, as one merely obtains a standby unit.

The terminal must be artificially made by man, and be well designed to ensure the most efficient operation/utilization of the transport unit using it. This is particularly important today when more and more emphasis is on more intensive unit operation. Basically, the terminal is the link in the transport chain and merges at an interchange point involving one or more forms of transport, to offer through transit such as airport or seaport. Terminals require adequate area for expansion and a good layout to permit an unimpeded flow of traffic passing through it.

To sum up, the essential elements of a transport system are the way route, the vehicle, its motive power and the terminal. All must be so designed as to produce an efficient system, preferably capital intensive with a low labour content, to encourage low tariffs and thereby facilitate traffic development to contribute to economic expansion and social development. A study of the individual forms of transport now follows.

3.2 Canals and inland waterways

The canal network in the UK extends to only 2000 route miles compared with 200 000 route miles of roads, some 1200 miles of motorway and 11 000 route miles of railway. Consequently, the UK canal network makes little impact on the international trade scene particularly since the era of lighterage serving break-bulk cargo has ceased in many ports, such as London, following the development of deep-sea container services, and Ro-Ro (Roll on-Roll off) services from the UK and Europe to Asia, and the Channel Tunnel.

In Continental Europe, we must bear in mind that the canal network is very modern and extensive, and serves most major ports. It forms a major transport distributor in Europe, involving transits of considerable distances and covering a wide range of cargoes embracing general merchandise, bulk commodities and dangerous-classified products such as oil.

Moreover, the increasing acuteness of the energy situation is forcing countries to reduce their consumption of imported energy and develop lower energy-consuming modes of transport. This strongly favours the development of inland waterways where suitable conditions obtain.

A study by MDS Transport consultants embracing EU and non-EU countries published in 1998 reveals that barge transportation is the fastest growing transport mode quadrupling its market share from 2 per cent in 1982 to 8 per cent in 1996. Waterways conveyed over 2 million TEUs of the 23.9 million TEUs total European inland container flows in 1996. Modernization of the canal system in these countries permits an increase in the capacity of barges using the network and leads to an extension in services.

Rotterdam port is a focal point in the extensive network of inland waterway services and features strongly in the 'just in time' strategy adopted by the shippers who use it. The area is served by 30 terminals on the Rhine. Apart from the cost savings achieved through the large-scale barge operation, the additional logistics benefits are paramount. These include flexibility of services and the close proximity of the terminals to the shippers' premises.

The Rhine corridor between Rotterdam, Antwerp and on to Germany offers cheap and efficient container transport. In 1997 between 35 and 40 per cent of all containers moved out of Rotterdam, Antwerp and Amsterdam were transported by barge and the market share is growing. The barge network acts as a feeder service to the ports of Rotterdam, Antwerp and Amsterdam and is very economical. An example is the Container Terminal Nijmegen on the River Waal and a barge terminal at Born on the River Maas between Maastricht and Roermond. At Born catchment areas extend beyond the borders of South Lumburg and include container movements from the neighbouring industrial areas of Germany, Belgium and the more distant markets of Luxembourg. The containers are moved by barges in units of four operated by a push boat and generate an overall capacity of 360 TEUs.

A container movement which has grown considerably in the lower region of the Rhine is operated by Haeger & Schmidt, Haniel Reederei and Rhine-container. Each vessel has a capacity of 156 TEUs and the consortium operate 19 sailings per week between Rotterdam and Duisburg. The sailings run from Rotterdam and Antwerp to Nijmegen, Emmerich, Duisburg, Neuss, Stuizeberg, Düsseldorf, Cologne and Leverkusen.

An example of the most recent new waterway completion emerged in 1992 when the Rhine and Danube were finally joined by the new Rhine Main–Danube

(RMD) link canal. It will open up a 3500 km cheap inland waterways route between the North Sea and the Black Sea, and will serve nine east and west European countries. The RMD route runs through Holland and Germany to Mainz, and up the Main to Bamberg, the northern canal entrance. On the other side of the Franconian Jura, the canal joins the Danube at Kelheim. That river flows through Austria, clips the former Czechoslovakia and continues south through Hungary and Yugoslavia. Turning east again, it forms the border between Bulgaria and Romania before turning north to touch in Romania the southern tip of the CIS and finally empties itself into the Black Sea.

Inland waterways barge distribution acting as port feeder services operates in many developing and less developed countries. Such services are long established and examples are found in the markets of Africa, the subcontinent and the Far East. Examples are found too in the ports of Bangkok and Klang which permit overside loading thereby speeding up the turnround of vessels. They tend to be in the bulk and consumer unitized markets, and such business is tending to be transferred to the containerized network as the infrastructure is modernized and markets expand with modern methods of handling and distribution.

The UK canal system, in comparison with the Continental network, is very antiquated and no extensive modernization has taken place for many years. Undoubtedly a major reason for this is the competitive vulnerability of the network to road or rail – particularly the former. This applies not only to overall rates, but also to transit time. A significant factor overall is the time consuming and expensive process of transshipment both at the port and alongside the canal-situated destination warehouse. Moreover, few traders have warehouses situated on the canal network which again discourages use of the system. A further aspect is that the average transit in UK is 60-70 miles compared with up to 1000 miles or more in Europe.

3.3 International air transport

Air transport is one of the youngest forms of transport and undoubtedly continues to make a major contribution to the exploitation of world resources. At the moment air freight constitutes 1 per cent in volume and about 20–30 per cent in value terms of total world trade.

The development of civil aviation was particularly fostered during the Second World War which considerably aided the advancement of this mode of transport in technical terms. Initially, the passenger sector was developed, but from the mid-1950s air freight began rapid annual growth until 1973 when there was a significant escalation in fuel costs. Air freight rates were increased to offset the additional operator's cost and, coupled with the subsequent world trade recession, the annual growth rate of some airlines diminished. During the past few years major changes have emerged in the air freight industry, and by 1993 the global air freight market could be divided into three broad sectors: express, special commodities and traditional air cargo.

To examine the express market first, this is now dominated by integrators such as Fedex, TNT, United Parcels Service (UPS) and DHL. Hence the main role for most international air express markets is as carriers acting for the integrators or wholesalers. British Airways cargo, for example, has now developed a strong 'on board' courier network under the name 'Speedbird Courier'. Currently it serves 70 international routes and has some 124 couriers flying daily, serving 150 countries.

The 'Speedbird' service operates on the basis of a published timetable, detailing all the flights on which a Speedcourier travels. Space is sold to both retail and wholesaler courier companies, including the big four: Fedex, TNT, UPS and DHL. The courier service handles documents, parcels and express freight, operating from the airport of departure to the consignee's premises. Express freight includes computer diskettes, computer printouts, brochures, tapes, books, annual reports, etc. The rates are based on four zones, with each country being allocated a zone. The rate is inclusive of export processing, international carriage, import processing, international processing, customs clearance and delivery to city centres. The consignment is accompanied by the 'Speedbird' consignment note, completed by the shipper, and which usually avoids the additional provision of a pro-forma invoice. The consignment is monitored throughout its transit and confirmation and proof of delivery is provided.

Other airlines have tackled the express market, particularly Lufthansa and Japan Air Lines, which have up to a 25 per cent stake in the air express company DHL. The air express market within Europe is highly vulnerable to the surface courier services involving EuroTunnel Freight and neighbouring countries. Competition is keen on rates and transit times are guaranteed.

A further division is found in the international air freight services. This involves special commodities such as perishable products, live animals, project outsized cargoes and hazardous goods. This business is primarily orientated towards the traditional carriers, the airlines and freight forwarders.

The third sector is the traditional air cargo. This embraces the transportation of normal industrial and commercial shipments moving in parcel, container or pallet form. The integrators are already making substantial inroads into that market, forcing the airlines and forwarders to look at ways of improving their services. A large volume of this trade is represented by the consolidation market under agents' sponsorship. Attention will be directed to improve product quality. In particular, it must strive to develop an unmistakable performance profile through product enhancement of which improved information systems will be an integral part.

3.3.1 Advantages of air freight

(1) High speed and quick transits.
(2) Low risk of damage/pilferage with very competitive insurance rates.
(3) Simplified documentation system – one document, an air waybill, is used for throughout air freight transit and is interchangeable between IATA accredited airlines. The IATA air waybill is, therefore, acceptable on any IATA airline

permitting flexibility of through routeing with no transshipment documentation problems at airports en route.

(4) Common code of liability conditions to all IATA accredited airlines.

(5) Virtually eliminates packing cost. This is an important cost saving attributed to air freight and the shipper may find it worthwhile to engage professional packaging services to ensure the merchandise has the correct packing specification for this mode of transport. Significant packaging cost savings can be realized to offset the higher air freight rate compared with surface transport.

(6) Ideal for palletized consignments. A substantial volume of merchandise is now moving on pallets which aids handling, reduces packing needs, facilitates stowage and lessens the risk of damage/pilferage. Again for the shipper new to the export business, it may prove worthwhile to establish whether it would be advantageous to have the merchandise palletized. Many such palletized consignments are using the shrink-wrap packaging technique (p. 152).

(7) Quick transit reduces the amount of capital tied up in transit. This facilitates prompt financial settlement of individual consignments thereby aiding the exporter's cash flow situation. On this point much depends, of course, on the export sale contract terms of delivery.

(8) Quick, reliable transit eliminates the need for extensive warehouse storage accommodation provided by the importer, reduces the risks of stockpiling, that is, obsolescence, deterioration, and the capital cost tied up in warehouse/stock provision. Moreover, it enables the importer to replenish his stock quickly, such as when demand for a commodity has become exhausted more rapidly than forecast.

(9) Ideal for a wide variety of consumer-type cargoes, particularly consignments up to 1500–2000 kg. In addition, the average consignment size is increasing as larger air freighters are introduced (p. 51).

(10) The existing very extensive international air freight network continues to expand which aids its development and increases its share of the international trade market. This in turn encourages new markets to the air freight sector thereby aiding international trade development. For example, in some large countries major car manufacturers guarantee a replacement spares service through the medium of air freight, which in itself has a status symbol and thereby aids the exporter's sales. Likewise air freight services generate new markets to the exporter such as day-old chicks being transported 3000 miles which obviously would not be possible or practicable by sea transport.

(11) Parity obtains on rates on IATA scheduled international services and competition exists only on service quality. This, in the long-term, benefits the shipper as no rate wars, which would be detrimental to the service and trade, arise.

(12) Services are reliable and to a high quality.

(13) Major airports worldwide – compared with major seaports – tend to be situated in the centre of commercial/industrial areas. In consequence the airport is, in many situations, more closely situated to the industrial/commercial market, giving it a competitive advantage in terms of lower collection/distribution cost.

(14)   Air freight facilitates the 'just-in-time' concept, with the air freight distributor forming the link between the central warehouse or manufacturing plant and the 'point of sale'. Goods are simply replenished as they are sold at the importer's premises. Examples are fashionable goods and perishable products.

(15)   The air freight network worldwide is more extensive and offers more frequent flights than the maritime services.

(16)   The 'value added benefit' found in fast transits and service frequency is profound. For example, the spares replacement market serving factory plant or the computer software and hardware industries are good examples. The sooner the goods arrive, the greater is the financial benefit to the importer.

(17)   Services are continuously being improved and new ones developed through the 'combined transport operation' concept. An example is the sea–air hubs which are slowly being developed on a global basis. A comparison of sea–air services in various hubs is found in Table 3.1. The transfer hub is totally reliant on whether the operation can offer a relatively faster transit time and lower transportation cost. In marketing the sea–air product via multi-modal services, a comprehensive sailing programme covering all possible origins and destinations on a monthly basis is required. A 'hot box' arrangement is essential in which sea–air containers on transfer hubs have priority of discharge otherwise containers are delayed. Overall, it is a multi-modal logistics operation.

TABLE 3.1 Comparison of sea–air services in various major transfer hubs

Transfer hub	Cargo origin	Destination	Total transit time
UAE	Hong Kong	Europe	15–16 days
Dubai/Sharjah	Taipei	Europe	14–15 days
Abu Dhabi	Singapore	Europe	8–9 days
	India	Europe	7–8 days
Khor Fakkan			2 days less
West Coast (Seattle/Vancouver)	Hong Kong	Europe	15–16 days
	Taipei	Europe	14–15 days
	Japan	Europe	11–12 days
	Korea	Europe	14–15 days
	China (North)	Europe	17–18 days
Korea (Seoul)	China (North)	Europe/USA	6–7 days
West Coast (Los Angeles)	Taipei	America	15–17 days
	Korea		14–16 days
	Japan		13-15 days
Russia (Vostochny)	China (Shanghai)	Europe	14-15 days

(18) Air freight capacity is continuously increasing as the latest generation of aircraft emerge. Air freighters are now becoming more common. Overall, airline operation costs are being reduced.

(19) New airports continue to be introduced globally. Hong Kong, Malaysia, Kuala Lumpur and Japan, for example. All are hub airports which offer feeder air freight services within the region.

(20) An example of the growing development of the cargo village is the expansion plan announced in 1998 to provide a new 200 000 tonne capacity cargo village at Oman's Seeb International Airport in the Middle East. The long-term plan is to facilitate the speedy transfer of freight from Muscat's port Mina Sultan Qaboos to Seeb International.

3.3.2 Disadvantages of air freight

(1) Limited capacity of air freighter and overall dimensions of acceptable cargo together with weight restrictions.

(2) Very high operating expenses and initial cost of aircraft when related to overall capacity – average capacity is in the region of 20 000–25 000 kg. It is for the latter reason that many air freighters are converted passenger aircraft. Moreover, some 80 per cent of air freight is conveyed on passenger scheduled services.

(3) The service is vulnerable to disruption by the weather, for example fog and ice, particularly at airports with less modern traffic control equipment.

(4) Airline operation today is very sophisticated in all areas including air freight. It is vulnerable to rates and transit time competition in short hauls by surface transport, due to the high airport cost and landing fees which inflate terminal costs. Consequently, most major operators with air freight from London for Paris and Brussels rely on surface distribution which is more economical in cost and also because the smaller aircraft operating the short hauls do not have capacity to carry the larger, more economical, pallet loads.

It must be recognized that an increasing volume of cargo is now conveyed on air freight charter flights and this latter market is tending to expand quite rapidly. Air freight is a growing market and the trend towards developing larger capacity air freighters will continue to meet such demand and facilitate optimum performance and operation. It is particularly ideal for the small exporter and this form of international distribution should be continuously borne in mind by the discerning shipper.

An interesting development emerged in the early 1990s with the Luxembourg-based carrier Cargolux Airlines International. It was the first airline to take delivery of the Boeing 747-400 freighters and by 1994 it had three in operation. It has a payload of up to 110 tonnes as recorded on a flight from Seattle to Luxembourg, whilst on the longer haul Luxembourg to Hong Kong it was 90 tonnes.

Moreover the role of the freight forwarder IATA agent in air freight development has now become extremely important. It involves the provision of a consolidated consignment. Under such arrangements, the freight forwarder markets the service and embraces in the tariff structure not only the air freight tariff, but also the collection and delivery charges and other ancillary rates such as documentation, customs clearance and so on. The freight forwarder would have a contract with the airline guaranteeing a specified cube space on a specified flight on a regular basis for which an overall freight rate is charged by the airline to the freight forwarders. In such circumstances, the freight forwarder is able to quote very competitive composite rates, whilst the airline operator no longer becomes involved in direct marketing and selling the service. The latter development has enabled many airline operators to achieve substantial labour cost savings. It has resulted in a market expansion on some airline routes through the freight forwarder offering more competitive composite rates coupled with a guaranteed service.

The growth of the international air freight market has been spectacular in recent years with an 8 per cent rise in 1996 followed by 11 per cent in 1997, involving a total of 15 million tonnes. This trend is likely to continue and is being driven by a more logistic internationally focused market. Many other factors contribute to this continuing growth, including the expansion of the integrator market and courier service, the development of Cargo Website and the new EDIFACT message to replicate the Cargo IMP FSA and FWB messages which pass information between airlines and freight forwarders and form an integral part of the EDI implementation programme.

A further factor is the continuing development of new airports as found in the Far East in Hong Kong and Japan together with the modernization and expansion of existing ones. An example of the latest high tech air freight terminal is the British Airways freight terminal found at London Heathrow which was opened in January 1999 and is a market leader in high tech provision.

Another example of a modern air freight terminal is located in Frankfurt. It is the largest air freight transshipment site in Europe and is operated by Lufthansa. It has a $25\,780\ \mathrm{m}^2$ freight transshipment hall which is linked to various warehouses of modular design. It handles 700 000 tonnes annually and processes 1900 tonnes daily, involving 6000 shipments. The heart of the cargo centre is the central monitoring station, where various computer systems control and monitor the flow of freight within the terminal. A conveyor system transports the pallets and stores them in the highbay warehouse while a box system transports medium-sized shipments to the box warehouse in special boxes. A mini-shipment system controls the storing of the small shipments. From the central control station, the storing and removal of freight from storage is controlled and monitored via computer-controlled conveyor tracks and automatically operated stacker cranes. The physical flow of freight is accompanied by the electronic flow of information. The systems communicate with one another and exchange data, enabling the retrieval of warehouse and air waybill data at any time. A computer controlled warehouse check is conducted daily. Furthermore, the direct link to the customs computer system guarantees that shipments cross borders quickly and without hitch.

A central master data processing system handles the processing of all freight data 24 hours a day. The structural centre of the Lufthansa Cargo Centre is the enormous freight transshipment hall. Here the containers and pallets are stacked and removed and the mixed cargo processed; the freight shipments are sorted into large, medium-sized and small shipments and then forwarded to the appropriate warehouses via automatically controlled conveyor systems. Large shipments are taken to the highbay warehouse, the capacity of which was more than doubled in the second stage of construction. In the six aisles of the five or nine storey highbay warehouse, special stacker cranes store items in and remove items from over 2000 storing places. Medium-sized shipments are placed in boxes and stored in the two-storey box highbay warehouse with its over 4800 storing places. In the mini-shipment system, small shipments are conveyed and distributed by computer control, then stored manually by destination in the handracking warehouse which holds more than 10 000 small shipments.

The reliable 'warehouse system' is employed in the box and pallet highbay warehouse, i.e. the individual storing places in use are merely placed in the computer memory as they are unimportant for the actual processing of the shipments; a computer-controlled warehouse check is conducted for added security. The rapid loading and unloading of aircraft, the transshipment from one Lufthansa jet to another, is achieved by using the latest loading devices such as standardized pallets and containers. Work alongside and in the aircraft is monitored using the Lufthansa ramp agent's precise loading diagram. Loading and unloading is conducted with time-saving mechanical loading systems, including highloaders and electrically driven conveyors.

Transit freight passes through Frankfurt in six to ten hours; direct transshipment of complete load units at the freight yard is handled in two hours, and the high-performance satellite near the passenger terminal can be handled in one to six hours. Here scheduled 'quick transfers', the transshipment of very urgent shipments, takes one hour. Not only are the direct transshipment of entire load units and quick transfers handled here, but also all airmail transshipments.

Today the air freight operator tends to formulate a global approach to the market using high tech means, involving the most advanced satellite and computer links available. An example of such a strategy is Thai Airlines: its operation is based on direct flights or via a worldwide system of cargo hubs covering different regions and customer priorities. Bangkok is the hub for Asia serving 46 destinations; Paris is the European hub which is linked to direct onward transfer by road to key industrial centres – it also serves 12 European destinations on direct flights; and finally, Seattle is the North American hub with three direct destinations. Australasia has no hub, but relies on seven direct destinations. Onward connections with the hubs in Paris and Seattle are quick and may involve either air or surface transport. Additionally, to supplement the Thai network, it has inter-line service and cooperation agreement with over 100 airlines. Computerized cargo control is exercised through ORCHIDS, the online Revenue Cargo Handling and Information Distribution System.

3.4 International road transport

The road vehicle is a low capacity but very versatile unit of transport which is most flexible in its operation. Since the early 1970s, the international road haulier has become increasingly dominant in the UK/Continental trade with some services extending to Asia and the Middle East. Road haulage has the following features.

(1) One of its most significant advantages is the road vehicle distributive ability. Overall it can offer a door-to-door service without intermediate handling.

(2) No customs examination arises in transit countries provided the haulier is affiliated to TIR as the cargo passes under bond when the unit is passing through one of their countries. Insofar as transit countries within EU are concerned, no customs examination arises.

(3) It is very flexible in operation which is particularly useful when circumstances demand a change in routeing through road works, a blockage or disrupted shipping services.

(4) It is very competitive within certain distance bands compared with air freight, both in terms of transit times and rates.

(5) Documentation is simple as, under CMR, a through consignment note is operative with a common code of liability conditions.

(6) The service tends to be reliable and to a high standard. Delays usually only occur when bad weather prevails or due to some other exceptional circumstances.

(7) The TIR vehicle may be 12.20 m (trailer) or 15.50 m (articulated vehicle) with an overall gross weight capacity of 42 tonnes (44 tonnes in Continental Europe). Hence, initial cost is low when compared to an air freighter. However, limited capacity imposes certain weight and dimensional restrictions on the traffic which can be carried.

(8) It is ideal for general merchandise and selective cargo in bulk in small quantities conveyed in a specialized road vehicle. The service is renowned for its groupage flow under a freight forwarder's sponsorship and, therefore, ideal for the small exporter. An increasing number of shippers are now using their own vehicles to distribute their own goods.

(9) Packing costs are less when compared with conventional shipping (break-bulk cargo) services.

(10) The driver accompanies the vehicle throughout the road transit thereby exercising personal supervision and reducing the risk of damage and pilfering. Accordingly, the operator can control his vehicle at all times as the driver usually 'reports in' to his company control office at staged points en route.

(11) A wide range of routes and types of service exist between the UK and the Continent. Services are frequent and many operators have a European operation which is highly sophisticated. An example is DANZAS, a global freight forwarder which has daily trailer scheduled services between 13 countries in Western Europe; the range is between 24–48 hours door-to-door, consignor and consignee or factory-to-factory schedules. Warehouse distribution centres in key industrial and commercial areas are located in each of the countries.

A wide-range of trailer units are used in the European road distribution network, usually operating warehouse-to-warehouse or factory-to-factory schedules; details are given in Table 3.2.

TABLE 3.2 Trailer units in use in European road haulage

Name	Description
Refrigerated semi-trailer	Triaxle 38–40 tonne operation – multi-compartment/dual temperature
Tail lift refrigerated semi-trailer	Triaxle 38–40 tonne operation – standard refrigeration fitted with roller shutter doors and 1500 kg tail lift
Dry freight van	Triaxle 38–40 tonne 24 or 26 pallet capacity
Step frame van	Triaxle 38–40 tonne – racking for garment carrying
Curtainsider	Triaxle 38–40 tonne – 24 or 26 pallet capacity, high-tension load restraining curtains and variety of optional cargo control systems
Insulated curtainsider	Triaxle 38–40 tonne – 24 or 26 pallet capacity, designed to carry chilled produce at maximum thermal efficiency
Tilt semi-trailer	Triaxle 38–40 tonne – 24 or 26 pallet capacity, four or five dropsides per side, sliding roof
Step frame tilt semi-trailer	Triaxle 38–40 tonne – 24 or 26 pallet capacity, three dropsides on lower deck and two on upper deck
Bulk tipping semi-trailer	Triaxle 38 tonne with 42–55 cubic yard capacity – hinged rear tailgate and grain hatch
Bulk liquid tanker	Triaxle 38–40 tonnes – foodstuffs, chemicals, spirits
Platform skeletal	Triaxle 38–40 tonnes – detachable headboard
Platform semi-trailer	Triaxle 38–40 tonnes – option for brick crane
Extendable flat platform	Triaxle 38–40 tonnes – designed to convey overlength indivisible loads. Extends between 40 ft (12.20 m) and 60 ft (18.30 m).
24 ft (7.20 m) skeletal	Two axle 32 tonne, conveyance 1 TEU.
Step frame skeletal	Triaxle 38–40 tonnes – designed to convey 1 TEU tank container.
40 ft (12.19 m) skeletal	Triaxle 38–40 tonnes, conveyance 2 TEUs.
Extendable semi-low loader	Broshuis semi-low loader – 27 ft (8.50 m) well extends to 45 ft (13.50 m) – overall 45 tonne gross combination weight, option rear steer.
Dual-purpose coil carrier	Triaxle 38–40 tonne – conveyance steel coils, option curtainsided.

(12) The trailer service is very flexible and this helps to develop business. In many situations, it can be customized to meet the shipper's needs aiding cost efficiency and improving substantially the quality of service.

During the past 20 years, roll on-roll off traffic between the UK and the Continent has developed very substantially under CMR/TIR conditions conveyed on vehicular ferries. The freight forwarder has featured greatly in this development offering groupage services to many countries under scheduled services usually working in correspondence with a Continental-based freight forwarder. Such services have developed much faster than originally envisaged and in some cases to the detriment of air freight, and container services in the UK/Continental trade. In some countries, the environmental lobby has slowed down the expansion of the European trailer network and some Continental countries restrict the times/periods/routes over which such traffic may be conveyed. A problem for the road operator is to obtain balanced working, that is, a full profitable load in each direction.

The trailer operation is ideal for a small exporter and it is worth making an enquiry to a freight forwarder for a particular stream of international consumer type traffic, insofar as rates, transit times, routeing, schedules, etc. are concerned (p. 417).

As we progress into the twenty-first century, the pattern of the European truck network will change to meet market conditions. The Channel-Tunnel (pp. 61–2) has resulted in many hauliers centralizing their services in the two portals. Many of the larger hauliers tend to dispatch their trailers unaccompanied on the Eurotunnel freight trains and thereby improve the productivity of the drivers who work to and from the portals.

The EC Single Market will further stimulate trade and greater competition will result. Undoubtedly, more emphasis will be placed on cost efficiency in the European distribution strategy, with quicker schedules and development of the 'just-in-time' concept by the larger shippers. An increasing number of the larger industrial companies will be reviewing their European distribution strategy and relocating their distribution and warehouse centres closer to their markets, thereby reducing haulage and distribution costs. Key distribution centre areas could be northern France near Dunkerque, the Iberian peninsula, southern Germany and northern Italy.

The liberalization of the former communist countries (COMECON) in central and Eastern Europe has produced new markets. In addition, today, there is a greater emphasis on a logistic driven pan-European distribution network with no national frontiers. Expansion will be further stimulated as the Czech Republic, Hungary, Poland and Slovakia seek membership of the EU.

The EU strategy towards the road haulage market, however, is not favourable as it is not an environmentally friendly mode of transport. Nevertheless, against such a background, a survey by MDS Transmodal confirmed that road transport remains the dominant transport mode growing from 70 per cent in 1982 to 74 per cent in 1996 throughout both EU and non-EU countries. (see pp. 428–36 and 441–4).

Our evaluation of international road transport would not be complete without stressing that the European trailer network could be developed in other parts of the world. Trucking between Canada–USA and USA–Mexico is firmly established and will grow under NAFTA (p. 10). It could also be developed more extensively in the area of South East Asia in the next decade. This would depend on the scale and pace of infrastructure development and the provision of adequate Ro-Ro services. Rail services in this region are gradually being improved and developed but primarily on the basis of existing routes, with no new routes being built. The tendency is to develop motorway networks between major industrial and commercial centres involving major ports and places of tourism. The topographical features of the region present problems in developing the transport infrastructure. A major factor will be the development of trade amongst South East Asian countries.

The first ten years of the new century will witness continuous expansion of the international road transport service as its flexibility and cost factors remain dominant factors among the selection criteria of transport modes. This will be evident in all developed and developing markets.

3.5 International rail transport

In the UK, the railways developed in the 1850s in an era of steam traction. Today's modern railway system is a high-capacity form of transport operating on a disciplined, controlled, reliable, and exclusive artificial way route. It is capable of attaining relatively high speeds and is most economical under the complete train load concept as distinct from the individual wagon load involving frequent marshalling.

International rail distribution in Europe has been stimulated by the EuroTunnel. It has highlighted the social and economic benefits of offering trans-European rail freight services in three sectors: the wagon or train load movement; the inter-modal system relying on rail for the main leg, and road for the feeder units; and finally maritime containers. The question posed is whether rail freight and combined rail/road transport will be viable for a wide range of goods in addition to the former traditional bulk traffics. Crucial factors will include the development of efficient transshipment operations and good consignment control capabilities. In fact, good information technology systems – increasingly including EDI – are already playing an important role in general distribution service development. The EU has become increasingly conscious of the need to develop a trans-European rail network to aid economic development.

Historically, most European road and rail infrastructure was built to serve mainly, if not solely, national interest. Formation of the EU and its subsequent growth from six to 15 member states increased the importance of the international transport network dimension; the prospect of eastward enlargement of the EU has further strengthened it. Moreover, most transport infrastructure was financed from taxation on a nationally focused basis with little regard to the need to provide a fully integrated trans-European transport network.

The growth of intra-EU trade was accompanied by an increase in congestion on major international routes resulting in bottlenecks. Subsequently, the single European Act 1986 and the emergence of the Single Market in 1992 throughout 15 states presented new opportunities and also new problems. Ultimately, the Maastricht Treaty accepted the earlier published guidelines produced by the European Commission. This was on the basis of EU governments calling for the development and inter-connection of trans-European networks including 'the most efficient surface communications links'. In late 1994 the EU summit in Essen adopted 14 priority projects, spread both geographically and across all transport modes (see Table 3.3).

This programme demonstrates the EU commitment to an integrated transport network so essential in the economic development of a Single Market. A further ten projects to feature in the next phase have been formulated including new airports at Athens and Berlin; 37 combined transport projects in Germany, Italy, Belgium and

TABLE 3.3 TENS (Trans-European Network): Priority Projects

Project	Distance	Cost
Oresund Denmark–Sweden fixed road/rail link	52.5 km	ecu4.148bn (£2.75bn)
Nordic triangle	1800 km	ecu10.070bn (£6.7bn)
Ireland–United Kingdom–Benelux road link	1530 km	ecu3.629bn (£2.4bn)
United Kingdom West Coast main railway line	850 km	ecu3bn (£1.99bn)
Rail link Cork–Dublin–Belfast–Larne–Stranraer	502 km	ecu357m (£235m)
Rail freight/combined transport Betuwe line Rotterdam–Dutch/German border	160 km	ecu4.094bn (£2.7bn)
High speed/combined transport rail line Lyon–Turin–Milan–Venice–Trieste	734 km	ecu18.260bn (£12bn)
High speed/combined transport rail line Berlin–Munich–Brenner–Verona	958 km	ecu15.102bn (£10bn)
Pathe and Via Egnatia motorways in Greece to Bulgarian/Turkish borders	1580 km	ecu9.242bn (£6.1bn)
LisbonValladolid (Portugal–Spain) motorway	details not yet finalized	
High speed rail line London/Paris–Brussels–Cologne/Amsterdam	1176 km	ecu17.232bn (£11.5bn)
High speed rail line Madrid–Barcelona–Perpignan–Montpellier	1601 km	ecu14.072bn (£9.3bn)
High speed rail line Paris–Metz–Strasbourg–Karlsruhe	551 km	ecu4.777bn (£3.1bn)
Malpensa airport Milan		ecu1.047bn (£700m)

List approved by EU Essen Summit, December 1994

Portugal; a high speed rail/combined transport Danube Axis Munich/Nuremberg–Vienna–Budapest; a high speed rail in Denmark; a Trans-Appenine Bologna–Florence highway and two motorway projects in France and Portugal–Spain.

Details of the general cargo and steel rail wagons operating on the Anglo-Continental network are given in Table 3.4.

An example of the use of purpose-built wagons operating in train load formation is the movement of cars from factory to destination rail-head. This includes Amsterdam, Cologne, Brussels, Lille, Paris, Basle, Munich, Turin, Port Bout and Hendaye. STVA is the leading European rail transporter.

The second division is the inter-modal system involving rail and road. This embraces the swap-body concept and the development of the inter-modal system providing a door-to-door service; it involves road, rail and sea. Overall, this is a growth market as more dedicated services and facilities are introduced. A description of a number of swap-bodies is given in Table 3.5. All are suitable for road/rail/sea movement and transshipment by lift truck and top loading crane. The swap-bodies can also be mounted/demounted on/off draw bars and semi-trailers giving a quick turnaround time; most swap-bodies can be stocked up to three high.

TABLE 3.4 Wagons operating on the European rail network

Wagon type	Description
Covered freight/wagon – general cargo	Two axles – capacity 28 000 kg, two sliding doors per wagon side, capacity 34 Euro-pallets; ideal for high-volume palletized or break bulk goods
Covered freight wagon – general cargo	Bogie – capacity 33 000 kg, three sliding doors per wagon side, capacity 48 Euro or 38 industrial pallets; ideal for heavy or high-volume palletized or break bulk goods, each door gains access to one-third of area
Covered freight wagon – general cargo	Bogie – capacity 52 000 kg, two sliding doors per wagon side; provides wider access to the load area, capacity 51 Euro or 40 industrial pallets; ideal for heavy or high-volume palletized or break bulk goods
Covered freight wagon	Bogie – capacity 60 500 kg, five wells set into wagon floor can accommodate steel coils; for transport of steel sheets, plates and other heavy goods, wells covered by integral drop flaps to give completely flat loading surface
Covered freight wagon	Bogie – capacity 6500 kg, five wells set into wagon floor for transport of steel coils

TABLE 3.5 Swap-bodies

Swap-body type	Distribution
Steel swap-body (DTY van)	Corrugated steel with grappler pockets with roller rear door and/or side door and mounted on four adjustable legs. It has a payload of 13 680 kg, length 7.15 m, width 2.5 m and height 2.67–2.75 m. Also available in lengths of 7.45 m and 7.82 m and 3 m high
Full-side access swap-body	Corrugated steel with grappler pockets with full width or 2.50 m side doors and mounted on four adjustable legs. It has a payload of 12 620 kg, length 7.15 m, width 2.5 m and height of 2.67–2.75 m. Also available in lengths of 7.45 m and 7.82 m and 3 m high
Refrigerated swap-body	Pallet wide ATP/FRC insulated with grappler protection plates – refrigeration unit and mounted on four adjustable legs. It has a payload of 12 930 kg, length 7.15 m and width 2.6 m. Also available in lengths of 7.45 m, 7.82 m and 13.6 m
Curtainsiders access swap-body	Steel construction with end door of ply metal construction and one piece aluminium roof and curtains running each side throughout its length. It is mounted on four adjustable legs. It has a payload of 16 000 kg, length 7.15 m, width 2.480 m, height 2.36/2.44/2.69 m and side opening length 6.86 m. Also available in 7.45 m and 7.820 m length. Ideal for automotive and drinks industries

Swap-bodies provide complete flexibility for distribution by rail, road and inland waterway. The units can be handled at existing container and rail terminals involving a lift on/lift off crane operation, whilst the truck driver can self-load/unload the unit using the vehicle's own hydraulic air system at the shipper's premises. The flexibility of self-loading/unloading avoids the need for expensive mechanical handling at pick-up points. Moreover, driver and vehicle productivity is improved as they do not have to stand by and wait whilst goods are loaded or unloaded, but simply drop off the swap-body and collect it again later when it is ready.

A further example of combined transport operation is the piggyback system. This involves rail conveying the road trailer throughout the major part of the transit and the road vehicle collecting and delivering the goods. The trailer is either driven on and off the rail wagon or may be loaded/unloaded by a lift on/lift off crane operation.

In the longer term, it is envisaged that the European market will grow in such a way that international road haulier/freight forwarders will service 'block train movements' of hauliers' vehicles including dismountable bodies in purpose-built wagons. Hence rail will convey the trailers over the greater part of the total journey. Such services will operate between key centres in Europe.

The final category is the movement of maritime ISO containers to and from the seaports. This may involve an international movement between the major ports such as Felixstowe, Liverpool, London, Southampton and the 40 purpose-built terminals including eight situated at ports. The trains are run in fixed formation between terminals to a prescribed timetable in the same way as a passenger train. The wagons are tailor-made to carry only containers. The transfer from road to rail (or ship) is carried out at specially built terminals and it is smooth, safe and fast. The method of transfer is by means of 'portal'-type cranes which can operate over the whole length of the specially laid rail sidings. Each of the rail-served container bases has a direct distribution facility which eliminates intermediate warehousing. This rail operation has been established for over 25 years and is very reliable and cost effective. Individual major container/shipowners have contracts with Freight Liner Ltd for the charter of complete trains on a regular basis. This is completely integrated with the sailing schedules and container base operation – the latter managed by an international consortium of international trade interested parties.

The opening of the Channel Tunnel railway has provided a potential market for the international containerized rail movement between major container ports such as Rotterdam, Antwerp, Hamburg, Dunkerque, Cherbourg, Zeebrugge and the UK container bases; Rotterdam could become a major distribution point.

The movement of containers by train is very much a growth movement in all parts of the world. Overall, it is quicker and cheaper compared to road, subject to movement being in complete train formation on a regular scheduled basis and thereby attaining good infrastructure utilization.

In Malaysia, Port Klang is served by an inland container base at Ipoh. It is called a 'dry port' and has played a major role in developing the Malaysian economy and Port Klang (p. 85).

Another example is the movement of rail-borne containers from the west to east coasts of North America, plus of course the hinterland market distribution. An example is the Port of Seattle which has six container trains daily stacked two high in 'low-loader' railway wagons with a capacity of 280 TEUs. Transit time to Chicago is 62 hours, and to New York five days. Similar services operate from the ports of Oakland, Los Angeles and Long Beach, including direct to the east coast and New York. Such a container movement is called a 'land-bridge' with much of the traffic originating in Japan, Singapore and Hong Kong. It has resulted in a decline of the North American east coast ports and a speeding up of container transits, from the Far East and Europe, with lower freight rates. Undoubtedly, the rail container movement will grow in the next decade, especially in the EC.

3.6 EuroTunnel

In 1994 the Channel Tunnel was opened, linking the British Rail network with the European rail system which extends to 150 000 route miles. Ultimately, it will have a profound impact on the pattern and development of freight distribution between the UK and Europe, with a higher volume of rail-borne movement currently moving in the road trailer network. Moreover, the project has resulted in a severe curtailment or closure of nearby shipping routes operating from Newhaven to Sheerness seaboard.

Furthermore, major container operators are likely to review their pre-Channel Tunnel sailing schedules with a view to having fewer European ports of call and centralizing their services on one or two major ports, relying more on rail as the distributor/feeder. The ports of Rotterdam, Antwerp, Hamburg, Dunkerque and Cherbourg could feature in this hub and spoke strategy.

Many factors are involved, including the development of shippers' business in the Single Market with no trade/customs barriers; however, the shipper will be looking at the most cost-effective distribution system with an emphasis on reliability, cost, frequency, quality of service, technology and overall transit time. The issue has become one which is logistically driven. A fundamental point is that rail transport with modern technology and volume business attaining good infrastructure utilization is quicker and cheaper than sea transport. A salient feature will also be the targeting by shippers at their distribution centre. Major seaports, their infrastructure and environs are very attractive and cost effective.

The Euro-Tunnel is a 31-mile subterranean rail tunnel between Folkestone (UK) and Fréthun near Calais (France). It is built below the seabed in the English Channel and comprises of three tunnels – two of which are 7.6 m diameter to convey trains, and one of 3.3 m which is a service tunnel. Terminals with road and rail access are provided at both portals (Ashford and Calais).

Two types of trains use the tunnel. Cars and coaches at the portals drive onto a special shuttle train service. Cars use double-decker wagons and coaches single-deckers. Passengers stay with their vehicles or stroll around the train. Road haulage vehicles drive on to a separate single-decker shuttle train service. The other type of train is the through international service involving passengers, freight wagons and maritime containers. Such services are operated by the BR/SNCF rail personnel linking key UK and Continental destinations situated in industrial and commercial centres.

Ultimately it is planned to operate express passenger services from Birmingham, Manchester, York and Glasgow to European destinations such as Brussels, Cologne, Paris, Amsterdam and other major European cities. Initially, the bulk of the services will be between London (Waterloo) and Paris/Brussels. EuroTunnel has had a severe impact on the air passenger short-haul business between London/Paris and Brussels.

The freight train services convey through Anglo Continental RIV freight wagons involving cars, steel and general merchandise. However, at the moment the bulk of the freight business is found in the inter-modal market involving swap-bodies, containers and trailers which were previously carried on the cross-channel ferries. All the freight services through the tunnel are operated by EuroTunnel Freight. Dedicated through freight wagon services operating inter-modal business, involving swap-bodies, containers and trailers will operate from the eight UK freight terminals to Basle, Perpignan, Milan, Stuttgart, Bordeaux, Vienna, Mannheim and Munich; overall, 120 European destinations are involved. The services will be dedicated, thereby guaranteeing transit times, and modern technology will be used to monitor each cargo wagon consignment. Details of the transit times are given in Table 3.6 Additionally, there are fully customerized trains involving car transporters, bulk commodities and foodstuffs.

The other rail freight market through the Channel Tunnel is the movement of maritime ISO containers to and from UK container bases and major European ports such as Rotterdam, Zeebrugge, Antwerp and Dunkerque. This traffic will eliminate the reliance on the existing shipping feeder services and/or result in major container operators having fewer ports of call on their European schedules (pp. 63–81).

Overall, some 50 per cent of all the trains passing through the tunnel are through services involving BR/SNCF/SNCB. The project was built by EuroTunnel, an Anglo-French company at a cost of $6000 million. Undoubtedly, exporters must consider the EuroTunnel very strongly in their planning of a European distribution network.

TABLE 3.6 EuroTunnel transit times

UK Terminal	Destination	Transit time (hours)
Glasgow (Mossend)	Basle	27
Cleveland (Wilton)	Perpignan	33
Manchester (Trafford Park)	Milan	32
Liverpool (Freeport)	Stuttgart	22
Wakefield (Port Wakefield)	Bordeaux	22
Birmingham (Landor Street)	Vienna	31
Cardiff (Pangam)	Mannheim	18
London (Willesden/Stratford)	Munich	24

4

■ □ ▨ ■ 4

Characteristics of international transport modes: 2

4.1 Containerization

Containerization is a method of distributing merchandise in a unitized form thereby permitting an inter-modal transport system to be evolved providing a possible combination of rail, road, canal and maritime transport. The system is long established and was in being at the turn of the century, albeit in a somewhat modified form to that which exists today. It became particularly evident in the North American coastal trade in the 1930s when the vessels were called 'Van ships'. Today, we have the sixth generation of container ships, of 8000 TEUs, in service, operated by the Maersk line. It is likely the 8000 TEU ship, which costs around US$120 million, will dominate the Europe–Asia trade routes by 2010 as the benefits of containerization become more attractive in a large number of countries, thereby aiding the rising living standards and facilitating trade expansion.

There is no doubt that the expansion of containerization will continue beyond the millennium. By the year 2005 containerized cargo will account for some 60 per cent of all cargo moved by sea. In 1990 it was 40 per cent. The growth is emerging from two sectors: (a) the transfer from the bulk cargo division, particularly the reefer and fruit carriers and (b) organically, as the benefits of containerization through multi-modalism and logistic focus accelerate trade development.

An example of continuing growth is found in China which plans to build 16 coastal container terminals linked to the interior by dedicated rail shuttles. A further example is the growth of global transshipment. This is entirely driven by the hub and spoke system. Under this system the largest hub ports like Singapore, Hong Kong and Rotterdam rely on smaller spoke ports to feed containers into the mega-container service. An analysis of the global transshipment growth 1995–2005 is found in Table 4.1.

The massive growth in world container trade in the next eight years will require investment in ports and terminals of up to US$29 billion. This involves the provision of an extra 100 million TEU handling capacity by 2005 – a 60 per cent increase in global container activity requiring an extra 200 terminals to be built involving the continuing expansion of the hub and spoke system.

TABLE 4.1 Forecast global transhipment by region ('000 TEU port of handling)

	1995	1996	1997	1998	1999	2000	2005
N. Europe	5 238	5 649	5 967	6 263	6 556	6 873	9 301
S. Europe	2 970	3 654	4 306	4 910	5 478	6 038	8 469
Middle East	2 235	2 421	2 613	2 976	3 480	4 050	5 787
S. Asia	703	974	994	1 019	1 029	1 076	2 147
SE Asia	9 455	10 615	11 680	12 958	14 353	15 804	24 325
Far East	7 724	8 288	8 865	9 522	10 171	10 809	14 048
N. America	1 604	1 672	1 699	1 707	1 713	1 742	2 035
Carib/C. America	781	982	1 355	1 755	2 092	2 405	3 181
S. America	89	103	115	213	365	557	2 202
Oceania	81	88	95	102	109	117	162
Africa	1 177	1 216	1 286	1 382	1 474	1 565	1 988
World Total	31 886	35 471	38 975	42 827	46 820	51 034	73 645

Note: Eastern Europe assumed to develop no meaningful transhipment activity.

Source: Drewry Shipping Consultants

The growth of containerization is further stimulated by the accelerating expansion of the integration of containerized shipping movement with either air freight or a rail land-bridge. An example of the land-bridge is the North American double-stack container trains between the west and east coast ports (p. 70), and Dubai and Singapore (p. 93) offer an example of the air freight bridge to Europe involving cargoes from the Far East. Furthermore, the development of the high-cube container market continues to expand to meet the growing business needs of the high-cube low-weight ratio cargoes such as garments, foodstuffs and light machinery especially those goods originating from the Far East. This involves containers of 13.75 m (45 ft), 14.65 m (48 ft) and 16.20 m (53 ft) length and 2.9 m (9 ft 6 in) in height (p. 71).

Details of the 29 major container ports are given in Table 4.2 and it is significant that five of the top six are located in the Far East.

A further development of containerization is the feasibility of design vessels of 5000 TEUs to transit the Panama Canal which currently has a limitation – caused by a restriction on vessel width – of 4600 TEUs. This would considerably increase the productivity of routing more container ships through the Panama Canal.

Details are given in Table 4.3 of the top 20 container lines which represent about 48 per cent – 2.6m TEU – of world available capacity in 1997 and this figure will grow beyond 50 per cent through mergers and acquisitions as we pass the millennium.

Undoubtedly, long-term containerization will be virtually the only method of general merchandise distribution in major deep-sea trades, and already some 90 per cent of such trades are containerized. These developments have heralded a new era in international trade distribution to both the small and large exporter. The exporter may use a complete ISO (International Standards Organisation) container (full container load – FCL) or despatch his merchandise to a container base or an inland clearance

TABLE 4.2 Major container ports

No.	Port	1996 TEU	1995 TEU	(No)	Country/Region
1	Hong Kong	13 460 343	12 549 746	(1)	PRC
2	Singapore	12 943 900	11 845 600	(2)	Singapore
3	Kaohsiung	5 063 048	5 232 000	(3)	Taiwan
4	Rotterdam	4 935 616	4 786 577	(4)	Netherlands
5	Busan	4 725 206	4 502 596	(5)	South Korea
6	Yokohama	3 911 927	2 756 811	(7)	Japan
7	Hamburg	3 054 320	2 890 181	(6)	Germany
8	Long Beach	3 007 425	2 389 533	(9)	USA
9	Los Angeles	2 682 803	2 555 204	(8)	USA
10	Antwerp	2 653 909	2 329 135	(10)	Belgium
11	Keelung	2 320 397	2 169 893	(13)	Taiwan
12	Tokyo	2 311 453	2 177 407	(12)	Japan
13	New York/New Jersey	2 269 145	2 275 690	(11)	USA
14	Dubai	2 247 024	2 073 081	(14)	UAE
15	Kobe	2 229 320	1 463 515	(23)	Japan
16	Felixstowe	2 042 423	1 898 201	(15)	UK
17	Manila	1 971 524	1 668 031	(16)	Philippines
18	Shanghai	1 930 000	1 527 000	(19)	PRC
19	San Juan	1 600 000	1 593 000	(17)	Puerto Rico
20	Bremen/Bremerhaven	1 543 405	1 526 421	(20)	Germany
21	Oakland	1 498 202	1 549 886	(18)	USA
22	Seattle	1 473 562	1 479 076	(21)	USA
23	Nagoya	1 469 186	1 477 359	(22)	Japan
24	Tanjung Priok	1 421 693	1 300 126	(25)	Indonesia
25	Port Klang	1 409 491	1 133 811	(28)	Malaysia
26	Colombo	1 356 301	1 028 746	(32)	Sri Lanka
27	Algeciras	1 306 825	1 154 714	(27)	Spain
28	Bangkok	1 232 610	1 432 843	(24)	Thailand
29	Charleston	1 151 401	1 030 662	(31)	USA

depots (ICD) for it to be consolidated with other compatible cargo en route to a similar destination country or area for despatch as a less than container load (LCL).

Features of containerization can conveniently be summarized as follows:

(1) It permits a door-to-door service which may be from the factory production site to the retail distributor's store – an overall distance of some 6000 km. Or it may be an FCL or LCL movement.
(2) No intermediate handling at terminal transshipment points, namely rail/road terminals or seaport.

TABLE 4.3 Top 20 container service operators

Rank	Carrier	Vessels	TEU
1 (3)	Maersk	106	232 257
2 (1)	Evergreen/Uniglory	108	228 248
3 (6/8)	P&O/Nedlloyd	106	221 531
4 (2)	Sea-Land Service	95	215 114
5 (4)	Cosco	139	201 593
6 (8)	Hanjin Shipping Co[1]	62	174 526
7 (9)	Mediterranean Shipping Co	100	154 185
8 (6)	Mitsui OSK Lines	62	115 763
9 (5)	NYK Line/TSK	68	128 154
10 (11)	Hyundai Merchant Marine	36	112 958
11 (12)	Zim Israel Navigation Co	59	98 086
12 (16)	Yangming Marine Transport Corp	42	96 145
13 (20)	CMA-CGM[2]	64	89 658
14 (18)	OOCL	30	85 940
15 (16)	Neptune Orient Lines[3]	36	85 664
16 (35)	CP Ships[4]	46	85 016
17 (14)	K Line	45	84 198
18 (15)	APL	38	79 918
19 (14)	Hapag-Lloyd Containerline[5]	23	73 372
20 (24)	Cho Yang Shipping	30	55 882

Source: *Containerisation International Yearbook* data and carriers

Note: Last year's figure in brackets.
1 Includes Hanjin's 70 per cent shareholding in DSR-Senator
2 Includes CGM's 50 per cent shareholding in Horn Line
3 Includes NOL's equity interests in PUL International Lines, Lorenzo Shipping, Centenary Shipping and Nepline
4 Encompasses the containership fleets of Canada Maritime, Cast, Contship Containerlines and Lykes Lines
5 Excludes the Rickmers Line fleet

(3) Low risk of cargo damage and pilferage enables more favourable cargo premiums to be obtained compared with break-bulk cargo shipments and individual airfreight consignments.

(4) The absence en route of intermediate handling plus quicker sea transits compared with break-bulk cargo shipments permits less risk of damage and pilferage.

(5) Elimination of intermediate handling at maritime terminal transfer points, that is, seaports, enables substantial dock labour savings to be made. In industrial countries, where there is a high income per capita, this can realize considerable financial savings.

(6) Less packing needs for containerized consignments. In some cases, particularly with specialized ISO containers such as refrigerated ones or tanks (liquid or

powder), no packing is required. This produces substantial cost savings and raises service quality.

(7) The elimination of intermediate handling coupled with the other inherent advantages of containerized shipments tends to permit the cargo to arrive in a better condition thereby enhancing the quality of service.

(8) Emerging from the inherent advantages of containerization, rates are likely to remain more competitive. A significant reason is that containerization is, in the main, a capital-intensive transport network, compared with the individual consignment distribution system which tends to be more labour intensive. This is particularly so with maritime container distribution which has produced substantial labour cost savings.

(9) Maritime container transits are much quicker compared with break-bulk cargo. This is usually achieved through a combination of circumstances, namely faster vessels, a rationalization of ports of call and substantially quicker transshipments. For example, the Europe to Tokyo sailing time is 24 days.

(10) As a result of faster transits and the advantages under items (7) and (8), containerization encourages trade development and permits quicker payment of export invoices.

(11) Maritime containerization has permitted maritime fleet rationalization producing substantial capital cost replacement savings as fewer ships are needed. However, these ships must be more intensely operated and of an overall larger capacity. On average, one container ship – usually of much increased capacity and faster speed – has displaced up to six break-bulk cargo vessels on deep-sea services. This development has been facilitated by the rationalization of ports of call. Overall, a container vessel spends less than 10 per cent of her time in port.

(12) Container vessels attain much improved utilization and generally are very much more productive than the break-bulk tonnage.

(13) Faster transits, usually coupled with more reliable maritime schedules and ultimately increased service frequency, is tending to encourage many importers in selective shipping trades to hold reduced stocks and spares. This produces savings in warehouse accommodation needs, lessens the risks of obsolescent stock and reduces importers' working capital. It exploits the benefits of the 'just-in-time' concept and improves inventory stock control and warehouse management results. These are good selling points to be borne in mind by the shipper when deciding on the mode of transport to be used.

(14) Containerization produces quicker transits and encourages the rationalization of ports of call. This, in many trades, is tending to stimulate trade expansion through much improved service standards. This is resulting in increased service frequency which will aid trade development.

(15) Provision of through documentation or combined transport bill of lading, involving a common code of liability for the through transit.

(16) Provision of a through rate. For example, this embraces both the maritime and surface transport cost of the ISO container. Again, this aids the marketing of the container concept.

(17) More reliable transits – particularly disciplined controlled transit arrangements in maritime schedules. Most major container ship operators have computer equipment to facilitate the booking, stowage, and control of containers throughout the transit.

(18) New markets have emerged through container development and its inherent advantages.

(19) Maritime containerization is a capital-intensive project and as such is beyond the financial limit of many shipowners.

(20) Not all merchandise can be conveniently containerized. However, the percentage of such traffic falls annually as new types of maritime containers are introduced.

(21) Maritime containerization has greatly facilitated the development of consolidated or break-bulk consignments. This particularly favours the small exporter unable to originate a full container load which is consolidated through a container base.

(22) Containerization facilitates the maximum use of computerization in many areas, especially container control, customer billing, container stowage in the vessel, documentation processing, and so on.

(23) The international maritime container network expands annually as ports/berths are modernized, together with their infrastructure. This involves the development of the dry port such as Ipoh (p. 85); the development of new container berths; the relocation of container berths to accommodate larger vessels such as in the ports of Bangkok and Klang; the development of air freight and land-bridges (p. 93); electronic data interchange (p. 373); the development of feeder services to serve the major ports; and the new generation of high-capacity containers (p. 72). All these factors improve the 'value added benefit' which the shippers obtain from the use of the container network.

Finally, Tables 4.4 and 4.5 present a cost analysis of the standard service profitability on the transatlantic and Europe–Far East trade based on 1996 data. A comparison of the data on the two trades produces a useful analysis.

There is no doubt multi-modalism (Chapter 5) and logistics (Chapter 6) are driving the accelerated growth of containerization together with the fast expanding hub and spoke system. The two mega-carriers (Table 4.2) will continue to be under pressure from Shipper Councils to improve service quality and offer more competitive rates. Countries which are not part of the global container network will be severely disadvantaged in terms of their growth and development.

4.2 Container distribution

Today, there are 8.5 million containers in circulation. Some 50 per cent are owned by shipping companies and the residue are leased or industrially owned. A leading container leasing company is Ge Seaco which has 30 per cent of the global market share. The lease price is determined by the container type, the length of lease – one or

TABLE 4.4 Estimated 1996 standard service profitability on the transatlantic trade

Revenue	US$000/rv	%
Eastbound	2026	52.7
Westbound	1816	47.3
Total	3842	
Costs		
Fixed costs		
Bunkers	109	3.2
Ports	209	6.0
Capital	373	10.8
Operating	186	5.4
Administration	531	15.4
Sub-total	1408	40.8
Direct costs		
Terminals	815	23.6
Transport	455	13.2
Depots	61	1.8
Refrigeration	28	0.8
Sub-total	1358	39.3
Indirect costs		
Equipment provision	288	8.3
Empty containers	96	2.8
M&R	228	6.6
Cargo claims & insurance	76	2.2
Sub-total	687	19.9
Fully built-up service costs	3453	
Voyage result	388	
Margin on revenue		10.1

Source: Drewry Shipping Consultants

TABLE 4.5 Estimated 1996 standard service profitability on the Europe/Far East trade

Revenue	$000	%
Eastbound	2483	35.2
Westbound	4581	64.8
Total	7064	
Costs		
Fixed costs		
Bunkers	500	6.6
Ports	893	11.8
Capital	1424	18.9
Operating	539	7.2
Administration	755	10.0
Sub-total	4111	54.5
Direct costs		
Terminals	1325	17.6
Transport	883	11.7
Depots	76	1.0
Refrigeration	48	0.6
Sub-total	2332	
Indirect costs		
Equipment provision	401	5.3
Empty containers	185	2.5
M&R	378	5.0
Cargo claims & insurance	126	1.7
Sub-total	1090	14.5
Fully built-up service costs	7532	
Voyage result	−469	
Margin on revenue		−6.6

Source: Drewry Shipping Consultants

more years – and the route it will ply. Some routes generate a high intensive user such as the short sea, whilst the deep-sea route is less intensive. The location to where the container must be returned also determines the price. The container life is about ten years depending on the trade assigned and the user.

The reason why the container lease market is so large is that containers represent a high capital investment which the shipping company prefers to entrust to a leasing company. A dry cargo container costs US$2000 whilst for a reefer the figure is US$28 000.

A major problem with containers today is the repositioning of empty containers. It is very costly and arises through economic and political developments. The Far East currency crisis has exacerbated the situation. It is a long-term problem and varies with trade route and container type. In the Europe–Far East trade – heavy cargo – raw materials and semi finished goods are imported in 6.10 m (20 ft) containers, whilst Asia exports light cargo – consumer goods in 12.20 m (40 ft) containers. Repositioning the containers or transporting them to the right place is costly and reduces profit margins both on shipping lines and leasing companies.

A number of possible solutions exist:

(1)   The container owner shifts the boxes to where they are most needed at the lowest possible cost. This may involve despatching them by a circuitous route, adopting a policy of cabotage, or renting them out at a reduced rate or even lending them free of charge.

(2)   The lease company prefers the container to be returned to a strategic location, so the return location is written into the contract, even if it is a five-year contract. This strategy also influences the lease price.

(3)   In situations where a serious imbalance arises as in the Far East trade, the best option is to charter shipping space to reposition the boxes.

A case study of the Port of Rotterdam manifests the problem. An analysis of the data below focuses on the situation in 1997 which was worsened by the Far East currency crisis.

To:	Rotterdam empty containers		
From:	Europe	24.4 per cent	(270 250)
	Africa	55.9 per cent	(31 000)
	North America	7 per cent	(29 500)
	Central and South America	25.5 per cent	(38 250)
	Middle East	30.8 per cent	(14 750)
	Asia	7.8 per cent	(84 750)
From:	Rotterdam empty containers		
To:	Europe	9.2 per cent	(106 000)
	Africa	6.2 per cent	(4 500)
	North America	9.5 per cent	(36 750)
	Central and South America	12.9 per cent	(11 000)
	Middle East	5.2 per cent	(6 250)
	Asia	8.7 per cent	(72 000)

Because Europe has always exported more containers than it imports, Rotterdam has acted as both supply source and store port for empty containers; thus fulfilling a balancing function in empty container logistics. The position is worsened as over 50 per cent of the container movements are empty within Europe. Rotterdam has fifteen depôts which can store about 25 000 containers to meet the increasing demand in the European hinterland. Rotterdam also stores feeder containers for smaller ports that have no depôts themselves such as Norway. Empty containers are consigned to a port as without these empties there would be no full ones.

A number of areas are being examined to reduce box repositioning. The Internet provides the opportunity to match supply with demand in a revolution in the method of working in transport and logistics. The interchange of containers between shipowners and leasing companies does offer flexibility and optimizes use of containers and equipment. Central planning units and collaborative agreements amongst carriers and owners present a further solution. All the foregoing concepts are in the process of operation and development, often based on a localized port or trade. Overall, it improves profit margins and ship productivity, as is evidenced in the Port of Rotterdam which is applying these strategies.

Finally, with regard to future developments in container tonnage, a high speed service by fast ship is planned to start in 2001 between Philadelphia in the USA and Cherbourg in France. The voyage time is scheduled for four days, giving seven days door-to-door for freight between the USA and Europe, compared with 17 to 21 days at present. Freight rates will attract a premium of 30 per cent. The high speed container ship will have a speed of 35–40 knots and a total of 1432 TEUs conveyed on two decks, all under cover. The vessel has a beam of 40 m, an overall length of 265 m, a draught of 10m and 30 700 d.w.t. The cost is US$220 million. The vessel, when launched and operational, could herald a new era in container maritime distribution and stimulate trade expansion. It could bring similar benefits to shippers as those which emerged with the Fast Ferry (see p. 88).

4.3 Container types

It would be appropriate to examine the size and types of both ISO and International Air Transport Association (IATA) containers, which now follows.

The range of ISO container types tends to expand annually to meet the increasing market demands on this fast-growing primarily deep-sea international method of distributing merchandise. Basically, the majority of containers used are built to ISO specification thereby permitting their ease of ubiquitous use on an international scale. Many of the containers are built to a standard outlined by one of the major ship classification societies such as Lloyd's Register of Shipping. The basic container most commonly built of steel or aluminium modual size is 2.45 m (8 ft) × 2.45 m (8 ft) but there exist some of 2.45 m (8 ft) × 2.60 m (8 ft 6 in) which tend to be applicable to the North American trade. Their length is 3.05 m (10 ft), 6.10 m (20 ft), 9.15 m (30 ft), 10.70 m (35 ft), or 12.20 m (40 ft). The 3.05 m (10 ft) and 10.70 m (35 ft) are not very common and the former is usually found in the short sea trades.

The most popular size is the 6.10 m (20 ft) or 12.20 m (40 ft) length with a module of either 2.45 m (8 ft) × 2.60 m (8 ft 6 in) or 2.45 m (8 ft) × 2.45 m (8 ft). More recently, containers of a module of 2.45 m (8 ft) × 2.75 m (9 ft) or 2.45 m (8 ft) × 2.90 m (9 ft 6 in) have emerged but their use is limited due to the extra height clearance, particularly by rail. The 6.10 m (20 ft) and 12.20 m (40 ft) length containers with a module of 2.45 m (8 ft) × 2.45 m (8 ft) have a cubic capacity of 30 m^3 and 66.5 m^3 and a maximum load weight of 18 000 kg and 27 070 kg respectively. The 2.45 m (8 ft) × 2.60 m (8 ft 6 in) module have a cubic capacity of 31 m^3 and 68.1 m^3, with a maximum load capacity of 18 720 kg and 27 580 kg. In some countries, the 12.20 m (40 ft) container cannot be used to the full capacity due to road weight restrictions. An increasing number of the 6.10 m (20 ft) containers currently built have a maximum load weight of 21 600 kg, and the 12.20 m (40 ft) have a maximum 32 210 kg load weight (see Figure 4.1).

Cargo is usually stowed in the air freighter under a unit load device (ULD). This may involve a pallet, container or igloo. Details of the range of ULD used on the Boeing 737F (cargo capacity, 16 tonnes) and 747F (cargo capacity, 102 tonnes) are given in Table 4.6. These containers are used by Lufthansa Boeings 737F and 747F, and similar pallets and containers are used by other major air freight carriers. The 6.10 m (20 ft) and 3.05 m (10 ft) containers may be used for combined transport schedules which is a growth market in air freight consolidation.

The Shipping Companies and Container Leasing Companies are very conscious of the need to keep ahead of the market requirement. An example is the high-cube container (HCC) which has a height in excess of 2.59 m, a length over 12.19 m and width over 2.44 m. The increased cube has been designed to meet strong market needs to despatch more economically worldwide the expanding range of commodities which have a high volume and low weight ratio. These include light machinery, foodstuffs, furniture and so on. Such markets are very strong in the Orient where low-cost labour, aggressive marketing and high technology have facilitated a major export region for such products.

The container specifications tend to fall into the following categories:

Height (m)	Width (m)	Length (m)
2.90	2.59	12.19
2.90	2.59	14.93
2.90	2.59	16.15

The cost benefits of the high-cube and oversize containers include a reduction in the number of boxes handled, attained through higher load factor. Also under certain tariff conditions, the port handling charges per unit of product may be reduced. There is reduction in the number of container movements in the port area, which reduces road congestion in the area; and fewer boxes will reduce the level of documentation and administration, and overall distribution costs will fall, thereby permitting a lower market price.

The development of the high-cube and oversize container will have a profound effect on the international distribution infrastructure. This involves container ship specification, including lifting apparatus, port equipment and straddle carriers, fork lift trucks, gantry cranes, road transport trailers, railway wagons and the relative regulations.

The trade in which they feature strongly is primarily based in the Orient, especially the ports of Hong Kong, Japan and Singapore and the feeder ports they serve, and it involves the seaboards of North America and Europe.

A wide range of ISO containers exists today and the more common ones are detailed in Figure 4.1. A brief description of container types is given below:

(1) General purpose dry cargo containers are closed and are suitable for the carriage of all types of general merchandise and, with suitable temporary modification, for the carriage of bulk cargoes, both solid and liquid. A popular container ideal for both the FCL and LCL markets.

(2) Insulated containers protect against heat loss or gain and are used in conjunction with a blown-air refrigeration system to convey perishable or other cargo which needs to be carried under temperature control. An ideal container for the movement of foodstuffs which is a rapidly expanding international market.

(3) The fruit container has been developed to carry fresh deciduous and citrus fruit, the internal dimensions being slightly larger than the standard insulated container to accommodate the packing of standard fruit pallets and cases.

(4) Refrigerated containers are designed to operate independently of a blown-air refrigerated system and are fitted with their own refrigeration units which require an electrical power supply for operation. Each container is capable of being set at its own individual carriage temperature. Ideal for meat, dairy products and fruit.

(5) Bulk containers are designed for the carriage of dry powders and granular substances in bulk. To facilitate top loading three circular hatches (500 mm diameter) are fitted in some containers in the roof structure. For discharge a hatch is fitted in the right-hand door of the container.

(6) Ventilated containers are broadly similar to the general purpose container specification except for the inclusion of full length ventilation galleries sited along the top and bottom side rails, allowing the passive ventilation of the cargo. Ideal for products such as coffee.

(7) Flat rack containers are designed to facilitate the carriage of cargo in excess of the dimensions available in either general purpose or open top containers. Such containers have a collapsible end. A combination of two or more flat rack containers can be used to form a temporary break-bulk space for uncontainerable of cargo moved on a port to port basis provided the total weight and point loading of the cargo does not exceed the static capabilities of the flat racks. Overall a container ideal for the carriages of oversized, awkward and heavy cargoes.

(8) Open top containers with their top loading facility are designed for the carriage of heavy and awkward shaped cargoes and those cargoes whose height is in excess of that which can be stowed in a general purpose container. It may also be described as an open sided/open top container. Tarpaulin tilts are available to protect the cargo. The container is ideal for sheet glass, timber and machinery.

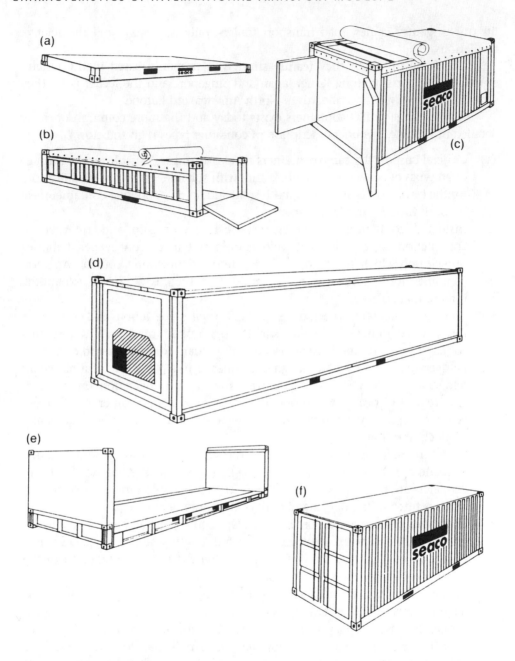

FIGURE 4.1 Container types

(a) 20 ft platform flat (bolster) – 40 ft size available – for building materials, vehicles, indivisible loads, lumber, etc.
(b) 20 ft half height with ramp end door – tarpaulin roof – for heavy loads, building materials.
(c) 20 ft open top – 40 ft size available – for large awkward items such as machinery – tarpaulin roof for water tight integrity – door header swings to assist loading of high items.
(d) 40 ft refrigerated container with integral refrigeration machinery for chilled and frozen cargoes.
(e) 20 ft spring assisted folding end flat rack – 40 ft size available – can be provided with built in interlocking mechanism for multiple empty transportation.
(f) 20 ft covered container – 8 ft 6 in high – 40 ft available.

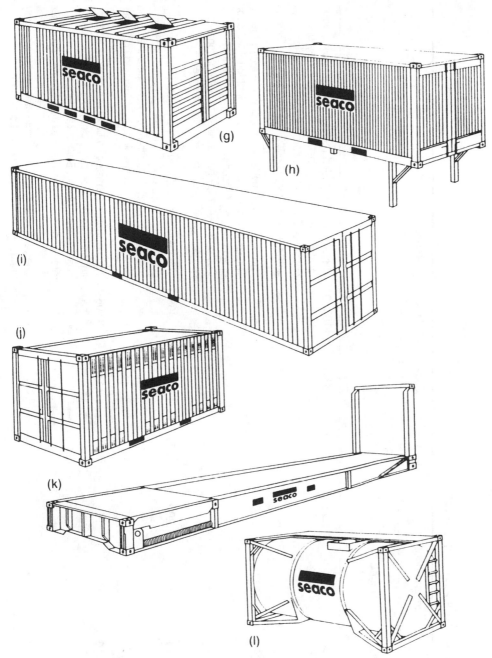

FIGURE 4.1 *continued*

(g) 20 ft bulk container for grain, powders, etc.
(h) 7.15 m swap body with demountable legs – 2.5 m width for two pallet wide European operation.
(i) 40 ft high cube 9 ft 6 in high – 45 ft also available – for cargoes that cube out.
(j) 20 ft ventilated container for cargoes such as coffee and cocoa that experience condensation damage.
(k) 40 ft sea deck style combination flat rack and platform flat – 20 ft size available for large items of machinery, construction equipment, etc.
(l) 20 ft tank container for bulk hazardous and non-hazardous liquids. (Reproduced by kind permission of Sea Containers.)

TABLE 4.6 Range of ULD on Boeing 737F and 747F

Container type	Loading capacity			Tare weight (max.) (kg)	Cubic capacity	Max. load	Description
	Length (cm)	Height (cm)	Width (cm)				
6.10 m (20 ft) container with ISO fittings	594	230	228	1000	33.0	10340	The container is loaded through a double-wing door located on its front panel. Customs seals may be obtained. Surface transport is possible. Built-in garment racks are provided
3.05 m (10 ft) container	293	237	220	255	16.5	6549	The container is made entirely of light-weight metal. The container is loaded through a double-folded door or an opening (closed by a net and tarpaulin). Customs seals may be obtained for international cargo. Built-in garment racks are provided
LD 7 container-igloo shell	294	153	200	225	9.6	5808	The igloo shell is affixed to the pallet. The load opening is closed with a net and tarpaulin. Surface transport is possible. Built-in garment racks are provided. It is also available as a refrigerated container
LD 3 container	146	160	144	80	4.0	1508	The container consists of a box-type construction of light metal. The opening is closed by a flexible door of coated fabric plastic. Built-in garment racks are provided. It is also available as a refrigerated container
Pallet	592	230	–	–	–	–	The pallet consists of an aluminium case (the loading surface) and surrounding sectional frame

Type						Description
Car transport	485	–	230	–	–	The pallet consists of an aluminium case (the loading surface) and surrounding sectional frame. Additionally, it features special tie-down tracks for securing car transport racks and wheel lashing belts
Pallet	304	–	230	–	–	The pallet consists of an aluminium case (the loading surface) and surrounding sectional frame
Pallet	304	–	210	–	–	The pallet consists of an aluminium case (the loading surface) and surrounding sectional frame. Installed in the frame is a tie-down track on which pallet nets, tension belts and lashing rings are secured. For better utilization of lower-deck capacity the pallets in the standard 304 cm length can be equipped with side extensions
Pallet	304	–	139	–	–	The pallet consists of an aluminium case (the loading surface) and surrounding sectional frame. Installed in the frame is a tie-down track on which pallet nets, tension belts and lashing rings are secured. For better utilization of lower-deck capacity the pallets in the standard 304 cm length can be equipped with side extensions
Container – for 3 horses – open with front doors	208	208	228	510	3 horses	An aluminium assembly on a 304 cm × 210 cm pallet. The watertight floor pan and ramp are equipped with slip-proof, noise clamping floor covering. The horses' head area features bite-guards and tarpaulins; inner walls are padded

(9)   The half height open top container is designed for the conveyance of heavy, dense cargoes such as steel, pipes, tubes, metal waste, ingots, copper bar, marble, stone and heavy drums. It is ideal for shippers whose premises have a restricted height for loading or discharge.

(10)   One of the most important developments in container technology in recent years came with the tank container. Ge Seaco remains the market leader and offers five types:

(a)   The IMO type 1 for chemicals involving hazardous cargo and a capacity ranging from 12 000 litres to 26 000 litres.

(b)   Lightweight tanks offering reduced tareweight for increased payload. Designed for a range of chemical and bulk liquids with a capacity of 21 000 litres.

(c)   Food grade tanks for edible cargo with a gross weight of 34 000 kgs and tare weight of 3300 kgs.

(d)   New insulated tanks for liquids which are non-heat sensitive with a gross weight of 34 000 kgs and tare weight of 3345 kgs.

(e)   Special tanks for highly hazardous liquids and gases with a capacity ranging from 12 000 litres to 25 000 litres.

Overall, the tank container offers a safe and simple method of controlling cost while using a recyclable resource. On arrival the tank discharges directly into the production process, saving both valuable time and costly handling and heating charges. Shippers not only save time and money, but the tank unit provides up to 35 per cent additional cargo over drums in each ISO shipment, with wastage from drums through spillage or damage at an estimated 5 per cent per journey; annual savings are significant. Also other cost savings include the drum provision and its disposal in an environmentally conscious global society.

(11)   Artificial between deck containers are without end walls, side walls, or a roof and are also known as platform carriers. These units are used for oversize and overweight cargo which cannot otherwise be containerized. They are 6.10 m long and 2.4 m wide or 12.20 m long and 2.4 m wide.

(12)   The larger cube containers were introduced in the late 1980s and are used for dry cargo and equipped with removable beams in the upper part. They are used especially for garments on hangers and are very popular in some trades. The container is 12.20 m long, 2.4 m wide and 3.0 m high, or 6.10 m long, 2.4 m wide and 3.0 m high.

(13)   Bin containers have a cargo capacity of 21 600 kg and a tare weight of 2400 kg and a length of 6.06 m, a width of 2.44 m and a height of 1.30 m. They are ideal for heavy dense cargoes such as steel pipes.

(14)   Bolster flat containers have a capacity of 23 000 kg and a tare weight of 1040 kg, a length of 6.06 m, width 2.44 m and height 0.23 m. They are ideal for heavy cargoes.

(15)   The Stak bed container is a piece of equipment that offers the three-in-one capability of being a cargo platform (or flat), a fixed-end flatrack and a folding-end flatrack. It has vertical corner posts with horizontal bracing pieces. Recesses

in the cargo platform permit the end-frame to stow when folded, flush with the deck, to provide an unrestricted surface area for cargo loading.

(16) Sea Cell container has been recently developed by Sea Containers to meet the growth market needs of palletized cargo. The 6.10 m (20 ft) Sea Cell has 1.5 m^3 and the 12.20 m (40 ft) box 3 m^3 extra capacity and both carry 27 per cent more pallets than a standard box container.

As we progress through the millennium, it is likely more container types will be introduced.

An example of a modern third-generation Ro-Ro container ship is operated by the Atlantic Container Line. It has a capacity of 2911 TEUs, and trailer lane capacity of 3839 m. Such a vessel is highly versatile in terms of the cargo mix, and conveys containers, road trailers, 20 ft (6.10 m) and 40 ft (12.20 m) dry vans, special heavy lift equipment for abnormal loads, extendable road trailers, railway rolling stock on road bogies, 12.20 m (40 ft) full high open-top trailers, 'U' beam frames on pier-to-pier trailers for steel products, block-stowed cargo such as logs, neo-bulk cargo on 6.10 m (20 ft) bolsters such as woodpulp and paper rolls, 6.10 m (20 ft) and 12.20 m (40 ft) flats and so on. Such a vessel exploits the advantages of combined transport. The vessel has a 52 000 d.w.t. and speed of 20 knots.

An example of the latest generation of container tonnage is operated by Evergreen International Ltd with east- and west-bound round-the-world services. Two types of vessels are provided, In 1998 the shipowner ordered for the west-bound round-the-world service, five 5364 TEUs of the U class container vessel with a speed of 23 knots and scheduled for delivery in 2001. This will displace existing smaller tonnage.

Over 50 per cent of containers are owned by the world's container leasing companies. Details are given below and feature leasing companies Clou, Flexi-Van, Genstar, IEA, and Ge Seaco:

	1991 ('000)	1991 ('000)
Dry van	1824	2050
High-cube	122	133
Tanks	6	8
Reefers	63	70
Open tops	68	74
Flat tops	40	44
Bulkers	4	3
Others	10	10
Total	2236	2392

The annual growth rate is 5–7 per cent.

4.4 Container bases

The container base forms an important part of an integrated international transport system designed to link container terminals where ships are handled, with inland centres, using a rail system or road haulage distribution network. In some countries they are called container freight stations (CFSs). Usually they are under the management of a consortia of ship operators; a consortia of container operators engaged in the freight forwarding business; or a consortia comprising freight forwarders, road hauliers, etc. and others engaged in such businesses, e.g. a local port authority. It can be situated in the port itself, or the seaport or airport environs, or an industrial area which can support the facility in generating adequate quantities of containerized import/export traffic through it, involving both LCL and FCL. A summary of the services offered is given below:

(1) Container handling and storage. A range of comprehensive container handling and storage facilities which cover all types, both loaded and empty, together with purpose-built stacking areas and on-site repair and maintenance resources for containers and related equipment.

(2) Specialist cargo resources to handle dangerous cargo; consignments 'over height', 'over width' and 'out of gauge'; and container stowage of all types of cargo.

(3) Export and import LCL. Container bases are used by consolidators NVOCCs particularly for the following needs or reasons: cargo handling; professional container packers; efficient de-vanning checking and customs clearance of imports; and quick vehicle turn-round when collecting or delivering cargo.

(4) On-site customs clearance. Full customs and port health facilities including the direct trader input system for computerized preparation and handling of customs entries. Such a customs facility enables any problem to be resolved quickly and locally, not at a seaport or airport distant from the importer's or exporter's premises.

(5) Adequate security of the goods through on-site guards, CCTV, perimeter alarms and cargo systems and procedures.

(6) FCL cargo handling. An increasing number of exporters and importers use the container base for the full container load.

(7) Customs warehousing. This yields savings to the importer on VAT payment and import duty as the payment is only made when goods are withdrawn from the bonded warehouse.

(8) Office accommodation for tenants using the container base on a regular basis.

(9) Workshops for vehicle maintenance and repair, washing and steam-cleaning services for the containers.

The major advantages of container bases are to provide a service to the importer/exporter situated in the container base hinterland and relieve the port authority of local customs clearance of import/export cargoes. This latter advantage tends to reduce the problems of port congestion, that is, containers awaiting clearance due to non-availability of documents, and enables the throughput of the container berth to be maximized. Ultimately, it speeds up the transit, as no inordinate delay is usually experienced at the port, and thereby the development of international trade is encouraged. Undoubtedly, the number of container bases will increase as the container trade expands.

4.5 Non-containerizable cargo

As we progress through the millennium the development of intermodalism will grow, especially in deep-sea shipping services. This involves the provision of a door-to-door service to the shipper.

An example of tonnage offering such a service is operated by the Atlantic Container Line. It involves the third-generation Ro-Ro container vessels conveying containers, Ro-Ro, trailers cars and non-containerizable cargo. The combined cellular and roll-on/roll-off vessels operate on Europe-North America trade and serve the ports of Bremerhaven, Gothenburg, Le Havre, Liverpool, Rotterdam, Baltimore, New York, Philadelphia, Portsmouth and Halifax.

Non-containerizable cargo can be divided into four categories (Table 4.7). These are:

(1) Rollable cargo with its own wheels or tracks that can be driven onboard or towed. Road vehicles and agricultural machinery are examples.
(2) Cargo that is carried on trailers. This involves 'maafi' and heavy-duty trailers for pier-to-pier movements; flatbed trailers for door-to-door transportation; and trailers for the movement of exceptionally large or heavy loads door-to-door.
(3) Special project cargo that requires experience and expertise to find a cost-effective solution. This includes, for example, the conveyance of trains in the Ro-Ro decks by laying rail lines into the ship; developed purpose-built road bogies to carry subway cars door-to-door and special extendable flatbed trailers for the carriage of 22 m (72 ft) long aircraft wings.
(4) Neo-bulk cargo, a term given to a wide range of staple products that can be efficiently carried in the Ro-Ro decks as unitized break-bulk (e.g. wood-pulp, board, paper, logs and steel). Details of the range of equipment used for non-containerizable cargo are given below and in Table 4.8:

Capacity (tonne)	Length (mm)	Width (mm)	No. of axles	Commentary
Roll trailers				
20	6096	2438	1	Units with capacities of up to 180 tonne
30	12 190	2438	2 bogie	are available for pier-to-pier movements.
40	12 190	2438	2 bogie	Operational advantages include low
55	12 190	2438	2 bogie	timber surfaced cargo platforms, multi-
60	12 190	2438	2 bogie	wheel bogies for extreme manoeuvrability,
100	12 190	3048	4 bogie	separate lashing points for cargo and
180	12 954	3454	8	trailer, and high degree of stability, even when carrying oversize units

TABLE 4.7 Non-containerizable cargo

Rollable	Trailer/'maafi'	Special projects	Neo-bulk
Maximum weight varies according to machine. Items over 60 tonne (132 275 lb) are considered special projects. Please refer to the vessel's cargo specification on weight and dimension	Road Trailers for door-to-door transportation	The shipowner defines special projects as cargo where any one of the following dimensions is exceeded: L 12.19 m (40 ft) × W 3.05 m (10 ft) × H 3.05 m (10 ft), or where the weight exceeds 55 tonne (121 252 lb). Rollable cargo is classed as a special project when the weight exceeds 60 tonne (132 275 lb)	Maximum dimensions for a consignment loaded on a 6.10 m (20 ft) bolster are: L 6.10 m (20 ft) × W 2.43 m (8 ft) × H 2.59 m (8 ft 6 in). Payload maximum is 20 tonne (44 000 lb)
Items may be towed or driven under their own power into the ship.	Consignments may be considered 'in gauge' where dimensions do not exceed L 12.19 m (40 ft) × W 2.43 m (8 ft) × H 2.59 m (8 ft 6 in)		Cargo may be loaded on a 6.10 m (20 ft) bolster or on a 12.20 m (40 ft) flatbed trailer. In some cases, the cargo may be blockstowed on the Ro-Ro decks of the ship
Cargo is normally delivered to the port of loading by the shipper or his agent and collected at the port of discharge by the consignee or his agent	Maximum payload without additional charges for 'in gauge' cargo is 18 tonne (39 682 lb). Heavier, indivisible loads can be carried, but prior arrangements and clearance must be obtained	Note that any cargo, regardless of weight which is exceptionally dense will require prior clearance before carriage by shipowner	Equipment may be loaded or discharged at the shipper's or consignee's factory, or at the ACL ocean terminal
The normal ship's securing system using chains, etc. is employed onboard the vessel	Normal available equipment is the 12.20 m (40 ft) flatbed trailer with side-pockets for stanchions	Roll trailers are available for payloads up to 55 tonne and 60 tonne; heavy duty trailers for up to 100 tonne and 180 tonne. Leased trailers, including drop frames, well trailers and extendables are available on a one trip basis from the shipowner	For inland transportation of door-to-door cargo on a 6.10 m (20 ft) bolster or a 12.20 m (40 ft) flatbed trailer, container rules apply
Shipowner does not supply tarpaulins	Equipment may be loaded or discharged at the shipper's or consignee's factory, or at the ACL ocean terminal	Roll and heavy duty trailers are for pier-to-pier cargo only but leased trailers may move over the road with permits if required	Web lashing, signode steel banding, tarpaulins and shrink-wrapping are used to secure the cargo. Tarpaulins are normally supplied by the trucker or shipper
	For inland transportation of 'in gauge' cargo normal container rules apply, but 'out of gauge' cargo requires prior clearance	Securing is achieved by chains, steel banding, wire and bottlescrews (turnbuckles) as necessary	
	Chains, nylon web lashing and signode banding may be used to secure the cargo	Shipowner does not supply tarpaulins	
	If required, tarpaulins must be supplied by the shipper or trucker		
	Shipowner does not supply tarpaulins		
	'Maffi' trailers for pier-to-pier transportation		
	The maximum dimensions of cargo should normally not exceed L 12.19 m (40 ft) × W 3.05 m (10 ft) × H 3.05 m (10 ft)		
	Normal maximum weight is 55 tonne (121 252 lb). Cargo in excess of this is considered a special project		
	Roll trailers are available to carry up to 20 tonne, 30 tonne, 40 tonne, 55 tonne and 60 tonne		

Capacity (tonne)	Length (mm)	Width (mm)	No. of axles	Commentary
Flatbed trailers				
20	12 190	2438	2	Special house-to-house trailers for through transport of machinery and other outsize and/or high cargo units. These are either owned by the shipper or available on lease. Special heavy-lift trailers for house-to-house movement of extra heavy loads available from shipowner
Bolsters – flats without hardboards				
20	6000	2438		This is a unit constructed with a strengthened floor which can be stowed from either the top, sides or ends

TABLE 4.8 Types of cargo

Rollable	Trailer/'maafi'	Special projects	Neo-bulk
Tractors	Boats	Subway cars and rolling stock	Woodpulp
Backhoes	Yachts	Fixed-wing aircraft, Aircraft wings	Linerboard
Trucks	Machinery	Helicopters	Plywood
Cars	Linerboard	Forging machines and presses	Newsprint
Earthmovers	Cotton liner pulp	Crankshafts	Lumber
Mobile cranes	Flowerbulbs	Transformers	Waferboard
Combine harvesters	Mining shields	Boilers	Particle board
Buses	Hay balers	Pipe mills	Press board
Bulldozers	Specialized steel products	Dryers	Iron and steel products
Excavators	Crane parts	Press rolls	Logs
Wheel-loaders	Injection moulds	Steel rolls	
Trackloaders	Compressors	Converters	
Motorgraders	Cranes	Military vehicles	
Air compressors	Alternators	Street cars	
	Rotors	Oilrigs	
	Turbines	Earthmovers over 55 tonne	
	Constructionals	Railway locomotives	
		Ballast cleaners	
		Metal working machinery	
		Large boats and yachts	
		Long and wide loads	

The Ro-Ro container vessels are large and very flexible, with the ability to carry a variety of cargo mixes. The Ro-Ro decks incorporate hoistable car decks which can be raised or lowered according to market demand at the time. Even in the lowered position, the space underneath these car decks allows the blockstowing of a wide range of neo-bulk commodities and the stowage of normal Ro-Ro cargo. With the car decks raised, the height permits the carriage of out-of-gauge Ro-Ro cargo, which can be on trailers or wheeled or tracked. Examples include heavy machinery, locomotives, yachts, aircraft, earthmovers, automobiles and caravans. Alternatively, blockstowing in several layers is possible and therefore a high utilization can be achieved in such tonnage.

The vessel is fitted with a 'jumbo angled stern ramp' which permits the simultaneous two-way movement of roll trailers and other Ro-Ro cargo. Loading and discharging of Ro-Ro or blockstowed cargo at the same time as cars is achieved by providing separate ramp systems within the vessel.

TABLE 4.9 Shipper's check-list

(1) Name of Shipper	(1) Name of shipper	(1) Name of shipper	(1) Name of shipper
(2) Name of Forwarder	(2) Name of Forwarder	(2) Name of Forwarder	(2) Name of consignee
(3) Name of Consignee	(3) Name of consignee	(3) Name of consignee	(3) Type of commodity
(4) Type of Commodity	(4) Type of commodity	(4) Type of commodity	(4) Origin of cargo
(5) Measurements of cargo	(5) Dimensions of cargo	(5) Dimensions of cargo	(5) Port of loading
(6) Weight of cargo	(6) Weight of cargo	(6) Weight of cargo	(6) Final destination
(7) Is it self-propelled? Is it wheeled or tracked?	(7) Type of packing	(7) Final destination	(7) Port of discharge
(8) Port of loading/port of discharge	(8) Date of shipment	(8) Port of loading/port of discharge	(8) Projected volume/per week/per month/per year
(9) Date of move	(9) Origin of cargo	(9) Date(s) of shipment	(9) Measurement of cargo
(10) Is shipowner to be involved on inlands distribution?	(10) Port of loading	(10) Is a drawing, shipping diagram or sketch plan available?	(10) Weight of cargo
(11) If wheeled: No. of wheels per axle No. of axles Distance between front axle and rear axle If tracked: Ground contact area of tracks (i.e. length and width actually on ground); internal distance between tracks	(11) Final destination	(11) Any additional information, for example, configuration of cargo, configuration of base, accompanying cargo such as parts and accessories	(11) Present method of transport
	(12) Port of discharge		(12) Inland arrangements
	(13) Is cargo 'in gauge'? i.e. measurements do not exceed L 40 ft × W 8 ft × H 8 ft 6 in		(13) Can cargo be double-stacked?
	(14) Can shipper/consignee accept 40 ft trailers at plant?		(14) Does shipper/consignee have clamp truck?
	(15) Will cargo be loaded/discharged under cover?		(15) Will cargo be loaded/discharged under cover?
			(16) If woodpulp (a) are bales unitized? (b) are bales 6 or 8 packed?

4.6 Inland clearance depots

Inland clearance depots (ICDs) are situated at convenient points – usually in industrial and commercial areas outside the limits of any port or airport. They are operated by a consortium or other approved body and provide facilities for the entry, examination and clearance of goods imported or exported in containers, railway train ferry wagons, unit loads or other approved methods. This facility has been inaugurated in recent years to reduce to a minimum the formalities that have to be observed at ship's side. It enables importers and exporters to gain full advantage of the use of such services as Ro-Ro vessels and containerization cargoes involving the trailer or container travelling under Customs Bond to and from the port. It may be road or rail borne. Overall the ICDs have taken over the traditional role of the conventional port, being served by customs facilities and sheds and accommodation for stuffing and stripping LCLs (less than container loads: shippers/consignees not having sufficient cargo to justify a full container load (FCL) can bring their traffics individually to the ICDs for consolidating, with other traffic into LCL containers for forwarding to/from the goods' ultimate destination/source).

It will be appreciated that the inland clearance depot is essentially a customs term used to identify where customs clearance facilities are provided away from the airport and seaport and for public use. Many are container freight stations dealing with exclusively containerized cargo, and others may be a freight village (p. 57) or dry port (p. 86); the Customs bond is usually TIR (Transport International Routier). They are usually managed by a consortium.

4.7 Dry ports

The development of multi-modalism internationally has seen the emergence of the inland situated dry port. Basically, it is a rail terminal located in an industrial and/or commercial region providing a direct rail link with one or more container ports. It is served by dedicated container trains with the import/export cargo being cleared by customs at the dry port. It handles both LCL/FCL cargoes and overall has all the facilities and logistics provided by the seaport. This includes cargo handling warehousing and open storage; port services documentation and clearance; shipping arrangements, for example freight arrangements; booking of cargo shipping space and through bills of lading; customs brokerage documentation and clearance; insurance; and cargo consolidation.

An example of a dry port is found at Ipoh which serves the ports of Klang (260 km) and Penang (180 km) in Malaysia. The project was developed by the Malayan railway and Port Klang and deals with LCL/FCL container export/import cargoes. The dry port of Ipoh acts as a multi-modal transport operator and provides a comprehensive service. This includes road transport to/from shippers' premises; booking of shipping space and provision of related documentation; road haulage to/from the dry port; and customs brokerage and freight forwarding thus avoiding the need to have agents at the port to handle the shippers' cargo. Daily dedicated container trains operate between Ipoh and the two ports completely integrating with the container shipping schedules and thereby providing a total service.

The dry port occupies an area of 6 ha embracing a container yard for heavy stacking, empty boxes and open storage; additionally, there are import and export sheds. Handling equipment includes fork lifts, cranes and container trailers. Ipoh is managed by the Malayan Railway and Port Klang, whilst all the services are contracted out, including handling, freight forwarding, road haulage, customs, security and maintenance. In 1992 it handled 10 000 TEUs. A major factor in the success of the project is the unimpeded flow of containers to/from the two ports thereby speeding up the transit time. The dry port has made a major contribution to the acceleration of the industrial and commercial growth in the region of central Malaysia which it serves.

4.8 Sea transport

During the past 25 years, there has been a radical change in the techniques adopted in the distribution of international trade insofar as maritime transport is concerned. Basically, some 98 per cent of world trade in volume terms is conveyed by sea transport and the following developments have emerged since the mid-1960s which have aided a more economical distribution thereby encouraging the exploitation of the world resources:

(1) Containerization displacing the conventional 'tween deck tonnage has transformed the international distribution of general merchandise introducing a door-to-door service. Moreover, it has substantially improved transit times and raised service quality. Progressively over the next few years the shipping industry will witness the gradual introduction of containerization in the remaining 10 per cent of the general cargo trades.

(2) Ro-Ro services conveying road haulage vehicles on international transits again offer a door-to-door service. Likewise, the Ro-Ro service speeds up transits and has raised service standards. This mode of distribution is very popular in the fast expanding UK–Continental trade.

(3) Provision of numerous types of purpose-built specialized bulk cargo carriers. These include liquefied natural gas carriers (LNGs), vehicular carriers for shipment of trade cars, cab chassis, lorries, banana carriers, cement ships, chemical barriers, etc. Moreover, existing long-established vessel types such as oil tankers, ore carriers, timber vessels, have been dramatically improved in terms of their design with a particular emphasis on speed of handling, cargo transshipment, and quick turn-round time in port.

(4) To cater for the need to improve ship turn-round time, versatility of vessel employment, and to contain operating cost, an increasing number of vessels have been introduced, including combi carriers. This vessel is basically a unitized type of cargo carrier combining container and vehicular shipments, including Ro-Ro (p. 53).

(5) The development of the multi-modal or combined transport service is very much on the increase (pp. 94–9). It entails the use of more than one mode of transport on a particular journey offered by a single operator acting as principal for the entire journey. The prime advantage is the door-to-door or warehouse-to-warehouse service.

(6) Logistics and high technology is now driving container expansion coupled with the growing expansion of the hub and spoke global container network.

Sea transport is basically a capital-intensive method of distribution and involves vast investment sums. Consequently, the life of the ship spans some 15–20 years but, as vessels become more intensely used coupled with the advancement of marine engineering technology, the ship's life is tending to become 10–15 years. The problem facing the shipowner, and to a lesser degree other types of transport, is the degree of inflation inherent in ship replacement and the level of freight rates yield.

It is appropriate to mention that vessels generally in the past decade have tended to become modestly faster; of a much increased capacity; rather more specialized and purpose-built for particular cargoes; much more intensely used with overall rather small crew complements; and finally, offering a much improved quality of service. Moreover, full advantage is now being taken of computerization in all areas of international trade distribution involving electronic data interchange (EDI). All these factors have aided the development of international trade and in so doing have enabled sea transport to remain competitively priced. An examination of the more important types of vessels follows, but the reader who wishes to know more about these aspects should study Chapters 2, 3 and 4 of *Elements of Shipping*.

(1) The oil tanker represents about one third of the world merchant fleet in deadweight capacity terms. In fact, some of the world's larger vessels are tankers, some of which exceed 500 000 d.w.t. Crude oil is transported from the oil fields to refineries, and petroleum and fuel oil from refineries to distribution centres and bunkering ports, so that there is a worldwide network of tanker routes. Vessels exceeding 200 000 d.w.t. are called very large crude carriers (VLCC) and those above 300 000 d.w.t. ultra large crude carriers (ULCC). As a result of the reduced world demand for oil, the future oil tanker is more likely to be about 200 000 d.w.t., as the larger specifications have proved rather inflexible in their operation especially in times of economic depression.

(2) Coasters are all-purpose cargo carriers operating around our coast.

(3) A container vessel is basically a cellular vessel with crew and machinery situated aft. Each hold of a cellular ship is fitted with a series of vertical angle guides adequately crossbraced to accept the container. The sixth-generation container vessel has a speed of 23 knots with up to 4400 container capacity. Prominent shipowners are P&O Nedlloyd Lines, Maersk Line, Atlantic Container Line, Hamburg – Süd, DSR – Senator Lines, Hapag-Lloyd, Andrew Weir Shipping and Evergreen.

(4) LASH. Lighter aboard the ship. This type of vessel enables lighters to be conveyed from one port to another thus combining inland waterway with

ocean transportation. This type of vessel is in decline, overtaken by the development of multi-modalism.

(5) LNG. The liquefied natural gas carrier fleet is an important part of the world mercantile fleet – and is a growth sector. This product is an important form of world energy.

(6) OBO. Ore/bulk/oil ships are multi-purpose bulk carriers designed for switching between bulk shipments of oil/bulk grain, fertilizer and ore trades. Many such vessels exceed 200 000 d.w.t.

(7) Ro-Ro type vessels are designed to carry private cars with passengers, coaches, road haulage vehicles and non-motorist passengers. Such vessels are also termed multi-purpose vehicle ferries and operate in the UK–Continental, the Baltic and Mediterranean trades. The important feature of the Ro-Ro vessel is that the vehicles are driven on or off the ship by means of a ramp at the port/berth thereby permitting an unimpeded transshipment movement. This type of vessel has become very popular in the short sea trades around the world, especially in the Mediterranean market; a large number of them are designed to convey only freight, involving the accompanied or unaccompanied trailer, containers, 'maafi', and 'out-of-gauge' indivisible loads conveyed on purpose-built trailers.

(8) Train ferry vessels carry railway passenger and freight rolling stock. Access to and from the vessel is over a ramp thereby permitting an unimpeded transshipment offering through rail transits.

(9) The 'tween deck vessel is a general cargo vessel engaged primarily on deep-sea liner cargo services. This type of vessel has other decks below the main deck called 'tween decks and all run the full length of the vessel. Currently, this type of vessel is being displaced in many trades by the container ship and combi-carrier. The Chinese and Indian fleets have a larger number of such vessels secured on the second-hand market.

(10) The combi-carrier is a unitized cargo carrier combining container and vehicle shipment including Ro-Ro. It is tending to displace 'tween deck tonnage and is particularly ideal in Third World country trades where port transshipment facilities are rather inadequate.

(11) The introduction of the high speed ferry in 1996 involving the monohull and catamaran is displacing the slower multi-purpose ferries and hovercraft. The latest generation of high speed ferry has a speed of 40 knots and can carry 1500 passengers with cars and trailers. Examples where these services have been introduced include Vancouver Island, Tasmania, Irish Sea, North Sea, Greek–Italian trade and other intra-Mediterranean ferry and Ro-Ro routes.

(12) The hydrofoil offering fast passenger ferry services is found in the Greek Islands the Swiss–Italian lakes and other lakes and estuarial areas of the world.

The type of merchant vessel employed on a trade route is determined basically by the traffic carried. Broadly there are three main divisions: liners, tramps and specialized vessels such as tankers.

The liner vessel operates on a scheduled service between a group of ports. Such services offer cargo space or passenger accommodation to all shippers and passengers who require them. The ships sail on scheduled dates/times irrespective of whether they are full or not. Container vessels in deep-sea trades and Ro-Ro vessels in the short sea trades feature prominently in this field. The passenger market is found in the high speed and multi-purpose ferries found in the Baltic, Mediterranean, Vancouver Island, Irish Sea, North Sea and Greek–Italian trade. The deep-sea liner services provide regular services serving a group of ports situated in different countries. Examples include the Europe–Asian, Europe–North American and round-the-world services. Some services operate under a liner conference system which is highly regulated but in decline (see p. 464). However, the bulk of liner services are deregulated and operate outside the liner conference system. The bill of lading features very prominently as the consignment note used in the liner cargo service, with the exception of the international road haulage shipment which involves the CMR document and rail which involves the CIM consignment note.

The tramp or general trader, as she is often called, does not operate on a fixed sailing schedule, but merely trades in all parts of the world in search of cargo, primarily bulk shipments. Such cargoes include coal, grain, timber, sugar, ores, fertilizers and copra which are carried in complete shiploads. Many of the cargoes are seasonal. Tramp vessels are engaged under a document called a charter party on a time or voyage basis. Such negotiations usually are conducted by shipbrokers on behalf of their principals. The fixture rate is determined by the economic force of demand and supply insofar as cargoes seeking shipping space and the availability of vessels is concerned. Such vessels are occasionally chartered to supplement existing liner services to meet peak cargo-shipment demands, or by the shipper with a substantial shipment of cargo, that is, trade cars/chassis.

The specialized vessel such as the oil tanker, ore carrier and timber carrier may be under charter or operated by an industrial company, that is, oil company, motor manufacturer, etc. to suit their own individual or market needs. Most oil companies operate chartered tonnage involving oil tankers on long-term charter.

4.9 Pipelines

Pipeline networks in the UK are mainly confined to oil and gas distribution. In the case of oil, the pipelines link the oil refinery – usually a port terminal – with various distribution depots.

The basic advantage of a pipeline is the low cost of distribution with virtually no labour content in the distribution network. Costs of installing the pipeline system may be moderately high, but are relatively low insofar as distribution is concerned. A further basic advantage is the 24-hour availability of the pipeline and its low maintenance. Conversely, the pipeline has a fixed capacity which inhibits market growth unless a further pipeline is installed. It has many advantages from an environmental point of view with virtually no noise or fumes. Little disruption is caused to the environment during installation compared with road or rail development. Moreover, it permits more than one type of product to be distributed through it.

Pipelines feature more prominently in the USA where they account for some 8 per cent of the proportion of freight/merchandise distributed. They distribute a wide range of bulk commodities, and a number of the pipelines are so designed to distribute more than one commodity type following completion of the cleansing process. By the year 2000 it is forecast that the length of the global pipeline network – (for the transport of oil, gas and liquefied petroleum gas) – will exceed 15 000 km.

4.10 Palletization

Palletization is the process of placing or anchoring the consignment to a pallet or base made of wood or metal. It is a very common technique in air freight where the pallet accompanies the consignment throughout the transit from the factory premises to the retailer. A shrink wrapping technique is frequently used (p. 152). It may be a stillage involving base plates; the box pallets where one side can be dropped; or the skeleton pallet for lightweight cargoes.

Palletization is a growth market in container shipment involving multi-modalism. Accordingly, Ge Seaco have recently introduced the Sea Cell container (see p. 79). Basically, palletization aids cargo handling, reduces packing, facilitates stowage, and mechanizes the technique of cargo handling involving the pallet truck and fork lift truck. To the shipper involved in general merchandise distribution, an enquiry into the possible use of pallets may prove worthwhile. Some shipowners and port operators offer rate concessions on palletized cargo.

4.11 Seaports

The role and significance of ports has changed dramatically during the past decade and this will accelerate into the twenty-first century. Today they have a higher profile both economically and technically in maritime and international trade. Ports today are not only a link in a transport chain but are also trade and distribution centres. Such changes are being driven by the expanding global container network involving the hub and spoke system and increasing volume of container transshipment (see pp. 63–8). Logistics is also playing a major role in international trade distribution (see Chapter 6) in a high tech environment together with privatization as governments opt out of state ownership and investment in their ports. Today shippers are looking for dedicated schedules door-to-door with the customs examination being undertaken at the consignor/consignee premises or at a nearby container freight station/dry port/freight village. Hence an increasing volume of business passing through the port will be customs examined outside the port environs thereby reducing the risk of congestion. Other benefits will include a reduction in infrastructure needs in terms of warehousing and a speeding up of transit. Moreover, it will intensify berth utilization and its infrastructure thereby increasing the throughput of the port. With the elimination of customs examination, the dock labour force will be substantially reduced and this will be accentuated by the provision of high tech computerized cargo handling equipment.

An increasing number of major ports are becoming trade distribution centres, with such developments being concentrated in the port environment. Examples include the ports of Singapore and Rotterdam. The trading areas are called 'Distriparks' and provide industrial companies with a central distribution location with the major benefits of the nearby port infrastructure and prosperous hinterland. Goods are imported and exported through the port and processed through Distripark units involving a warehouse and distribution centre. Companies lease the site and/or warehouse and import the products for assembly, processing, packaging and labelling to serve the nearby markets. This provides enormous cost savings in customs duties, including international cargo distribution; often lower labour and handling costs; the development of customerized products to serve the local market; lower local market distribution costs; an integrated logistics approach to the flow of goods involving 'just-in-time' deliveries; lower inventory costs, due to better control and less inventory; centralized distribution; stuffing and stripping of containerized general cargo; and continuous access to the port infrastructure. The range of products is large, including foodstuffs, garments, machinery, consumer goods, industrial products and so on. Goods leave the Distripark by sea, road, air and canal. An increasing number of exporters are now adopting a policy of purchasing component parts of their products in different parts of the world and undertaking all the assembly work at the Distripark, with each Distripark reflecting the needs of the hinterland it serves. It is very cost effective and will develop especially in regions which have free trade agreements such as the EU, ASEAN, NAFTA and so on.

Three such Distriparks exist in Rotterdam port, and the one at Botlek has a site of 86 ha. The Schenker Integrated Logistics Center will be operational in Distripark Botlek at the beginning of the year 2000. Schenker Integrated Logistics has more than a thousand branches worldwide, employs 27 000 people and has an annual turnover of about DM10 billion. Schenker is one of the world's leading forwarders and logistics service providers. The company announced that it wanted to set up a branch in Distripark Botlek halfway through 1998. On its 50 000 m^2 site Schenker can offer its customers a complete package of logistic services. 'From cross-docking to groupage and the despatch of hazardous material, from temporary storage and value added services to highly specialised logistic projects,' is how Schenker's Rotterdam manager Ebi van Snek describes the company's services. For Schenker the new premises will be an important link in the company's worldwide network. 'We are currently creating a number of junctions worldwide where we can concentrate cargo for our customers,' says Ebi van Snek. 'In Asia, that is Singapore. In Europe that will of course be Rotterdam, as well as a possible second European location. There are also another two of these junctions in the United States.' Here Schenker is anticipating the wishes of several of its customers to be active on several continents as companies want to be able to keep their stock on the spot in order to be able to serve the market better. Schenker's investment in the Distripark Botlek project will amount to more than 10 million dollars.

However, Singapore's port is the market leader in the provision and development of the Distriparks concept. It stems from its being a trading centre and over 500 multinationals and international trading companies use Singapore as their central physical distribution base and logistics centre for the Asia–Pacific region. Distriparks are provided at Alexandra and Pasir Panjang; and a Distribelt embracing a 3700-ha distribution zone runs alongside a 20-km stretch on the southern coast. It embraces the Container Terminal, Keppel Terminal, Pasir Panjang Terminal, cargo consolidation, Alexandra Distripark and Pasir Panjang Distripark. With shipping infrastructure and support, multinational corporations and international freight forwarders operate from this base.

The Pasir Panjang Distripark has ten single-storey centres involving a 162 000 m^2 space with purpose-built ceilings. Additionally, at Pasir Panjang Districentre a three-storey building is provided with 45 000 m^2 including office space of 2000 m^2. It is an ultra-modern warehouse, with each unit able to offer a customerized service in consolidation, repacking, labelling and sorting centres. Round-the-clock security, fire services, fork lift accessibility to every floor, high ceilings, specialized facilities, CCTV security and PA systems are provided. Overall, the Port of Singapore has 14 Districentres within the Distriparks; all have EDI and are fully computerized and automated.

A total of over 750 free trade zones (FTZs) now exist worldwide. The sites are usually situated in the port environs and are free of customs examination and duty until leaving the area. It enables companies to import products and components for assembly, processing, labelling and distribution to neighbouring markets or be despatched to more distant ones. Examples of FTZs are found in the ports of Liverpool, Southampton and Hamburg.

Dubai and Singapore are two major ports which have developed the fast-growing sea/air market to Europe and North America using the nearby airport (p. 93). Singapore port is regarded as the major trading centre of the Far East and more recent facilities include a conference centre.

A new generation of container berths are emerging and an example is found at the Brani terminal at the Port of Singapore. It has an area of 80 ha and a handling capacity of 3.8 million TEUs. It has 15 000 TEU ground slots and five main berths, together with four feeder berths. Total berth length is 2600 m and the minimum depth alongside the main berth is 15 m and the feeder berth 12 m. It has 1000 power points for reefer containers and 20 single-trolley and four double-trolley quay cranes; some 96 rubber-tyred yard cranes are provided. Overall, 100 prime movers are available, and likewise 100 double-stacked container trailers; it has 14 lanes. Brani terminal, situated on an island just across Tanjong Pagar terminal, is linked to Tanjong Pagar terminal and Keppel Distripark by a four-lane causeway. It is equipped with the Computer Integrated Terminal Operations System (CITOS) which integrates and automates Brani planning, control and documentation procedures.

The container freight station (CFS) is an inland depôt handling containers. It is usually identified with one or more ports and has all the facilities to handle the container import/export; stuffing/unstuffing; container servicing, cleaning, main-tenance and repair; and road/rail served with customs facilities. Such facilities are found in Australia and the Middle East, and in other parts of the world where they are known as container bases/container yards.

The development of multimodalism (Chapter 5) in the current decade means that the role of ports will change further, with greater emphasis on trading centres becoming a focal point in terms of resources, infrastructure and professional services for the markets served. It will involve port authorities becoming more closely involved in the markets they serve, embracing both local and international communities. Also, an increasing number will become privatized as governments opt out of state ownership and investment of their ports.

Finally, one must stress that the shipper will focus on the strategic location in the criteria of port selection and the added value such a port offers in the distribution network.

4.12 Sea/air concept

It is significant that Dubai and Singapore are both the primary trading centres of their regions. Such ports are regarded as 'one-stop ports' as shipowners rely on feeder services to generate cargo. Dubai is strategically placed at the crossroads of Asia, Europe and Africa. Singapore is regarded as the trading hub of the Far East market. Manufacturing and trading companies around the world increasingly recognize that efficient production and marketing must be matched by an equally efficient system for shipping goods from the factory to the customer. Hence, Singapore and Dubai are the distribution hubs of their regions (Table 3.1, p. 50).

The sea/air development/transfer at Dubai and Singapore are both growth markets. A range of established air freight consolidators serve the airports, offering daily services to a range of destinations. Cargo transfer from ship's deck to aircraft take-off takes less than five hours, involving the minimum of customs formalities, with only one custom document for the entire transshipment. Cargo handling facilities and services are provided continuously. The sea/air connection is fast, cost-saving and a reliable mode of transshipment. Repacking services are also provided for goods in transit. Substantial savings can also be made in many subsidiary costs of sea freight, warehouse fees, handling, wharfage, haulage cost and insurance. Overall, transit time of transshipment cargo is guaranteed and insured against delay.

Singapore's port is served by 700 shipping lines and linked to 300 ports worldwide. The airport has 52 airlines serving 110 cities in 54 countries. Dubai's international airport is served by 53 airlines serving over 100 destinations. The new cargo complex is one of the most modern in the world, handling both FCL and LCL TEUs, with the latest technology including computer controlled temperature warehouses and handling 250 000 tonnes annually. The seaport is essentially a transshipment point, with over 60 per cent of import cargo destined for re-export; it handles over 12.9 million TEUs annually. The port is served by over 100 shipping lines.

5

Multi-modalism

Multi-modalism is the process of providing a door-to-door or warehouse-to-warehouse service to the shipper which embraces two or more forms of transport, and involves the merchandise being conveyed in a unitized form in the same unit throughout transit. It involves a scheduled and/or dedicated service. Forms of multi-modalism are:

(1) Containerization – FCL/LCL/road/sea/rail.
(2) Land-bridge – trailer/truck – road/sea/road.
(3) Land-bridge – pallet/IATA container – road/sea/air/road.
(4) Trailer/truck – road/sea/road.
(5) Swap-body – road/rail/sea/road.

A development which has emerged in recent years from combined transport operations, multi-modalism is the term used for non-vessel operating carrier (NVOC) operations or non-vessel operating common carrier (NVOCC) operations. Multi-modalism may arise in a container (FCL or LCL) movement or trailer transit. In such a situation, carriers issue bills of lading for the carriage of goods on ships which they neither own nor operate. A freight forwarder will usually issue the FIATA Multi-modal Transport Bill of Lading (see p. 308) for a container or trailer movement or, if the trailer movement is in the UK–Continental trade, a CMR consignment note. For shippers requiring a cargo receipt the freight forwarder will issue a FIATA Forwarders Certificate of Receipt (see p. 309).

An example arises where a freight forwarder offers a groupage service using a nominated shipping line and shipping line equipment. The freight forwarder offers his own tariff for the service but buys from the shipping line at a box rate. NVOCC allows shipping companies to concentrate on ship management and the freight forwarder to utilize his expertise in marketing and consolidating cargo. It is particularly evident in the USA, Far East and Africa trades.

All forms of multi-modalism involve a dedicated service usually under non-vessel operating common carrier (NVOCC) or non-vessel operating carrier (NVOC) arrangements.

5.1 Rationale of development of multi-modalism

Today multi-modalism has become the prime method of distribution in a competitive market. Shippers are looking to the carrier to provide the optimum route for their buyers at a competitive tariff and an acceptable throughout transit time. The development of multi-modalism has arisen due to the following reasons:

(1) Development of the 'just-in-time' strategy requiring dedicated and integrated schedules within shippers' warehouse and distribution arrangements.

(2) Shippers demanding continuous improvements in the distribution network and a quickening of the supply chain.

(3) The documentation involving the carriers' liability and code of practice relative to multi-modalism is now in place through the auspices of the International Chamber of Commerce (ICC) and other international bodies.

(4) World markets are changing rapidly from the primary products to the industrialized scene, as found in Malaysia. Value added benefits have become closely involved with the distribution chain.

(5) Containerization and its infrastructure through the seaport network continues to expand (pp. 63–71).

(6) The development of Distriparks, Districentres and Free Trade Zones (pp. 90–3) continues to grow.

(7) Markets are becoming more global and marketeers follow the strategy of manufacturing/processing/packaging in low labour-cost markets and rely on such centres to distribute to nearby growth markets. This is reducing the supply chain timescale and improving the service to the buyers and importers.

(8) Operators such as P&O Nedlloyd, Container Line and Atlantic Container Line have customerized logistics departments which counsel their clients to provide the most cost-efficient methods of distribution, packaging and routeing.

(9) The development of EDI has greatly facilitated international physical distribution management and control with no boundaries and time zone problems (Chapter 16). This extends to customs clearance.

(10) Air/rail/sea/canal/seaport operators are working more closely together to keep pace and facilitate trade development. Examples include the sea/air bridge from Singapore and Dubai (p. 93) and the sea/rail land-bridge in North America (pp. 90–3).

(11) Governments are taking a keener interest in the development of their nation's economy by encouraging a global trade strategy, and providing the infrastructure to facilitate this objective.

(12) The European market for example, regards the development of a European combined transport network essential to its economic development, and in 1990 the Transport Council adopted a resolution to set up a high-level working group to identify the measures necessary to achieve this objective.

Overall, the foregoing factors demonstrate how multi-modalism is leading the growth of worldwide markets.

5.2 Factors driving multi-modalism into the twenty-first century

There is no doubt, in an era of continuing international trade growth varying from 1 to 5 per cent annually, that strategically the role of distribution will become increasingly important. Markets continue to develop globally in line with the efficiency of their infrastructure in an increasingly competitive high tech environment. The pressure to develop multi-modalism is economically driven by industry and politically driven by government. The transport operator as provider of the service has the responsibility of working with other carriers and resource providers to provide a dedicated high tech multi-modal network at a reasonable tariff. This requires terminal operators – shipping/rail/canal/road/pipeline carriers; international agencies ICC, IMO, IATA, UNCITRAL, WTO – and freight forwarders, agents and transport equipment manufacturers who can provide a uniform global liberalized framework in which to operate on a transparent basis; and finally requires an environment completely deregulated from national prejudice or culture and from any one government's regulations. Innovation and adoption in response to opportunities and threats, both short- and long-term, are key elements in the ongoing development of multi-modalism.

Overall multi-modalism involves a team of providers in a transport chain where all the constituents work closely together in accord with market needs and objectives. It requires each party to the multi-modal operation, including both the provider and user, to take up a strategic position with a view to focusing on the long-term benefits in a fast moving and changing global high tech infrastructure. Planning is the central key to such strategies if they are to add value to the multi-modal transport chain. This involves improving transit times, reliability, volume throughput, interchangeability – involving swap-body/container transshipments; quality of service and professional management. The development of computerized technology enables management to monitor performance with a view to raising standards.

An examination of the European infrastructure environment in 1998 identified the features driving the intermodal expansion. These included a dissatisfaction with operating conditions and practices; shippers, containership operators and forwarders all confronting a range of problems including over tonnaging, high cost and low rates imposed on the shipping lines by global shippers who in turn were demanding more and more sophisticated services. Solutions to such problem areas include deregulation; the provision of an integrated coherent European network and the development of a service orientated and cost reducing culture.

Accordingly, developments now sought in the European intermodal network include the following:

(1) Container lines taking over control of their own inland services, quality and costs.
(2) Traditional operators striving to keep or win their share of the market through a more multi-modal focused strategy.

(3) Ports and terminals competing through their hinterland links for more multi-modal orientated business.
(4) A new international cooperative forum.
(5) Formulation of global logistics operators and intermodal marketing companies.
(6) The need for a single European infrastructure strategy (see pp. 441–44).
(7) The need for a single transport market with harmonization of regulations and competition rules.
(8) The identification and elimination of any obstacles to intermodality.
(9) The continuous exchange of relevant data amongst intermodal carriers to facilitate service improvements both on a day-to-day basis and when planning short- and long-term improvements.

Europe operates a short distance transport market and has a complex coast line. It has a liberalized trucking industry but the railway network is highly regulated on a national basis. This impedes the development of intermodalization. For example severe restrictions exist not only for private operators to operate trains over national networks but also to manage and transship swap-bodies and containers at rail served freight terminals. Such operating restrictions which are union influenced are in complete contrast with the United Kingdom network which is fully privatized and operates on a free market access basis with no direct government intervention. A further significant factor is that the European rail network is state funded and accountable, whilst in the United Kingdom it is in the private sector.

In contrast North America is, like Europe, an industrialized economy which is high tech and highly developed especially in the USA and Canada. Both are economic blocs as found in NAFTA (see p. 10) and EU (see p. 428). The geographical and political differences are very significant. North America operates in a liberalized free market environment. Overall, the average freight haul is very much longer. The east and west coasts of America have a trade interface with Europe and with Asia and the Far East respectively. This opens up enormous intra-trade route opportunities which have been grasped by the ports and railways to provide land-bridge (sea/rail or sea/rail/sea) services (see pp. 90–3). Such developments are strategically wide ranging, involving market partners, investment patterns and strategic operational alliances, based on competition and the volume of business involved. Overall, it reflects a different management culture of deregulation compared with Europe which tends to be a highly regulated market.

We have already mentioned the changing role of seaports globally and the growing trend towards privatization and the movement away from the state controlled Port Authority (see p. 90). At the same time container ship operators are extending their hub and spoke systems (see pp. 63–71). All these port developments are generating more investment in the industry and at the same time provide opportunities to extend multi-modalism to the port hinterland by rail or road. Such developments are global in developed and developing countries, newly industrialized countries (NICs) and less developed countries (LDCs). Each have a different economic profile, but all have the opportunity to develop their economies through such investment. It brings together, through trade, high and low cost labour markets of varying skills featuring industrial and agricultural economies.

5.3 Features of multi-modalism

Given below is a broad analysis of multi-modalism:

(1) It provides a dedicated service with each operator or carrier committed to the schedule.

(2) It operates under NVOCC or NVOC arrangements (p. 94).

(3) A strong feature is its provision of a regular, reliable, competitively priced quality door-to-door service with acceptable transit times. Hence the value added benefit is considerable to the multi-modalism users; and it is usually fully computerized involving EDI, thereby enabling the operator to monitor the package throughout its transit. Overall, it places the multi-modal user in a strongly competitive situation.

(4) It develops and coordinates the best features of the transport modes to the advantage of the shipper.

(5) It is an ideal environment for EDI and, undoubtedly, as EDI expands on a global scale, the multi-modal network will move with it.

(6) The multi-modal network is very extensive and fast growing. The wide range of services it can offer stimulates the development of markets worldwide.

(7) It is consumer led and market driven in its development in a logistic environment. Overall, it is bringing markets and the buyer and seller closer together, and especially so in the high tech and fast-moving consumer markets including foodstuffs.

(8) An increasingly large number of operators are providing logistics departments to customize their clients' needs (pp. 101–21).

(9) Good asset-utilization of multi-modal infrastructure permits competitive door-to-door or warehouse-to-warehouse through rates to be offered. Thus it exploits the economies of scale and yields a favourable return on transport investment. Basically, it is a high tech operation.

(10) Under the auspices of the ICC and other international bodies a common code of liability and processing of documents is now permitted. This has created confidence in the market and the handling of all the multi-modal documents by banks, carriers, agents, buyers, sellers and port authorities. It has also permitted a through door-to-door or warehouse-to-warehouse rate to be quoted.

(11) Operators are strongly committed to multi-modalism, and as time moves on, its extension will gather momentum and the existing networks will be further improved and diversified. It will be market and technology driven, aided by an increasingly discerning shipper.

(12) Multi-modalism is giving a new impetus to the role of seaports and airports, especially the former. Port authorities worldwide are developing not only the port enclaves through Districentres and free trade zones, but also initiating and

encouraging the infrastructure operators on which they rely, to develop and improve existing multi-modal networks. Examples include the ports of Singapore, Dubai, Klang and Rotterdam. Overall, port authorities are tending to coordinate the activities and develop their strategy on an unprecedented scale. Many are being privatized and have an enhanced role through the development of the hub and spoke system (see pp. 63–8). The port authority of today is only a part of the total product network (pp. 90–3).

(13) Associated with item (12), the changing pattern of international distribution is resulting in less port-to-port cargo and the accelerated growth of multi-modalism. This relieves port congestion and develops ICDs, dry ports, free trade zones and the use of local import control and export control customs arrangements. It encourages the development of a new vision and enthusiasm at all levels of the supply chain to improve the value added benefits which accrue to the exporter and importer in using the network system (see Chapter 5).

(14) As indicated earlier, many multi-modal operators have a logistics department to counsel and develop shippers' needs. This is encouraging closer harmony between the shipper and operator and ensures an ongoing market-led commitment from both the user and provider of the multi-modal network.

(15) Market research is an essential ingredient to develop the system involving a continuous monitoring of the network.

(16) Multi-modalism develops new markets, improves commodity quality, raises loadability and lowers transit times, reduces packing and aids the development of consumer high tech fast-moving markets. Moreover, it brings cultures and the international business world closer together both in their objectives and ideology.

(17) The system favours both the large and small shipper by involving the full load or consolidated consignment.

To conclude our analysis, there is no doubt that multi-modalism will contribute significantly to a changing international trade pattern. It will open up countries with low labour-cost skills to the industrialized westernized markets with great buying power. Such industrialized high labour-cost countries are increasingly reliant on the development of their global manufacturing business by producing within the low-cost markets and relying on multi-modalism to distribute the goods in a cost-effective manner to high GDP markets.

5.4 Multi-modalism strategy

The strategy to adapt to multi-modalism is essentially market and technology led. It is an ongoing strategy, with market growth providing the cash flow necessary to fund the continuing investment. Moreover, as the system develops, the economies of scale will lower development costs, as has been experienced in computerization. It is an exciting time and one full of opportunity, but it is a strategy which requires complete

professionalism and high quality training at all levels. We will briefly consider some of the aspects which require special attention.

(1) Shippers and operators must continuously study trading patterns and trends to identify and develop new opportunities for multi-modalism. Existing systems must be continuously evaluated and improved as the trading pattern changes.

(2) Trading blocs such as ASEAN, NAFTA, EU and EFTA need to review both their internal market and external market multi-modal systems structure. The closer trading blocs work together, the greater will be the benefit in terms of market growth and distribution improvement. Strategies of empathy must prevail, involving all parties, to the total distribution product.

(3) The Pacific Rim continues to house a number of important markets and will require particular attention in terms of opportunities.

(4) Major shippers, particularly multinationals, are companies with great investment resources and high calibre personnel who are leading the way in the development of multi-modalism in many markets. The smaller shipper, who may be a subcontractor, is benefiting from such developments.

(5) Multi-modalism strongly favours the 'just-in-time' strategy.

In the next 10 years the multi-modal network will be much extended and will become virtually global. Continuing port investment and development of the hub and spoke system, coupled with the annual growth of containerization in a logistics driven environment will all play major roles. Consumer markets in particular will no longer rely on the seaport-to-seaport or airport-to-airport network, but rather the door-to-door or warehouse-to-warehouse system. The 'just-in-time' strategy together with the role of Distriparks, Districentres, FTZ, ICD/dry ports, air and land-bridges, LEC and LIC, and the industrial plant transplant, will all become established on a global basis. The ramifications of multi-modalism will contribute significantly to raising living standards worldwide.

■ □ ■ ■ 6

Logistics and globalization

6.1 Role of logistics

Logistics can be broadly defined as the time-related positioning of resources, ensuring that materials, people, operational capacity and information are in the right place at the right time in the right quantity and at the right quality and cost.

Today the world is a single integrated market place in which supply chain efficiency has become a competitive necessity. Manufacturers and retailers have sought cost savings and service improvements to enhance their competitiveness by supplying larger markets with fewer production and distribution centres.

The multinational industry or company is now logistically driven and managers must be logistically literate. This has placed new demands on the logistics industry and in order to meet these demands a new industry of global supply chain services is developing. The gains that can be made from inventory reduction due to quick response and just-in-time have been the basis of widespread industry reform.

Logistics is a corporate function and a strategic part of business planning. Many companies now see logistics management as part of the marketing discipline designed to improve customer service and sales. For a logistics operation to be successful on an international scale, two main criteria have to be satisfied: there needs to be an integrated network of professionals throughout all countries concerned to ensure the smooth passage of goods; and secondly there has to be a high level of specialist expertise and knowledge relating to the multitude of laws, conventions and regulations inherent in the conduct of the international trade environment. A further point, transparency of data communication, must be evident at all times between parties in the supply chain. The trend in the past decade has been for international companies to rationalize their business by integrating production, sales and marketing operations across frontiers. Their suppliers have followed suit and in the logistics industry there has been a strong move towards creating international networks either through merger and acquisition, or through confederations of independent professionals. Hence, there is no established pattern of international logistics networks at present. Each logistics company will have its own particular type of network with its own strengths suitable for some types of customers and not others.

The demand-focused international trade industry does increasingly rely on satellite production, encourage suppliers to have shorter product lifecycles through fashion and technology advancement, and develop in the food industry, through technology, longer shelf life. All these factors help to drive logistics in a shrinking world of global sourcing.

Few service industries have changed more dramatically than international transport in the last decade. The impact of logistics has turned transport on its head. An activity long regarded as a self-defining but unavoidable cost centre is now seen as a means of reducing inventory, cutting costs and improving customer service. Exporters and importers have the tools by which they can become more efficient, more customer focused and more profitable. The many small firms that do not need a customized logistical service can call on the integrators (see p. 48). Led by a handful of mainly US owned multinationals, these companies have been winning market share as their operational ambitions have been extended.

Similarly, information technology systems have equipped transport providers to upgrade their services to improve utilization and yield. Whether it is the transport industry, the port industry, international rail freight or aviation, the current common denominator is to aim for optimal use of capacity and resources, irrespective of whether the equipment is a container gantry crane or a Boeing 747 freighter. To take an example from shipping, major container lines give a shipper or consignee the ability to track his or her container from the start to the finish of its journey. In an ideal world the container would arrive exactly when the consignee wants it and he or she could ignore its journey. But in the real world delays occur. To be able to know 24 hours a day the precise location of the container and maybe altering its estimated time of arrival, is a tremendously powerful tool for adjusting other elements in the business around it. At the other end of the scale, deciding on behalf of a European-wide supermarket chain how many distribution centres it should build and where they should be located to optimize the delivery operation is a complex numerical evaluation aided by computer analysis.

In consequence a growing number of businesses are outsourcing part or all of their logistics management. A number of shipping lines like P&O Nedlloyd (see pp. 104–8), and CSX/Sea Land have logistics subsidiaries to bid for this third party business.

Multinationals are driving the logistics expansion as big companies stipulate quality of service and the medium sized and small firms are simply having to comply. Medium and small companies are changing their organizational structure and what were once standalone shipping departments are becoming part of a larger customer service organization (see p. 30). Multinationals have built partnerships with their logistics suppliers. Large companies sourcing their materials on a global basis insist on dealing with a logistics company with a worldwide network. Major shippers are looking for cost benefits and the opportunity to add value. Manufacturers are looking to reduce inventory, improve operational performance and enhance customer service.

Logistics generates competitive advantage in the market place and achieves cost reduction. Moreover, it introduces a logistics management culture in a company which in turn raises the quality of service which can be further improved by adding value to the service through a variety of options (see p. 109). The key to it is adaptation and transparency whereby all parties in the supply chain have complete integrity through the continuous exchange of data.

An analysis of the logistic needs for the European focused company is given below.

European companies require a European service from logistics service providers. They do not want:

(1) a plethora of service providers when they are consolidating;
(2) to manage distribution at a national level when they are operating at the European level;
(3) different computer systems throughout Europe when they have introduced European-wide integrated systems;
(4) varying reporting methods and measures in different markets.

European companies do not need:

(1) a single service provider operating in all markets and geographies;
(2) assets owned and managed by the same company in all markets.

They do need:

(1) a single management interface for all European operations;
(2) a common standard of measures and reports provided centrally by the European logistics service managers;
(3) a single systems interface giving visibility of stock movements and locations;
(4) a common billing standard;
(5) a single agreement.

It is argued that logistics service providers must meet this challenge and must also provide:

(1) a consistently high standard in the basic services of transport and warehousing;
(2) a visionary approach with new ideas, concepts and approaches;
(3) access to best practice from different sectors and national approaches;
(4) a clear chain of command with national and locations operations treating all customers as 'ours' and not treating some as 'theirs' and therefore as second-class.

The global and European logistics services market, it is predicted, will undergo 'a significant change' in the next few years. These changes could include:

(1) more mergers and acquisitions to reduce excess capacity and increase scope;
(2) joint ventures between different types of service providers;
(3) joint ventures and operating networks across European and global markets;
(4) a move to provide chain management services with 'basics,' such as transport and warehousing outsourced;
(5) joint ventures between logistics and other service providers, including systems houses and consulting groups;
(6) joint ventures between logistics service companies and niche market clients.

A key factor in logistic management internationally is the channel of distribution (see p. 394). The degree to which the channel is simple or complex, will depend on the nature of the goods and the channel strategy. A channel of distribution which involves numerous stages is likely to add considerably to the final price of the goods as each intermediary adds a percentage for profit. Hence, determining the channel of distribution strategy for a logistics operation is one of the most important factors in the whole process. It must reflect the need to maximize sales opportunities, achieve high levels of customer service, minimize cost and ensure accurate information flows. Many companies use a third party logistics specialist.

Warehousing and storage systems play a decisive role in international logistics. It includes the FTZ and Distriparks (see pp. 90–3) as found in seaports and their environs. It epitomizes the role of the seaport today as the trading centre. Effective warehouse management ensures a smooth level of supply to customers. Additionally, it yields the following benefits: economies of scale permitting long production runs and bulk cargo shipments; the ability to build up stocks in anticipation of seasonal or new product demand; improved customer service by, for example, the quick replacement of faulty goods or components; it facilitates break-bulk and other assembly operations as found in Distriparks and FTZ for onward shipment to customers; and finally it provides a secure and good environment to protect goods from damage, deterioration and pilferage internationally. Logistically, focused warehouse management is found in the ports of Singapore, Dubai and Rotterdam where goods are assembled, processed and packaged for distribution to an international market. All the warehouses in these ports are computer controlled.

The foregoing developments are driving many carriers who operate global services to develop a specific logistics product essentially offering a portfolio of integrated services. This applies both to shipowners and airlines.

6.2 P&O Nedlloyd Container Line – Logistics Division

A leading player in the field of global logistics operation is the mega container carrier P&O Nedlloyd Container Line. It has the world's largest number of standing container slots of 224 000; a fleet of 112 vessels including four vessels of 6674 TEU – the latest container tonnage generation; a 540 000 TEU fleet of containers; a genuine global network; a US$4 billion annual turnover; a well-developed EDI system (see pp. 373–5) and in 1997 it carried 2.3 million loaded TEUs. Formed in 1996 with 600 specialist staff working in 44 offices in 19 countries, spanning Europe, the Gulf, the USA, the Far East and the Indian subcontinent, it identifies the following six key areas sought by customers.

(1) Strategic solutions to the problems of long-distance product sourcing and movement. This is achieved by matching the client's business needs to the latest techniques and expertise to formulate solutions to the problems of long-distance product sourcing and movement. An example is the European-based departmental stores buying a range of consumer products from the Far East. Key

factors are quality control, coping with variations in consumer demand and distributing supplies in a cost-effective manner.

(2) Companies which can provide capabilities interfaced across a range of different transport modes including sea, road, rail, canal and air as found in multi-modalism.

(3) Improvements in quality of service to end customers. This basically centres on customer asset management – ensuring the goods arrive in a quality condition to a prescribed schedule with zero failure rate.

(4) Improvements in profits realized through all the marketing and financial benefits inherent in the global logistic system to the user.

(5) Management of 'trade-offs' within the supply chain.

(6) A fully outsourced logistics management service.

Users of the service include automotive manufacturers, high-street retailers, wines and spirits producers, footwear, fashion garments, sports goods and electronic manufacturers.

The global logistics operators focus attention on the four key service areas detailed below.

(1) *Supply chain management.* This requirement may be illustrated by the leading retail chains sourcing their merchandise from suppliers in Europe, the Far East and the USA. The logistics operator's task is to ensure that goods of a saleable quality are manufactured and transported safely and cost effectively and are delivered on time. This key service covers three aspects:

   (a) vendor management, involving the processing of customers' orders direct to their suppliers and monitoring the production process;

   (b) information, featuring receipt of customers' orders via EDI download (this leads to 24-hour monitoring and reporting of status and cost down to item level);

   (c) communication, permitting customers to receive advance notice of shipments which are off schedule via international e-mail links.

   The key benefits are reduced inventory levels, improved visibility of all costs to item level, improved delivery on time and clearer management responsibility. Study the supply pipe line in Figure 6.1.

(2) *Delivery and customs clearance.* An example of this requirement is provided by a leading drinks company with over 50 brands worldwide. The objective is to receive and handle stock and to arrange transport and overseas shipment. The four main features of the service include:

   (a) inventory management, featuring direct data exchange to provide on-line reporting;

   (b) order picking, embracing maximizing deliveries of export shipments direct to the end customer;

   (c) quality control including checking on arrival, arranging, relabelling and repacking as required;

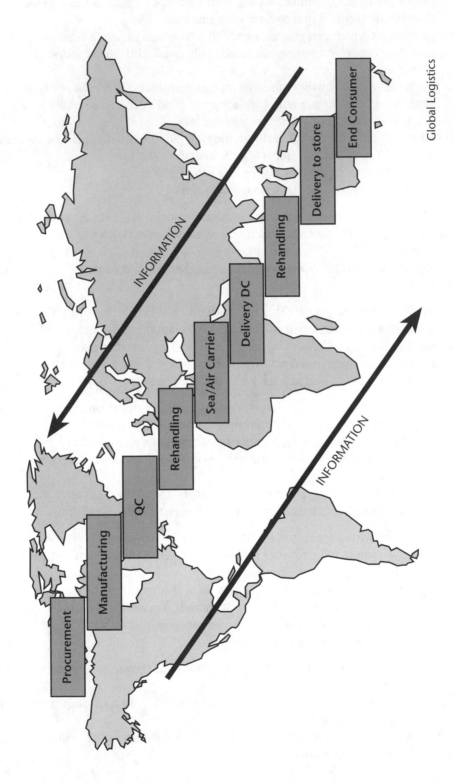

FIGURE 6.1 Global logistics supply pipe line reproduced courtesy P&O Nedlloyd

(d) security, the adoption of sophisticated arrangements suitable for a high-value commodity.

The key results include delivery only when market demand dictates, secure and cost-effective storage and efficient onward distribution services.

(3) *Distribution management.* This is the requirement of a major sportswear company which imports merchandise from suppliers in the Far East. The objective is to improve upstream process controls and maximize direct delivery to high-street stores in Europe. The three main features of the service include:

(a) quality control, embracing collecting goods from suppliers and ensuring compliance with specified quality standards;

(b) consolidation and delivery, embracing sorting, labelling and packaging goods according to end-customer order requirements and providing delivery direct to the customer;

(c) information, embracing full integration via EDI between the customer's purchase order system, their financial and distribution systems and the global supply chain management system.

The ultimate results were improved supplier quality standards, reduced warehousing and handling costs and shortened order cycle times.

(4) *Import logistics and outbound distribution.* This is illustrated by a manufacturer of electronic goods which sources components in the Far East for manufacture in Europe. The objective is to manage the inbound supply of components to exacting production schedules and distribute the finished products across Europe. The three main features of the service include:

(a) supply chain management, embracing the despatch of orders, the monitoring of production, consolidation and delivery on time to the manufacturing plant;

(b) information, embracing tracking progress in the supply chain so that customers can accommodate changes to the production plan;

(c) consolidation/distribution, featuring maximizing container usage to cut costs and distribution 'on time' to retailers.

The key results are proactive control of delivery schedules and reduced shipment costs from the consolidation and integration of inward and outward distribution.

Overall, the global logistics company concentrates on six core products: supply chain management, warehousing, customs clearance, air freight, consolidation and project cargo. It will improve supply chain visibility by developing tailored processes and tracking systems. This will lead to improved buying processes and decision-making, reduced stock levels and improved reaction times in delivering to end users. Overall, it will reduce supply chain costs, thus cutting lead times, creating fast-flow procedures and introducing upstream controls.

6.3 Factors contributing to the development of logistics

The factors influencing the development of global logistics are numerous. The most salient are detailed below.

(1) The development of information technology (IT) has enabled a transformation to take place in communication and data transmission opening up markets and re-focusing strategies in distribution and manufacturing outsourcing and assembly. It has no culture or language barriers, no time zones and is available continuously, bringing together the low and high labour cost nations and their skills for the exchange of goods and services.

(2) The globalization of markets with their infrastructure and international trade environment generating business confidence internationally. A major contributor is the WTO (see pp. 22–8).

(3) The accelerating development of the global container network has offered a new challenge to the global trader. It has placed a fresh focus on global distribution with an emphasis on added value in the distribution chain. The question posed by the international entrepreneur is how can we further improve and extend the conventional multi-modal container service to the benefit of the shipper and in the interests of efficiency. Shippers are already being offered the option of independent software and systems as an alternative to those available from the carrier. This allows suppliers, carriers, manufacturers and retailers to make optimum routeing decisions and increases the transparency of goods flows. The financial efficiency of the supply chain network is also being examined. This involves developing a product to coordinate the flow of funds more efficiently with the movement of goods thereby allowing the importer and exporter access to cheaper sources of money.

(4) The continuous expansion of the integrators TNT and DHL. This has opened up new markets in both the manufacturing and service industries.

(5) The decline of the end-to-end/port-to-port liner conference system and the development of the hub and spoke global container network (see p. 63) coupled with the expansion of multi-modalism.

(6) The emergence of the mega container operator (see p. 104) which exploits the economies of scale and provides the mega operator the opportunity to provide the 'in-house' global logistics resources such as found in P&O Nedlloyd.

(7) The decline of the freight forwarder has emerged as the mega container carriers develop in-house global logistic operations. This has encouraged the trade to entrust the entire distribution arrangement to the shipowner thereby bypassing the freight forwarder.

(8) The development of the freeport, free trade zones and Distriparks (see pp. 90–3) in the port environs has opened up new opportunities of trade distribution for the international entrepreneur. Such designated areas are immune from customs examination and revenue collection until they enter the domestic market in question. They enable the global trader to outsource the product and focus on such areas as the component assembly point, the packaging and

distribution point, and the mixing and blending unit for powdered cargoes such as spices.

(9) Value is added to the product through the global logistic network. It may be through better packaging arrangements, more outsourcing of componentized products which offer lower costs and better quality, or through the blending and mixing of food products as found in the Distriparks in the Port of Rotterdam.

(10) Companies, particularly multinationals, are being driven by their logistics departments. Moreover, the multinationals now focus on a simultaneous global product launch across all markets to ensure an early cash return on capital expenditure rather than concentrating on a regional launch over a period of time, for example, phase one Europe, phase two North America and phase three the Far East. This favours the logistic operation.

(11) Following on from point (10) is the intense competition emerging in the global product market. Hence, to remain competitive the trader must adopt a global logistic strategy.

(12) Satellite production demands a logistic network. It is computer driven.

(13) Shorter product lifecycle driven by a fashion conscious international market and continuous technical advancement favours logistic efficiency.

(14) The ongoing technological developments providing a longer shelf life for many consumer products, especially foodstuffs, needs a logistically based distribution sourcing mechanism.

(15) The global logistic facility offers a one-stop operation and the opportunity to deal with one person, the account executive. Hence, both the importer and exporter develop empathy with the global logistics operator on a tailor-made basis, taking full advantage of their professionalism and experience coupled with a competitively priced operation. Traders can therefore concentrate on their core business of marketing, product development, investment and production.

(16) The global logistic operation encourages the rationalization of distribution networks. This will accelerate as the hub and spoke system develops through the mega carrier operations.

(17) Continuing improvements in the global infrastructure, e.g. port modernization, the development of inland clearance depots and free trade zones, the provision of new and enlarged airports, the development of road and rail networks serving the ports and airports, all favour the global logistic operation. The development of multi-modalism involving a stronger interface and integration between transport modes and the emergence of dedicated services also favours global logistics.

(18) Undoubtedly, the rapid expansion of information technology has been a major driving factor as the global logistic operation is computer driven.

(19) Companies today demand responsiveness from the global operator. The discerning international entrepreneur is demanding the 'total logistics product service' (see item 17). When a trader purchases a service, the trader expects the consignment to be delivered or to be informed of delays or challenges encountered. As trade expands and companies move from a regional to a

global market basis to exploit the economies of scale, to remain competitive in price and product specification, and to make further market penetration, the quality of the service becomes paramount. Moreover, the global logistics operator, through experience and professionalism, facilitates the trader's expansion from a regional to a global market base. The global operator will be able to help the trader in planning such market expansion and provide data on the culture, the market environment, import restrictions, customs regulations and the best-practice global logistics operation feasible. Today, traders are logistically literate and demand accreditation to product quality control – which includes distribution through global logistics. Moreover, traders demand a quick response to changing and volatile order levels with cycles of peaks and troughs. Again, the mega logistic carrier can best respond to such a challenge.

(20) Market research confirms that only 30 per cent of changes in suppliers are motivated by a better or cheaper product. Most changes occur due to a poor service quality or inadequate attention to the individual customer. This also favours the mega logistics global operator.

(21) The manufacturer/producer striving to achieve a shorter production cycle realized with the facilitation of many of the ingredients offered by the logistics system.

(22) The development of third party logistic contractors such as Wincanton Logistics and Exel Logistics.

(23) The continuous improvement in supply chain software. The most important concept underlying management of supply is that of integration. This embraces manufacturing resource planning, inventory management and supply chain design. Goods must be able to flow in a highly organized manner between each stage of the supply chain while at the same time achieving the most desirable balance between sales – stocks – production and customer service – cost – working capital. Every supply chain will have a different set of emphases. For example, a manufacturer of high specification value goods may be more interested in speed and security of delivery than achieving the lowest cost. It is essential all parties involved in the supply chain have an agreed set of priorities. Moreover, effective transparent communication and understanding needs to be created of what the supply chain is designed to achieve. Logistic systems are important to be able to send data to where the decisions are taken and to keep all the international business managers and sectors informed about the flow of goods. Figure 6.2 features the supply chain software. Software advances have been accelerated through the rapid globalization of manufacture and distribution.

(24) The development of time sharing with the logistics contractor. This involves the contractor being linked to the customer's own IT system – receiving order picking and delivery instructions, implementing them and feeding back the results for processing and evaluation. However, this limits their ability to take a proactive approach to their customer's needs.

(25) Economic and trading blocs as found in Europe, North America and the Far East are continuing to develop as member states realize their benefits. Such blocs

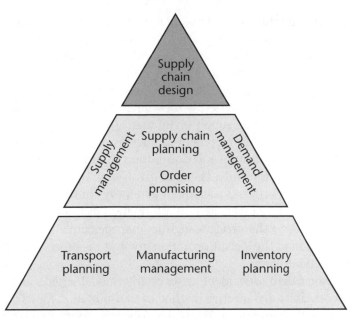

FIGURE 6.2 A focus of the supply chain software
Reproduced by courtesy of Synquest

favour particularly the global logistic trader who can adopt the strategy of selling a single product in a single market such as the European Union which has no culture or trade barriers and permits the free flow of goods. Supply chain efficiency is here a key factor in sales performance and market penetration.

To conclude our analysis the specific reasons for the increasing interest in supply chain management and global logistics can be summarized as follows:

(1) *Concept*. Companies are primarily concerned with reducing delivery times and improving responsiveness to customers, reflecting the shorter product lifecycles they face.
(2) *Value*. Equal emphasis is placed upon cost savings (from reduced inventory levels, economies of scale and a reduction in fixed assets) and improved service quality (through reliable delivery, improved stock availability and response times).

To achieve improvements in the management of a supply chain, keeping track of goods at all times is the key. This can be achieved through manual methods or sophisticated EDI tools. (see pp. 373–93)

6.4 The logistic freight forwarder

Advances in information technology and the relaxation in Europe of customs barriers have greatly facilitated the emergence of new strategies in trans-European distribution. Gone are the national boundaries as impediments to quick distribution with their attendant customs examination. Today, traders treat the 15 European states as a single market with no trade, distribution, culture or product specification barriers. Consequently, traders are outsourcing their non-core functions and entrusting the pan-European distribution operation to the logistic freight forwarder. This involves the freight forwarder taking over every subsequent function from production line to final delivery and focusing on supply chain management.

A further industrial development is the move to product outsourcing and spreading points of manufacture and distribution throughout a variety of countries. Accordingly, the freight forwarder becomes involved in managing the flow of goods, from warehousing, picking and packing to inventory control and product repairs. A global network and heavy investment in information technology is required. Freight forwarders offer added-value services, logistics management and reliable information to their clients. In short the logistic operation involves the process of order acceptance to the stage of end delivery.

The logistic freight forwarder focuses on intermodal services and endeavours to formulate a cost- and time-effective method of transportation for its customers and a single rate for the through transit. The freight forwarder concentrates on supply chain management and works towards forming partnerships covering parts of the supply chain with its major customers.

Overall, the logistically focused freight forwarder provides value added services including inventory control, sorting, deferred manufacturing, assembly, testing, badging, packaging, labelling and bar-coding. The benefits to the shipper include improved cash flow, lower running costs, reduced capital expenditure, released management time and flexibility.

To conclude, the successful logistic freight forwarder must be prepared to adapt to a changing global logistic scene and invest heavily in EDI and good quality, trained and committed staff. Undoubtedly, this is an opportunity for the mega freight forwarder.

6.5 Greater Columbus – an inland logistic port, USA

Basically, the art of logistics is the ability to get the right product at the right place at the right time. In short it is the planning, organization, control and execution of the flow of goods from purchasing through production and distribution to the final customer in order to satisfy the requirements of the market. In international distribution terms this is the process of warehousing, transporting and distributing goods and cargo and the positioning of containers and/or equipment. It requires, therefore, an integrated and high-quality package of services in which the emphasis is focused on care of the cargo and provision of the most efficient coordination and management of the transport process. It comprises transport forwarding, storage and distribution, all of which are adapted to the specific requirements of the product, the supplier and the buyers: a total package covering all the links in the logistic chain but where the different components can also be offered individually.

It combines production, warehousing, distribution and transport for shippers on a global basis.

An interesting inland port featuring a new era in logistics is Greater Columbus situated in the state of Ohio, USA. It was set up in 1992 and is surrounded within a 250-mile radius by major metropolitan areas such as Cleveland, Cincinnati, Pittsburgh and Indianapolis. Columbus enjoys a favourable geographic location and within a 500-mile radius is 58 per cent of the nation's population and disposable income and 50 per cent of the nation's manufacturing capacity. Within 250 miles, over $170 billion of international trade is conducted and over 22 per cent of the nation's GDP generated. Details of Columbus's competitive situation regarding access to the population and transportation time are featured in Table 6.1.

In short, Columbus is situated in the heart of the USA. Hence, strategically it is very favourably situated, a factor enhanced by the development of marketing partnerships with the seaports of New York, New Jersey, Virginia and Los Angeles. Air cargo services are available at Rickenbacker International Airport and partnerships are in place to cater for international air freight with a number of airlines using wide-body aircrafts such as Boeing 747s and DC 10s. Door-to-door transit times to and from the Far East and Northern Europe are shown in Table 6.2.

An outstanding feature of Columbus is its competitiveness with other major US distribution cities such as New York, Chicago, Atlanta and Los Angeles. This is demonstrated in Table 6.3 which compares warehousing, labour and redistribution costs.

A major aspect of the successful logistics operation is supply chain management. This involves the integration of all parties involved in the logistics channel. The supply chain may be represented by a series of loops, with each loop representing a

TABLE 6.1 Competitive situation of Columbus

City	% of population reached in two days	Average time to service US markets
Columbus	53	2.71 days
New York	34	2.83 days
Chicago	41	2.99 days
Atlanta	35	3.21 days
Los Angeles	15	4.16 days

TABLE 6.2 Columbus: transit times

Destination	Air cargo	Ocean expedited service
Far East	21 hours	15–18 days
N. Europe	10 hours	10–12 days

TABLE 6.3 Comparison with other major distribution centres

	Warehouse \$/sq.ft[1]	Warehouse \$/sq.ft annual increase[2]	Warehouse labour \$/hours[3]
Columbus	2.50	0%	11.57
New York	3.50	8%	11.57
Chicago	3.30	8%	23.50
Atlanta	2.75	13%	12.72
Los Angeles	3.90	8%	12.09

1 Recent estimates of net lease cost for suburban sites.
2 Represents estimated annual increase in warehouse space costs for the next 12 months.
3 Represents average wage estimates for material handler/fork truck operator.

member in the channel, from suppliers to the end customer. In the past, channel members often operated independently without sharing information and coordinating material flow. Relationships between channel members were often adversarial. The modern supply chain connects these loops into an integrated chain, with material flow closely coordinated between channel members and facilitated by the sharing of information. Partnerships among channel members replace formerly adversarial relationships, and the result is a more efficient flow of goods and information across the channel. The implementation of information technology has facilitated much of this transformation in the supply chain. Utilizing such tools as POS data acquisition, EDI document transmission, JIT materials management and ECR/QR replenishment, channel members can become more efficient by removing time from the cycle. The result is a streamlined supply chain which delivers enhanced value to the consumer and improves the competitive position of channel members.

To build a high-performance global supply chain through an inland port is a complex operation. As the supply chain increasingly becomes international in scope, the logistical complexities multiply. Columbus is well suited to serve as an inland hub for European shippers trying to reach the US market, as well as for US shippers trying to reach the European market. Columbus boasts excellent air cargo capacity with Rickenbacker International Airport, a former military base now converted primarily to commercial use. Rickenbacker is capable of landing any size of aircraft, and is supported by the services required to efficiently process air cargo. In addition, Columbus possesses the necessary rail infrastructure to allow efficient intermodal connections to coastal port cities. Columbus has established formal partnerships with three of these: New York/New Jersey, Los Angeles and Norfolk. These partnerships provide shippers with enhanced service levels between the port cities and Columbus. Taken together, the logistical benefits of Columbus provide an attractive alternative to moving cargo through the busy and congested ports of larger US cities. In terms of market access, Columbus is within a one-day truck drive of over 50 per cent of the nation's purchasing and manufacturing capacity. In assessing the numerous benefits that Columbus has to offer, it makes sense to include Columbus as a link in a global supply chain.

Thus we can see that Columbus has developed an effective transportation and logistics infrastructure allowing it to become a premier trade centre and modal inland port. It provides a multi-modal transportation system and information system within its region, making it the logical choice of location for companies looking to serve US and Canadian markets from a single distribution, manufacturing or assembly operation.

6.6 Logistic case studies

A wide range of industries now benefit from the international logistic focus. Two examples of different industries featuring automobiles and office furniture are given below courtesy of Kay O'Neill Logistic Professionals, Colnbrook, Slough SL3 0AT.

General Motors: When General Motors began to source components from Europe for its Brazilian car and truck plants, Kay O'Neill was assigned to handle the logistics operation in the UK. In partnership with J.H. Bachmann, part of the Krupp organization, they have been responsible for coordinating supplies from 40 components manufacturers and ensuring their safe, on time delivery to Brazil. Technological support includes EDI links with the factories and on-line shipment data.

The products range from tiny items like door rubbers to whole sub-frames. Part of Kay O'Neill's expertise is employed in devising original packaging solutions to meet these wide ranging requirements. For example, they designed a disposable crate which could be fitted on to the end of the production line.

The volumes are considerable. Kay O'Neill ships over a thousand containers every year and air freights hundreds of thousands of kilos of more urgent parts. The customs regulations are particularly complex.

The relationship between Kay O'Neill and GM has grown closer over the years not only because of the benefits of shared knowledge and experience, but also because they have enabled a major customer to improve the cost-efficiency of their logistics operation and helped to reduce downtime at the plants. This has created more opportunities for the two companies to work together.

Haworth UK: For over eight years Kay O'Neill has provided a full range of logistics services to Haworth UK, the British arm of the fast growing global office furniture company. Each year has seen the challenges grow bigger and bigger as Haworth's activities have expanded in the UK, Ireland and mainland Europe. During this time Kay O'Neill have continued to redesign their services to meet this customer's rapidly changing requirements. For Haworth, Kay O'Neill process around 50 trailers and containers every month.

The products, which comprise systems furniture, seating, storage and desking lines, travel lightly packed, particularly in Europe. This means that extra special care must be taken throughout the physical handling process to protect the valuable merchandise from any kind of damage. This is where their special expertise in handling and protecting high value goods really pays off.

Use is made of the latest communication systems. Kay O'Neill has set up an EDI network with Haworth's manufacturing facilities in America, Canada and Europe. Consequently they have become an integral link in Haworth's international distribution chain to the point where Kay O'Neill can often anticipate problems and provide guidance on difficult decisions.

6.7 Criteria of logistic supplier selection

As suppliers to the logistics industry have developed their organizations and widened their range of services, the possibility for companies to outsource their logistics operations has increased dramatically.

There are many reasons for outsourcing but the most common include accessing economies of scale, increasing flexibility, refocusing of business on 'core' activities, reducing overheads and simplifying organizations.

The first stage in the selection task is to consider the implications of distribution strategy for the achievement of business plan goals including the effect on cost, quality and flexibility. This will probably involve an in-house evaluation of the activities involved. The next step is to conduct a full costing exercise taking into account the type of service to be provided, the price of the service, the net revenue released by reducing the in-house resource and the cost of switching. The final stage is to identify the number of viable suppliers in the market bearing in mind that no two logistic companies are exactly the same. All have their own areas of specialization. Particular attention should be given to the professional qualifications of the directorate; membership of a trade association; the company's track record; the level of commitment, interest and experience in the area of logistics sought; and their contract terms, resources and client base. Adequate time should be devoted to supplier selection and meaningful discussions conducted with potential candidates.

6.8 Globalization

It is appropriate that logistics and globalization are examined simultaneously, as one feeds off the other in terms of their development.

During the past 20 years, the pattern of international trade has changed dramatically. This is due to a variety of factors, in particular technology, politics, economics, cultural and legal considerations. Trade does not pass unless there is business confidence but the legal framework and infrastructure in which trade is conducted today is very different from two decades ago. The world is opening up with faster travel, common mass media and open communication systems.

There are, of course, numerous other factors which we will examine subsequently but a book of this nature would not be complete without a focus on globalization. To define a global company we could say that it represents the process of the whole organization targeting the selection and development of market opportunities and building up the infrastructure essential for that objective to be realized; such a process being conducted on a global basis.

Globalization of markets and trade results in the provision of a product or service which can be sold virtually in any market of the world providing the economic infrastructure and culture can support it. The key to it is the design and specification of the product or service and the added value it provides to the user or consumer. The product may be produced on a regional basis such as in Europe, Asia, North America, South America, etc. to serve those markets on a customerized basis but with the same core specification. For example, cars produced for cold climates would have heaters, whilst those for hot climates would have air conditioning.

6.8.1 Advantages of globalization

In a highly competitive world market environment, driven today by logistics and computer literacy in management and consumer needs, some of the benefits globalization of trade brings to world markets are detailed below.

(1) World living standards are raised. This is in the earliest stages of its realization, as globalization of an economy will only benefit those parts of an economy or region which globalization has reached, such as in India and China.
(2) Globalization brings cultures closer together through the added value products or services offered to their consumers and users. This may be through films, technology, etc.
(3) Overall, globalization develops world resources.
(4) Greater integration via economic blocs or customs unions bring countries closer together to exploit their economic well-being. Such cooperation is usually based on the development of those products which have the greatest economic potential in world markets.
(5) Globalization encourages investment globally.
(6) Emerging from item (5), governments which are stable and subject to the democratic processes are more likely to attract trade and investment.
(7) Global trade encourages the development of the infrastructure within a country, as a high standard of infrastructure is an essential ingredient to that country's participation at a global level. This includes airports, seaports, transport multi-modalism, banking systems, information technology, education and training, energy resources and an acceptable legal environment. Examples of such countries are South Korea, Malaysia, Thailand, Southern China and so on.
(8) Globalization encourages tourism which brings wealth, cultural understanding and economic and social development in many regions of the world.

6.8.2 Factors driving globalization

A wide range of factors are driving globalization and these are detailed below:

(1) It reduces trade barriers (see pp. 412–3).

(2) It encourages standardization of products as distinct from adopting the product to meet the needs of a particular culture or group of customers.

(3) Standardization of products lowers production costs and design expenses, and enables goods to reach the market sooner as the lead time is much reduced.

(4) It favours strong brand management such as Ford Motors, NIKE, Chanel, Kodak and Sony.

(5) It exploits logistics (see pp. 101–20).

(6) Information technology stimulates globalization as it has no time zones, language barriers or culture impediment.

(7) Quicker and more efficient distribution is a key factor to develop global markets. (see also item 5) Examples include development of the hub and spoke system (see p. 63), port privatization, development of multi-modalism and continuing expansion of new or modernized airports and seaports.

(8) International agencies who provide the framework for international trade and greatly facilitate its globalized development are playing an increasingly important role. Examples include ICC, WTO, UNCTAD, UNCITRAL, OECD, IMF and INMARSAT.

(9) It is opening up global financial markets such as Stock Exchanges in Africa.

(10) Economic blocs stimulate globalization of their products and services, as found in the EU and NAFTA. Also, the EU constitutes a Single Market and encourages both economic and monetary union as found in the launch of the euro in January 1999 (see pp. 273–9).

(11) Companies which wish to compete in global markets must remain competitive and profitable to generate investment. Hence, the need to drive down costs, especially in areas of research and development, a move towards having fewer layers of administration resulting in a flatter organization structure; more regional autonomy structures; a greater focus on the customer; more out-sourcing of components – global sourcing; shorter product lifecycle; satellite production; reduced financing costs; proactive marketing anticipating customer needs; technological developments providing longer shelf life; and a shorter lead time in design and product development aided by technology. All these factors focus on the need for the multinational industries (MNI) to remain competitive and result in buoyant merger and acquisition markets or strategic operating alliances. Such strategies reduce costs, attract continuing investment, improve profitability and provide a wider market share.

(12) The MNI is driving the global market and overall today accounts for over 60 per cent of world trade.

(13) Globalization is developing a wide range of global service industries in mega container operators, airlines such as British Airways, management consultancies, banks and fast foods – McDonalds, Burger King, etc.

(14) The youth culture involves the younger generation favouring globalization. This emerges through travel, education, especially higher education, involving studying overseas, the impact of the media and availability of high technology through the Internet, e-commerce, etc.

To conclude this analysis one must stress that the MNI must continually review its position in the market place and especially in the area of focusing on customer needs and developing them on a global basis.

6.9 Global village

Emerging from the globalization concept is the global village. This is basically where all the major global brands are available especially in the consumer market. It includes cameras, restaurants, perfumery, clothes, hi fi equipment, radio, televisions, shoes, petrol, cars, white goods, medical needs and so on.

The global village concept may be found at major airports and major cities and tourist and commercial centres worldwide. Annually, the range of global village products is extending and likewise their location.

6.10 Factors obstructing globalization

There is no doubt that market globalization is favouring countries which wish to participate in the economic and social benefits it yields. Conversely, there are many parts of the world where inhabitants resent globalization strongly for a wide variety of reasons which we will briefly examine.

(1) It changes the culture and social standards of a country. Cultures and religion are very deep-rooted in many areas of the world and globalization, embracing the global village, represents an intrusion into heritage and deep-seated cultures and beliefs, extending to many generations. Improved education and more travel can help bring change to such situations in the long term.

(2) Globalization develops a homogeneous consumer rather than a heterogeneous client. Overall, it restricts choice and can encourage a quasi monopolistic situation which may not always operate in the interests of the consumer. Hence, the need in some countries to provide legislation for more consumer protection.

(3) The arrival of the global village, particularly with the franchise concept (see p. 405), involving rigid retail outlet design, may alienate the culture and local architect philosophy. This needs to be handled with care and understanding.

(4) The global player, the MNI, has a larger income often in excess of a less developed country. This tends to place the MNI in a strong position when entering a less developed market, which can be exploited if not handled with care and empathy.

(5) The globalization of markets can destroy local manufacturers and alienate the populace. Alternatively, the arrival of a large MNI will raise standards, bring new economic prospects to a region and improve a country's trade balance. Such situations require continuous dialogue to ensure both parties benefit from the venture and the social implications are not disregarded. Careful planning and the development of improved living standards must be sought.

(6) Distribution plays a major part in the globalization of markets. This does result in many countries not featuring in such globalization. For example, countries which are not on a global container network are seriously disadvantaged in the development of their trade in a multi-modal logistic international trade environment.

(7) Finally, politics play a major role in the globalization of markets. An example is the G8 group and major economic blocs such as EU, NAFTA and MERCOSUR.

6.11 Developing the global economy

The dynamic ideal based on a new global economy offers the possibility of lifting billions of people into a worldwide middle class. But it also contains within it the seeds of new instabilities, new inequalities and new threats of the global economy. The challenge to the millennial generation, therefore, is to create a world trading system attuned to the pace and scope of the new global economy, one that offers an opportunity for all our people and one that meets the profound environmental challenge we share.

The international agency driving world trade is the World Trade Organisation (see p. 22). Formed in 1995 as a successor to GATT at the Uruguay Round of talks, the WTO has generated, in four years, an increase of 25 per cent in world trade. It has helped to build the infrastructure for the global economy and formulated agreements on information technology, telecommunications and financial services affecting trillions of dollars in global commerce each year.

Discussed briefly below are the essential ingredients to develop globalization in the twenty-first century, many of which were discussed at the 50 year anniversary of GATT/WTO in Geneva in 1998.

(1) The development of an ever more open global trading system. Economic freedom and open trade have brought unprecedented prosperity in the twentieth century. It is essential that the circle of opportunity is widened in the twenty-first century. For example, in the USA one-third of the strong economic growth achieved in the period 1992–97 was generated by exports. For every country engaged in trade, open markets dramatically widen the base of possible customers for goods and services.

(2) Countries must recognize that in the new global economy, the way we conduct our trade affects the lives and livelihoods and the health and safety of families around the world.

(3) There is a need to harmonize the goal of increasing trade with the goal of improving the environment and working conditions. Enhanced trade can and should enhance the protection of the environment. Hence, international trade rules must permit sovereign nations to exercise their right to set protective standards for health, safety and the environment and biodiversity. Nations have a right to pursue these protections – even when they are stronger than international norms.

(4) The WTO must modernize by opening its doors to the scrutiny and participation of the public. Thus, the need to take every feasible step to bring

openness and accountability to its operations. Hence, the need to conduct all hearings by the WTO in public, and not, as at present when one nation challenges the trade practices of another, behind closed doors.

(5) There needs to be a trading system that taps the full potential of the information age. Today, there are no customs duties on telephone calls, fax messages, e-mail or computer links when they cross international borders. Hence, the need to continue liberalization of the electronic global commerce with no trade barriers.

(6) There should be a trading system for the twenty-first century which comprises governments that are open, honest and fair in their practices. This embraces government procurement being based on open and fair bidding and not on national prejudices. Another area is the need to adopt the anti-bribery convention developed by the OECD in 1997.

(7) There should be provision for an open global trading system that moves as fast as the market place. This embraces quicker ways of eliminating trade barriers, without resorting to meticulous evaluations, which are often inspired by time delaying tactics. Such an area is agriculture with its subsidies and quota systems. It is a fast growing market with yet greater potential, which could be realized through greater liberalization. Indeed, another fast growing industry area, is the service sector – banking, tourism, transport, insurance, energy, express delivery, audio-visual, consultancy, professional services, etc. It is the area least disciplined by WTO rules.

(8) There is a need to spread the benefits of globalization. This embraces the need to help developing countries integrate into the global economy and thereby gain from the benefits of globalization.

(9) Trade liberalization should be extended.

(10) World trade expansion should be developed but not at any cost. The paramount need is to protect the environment. Governments need to consider the environmental impact of everything they do, including the trade sphere. Trade rules should not be used to impose unfair standards on developing countries, nor to discriminate against their exports.

(11) To help cash flow management of the export order an increasing number of sellers are opting for stage payments of the export sale contracts. This involves a 20 per cent down payment on confirmation of the order, followed by four subsequent payments on a timescale agreed between the seller and the buyer. This practice is long established in major contracts but extends to the SME trade finance strategy.

Undoubtedly, the foregoing criteria of ingredients to accelerate globalization of trade will be constrained by political and economic considerations. The reader may wish to monitor the extent to which these proposals are developed.

Recommended reading:

WTO Focus – Newsletter 50th year GATT/WTO – 18–19 May 1998, No 31 June 1998.
Freight Management International.
International Freighting Weekly.
Distribution Business.

7

Freight rates

7.1 Theory of freight rates

Freight is the reward payable to the carrier for the carriage of goods in a mercantile or recognized condition ready to be delivered to the merchant

The pricing of air or sea transport services, usually in combination with land transport services, is dependent on the forces of supply and demand, but the factors affecting both supply and demand are perhaps more complicated than is the case of most other industries and services. The demand for a particular international transport service mode(s) is basically derived from the demand for the commodities carried and is, therefore, affected by the elasticity of demand for these commodities.

The demand for sea or air transport is affected by both direct competition between carriers and, because it is a derived demand, by the competition of substitutes or alternatives for the commodity carried. On any particular route, the shipowner or airline is subject to competition from carriers on the same route, and also from the carriers operating from alternative supply areas. The commodities carried by the latter may be competitive with the commodities from his or her own supply area and, to that extent, may affect the demand for his or her services. On many routes there is also competition from more than one form of transport.

The elasticity of demand for sea or air transport varies from one commodity to another. In normal times, an important factor affecting elasticity of demand for sea or air transport, is the cost of transport in relation to the market price of the goods carried. Although it may be small, the cost of sea or air transport is often a significant element in the final market price of many commodities. It can vary from 3 to 15 per cent depending on the transport mode and the commodity. (See pp. 205–7 *Maritime Economics, Management and Marketing*).

The price eventually fixed for a chartered vessel or aircraft depends largely on the relationship between buyers and sellers. Where both groups are numerous and have equal bargaining power, and where demand is fairly elastic, conditions of relative perfect competition prevail. Under these conditions for chartered tonnage, prices are fixed by the 'haggling of the market' and are known as contract prices. The market for tramp charters operates under such conditions and the contract is drawn up as a agreement known as a charter party.

Under these conditions, the rate structure for tramps is a very simple product and emerges from the competitive interplay of supply and demand. From the economist's point of view, rates made in this way represent the most efficient method of pricing; for when price is determined under conditions of perfect competition, production is encouraged to follow consumer wishes and price itself does not deviate to any great extent from average total cost. A similar criterion applies to air freight charterers. It must be borne in mind, however, that the air charter market extends both to the very large shipment offering, for example, an indivisible load urgently required such as a ship's propeller, and the smaller split charter involving consignments of 500–2500 kg. Some air freight forwarders have their own charter subsidiaries.

Chartering can also extend to Ro-Ro vehicles in the trades and markets beyond. The shipper/freight forwarder can charter a portion of the vehicle from the road operator either on a regular or spasmodic basis. In general terms the shipper must critically examine, including alternatives, the total freight cost of the transit and reconcile it with the distance. Generally, the shorter the total journey distance, the greater the need to ensure the cost is proportionate to the distance, otherwise it could quickly price the goods out of the overseas market. Generally too, documentation and customs entry cost do not vary greatly. Liner cargo services are now dominated by container tonnage with rates broadly reflecting market conditions whether on an FCL or LCL basis and determined by the shipowner. In contrast, a few container trades are under the aegis of the liner conference (see p. 464).

Air freight rates operative on regular scheduled international services are decided collectively by the airlines through the IATA mechanism which adopts a policy of parity on the level of rates on individual services/routes. The rates reflect market conditions and service cost. A major share of the air freight market is now conveyed under agent sponsorship involving consolidation arrangements and integrators (see p. 48).

Overall, a properly compiled tariff should encourage the movement of all classes of cargo to ensure the best balance between revenue production and the full utilization of the transport unit.

7.2 The constituents of the freight rate

Rate making has changed significantly in recent years as a result of the development of multi-modalism (Chapter 5). No longer is the rate based on one carrier on a port-to-port or airport-to-airport basis; it also involves two or three carriers providing a dedicated door-to-door service featuring one overall composite rate and the sea/land-bridge from the Far East to North America using the gateway ports of Vancouver, Los Angeles, Seattle and double-stack container trains (p. 64). For example, a consignment from Malaysia to industrial Europe via Dubai would embrace three major legs of the transit: (a) the rail journey from the dry port of Ipoh (p. 85) to Port Klang; (b) the maritime trip between ports Klang and Dubai; and (c) the flight from Dubai (p. 90) to Frankfurt (p. 92). Additionally, it would feature the collection and delivery charges which may involve a 40-mile road journey to Ipoh and a 70-mile rail journey to the consignee warehouse from Frankfurt. Furthermore, the transshipment and handling charges at the ports of Klang and Dubai, and Dubai airport will be included. Overall, the rate would feature the following:

(1) Consignor premises and collection to Ipoh, based on zonal road rate charge.
(2) Processing of cargo/handling/packaging/documentation at Ipoh.
(3) Agents' charges including customs formalities.
(4) Rail journey Ipoh to Port Klang.
(5) Handling charges to Port Klang raised by the port authority to cover transshipment costs.
(6) Shipowner's freight costs Port Klang to Port Dubai.
(7) Handling and transshipment charges at Port Dubai to convey goods from port to airport; these are raised by the port authority and agent.
(8) Handling charges at Dubai Airport, including documentation and the agent; these are raised by the airport authority and agent.
(9) Air freight charges from Dubai to Frankfurt raised by the airline.
(10) Handling/documentation/customs import duty at Frankfurt Airport. These are raised by the airport authority and the agent.
(11) Delivery by rail or road to consignee's warehouse; rail charges raised by the German railways; and road charges raised by road hauliers.

The foregoing use of freight forwarders demonstrates their role as one of coordination and facilitation. The rate from Ipoh to Frankfurt will not feature any import duty as this is a local charge for the importer at Frankfurt. Overall, the above demonstrates the complexity and range of parties involved in developing a multi-modal rate; it excludes cargo insurance and provision made for CAF. The freight rate for the three major legs would be based on the W/M (weight/measurement) criteria (p. 140) and the consignment under notice would be consolidated into an LCL container at Ipoh, which would be unstuffed at Dubai port for transshipment to the nearby airport.

Basically, the tariff raised for a consignment can embrace a number of elements other than the sea, air, plus inland transport tariff and these are listed below.

(1) Tariff cargo rate. In the case of air freight, this will be between the relevant airports for the airline rate. In the case of the agent's consolidated rate, the charge could be a through tariff from the shipper's factory to the importer's distribution warehouse. Likewise for maritime transport, it will be the port-to-port container, Ro-Ro vehicle, or general cargo rates. The same criterion applies to a chartered aircraft or ship. The charter party will determine the extent to which the charterer bears the cargo handling transshipment cost included in the overall fixture rate. It should be noted that there is an increasing tendency to develop the combined transport operation concept with through rates and documentation. This is particularly true of containers and Ro-Ro traffic.

(2) The customs clearance charge is usually based on the local port authority or airline tariff. Charges vary between import/export, commodity type, quantity, and the degree of ultimate customs physical turn out examination of the consignment. The latter is usually a separate charge. It includes the presentation of the requisite documents/entry to customs. HM Customs have the legal authority to examine all imported consignments originating outside the EU, but, in reality, only random inspections are made at the discretion of the local customs officer. Customs clearance may be undertaken at an inland clearance depôt or the shipper's premises (LEC/LIC) by prior arrangement, with the goods travelling under bond to and from the seaport. The actual presentation of the goods to customs and their ultimate clearance will be undertaken on behalf of the shipper by the port authority or airline, or the freight forwarder acting on behalf of his client.

(3) Freight forwarder's commission. Many small exporters engage the services of a freight forwarder to look after the distribution arrangements of the consignment. The role of the freight forwarder is explained on p. 417, and accordingly raises a commission charge with the exporter/importer. This is usually between 2.5 and 5 per cent of the total freight account.

(4) Customs duty will vary according to commodity specification and applies to imported consignments. It also extends to value added tax or something similar depending on the importing country.

(5) Disbursements. These embrace a variety of items including freight services, telephone calls, e-commerce messages, currency surcharge, fuel surcharge, cost of feeding livestock, additional cost to police a valuable consignment, etc. Again it will depend on the nature of the cargo and the particular circumstances obtaining at the airport, seaport, or inland clearance depôt.

(6) Cargo insurance premium. Usually the premium is lower for air freight than for sea transport but much depends on the latter method of forwarding, namely container, Ro-Ro, or general freight in break-bulk 'tween deck tonnage.

(7) Delivery/collection charge. The collection and delivery of the cargo is usually undertaken by road transport. The rate is normally assessed on distance within a zonal rating. This is related to the weight or cubic measurement of the consignment. This task may be undertaken by the exporter and/or importer's own vehicles. In other circumstances, the delivery and/or collection may be included in the through rate.

(8) Transshipment charge. This arises when cargo is transshipped en route to continue its transit. It may occur at an airport or seaport. Again it could be an inclusive charge within the through rate, but much depends on the circumstances. When the cargo involves special arrangements being made to transship it, due to its awkward shape, excessive weight or size, or the general nature of the commodity (e.g. livestock), additional charges are normally raised.

(9) Documentation charge. Circumstances arise when it is necessary to obtain a certificate of origin to accord with the importing country customs' requirement to establish or verify the place of manufacture of the goods. This document, to be obtained by the exporter, is available from the local Chamber of Commerce,

or if a consular invoice is required, from the consulate of the importing country. A charge is raised by the consulate office for this service which can be as much as £75 in some cases.

(10) Demurrage. Cargo detained at an airport, seaport or inland clearance depôt beyond a prescribed period attracts a daily demurrage charge. The cargo may be delayed due to wrong presentation of customs clearance documents, non-availability of an export/import licence, pending payment of customs duty, awaiting collection by consignee, etc.

(11) Handling cost. This embraces cost of handling the cargo at the terminal. It is sometimes included in the through rate. In the case of containers, it is usually based on a tariff per container lift, ship to shore and vice versa. It can vary by container type, empty or loaded. Extra charges are raised for special lifts, i.e. indivisible loads.

(12) Wharfage charge. This is a charge raised by the port authority for cargo transshipment.

(13) Cargo dues. Again a cost raised by the port authority for goods passing over the quay.

(14) Rebate. In the case of sea freight, exporters originating substantial quantities of traffic are granted a rebate provided they adhere to the shipowner/liner conference conditions. It may be an immediate rebate offering 10 per cent on the published tariff or possibly 10.5 per cent on a deferred rebate payable six months after the traffic has passed. Basically, a deferred rebate is a device to ensure that shippers will continue to support a conference or shipping line. Hence the shipper has an inducement to remain loyal to the liner conference or shipping line insofar as he stands to lose the rebate by using a non-conference vessel.

(15) Bunker or fuel surcharge (bunker adjustment factor, BAF). In an era when fuel costs now represent a substantial proportion of direct voyage cost, shipowners are not prepared to absorb the variation in fuel prices. They take the view that price variation of bunker fuel tends to be unpredictable, bearing in mind that it is usually based on the variable dollar rate of exchange, and that it is difficult to budget for this cost realistically and reflect it adequately in their rate formulation. Moreover, an increase in the bunkering price erodes the shipowners' voyage profitability.

(16) Currency surcharge (currency adjustment factor, CAF). This arises when the freight rate is related to a floating currency such as sterling. For example, if the rate were based on French or Belgian francs which both operate fixed rates of currency, then the sterling rate of exchange in January would probably be different to the situation the following July. For example, when sterling is depressed, it would probably earn more French and Belgian francs per £1 sterling in January than in the following July. Accordingly, a currency surcharge is imposed to minimize losses that the shipowner would incur, bearing in mind the shipowner obtains less sterling equivalent in French or Belgian franc rated traffic whilst, at the same time, port expenses in Belgium and France would be greater due to the depressed sterling rate of exchange.

An example of a currency surcharge scale is given below, involving the Anglo–French trade. The freight tariff is sterling based on 9.90 French francs to £1, and the rate per tonne is £20 or FF198:

When charges are to be paid in French francs to £1	Surcharge in French francs (per cent)
10.82 to 11.04	5
10.59 to 10.81	4
10.36 to 10.58	3
10.13 to 10.35	2
10.02 to 10.12	1

No surcharge 9.78 to 10.01 (void area) nil (no surcharge).

When charges are to be paid in sterling; French francs to £1	Surcharge in sterling (per cent)
9.66 to 9.77	1
9.43 to 9.65	2
9.20 to 9.42	3
8.97 to 9.19	4
8.74 to 8.96	5

The percentage of surcharge will be determined each week by reference to the average rate as published in *Le Monde* and the *Financial Times* on Saturdays (i.e. Friday's closing prices):

		£
(a)	Payment in sterling – exchange rate FF9.18 to £1	
	10 tonnes at £20 per tonne	200
	4 per cent surcharge based on exchange rate of FF9.18	8
		208

		FF
(b)	Payment in French francs – exchange rate FF 11.02 to £	
	10 tonnes at 198 French Francs per tonne	1980
	5 per cent surcharge based on exchange rate of 11.02 FF	99
	Total French francs	2079

(17) Surcharges are usually raised for heavy lifts such as indivisible consignments and on excessive height or length of Ro-Ro rated traffic, together with any other traffic where special facilities are required.

It will be appreciated that special rates exist for particular cargoes. These include indivisible loads such as a transformer; antiques such as furniture of high value; household effects requiring special packaging for international transit; and livestock involving special facilities on the transport unit. The level of rebate is usually negotiated between the shipper and shipowner. Obviously the ultimate rate, mode of transport and route will be much influenced by the export sales contract and the delivery terms contained therein.

7.3 Factors influencing the formulation of freight rates

We will now examine the salient factors which influence the formulation of freight rates.

(1) Competition. Keen competition on rates exists among various modes of transport. For example, in the UK–Europe trade, competition exists amongst air freight agents offering consolidated services, Le Shuttle (EuroTunnel), ISO containerization and international road haulage.

(2) The nature of the commodity, its quantity, period of shipment(s) and overall cubic measurements/dimensions/value.

(3) The origin and destination of the cargo.

(4) The overall transit cost.

 5) The nature of packaging and convenience of handling.

(6) The susceptibility of the cargo to damage and pilferage.

(7) The general loadability of the transport unit.

(8) Provision of additional facilities to accommodate the cargo, namely heavy lifts, strong room, livestock facilities, etc.

(9) The mode(s) of transport.

(10) Actual routeing of cargo consignment. Alternative routes tend to exist, particularly in air freight, with differing rate structures and overall transport costs.

The factor which has come to prominence in recent years in rate assessment is the 'value added benefit' the shipper derives from the mode(s) of distribution used (Chapter 13). The overall rate may be high, but it enables cost savings to be realized in lower inventory cost; improved service to the importer's clients; much reduced down time on unserviceable machinery undergoing repair; replenishment of stocks to meet consumer demand; assembly of component parts undertaken in low labour-cost markets, and with suppliers sourced worldwide; and the benefits the high-profile quality distribution network gives to the shipper. Reliability, frequency and transit time, and the overall quality of the service which involves the total product concept embracing all the distribution ingredients, are major and decisive factors. An increasing volume of air freight is now consigned under a logistics driven programme (see pp. 101–20).

We will now examine the varying methods of available freight rates by mode of transport.

7.4 Air freight rates

The formulation of air freight rates is controlled by the International Air Transport Association (IATA) insofar as major world airlines are affiliated to it, representing approximately 98 per cent of international air freight services. IATA has no influence on internal – for example, Glasgow–London – domestic flight air freight tariffs or charter flights. The significant aspect of the IATA affiliated airline is that no competition is permitted on air freight rates, that is, parity obtains, and competition is permitted only on service quality, frequency, etc.

Basically there are seven types of air freight rates in existence, each of which is designed to stimulate traffic in various ways. Moreover, it is relevant to say the same individual rates do not necessarily apply in both directions thereby reflecting the differing market situations. For example, a commodity rate for product type A may exist from London to New York but not in the reverse direction. Moreover, routeing of cargo is significant both in terms of transit time and tariff. If two routes are available, the shorter route in distance terms is likely to be the cheapest, but may be the longer in transit time due to the less frequent and slower schedules or connections.

International air cargo is charged by weight, calculated either as actual gross weight or in equivalent volumetric units, whichever is the greater. Thus air cargo is charged by weight except where the volume is more than 366 in^3/kg. In such cases, volumetric charges apply and each unit of 366 in^3 is charged as 1 kg. To calculate this, the maximum dimensions of the piece should be multiplied together to give a volume in cubic inches. This volume must be divided by 366 and the result will be the volumetric weight. If this is more than the actual weight, then the volumetric weight will be the chargeable weight. Where the consignment consists of pieces varying in density, the volumetric calculation will be based on the whole consignment. For metric measurements, 6000 cm^3 = 1 kg (see example, p. 140).

Air cargo rates are quoted per kilogram (gross weight or volume equivalent) and apply from airport of departure to airport of destination; they do not include charges for cartage, customs entry and clearance, etc.

A brief examination of each air freight rate classification now follows:

(1) Specific commodity rates. These reduced rates apply to a wide range of commodities and to qualify the shipper must comply precisely with the commodity specifications as found in the tariff. Likewise, the rate will apply only between specified airports of departure and arrival – it is not possible to send goods at these preferential rates to alternative destinations, even where the alternative airport is on the same route and nearer to the airport of origin. The minimum quantity allowed at each rate is 100, 300, 500 and 1000 kg (shipping above the limit is allowed but not below it). Hence a consignment of 85 kg would be charged at the minimum kilogram rate, that is, 100kg at 95p which equals £95. This type of rate has done much to stimulate air freight development, and by encouraging quantity shipments, has produced cost savings in documentation, handling and packaging. In the event of the merchandise not qualifying for the reduced commodity rate, the shipper is advised to contact the agent or airline who may be able to introduce a special rate when regular and substantial shipments are involved.

(2) Classification rates (surcharges and rebates). Classification rates apply to the following commodities where no specific commodity rate is available:

(a) Newspapers, periodicals and books. Consignments of newspapers, periodicals, magazines, books, catalogues, talking books for the blind and Brailletype equipment are carried at reduced rates. Special rates are available on application to the airline.

(b) Human remains. The regulations governing the carriage of human remains vary from route to route. Prior application is necessary to the airline.

(c) Valuable cargo. Certain types of gold and platinum, diamonds (including industrial), rubies, emeralds, sapphires and pearls (including cultured pearls), legal bank notes, travellers cheques, securities, shares and share coupons and any article having a declared value for carriage of £450 or more per gross kilogramme are charged at the normal air cargo rate plus a 100 per cent surcharge. The minimum charge for valuable cargo is the normal applicable minimum charge plus a surcharge of 100 per cent, but not less than US $50 (operative rate October 1992). Quantity rates are not applicable.

(d) Live animals. Collection charges are not normally available for the carriage of live animals except under special circumstances. Prior arrangements must be made for the carriage of animals. Stringent regulations apply regarding documentation and travel facilities and conditions. Special rates are applicable for the conveyance of live animals, usually at normal general cargo rates (i.e. the under 45 kg or under 100 kg rate as applicable); quantity rates are not applicable. The minimum charge for the carriage of live animals is the normal minimum charge increased by 50 per cent. Every consideration will be given to flight conditions such as altitude and temperature, but no responsibility can be accepted by the airline in the event of death or injury to the live animals due to atmospheric or climate conditions or to natural causes. A shipper's certificate for live animals is required.

(3) Valuation charge. Where consignments are offered for international carriage, a declaration of value must be made. It is permissible to make the statement 'no value declared'. Where goods have declared a value for carriage per kilogram higher than a certain level, a valuation charge will apply in addition to the freight charges.

(4) General cargo rates. These are the basic rates and fall into three categories as below:

(a) minimum charges;
(b) normal rate – the '100 kg' rate.
(c) quantity rate – applicable on the various minimum quantities shipped, called break-points. It is permissible to charge a consignment at a higher weight rate if a lower charge results overall.

(5) Unit load device (ULD) rates. This applies to any type of container, container with an integral pallet, or aircraft pallet whether or not owned by an IATA member, and whether or not considered to be aircraft equipment.

(a) Aircraft ULDs. These are units which interface directly with an aircraft loading and restraint system, and meet all restraint requirements without the use of supplementary equipment. Such units are an integral part of the aircraft. Aircraft ULDs can be loaned to shippers and agents for loading purposes provided the shipper or agent can prove that he is equipped to handle them.

(b) Non-aircraft ULDs. These units do not interface with the aircraft restraint system. They must be registered with IATA and conform to IATA standard specifications. Non-aircraft ULDs, in order to be eligible for rating incentives, must be owned by a shipper or agent.

Rating of ULDs: two rating method exist – 'method A' and 'method B'.

Method A. On certain routes, rating method A charges shall apply at the request of the shipper for consignments carried from airport of departure to airport of destination entirely in ULDs. In order to qualify for bulk unitization rates, the cargo must be carried from origin to destination in the same ULD. The charge for the consignment shall consist of a flat minimum (pivot) charge for a specified pivot weight above which an additional charge (over-pivot rate) per kilo or pound will apply. Charges for airline-owned aircraft ULDs shall be based on the actual gross weight less the actual tare weight of the ULD. Charges for shipper- or agent-owned aircraft ULDs or non-aircraft ULDs shall be based on the actual gross weight less the actual tare weight, but not more than the IATA tare weight allowance for the particular ULD.

Method B. Discounts and tare weight allowances only apply when shipments are delivered to the airline packaged in registered shipper-owned, standard size non-aircraft units. Charges are based on the actual weight of the shipment, less the tare weight allowance, but not less than the minimum chargeable weight for the particular container used. The tare weight allowance is always that which is printed on the actual container. A discount is also granted under this programme, which refers to each type of non-aircraft ULD. The amount of discount can be deducted from the weight charge, but shall not exceed 10 per cent of the charges applicable to the consignment carried in the ULD. In no case shall the charges established under method A be applied cumulatively with the discount authorized under rating method B.

Dangerous goods, live animals, or human remains will not be accepted in a ULD, rated under either method A or method B.

(6) Cabotage. United Kingdom cabotage is the term used for goods carried when points of origin and destination are both within the sovereignty of the UK, where special non-international rates may apply. The carriage of UK cabotage traffic is reserved for UK airlines, and the airlines of the Colonies, Protectorates, Trust Territories or Protected States listed below. Traffic between the UK and the listed territories, or between any of the territories is 'United Kingdom cabotage', and cannot be carried by foreign airlines without special permission. The listed territories are: Anguilla, Ascension Islands, Bermuda, British Virgin Islands, Caicos Islands, Cayman Islands, Falklands Islands, Gibraltar, Hong Kong, Montserrat, St Christopher, St Helena, St Vincent, Turks Islands.

(7) Express handling units. These provide a fast and flexible handling service for cargo shipments and courier traffic. A well-established unit is British Airways' Speedbird Express door-to-door service (as described below). Export shipments up to 100 kg, with individual package weights under 30 kg, can be handled up to 45 minutes before scheduled flight departure time.

The Speedbird courier is a wholesale courier operator. It involves a wholesale airport-to-airport courier service for freight forwarders and air express companies guaranteeing discretion and impartiality with the British Airways on board courier. Packages must not exceed 32 kg. Presentation of documents to customs is available on request to expedite clearance. 'Through tagging' is a through bag service from place of origin to final destination, avoiding the problems of customs clearance and representation. The Speedbird courier service tariffs are available from the courier companies. All consignments must be accompanied by a Courier Baggage voucher.

7.4.1 Charges

(1) Payment of charges. Charges can be paid at the time of despatch by cash, cheque or credit card (most major credit cards are accepted). However, regular shippers make use of credit facilities which are usually available from most major airlines. This enables their air freight charges to be billed for settlement on a monthly basis.

(2) Charges forward. Goods despatched to most countries may be sent 'charges forward', i.e. cartage, export fees and freightage payable by the consignee. Consignments cannot be sent with carriage and valuation charges partly prepaid and partly forward. Charges forward facilities are not available on domestic routes, when all charges must be prepaid. This service is not normally available for perishable goods or live animals.

(3) Cash on delivery. No COD consignments can be accepted on most airline air waybills or services.

(4) Disbursements. Most airlines will charge 10 per cent with a basic minimum fee of US $20 (valid, October 1992) for collection from a consignee of any disbursement shown on the air waybill. This charge will be made when collection is on behalf of any shipper or agent. Disbursements will not usually exceed the freight charges shown on the air waybill. When the issuing carrier cannot collect the amount to be collected from the consignee for any reason, the amount will be charged to the shipper or agent.

(5) Perishable cargo. Air freight charges for perishable cargo must normally be prepaid. If required, a deposit to cover surface reforwarding charges from the airport of arrival will be collected from the consignor.

(6) Mixed cargo. A mixed consignment is one which contains a number of different commodities which do not qualify for the same rate and conditions. Charges for mixed consignments are based on the applicable general cargo rate. Where the shipper declares separately the weight, or volume and contents of each package

in the consignment, charges are based on either the appropriate commodity rate or the general cargo rate for each package.

(7) Packaging of the consignment will be charged on the basis of the highest rated article in the consignment. Articles which cannot be included in mixed consignment are: live animals, perishable goods, human remains, diplomatic bags, baggage shipped as cargo, and valuable cargo which includes articles with an actual value of US$20 000 (valid October 1999) or equivalent, or more per gross kilo.

(8) Cargo subject to regulations relating to the carriage of dangerous goods must be offered separately, and clearly indicated in the Shipper's Declaration (pp. 160–81).

All these air freight rates exclude customs clearance charges duty, road or rail collection and distribution, warehousing, demurrage, etc. In addition to the foregoing, for special or large consignments, an aircraft can be chartered. Rates vary according to market conditions and other factors. The shipper conducts his negotiations through an air charter broker found on the Baltic Exchange or directly with an airline or air freight forwarder. As indicated earlier, a certain degree of bargaining can emerge to settle the ultimate charter rate for the larger air freighter. Much depends on whether prospects exist for the aircraft to be chartered on the next flight, otherwise the operator will be faced with an empty aircraft to fly to the next assignment. Little room exists for bargaining for split charters for small consignments varying between 500 kg and 3 tonnes. The charterer may need to wait a few days in such circumstances to combine with other cargo thereby obtaining a favourable rate based on a full aircraft.

7.4.2 Air freight consolidation

Our study of air freight rates would not be complete without consideration of air freight consolidation.

The ongoing development of air freight consolidation shows no abating as we progress through the early years of the twenty-first century. Growth may, however, be slowed down as the logistics market focuses more on air freight. Air freight consolidation involves the freight forwarder – usually referred to as the agent – who has a contract with an airline on specified flight(s) to provide consolidated cargo for allocated cargo hold space which the agent undertakes to fill. Thus the agency agreement involves the forwarder offering a consolidation (CONSOL) service on specific regular flights. The consolidated consignment is under agent sponsorship and may involve up to 30 consignments including differing consignees and consignors. Each consignment tends to be destined for the same or similar destination, area or region which enables the shipper to take advantage of the favourable competitive rate and convenient regular quality service. The cargoes are mixed subject to their compatibility except that dangerous classified cargo is exempt from such a facility (p. 168). Limitations are imposed on weight and general dimensions of the cargo. The agent is responsible for the overall consolidated consignment of some 30 consignments and sponsors them. The agent prepares a cargo manifest to accompany the master air waybill (MAWB) throughout the flight and issues house air waybills (HAWB) to individual shippers. The MAWB is prepared by the airline who issues it. The HAWB is produced and issued by the agent. The agent's responsibility includes cargo collection and/or delivery, payment of all reasonable costs throughout the transit including collection or delivery charges (usually involving the agent's own vehicles), air freight, airport/airline disbursements, documentation, customs and so on. The agent is able to charge an inclusive rate throughout which is usually much lower when compared with a package or consignment sent as an individual parcel. Usually the agent works in close liaison with a corresponding agent in the destination area or region, and the two agents work on a reciprocal basis, developing the consolidated air freight business in both directions.

Details of the scheme are given below:

(1) It is particularly attractive to the exporter/shipper engaged in despatching small consignment(s) which can be conveniently accommodated into a ULD subject to its compatibility with other cargo shipped. If there are any queries on weight or dimension limitations, the shipper should contact the agent.

(2) Documentation is simplified and all the documentation needs relative to the transit are usually taken care of by the agent. The agent issues at the time of flight departure a 'house air waybill' (HAWB) which is identified with the master air waybill (MAWB) including number and cargo manifest details.

(3) The promotion of the consolidated service is undertaken by the agent who takes care of all the transit needs of the consignment including documentation. This enables the airlines to concentrate on providing a quality air freight flight service and to become less involved in marketing the service involving contact with individual shippers.

(4) The rate is calculated on a W/M (weight/measurement) basis (pp. 140–1).

(5) The agent promotes the service – a feature of it is the competitive inclusive rate structure compared with an individual package despatched under IATA fare structure arrangements (pp. 132–3).

(6) The scheme enables the airlines to obtain the maximum income from the allocated aircraft hold accommodation earmarked for the agents and thereby improves the airline profitability through good capacity utilization.

(7) It enables the airline to plan ahead with confidence in the knowledge that air freight consolidated consignments are being developed by the agent and in so doing facilitates the guarantee of traffic to the airline.

(8) The agent agreement with the airline usually permits the agent to vary, cancel or reduce his pre-booked cargo hold space up to 36 hours before flight departure time, thereby permitting the airline to use the cargo hold space for other shippers.

(9) The air freight consolidation facility does not exist on every air freight service, which tends to restrict the user. However, it is a fast-growing market and the initiative for its expansion in terms of extending the range of flights and services on which it is available rests with the agent in consultation with the airline.

(10) The rates structure is inclusive of collection and/or delivery charge, documentation, customs clearance, airline disbursements and so on, which is a good selling point of the service. It permits the shipper to avoid the minimum freight rate regulations found in the airline (IATA) approved rate structure (pp. 128–32).

(11) Packing costs are substantially reduced and the risk of cargo loss and/or damage is minimized, thereby lowering insurance premiums.

(12) Consolidated consignments tend to result in quicker customs clearance.

(13) It encourages the freight forwarder to maximize profitability through an equal spread or mix of high-and low-density cargoes.

(14) It encourages the use of ULDs with all the attendant advantages.

(15) It enables the agent to offer guaranteed services, thereby aiding quality of service and development of the market.

(16) Its general competitiveness and favourable quality of service facilitates the development of international trade.

(17) Quicker and reliable transit times are offered which is a good selling point of the service.

(18) A major benefit to the industry and shippers is the extensive network of consolidator services worldwide. An increasing number are involved in the sea/air package (p. 93). Such frequency of service and a global network substantially increases the 'value added benefit' to the shipper and develops the just-in-time concept through quicker transit times and more competitive rates.

(19) An increasing number of consolidators tend to specialize in certain commodities which encourages the development of overseas markets on a low-cost international distribution basis.

(20) Most air freight consolidators operate on a minimum consignment weight basis and, accordingly, regular shippers of the consolidators' service usually build up a collection of consignments over several days to take advantage of the most economical rate rather than despatching daily and being charged a 100 kg rate for a commodity of 15 kg.

(21) The airline system is fully computerized (p. 133).

Air freight consolidation services exist worldwide and there is every evidence to suggest that its growth will continue. It is ideal for the smaller exporter and through its competitiveness and quality of service is aiding the development of international trade by air.

7.5 Canal and inland waterways freight rates

The portion of the international transit conveyed by canal will have a tariff based on distance, commodity type, transshipment cost, handling charges and any other miscellaneous charges. For example, if the consignment is an indivisible load, it may involve some special, heavy lifting equipment. Special rates usually exist for containers, palletized cargoes and special contract tariffs are available for regular shipments. The tariffs and range thereof vary by individual country and canal authority. They exclude customs clearance charges. The rates are based on either a weight or measurement assessment.

Distribution of international trade by inland waterway based on the major European ports is very extensive on the Continent for a variety of reasons. Rates are based on weight or cubic measurement and vary by commodity and trade. It is a highly competitive method of distribution for certain commodities and/or trades and one which is likely to continue to expand as the system is modernized and further developed.

The integration of inland waterways with deep-sea services, especially in the field of containerization and bulk commodities, is being developed at many European ports, principally Dunkerque, Antwerp, Rotterdam and Hamburg (pp. 57–61). The rates are usually inclusive under the intermodal combined transport system. For containers, it is based on TEU criteria.

7.6 International road haulage freight rates

The development of the international road haulage market UK/Europe–Asia–Middle East has been outstanding in recent years, particularly for the UK–Continent under CMR conditions. Undoubtedly the fixed links involving Le Shuttle and those in Scandinavia (see pp. 61–3) has facilitated this development.

The rates charged to the international road freight forwarder to convey the vehicle and/or trailer on the vehicular ferry are based on the trailer/vehicle length, and whether it is empty or loaded, accompanied or unaccompanied. Additional charges are raised for excessive width and/or height. Special rates usually exist for declared valuable cargoes. Rebates are given to hauliers and agents who originate substantial quantities of traffic annually to an operator for a particular route or service. These rates are exclusive of customs clearance charges, etc. Keen competition exists amongst operators particularly on rates and fringe benefits, namely free cabins or meals for drivers, together with free passage for drivers. An increasing number of large, and indeed medium sized, exporters now undertake their own international distribution by road. It has many advantages particularly if the cargo flow can be balanced in each direction.

To the shipper using the international road freight forwarders service – much of which is groupage traffic – the actual rate is based on the cubic measurement or weight of the cargo, whichever produces the greater revenue. This is related to the commodity classification, and origin and destination of the cargo. The cargo measurement 3 m^3 (three cubic metres) equals 1 tonne (1000 kg). The calculation is based on the W/M option (p. 140). Rates are very competitive particularly compared with air freight for merchandise destined outside the European Community. To improve vehicle crew utilization in an era of rising cost, an increasing number of the larger road haulage operators despatch their vehicles unaccompanied on the vehicular ferry. This enables the driver to deposit his trailer at the ferry terminal and collect another one waiting. It avoids driver lodging allowance cost being incurred and enables better vehicle control to be achieved with improved reliability and lower cost. Shippers using the road trailer unit network may opt for the EuroTunnel rather than a cross-Channel ferry.

7.7 International rail services rates

Details of the international rail service rates are given below:

(1) Cargo wagons (Table 4.7) containers, and road trailers (Table 4.7), are available for contract hire from one month to several years thereby forming part of a shipper's in-house transport operation throughout the European rail network.

(2) Groupage services offering collection and delivery between UK freight villages and key industrial and commercial centres. Rates are based on the W/M concept and are available from leading rail freight forwarders such as MAT Transport and Danzas. This involves the cargo wagon (Table 4.7) and palletized merchandise.

(3) Purpose-built car transporter wagons in complete train load formation (p. 57–61). Rates are negotiated direct with suppliers to move the cars between factories and distribution points.

(4) Maritime ISO container trains. Rates are negotiated with the container operators to convey TEUs between seaport and container terminals usually in complete train load formation.

(5) Intermodal services, the UK and the Continent. This involves 1200 intermodal wagons operating between UK-based rail Euro terminals and 15 Continental industrial centres. The wagons are 2.77 m high and 2.5 m wide and refrigerated units are 2.75 m high and 2.6 m wide. They can accommodate swap-bodies (Table 4.7) and containers in the form of tilts, tanks, reefers, flats, dry boxes, etc. Rates are based on a range of options to meet shippers' needs including the chartering of wagon space on a regular or irregular basis, to the chartering of a complete train. Allied Continental Intermodal (ACI) and combined Transport Ltd operate the services.

(6) The Channel Tunnel rate for the road haulage vehicle travelling between the portals will be based on the vehicle unit. Hauliers who can guarantee a certain volume of business annually will be given a discounted rate.

7.8 Maritime container rates

The general practice is to formulate individual rates by container type, capacity, and the actual origin and destination of the merchandise. The through rate will embrace the inland transportation cost known at the time of despatch, embracing collection and terminal handling expenses, but it will usually exclude customs clearance charges, demurrage, etc. Much of course depends on the trade. This practice applies to full container load (FCL) traffic. Some of the containers are stuffed and unstuffed at the container base, which may be an inland clearance depôt (ICD).

The mega container operator with a fleet in excess of 250 000 TEUs tends to formulate their rate structure on three factors:

(1) the cost of the service;
(2) the value added benefit the service provides to the shipper;
(3) the opportunities in the market place for containerized goods.

The rate structure and level of rates is very flexible. The bulk of the container services globally operates outside the liner conference system constraints. Some large multinational companies own/lease ISO containers. They are usually of a specialized type offering a two-way traffic flow. The tariff for such traffic is usually a specially negotiated contract rate.

A very substantial volume of traffic which is conveyed in containers is less than container load (LCL) traffic involving the NVOCC concept (pp. 94–5). The cargo is assembled and stuffed into a container at a container base or inland clearance depôt with each individual consignment attracting separate rates. Such rates are calculated on a weight or cubic measurement basis whichever produces the greater revenue. They naturally reflect the origin and destination of such merchandise, together with, when practicable, likely disbursement charges, namely handling, customs clearance, etc. The LCL rate is based on W/M. Volume shippers who guarantee a specified tonnage annually are granted discounted rates.

Rates parity is unlikely to exist in each direction between two seaports and the reasons are numerous. Major factors include the imbalance of the traffic flow, and differing types of cargo and the varying specifications of containers used. An imbalance of cargo flow is very common and generates problems for the shipowner. For example, a country may have a severe imbalance of exports compared with imports shipments. It may export primarily industrial manufactured goods, involving covered containers, and import foodstuffs, requiring reefer containers.

An illustration of the consolidator rates strategy under NVOCC is given below:

Shipowner rate
(1) 50 individual shipments of 2 tonne at LCL rate of US $60 per tonne charged by the shipping line (US $60 * 100 tonne)   US $6000

Consolidator rate
(2) 50 individual shipments of 2 tonne at consolidator rate of US $30 per tonne (US $30 * 100 tonne)   US $3000

        Total Rate Difference   US $3000

(3) Rate per tonne charged by consolidator to individual shippers (50 shipments at 2 tonne = US $5000)   US $50
(4) Saving per tonne to shippers (i.e. US $60 – US $50)   US $10
(5) Margin of profit per tonne to consolidator (i.e. US $50 – US $30)   US $20
(6) Saving to shippers (50 shipments at 2 tonne US $6000 shipowner's rate – 50 shipment at 2 tonne US $5000 consolidator rate)   US $1000
(7) Profit to consolidator   US $2000

The above demonstrates a situation where the shipowner's LCL rate per tonne is US $60, whereas the NVOCC consolidator rate to shippers is US $50, yielding a profit to the consolidator of US $20 per tonne on the basis that the wholesale rate is US $30 per tonne quoted by the shipowner.

For consignments requiring special facilities such as livestock or indivisible loads requiring heavy lifts, additional charges are raised.

Maritime container rates are very competitive and this mode of transport now constitutes a substantial volume of deep-sea worldwide general merchandise cargo.

7.9 Sea freight rates

We will now examine the sea freight tariff formulation relative to liner cargo rates involving break-bulk cargo, LCL container shipments and ship chartering. It should be mentioned that the terms tariff and rate are synonymous inasmuch as various forms of transport use either, according to circumstances.

Liner rates are based partly on cost, and partly on value. Many freight rates are quoted on a basis of weight or measurement at ship's option. This means that the rate quoted will be applied either per ton of 2240 lb (weight) or on 40 ft^3 (cubic measurement) per ton, whichever will produce the greater revenue. The reason for this method of charging is that heavy cargo will bring a vessel to her loadline before her space is full, while light cargo will fill her space without bringing her down to her maximum draught. To produce the highest revenue a vessel must be loaded to her full internal capacity, and immersed to her maximum permitted depth. In most trades, cargo measuring under 40 ft^3/ton weight is charged on a weight basis, whilst cargo measuring 40 ft^3 or more per ton is charged on a volume measurement basis. With the spread of the metric system, many freight rates are quoted per 1000 kg or m^3 (ICBM – one cubic metre) (p. 141).

Liner tariffs quote rates for many commodities which move regularly. These rates are based on the stowage factor (rate of bulk to weight), on the value of the cargo and on the competitive situation. Many tariffs publish class rates for general cargo not otherwise specified. Some tariffs publish class rates whereby commodities are grouped for charging into several classes. On commodities of very high value, *ad valorem* rates are charged at so much per cent of the declared value. When commodities move in large quantities, and are susceptible to tramp competition, shipowners often employ 'open rates', that is, the rate is left open, so that the shipping line can quote whatever rate it determines. For heavy lifts and extra lengths it is usual to make additional charges in order to cover the special handling of such cargo.

Insofar as chartered vessels are concerned the negotiation is usually undertaken by a shipbroker, who may be on the Baltic Exchange communicating with other shipbrokers having a vessel available to hire. Alternatively, the shipbroker may go direct to the shipowner.

The rates are not pre-determined but are based on economic forces of supply and demand. A voyage charter is a contract for a special voyage, while a time charter is a contract for a period of time which may cover several voyages. Therefore, the voyage charter rate is a short-term rate, while the time charter rate is often a long-term rate. When trade is buoyant and voyage rates are rising, charterers, in anticipation of further rises, tend to charter for longer periods to cover their commitments; when rates are expected to fall, they tend to contract for shorter periods. Therefore, the current time charter rate tends to reflect the expected trend of voyage rates in the future. If rates are expected to rise, it will tend to be above the current voyage rates; if they are expected to fall, it will tend to be below the current voyage rates. Generally speaking, the two rates move in the same direction, but because time charter rates depend on market expectations, they tend to fluctuate more widely than voyage rates. When conditions are improving, long-term rates tend to rise more rapidly than voyage rates; when conditions are deteriorating, voyage rates tend to fall more rapidly.

In more recent years there has been a tendency in an increasing number of liner cargo trades to impose a surcharge on the basic rate. This includes bunkering or fuel surcharge, currency surcharge and finally surcharges raised on heavy lifts such as indivisible consignments or on excessive height or length of Ro-Ro traffic (pp. 53–7).

It is relevant to mention that the bill of lading is the document usually associated with liner cargo and the charter party with chartered vessels.

7.10 Calculation of freight rates

To illustrate the calculation of the freight rate applicable to all transport modes, an example is given below.

Consider the despatch of the following luxury food items from Birmingham to Milan; all items are packed in tri-wall cartons:

6 cartons $120 \times 80 \times 80$ cm; weight of each carton 50 kg

Freight rates are:
Air £2.50 per chargeable kg
Sea US $150 per tonne W/M (assume $1.8 = £ 1$)
Road £200 per 1000 chargeable kg

Chargeable weight/volume ratios for each mode should be assumed to be:
Air 6 CBM = 1000 kg
Sea 1 CBM = 1000 kg (CBM = cubic metre)
Road 3 CBM = 1000 kg

Air – Volumetric –

$$\text{One carton} = \frac{12 \times 80 \times 80}{6000} \text{ kg}$$

$$\text{Six cartons} = 6 \times \frac{12 \times 80 \times 80}{6000} \text{ kg} = 768 \text{ kg}$$

Air freight rate – £2.50 per kilogram
Total air freight volumetric – 768 kg $\times$ £2.50 = £1920

Weight

  1 carton 50 kg

  6 cartons, 6×50 kg = 300 kg

  Air freight rate – £2.50 per kilogram

  Total air freight – weight = 300kg $\times$ £2.50 = £750

Sea – rate – US \$150 per tonne (1000 kg)

  Rate sterling US \$150 ÷ 1.8 = £83.33 per tonne

  Rate sterling per kilogram £83.33 ÷ 1000 = £00.08

 Volumetric

 1 carton $= \dfrac{12 \times 80 \times 80}{6000}$ kg

 6 cartons $= \dfrac{6 \times 12 \times 80 \times 80}{6000}$ kg = 4608 kg

Sea freight rate – £00.08 per kilogram

Total sea freight rate volumetric 4608 kg $\times$ £00.08 = £368.64

Weight

  One carton = 50 kg

  Six cartons, 6×50 kg = 300 kg

  Sea freight rate – £00.08 per kilogram

  Total sea freight rate = 300 kg $\times$ £00.08 = £24.00.

In some trades the rate would be based on the nearest tonne, in which case the volumetric rate would rise from 4608 kg to 5000 kg and yield £416.65, and the weight from 300 kg to 1000 kg to produce £83.33.

Road

  Rate £200 per chargeable 1000 kg

  Road rate per kilogram £200 ÷ 1000 = £00.20

 Volumetric

 1 carton $= \dfrac{120 \times 80 \times 80}{3000}$ kg

 6 cartons $= \dfrac{6 \times 120 \times 80 \times 80}{3000}$ kg = 1536 kg

Road freight rate £00.20 per kilogram

Total road freight 1536 kg $\times$ £00.20 = £307.20

Weight

  1 carton 50 kg

  6 cartons, 6×50 kg = 300 kg

  Road freight rate £00.20 per kilogram

Total road freight rate 300 kg $\times$ £00.20 = £60.

Most carriers would calculate the road freight when mention is made of 'per 1000 kg' chargeable on the basis of rounding up to the nearest 1000 kg. Hence the volumetric would rise from 1536 kg to 2000 kg yielding £400, and the weight from 300 kg to 1000 kg producing £200.

The carrier would charge the volumetric or weight rate which will yield the highest income. Accordingly, in the example the answer would be as follows:

Air (volumetric)	£1920	
Sea (volumetric)	£364.64	(£416.65, nearest tonne)
Road (volumetric)	£307.20	(£400, nearest 1000 kg).

An alphabetical list of salient freight rates is given below:

Ad valorem. This is based on the declared value of the cargo whereby merchandise declared at £1000 with 2.5 per cent *ad valorem* rate would be charged £25.

Antiques. Antiques including art treasures require special packaging by an accredited company and special freight rates apply. Freight forwarders tend to specialize in this business.

Bloodstock. This involves the movement of racehorses. Special arrangements and rates apply by air and Ro-Ro ferry. All must be accompanied by a groom.

Box. A container rate (pp. 137–40).

Commodity. See p. 129.

Commodity box. A container rate.

Consolidated. The rate is for consolidated consignments usually based on W/M option. Also termed the 'groupage rate' (p. 140).

Dangerous cargo. Conveyed under ADR, RID, IMO and IATA regulations, involving a rate about 50 per cent above the general cargo rate (pp. 160–81).

Dead freight. This usually arises when a charterer fails to provide a full cargo for a ship.

Express Air Freight Service. For packages, documents, usually involving couriers (p. 132).

FAK (freight all kinds). This rate applies to all types of cargo irrespective of commodity type.

Fixture. Chartering a vessel (p. 140).

Groupage. See consolidated entry (pp. 133–5).

Household effects. Removal of household furniture. Special packaging and rates apply. Some agents specialize in this business.

Indivisible loads. Such consignments are of excessive weight or dimensions and require special handling equipment and arrangements (p. 136).

Livestock. Special rates and arrangements apply.

Lump sum freight. This is an amount payable for the use of the whole or portion of a ship.

Pallets. Rates applicable to palletized cargo (p. 152).

Postal. There is a wide variety of postal services ideal for documents, small packages and samples (p. 137).

Project forwarding. This involves the coordination through a freight forwarder of all the international transportation arrangements of all products relative to a major capital project such as a new airport terminal, power station, etc.

Rebate. A discount on a published rate attained through negotiation on a guaranteed volume over specified period, etc. (p. 126).

Ro-Ro rates. Applicable to road haulage movement (p. 136).

Trade vehicles. Rates involving the movement of trade cars, lorries, buses, etc.

W/M. Option weight/measurement ship option based on weight or measurement evaluation (pp. 140–42).

7.11 Overseas postal service tariffs and services: Royal Mail International

Royal Mail International (RMI) operates a strategic business within Royal Mail. Overall, it is the foremost UK based international carrier and has effective links with the world's postal administrations and delivers direct to over 300 destination nations worldwide. It offers the following range of services.

7.11.1 International Unsorted Service

The International Unsorted Service is designed as a contract airmail service. The service is split into two streams: letters for all correspondence and print/packets for all other mailing items. There is also an 'on demand' option for one-off postings. Collection is free, and it offers a worldwide distribution service with direct delivery to more than 280 points of entry. All items carry a UK postmark and a UK return address. The service is monitored to 16 countries within Europe and six in the Rest of the World including all major business centres. Commercial value items of up to £270 require a green CN22 customs document and merchandise over £270 requires form CN23. Items up to 2 kg embracing invoices, magazines and newspapers may be despatched and also books up to 5 kg.

7.11.2 International Sorted User Service

The Royal Mail International Sorted User Service is a cost effective method to mail multiple printed matter items abroad. This includes books, magazines, newspapers, direct mail, CD-ROMs and disks. The service is simple – the sender sorts and bags the mail whilst Royal Mail International collects and distributes it. There are three services: priority – the quickest and most efficient distribution method; standard – available for countries outside Europe and combines value for money with speed – mail is flown to the destination country and then distributed economically; and finally economy which is the cheapest using surface mail methods of ship and rail. Customs documents are either CN22 or CN23.

7.11.3 International Direct Entry Service

The International Direct Entry Service enables users to send direct mail, publications and packages through the domestic mail services of countries in Europe, North America and Australasia. It is ideal for specialist publications. The mail goes directly into the destination country's postal service complete with a local printed postmark and return address.

7.11.4 International Response Service

International Response Service extends the principles of the UK reply paid system to items mailed overseas. There are two services: the international business reply carries a response mechanism with a prepaid UK address so recipients can respond by airmail at no cost, and international admail involving a reply device which is prepaid with a local return address. An annual licence fee is involved and there is a charge per item returned.

Additionally, an International Stamped response service exists involving offering a local return address for mailings that are not prepaid or pre-addressed. Customers can send their own items to a local PO Box using their national stamps. It is ideal for an 'off the page' advertisement.

7.11.5 SWIFTAIR and Signature Services

Swiftair offers a priority airmail service for urgent items. There are three options:

(1) Swiftair – for more urgent items. This offers priority handling with an express delivery service that is particularly cost effective.
(2) Swiftair plus recorded gives the speed of Swiftair plus the reassurance of a signature on delivery.
(3) Swiftair plus registered – gives the speed of Swiftair plus the reassurance of a signature on delivery and compensation in the event of loss or damage.

Swiftair is tracked to the point of departure to all countries, to the point of arrival in most western European countries and to end-delivery in the Republic of Ireland.

■ □ ■ ■ 8

Export cargo packaging, stowage, marking and dangerous cargo shipments

8.1 Factors influencing type of cargo packaging

Packaging techniques today are becoming increasingly sophisticated to meet a market which is seeking continuous improvements in the following areas:

(1) Improved standards to reduce risk of damage and pilferage. This in turn encourages competitive cargo insurance premiums and maintains good relations with the importer. Cargo received in a damaged condition seriously impairs the exporter's product overseas market prospects as it loses goodwill with the importer. Moreover, the exporter is ultimately obliged to replace the damaged goods, which can be a costly task.

(2) A better utilization of transport capacity to lower distribution cost. This is particularly relevant to ISO container use when suitably sized packaged cargo can be firmly stowed in it with no broken stowage. Full advantage should be taken of high-capacity containers for volume cargoes, and use made of a stowage plan. This reduces the risk of damage, and ensures all container capacity is utilized, subject to the total weight limitations not being exceeded. Moreover, it reduces the need to use dunnage and, by attaining higher utilization/load factor of container capacity, lowers the freight cost of each unit distributed.

(3) Improved cargo handling. Cargo packaging in design, namely dimension and configuration, should facilitate the most economical method of handling. This is particularly relevant to awkward shaped cargo. Moreover, it applies from the time the goods are packaged, which may be in the factory, until it reaches the importer's warehouse/distribution centre. Mechanical and computerized and high tech cargo handling equipment is now in extensive use to reduce labour cost and speed up cargo handling.

(4) Packaging costs amongst various manufacturers are now very competitive. The shipper is very conscious of containing packing costs and the exporter is well advised to engage a specialist packaging company to obtain professional advice and gain the best results.

Two sizes in common use are the Euro-pallet 800 mm × 1200 mm and the industrial pallet of 1000 mm × 1200 mm which has a capacity of 2 tonnes. Additionally, a wide range of pallet sizes are constructed which are tailor-made to the unit load. It may be white furniture, cartons, etc. The pallets are affixed to the goods using stretch-wrapping techniques.

An increasing number of global transport operators provide a complete range of packing services. Nedlloyd Districentres of the Netherlands provide such a service. It operates in 40 countries and specializes in warehousing, stock control, order processing, assembly, modification, packing, domestic and international distribution and customs documentation. It provides multilingual instructions such as shipment to Italy in Italian; consolidation of a range of small products from a shipper; despatch of promotional material using plastic film; product test; product assembly; shipment of goods on fixed units or pallets or other techniques; and packing in shock-absorbent polyurethane foam or plastic foil on pallets using stretch-wrapping techniques. Packaging specifications vary by transport mode, type of pallet commodity and transit routeing. Each overseas sales contract cargo needs to be individually considered to obtain the best results and sustain/develop overseas markets. Moreover, one must bear in mind that packaging not only protects but also gives the shipper's product added value.

An examination will now be made of the various factors influencing the nature of packaging for an international consignment.

(1) Value of the goods. In the main the high-value consignment usually attracts more extensive packing than low-value merchandise. Much, of course, depends on the nature of the commodity. If packing is inadequate, bearing in mind transit and declared cargo valuation, problems could be experienced in carriers' liability, acceptance and adequate cargo insurance coverage. Moreover, high-value consignments, such as a valuable painting, require adequate security and likewise attract higher freight rates. Such packing must be done professionally.

(2) Nature of the transit. The type and length of transit. Is the movement national, European or transglobal? What form of transport will be used during the transit – road, rail, short sea, deep-sea or air? All have varying characteristics which make varying demands of the packaging of the goods. Moreover, one must consider the method of shipment; it may be break-bulk, LCL or FCL. The more handling goods must endure, the stouter the packaging required; furthermore, the greater the degree of overstowage that the goods must endure, then the stronger the packaging needed. Certain forms of transport, particularly air and ISO containerization, usually require less extensive packing. This is a strong marketing feature of their service. Air transport particularly encourages palletized consignments with cargo strapped/anchored throughout the transit. Fibreboard cartons for consumer products are very popular with both air and ISO container shipments. For break-bulk shipments involving several transshipments at the ports and other points en route, more elaborate, robust packing is required. Such traffic movement is found in general cargo non-containerized shipments from China and India. Cargo wagon and Ro-Ro consignments have

modest packing requirements, but much depends on their collection and delivery arrangements and the degree of robust packing needed. Packing needs for cargoes despatched in purpose-built transport units are usually minimal. This is particularly so with containerization. Packing needs are obviously modest for transport services offering a door-to-door service with no transshipment en route.

(3) Nature of the cargo. This concerns the characteristics of the goods concerned and their susceptibility to various loss/damage. It is important to bear in mind that packaging offers protection against pilferage as well as damage. This factor together with item (2) are the two major factors which determine the type of packing for an individual consignment. Cargo shipped in bulk requires little or no packing, whilst general merchandise needs adequate packing. For example, apples can be consigned in cases, boxes, cartons or pallet boxes. Cement on the other hand may be shipped in five- or six-ply paper bags, containers or in bulk. Motor vehicles are usually shipped unpacked to reduce freight, with each vehicle being individually secured and stowed. Grain, ores and coal are all shipped in bulk. Electrical equipment such as cathode ray tubes would be accommodated in a skeleton wooden case and usually conveyed by air. Computer equipment falls into a similar category.

(4) Compliance with customs or statutory requirements. This is particularly relevant to dangerous cargo where strict regulations apply both by air and sea concerning the carriers' acceptance, packing, stowage, documentation, marking and carriers' liability. This aspect will be examined later in the chapter. Statutory regulations also apply to the transportation of foodstuffs involving the temperature enforcement of the food. Such regulations are found in the Food Hygiene (Amendment) Regulations 1990.

In some countries, straw is an unacceptable form of packing due to the risk of insects being imported. Quarantine regulations are particularly extensive in Australasia where materials such as wood products, rice husks, straw and similar plant material may not be used as packaging material or dunnage. This ensures that all packing materials are free from soil and contamination from animal products which can harbour pests, particularly insects, which are capable of causing wholesale devastation in forests. If the exporter does use wood it is advisable to have it suitably treated, namely by fumigation, kiln drying or impregnation, and to obtain a certificate to this effect for despatch to the importer. If in doubt the exporter is advised to consult his agent.

(5) Resale value, if any, of packaging material in the importer's country. In some developing countries, large drums, wooden cases, or bags have a modest resale value. This helps to offset the packaging cost.

(6) General fragility of cargo. In the main, the more fragile the cargo becomes, the greater the degree of packaging required. This is very much related to the mode of transport, particularly air freight which has only limited packaging needs and low value of consignment. A judgement must be made on the most acceptable form of packaging to adopt and if in doubt advice must be sought.

(7) The international consignment delivery terms of sale (Incoterms 2000, p. 333). Again the actual packing specification may be contained therein and it is important to take into account who will bear the cost. This is usually the exporter.

(8) Variation in temperature during the course of the transit. Temperature variation can be quite extensive during transit and packaging must take account of this to permit the cargo to breathe and avoid excessive condensation/sweating, see item (4) above. Again advice should be sought when necessary from the airline or shipowner.

(9) Ease of handling and stowage. Awkwardly shaped cargoes packed in cartons or containers can greatly facilitate stowage, particularly in a container and using mechanical cargo handling equipment. Cargo stowage and obtaining the maximum practicable utilization of available transport unit capacity are areas worthy of study to lower unit distribution cost. Likewise, if awkwardly shaped cargoes are conveniently packed this will speed cargo handling. Moreover, cargoes of an awkward shape can attract additional handling charges and a freight surcharge in some circumstances. Furthermore, such cargoes are more vulnerable to damage and could therefore attract higher cargo insurance premiums.

(10) Insurance acceptance conditions. Cargo which is particularly fragile or which has a bad record in terms of damage/pilferage may be subject to a prescribed packing specification. Otherwise, the insurance company or underwriter will refuse to cover them at a competitive cargo insurance premium. Insufficiency of packaging is usually an adequate defence in most carriers' contracts of carriage to claims of certain kinds.

(11) The size of the cargo and its weight. Basically there are three main considerations to be observed when determining the form that a package should take and these include size, shape and strength.

    (a) The size of the package will be governed by the size of the marketable unit as, for example, a sliced loaf and a packet of 20 cigarettes. Comparison between the sizes of marketable units of various products frequently reveals the phenomena that products of low bulk command relatively higher prices than those of greater bulk. The reasons for this are two-fold. First, a readily saleable unit of an expensive product tends to be small in order to come within the means of the average consumer, for example, ladies' perfume. Secondly, the purchase of a large quantity of a product normally results in an overall reduction in the cost per basic marketable unit. This means that the customer pays less for the product, or alternatively is able to buy a larger quantity for the price he or she is prepared to pay. An example is found in the retail shop when the basic-sized package of a household product may cost 90p, while the family size containing almost twice the quantity costs 140p.

    (b) Shape to a large extent is determined by the shape of the goods to be enclosed within the package. Loose goods, the shape of which is flexible, may be accommodated within a package designed to meet one or more of a range of requirements, for example, the cylindrical shape of the package containing a household bleach cleaner makes it convenient to use with one hand, yet the package is self-balancing upon a flat and stable base. More rigid products, such as a pair of tailor's scissors must be packaged within a container of a more regular shape – in this instance, an oblong package.

(c) Associated with size and shape is strength. Some products by their very nature need protection provided by the package, for example eggs, while others lend support to the package material, for example, metal ashtrays. Some products possess a rigid natural shape, but need cushioning by the package to protect a delicate mechanism, for example, a model electric train, while others rely upon the package for protection and retention of shape, for example, tinned fruit.

Finally, one must bear in mind that the final shape, dimension and weight of consignment, will determine level of freight rate.

(12) Marketing considerations. An overriding consideration, certainly for consumer goods and increasingly so for industrial products, is that the package should fit into the overall marketing concept. On a company strategic level, it must enhance and reinforce the company's image with the customer, whilst, on a lower level, it must sell positively by putting across three cardinal points: the nature, the price and the advantages of the product. Moreover, it must endeavour to generate further sales with the same customer by performing satisfactorily whilst the product is in use. Additionally, one must bear in mind any advertising motif to be accommodated on the packaging.

(13) Facilities available at the terminal; namely airport, seaport, one-stop and feeder ports, container base, inland clearance depot, warehouse, districtparks, free trade zones, dry ports, container freight stations, freight villages, etc. Lifting equipment at some seaports and particularly airports may be of limited capacity. Accordingly, relative to an indivisible load, the shipper may be compelled to despatch it in two parts instead of one integral unit. Moreover, not all airports have Customs clearance facilities and this could lead to an alternative air terminal being used with differing handling equipment capacity.

(14) Type and size of container, cargo wagon, pallet, Ro-Ro vehicle or aircraft. The configuration of the transport unit together with access thereto will influence the actual ultimate dimension of the packaging, its maximum weight and shape.

(15) Marking of cargo packaging. Each package must bear a marking code and use a symbol to ease handling (Figure 8.1).

(16) Cost of packaging. This is becoming an increasingly important aspect in deciding on the type of packaging. In a world where overseas markets are becoming more competitive the exporter is constantly exploring ways and means of reducing distribution cost and improving marketing techniques. Packaging features very much in this evaluation.

Packaging, therefore, is not only designed as a form of protection to reduce the risk of goods being damaged in transit, but also to prevent pilferage and aid marketing. It is, of course, essential to see not only that the right type of packing is provided, but

FIGURE 8.1 Recognized international cargo marking symbols

also that the correct quality and form of container is used. There are numerous types of packing and a description of the more important forms follow.

8.2 Types of packaging

Many goods have little or no form of packing and are carried loose. These include iron and steel plates, iron rods, railway rolling stock, and steel rails. Such cargoes are generally weight cargoes with a low stowage factor. Heavy vehicles, locomotives and buses are also carried loose, because of the impracticability and high cost of packing.

Baling is a form of packing consisting of a canvas cover often cross-looped by metal or rope binding. It is most suitable for paper, wool, hay, peat, cotton, carpets and rope. Basically, it is a cheap and effective form of packing which aids handling. It affords limited protection to cargo.

Bags made of jute, cotton, plastic, or paper are a cheap form of container and are ideal for a wide variety of products including cement, fertilizer, flour, oil cakes, animal feeding products, chemicals and many consumer products. Their prime disadvantage is that they are subject to damage by water, sweat, leakages or, in the case of paper bags, breakage. The bags can be stacked on pallets to facilitate handling.

Barrels, hogsheads and drums are used for the conveyance of liquid or greasy cargoes. The main problems associated with this type of packing are the likelihood of leakage if the unit is not properly sealed, and the possibility of the drums becoming rusty during transit. Acids can also be carried in plastic drums and bottles. Such a form of packing, particularly drums, can have a resale value in certain countries overseas, whilst others are used indefinitely in numerous transits, particularly hogsheads.

Boxes, cases and metal-lined cases are also used extensively particularly in break-bulk and LCL cargoes. It is an expensive form of packing but it has some resale value in certain countries overseas. Overall, this type of packing gives complete protection and lessens the risk of pilferage plus it is an aid to handling. Basically, this form of packing is wooden in construction and varies in size and capacity. Moreover, it may be strengthened by the provision of battens and metal binding. Many of them, such as tea chests, are lined to create airtight packing which helps to overcome the difficulties that arise when passing through zones of variable temperature. This form of packing is particularly prominent in surface transport and is used for much machinery and other items of expensive equipment. However, it is becoming less popular as the cost of timber has risen sharply in recent years and containerization has lessened the need for such elaborate robust packing in certain trades.

Carboys, or glass containers enclosed in metal baskets have a limited use and are primarily employed for the carriage of acids and other dangerous liquids transported in small quantities. Again, it is a packing form found primarily in sea transport.

Cartons are a very common form of packing in all modes of international distribution involving in particular consumer products. They may be constructed of cardboard, strawboard or fibreboard. This form of packing is very much on the increase as it is relatively inexpensive, expandible, aids marketing, handling and stowage. It is particularly ideal for containerization and palletized consignments – the latter featuring prominently in the air freight field with the cartons affixed by metal bands to the pallet. The principal disadvantage is its susceptibility to crushing and pilfering. It is a very flexible form of packing and, therefore, prevents the breakage which may occur if rigid containers are used. Polystyrene now features more and more as a packing aid in cartons.

Crates or skeleton cases are a form of container halfway between a bale and a case. They are of wooden construction. Lightweight goods of larger cubic capacity such as machinery, domestic appliances like refrigerators, cycles and certain foodstuffs, for instance oranges, are suitable for this form of packing. It is used both in air and sea transport, including containerized shipments for skeleton cases.

Aluminium transport and storage containers are globally used. Constructed of aluminium, they are lightweight and can be both stacked and interstacked. A leading supplier is Bott Ltd who manufacture the Bott Ali Container range. They have a tare weight range from 5.6 kg to 26.0 kg spanning seven sizes. Examples are given below:

Length (mm)	Height (mm)	Width (mm)	Tare weight (kg)
600	400	240	5.6
800	400	330	8.0
800	600	400	12.5
800	600	600	12.5
1200	800	500	26.0

All are compatible with the pallet sizes 800×1200 mm or 1000×1200 mm.

Two new packing techniques have emerged in recent years. The first one is the bulk liquid bag or container. It can store various kinds of liquid cargo. When not in use the bag can be folded to 2 per cent of its volume. Other cargoes can be conveyed in the unit on the return trip. It costs about one-sixth of the price of a steel drum and one-quarter of a tank container. Each bulk liquid bag can carry a volume of liquid cargo equivalent to 210 large-capacity steel drums.

The second development is shrink-wrapping. It is very popular with air freight consignments, and consolidated consignments whether conveyed by air or surface transport. The cost is much less than the wooden case and similar relatively high cost material. The shrink-wrapping is provided by placing the goods to be covered on a base – usually a pallet for ease of handling – and covering it with a film of plastic. This is shrunk to enclose the items by the use of hot-air blowers (thermo-guns). It is a relatively cheap form of packing, particularly in relation to timber and fibreboard cartons. Moreover, it gives rigid protection to the cargo and its configuration follows the outline of the goods.

An interesting recent development in materials handling has been provided by Bel-O-Pak (UK) Ltd of London. It offers potential improvements in the space, weight, safety, methods and costs aspects of in-plant, storage and transit operations. This involves a variety of materials handling units. These are primarily based upon a collapsible expendable device, normally of recycled paper based fibreboard. Such a product when used in an assembly upon which a unit, unitized or intermediate bulk load is carried provides a facility whereby such loads may be mechanically handled by fork lift trucks or hoist slings. This may be the pallet box which is an expendable or reusable IBC/silo of heavy-duty corrugated board for transit and storage of powders and products which are best protected by a rigid casing. It provides up to 15 per cent increased volumetric capacity. Another product is the BOP sheet which is an expendable load-unitizing and handling facility on a base handling device for a one-piece load. Its slimness enables improved space utilization to be achieved as the open-ended sleeve/aperture with a pleated structure collapses under the weight of a unit load. However space is formed inside the length of each sleeve/aperture to give access to the fork lift truck when handling the unit.

Palletization is closely associated with packing and becoming increasingly popular with the sea cell container developed by Seaco (see p. 79). The pallet may be of steel or wooden construction. The pallet, in appearance, is like a platform on which the cargo is placed. An aperture is provided at each side to enable the fork lift truck to mobilize/handle the pallet. Wooden pallets, by which the cargo is anchored, are very common in air freight thereby facilitating cargo handling on a unitized basis. The

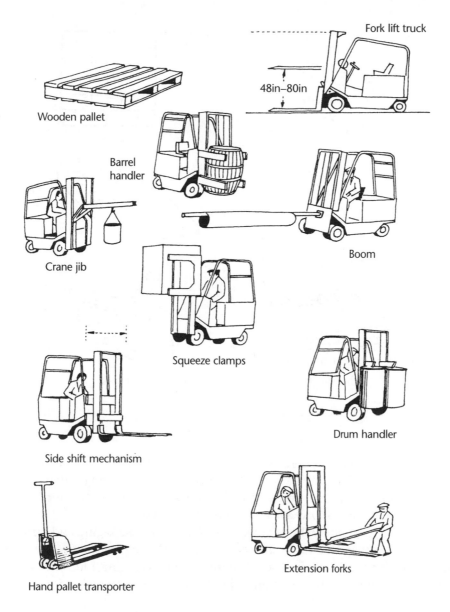

FIGURE 8.2 (a) Cargo handling equipment – fork lift trucks and pallet

pallet accompanies the cargo throughout the transit. Wooden pallets are regarded as expendable equipment when provided by the shipper who anchors the cargo to it. The pallet is manoeuvred by one of the fork lift trucks described and illustrated in Figure 8.2.

Packaging is now universally recognized as a decisive selling point in the realm of household consumer goods and similar products. Mass production, marketing, consumer advertising, display, design, presentation, protection hygiene and self-service retailing have made mechanical wrapping an almost universal necessity for

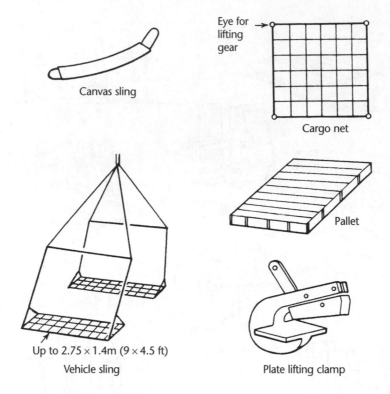

Canvas sling

Eye for lifting gear →

Cargo net

Pallet

Up to 2.75 × 1.4m (9 × 4.5 ft)
Vehicle sling

Plate lifting clamp

FIGURE 8.2 (b) Cargo handling equipment

small consumer goods. Modern packaging materials combine with modern handling equipment to make stacking at a greater height possible resulting in saving of floor space. Improvements are constantly becoming possible in the durability and protective quality of the package as technology progresses.

To the UK exporter who is anxious to improve his packaging and distribution technique, it is suggested he or she consults the Packaging Division of the Research Association for the Paper and Board, Printing and Packaging Industries (PIRA) of Leatherhead, Surrey. This organization provides services for which a fee is charged; details are given on p. 471.

Finally, the shipper must continuously review the form of packaging used in the light of the foregoing factors and the need to remain competitive coupled with rising standards.

8.3 Stowage of cargo

To the exporter, it is important he or she is aware of the principle of cargo stowage, particularly in an era where more shippers are stuffing containers or operating their own TIR international road haulage vehicle or inter-modal service between the UK and the Continent, and beyond. Overall, the prime consideration is the safety of the transport unit employed which may be a container, vessel, aircraft or road vehicle. It is the overriding factor to be borne in mind throughout the transit that the merchandise does not impair the general safety of the transport unit and likewise is not a danger to others. Moreover, one must bear in mind that stowage standards are rising all the time and the shipper should always seek prior advice if in doubt. This is particularly relevant to containerization where most major container operators provide a free advisory service on the principles of container stowage.

Basically there are four main factors to consider in the stowage of cargo.

(1) The best possible use should be made of the available dead weight or cubic capacity. It may be a container, road vehicle, ship or aircraft. Broken stowage, which is space wasted by cargo of irregular-shaped packages or irregularity of cargo spaces, should be kept to a minimum, consistent with the general stability of the transport unit. Generally 10–15 per cent of the total cubic capacity is allowed for broken stowage. A stowage plan detailing the cargo location can greatly facilitate achieving a good utilization of available space compatible with safety standards and is therefore used extensively in shipping, air freight cargo hold distribution, containerization and the large TIR international road haulage vehicle used by freight forwarders. Then, as far as practicable, full use should be made of the cubic capacity of the transport unit. An uneven distribution of cargo can result in an unstable load and encourages cargo movement throughout the transit. In the case of a vessel, uneven distribution of cargo can be compensated by ballasting the portion of the ship empty of cargo.

(2) Allied to the previous item is the need to prevent damage to the ship, road vehicle, aircraft or container. Not only must there be a proper distribution of cargo to ensure adequate stability and trim, but it must also be properly secured to prevent shifting. If there is a movement of the cargo during the transit, it will tend to cause the transport unit to become unstable thereby creating a serious hazard. In the case of a vessel, she will tend to list, which is particularly relevant to movement of bulk cargoes such as grain, small coal, flintstone or iron ores. The situation is more serious when dangerous cargoes are involved irrespective of the transport mode. To reduce the risk of cargo movement, dunnage is provided. This takes the form of foam rubber, polystyrene, timber boards, mats or inflatable bags which are placed between the cargo to prevent movement during transit. The shipper must be careful which type is chosen for some countries, particularly Australasia, where stringent regulations exist prescribing which dunnage material may not be used, for example, timber. Again one cannot stress too strongly the need to have total regard to the safety of the transit which is the prime consideration.

(3) Similarly, cargo which is fragile, taints very easily, is liable to leakage, scratches easily, has strong odours, or is liable to sweat requires proper segregation, otherwise the carrier will be faced with heavy claims and possible loss of goodwill amongst shippers. Obviously a crate of oranges with a penetrating odour cannot be stowed adjacent to a consignment of tea, which taints easily, and machinery cannot be placed on top of chinaware.

(4) Finally, a proper segregation of different consignments for various destinations, areas, ports and countries must be made to prevent delay in distribution and avoid double handling. This is a task primarily for the shipowner, airline, container operator or freight forwarder – the latter two being particularly involved in consolidated and groupage consignments. Again the stowage plan has a significant role to play in such a situation.

Our study of cargo stowage would not be complete without an examination of the principles of ISO container stowage, which is an increasingly popular method of international distribution, the container specification is found on pp. 72–3, see also Figure 4.1. Moreover, an increasing number of exporters are using the full container load consignment and undertaking their own stowage. The principles of container stowage are as follows. Again it cannot be stressed too strongly that safe container transport depends primarily on a correct and immovable cargo stow and an even weight distribution.

(1) The container must be stowed tightly so that lateral and longitudinal movement of the cargo within is impossible. Tight stowage can be achieved by making the shape and the dimensions of the package an optimum module of the container. Alternatively, if a unit load is being used such as a pallet, the base of it must form a module of the container.

(2) As an alternative to item (1), the cargo must be effectively restrained within the container. This is necessary for a variety of reasons including: (a) to prevent collapse of the stow while packing, unpacking, or during transit, for example, rolls of felt on end; (b) to prevent any movement during transit of part-loads or if single heavy items, for example, large pieces of machinery (the heavier the item the more damage it will do if allowed to move); and finally, (c) to prevent the 'face' of the stow collapsing and leaning against the container doors, that is, to prevent it from falling out when the doors are opened at final destination or for customs inspection.

(3) The consignment must be adequately secured. Details of the various techniques are given below:

   (a) Shoring – bars, struts and spars located in cargo voids to keep the cargo pressed against the walls or other cargo.
   (b) Lashing – rope, wire, chains, strapping or net secured to proper anchoring points within the container and tensioned against the cargo.
   (c) Wedging – wooden distance pieces, pads of synthetic material, inflatable dunnage to fill voids in the cargo and keep it immobile against the container walls.
   (d) Locking – cargo built up to give a three-dimensional brick wall effect.

Overall, a container safely transported depends chiefly on a correct and immovable stow and an even weight distribution.

Basically, there is no simple formula to apply when securing cargo in a container and only experience can aid perfection and solution. Each cargo must be treated on its merits – the type of cargo, the way in which it is stowed, the cargo handling equipment available and the permanent fittings in the container. The built-in securing points, dunnage brackets, etc. should be used extensively. Any timber dunnage used must be dry and comply with any quarantine regulations. Any shoring which presses against the container wall should have extra timber laid longitudinally between the wall and point of support to spread the weight over two or more side posts. Useful filler pieces for wedging or preventing chafe include old tyres, polyurethane slabs, macerated paper pads and, for light packages, rolled-up cardboard. Unless an identical stow is anticipated on the return container journey, it is best if the lashing equipment chosen be considered as expendable. Where synthetic strapping material is used, terylene is preferable to nylon for heavy loads as it is less liable to stretch.

To restrain cargo various techniques exist. Again it depends on the commodity involved. Top-heavy articles should be wedged, shored and lashed to prevent toppling. Heavy weights should be secured to stout ring-bolts (sited in the container floor and side walls) and/or be shored with timber. Chain or wire with bottle screws may be used. Wheeled vehicles should be chocked, and lashed with Spanish windlasses, with the chocks chamfered or padded to protect the tyres. If the floor is of extruded aluminium, portable securing devices must be used. Resilient loads can cause lashings to slacken. This may be overcome by introducing elasticity, for example rubber rope, into the lashing pattern. No securing of pallets is necessary, provided the load is properly secured to the pallet, if the distance between pallets and container walls is 100 mm (4 in) or less. Pallets must not be allowed any longitudinal movement. If securing is necessary, stow pallets against container walls and wedge wood blocks between pallets. It may be necessary to insert sheets of board between pallet loads to protect against chafe and prevent bags, cartons, etc. interweaving and jamming the stow.

In many instances there is a space 400–2400 mm (4–9 in) remaining between the face of the cargo and container doors. Cargo must be prevented from collapsing into this space. It can be achieved in a variety of ways detailed as follows:

(1) Use of suitably positioned lashing points with wire, rope, strapping, etc. woven across.
(2) A simple wooden gate for the wider gaps and heavier cargo.
(3) Use of filler pieces, that is macerated paper pads, polystyrene, wood, wool pads, etc. for the narrower gaps and lighter cargoes, for example cartons of biscuits.

Care must be taken to ensure that there is no 'fall out' when the container doors are opened. This is particularly relevant to a container which has been completely packed with cartons or sacks. Although this can sometimes be achieved by interlocking tiers of packages, it is better to make sure by using any fixing points located in the door posts of the container. Nylon strapping, polypropylene or wire threaded through such points forms an effective barrier.

To ensure there is adequate and correct overall distribution of cargo within the covered container, the goods must be secure within their packages. Moreover, the pack itself must be as full as possible so as to resist pressures external to it. Packages must be sufficiently rigid to withstand the weight imposed upon them when stacked, usually to a minimum height of 2.10 m (8 ft). If more than one type of cargo is stowed in the container, it is essential they are all compatible and cannot contaminate or be contaminated. Heavy items and liquids should be placed at the bottom with light and dry ones on the top. Within practical physical limitations of handling, the unit package should be as large as possible since this can reduce costs by up to 20 per cent and increase volumetric efficiency by up to 10 per cent. Consult when practicable the consignee about the proposed method of loading and sequence. This will facilitate discharge at the destination. Where relevant, stowing should be carried out in sequence which will permit rapid checking and stowage operations during and subsequent to unloading. In the event of the consignment being subject to customs pre-entry procedures, it would facilitate customs examination, should this occur and obviate unloading, if such cargo were stowed at the door end of the container. Shippers should avoid having a gap in the stow along the centre line of the container or at the sides as this will generate cargo movement in the transit and possible cargo damage.

Undoubtedly much of the foregoing cargo stowage principles relative to ISO covered containers can likewise be applied in many areas to stowage in other transport modes particularly in cargo wagon and the TIR international road haulage unit conveying consolidated and groupage cargo in a covered enclosed transport unit and inter-modal transits.

It would be appropriate to deal briefly with the equipment used in container stowage and discharge particularly as many exporters/importers have such cargo handling equipment in their factory or warehouse. Basically, the handling method used should be the one which gives the greater efficiency, with economy, and makes full use of any existing facilities and the equipment available.

The most versatile tool for tiering or stacking cargo in a warehouse or container base, etc. and for transporting loads up to a maximum of 2000 kg is the fork lift truck. Its general characteristics such as capacity, height of lift, speed, etc. will depend on overall work factors. The fork lift truck specification required for container work includes: a maximum collapsed mast height of 80 in; a free lift minimum of 48 in; its motive power must be either battery, electric or gas depending on circumstances; the mast tilts must be as large as possible; the gradient capacity laden minimum 1 in 10, cushion tyres, and spot light and wheel loadings in accord with maximum permitted load.

A wide variety of fork lift trucks exist and these include the following which are illustrated in Figure 8.2:

(1) Side shift mechanism. This moves the forks laterally either side of centre and thus considerably reduces the necessity to manoeuvre the fork lift truck inside the container.
(2) Extension forks. These are used for handling awkward loads and to obtain extra reach. They are particularly useful, if the fork lift truck is of sufficient capacity, for clearing a space equivalent to the depth of the pallets on each side of a trailer mounted container, thus providing easy operation of the pallet transporters.
(3) Boom. Ideal for carpets, pipes, etc.

(4) Barrel handler. In addition to clamping the barrel with two sets of upper and lower arms, it also revolves so that the barrel can be picked up and handled in the roll, or in the upright position.

(5) Crane jib. This converts the fork lift truck into a mobile crane.

(6) Drum handler. This permits the fork lift truck to handle one or two drums at a time.

(7) Squeeze-clamps. This is used for handling unit loads and individual items without the aid of pallets. The design and application of this attachment must be selected carefully since the operation of the clamp arms may be impeded by the container walls.

The foregoing types demonstrate the versatility of the fork lift truck.

8.4 Marking of cargo

Associated with packing is the marking of cargo. Basically, the export shipping mark and number is vital in the correct identification of the shipment irrespective of the transport mode. Moreover, it must be simple, easily identifiable and not masked with irrelevant information or old markings.

When goods are packed, they are marked on the outside in a manner which will remain legible for the whole of the transit. First of all, there is some mark of identification and then immediately underneath this for a maritime consignment, the port mark is shown. For example the merchant may be S. K. Winter Ltd and the goods are being shipped in the mv Suffolk to Gothenburg in which case the marks will be as follows:

S. K. W.
O/no. 1725
BORAS
Via GOTHENBURG
Nos 151-157

The consignment is identified, first, by a neutral abbreviation of the consignee's name; this reduces the risk of pilferage as potential criminals or receivers cannot easily relate the contents as they could if the full name of the customer were shown. The second line is the consignee's order number, and by this he or she can identify the consignment without having to open the packages; this is especially useful if he or she buys from a number of suppliers, or in cases where goods may be stored before use. The final delivery point is shown in the third line, whilst the fourth clearly shows the port of entry, thus helping to reduce the risk of the goods being routed incorrectly. Finally, the package numbers are shown – very useful to a supplier if kept in a strict sequence as it can be seen at a glance where a particular manufacturing run has been allocated, and equally useful to the consignee if this set of numbers is peculiar to one particular supplier.

Marks and numbers are the only common identification factor of any particular consignment after it has been packed for despatch. It is this detail which is shown in invoices, customs documents, bills of lading or air consignment notes, insurance certificates and collection/delivery notes. If the mark is interpreted wrongly on any of these documents, it is possible that mis-delivery or loss of the goods will occur and it follows that the marks or numbers must be shown clearly and indelibly on all the packages by means of stencil or secure tie-on labels. In addition to the mark, all goods should be labelled by the supplier showing the ship-berth, dock and loading brokers and sender's name and address.

In some trades, the practice is to give the dimensions of the package in metres which may be used in assessing the freight. Moreover, it is preferable for the gross and net weights to be likewise shown. Overall, it is desirable that the foregoing markings should be portrayed on three faces of the package – preferably side, end/or ends and top – with all markings clearly shown using large, clear lettering. All of the above criteria of cargo marking apply to other international transportation distribution modes such as air freight, road haulage, cargo wagon, and containerization, but it must be borne in mind they vary by individual trade and circumstance. It is also important to mention that the cargo markings correspond exactly with those on the bill of lading or other consignment note, such as CMR, CIM, air waybill used according to transport mode. In regard to containerized shipments both for FCL and LCL cargoes, especially the latter which are subject to break-bulk movements, all packages should be marked as under:

(1) container operator's/shipowner's booking reference number;
(2) intended ship or voyage;
(3) name of combined transport operator.

In no circumstances should marks be used as advertising as they encourage pilferage.

To facilitate handling and to overcome differing language problems a recognized international marking symbol code is used, such as, 'this way up', 'keep dry', etc. These are printed on the exterior of the packing and a selection of them which have been accepted by the International Standards Organization is given in Figure 8.1.

Finally, it must be mentioned that the consignment must be adequately labelled giving the delivery address details. Nevertheless, it is relevant to note that the export shipping mark forms the principal identification for the movement of the goods.

8.5 Dangerous cargo

Dangerous goods have been defined as those substances so classified in any Acts, rules or by-laws or having any similar properties or hazards. The legislation applicable to all British-registered tonnage or other vessels loading in British ports are contained in the Merchant Shipping (Dangerous Goods and Marine Pollutants) Regulation 1997. Other regulations include Dangerous Substances in Harbour Areas Regulations 1987, the Health and Safety at Work Act 1974, the Environment Protection Act 1990,

Carriage of Dangerous Goods (Classification, Packaging and Labelling) Regulations 1996 and Management of Health and Safety at Work Regulations 1992 (as amended). These require that all packaged goods are:

(1) Classified and declared by the shipper to the Master.
(2) Packaged in a manner to withstand the ordinary risk of handling and transport by sea, having regard to their properties.
(3) Marked with proper shipping name and indication of the danger.
(4) Properly stowed and effectively segregated from others which may dangerously interact.
(5) Listed in a manifest or stowage plan giving stowage details. This must be aboard the ship.

The requirements of the Merchant Shipping (Dangerous Goods and Marine Pollutants) Regulations reflect the International Maritime Dangerous Goods Code (IMDG), produced by the International Maritime Organization (IMO). The Code has been adopted by 50 countries, representing 85 per cent of world tonnage. A consolidated four-volume 1990 edition produced by IMO incorporates extensive revisions adopted by the IMO Maritime Safety Committee at its 1989 session and effective from 1 January 1991. The latest IMDG Code is the 27th amendment effective from 1 July 1995. A supplement to the Code contains emergency procedures, Medical First Aid Guide, Code of Safe Practice for Solid Bulk Cargoes, Reporting Procedures for Incidents, IMO/ILO Guidelines for Packing Cargo in Freight Containers and recommendations for the safe use of pesticides in ships.

It is estimated that more than 50 per cent of the cargoes transported by sea today can be regarded as dangerous, hazardous and/or harmful (marine pollutants) under the IMO classification, designation or identification criteria. Some of them are dangerous or hazardous from a safety point of view, but are also harmful to the marine environment; others are harmful to the marine environment alone. The cargoes concerned include products which are transported in bulk such as solid or liquid chemicals and other materials, gases and products for and of the oil refinery industry. Between 10 per cent and 15 per cent of the cargoes transported in packaged form, including shipborne barges on barge-carrying ships, freight containers, bulk packagings, portable tanks, tank-containers, vehicles, intermediate bulk containers (IBCs), unit loads and other cargo transport units, fall under these criteria.

As the world becomes increasingly industrialized and as industry itself becomes even more complex, so the transport by sea of these cargoes will continue to rise and the lists of products will grow. It is essential, if shipping is to maintain and improve its safety record, that these cargoes are stored, handled and transported with the greatest possible care.

Volume I of the IMDG Code also contains the alphabetical General Index of dangerous substances, materials and articles, and the marine pollutants. This index is followed by the Numerical Index (the table of UN numbers with corresponding IMDG Code page numbers, EmS numbers and MFAG table numbers) and a list of definitions, including commonly used abbreviations.

8.5.1 Revised Annex I to the IMDG Code, containing the packing recommendations

Revised Annex I to the IMDG Code contains recommendations on the packing of dangerous goods, and on the construction and testing of packagings. Annex I was adopted by the Maritime Safety Committee in 1984 and is included in Volume I of the IMDG Code. From 1 January 1991, only tested and marked packagings should be used for the transport of dangerous goods.

The recommendations take into account the mandatory requirements on packing set forth in regulation 3 of Chapter VII of the 1974 SOLAS Convention, as amended. Regulation 3 requires packages containing dangerous goods to be capable of withstanding the ordinary risks of handling and carriage by sea and lays down other specifications.

Annex I closely follows the United Nations Recommendations in respect of the packing of dangerous goods, as contained in Chapter 9 of the Orange Book.

The principle of dividing dangerous goods, other than those covered by classes 1, 2, 6.2 and 7, into three packaging groups according to the degree of danger they present, i.e.

packaging group I: goods presenting great danger;
packaging group II: goods presenting medium danger; and
packaging group III: goods presenting minor danger

is reflected in the recommendations of Annex I and has an impact on the detailed provisions for the construction and performance testing of types of standard receptacles, packagings and packages ready for shipment.

The recommendations of Annex I are intended for manufacturers of dangerous goods and of packagings for these goods, the shippers and carriers as well as competent authorities, and are to be used in conjunction with the IMDG Code.

8.5.2 General Index of the IMDG Code

All substances, materials and articles which appear in the IMDG Code are listed in alphabetical order of the proper shipping name (correct technical name) in the General Index of the IMDG Code, which also gives the product's UN number, its Emergency Schedule number (EmS No.), Medical First Aid Guide Table Number (MFAG Table No.), the IMDG Code page number of the individual schedule, class, packaging group and subsidiary risk label(s).

A number of dangerous goods are not listed by name in the Code and, therefore, will have to be shipped under a generic name/entry or a Not Otherwise Specified (NOS) entry. These entries have also been included in the General Index. For some goods, secondary names and synonyms also appear.

Following the General Introduction, Annex I and the indices, the IMDG Code then details the nine classes of dangerous goods, divided as follows:

Class 1.1 – Mass Explosion Hazard

Class 1.2 – Projection Hazard

Class 1.3 – Fire Hazard

Class 1.4 – No Significant Hazard

Class 1.5 – Very Insensitive Substances with Mass Explosion Hazard

Class 1.6 – Extremely Insensitive Articles with No Mass Explosion Hazard

Class 2.1 – Flammable Gas

Class 2.2 – Non-Flammable Compressed Gas

Class 2.3 – Toxic Gas

Class 3.1 – Flammable Liquid – Flash-point below –18°C

Class 3.2 – Flammable Liquid – Flash-point between –18°C & +23°C

Class 3.3 – Flammable Liquid – Flash-point between +23°C & +61°C

Class 4.1 – Flammable Solid

Class 4.2 – Spontaneously Combustible

Class 4.3 – Dangerous When Wet

Class 5.1 – Oxidising Substance

Class 5.2 – Organic Peroxide

Class 6.1 – Toxic Substance

Class 6.2 – Infectious Substance

Class 7   – Radioactive Material

Class 8   – Corrosive Substance

Class 9   – Miscellaneous Hazard Substance

8.5.3 Non-classified materials

A list of materials hazardous only in bulk (MHB) is included in section 24 of the General Introduction to the Code. Each class or category of goods is identified by a distinctive mark, label or placard. The marks, labels and placards are shown in Annex 4. Where appropriate, each individual schedule (page) in the Code shows the label or labels (100 mm × 100 mm) and, if applicable, the Marine Pollutant mark to be affixed to a receptacle, package, article, unit load or IBC, or as placards (enlarged labels of 250 mm × 250 mm) to be affixed to portable tanks, freight containers, vehicles or other cargo transport units, as provided for in the IMDG Code. Some consignments of dangerous goods should have the UN number of the goods displayed in the lower half of the placard or on a rectangular orange panel (120 mm × 300 mm) to be placed immediately adjacent to the placard.

All placards, orange panels and Marine Pollutant marks should be removed from cargo transport units or masked as soon as both the dangerous goods or their residues, which led to the application of those placards, orange panels and marine pollutant marks, are discharged.

The individual schedules of the Code follow a similar pattern. The substance's, material's or article's proper shipping name (correct technical name), and any known and commonly used alternative names (synonyms) appear at the top left of the schedule. To the right of this, other relevant information or observations are given, such as the UN identification number (UN No.) assigned to a substance or article by the United Nations Committee of Experts on the Transport of Dangerous Goods, its chemical formula, explosive limits, flash-point and so on. As an example, the schedule for 1,1,1 – Trichloroethane (Methylchloroform) (UN No. 2831), which is given with Trichlorobutene (UN No. 2322) on IMDG Code page 6272, is reproduced in Annex 5. 1,1,1 – Trichloroethane is widely used as typewriter cleaning fluid and thinner, 'Tipp-Ex'.

The other headings used in the individual schedules include properties or descriptions (such as the substance's, material's or article's state and appearance), special observations, packing, stowage and segregation. The schedule also shows the label(s) or placards and, if applicable, the Marine Pollutant mark, as appropriate to the substance, material or article. This is basically one of the marks, labels or placards shown in Annex 4, but a label or placard may also contain additional information. Those used for explosives, for example, also give the substance's or article's division number and compatibility group. Class 3 labels or placards sometimes contain a reference to the flash-point or flash-point group. For class 7 labels or placards additional information on the contents, activity and transport index is required.

Details of the salient points emerging from the IMO regulations, relative sea transport and RID (see p. 181) and ADR (see p. 180) international rail and road regulations are as follows:

(1) Dangerous goods to be declared by their correct technical name and their principal hazard to be shown by reference to their dangerous-goods class.
(2) Persons responsible for loading vehicles or containers to complete a container or vehicle packaging certificate.
(3) Packagings, vehicles, containers, etc. to be marked to indicate the hazard or hazards presented by the contents.
(4) The goods to be packed in an adequate manner.
(5) The goods to be stowed so that they do not give rise to a hazard.
(6) The employer/employee to ensure health and safety as far as possible of those involved in transport of dangerous goods.
(7) The ship's Master to have a record of dangerous goods on board and where they are stowed.
(8) Regulations apply to all UK ships and other vessels while they are loading or discharging cargo within the UK.
(9) Prohibition for certain dangerous goods on passenger ships.
(10) On-deck only stowage on passenger vessels when specified in IMDG Code or Department of Trade Blue Book must be strictly applied.
(11) Powers described for prosecution for non-compliance with statutory requirements.

The International Maritime Dangerous Goods Code, and Department of Trade Blue Book, are recommendations on how the requirements of the dangerous goods regulations can be satisfied.

In fact the regulations state in a number of places that in the event of an incident, if it can be shown that the recommendations of the Blue Book and IMDG Code have been met then the requirements of the regulations have been complied with. Some elements apply to all dangerous goods and some apply only to certain substances or articles. These include:

(1) Class
(2) Proper Shipping Name (PSN)
(3) UN Number
(4) Packaging Group (PG)
(5) Subsidiary-Risk (sub-risk)
(6) Flash-point (F/P)
(7) Marine Pollutant (MP)
(8) Control Temperature (C/Temp)
(9) Emergency Temperature (E/Temp)
(10) Net Explosive Content (NEC)/Net Explosive Quantity (NEQ)
(11) Hazard Division
(12) Compatibility Group
(13a) Radioactive Schedule Number
(13b) Radiation Dose Rate
(13c) Transport Index (TI)
(14) Limited Quantities (LQ)
(15) Waste
(16) Empty Packagings

The shipowner like the airline will only handle such dangerous cargo by prior written arrangement and on the express condition the shipper provides a very full and adequate description of the cargo. If accepted, a special stowage order – often referred to as a dangerous-goods form – will be issued which will indicate to the Master that the cargo conforms to the prescribed code of acceptance laid down by the shipowner. It cannot be stressed too strongly that shipment will not take place until a special stowage order has been issued by the shipowner, which is the authority for shipment. Moreover, the shipper must fully describe the cargo and ensure it is correctly packed, marked and labelled. This he can do through a freight forwarder, which is often the practice.

Before dangerous goods can be authorized for shipment the following information is required:

(1) Name of sender.
(2) Correct technical name of dangerous goods (the trade name may not be sufficient to identify the hazard) followed by the words 'Marine Pollutant' (if applicable).
(3) Class of dangerous goods.
(4) Flash-point (where applicable).
(5) UN No. to identify substance.
(6) Details of outer packing.
(7) Details of inner packing.
(8) Quantity to be shipped in individual packages and in total.
(9) Additional information for radioactive materials, explosives and consignments in bulk (e.g. tank containers, road tankers, etc.)

A flow chart courtesy of Felixstowe Dock and Railway Company relative 'export dangerous goods' declaration is found in Figure 8.3.

The dangerous-goods authority form will bear a reference number and will show the sailing details including port of departure and destination on which consignment is authorized: the hazard class, UN No., labels, key number (for emergency in event of

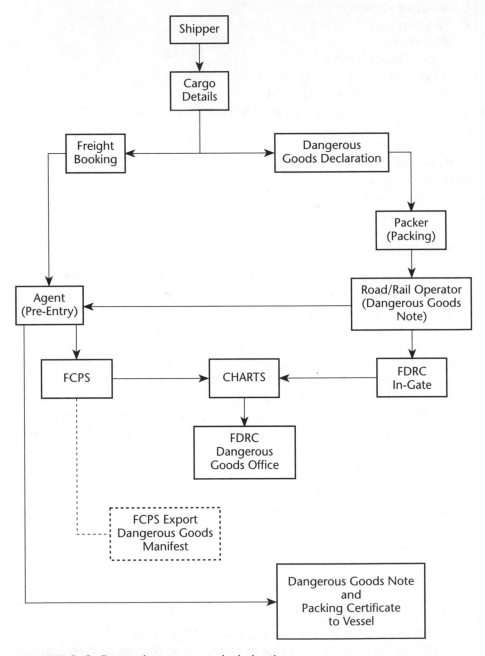

FIGURE 8.3 Export dangerous goods declarations
Reproduced courtesy Felixstowe Dock and Railway Company

any incident, spillage, etc), and any special instructions (i.e. special Department of Trade approval or restrictions on stowage, i.e. on deck only (passenger ship), freight vessel only, etc.).

On arrival of the goods at the departure port, the goods and authority to ship are submitted to the Master of the ship for ultimate approval prior to loading and customs clearance.

A further example is found in the deep-sea container shipment. It is the responsibility of the person loading the vehicle or freight container to ensure the packaged goods are correctly stowed, segregated and secured in accordance with the IMDG Code. It is ideal for the shipment of dangerous cargo particularly as it avoids multiple handling, protects the goods from interference by unauthorized persons and eliminates the risk of damage from the use of inappropriate methods of slinging. The following information is required at the time of booking the container:

(1) name of vessel;
(2) port of loading;
(3) port of discharge;
(4) number, kind and size of individual packages (including inner packages if valid) and total quantity – i.e. gross and net weight in kilos;
(5) correct technical name of substance, as defined in IMDG code;
(6) classification of substance (IMO);
(7) UN No. of substance;
(8) marine pollutant – if applicable;
(9) packaging group;
(10) flash-point – if any;
(11) EmS Number (as listed in IMDG Code);
(12) MFAG Table Number (as listed in IMDG Code).

With 'tween deck or bulk cargo shipments the loading of the ship is undertaken by stevedores, but with containerization this is done by container packers who are usually container operators or freight forwarders. Accordingly, with regard to the latter, a 'packing certificate' must be completed which certifies the following:

(1) The container was clean, dry and fit to receive the cargo.
(2) No cargo known to be incompatible has been stowed therein.
(3) All packages have been inspected for damage, and only dry and sound packages loaded.
(4) All packages have been properly stowed and secured and suitable materials used.
(5) The container and goods have been properly labelled.
(6) A dangerous-goods declaration has been received and completed for each dangerous consignment packed in the container.

It is paramount that the packing certificate is duly completed and signed by the shipper as it confirms to the shipping line and the Master that the task of packing the container has been properly carried out. The document accompanies the goods throughout the voyage. In regard to FCL containers, the Dangerous Goods Packing Certificate is incorporated in the IMO Dangerous Goods Note.

To comply with Classification, Packaging and Labelling of Dangerous Substances Regulations 1984, and the Road Traffic (Carriage of Dangerous Substances in Packages, etc.) Regulations 1986, a Transport Emergency Card (Tremcard) or equivalent must be supplied for substances within the following groups:

(1) Any quantity of an organic peroxide or self-reactive flammable solid which has a self-accelerating decomposition temperature of 50°C or below, or where it is required to be conveyed below a specified temperature.

(2) In receptacles with a capacity of 51 kg or more where the substance is an organic peroxide (not subject to the above paragraph), a flammable or toxic gas, asbestos or asbestos waste, certain other hazardous wastes and any other substance allocated to Packing Group I of CPL/IMO regulations.

(3) In receptacles with a capacity of 2001 kg or more where the substance is allocated to Packing Group II of CPL/IMO regulations.

(4) In receptacles of 2001 kg or more where substance is allocated to Packing Group III of CPL/IMO regulations.

Basically the code of 'one class–one container' must be observed unless the container operator has expressly agreed to a relaxation. Substances which fall into the same class but are incompatible must also be stowed in different containers, for example, peroxides and permanganates (both oxidizing substances). Dangerous goods may be incompatible with certain non-dangerous substances. Examples are poisons and foodstuffs, or those which react in contact with harmless organic materials, such as nitrates, chlorates, etc.

A container in transit is subjected to acceleration and deceleration factors in a longitudinal and to some degree, a lateral direction when travelling overland, and in a vertical and lateral direction at sea. At all times it is subjected to some degree of vibration. Hence, the contents must be firmly stowed and secured against movement and chafing. Particular care with dangerous cargoes must be taken to ensure that the contents will not fall outwards when the doors are opened. Dangerous cargoes forming only part of the load must be stowed in the door area of the container for ease of access and inspection. In the case of non-dangerous goods, damage arising from poor stowage is usually confined to the container concerned, but in the case of dangerous goods the effects could be widespread.

A dangerous goods note (DGN) (see p. 479) and Container Vehicle Packing Certificate (see p. 169) is required to be completed. This document must always accompany the goods and the Container/Vehicle Packing certificate section must be completed for any Shipper-packed FCL container and must be signed by the Shipper. It is relevant to note that obnoxious/irritant substances are classified as non-hazardous, but must be stowed and treated as dangerous cargo. Hence, any cargo having such substances must be clearly labelled prior to shipment and the carrier notified.

Labels and placards (Figure 8.4) are assigned to each class of dangerous goods in the IMDG Code, and denote the hazards involved by means of colours and symbols. Colours and symbols should be as illustrated, except that symbols, texts and numbers on green, red and blue labels and placards may be white. It is a legal requirement that the labels are affixed to the container.

DANGEROUS GOODS
Incorporating IMDG Code Amendment 28 (Jan 1997)

LABELS (for packages) (MINIMUM SIZE 100mm X 100mm) **AND** PLACARDS (for transport units) (MINIMUM SIZE 250mm X 250mm)

IMO 1
*THE APPROPRIATE DIVISION NUMBER AND COMPATIBILITY GROUP ARE TO BE PLACED IN THIS LOCATION e.g. 1.1D.
**THE APPROPRIATE COMPATIBILITY GROUP IS TO BE PLACED IN THIS LOCATION

IMO 1 SUBSIDIARY RISK   IMO 2.1   IMO 2.2   IMO 2.3

IMO 3.1 (F/P-below-18°c)
IMO 3.2 (F/P-18°c>+22.9°c)
IMO 3.3 (F/P+23°c>+61°c)

IMO 4.1

IMO 4.2

IMO 4.3

IMO 5.1

IMO 5.2

IMO 6.1

ELEVATED TEMPERATURE

CONTAINER UNDER FUMIGATION

Port of Felixstowe

THE HAZARDOUS CLASSES AND THEIR SUB-DIVISONS

Class 1.1 Mass Explosion Hazard
Class 1.2 Projection Hazard
Class 1.3 Fire Hazard
Class 1.4 No Significant Hazard
Class 1.5 Very Insensitive Substances with Mass Explosion Hazard
Class 1.6 Very Insensitive Articles with No Mass Explosion Hazard

Class 2.1 Flammable Gas
Class 2.2 Compressed Non-Flammable Gas
Class 2.3 Toxic Gas

Class 3.1 Flammable Liquid - Flashpoint Below - 18°C
Class 3.2 Flammable Liquid - Flashpoint Between - 18°C and + 23°C
Class 3.3 Flammable Liquid - Flashpoint Between + 23°C and + 61°C

Class 4.1 Flammable Solid
Class 4.2 Spontaneously Combustible
Class 4.3 Dangerous When Wet

Class 5.1 Oxidising Agent
Class 5.2 Organic Peroxide

Class 6.1 Toxic Substances
Class 6.2 Infectious Substances

Class 7 Radioactive

Class 8 Corrosive

Class 9 Miscellaneous

IMO 6.2
IMO 7
IMO 8
IMO 9

NO LABEL OR PLACARD REQUIRED: WHERE INDIVIDUAL SCHEDULES WITHIN THE IMDG CODE STATE NO LABEL OR PLACARD IS REQUIRED, IT IS IMPORTANT TO NOTE THAT TRANSPORT UNITS CARRYING SUCH COMMODITIES ARE REQUIRED TO HAVE THE U.N. NUMBER AND PROPER SHIPPING NAME DISPLAYED ON EACH SIDE AND END(S) OF THE TRANSPORT UNIT.

A member of the Hutchison Port Holdings Group

PLACARDS TRANSPORT UNITS CARRYING A SINGLE HAZARD, EXCEPT CONSIGNMENTS OF IMO 1, MUST HAVE THE SUBSTANCE'S UNITED NATIONS NUMBER DISPLAYED * IN BLACK DIGITS, NOT LESS THAN 25mm HIGH ON A WHITE BACKGROUND (IF USING ALTERNATIVE 1) OR ON AN ORANGE RECTANGULAR PANEL NOT LESS THAN 120mm HIGH AND 300mm WIDE WITH A 10mm BLACK BORDER AND THE UNITED NATIONS NUMBER IN BLACK DIGITS NOT LESS THAN 65mm HIGH TO BE PLACED IMMEDIATELY ADJACENT TO THE PLACARD (IF USING ALTERNATIVE 2)

MARINE POLLUTANT MARK:

SUBSIDIARY RISK LABEL/PLACARD
MUST NOT DISPLAY THE CLASS NUMBER

TEXT MUST ALWAYS APPEAR FOR IMO 7
 (ALTERNATIVE 1)
  (ALTERNATIVE 2)

FIGURE 8.4 IMO dangerous goods labels and the associated dangerous goods classifications
Reproduced courtesy IMO

Class 1	**Explosives**	This class is comprised of the divisions; 1.1, 1.2, 1.3, 1.4 and 1.5. Explosives also have a compatibility group letter. **Usually, only explosives of Class 1, Division 4, compatibility Group S are acceptable for carriage on passenger aircraft.**	
Class 2	**Gases**	This class comprises three divisions: 2.1 Flammable gases, 2.2 Non flammable, Non toxic gases and 2.3 Toxic gases.	
Class 3	**Flammable liquids**	Remember that the *flash point* of a Flammable Liquid is the temperature at which a vapour from the liquid could be ignited by a flame or spark. *It is not* the temperature at which it would ignite spontaneously.	
Class 4	**Flammable solids Spontaneously combustible substances Water reactive**	This class comprises three divisions: **4.1** Flammable solids, **4.2** Substances liable to spontaneous combustion, and **4.3** Water reactive substances which in contact with water, either emit flammable gases or become spontaneously combustible. (Also known as 'Dangerous When Wet').	
Class 5	**Oxidising substances; Organic peroxides**	This class comprises two divisions: **5.1** 'Oxidising Substances and **5.2** Organic Peroxides'.*	
Class 6	**Poisonous (toxic) and Infectious substances**	This class comprises two divisions: **6.1** Poisonous substances, and **6.2** Infectious substances.	
Class 7	**Radioactive materials**	This class has no divisions, but there are three categories for non-fissile materials which are determined by the radiation level of the complete package. **Fissile materials are not usually acceptable for air carriage without special arrangements.**	
Class 8	**Corrosives**	Substances in this class cause damage to the skin and/or metal.	
Class 9	**Miscellaneous dangerous goods** (including magnetized materials)	This class comprises substances whose properties do not match those of any of the other eight classes, but would pose a risk to safety if not properly prepared for carriage.	
NOTE:	**Subsidiary Risk**	Some Dangerous Goods have properties which meet the definition of more than one hazard class or division. The less serious hazard of such substances is described as a subsidiary risk.	

FIGURE 8.5 IATA dangerous goods labels and the associated dangerous goods classifications
Reproduced courtesy British Airways

The class number should appear in the bottom corner of the label or placard. The use of the texts shown on the illustrations and of further descriptive texts is optional. However, for Class 7 the text should always appear on the labels and the special placard. If texts are used for the other classes, the texts shown on the illustrations are commended for the purpose of uniformity.

Dangerous goods which possess subsidiary dangerous properties must also bear subsidiary risk labels or placards denoting these hazards. Subsidiary risk labels and placards should not bear the class number in the bottom corner.

Labels for packages should not be less than 100 mm × 100 mm, except in the case of packages which, because of their size, can only bear smaller labels. Placards for cargo transport units should not be less than 250 mm × 250 mm; correspond with respect to colour and symbols to the labels; and display the number of the class in digits not less than 25 mm high.

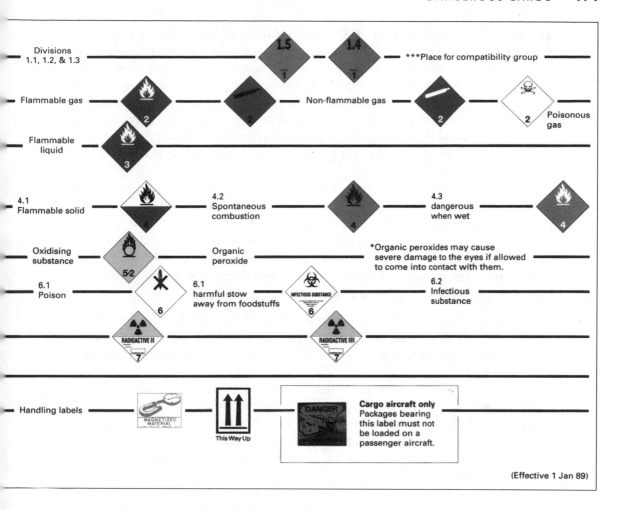

Divisions 1.1, 1.2, & 1.3 — 1.5 — 1.4 — ***Place for compatibility group —

Flammable gas — Non-flammable gas — Poisonous gas

Flammable liquid

4.1 Flammable solid — 4.2 Spontaneous combustion — 4.3 dangerous when wet

Oxidising substance — Organic peroxide — *Organic peroxides may cause severe damage to the eyes if allowed to come into contact with them.

6.1 Poison — 6.1 harmful stow away from foodstuffs — 6.2 Infectious substance

Handling labels — MAGNETIZED MATERIAL — This Way Up — Cargo aircraft only Packages bearing this label must not be loaded on a passenger aircraft.

(Effective 1 Jan 89)

Some consignments of dangerous goods should have the UN number of the goods displayed in black digits not less than 65 mm high, either against a white background in the lower half of the placard or on a rectangular orange panel not less than 120 mm high and 300 mm wide, with a 10 mm black border, to be placed immediately adjacent to the placard.

All labels, placards, orange panels and marine pollutant marks for subsidiary dangerous properties should be removed from cargo transport units or masked as soon as the dangerous goods are unpacked and any residue removed. The detailed requirements regarding marking, labelling and placarding are contained in the IMDG Code.

The universal adoption of the International Maritime Dangerous Goods Code (IMDG) has greatly facilitated the movement of dangerous goods between countries. Accordingly, a dangerous goods labelling code for maritime consignments exists and some codes are given in Figure 8.4.

With regard to dangerous classified cargo conveyed by air, it is the legal responsibility of every person involved in the shipping of dangerous goods to be aware of and to comply with the ICAO Technical Instructions for the Safe Carriage of Dangerous Goods and the IATA Dangerous Goods Regulations which govern the carriage of these goods. The technical instructions are a set of international regulations governing the carriage of dangerous goods by air. They are published by the International Civil Aviation Organization (ICAO) and are based on the United Nations recommendations for the safe transport of dangerous goods. They contain a dangerous goods list showing which goods may be carried by air and giving details of the requirements for carriage including quantity limits, packing, marketing, labelling and documentation requirements.

The air transport regulations for dangerous classified cargo acceptance are more severe than those for maritime transport. Some substances are entirely prohibited, others may only travel in all-cargo aircraft, whilst some are permitted to be conveyed in passenger aircraft. All those which may travel by air require special packaging, labelling and documentation. Moreover, quantity restrictions are also applied per flight in the interest of safety. Details of the air freight dangerous-cargo classification – formulated by IATA – are given below:

Class 1: Explosives – this class is comprised of the divisions: 1.1, 1.2, 1.3, 1.4, and 1.5. Explosives also have a compatibility group letter. Only explosives of Class 1, Division 4, compatibility Group S are acceptable for carriage on passenger aircraft.

Class 2: Gases – this class comprises three divisions: 2.1 flammable gases, 2.2 non-flammable and non-toxic gases and 2.3 toxic gases.

Class 3: Flammable liquids – remember that the flash-point of a flammable liquid is the temperature at which the liquid emits a vapour which would be ignited by a flame or spark. It is not the temperature at which it would ignite spontaneously.

Class 4: Flammable solids – spontaneously combustible substances – water reactive. This class comprises three divisions: 4.1 flammable solids, 4.2 substances liable to spontaneous combustion and 4.3 water reactive substances which, in contact with water, either emit flammable gases or become spontaneously combustible. (Also known as 'Dangerous When Wet'.)

Class 5: Oxidizing materials, organic peroxides – this class is comprised of two divisions: 5.1 – oxidizing materials, and 5.2 – organic peroxides.

Class 6: Poisonous (toxic), and infectious substances – this class is comprised of two divisions: 6.1 – poisonous substances, and 6.2 – infectious substances.

Class 7: Radioactive materials – this class has no divisions, but there are three categories for non-fissile materials which are determined by the radiation level of the complete package. Fissile materials are not usually acceptable for air carriage without special arrangements.

Class 8: Corrosives – substances in this class cause damage to the skin and/or metal.

Class 9: Miscellaneous dangerous goods (including magnetized materials) – this class is comprised of substances whose properties do not match those of any of the other eight classes, but would pose a risk to safety if not properly prepared for carriage. Details of IATA labels for dangerous cargo are found in Figure 8.5.

Subsidiary risk – some dangerous goods have properties which meet the definition of more than one hazard class or division. The less serious hazard of such substances is described as a subsidiary risk.

The nature of the flight conditions the package is likely to encounter will vary and falls under three main areas: temperature variations, pressure variations, and vibrations. We will now examine each briefly.

The extremes of temperature which may be encountered in all transportation are in the order of –40°C and +55°C (–40°F and +130°F). Modern pressurized aircraft cabins and cargo holds are pressurized at the equivalent of about 3050 m (10 000 ft) altitude, irrespective of the actual flight level, which might be as high as 13 720 m (45 000 ft). 3050 m (10 000 ft) is equivalent to a pressure of 0.7 bar (10.1 lb/sq. in) and represents a difference of 0.3 bar (4.7 lb/sq. in) between the ground atmospheric pressure and cabin pressure. In certain extreme circumstances, this may rise to a difference of about 0.65 bar (9.4 lb/sq. in). In older-type non-pressurized aircraft, which may still be in use in certain parts of the world for cargo purposes, the differential may also be as high as 0.56 kg/sq. cm (8 lb/sq. in).

Vibrations in commercial aircraft to which packagings may be exposed range from 5 mm amplitude at 7 Hz (corresponding to 1 g acceleration) to 0.05 mm amplitude at 200 Hz (corresponding to 8 g acceleration).

Most packagings for dangerous goods must be subjected to performance tests designed to ensure that the contents of the packaging can be carried safely under normal transport conditions. The approval of packagings is by national authority testing organizations and only packaging identified as meeting the specifications required can be used for the carriage of dangerous goods. For the precise requirements for the packagings for dangerous goods always refer to the applicable sections in the dangerous goods regulations.

Given below are some guidelines:

Breakable or puncturable containers.	Glass, earthenware and plastic must be well-cushioned in absorbent material and packed in strong, approved containers.
All packaging must be resistant to its contents.	Make sure that the packaging contains nothing which could be eroded by its contents, or could form a hazardous compound with them. Certain types of plastics are unsuitable for packing some ethers, mineral oils and acids. You will find that most plastic container manufacturers publish compatibility lists.
Absorbent materials must be chosen carefully.	It must not react dangerously with the contents.
Do not exceed the net quantity per package limitations.	Remember that the type of packaging employed may impose additional limitations.

Some different dangerous goods must be packed individually (unless otherwise permitted). Outside containers must not enclose inside containers of substances which, when mixed, would cause a dangerous evolution of heat or gas, or produce corrosive substances.

Packages must be marked on the outside with:

(1) the proper shipping name and corresponding UN or ID number;
(2) the full name and address of shipper and consignee;
(3) if required, the specification packaging markings.

The correct hazard labels must be attached to each dangerous goods package. If possible, the labels should be placed next to the shipper or consignee's address. 'This Way Up' labels must be used on combination packagings containing liquid dangerous goods, excluding flammable liquids in inner receptacles of 120 ml or less. Where freight is restricted to carriage on cargo aircraft only, the 'Cargo Aircraft Only' label must be affixed to the package.

Most packaging for dangerous goods must be subjected to performance tests designed to ensure that the contents of the packaging can be carried safely under normal transport conditions. The approval of packagings is by national authority testing organizations and only packaging identified as meeting the specifications required can be used for the carriage of dangerous goods. The precise requirements for the packaging for dangerous goods is found in the applicable sections of the IATA dangerous goods regulations.

Documentation relative to restricted air cargo is most important and must be strictly adhered to. The shipper's declaration for dangerous goods must be completed in duplicate by the shipper. Under no circumstances shall it be signed by an IATA cargo agent, consolidator or forwarder.

8.6 The air waybill

The 'Nature and quantity of goods' box of the air waybill should show a general description of the goods and the 'Handling information' box should include the statement 'Dangerous Goods as per attached Shipper's Declaration' or 'Dangerous Goods as per Transport Document for Dangerous Goods'. If the shipment is acceptable only on cargo aircraft, the words 'Cargo Aircraft Only' should be added.

If a Shipper's Declaration is not required for dangerous goods, the 'Nature and quantity' box of the air waybill should show a description of the goods followed by, in sequence, the proper shipping name, class or division number; UN or ID number; subsidiary risk, if any; number of packages; net quantity per package; the packing instruction; and the UN packing group. The words 'Dangerous Goods – Shipper's Declaration Not Required' should be shown in the 'Handling information' box.

The same air waybill may cover other articles, whether dangerous or not, but the dangerous goods must be stated separately by showing them, first, on the air waybill.

If the shipper is not sure that the goods are not classified as dangerous but they are described on the documents in a way that might indicate a restriction (e.g. chemicals, toiletries, etc.), add after the description of goods the statement 'Not Restricted'.

Before accepting a consignment containing dangerous goods, the airline requires the shipper to complete an 'Acceptance Check-list' consisting of a set of questions relating to the information given by the shipper on the documents, and to the condition of the packages. There are separate lists for non-radioactive materials and radioactive materials.

Dangerous goods acceptance check-list – non-radioactive materials

(1) Complete this check-list in duplicate.
(2) Answer all questions as appropriate.
(3) If goods are acceptable, sign the check-list and attach the original copy to the AWB and retain duplicate on station file.
(4) If any question is answered 'No', do not accept the shipment but give the original to the shipper and pass a copy to the locally designated official.

(A) Shipper's Declaration

(1) Are there two copies in English and in the IATA format?
(2) Has any amendment or alteration been signed by the shipper?
(3) If the AWB number and places of destination and departure are not shown, enter them.
(4) If the number of pages is not shown, check with the shipper and enter them.
(5) Are the names and full addresses of the shipper and consignee shown? – For Division 6.2, is the emergency contact name and telephone number shown?
(6) Has the 'non-applicable' aircraft limit and 'Radioactive Shipment' type been deleted?

Is the following information correct for each entry:

(7) Proper shipping name, supplemented with technical name(s) when applicable?
(8) Class or division number? For Class 1 the compatibility group also?
(9) UN or ID number?
(10) Subsidiary risk(s) corresponding to the subsidiary risk label(s) applied to the package?
(11) Number and type of package(s)?
(12) Quantity of each package?
(13) If relevant, is the 'Q' value shown?
(14) Indication that an 'Overpack Used'?
(15) Packing group?
(16) Packing instruction number?
(17) If applicable, indication that shipment is 'Limited Quantity'?
(18) If applicable, the special provision number?

(19) If applicable, indication that government authorization is attached? If so, is there a copy in English?

(20) If appropriate, is the 'Emergency Response' telephone number(s) shown?

(21) Are the name, title, place and date shown?

(22) Is the declaration signed?

(B) Air Waybill

Does the 'Handling Information' box show:

(23) 'Dangerous Goods as per Attached Shipper's Declaration'?

(24) If applicable, the words 'Cargo Aircraft Only'?

(25) If no Shipper's Declaration required, is the applicable information shown in the 'Nature and Quantity' box?

(C) Packages

(26) Do the number of packages delivered agree with the number shown on the Shipper's Declaration?

(27) Does the type of packaging correspond with the type shown on the Shipper's Declaration?

(28) Are the package(s) free from damage and leakage and in a proper condition for carriage?

(29) Are the specification markings correctly marked?

(30) Are the Proper Shipping Name, including technical name where required and the applicable UN or ID numbers, on the package(s)?

(31) Are the names and addresses of Shipper and consignee shown on each package?

(32) If 'Overpack Used', and specification marks not visible, has the overpack been marked: 'Inner Packages Comply with Prescribed Specifications'?

(33) Are the correct hazard label(s) and when applicable the subsidiary risk label(s) on the package(s) as prescribed?

(34) If special markings are required, are they on each package?

(35) Is the 'Cargo Aircraft Only' label affixed as required?

(36) Are the handling label(s) affixed as required?

(37) For liquids in combination packagings, is the package orientation properly indicated on two sides?

(38) Have all irrelevant marks or labels been removed or obliterated?

(D) General

(39) Have all applicable special provisions been complied with?

(40) Have all applicable state and operator variations been complied with?

(41) Where necessary, have advance arrangements been made and confirmed?

Comments ....
....
....
....
Checked by ....
Signature   Time   Date
....
Name (block capitals)   at (station)

Dangerous goods acceptance check-list – radioactive materials

(1) Complete this check-list in duplicate.
(2) Answer all questions as appropriate.
(3) If goods are acceptable, sign the check-list and attach original copy to the AWB and retain duplicate on station file.
(4) If any question is answered 'No', do not accept the shipment but give original to the shipper and pass a copy to the locally designated official.

(A) Shipper's Declaration

(1) Are there copies in English and in the IATA format?
(2) Has any amendment or alteration been signed by the shipper?
(3) If the AWB number and places of destination and departure are not shown, enter them.
(4) If the number of pages is not shown, check with the Shipper and enter them.
(5) Are the names and full addresses of the Shipper and consignee shown?
(6) Has the 'Non-applicable' aircraft limit and 'Non-Radioactive Shipment' type been deleted?

Is the following 'Nature and Quantity' information correct for each entry:

(7) Proper shipping name, Class 7 and UN number?
(8) If applicable, subsidiary risk?
(9) The words 'Radioactive Material', if not included in proper shipping name?
(10) Name or symbol of radionuclide(s)?
(11) Physical and chemical form or, if relevant, special form, if not included in proper shipping name?
(12) If relevant, the group for LAS material or SCO using terms 'LSA-I', 'LSA-II', 'LSA-III', 'SCO-I', 'SCO-II', 'SCO-III' as appropriate?
(13) Number and type of package(s)?
(14) The activity in each package specified and within limits?
(15) Indication that an 'Overpack Used'?
(16) Category of the package(s)?

  – for Category II and III only, the Transport Index and dimensions of each package?
  – for fissile material, the words 'Fissile Excepted'?

(17) The identification mark for each applicable competent authority certificate and are copies of such certificates attached? If so, is there a copy in English?

(18) If appropriate, is the 'Emergency Response' telephone number(s) shown?

(19) Is the name and title of the signatory and place and date of signing shown?

(20) Is the declaration signed?

(B) Air Waybill

Does the 'Handling Information' box show:

(21) 'Dangerous Goods as per Attached Shipper's Declaration'?

(22) If applicable, the words 'Cargo Aircraft Only'?

(23) If no Shipper's Declaration required, is the applicable information shown in the 'Nature and Quantity' box? (Note: This also includes 'Dry Ice' requirements.)

(C) Packages

(24) Do the number of packages delivered agree with the numbers shown on the Shipper's Declaration?

(25) Does the type of packaging correspond with the type shown on the Shipper's Declaration?

(26) Are the package(s) free from damage and leakage and in a proper condition for carriage with the sealing intact?

(27) Are the proper shipping name and UN number shown? Are the proper shipping name, including technical name where required and the applicable UN or ID numbers, on the package(s)?

(28) Where applicable, is each package marked either 'Type A' or 'Type B(U)' or 'Type B(M)'? (Note: All 'Type B' packages must be complete with the identification mark, serial number and embossed trefoil symbol.)

(29) Are the names and addresses of shipper and consignee shown on each package?

(30) If 'Overpack Used', and 'Type A' or 'Type B' markings not visible, has the overpack been marked: 'Inner Packages Comply with Prescribed Specifications'?

(31) If gross weight exceeds 50 kg, is it marked on the package?

(32) Are all required radioactive materials and subsidiary risk labels correctly affixed?

(33) Is each radioactive label marked with:

  (a) the radionuclide symbol (except for 'LSA-I')?
  (b) the 'LSA-I', 'LSA-II', 'LSA-III', 'SCO-I', 'SCO-II' markings as applicable?
  (c) Activity? (or the mass if fissile material).
  (d) For Categories II and III, the transport index?

(34) If applicable, the 'Cargo Aircraft Only' label?

(35) Have all irrelevant marks or labels been deleted?

(D) General

(36) Have all applicable special provisions been complied with?

(37) Have all applicable state and operator variations been complied with?

(38) Where necessary, have advance arrangements been made and confirmed?

Given below is a list of commodities which are hazardous and need special packaging, labelling and documentation when conveyed by air transport.

Aerosols

Ammunition

Arcton (trade name for compressed non-inflammable gas)

Automobile parts (could indicate batteries, cellulose paints, etc.)

Barometers (may contain mercury)

Batteries (may contain acid)

Bleach

Breathing apparatus (may indicate compressed gas cylinders)

Bull semen (refrigerants such as liquid nitrogen are used)

Butane

Chemicals or 'harmless chemicals' (often found to be hazardous)

Cryogenic liquid (liquid gases used as refrigerants – e.g. liquid nitrogen)

Cylinders (may contain compressed gases)

Dental apparatus (may indicate gas cylinders, alcohols, resins, etc.)

Dry ice (solid carbon dioxide, used as a refrigerant)

Electrical equipment (may contain magnetized material or mercury)

Electrical powered apparatus (may contain batteries)

Electron tubes (may contain mercury)

Engines (may contain fuel)

Freon (trade name for compressed, non-flammable gas)

Frozen food (may be packed in dry ice)

Gas(es) – 'gaseous' (may be a hazardous chemical; check proper name in IATA regulations)

Hair tonic (may be flammable)

Household goods/personal effects (may contain hazardous materials)

'Inhibited' or 'uninhibited' materials (may be hazardous)

Insecticides (may be flammable, poisonous or corrosive)

Laboratory equipment (may contain hazardous chemicals)

Lacquer (may be flammable)

Lighters – cigarette (may contain liquid fuel)

Lightmeters

Machinery (may have compressed gases, flammable liquids, batteries, radioactive materials, etc.)

Magnets, magnetized materials

Manometers (may contain mercury)

Medical supplies

Motorcars or cycles or parts thereof (may contain fuel or indicate batteries or cellulose
   paints)
Oil drilling equipment (may contain mercury)
Paint, enamel, etc. (may be flammable)
Perfume (may be flammable)
Pesticides (may be flammable, corrosive or poisonous)
Pharmaceuticals (may contain hazardous chemicals)
Polymerizable materials
Rectifiers (may contain mercury)
Refrigerators (may contain compressed gases)
Repair kits (may contain adhesive, cellulose paints, solvents, etc.)
Sample for testing (may contain hazardous materials)
Soda-water makers
'Stabilized' or 'unstabilized' substances (may be hazardous)
Switchgear (may contain mercury)
Toys (especially those made of cellulose)
Vaccines

Finally, in regard to the movement of dangerous goods by road within Europe, the
relevant conditions are found in the European Agreement concerning the
international carriage of dangerous goods by road (ADR). This came into force
on 29 July 1968 in the territories of those countries which had notified or acceded
to the Agreement. At present these countries are Austria, Belgium, Czechoslovakia,
Denmark, Finland, France, Germany, Hungary, Italy, Luxembourg, the Netherlands, Norway, Poland, Portugal, Spain, Sweden, Switzerland, the UK, and
Yugoslavia. The purpose of ADR is to ensure that dangerous goods being conveyed
by road are able to cross international frontiers without hindrance, provided such
goods are packaged, marked, documented and labelled in accordance with
regulations and likewise the vehicles. This includes vehicle marking, equipment,
training, tanker requirements and Tremcards. Most countries insist that Tremcards
which accompany the goods on their international journey are in the language of
the importing country. The dangerous goods classification under the ADR
transport regulations is the same as for sea transport in the IMDG code. The nine
classifications are listed on p. 169. The packaging, labelling, vehicle, tank vehicle
and tank container requirements are thus dependent on the class, item number
and properties of the goods to be carried.

An important feature of ADR is that tank vehicles and certain other vehicles
carrying explosives are subject to technical inspection and a certification procedure in
their country of registration to ensure that they conform with ADR requirements and
with the normal safety regulations in force in the country of origin governing brakes,
lighting, steering, etc. The competent authority (the Department of Transport in the
case of the UK) will issue a certificate of approval for vehicles which pass this
inspection. The ADR certificate is therefore acceptable by other contracting parties
during its period of validity, which will not be longer than one year. The term 'tank
vehicles' in this context means vehicles with fixed tanks intended for the carriage of

liquids or gaseous, powdery or granular substances, and does not include demountable tanks, tank containers or fixed tanks intended for the carriage of solids.

Our study of dangerous cargo would not be complete without a mention of the movement of such cargo internationally by rail throughout its transit. The merchandise is primarily bulk cargo and regulations are very stringent. Within Europe they are found in the International regulations concerning the carriage of dangerous goods by rail (RID) 1978 and subsequent amendments. The dangerous goods classification under the RID transport regulations is the same as for sea transport in the IMDG code. The nine classifications are listed on p. 169.

To conclude our study of dangerous cargo one cannot stress too strongly the need to ensure the relevant regulations are complied with at all times and shippers and exporters are advised to contact their freight forwarder or shipowner and/or airline when in doubt.

Recommended reading

Felixstowe Dock and Railway Company Customer Guide to procedures for handling
    dangerous goods 1999
British Airways Dangerous Goods brochure

■ □ ■ ■ 9

Export customs practice

9.1 Introduction

This chapter examines the customs procedures adopted in the United Kingdom which are laid down by HM Government. The UK is a member of the European Union (EU) and accordingly goods are in free circulation for those commodities which originate and are manufactured in any of the 15 states forming the single market – see Chapter 18. Goods which are exported or imported from a third country which is outside the single market such as the USA, the Far East, Switzerland, etc. are subject to rigorous customs procedures.

Customs procedures and legislation are subject to government policies and the political climate both nationally and internationally. Countries which are members of an economic bloc or Customs Union such as ASEAN are subject to the customs policies agreed within the membership.

It is appropriate at the commencement of this chapter to focus on customs policy in the next millennium covering the international movement of goods, excluding intra-EU trade. This involves an evaluation of the following major international initiatives and developments in the business world which are driving further changes in the business and customs environment.

(1) Growth and globalization of international trade involving the global village and product outsourcing on a logistic basis (see Chapter 6).
(2) Exploitation of new markets through new technology and continuing improved international distribution networks through multi-modalism (see Chapter 5).
(3) World liberalization of trade realized by the WTO initiatives and strategies (see pp. 22–8).
(4) Falling customs duty rates emerging from the GATT Uruguay and WTO Singapore agreements.
(5) The continuing international simplification/harmonization of customs requirements and procedures.
(6) The continuing mergers and overall growth of multinationals. This exploits the economies of scale.

(7) The rapid advances in technology and developments in electronic commerce. This involves the development of electronic commerce to produce 'seamless' international trade transactions.
(8) The growing influence of the EU and its enlargement coupled with the growth of other economic blocs and Customs Unions globally.
(9) The internationalization of criminal activity.
(10) The growing demand for environmental restrictions.

To facilitate the realization of effective customs strategies within the context outlined, it must be recognized that global competition will intensify – a factor recognized by the WTO. Additionally, other critical success factors of implementation are more customer focused: the appropriate international legal framework, the further development of efficient and effective customs procedures and systems and finally the maintenance of effective frontier admissibility controls.

Undoubtedly, the foregoing developments will be facilitated by the World Customs Organisation (WCO) which is an inter-governmental organization with worldwide membership whose mission is to enhance the effectiveness and efficiency of customs administrations. It is based in Brussels.

One of the important instruments developed by the WCO was the Harmonised System Commodity Description and Coding system known as the Harmonised System or HS (see p. 188). The HS was implemented in 1988 by an International Convention known as the 'International Convention on Harmonised System Commodity Description and Coding system'. It is administered by the WCO – more specifically the Harmonised System Committee: its goods classification system nomenclature is applied by more than 150 countries (including 88 contracting parties to the HS convention) for Customs tariffs and trade statistics, thereby facilitating international trade.

Overall, the main work of the WCO is the revision of the Kyoto Convention – the convention for the simplification and harmonization of customs procedures. A significant development is a change in emphasis from consignment based controls at the frontier to control, inland, using traders' records.

Currently the role of the HM Customs and Excise embraces five areas which are dealt with below: landing and shipping; warehousing; excise; value added tax; and preventive duties.

Landing and shipping officers are the people who directly control the importation and exportation of goods. They are responsible for ensuring that correct documentation is produced to cover the transaction, that all governmental requirements are fulfilled and that all revenues due are collected.

The lodgement of goods into a bonded warehouse is a method by which traders may defer payment of duty, or at times, reclaim duty already paid. The term 'bonded warehouse' indicates accommodation for which the owner has given his or her written promise under bond to comply with certain conditions laid down when the Commissioners approved the premises for 'Customs' business. Bonds may be given as security for a number of different transactions and will be described fully later in the chapter. The warehouse officer is responsible for the control of all receipts into the warehouse, operations within the warehouse, for example bottling of wines, and deliveries of goods from the warehouse. He or she is also required to ensure that duty is paid on all goods delivered from warehouse to a dutiable use.

9.2 Value Added Tax

From 1 January 1993, following the completion of the Single Market, there were important changes in the way that VAT is charged and accounted for on goods moving between Member States of the European Community (EC – now EU). For VAT purposes, the terms 'imports' and 'exports' for intra-EU movements of goods disappeared. They were replaced by new arrangements for zero rating intra-EU supplies of goods. VAT on goods traded between EU Member States is not collected at the frontier on importation. Instead, goods supplied between VAT registered traders are zero rated on despatch and any VAT due is payable on acquisition of the goods by the customer. The customer accounts for any VAT due on their normal VAT return at the rate in force in the country of destination of the goods. When VAT registered traders despatch goods to unregistered traders or private individuals in another EU country, the supplier must usually charge VAT at the rate in force in the country of despatch.

There are also special rates for freight transport and associated services. Special rules were introduced from 1 January 1993 for determining the place of supply of freight transport services, ancillary transport services and the services of intermediaries arranging freight transport and ancillary transport services. When the services are supplied to customers registered for VAT in EU Member States, the place of supply is the supplier's Member State when the suppliers belong in the Member State of the customer. The supplier will charge and account for VAT on the supply at the domestic rate. The customer will be able to recover input tax subject to the normal rules. Conversely, when the customer's Member State of the supplier does not belong in the Member State of the customer, the customer gives the supplier a valid VAT registration number. The supplier will not charge VAT on the supply but will still be able to recover any input tax incurred in making the supply subject to the normal rules. The customer must account for VAT under the 'reverse charge' procedure.

If a customer has not given a valid VAT registration number or the supply is to a private individual, the supplier will have to tax the service in the EU member state in the case of the following: the transport of goods where the transport of the goods originates; ancillary services where they are physically performed; the services of intermediaries arranging freight transport connected with the movement of goods between EU Member States – where the transport of the goods originate; or the services of intermediaries arranging ancillary services connected with the movement of goods between EU Member States – where the ancillary services are physically performed.

VAT goods purchased from other EU countries are immune from any VAT payment at the time of import. However, for most transactions between VAT-registered businesses, VAT will become due on acquisition of the goods by the customer and will be accounted for in the normal VAT return.

When non-VAT-registered businesses or private individuals in the UK purchase goods from a VAT-registered trader in another EU country, they will normally be charged VAT by the supplier at the rate applicable in that country. However, to avoid distortions of tax once the value of goods purchased from other EU countries exceed a certain threshold, the UK customer will, in certain circumstances, be liable to account for tax on the goods in the UK as acquisitions. Such persons will then have to register for VAT in the UK.

For VAT purposes, goods imported from outside the EC are treated as imported into the UK when:

(1) they arrive in the UK directly from outside the EU and the trader enters them for home use in the UK or customs duty otherwise becomes payable on them; or

(2) they have been placed in another EU country or in the UK under a duty suspension arrangement involving one of the following situations and the trader enters them for removal to home use in the UK, or customs duty otherwise becomes payable on them;

   (a) temporary storage,
   (b) free zones,
   (c) customs warehousing,
   (d) inwards processing relief (duty suspension system),
   (e) temporary importation (including means of transport) with total relief from customs duties,
   (f) external Community Transit (T1) arrangements,
   (g) goods admitted into territorial waters,
   (h) excise, warehousing.

The value for VAT-imported goods will be their customs value, plus the ancillary charges for freight ,etc. The customs computerized system for handling import entries (CHIEF) will allow VAT paid on the traders' imports under the government contractor, registered consignee, and bulked entry procedures to be included in VAT certificates. Basically, when Customs duty is due on goods, it coincides with VAT importation payment. Current import VAT arrangements are described in HM Customs Notice 700 and 725 (VAT imports and warehoused goods).

With respect to export under VAT terms, it will only take place when goods leave the territory of the EU, either directly or via another EU country. Goods which are despatched or transported to another EU country are not treated as export but are called 'despatches'.

When goods are received from outside the EU which are consigned to another EU country, the trader must put the goods into free circulation in the UK with payment of any customs duty and/or import VAT due, or place the goods under the external Community Transit (TI) arrangements. In this situation, any duty and/or VAT will be payable in the EU country of destination. Unless the traders' goods are warehoused in the UK for excise duty purposes, the trader will have to pay import VAT when the goods are put into free circulation in the EU country where that is done. Hence traders will not normally be able to put goods into free circulation in one EU country and pay import VAT in another. No import VAT will be payable, either in the UK or in the EU country of destination.

Generally speaking, the export transaction is zero-rated for VAT purposes subject to compliance with certain conditions, especially in the area of proof of the export transaction. Hence the goods are VAT zero-rated for goods transferred abroad, used for temporary exhibition or processing and exported on a sale or return basis. Proof of export is essential to qualify for VAT zero rating and consists of valid commercial or official evidence of export. In regard to sea freight, valid proof of export will include bill of lading, sea waybill and certificate of shipment; whilst for air freight, it embraces the air waybill. For groupage, the house air waybill or house bill of lading is acceptable, subject to it including the cargo description, sailing and/or flight details, seaport or airport of despatch and container or railway wagon number. In all cases such commercial and official evidence should be supported by other commercial documentation.

9.2.1 VAT distance selling arrangements

Distance selling arises when a supplier in one EU country supplies goods and is responsible for their delivery to any person in another EU country who is not registered for VAT; an example is the mail order. VAT on sales to non-VAT-registered customers in another EU country will, in principle, be charged and accounted for by the supplier in the country from which the goods are despatched, termed the 'country of origin'. So consequently, if traders supply goods under distance selling arrangements, they will not be subject to tax in this way until the value of the distance sales to another EU country in a calendar year reaches a threshold, currently at £70 000 per year.

9.2.2 VAT EU sales lists

Consequent on the abolition of the fiscal frontiers between member states of the EU, UK traders registered for VAT who make supplies of goods to traders registered for VAT in other EU countries will be required to send to Customs and Excise lists of their sales – usually called 'EU sales lists'. The lists are used to control the taxation of movements of goods within the EU. The EU sales list data submission is required when the trader makes supplies of goods to a person registered for VAT in another EU country; sends goods to a person registered for VAT in another EU country for process; returns goods after processing them to a person registered for VAT in another EU country; and transfers goods from the UK to another EU country in the course of that trader's business.

The EU sales list will contain the trader's VAT registration number, name and address, date of submission and period covered; the VAT registration number of the person in the other EU country to whom the trader has made supplies including a two-letter prefix identifying the country; the calendar quarterly aggregate (total) value of the goods which the trader has supplied to each customer; an indication where appropriate that the goods have been sent to another EU country for process; and an indication that the trader has returned the goods to another EU country after processing them, together with the value of the process.

9.2.3 Warehoused and free zone goods

Non-community goods received from other EC countries and warehoused under the customs warehousing arrangements or the Customs and Excise arrangements, if the goods are subject also to excise duty, will be subject to VAT when removed from warehousing to home use in the UK. The value for VAT will include the duties paid. Similar conditions apply for goods received direct from outside the EU for warehousing.

In regard to community goods received from other EU countries, only a limited range of goods placed in a warehouse will be subject to excise duty. Such goods will be warehoused under customs surveillance and include mineral oils, alcohol and alcoholic beverages, and manufactured tobacco. The value for VAT will include the excise duty paid.

In regard to free zones, goods will be zero-rated if they originate within the UK or one of the EU states. However, for goods received directly into a free zone from outside the EU, duty and import VAT duty will arise when the goods are removed into home use in the UK.

9.2.4 Freight transport and associated services

The cost of transport and insurance forms part of the value of goods for customs purposes. VAT will be due on the receipt or acquisition of the goods by the customer. Hence VAT will be accounted for in the same EU country as the one in which the customer has the right to recover the tax. The transport of goods between EU Member States is taxed either in the Member State where the customer is registered for VAT or if the customer is not a VAT registered person, which includes a private person, in the Member State from which the goods are removed, i.e. the place of departure.

Supplies of ancillary services and the services of intermediaries connected with the movement of goods between Member States are taxed according to the same rules as apply to intra-community transport services. However, when supplied to a customer who is not registered for VAT, ancillary services are taxed in the Member State in which they are physically performed and intermediary services are taxed in the Member State where the service which is being arranged is taxed.

9.2.5 Preventive duties

Though numerically small, the preventive staff or waterguard, as they are often called, are probably the best known members of the Customs and Excise Department. These are the people seen manning the ports and airports, and whose main task is the prevention of smuggling and the apprehension of smugglers. Besides these purely customs tasks, they are involved in the control of imported and exported goods, and are employed both for customs purposes and for local and central government purposes where they have an agency function. Further details of the Single Market customs legislation can be found on p. 428. In addition to the 15 Member States, associated and dependent territories which are treated as part of the customs and fiscal territory of the EC include: Azores, Balearic Islands, Isle of Man, Jungholz and Mittelberg, Madeira, Principality of Monaco and the Republic of San Marino. 'Special' territories which are part of the EU for customs purposes but not part of the EU for fiscal purposes include: Canary Islands (Spain), Channel Islands, French Overseas Departments (Martinique, etc.), Mount Athos – also known as Agion Poros (Greece), and the Principality of Andorra.

9.3 Customs tariff

All products exported are identified by the use of numerical codes as listed in the customs tariff. For statistical purposes and in connection with the enforcement of export licences, there must be a formal declaration of all commercial exports to the Customs authorities showing the tariff code of the product concerned. Each item has only one correct classification under the harmonized tariff system, which has been adopted by 85 per cent of the world's trading nations. It follows that the code used by the exporter should be the same (at either four or six digit level) as that used by the importer. If exporters use an incorrect code, they can mislead customers who may well pay more or less duty than is legally due. This can be avoided by effective customs planning (pp. 461–4).

The foregoing data required is found in the customs tariff published in three volumes by HM Customs. It includes a full list of goods with their various rates itemized. A supplement to the customs tariff is issued regularly in the form of an HM Customs Notice. Overall, the tariff includes 15 000 headings, set out in 97 chapters broken down into sections, headings and subheadings. The tariff is not used for intra-EC trade.

The present tariff based on the harmonized system (HS) should be studied closely to ensure the correct commodity code is adopted. It should be noted that the system adopted for collecting intra-EC trade statistics is called 'Intrastat'. Basically, Intrastat declarations are only necessary if the Intrastat threshold is exceeded (see p. 185).

9.4 Export controls

There are three main reasons for controlling the exportation of goods. These are as follows:

(1) revenue interests;
(2) prohibitions and restrictions;
(3) trade statistics.

9.4.1 Revenue interests

These interests (and the economy) may suffer if the following types of transaction are not controlled:

(1) Transshipment goods – should these goods not be transshipped, there is the possibility of loss of revenue.
(2) Goods for re-exportation after temporary importation.
(3) Goods exported from a bonded warehouse.
(4) Goods exported from an excise factory.
(5) Goods exported on drawback.
(6) Cars supplied free of VAT to overseas residents.
(7) Goods exported for process and subsequent re-importation.

Should these types of transaction not be controlled, there is a strong possibility of loss of revenue through dishonest people claiming that goods had been exported, etc. when in fact they had found their way on to the home market. The insistence on proper documentation of these transactions ensures that the revenue is safeguarded.

9.4.2 Prohibitions and restrictions

The regulations regarding prohibitions and restrictions change periodically but the latest information can always be found in Part 2 (ii) of the tariff and can include such items as a need for an export licence from the Department of Trade or the Intervention Board for Agricultural Produce (IBAP) and prohibitions on the exportation of certain animals and drugs.

9.4.3 Trade statistics

The introduction of the Intrastat system has important implications for the publication of trade statistics. Prior to the Single Market, trade statistics were produced monthly, but today the intra-EU trade figures are published some six months in arrears; the delay being dependent on the speed and accuracy with which traders supply data linked to the quarterly VAT returns. Estimates of trade with countries outside the EU will, however, continue to be published three or four weeks after the end of each month.

The supply of services is excluded from Intrastat. The system covers only those movements which represent trade in goods. In general these movements are equivalent to supplies made (and the corresponding acquisitions) under the arrangements for VAT on EU trade between Member States and they are recorded using the same rules, although there are exceptions such as the treatment of goods involved in process and repair.

9.4.4 Customs Handling of Import and Export Freight and the Abbreviated Entry (AE) Scheme

The HM Customs and Excise introduced in November 1992 an exports sub-system called Customs Handling of Import and Export Freight (CHIEF). It is the department's computer entry processing system. At those locations where the port system operator has developed special inventory systems which are linked to CHIEF Exports, exporters and agents may input the following pre-shipment and post-shipment information to CHIEF electronically:

(1) full pre-shipment declaration;
(2) low value pre-shipment advice;
(3) non-statistical pre-shipment advice;
(4) Abbreviated Entry (AE) pre-shipment message and completed entry; and
(5) Simplified Clearance Procedure (SCP) post-shipment declaration (prior approval required) (see p. 192).

At other locations when a pre-shipment advice or pre-shipment declaration is input to CHIEF a paper advice or declaration (on plain paper or pre-printed, but conforming to the SAD) must also be provided to the place where the goods are being declared for export. Alternatively, screen prints of the DTI input, taken after the entry has been committed to CHIEF, may be accepted in place of the SAD, except when a C88 (CAP) is required. A manually completed SAD must be presented for comparison purposes when a C88 (CAP) is required.

CHIEF will allocate a system generated export reference number (ERN) to each entry. The ERN is a 12-digit number consisting of the year (2 digits), the month (2 digits), a seven digit number and a check digit (e.g. 99 05 00000571). This number is used by the Tariff and Statistical Office, when keying the voyage information to CHIEF, to release data to their trade statistics system. The ERN will appear on the print but when a manually completed SAD is used it is essential that the ERN is also entered in Box B. Further information on CHIEF can be found in the Tariff Volume 3 parts 2 and 6 and the CHIEF User Guides.

The Abbreviated Entry (AE) facility will allow the build-up of an electronic entry on CHIEF. The AE is a two-part entry consisting of the input of the pre-shipment message and the build-up of information leading to the input of the completed entry. The AE message will require minimal information. In Electronic Data Interchange (EDI) transactions the user will be able to use his local system (e.g. a PC package) to build up the AE completed entry before submitting it to CHIEF. Using Human Computer Interface (HCI), an AE completed entry that cannot be completed may be stored until final details are available to the declarant.

Both the pre-shipment message and the completed entry must be input to CHIEF. The information required for the pre-shipment message must be input and the hard copy produced to customs at the place of export before the goods are shipped. The completed entry must be input no later than 14 days after shipment from the UK.

The AE cannot be used for goods which are dutiable or restricted, for example goods which are exported from bonded warehouses or which are subject to export charges or specific licensing requirements. These must be pre-entered.

9.4.5 Local Export Control

Local Export Control (LEC) permits an exporter, or freight forwarder who exports goods on behalf of others to have export consignments cleared by Customs and Excise at their own, or other nominated, premises inland. LEC procedures apply to: goods exported to destinations outside the customs territory of the European Union; goods to special territories which are not part of the European Union for fiscal purposes (Canary Islands, the Channel Islands, French Guiana, Guadeloupe, Martinique, Mount Athos, Reunion, St Pierre and Miquelon); and CAP goods to qualifying destinations within the European Union as provided for in Commission Regulation (EEC) 3665/87 Article 34.

The trader needs to assure the local customs staff that the shipper can meet the conditions for LEC authorization. The inland premises and/or the nominated inland premises of others will then be approved and a Customs Registered Number (CRN) be allocated to it. Accordingly, the trader will be able to have goods cleared inland and customs declarations will not need to be presented at the place of export for such consignments. Once the LEC has been approved, the control of a trader's export consignments will be based on the approved inland premises. The records will be inspected periodically and occasionally the goods will be examined.

If Community Transit (CT) documents are required to control the movement of the goods to those destinations specified in the above paragraph the trader will have to use the authorized consignor facility.

Goods covered by a LEC authorization do not have to be declared to customs at the place of export. However, before removing the export consignments from the approved inland premises the shipper must enter details of each consignment in the LEC records. The consignment will then move to the place of export accompanied by the appropriate removal document and, if necessary, authenticated CT documents for presentation to customs. Before entering the export consignment in the records, the shipper must give advance notice that goods are being exported. This advance notice can take one of two forms depending on the type of goods involved: individual notice or standing notice. The shipper must also submit the relevant post-shipment information to the Tariff and Statistical Office within 14 days using one of the available methods. LEC should normally be transported in secure containers and when required sealed by traders seals approved by Customs and Excise. See also Notice 482.

9.5 Export documentation and procedures

Goods presented by shippers for or at other places may do so at the following locations in the UK:

(1) an Inland Clearance Depot (ICD); or

(2) a port, airport or free zone (see p. 199) from which the goods will be removed under customs control to the port/airport of exportation; or

(3) shipper's own premises under LEC (see p. 191); or

(4) shipper's own premises under CAP scheduling; or

(5) inland grain premises approved for CAP purposes; or

(6) approved depositories (Retail Export Scheme goods). Full details of RES is given in HM Customs Notice 704.

The basic method of giving details of exports is by completion of an export declaration and presenting it with the goods to Customs and Excise before the goods are shipped, i.e. to make pre-entry. Alternatively, a registered exporter or his agent may use the simplified clearance procedure (SCP). The procedure tends to be used only when there is insufficient information to make a full export declaration using commercial documents or on an SAD at the time of export and should not be used routinely. Under SCP the export declaration may be lodged after shipment of the goods provided that a suitable pre-shipment advice, usually a copy of the document used for the commercial side of the export transaction, is presented in lieu of the export pre-entry.

The SCP may be used only for the exportation of goods which are not dutiable or restricted, for example goods from bonded warehouses or subject to export charges or specific licensing requirements or subject to CAP. Some goods are excluded from the export declaration requirements. The SCP is intended to be used when shippers do not have enough information to make a full export declaration on an SAD at the time of export and should not be used routinely.

Exporters and agents who regularly export and/or arrange despatch and documentation of goods of a kind not liable to duty or restriction may apply to their local Excise and Inland Customs Advice Centre for registration and allocation of a Customs Registered Number (CRN) to enable them to use the SCP.

Traders who so register may, subject to certain conditions, present a copy of a commercial document approved for use with SCP as a pre-shipment advice and deliver post-shipment export declarations at a date not later than 14 days after the date of sailing or flight of the ship or aircraft carrying the goods. Regardless of which document the exporter uses as a pre-shipment advice, the exporter must quote the unique reference number known as the Export Consignment Identifier (ECI). The ECI is made up of the CRN, plus a unique commercial reference of up to nine characters including any stroke or dash.

The commercial documents approved for use with the SCP are those in common use with all forms of transport being used to carry the export consignment to the port or place of exportation. Details are given below:

| National Standard Shipping Note Dangerous Goods Note | for conventional or containerized maritime traffic |
| Air waybill (including house air waybill) | for air traffic |

CMR Note	⎫
FTA Approved Own Account Transport Document	⎬ for Ro-Ro traffic
	⎭
Consignment Note CIM	rail traffic including express parcels
TIEx Note	for rail express parcels
Transfer Note	for rail Intercontainer traffic
Water Note	for the sea leg of other British Rail handled exports

The Commissioners of Customs and Excise will register an exporter or agent and allocate him or her a CRN – a five-digit number for use when exports are to be entered under SCP. Where required, a CRN will be issued for each address in the UK at which an exporter or agent keeps records of export transactions (such places need not be despatch points). It will be subject to the following conditions with regard to records, etc. An exporter or agent who is to be registered and issued with a CRN must:

(1) Maintain a business address in the UK.
(2) Keep records at that address of all export transactions for which he is responsible.
(3) Keep those records in the detail and form acceptable to the Commissioners of Customs and Excise so that their officers can, at any reasonable time, check on the accuracy, timely submission and completeness of customs documentation.
(4) Retain those records, available for inspection, for at least twelve months from the date of exportation of the goods.
(5) Retain, in those records for twelve months from the date of exportation of the goods, the Customs and Excise receipted 'Duplicate' of the export declaration submitted – form C&E1187 – or in the case of export declarations made through the DTI terminals, a screen print when the message has been committed to CHIEF.
(6) Advise Customs and Excise of any change of legal entity, address, or trading name.

The records referred to at (2) and (5) above must include the following information which must be readily identifiable to each export transaction.

(1) Advice of shipping instructions, dated and showing the trader's reference number and/or in the case of airfreight the air waybill or house air waybill number.
(2) The marks and numbers, and number of packages, or for bulk goods the quantity.
(3) Description of the goods.
(4) The name of the export ship or the flight number of the export aircraft.
(5) The date of despatch of the pre-shipment and post-shipment customs documents.
(6) Details of any relevant Community transit or ATR documents issued.
(7) Details of any action taken to amend documents.

To satisfy the requirements set out above certain minimum standards of record-keeping are expected of traders. The main requirement is the keeping of a day book, or similar record, showing export consignments cross-referenced to commercial records. The local Customs and Excise officer can advise on the kind of records which will be acceptable to ensure the regular and timely delivery of accurate export documents.

Local Export Control (LEC) allows eligible traders (i.e. exporters and freight forwarders) who regularly export goods to have them cleared at their own inland approved premises. Traders authorized under the scheme do not need to deliver normal pre-shipment documents at the place of export. All goods can be included in LEC apart from: goods covered by ATA carnet – goods moving via the UK 'under the UK transit' from port of entry to port of export in the UK (formerly transshipment) – and goods moving under CT documents raised in another Member State. The goods should normally be in secure containers and when required sealed by trader seals approved by Customs and Excise. For LEC purposes full Community Transit will be required only on all non-Community goods that have not been entered for home use in the Community. Full details on LEC can be found in HM Customs and Excise Public Notice No. 482.

A number of goods do not require export statistical declaration, and full details are found in HM Customs and Excise Public Notice No. 275.

It was mentioned earlier that all goods for exportation must be pre-entered unless the exporter is a registered person. There are, however, some types of export transactions which must always be pre-entered whether the exporter is registered or not. These are as follows:

(1) goods from a customs warehouse;
(2) goods from registered or entered excise premises;
(3) goods temporarily imported under a duty relief;
(4) goods imported under duty-free certificates or directions;
(5) goods not in accordance with the contract;
(6) goods exported subject to outward processing relief, the standard exchange system, or returned goods relief;
(7) goods for which excise drawback or repayment of duty is claimed.

For goods in the above categories the export declaration must be presented involving a control copy 1 of the SAD (headed in red Control Copy).

The Customs and Excise Tariff gives a good explanation of customs requirements at exportation and Notice 275 gives a box-by-box guide to the completion of Customs form C88 (see p. 204). Full details are not given here as both forms and requirements change periodically and one is best advised to consult sources currently appropriate.

Those goods which do not require to be pre-entered (that is, customs entry is presented before the goods are loaded for export) are entered on C88 which may be lodged with customs any time up to 14 days after the exporting ship leaves, where a specification or 'spec', as it is usually called, is sufficient. The SAD must be accompanied by any other documents required for controlled goods for example export licences or forms C88 (CAP) for the export of CAP goods. Before goods can be exported aboard a vessel, customs documentation for the vessel itself must be completed. This is referred to as outward clearance and forms an integral part of the customs control procedures. Additionally, there is the period entry facility for traders who regularly export large quantities of goods under a computerized stock control system. The system permits the export of goods by presenting a simplified pre-shipment advice similar to the SCP system and to submit the post-shipment declaration to customs on a computer tape or disk. The system can also be used with LEC.

To use the SCP system, for example, an agent would be allocated a CRN which is unique to that particular agent. The agent can then use the CRN when exporting cargo. This is done by putting the CRN number on an approved document such as a C88 form or a National Standard Shipping Note along with details of the cargo to be exported such as marks, numbers of packages, description of cargo and weight. However, with the CRN must be written the ECI number. This is the Export Consignment Identifier and this number must match up with the exporter's file reference. For example, on a C88 form may be written '31393 LGK 12635'. This means that the ECI is made up of the CRN 31393 and LGK 12635 (commercial reference). If a problem arose with this entry, HM Customs would be able to approach the agent who has this particular CRN and go to the file LGK 12635. It will be seen that the CRN/ECI should be totally unique to every job and consignment shipped from the UK under SCP.

The approved document is entered with HM Customs when the goods are exported. (It will be recalled that for certain goods such as transshipment goods, goods being exported under licence, or duty drawback goods it is not permitted to use the SCP.) After the goods have been shipped, the agent must do a full entry giving tariff code number, nett weight, value and any other information needed within 14 days of the confirmed date of sailing of the vessel. Late lodgement is treated by customs as non-lodgement and is therefore one of the major reasons for sanctions to be taken against traders. It is at this point that the worst problems seem to arise, as many agents appear to have problems with this aspect of the SCP.

To lessen such a problem the agent should, for example, keep a full and complete record of every job and consignment completed using the SCP so that he or she may ensure that a full entry is completed within 14 days. This record file should be kept to ensure that a copy of the full entry is received. The importance of these records cannot be stressed too much, as it is possible that the agent's CRN may be taken away if full entries are not completed, either late or not at all. Another serious problem is incorrect completion of full entries. For instance, to use the example quoted above, the SCP document may state '31393 LGK 12635'. However, if this is mistakenly altered, for example '31393 12635' or '31393 LGH 12635', the full entry and the SCP document will not match in the HM Customs computer at Southend. Therefore, it will appear that the agent has not completed a full post-entry.

Users of the SCP system are recommended to study Notice No 276 on the subject and particular attention should be given to the following check list.

(1) Before using an ECI make sure the goods do not require pre-entry.

(2) Allocate an ECI from the appropriate commercial records. Once allocated, do not change it.

(3) Ensure the ECI is correctly completed on the pre-shipment document, i.e. CRN number plus your commercial reference, and that it is in the right box.

(4) Ensure that all copies of the pre-shipment document are legible. Complete such documents by typewriter/machine whenever possible to ensure maximum clarity on all copies.

(5) Check your pre-shipment documents before they leave you. Their correct completion is an essential element in the efficient movement of your goods.

(6) Complete the C88 Export Declaration within 14 days of the confirmed sailing date ensuring the ECI quoted is the same as that shown on the pre-shipment document, and that all boxes are correctly completed. Delay in receiving shipping or flight details is not a valid reason for non-lodgement of the export declaration within the prescribed period. Also ensure lodgement to customs is within the prescribed time. Furthermore, chase up these important details when they are not received promptly.

(7) Post the declaration to HM Customs and Excise, Portcullis House, 27 Victoria Avenue, Southend on Sea, Essex SS2 6AL.

(8) Abbreviated entry (see p. 190).

9.6 Outward clearance of a vessel

Prior to the departure of a vessel the Master (or his agent) is required to attend before the Collector, or some other designated customs officer, to complete the necessary forms and deal with all questions relevant to the vessel's departure. The Master is not normally required to attend in person but may give written authority to an agent to clear the vessel on his behalf. The following documents are required to be completed or presented when application is being made for outward clearance.

(1) Form C13 in duplicate. A general declaration of the ship's departure must include details of any goods remaining on board for exportation.

(2) The ship's certificate of Registry.

(3) Light dues certificate. These dues are monies collected by customs on behalf of Trinity House and are for the maintenance of lighthouses, light vessels, buoys, etc. on the coast of the UK.

(4) Load line certificate. This certificate is issued by the Department of Trade in accordance with various international safety authorities. It gives details of the ship and its gross tonnage and details of the distance there must be between the load line of the ship and its free-board, dependent on its various situations throughout the world.

(5) Wireless certificate. All ocean-going passenger ships and cargo ships exceeding 500 gross registered tons must be equipped with a wireless, which must be surveyed annually.

(6) Safety equipment certificate. This indicates that the applicable Merchant Shipping Acts have been observed.
(7) Passenger certificate. This is only found on passenger ships authorized to carry 12 or more passengers. It gives details of the maximum total number of passengers which may be carried and confirms that the legal requirements in respect of safety equipment have been complied with.
(8) Form C14. This gives details of particulars of stores on hand at time of clearance.
(9) Inward clearance bill. Until a ship has been cleared inwards, that is, all goods, stores, passengers and crew properly accounted for as far as customs are concerned, an inland clearance bill will not be issued and without it outward clearance cannot be effected.

When all these formalities are completed to the satisfaction of the customs officer the ship will be allowed to leave port and proceed on her voyage. Within 14 days of clearance, the shipping company must present to customs a copy of the ship's manifest giving full details of cargo (including nature of goods, marks, shippers and consignees) and passengers' names. At times, the vessel clearing may have already cleared from another port and has carried goods from that port to the one where clearance is now being effected. In this case, clearance documents must include documents from the first port and, instead of an inward clearance bill, a transire (C196).

9.7 Customs reliefs

9.7.1 Inward processing relief

A range of duty reliefs are available for goods imported into the UK and their applicability is dependent on the goods being re-exported under control of the custom's authorities. An example is found in the inward processing relief whereby the goods may be processed or assembled in a componentized basis and subsequently re-exported. The customs regulations and procedures are stringent and adequate documentation must be provided to substantiate the imported merchandise. More-over, adequate pre-planning must be undertaken in consultation with customs. An increasing number of goods are now being treated in this way as global manufacturing strategies change. Overall, there are four types of authorization: simplified authorization (form C101); simplified authorization (form C&E 810); specific authorization; and community authorization. The simplified authorization (form C101) is granted at the time of import. Traders must hold the other authorizations before the goods may be imported under IPR – they cannot be issued retrospectively.

The trader must decide whether to use the suspension or drawback method of obtaining duty relief. With suspension the trader does not pay duty or import VAT as long as the shipper exports the goods or the products made from them or the goods are sold to another IPR trader or disposed of using one of the methods specified by HM Customs and Excise. In regard to drawback the shipper pays the duty and VAT at import. The trader claims the duty back only if the shipper exports the goods or products, and sells them to an IPR suspension trader or disposes of them using one of the methods specified by HM Customs & Excise. Details of the IPR are found in Notice No 221.

9.7.2 Outward processing relief and standard exchange system

Outward processing relief (OPR) permits partial or total relief from duty on goods that are exported for processing and subsequently re-imported. The regulations and procedures laid down by customs are stringent and prior arrangements must be made with customs. The standard exchange system (SES) is a variation of OPR and permits duty relief on items imported as replacements for Community goods exported from the Community for repair. Triangulation is a further method of OPR whereby goods are temporarily exported from one Member State and compensating products or replacements are imported into another Member State. Details of OPR are found in Notice No 235.

9.7.3 Returned goods relief

Another form of customs relief is found in the returned goods relief. It arises when goods which are exported for other purposes can also be relieved of duty if re-imported under the returned goods relief provisions, provided the re-importation takes place within three years of export (or within an extended time limit negotiated with the customs authorities), and that the goods have not undergone any process whilst outside the EC other than running repairs.

9.7.4 ATA carnets

ATA carnets may be used to simplify customs clearance of goods being temporarily exported. They replace normal customs declarations both at export and re-import. They also replace normal customs documents and security requirement in many countries worldwide into which the goods are being temporarily imported. Goods covered by ATA carnets are subject to normal export prohibitions and restrictions and licensing rules.

The carnets may not be used for goods which are: exported for process or repair; exported by post; not in free circulation before export from the UK. Certain Chambers of Commerce issue ATA carnets in the UK subject to receiving guarantees or deposits. For further information see Notice 104.

9.7.5 The TIR procedure

The TIR procedure allows goods in road vehicles or containers sealed by customs to cross one or more countries en route to their destination with the minimum of customs interference. TIR Carnets are used for this purpose. The arrangements for obtaining them and other conditions of the procedure are explained in HM Customs and Excise Notice 464.

Traders cannot use the TIR procedure for transit movements from the UK which are to be wholly within the EU. CT procedures must be used for these movements. Requirements to provide export declarations on the SAD are unaffected by the TIR provisions.

9.7.6 Customs warehousing and free zones

A customs warehouse is a system or place authorized by the customs authority for the storage of non-Community goods under duty suspension. It permits traders to delay duty and/or VAT payment on imported goods; to delay having a customs treatment applied to imported goods; to permit shippers to re-export non-Community goods (in which case import duty and/or VAT may not be payable at all), or to help traders who have difficulty at the time of import in meeting particular conditions such as certain import licensing requirements. It also caters for the storage and warehousing of goods originally imported into another customs regime, for example IPR or PFC. Overall, the customs warehouse can either be a place or inventory system authorized by customs for storing non-Community goods which are chargeable with import duty and/or VAT, or otherwise not in free circulation.

Depending on the circumstances and type applied for, i.e. premises based or system based, a customs warehouse may, for example, be the whole of a building, a small compartment in a building, an open site, a silo, a storage tank or an inventory system. A person who is authorized to operate a customs warehouse must take responsibility for the security and proper control of the warehoused goods. Customs carry out audit based checks on their activities to ensure the correct procedures are being carried out and that all the duties are paid on the due date.

There are six types of customs warehouse allowed under EC Regulations. These are classified as A to F in EC Regulation 2454/93, Article 504. At present the UK operates only types A, C and E as below.

(1) Type A is a public warehouse authorized for use by warehousekeepers whose main business is the storage of goods by other traders. The warehousekeeper is responsible for the security of the warehoused goods and undertakes to see that all customs obligations are met. In addition, the warehousekeeper is responsible for accounting for any shortage of warehoused goods. The warehousekeeper may also act as an agent and complete some or all of the official documentation as required.

(2) Type C is a private warehouse for use by individual traders for the storage of goods. The warehousekeeper need not necessarily own the goods but must be the depositor, i.e. the person bound by the declaration placing the goods under the customs warehousing procedure or to whom the rights and obligations of such a person have been transferred. The warehousekeeper must complete all official documentation relating to the warehousing activities.

(3) Type E is a form of private warehousing in which a company and its commercial accounting and stock control systems are authorized. The goods may be stored

at any notified storage site belonging to the authorized trader or in transit between such locations, with movements between one such site and another permitted without any official documentation. The authorization will be granted only to a private warehousekeeper who must be the depositor but not necessarily the owner of the goods. The authorized trader must complete all official documentation.

Any combination of these different types of warehouses described above is not permitted in the same premises or location. For example, goods within a Type E warehousing system cannot be stored on the premises of a Type A or C warehouse.

Goods which can be warehoused are:

(1) non-Community goods liable to customs duties and/or VAT (whether or not eligible for preference if put into free circulation);

(2) non-Community goods for which necessary supporting documents e.g. DoTI licences, are not available at the time of import;

(3) non-Community goods imported to another suspensive regime, e.g. IPR, temporary importations, etc. warehoused for export from the Community;

(4) non-Community goods processed for free circulation (PFC);

(5) non-Community goods not subject to a full rate of customs duty in the tariff, but liable only to import VAT;

(6) Community goods or non-Community goods in free circulation eligible for CAP refunds on export and warehoused in a specially approved warehouse under the CAP pre-financing arrangements.

Goods which cannot be warehoused are: carcasses and animal products unless the required import licence and/or health certificate is presented at the time of import; goods liable to excise duties unless excise duty is paid before the entry is made for customs warehousing. See HM Customs and Excise Notice 232.

A free zone is an enclosed area in which non-Community goods are treated, for the purpose of import duties, as outside the customs territory of the Community. Customs duty, import VAT or other import charges are not due provided the goods are not released for free circulation. Hence, payment of import duties (including agricultural charges) and import VAT is suspended when goods are placed in a free zone. The free zone regime can include goods originally imported into another system such as IPR. There are no special reliefs in free zones from other taxes, excise duties, or local authority rates in the UK. See Notice 334.

9.8 Duty preference and origin

The way an export is dealt with can determine whether an overseas customer is able to take advantage of the duty-free arrangements for certain exports from the EC; if it is not dealt with correctly, this may result in duty being paid unnecessarily. This point can therefore be crucial to retaining customers and to the continued health of an exporter's trade.

The European Union preference permits a UK exporter to help an import customer overseas to import the goods more cheaply, thereby enabling the exporter to become more competitive when competing in overseas markets. The import duty rate will be lower or nil. To qualify for the preference the goods must satisfy the customs rules regarding origin, transportation and export relief as explained in Notice 827.

Countries featuring in the export preference scheme include: (a) the countries of the European Free Trade Association (EFTA), that is, Iceland, Norway and Liechtenstein (covered by the EEA – European Economic Area) and Switzerland; (b) Bulgaria, Romania, Hungary, Poland, Czech Republic, Slovakia and Slovenia; (c) Baltic States – Estonia, Latvia and Lithunia; (d) Faroe Islands; (e) Cyprus, Israel and Malta; (f) Ceuta and Melilla; (g) 'Mashraq group' – Egypt, Jordan, Lebanon, Syria, 'Maghreb group' – Algeria, Morocco and Tunisia; (h) and some of the African, Caribbean and Pacific States (ACP), and Overseas Countries and Territories (OCT).

9.9 The Common Agricultural Policy (CAP)

The main purpose of the CAP is to provide stability of prices and supplies of agricultural products in the EU. Goods covered by the CAP include all basic and processed food products, whether or not for human consumption, including live animals.

When world market prices are lower than those in the EU, a levy charge brings the price of CAP goods imported from non-EU countries up to the level of EU prices, and refunds are paid to EU exporters to enable them to reduce prices and maintain their competitive position in the world market. Conversely, when world prices are significantly higher than those within the EU, or when EU supplies of a particular product are inadequate, export levies may be charged to deter the flow of such products out of the EU. Thus CAP goods provide a rare example of charges payable at export.

Levy and refund rates change frequently due to fluctuations in supplies and prices worldwide; for example, cereal levies can change daily, with a knock-on effect on processed products containing cereals. The rates also vary widely between different CAP goods. It is, therefore, vitally important that companies take these factors into account in determining where CAP goods are to be produced, processed and consumed.

A number of special arrangements are available for exporters of CAP products. Some offer simplified procedures which reduce compliance costs, whilst others can improve cash-flow.

9.10 The Community/Common Transit system (CT)

The Community Transit system is a customs procedure which allows goods not in free circulation and those few Community goods for which CT is required to move within the Community (see Chapter 18). Goods not in free circulation travel under the external transit (T1) procedure; Community goods travel under the internal transit (T2) procedure. The system is extended to EFTA and Visegrad countries (Hungary, Poland, Czech Republic and Slovak Republic), by virtue of a separate Convention, and this is known as Common Transit.

The CT procedure is based on the appointment of a principal who is responsible for the completion of the CT operation. These responsibilities include providing a guarantee and producing the goods intact at the customs office of destination within a prescribed time limit. The procedure is finalized on the return of an officially receipted copy of the transit document to discharge the movement and guarantee.

CT must be used for movements of: non-Community goods that have not been put into free circulation or another customs procedure which permits movement within the Community; and Community goods when they are: travelling via an EFTA or Visegrad country; goods travelling overland to an EFTA or Visegrad country. Use of the T2 procedure for transport by air or sea to an EFTA or Visegrad country is not compulsory when: travelling to or from one of the 'special territories' of the Community except for direct movements between the UK and the Channel Islands; subject to a Community measure involving their export to a third country, e.g. Common Agricultural Policy (CAP) goods; travelling to or from San Marino. Although San Marino is not part of the EC, a special customs union exists with the EC but excludes goods coming under the Treaty establishing the European Coal and Steel Community, and in chapters 25–97 of the Harmonised System that are travelling to or from the Principality of Andorra. Although Andorra is not part of the EC, a special customs union exists with the EC for the above mentioned goods.

The CT procedures must not be used for: movements of Community goods to other EC countries or territories except in specified circumstances; or movements direct to a non-Community country (other than EFTA or Visegrad countries), unless the goods are to cross a non-Community country under a single transport document issued in the Community and are to re-enter the Community during the course of the CT movement. A CT movement will be suspended during the passage of the goods through a non-Community country, for example movements to Finland via a Baltic country; or movements of either Community or non-Community goods in Chapters 1–24 of the Harmonised System that are travelling to or from the Principality of Andorra. Goods in these chapters which are not in free circulation will move under CT only to the French or Spanish border as appropriate; or movements of goods despatched as follows: by post; by the rail or the Intercontainer simplified CT procedure; under the TIR carnet procedure; by the ATA carnet procedure; under the NATO 302 procedure; using either the air or sea simplified CT procedures. The CT procedure works as follows:

(1) A person or firm known as the CT principal undertakes to transport goods from one point in the Community to another, or to an EFTA or Visegrad country, Hungary, Poland, Czech Republic and Slovak Republic, or, in certain circumstances, to San Marino or Andorra. The principal is responsible for providing a guarantee to cover the duties and taxes which may become due if

the movement is not satisfactorily completed and for producing the goods intact to the Customs office of destination within a prescribed time limit.

(2) The principal or representative completes a CT declaration on the SAD and presents it together with the goods and any other necessary supporting documents to customs at the office of departure.

(3) Customs at the office of departure carry out any necessary examination and/or control of the goods and documents and register the movement. If satisfied, the CT document is authenticated and a time limit for completion of the movement will be recorded in their SAD.

(4) Customs retain copy 1 of the SAD and return copies 4, 5 and 7 to the principal. The principal must ensure that copies 4, 5 and 7 travel with the goods.

(5) When goods transit through a non-EC country during a CT movement, the principal or their agent must complete a Transit Advice Note (TAN) (Form C1128). A separate TAN must be presented with the goods and transit document at the last and first EC offices when the consignment leaves and re-enters the EC.

(6) To complete the movement, the goods and CT documents must be presented at the office of destination within the prescribed time limit. Customs at the office of destination will certify that the goods have arrived safely or provide details of any discrepancies or irregularities and return copy 5 of the CT document to the office of departure or to a central office designated for this purpose.

(7) The movement is discharged when customs at the office of departure or the central office are satisfied that the movement has been satisfactorily completed or when any charges due for lost goods have been paid in full.

CT can be used for goods entering other countries or moving through all EFTA and Visegrad countries. These countries are not Member States of the Community, but Community goods may be entitled to preferential treatment in these countries and vice versa.

CT documents issued in EFTA and Visegrad countries show the status of the goods as it applied in the Community. This will be T1 unless the goods were previously imported from the Community, EFTA or Visegrad country under a T2 document, were controlled by customs and are being re-exported in the same state. Even so, the authorities in EFTA and Visegrad countries issue T2 documents only if the goods were in transit through their countries or were temporarily imported for exhibition or, subject to certain limitations, were warehoused there.

The term 'Common Transit' is used by, and in relation to, EFTA and Visegrad countries when referring to Community Transit. CT documents bearing either or both expressions are accepted in all Member States, EFTA and Visegrad countries. Community Transit can also be used for movements between the Community and San Marino and the Community and the Principality of Andorra. The Community has separate customs unions with these countries, and as a result goods in free circulation in San Marino or Andorra are regarded as also being in free circulation in the Community (with regard to Andorra these provisions apply only to goods in HS Chapters 25–97). See also Notice 750.

9.11 The Single Administrative Document

The Single Administrative Document (SAD) is a multi-copy form which is used throughout the Community, EFTA and Visegrad countries for the control of imports, exports and goods in transit. In the UK it is known as Form C88. It is an eight part document, although only the following copies are used for CT purposes:

Copy 1 Office of departure;
Copy 3 CT principal/consignor/exporter's copy;
Copy 4 Office of destination, or Community status (T2L) document;
Copy 5 Transit return copy;
Copy 7 Statistical copy for use in the member state of destination.

Copy 4 can be used as a Community status (T2L) document. Copy 7 is not required for UK Transit movements. The other copies of the SAD are for the following purposes:

Copy 2 Export declaration;
Copy 6 Import declaration;
Copy 8 Consignee's copy.

Customs and Excise provide various combinations of the eight copy set. For transit purposes, the following sets may be obtained: Export and transit (C88:Export/transit) comprising Copies 1, 2, 3, 4, 5 and 7; Status only (C88 Status) comprising Copy 4; for UK transit only (C88: UK Transit) comprising Copies 1, 4 and 5.

Alternatively, two sets of four copies, printed mainly for use when computerized declarations are made, can be used. Each copy has a dual function: 1/6, 2/7, 3/8, 4/5. The first set corresponds to copies 1–4, the second to 5–8. In each four-copy set the numbers of the copies used must be shown by deleting numbers of the copies not used.

The continuation sheet is a form used to supplement the transit document when more than one item is being despatched and there is insufficient room for details of all the goods. It may also be used when a consignment contains both T1 and T2 goods. A separate sheet is used for each status of goods, the SAD providing the common information and a summary of the sheets for each different status.

Goods which are exported: from Customs and/or Excise warehouses; or subject to OPR and/or OPT must be declared on separate SAD declarations, i.e. they must not be combined on a SAD with goods subject to other customs control procedures. Additionally, the information to be shown on partly completed SADs (copy 2) is used as pre-shipment advices for the SCP, the low value goods procedure and the non-statistical procedure. Overall, it forms a pre-shipment declaration made under the standard export declaration procedure; or a post-shipment statistical declaration under the SCP or LEC procedure.

When the document is being used as a pre-shipment declaration or a post-shipment statistical declaration under the SCP, enter after 'No' the exporter's TURN (Trader's Unique Reference Number) or equivalent as follows:

(1) for exporters registered for VAT enter the exporter's 12-digit TURN;

(2) for exporters not registered for VAT enter one of the following: UNREG for commercial exportations; PR for private exportations where there is no commercial purpose involved, e.g. household effects; for exportations by Government departments, which have been issued with 3-digit registration numbers in the range 001–499, enter 'GD' followed by the registration number; for exportations by health authorities, which have been issued with 3-digit registration numbers in the range 500–999, enter 'HA' followed by the registration number.

In the case of groupage consignments, where a single declaration is being made by an agent acting on behalf of several exporters whose goods are being sent to the same country of destination, the agent may show himself as the exporter. After 'No' enter 'GROUPAGE' but each individual exporter's TURN preceded by 'VAT' should be inserted in Box 44 for each item in the consignment.

Even when several exporters have goods of the same commodity code (Box 33) in the groupage consignment, a separate item is required for each exporter's TURN number.

10

Cargo insurance

Marine insurance is defined in the Marine Insurance Act 1906 thus; 'a contract of marine insurance is a contract whereby the insurer undertakes to indemnify the assured in a manner and to the extent thereby agreed, against marine losses, that is to say, the losses incidental to marine adventure'. Hence this includes cargo insurance involving the maritime conveyance of merchandise from one country to another.

Cargo insurance is an extensive subject and it would be wrong not to include a chapter on it in a book of this nature. Nevertheless, in so doing the reader must be reconciled to the fact that it is only possible to deal briefly with the salient parts of the subject. For further study the student is recommended to read one of the excellent cargo insurance textbooks available on the market.

This chapter deals with the practical considerations which affect export interest in terms of financial protection of goods in transit to overseas destinations. It is not an in-depth study of marine insurance as such; insurance and exporting can and do exist independently of each other. Furthermore, it is by no means coincidental that the insurance of ships and goods is the oldest form of insurance protection. Moreover, the advantages which accrue from a proper appreciation of the role cargo insurance plays in the transference to others of those risks to which goods consigned by sea and air are exposed, must be thoroughly understood by the exporter and shipper.

In its proper context, cargo insurance must be seen as an indispensable adjunct to overseas trade. Adequate insurance is vital to protect the interests of those with goods in transit. Accordingly, the student of the subject is well advised to obtain a copy of the Marine Insurance Acts of 1906 and 1909 available from HMSO, and study them closely. The 1906 Act contains the basis of all cargo insurance affecting export consignments, whilst the 1909 Act deals with the prohibition of gambling in maritime perils. Apart from the protection aspect, cargo insurance also plays a vital role in the financing of overseas trade by making it possible for banks to lend money against cargo in transit – a proposition they will only consider if the cargo is protected by insurance. It is appropriate to mention that this chapter will not be dealing with credit insurance as this will be found in Chapter 11.

It is important to indicate that in examining cargo insurance one must reconcile it with ship insurance insofar as maritime transits are concerned. The reason being that the voyage is still regarded as 'marine adventure' which involves both ship and cargo being at risk to maritime perils. This joint cargo/ship interest emerges when, for example, a general average contribution arises involving jettison of cargo to preserve the general safety of the marine adventure.

10.1 Cargo insurance market

There are no fixed rates in marine insurance and the actual premium for a particular ship or cargo is assessed on the incidence of losses in that trade and the risks that the ship and other conveyances transporting the cargo are likely to experience. This process of assessing the premium is known as 'underwriting' and the marine insurance contract is embodied in a document called a policy. Marine insurance is underwritten by Lloyd's underwriters and insurance companies.

Lloyd's is a society of underwriters which has its origins in the late seventeenth century when shipowners, merchants and underwriters met at Edward Lloyd's coffee house in the City of London. Edward Lloyd provided the facilities for the clientele of his coffee house to carry on the business of marine insurance. He personally had no involvement in this business and had no responsibility or liability in respect of the risks underwritten. Lloyd's was incorporated by Act of Parliament in 1871. Today the Corporation of Lloyd's performs the same function as that of Edward Lloyd 300 years ago, in so far as it provides the premises and the necessary services for the underwriting members to conduct the business of underwriting. The Corporation itself incurs no liability whatsoever in respect of the business accepted by the underwriting members. In effect, business is placed at Lloyd's and not with Lloyd's. Today the business written includes non-marine, motor and aviation insurance, as well as marine insurance.

For the purposes of transacting business, the underwriting members – or 'names' as they are more frequently known – are grouped into syndicates of varying sizes. Currently there are approximately 26 500 names grouped into some 400 syndicates. Whilst each syndicate is concerned primarily with writing one of the main classes of business (marine, aviation, non-marine or motor) it has become permissible, since the beginning of 1991, for a syndicate to accept risks in any of the other classes.

The monetary strength – or 'capacity' as it is known – of each syndicate is based upon the collective wealth shown by its underwriting members. The syndicate is managed by an underwriting agent, known as a managing agent, who appoints the active underwriter and supporting staff of the underwriting box of the syndicate in the Underwriting Room at Lloyd's. The underwriter, who is also an underwriting member of the syndicate, sits at the underwriting box of the syndicate and accepts risks on behalf of his members who bear the proportion of their particular share in the syndicate, i.e. each member receives his particular percentage share of all premiums and pays the same percentage of all claims emanating from the risks for which he or she has received premium. Each member has a separate and unlimited liability in respect of the risks written on his or her behalf by the underwriter of the syndicate.

In accordance with the provisions of the Lloyd's Act of 1982, which repealed many of the provisions of the earlier Acts, Lloyd's is now controlled by the Council of Lloyd's. This Council consists of 28 members – 12 elected from the working members and 16 from the external members. (A working member is a person who is primarily occupied with the conduct of business at Lloyd's either by a Lloyd's broker or an underwriting agent; an external member is a person who is not a working member of the Society.) A chairman is elected from the 12 working members who form the Committee of Lloyd's. The Council is responsible for the long-term planning and management of the affairs of the society, whilst the Committee is responsible for the day-to-day running of the business.

A considerable proportion of the business transacted in the London market is placed with insurance companies. Apart from the many British companies operating in the market there are also a large number of overseas companies. The basic difference between the Lloyd's underwriter and his company counterpart is that the liability of the former is 'several and unlimited', whereas the latter is a salaried employee of a limited liability company and has no personal liability in respect of the risks which he underwrites on behalf of his employer. Apart from this, generally speaking, the insurance companies transact business in a similar manner to that followed by Lloyd's underwriters. Certainly there is no difference at all as far as the underwriting of a risk is concerned, and it is quite usual for both Lloyd's and insurance company underwriters to participate in the same risk.

The great majority of the business transacted in the London market is handled through the intermediary of an insurance broker. Any individual or body corporate wishing to describe themselves as an 'insurance broker' must be registered with the Insurance Brokers' Registration Council in accordance with the provisions of the Insurance Brokers Registration Act 1977. The public does not have direct access to the underwriters at Lloyd's and business can only be presented to them by a Lloyd's broker. In addition to meeting the requirements of the Insurance Brokers' Registration Act 1977, the Lloyd's broker must also satisfy the rather more rigorous standards set by the Council of Lloyd's before he or she can operate in the market. The general – or non-Lloyd's broker – may possibly operate in the Lloyd's market via a Lloyd's broker with whom they enter into agreement for the handling of business.

The broker is the agent of the assured, his or her principal, and as such is subject to the common law of agency in so far as, if his or her principal is prejudiced as a result of negligence, then the principal may sue for damages. Effectively, brokers' services are provided without cost to the assured, whose remuneration, brokerage, is paid by the underwriters with whom the principal's business has been placed. Whilst a broking company may be a small organization of less than a dozen people, the large Lloyd's brokers of today are international organizations employing several thousand people worldwide.

The role of the broker is, first, to advise clients as to their insurance needs and, secondly, to comply with clients' subsequent instructions and obtain the cover required at the best possible rate of premium. The salient details of the risk are entered by the broker on a document known as a 'slip', which the broker presents to underwriters inviting them to accept all or a proportion of the risk specified thereon.

Unless the risk is a small one (i.e. of low monetary value), it will be placed with a number of underwriters in the market, each accepting a proportion (usually a percentage) of the sum insured. Upon completion of placing the risk, the broker issues a policy embodying the terms and conditions stated on the slip, having previously sent the principal a cover note informing him or her of the terms and conditions on which the risk has been placed and specifying the insurers participating. A further service provided by the broker on behalf of the principal is the negotiation and collection of any claims arising on insurances placed.

10.2 Lloyd's agents

In almost every port in the world will be found a Lloyd's Agent. These agents may be individuals or companies appointed by the Corporation of Lloyd's to serve the maritime community in their area. Like the Corporation which appoints them, they have no underwriting powers. Their main duties are:

(1) Protecting the interests of underwriters (Lloyd's or otherwise) according to instructions which may be sent to them, for example by endeavouring to avoid fraudulent claims.
(2) Rendering advice and assistance to Masters of shipwrecked vessels.
(3) Reporting to Lloyd's information regarding all casualties which may occur in their district and information as to arrivals and departures.
(4) Appointing surveyors to inspect damaged vessels and granting certification of seaworthiness when called upon to do so by Masters of vessels which have suffered damage.
(5) Notifying London headquarters of all information of relevant interest which may come to their notice.
(6) Surveying or appointing surveyors when called upon by consignees of cargo or by underwriters to survey damage and issuing reports stating the cause, nature and extent of all damage. Lloyd's agents will survey and issue reports in connection with damaged goods at the request of any interested party on the payment of a fee, quite apart from any question of insurance. All reports issued by Lloyd's agents are made 'without prejudice' and subject to the terms, conditions and amount of any policy of insurance.

10.3 Fundamental principles of insurance

Marine insurance is governed by the Marine Insurance Act 1906, which came into force on 1 January 1907. This Act did not create any new laws, but codified all the legal decisions which had been made during the preceding 300 years. The basic principles of insurance are specified in the Act. They are insurable interest; utmost good faith; indemnity and subrogation.

10.3.1 Insurable interest

The Marine Insurance Act 1906 provides that a person has an insurable interest in a marine adventure (any ship goods or other moveables exposed to maritime perils) where he or she stands in any legal or equitable relationship to the adventure or insurable property at risk therein in consequence of which he may:

(a) benefit by the safety or due arrival of the insurable property, or
(b) be prejudiced by its loss, or by damage thereto, or by the detention thereof, or
(c) incur liability in respect thereof.

It is important to understand the difference between the subject matter insured and insurable interest. Insurable interest is the financial interest of a person in the subject matter insured. Thus the insurable interest of the cargo owner is not the goods – the subject matter insured – but his financial interest in such goods and, accordingly, he should insure to the extent of that interest.

Whilst ownership of property – the subject matter insured – is the prime example of insurable interest, there are other circumstances in which a person may possess an insurable interest. For instance, persons responsible for goods while in their care, custody and control (e.g. a warehouseman), have an insurable interest in respect of their legal liability for such goods, even if the owner himself has effected insurance. Where goods are consigned to an agent for sale on commission, the agent has an insurable interest because, if the goods are lost, he will be precluded from earning his commission on their sale. In this instance, his insurable interest is his financial interest, i.e. the amount of his anticipated commission. The underwriter who insures goods has an insurable interest insofar as, if they are lost or damaged by one of the perils insured against, he will have to pay the claim made against him under the policy. Accordingly, he may limit his liability in respect of such a claim by insuring part of it with other underwriters. This is known an 'reinsurance'.

A policy effected without insurable interest is void, i.e. it has no legal value and is unenforceable at law. In all classes of insurance there is, therefore, a legal requirement that insurable interest exists at the time the insurance is effected. An exception to this rule applies in the case of cargo insurance. The Marine Insurance Act 1906 provides that the person entering into a contract of marine insurance must have an insurable interest or an expectation of acquiring one. This effectively covers the case of the buyer under a CIF contract who acquires his interest when the title to the goods purchased is transferred to him sometime after transit has commenced from the seller's premises.

Proof of insurable interest is not required at the time of effecting an insurance. But when making a claim, it is necessary for the assured to be able to show that he had an insurable interest at the time of loss. Cargo insurance effected in respect of CIF contracts of sale is invariably based on what is known as 'lost or not lost' conditions which means that the assured may recover any loss, even although he may not have acquired his interest until after the actual time of loss.

The most common forms of insurable interest in cargo insurance are:

(1) Ownership of the goods. The cargo owner has an insurable interest in the goods since he will benefit by their safe arrival or be prejudiced by loss of or damage thereto. Ownership usually involves two parties – seller and buyer, or consignor and consignee. The insurance requirements of these parties will depend upon the terms of the contract of sale.

(2) Charges of insurance (premium). The assured has an insurable interest in the premium paid in respect of any insurance he may effect. Whilst in hull insurance the shipowner effects a separate policy to cover the amount expended upon insurance premiums, in cargo insurance the sum insured reflects the cost of the goods plus the cost of insurance.

(3) Freight. This is the cost of transporting the goods from the consignor's premises to the consignee's premises and is either pre-paid or payable at destination. In most cases, it is advanced or pre-paid freight not returnable even if the goods are lost and not delivered. In these instances, therefore, the freight pre-paid is at the risk of the cargo owner and, as in the case of premium, is merged in with the value of the goods. Consequently, the sum insured reflects the cost of the goods plus the cost of insurance (premium) plus the cost of transportation (freight).

Other forms of insurable interest in cargo insurance are:

(1) Defeasible interest. This term describes an interest which may cease for reasons other than the operation of maritime perils. For example, the insurable interest of the seller of goods ends when the title to the goods passes to the buyer. The seller has a defeasible interest.

(2) Contingent interest. As the defeasible interest of the seller ceases the interest of the buyer commences. The contract of sale may contain a provision allowing the buyer to reject the goods in certain circumstances, e.g. delayed delivery. Where the buyer exercises this right of rejection, the interest immediately and automatically reverts to the seller. The seller has an insurable interest in respect of this contingency.

(3) Forwarding expenses. The contract of affreightment will probably include a clause allowing the carrier to discharge the goods at a port other than the one designated where, for some reason, they cannot be delivered or discharged at the destination port. For example, the destination port may be strikebound and the shipowner diverts the ship to another port. This would involve the cargo owner incurring 'forwarding expenses', i.e. the cost of getting his cargo on-carried to its intended destination. These charges are not covered under the standard cargo clauses, and when this situation occurs, it is usually too late for the cargo owner to effect insurance as the risk has already occurred. A prudent cargo owner would cover this interest by effecting an insurance on an annual basis for an amount sufficient to cover his possible expenditure in such circumstances.

(4) Commission. An agent may act for a cargo owner on a commission basis. The amount he or she anticipates earning will depend upon the arrival of the goods and he or she accordingly has an insurable interest to this extent.

Before leaving the subject of insurable interest, it is important for the reader to appreciate the relationship of this principle to the delivery terms specified in the contract of sale – i.e. where the individual insurable interests of the seller and the buyer attach and terminate – as this governs the extent of the insurance cover required by both. It is not proposed to consider here in any depth this aspect of the various forms of contract of sale as they are the subject of detailed examination elsewhere in this book.

As an example, however, under a Free on Board (FOB) contract the seller is required to arrange transport of the goods to the port and ensure that they are loaded into the vessel. At this point, when the goods pass over the ship's rail, this insurable interest ceases, and that of the buyer commences and continues until arrival of the goods at his or her premises. The seller, therefore, needs insurance cover from the time the goods leave his or her warehouse to FOB ship; the buyer needs insurance cover from FOB ship to arrival at his or her warehouse.

On the other hand, a Cost Insurance and Freight (CIF) contract places responsibility on the seller for arranging the transport of the goods from his or her warehouse to that of the buyer and paying the freight involved. He or she is also responsible for effecting insurance cover from 'warehouse to warehouse' in accordance with the buyer's instructions and paying the premium required. It is essential, therefore, that the insurance is arranged so that, in line with the transfer in title to the goods from the seller to the buyer, the beneficial rights of the insurance may be similarly transferred. This is known as assignment of the policy. Assignment of the insurance is effected by the seller (the assignor) endorsing the policy or certificate of insurance by blank endorsement to the buyer (the assignee). Blank endorsement means that the assignor signs his or her name above the company stamp on the back of the document and passes it to the assignee.

It is important to understand that assignment of the interest does not automatically assign the policy, and an agreement to assign the policy must exist before the seller parts with his or her interest. In practice, under a CIF contract there is an implied agreement that the policy will be assigned before the interest passes. By assigning the policy, the assignor passes to the assignee all the beneficial rights afforded by the insurance, thereby entitling the assignee to claim under the insurance as though he or she had had an insurable interest throughout the duration of the transit. It must be emphasized that the assignee cannot be in a better position than the assignor; his or her interest is derivative, i.e. he or she has exactly the same rights as the assignor. A breach of good faith or warranty on the part of the assignor would prejudice the assignee since the underwriter has exactly the same rights in relation to him or her as he had against the assignor.

10.3.2 Utmost good faith

The Marine Insurance Act 1906 provides that a contract of marine insurance is a contract based upon the 'utmost good faith' (uberrimae fidei), and if the utmost good faith be not observed by either party, the other party may avoid the contract.

It would not be practical or, indeed, possible for underwriters to check the accuracy or completeness of information submitted to them in respect of a risk to be insured. They have to rely upon the other party – the proposer or the broker acting on his or her behalf – observing the principle of utmost good faith which means a full disclosure of all material circumstances relating to the risk before the contract is concluded. A material circumstance is one which would influence a prudent underwriter as to the desirability of the risk. Where there is a non-disclosure of a material circumstance, the underwriter may avoid the contract. The underwriter may also avoid the contract if the broker is guilty of misrepresenting the risk during the placing negotiations. It is important to understand that avoidance of the contract does not render the contract void. A void contract is one which has no legal value and is, therefore, inadmissible as evidence in a court of law. If an underwriter avoids the contract, always provided that there is no fraud, the policy remains a valid document and the assured may contest the underwriter's action in a court of law. In practice, this situation usually arises where an underwriter refuses to pay a claim on the grounds that there has been a non-disclosure or misrepresentation at the time of placing the insurance. If the assured does not accept this allegation, he or she may challenge the underwriter's right to avoid the contract.

10.3.3 Indemnity

The purpose of insurance is to protect the insurable interest of the assured whereby, in the event of loss of or damage to the subject matter insured resulting from an insured peril, he or she is placed in the same position that he or she enjoyed immediately before the loss occurred. This is 'indemnity'. As will be appreciated, this basic principle of indemnity provides, in effect, that after indemnity the assured may not be in a better, or worse, position than he or she was in before the loss.

Whilst replacement is the means of effecting indemnity in some types of insurance, it would not be practical for marine insurers to replace ships and cargoes. The manner of indemnity is, therefore, a cash settlement. As explained above, the extent of this indemnity is the value of the insured property immediately before the loss occurs. This value is the insurable value and the basis for its calculation is specified in the Marine Insurance Act 1906. In the case of cargo, it is the prime cost of the goods, plus the incidental costs of shipping and insurance upon the whole. Where goods are, say, totally lost, this basis of indemnity would place the exporter of goods in the same position as if the goods had never left his or her warehouse and, therefore, conforms with the basic principle. Nevertheless, it falls somewhat short of the indemnity he or she would wish insofar as he or she would prefer to be in the same position as if the goods had arrived safely at their destination, i.e. realized his or her profit. The inadequacy of basing the indemnity upon the insurable value is further illustrated in the case of the frequently used CIF sales contract. Here the seller is responsible for arranging the shipment and insurance of the goods and his or her sales invoice to the buyer will accordingly reflect the freight and premium paid, in addition to the price charged for the goods, which will reflect the prime cost plus his or her percentage of profit.

The wise men who drafted the Marine Insurance Act at the beginning of this century were obviously very much aware of this problem and they accordingly worded the relevant section to overcome it. The section provides in its preamble to the bases for valuation 'Subject to any express provision or valuation in the policy the insurable value of the subject matter insured must be ascertained as follows.' Thus, the Act permits an agreed valuation, i.e. an insured value, to be declared in the policy, and only in the absence of such a valuation will the formula for arriving at the insurable value be used. The Act provides that a valued policy is one which specifies the agreed value of the subject matter insured and, in the absence of fraud, it is conclusive of the insurable value of the subject matter insured whether the loss be total or partial.

Consequently, cargo is always insured under a valued policy stating an insured value in line with the cargo assured's particular requirements. A valued policy will contain both a value – the insured value – and the sum insured. These may be expressed in different ways, e.g.:

> Sum insured £2 000 000 on
> 2000 cases merchandise, valued at £2 000 000
> or
> Sum insured £2 000 000 on
> 2000 cases merchandise, so valued.

The sum insured is the total of underwriters' subscriptions to the insurance and is, therefore, the maximum amount payable in respect of a claim. The sum insured is also the figure applied to the rate percentage, charged by the underwriter for writing the risk, to arrive at the premium due for the insurance. Effectively it represents the amount of insurance bought and it follows that, in the event of loss, one cannot expect to recover more than one has paid for.

In order for the subject matter insured to be fully insured, the sum insured and insured value must of course be for the same amount. If the sum insured is less than the insured value, this would mean that, for some reason, there is under-insurance or the assured has elected to bear a proportion of the risk himself. For instance, a sum insured of £1 600 000 on an insured value of £2 000 000 would indicate that the assured is bearing 20 per cent of the risk. In other words he will bear 20 per cent of every claim, recovering 80 per cent from his underwriters. In return for this he will save 20 per cent of the premium.

10.3.4 Subrogation

Subrogation is the corollary of indemnity in so far as its application prevents the assured defeating the principle of indemnity by recovering his loss from more than one party. For instance, insured goods may be damaged as a result of faulty stowage by the carrier. Under an 'all risks' insurance the cargo assured would be entitled to indemnity from his or her underwriters. He or she would also have recourse against the carrier. Whilst he or she may lodge claims against both, they may not recover and retain amounts received from both underwriter and carrier as this would defeat the principle of indemnity. In practice the underwriter, upon payment of the claim for the damage, would automatically be subrogated to all rights and remedies the cargo owner had against the carrier and, accordingly, may exercise these rights either in his or her own name or that of the assured for a recovery against the amount paid by him or her under the insurance. Any recovery the underwriter effects in this respect is limited to the amount of the claim paid under the insurance. It is possible, for example, where the insured goods have been undervalued, that the underwriter may recover more than the amount paid by him or her as a claim. In this event, he or she must pass the surplus proceeds to the assured.

The rights of subrogation pass to the underwriter upon payment of any type of claim. However, where the claim is in respect of a total loss, the underwriter is additionally entitled to proprietary rights in respect of whatever may remain of the insured goods and, accordingly, may dispose of these as is seen fit, retaining the whole of any proceeds even though these may exceed the amount of the claim paid.

10.3.5 Effecting Cargo Insurance

In the majority of international trade transactions, the contract will clearly state which party is responsible for arranging insurance for the goods being supplied and, in some cases, the point at which responsibility changes from supplier to buyer. This will be reflected in the Incoterm applied to the contract. Irrespective of the responsibility, it is important that the insurance cover is in force for the entire journey being undertaken, including any loading, unloading and temporary storage. Accordingly, insurance cover for the goods should embrace the following:

(1) Transportation of merchandise to the seaport or airport of departure.
(2) Period during which the goods are stored awaiting shipment or loading.
(3) The time whilst on board the ship, aircraft or other conveyance such as the international road haulage operation.
(4) The 'off loading' and storage on arrival at destination airport, seaport or other specified place.
(5) Transportation to the buyer's premises or address.

Where the supplier is responsible for arranging insurance, the insurance certificate or policy will be sent with the shipping documentation as evidence of cover. Insurance cover arranged by the supplier may end when the goods are landed at the port of arrival which can lead to problems such as the following.

(1) Cover needing to be arranged for the transit of goods from the port of arrival to the buyer's premises or those of the ultimate purchaser.
(2) Goods arriving damaged or incomplete at the port of arrival may lead to disputes between seller and buyer. Unless the goods are inspected immediately upon arrival, it will be difficult to prove where the loss or damage occurred.
(3) Settlement of claims may be delayed if insurance is arranged by an overseas insurer.

These problems can be circumvented by several mechanisms including:

(1) Extension of the seller's marine insurance cover to the ultimate destination, with the buyer assuming responsibility for the insurance premium relating to the period after arrival at the port of entry.
(2) Separate insurance cover being arranged by the buyer covering the final stages of the transit though this may not resolve demarcation disputes.
(3) The buyer taking responsibility for insurance from the supplier's premises to the ultimate destination.

10.4 Cargo insurance policy form and clauses

10.4.1 The SG policy form

A form of policy was included in the first schedule of the Marine Insurance Act 1906. This was the SG (Ship Goods) form adopted by Lloyd's on 1 January 1779. The insurance companies which developed in the nineteenth century never actually adopted the SG form of policy as specified in the Marine Insurance Act 1906, but preferred their own versions which, although including some slight variations, followed in general the same wording as the SG form and provided the same cover.

These company forms are now standardized in the form used by the Institute of London Underwriters (ILU) which signs policies on behalf of its member companies in the same way that Lloyd's Policy Signing Office signs policies on behalf of the syndicates at Lloyd's. Most insurance companies writing marine business are members of the ILU.

Subject to certain amendments and the attachment of clauses amplifying the cover to meet modern requirements, the SG form served the marine market for more than 200 years. Its strength and consequent retention for so long a time stemmed from the fact that during this period virtually every word and phrase has been the subject of litigation in the courts and its exact meaning established. Nevertheless, the archaic wording of the form together with the proliferation of clauses attached made it a complicated document, and following pressure from the United Nations Conference on Trade and Development (UNCTAD) for its replacement, a new form, the MAR Form (MAR being Marine), was introduced on 1 January 1982.

10.5 Cargo insurance rating

Premium rates are determined by numerous factors which are detailed below.

(1) The carrying vessel. The age, classification, flag, ownership, and management of the ship are an important consideration.
(2) Nature of the packing used. This has to be related to the mode of transport and its adequacy as a form of protection to the cargo. Air freight and maritime container shipments tend to require less packing.

(3) Type of merchandise involved. Some commodities are more vulnerable to damage than others. Additionally, one must relate this to the cover provided and experience, if any, of conveying such cargo.

(4) Nature of transit and related warehouse accommodation. Generally, the shorter the transit time, the less vulnerable the cargo is to damage or pilferage. Again the mode(s) of transport involved influence premium determination. Maritime containerization has tended in many trades and cargoes to reduce risk of pilferage, but the cargo still remains susceptible to damage.

(5) Previous experience. If the cargo involved has been subject to significant damage or pilferage the premiums are likely to be high. In the main, the shipper and broker tend to work well together in devising methods to minimize damage and pilferage and overcome inadequate packing.

(6) The type of cover needed. This is a critical area and obviously the more extensive the cover required, the higher the premium rate. Again the broker will advise the shipper on the extent of cover required, but much depends on terms of delivery.

(7) The volume of cargo involved. A substantial quantity shipment of export cargo may obtain a more favourable premium, but much depends on the circumstances, particularly transport mode and type of packing, if any.

Normally, alternative rates are available for different covers. For example, glassware may be insured at a high rate against all risks including breakage, or at a much lower rate excluding breakage, cracking or chipping. The degree of fragility is not the same for all commodities and obviously there cannot be a universal rate for breakage. To the exporter fresh to the business, it is wise to shop around to obtain the most favourable rates or seek advice from the freight forwarder.

10.5.1 The new Marine Policy Form and new Institute Cargo Clauses

On 1 January 1982 a new Marine Policy Form and new Institute Cargo Clauses were introduced in the London marine insurance market. As explained earlier the cargo insurance market is underwritten by Lloyd's underwriters and insurance companies. We will now examine a Companies Marine Policy subscribed to by insurance companies which are members of the Institute of London Underwriters.

The Companies Marine Policy serves as a contract of insurance for cargo and as detailed below there are three main types of policy: single shipment, annual and open.

(1) Single shipment or Facultative shipment.

    (a) Optional type of policy in that, having agreed to cover a specific shipment, there is no obligation to cover further shipments.

    (b) Used mainly for importers/exporters with occasional shipments, or can be used as a means of building up experience on a new venture prior to the issuing of a longer term contract.

(2) Annual policy

   (a) Issued for a twelve-month period subject to payment at inception of a minimum and deposit premium or deposit premium with a minimum retention.

   (b) Adjustable at the end of the period on the total value of sendings made declarable as either (i) an annual figure, or (ii) throughout the period, on an individual or monthly basis.

   (c) Suitable for risks where sendings are regular and low value goods are involved.

   (d) It ensures premium up front for the broker and underwriter.

(3) Open policy

   (a) Once issued this policy remains in force until no longer required, i.e. can be cancelled by either the Assured or the Insurer.

   (b) Annually reviewed to ensure that the Assured's requirements continue to be met.

   (c) Premium is normally payable in arrears, being calculated according to the value of shipments in a particular month.

Flexibility to meet each customer's individual requirements and variations in the latter two covers may be negotiated. The type of policy offered will depend on:

(1) frequency of shipments;
(2) annual value of shipments;
(3) ease of operation.

The above policies may be subject to Insurance Premium Tax.

Method of declaration

(1) Assured's typed declaration letter

   (a) No documentation issued usually by the assured.

   (b) Used where an annual value of sendings or turnover is required for adjustment purposes.

   (c) Usually utilized in small annual policies.

(2) Small declaration

   (a) Issued by assured companies to brokers/agents/assureds.

   (b) Used for declaring individual shipments on an import cover or as a request for a Claims Payable Abroad certificate to be issued on an export cover (where certificates have not been issued to a broker, etc.)

(3) Large declaration

   (a) Issued by assured companies to brokers/agents/assureds.

   (b) Used when there are regular multiple shipments involved, usually on an import cover.

   (c) Normally submitted on a monthly basis.

(4) Certificate of insurance

    (a) Issued by assured companies to brokers/agents/assureds.

    (b) Normally issued on export covers for individual shipments.

    (c) Usually submitted in monthly batches.

(5) Evidence of the contract of insurance

    (a) Freely assignable document.

    (b) Reflects cover of the master policy.

    (c) Indicates details of the claims settling agent to be used.

Scope of cover

Marine insurers use standard wordings known as Institute Clauses. Various clauses are used depending on the nature of the goods being carried. The three basic levels of protection offered are detailed as follows.

(i) Institute Cargo Clauses (A)

This represents the widest form of protection and provides all-risks cover against physical loss of or damage to the goods, including both total and partial losses. Exclusions are:

(1) wilful misconduct of the assured;

(2) ordinary leakage, loss in weight/volume or ordinary wear and tear;

(3) inadequate packing including stowage in a container by the assured;

(4) inherent vice;

(5) delay;

(6) insolvency or financial default of carriers;

(7) war and strikes and nuclear risks.

As well as these exclusions, some cargoes warrant more specific exclusions, e.g.:

(1) Machinery or electrical items – excluding electrical and/or mechanical derangement.

(2) Steel goods (if unprotected) – excluding rust, oxidization or discolouration.

(3) Tinned goods – excluding blowing and/or bursting of tins.

(4) Chocolates – excluding heating and/or sweating.

It is important to note that the only storage cover given is that given whilst in the ordinary course of transit. If the storage is intentional it is not covered. The equivalent cover is also provided by the Institute Cargo Clauses (Air) for sendings by air.

(ii) Institute Cargo Clauses (B)

These clauses are subject to the same exclusions as per the Institute Cargo Clauses (A). Protection, however, is limited to the major named perils listed below:

(1) Fire and explosion.
(2) Loss following upon a major accident to the ocean-carrying-vessel or over-turning or derailment of the land conveyance.
(3) Discharge of cargo at a port of distress.
(4) Earthquake, volcanic eruption or lightning.
(5) General average sacrifice.
(6) Jettison or washing overboard.
(7) Sea, lake or river water damage (not rain water).
(8) Total loss of any package lost overboard or dropped during loading/unloading.
(9) General average or salvage charges.

Cover can be extended to include theft or non-delivery if necessary. These clauses are used when underwriters are not prepared to give 'A' clauses as in the case of second-hand goods or packaged bulk cargoes.

(iii) Institute Cargo Clauses (C)

These afford the minimum protection available and are really only suitable for goods which are customarily insured against major casualties only or which are shipped in bulk, or where the condition of the goods is not known by the underwriter. The cover is loss or damage arising from any of the major perils listed under the Institute Cargo Clauses (B) except numbers 4, 7 and 8.

(iv) Additional Clauses

Institute War Clauses and Institute Strikes Clauses are usually added and give cover against the risks of war, strikes, riots and civil commotion. It should be noted that terrorism cover is granted by the strikes clauses whilst the goods are in the ordinary course of transit.

As mentioned previously, the preceding are the basic clauses which are used to cover most cargoes. There are, however, some commodities, goods and situations which are normally dealt with under special market trade clauses, e.g.:

Coal	Institute Coal Clauses
Frozen meat	Institute Frozen Meat Clauses
Cocoa, Coffee, Cotton, Fats and Oils not in bulk, Hides, Skins and Leather, Metals, Oil Seeds, Sugar (raw or refined) and Tea	Institute Commodity Trades Clauses (A)

Other aspects

The Companies Marine Policy is not valid unless it bears the embossment of the Policy Department of the Institute of London Underwriters. It is subject to English law and must contain an identical description of the cargo as found on the bill of lading, air waybill and feature the valuation and transportation details.

Check list, discrepancies (i.e. likely errors) and their consequences

If an insurance document is required check the following:

(1) It has been issued and/or signed by an insurance company or underwriter or an agent on their behalf.

(2) It is not a broker's certificate or cover note unless the presentation of such has been specifically authorized.

(3) If the insurance document indicates it is issued in more than one original, all originals are presented unless otherwise authorized in the credit.

(4) It is not dated later than date of shipment, despatch or taking in charge.

(5) It is issued in the currency of the creditor. If cover in a different currency is required, that it is presented in that currency.

(6) It provides sufficient cover and contains the same details in respect of special risks as stated in the credit terms. Unless otherwise stipulated, cover must be 10 per cent above the CIF or CIP value.

(7) It has been enclosed to the order of a specified party, issued in a transferable form, or endorsed by the insured if issued in the latter's name.

(8) It shows marks, numbers, weights and quantities and a description of goods that match the Bill of Lading and other documents.

(9) It does not show unauthenticated alterations.

(10) It shows the method of carriage of the goods, the point of loading on board, despatch or taking in charge, the name of the carrying vessel if appropriate and the port of discharge or place of delivery.

(11) It specifically covers transshipment when the transport document shows this will take place.

(12) It states a named place where claims are payable when required.

(13) It covers 'Loaded on Deck' when this is permitted within the Credit Terms or when despatch is effected in containers which may be loaded on deck – check appropriate jettison clauses.

10.6 Cargo insurance claims

Most insurance company policies require that immediate notice be given to the nearest branch or agency in the event of damage giving rise to a claim under a policy on goods. Lloyd's policies stipulate that a Lloyd's agent shall be called in should damage occur.

When notified of damage, the company's agent or Lloyd's agent proceeds to appoint a suitable surveyor to inspect the goods and to report on the nature and extent of the damage. A common practice is for a report or certificate of loss incorporating the surveyor's findings to be issued to the consignees, the latter paying the fee. This is the usual procedure relative to the Lloyd's agent. This certificate of loss is included with the claim papers and, if the loss is recoverable under the insurance cover, the fee is refunded to the claimants.

In some circumstances, the claim papers are returned to the place where the insurance was effected and subsequently presented to the underwriters. However, especially where goods are sold on CIF terms and the policy is assigned to the consignees, arrangements are made for any claims to be paid at destination. In such cases, the consignees approach the agents named in the policy for payment of their claims. Lloyd's agents undertake this service. The policy must be produced by the claimant when a marine claim is put forward because of the freedom with which the marine policy may be assigned. In circumstances where the policy or certificate of insurance has been lost or destroyed, underwriters are generally willing to settle the claim, provided that the claimant completes a letter of indemnity.

The presentation of claims is by negotiation on documents supporting the assured's case. It is very difficult to state with any degree of legal precision exactly on whom the onus of proof falls in every case, but generally speaking, the assured must be able to prove a loss by a peril against which he or she was insured. Once the assured has presented a prima facie case of loss by a peril insured against, the onus is on the insurers to disprove liability.

The following documents are required when making an insurance claim:

(1) The export invoice issued to the customer together with shipping specification and/or weight notes.
(2) The original bill of lading, charter party, air waybill, or CMR or CIM consignment note.
(3) The original policy or certificate of insurance.
(4) The survey report or other documentary evidence detailing the loss or damage occurred.
(5) Extended protest or extract from ships logs for salvage loss, particular average in goods, or total loss of goods for maritime consignments.
(6) Letters of subrogation for total loss or particular average on goods.
(7) Any exchange of correspondence with the carriers and other parties regarding their liability for the loss or damage.
(8) Any landing account or weight notes at final destination.
(9) Account sale (salvage) or invoice for reconditioning charges.

Having established the documents required to deal with the claim, it is important a code of procedure be devised to process it. Figure 10.1 features the 'cargo claim' and the main elements of it. In Figure 10.2 we have the 'development of the cargo claim' and its constituents from the factory to the buyer (consignee).

Brief details are given below of the claims procedure which involves a bulk shipment.

(1) Receiver notifies his agent of damage/loss and allows the ship's agent three days to examine cargo.
(2) When extent of damage is ascertained by receiver or shipowner's agent, the shipowner and P & I Club must be told.
(3) A large claim may require a P & I Club surveyor or a consultant to examine the cargo. An early examination is essential and the agent must establish from the

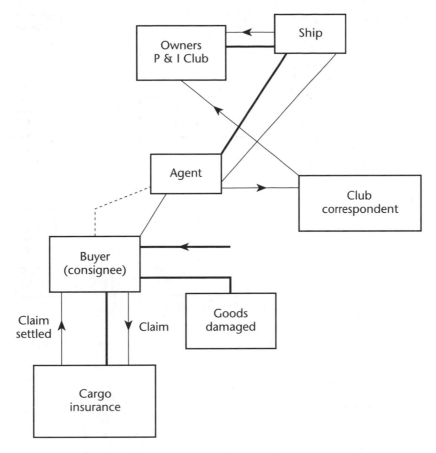

FIGURE 10.1 Cargo claim

ship's Master and confirm with the shipowner/P & I Club, the actual name of P & I Club involved.

(4) When the cargo claim facts are established, correspondence starts as detailed in Figures 10.1 and 10.2 involving interested parties: shipowner, receiver's agents, P & I Club, cargo receiver, shipowner's agent, cargo insurance company/Lloyd's, lawyers, etc.

(5) The receiver's agent's role is decisive in all stages to ensure prompt settlement is obtained and quick action is essential in the early stages.

It will be appreciated circumstances will vary. The claim could emerge at the factory warehouse of the buyer rather than at the destination port as found in the example above.

It is important to bear in mind that clean receipts for imported cargo acceptance should never be given when the goods are in a doubtful condition, but the receipt should be suitably endorsed and witnessed if possible, for example, if one package is missing. Furthermore, if the loss of damage incurred was not readily apparent at the

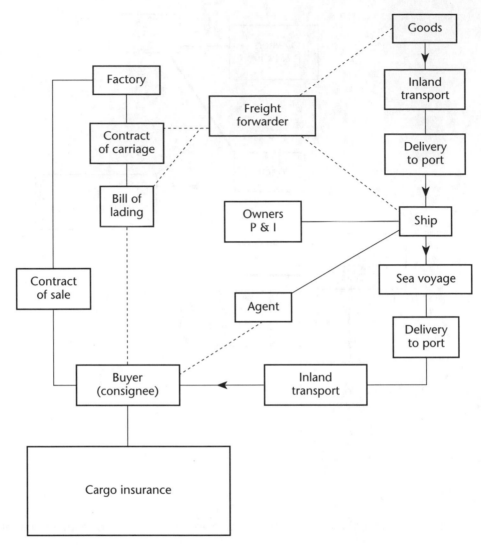

FIGURE 10.2 Development of cargo claim

time of taking delivery, written notice must be given to the carriers or other bailees within three days of delivery acceptance.

It is desirable the claim be progressed as quickly as practicable. It is advantageous for the exporter to have a good comprehension of the term general average (GA) which features in any standard maritime policy. It is defined as a 'loss arising in consequences of extraordinary and intentional sacrifices made or expenses incurred, for the common safety of the ship and cargo.' Examples of general average include jettison of cargo, damage to cargo, etc.

In the event of a shipowner declaring a general average loss occurring, each party involved in the voyage must contribute in proportion to their interest in the maritime venture. This, of course, involves shippers who may not have suffered any damage or loss to their cargo. The cargo is only released in such a situation when the shipper/importer has given either a cash deposit or provided a general average guarantee given by the insurers. Overall, this involves signing a general average bond which confirms the importer will pay his general average contribution following the average adjuster's assessment.

10.7 Cargo claims prevention

Claims prevention is the process of devising a system to reduce or eliminate the level of claims emerging from the carriage of goods on an international transit. It is important the exporter gives special attention to claims prevention and thereby maintains a good relationship with the buyer through the goods arriving in an undamaged condition with none missing (Figures 10.1 and 10.2). The circumstances which give rise to a cargo claim vary and the following is a broad summary of the situations:

(1) Missing goods.
(2) Damaged goods.
(3) Stained/mutilated/soiled goods.
(4) Non-saleable/marketable goods arising through frustration of the transit such as transit delays causing perishable goods to deteriorate beyond a marketable/saleable product.
(5) Failure of the goods to arrive on a specified date resulting in a compensation claim.
(6) Poor/inadequate packing.
(7) Inadequate/poor stowage.
(8) Poor handling/stacking of cargo resulting in damage, crushing, etc.

To minimize the level of cargo claims it is most desirable that adequate measures be taken. The following list should not be regarded as exhaustive but merely as a selection of the more important areas where measures can be taken to reduce claims:

(1) A transit test should be employed to determine where the delays, damage or pilferage were encountered and any remedial practical measures necessary should be instituted.
(2) Documentation should be continually improved to specify the circumstances of a claim and the reasons for a claim. Comprehensive claims reports permit a realistic analysis of causes and thereby produce a possible pattern of circumstances.
(3) Quality control of product, transport service and packaging should be improved. (See also item (4).)
(4) Packaging should be analysed for its adequacy, both for handling and stowage and for compatibility with atmospheric conditions, including weather exposure.
(5) Pilferage – aim to improve security and properly evaluate alternatives for routeing, packaging, cargo packing, marking identity, etc.

(6) Breakage – aim to improve packaging and better handling and stowage techniques and/or transport mode, i.e. break-bulk to containers.

(7) An evaluation of the cost of alternative means and/or remedies should be made and their likelihood of success assessed.

(8) Staff training should be provided, especially on the handling and stowage of cargo and on measures to lessen such cargo claims; this to include cargo claims report forms and their comprehensiveness and prompt submission.

(9) A code of procedure should be devised to report damaged or missing cargo, thereby ensuring that prompt action can be taken to lessen the prospect of further claims and to institute earlier enquiries in order to produce quick remedial measures.

(10) Adequate preventative claims staff resources should be provided to lessen such risk.

(11) All available modern technology should be used to lessen such claims.

(12) Produce a brochure on claims prevention and packaging, stowage and handling techniques.

(13) Initiate early discussions with the carrier(s) and other interested parties to devise remedial measures to resolve the difficulties and claims encountered.

It is most important that claims be kept to a minimum and thereby ensure cargo insurance premiums remain competitive and, at the same time, that the buyer is well-satisfied, with goods received in a quality condition. The need to deal with claims promptly and adequately cannot be overstressed.

10.8 International transport conventions

A brief review of the international transport conventions, by transport mode, now follows, but it is stressed there is a lack of uniformity between the different conventions.

The Carriage of Goods by Road Act 1965, which came into force in 1967, notified and enacted the provisions of the Convention on the International Carriage of Goods by Road (CMR). The Convention represents an attempt by the principal European nations to regulate the responsibilities and liabilities of carriers engaged in the international distribution of goods by road. Consequently, the Convention applies throughout the entire duration of the carriage, even if certain sections of the transit may be by sea, rail or air (although in the event of loss, liability would be determined according to the particular requirements of the law relating to the actual form of transportation involved, for example, Hague rules in respect of shipments by sea). The Convention applies to goods passing through the Channel Tunnel provided the merchandise remains on the road vehicle throughout.

Broadly speaking, the Convention applies to contracts for the carriage of goods in vehicles for reward between termini situated in two different countries, of which at least one is a signatory to the Convention. At the present time, 26 countries have signed, including all EC members, except Eire, together with Austria, Bulgaria,

Czechoslovakia, Finland, Hungary, Norway, Poland, Romania, Sweden, Switzerland, the CIS and Yugoslavia. The Convention does not govern carriage between the UK and Eire, or to internal dispatches within the UK, neither does it apply to postal sendings, funeral consignments, furniture removals and movement of own goods.

The contract of carriage is evidenced by a CMR consignment note, containing a description of the goods, carriage charges, and any special provisions such as agreed values, special interests, delivery instructions, etc. The consignment note states that the Convention is to apply, although it should be understood that the Convention would operate even if no document at all were issued.

Briefly the CMR Convention provides that the carrier shall be liable for the total or partial loss of the goods from time of receipt to time of delivery. In particular, the carrier is conclusively liable for loss if the goods have not been delivered within 30 days from the expiry of any agreed time limit, or 60 days after taking over the goods in the absence of such limit. Moreover, the carrier is responsible for the acts of employees and agents, including subcontractors and sub-bailees.

The carrier may be relieved from all liability if the loss is due to the wrongful act of the claimant, inherent vice of the goods or through circumstances the carrier could not avoid or prevent; but the onus of proof is on the carrier. On the other hand, the carrier discharges the onus of proof if it can be shown that the loss can be attributed to:

(1) Permitted use of open unsheeted vehicles.
(2) Improper packing, marking and numbering.
(3) Handling operations undertaken by the cargo owner.
(4) Nature of the goods (ordinary breakage, leakage, wastage).
(5) Carriage of livestock.

In the event of loss or damage, the carrier's liability is related to the market price of the goods at the place and time at which they were accepted for carriage, but not exceeding 25 Gold Francs/kg of gross weight, plus carriage charges, customs duties, and other charges incurred in respect of the carriage of goods, which are totally lost, or in proportion of partly lost or damaged goods. By arrangement between the carriers and consignor, a higher amount may be substituted for the convention limit if a special interest or higher value has been agreed between the parties. Should the consignee be able to prove that loss or damage has resulted from delay the carrier is required to pay compensation not exceeding the carriage charges (unless specially agreed).

In 1979 a protocol to CMR was promulgated by the EEC replacing the 25 Gold Francs by SDR (Special Drawing Rights) 8.33 per kilo. Nine countries have signed the protocol including the UK. This has had the effect of increasing the carrier's maximum liability. For example, taking the value of the pound in terms for Special Drawing Rights from the Financial Times on 4 June 1993, the conversion would be as follows:

    1 kg   = 8.33 SDRs
    1 SDR   = £1.0833
    1 tonne   = £9023.889

Notwithstanding the above limitations and immunities, the carrier is liable to pay full compensation if the loss, damage or delay is caused by the wilful misconduct or default of the carrier or his servants or agents acting within the scope of their employment.

The Convention regulates the procedures to be followed concerning claims against the carrier. The consignee must reserve the right to claim for any apparent damage not later than the time of delivery. If the damage is not apparent, the consignee must give written notice of damage within seven days. Claims for delay must be notified in writing within 21 days from the time the goods were placed at the disposal of the consignee. Legal action must be brought within a year but, in the case of wilful misconduct, the period of limitation is extended to three years.

Normally, the carrier in whose custody the damage occurred is liable to indemnify the claimant but frequently responsibility for loss or damage is difficult to determine. Furthermore, action may be brought only against the first carrier, the last carrier or the carrier in whose portion of carriage the loss occurred. The Convention, therefore, provides that the carrier who has paid compensation is entitled to recover from other carriers who may be primarily responsible, or alternatively, if liability cannot be determined accurately, responsibility may be apportioned according to each carrier's proportion of the total carriage charges and recovery made accordingly. If a carrier becomes insolvent, the other carriers bear his or her proportion of any outstanding claims.

From the exporter's point of view, it will be noted that the opportunities for recovery of losses sustained while goods are in the road hauliers' possession are quite extensive. The UK's accession to the EC has produced a dramatic increase in the volume and value of goods consigned to the continent. Sellers in this country who utilize the through transit facilities now provided by hauliers should be fully aware both of their own and the carrier's legal position if rights of recourse are to be successfully pursued.

To conclude, under this Convention the carrier is liable for loss or damage from the time he or she takes over until the time of delivery of the goods to the consignee, unless it can be proved that the loss or damage occurred because of one of the list of excepted perils. In short, these exceptions allow carriers to escape liability if they have not been negligent. Carriers are also liable for delay if the goods have not been delivered within the agreed time limit or, if there is no such agreement, within a reasonable time.

10.9 International rail transport COTIF/CIM

An international convention concerning the carriage of goods by rail has existed in some form since 1893. It permits the carriage of goods under one document; a consignment note (not negotiable) under a common code of conditions.

The COTIF Convention concerning international carriage by rail was signed in Berne in May 1980. It was given legal effect in the UK by section 1 of the International

Transport Conventions Act 1983 with effect from May 1985. COTIF abrogated the existing CIM convention which did not have force of law in the UK and an amended draft of CIM was attached to COTIF as Appendix 'B' to govern the carriage of goods. It should be noted COTIF has a wider application and covers passengers, etc. as well as goods.

Like CMR, COTIF/CIM applies only to international carriage and is not applicable to domestic traffic. The opening of the Channel Tunnel extended the application of the COTIF/CIM recourse. As a private company the Channel Tunnel operates an independent contract not subject to any mandatory law in which liability for delays is excluded and a limitation of SDR 8.33 (the same as CMR) is applied.

The terms and conditions of COTIF/CIM are similar to CMR but limitation is substantially higher at SDR 17 per kilo.

10.10 International air transport – Warsaw Convention

The international air carriage of goods is subject to either the Warsaw Convention 1929 or the amended Warsaw Convention 1955. Which of these Conventions applies depends on which Convention the countries of departure and arrival have ratified. For one of the Conventions to apply, both of the countries must have ratified the same Convention; if both have ratified the amended Warsaw Convention then, irrespective of whether they have both also ratified the earlier Convention, the amended Warsaw Convention applies.

Contractual Carriers (such as freight forwarders acting as principals) are also subject to the Conventions. Unlike other transport Conventions, both Warsaw Conventions require that certain information is stated on the air waybill, the absence of which will prevent the carrier from relying on both the exclusions and limitations of liability in the Convention and, in the case of the amended Warsaw Convention, will not entitle the carrier to rely on the limitations of liability. The limit of liability is 250 Poincare (gold) francs or, if the Montreal Protocols 1–3 of 1975 have been ratified, 17 SDRs per kilo.

10.11 Combined transport – International Conventions

10.11.1 ICC Rules for a Combined Transport Document

Some time ago an attempt was made to draft a Convention to cover loss or damage to goods carried under a combined Transport Document. Known variously at different stages as the 'Tokyo Rome Rules', the 'Tokyo Rules' and the 'TCM' Convention, it failed to secure general support. The International Chamber of Commerce took up the rejected draft and made various amendments to make it commercially more attractive. The final draft was published as the 'ICC Rules for a Combined Transport Document' (brochure No 298). These have found wide acceptance amongst Combined Transport Operators and most mega-maritime container operators apply terms and conditions which are based on ICC Rules, if not precisely complying with them.

10.11.2 UNCTAD MMO Convention

The United Nations Conference on Trade and Development (UNCTAD) was dissatisfied with the foregoing situation and decided to intervene with an international convention to govern Combined Transport. This was finally adopted at an international conference in Geneva in May 1980 at the United Nations Convention on International Multi-modal Transport of Goods (or UNCTAD MMO Convention as it is more commonly known). Like the Hamburg rules, if introduced it seems inevitably bound to increase carriers insurance costs.

This Convention will come into force 12 months after the deposit of the documents of ratification, acceptance, approval or accession with the UN in New York by the thirtieth country with no minimum tonnage qualification. To date (January 1999) it has been ratified by only eight countries: Chile, Georgia, Malawi, Mexico, Morocco, Rwanda, Senegal and Zambia.

10.11.3 UNCTAD/ICC Rules for Multi-Modal Transport Documents

As part of their continuing campaign to promote the Hamburg Rules and UNCTAD/ MMO Convention, UNCTAD sought the co-operation of the ICC for a combined Transport Document. The ICC Rules were in need of neither revision nor update and their general basic application worldwide attested to their acceptability to the parties concerned. Nevertheless, ICC joined forces with UNCTAD. Subsequently, a working party under Professor Jan Ramberg was asked to review these Rules and to formulate its draft based primarily on the Hague Visby Rules. The review has now been completed and the published UNCTAD/ICC Rules, which are voluntary, are unlikely to gain much recognition beyond a few NVOCCs for a variety of reasons.

11

Credit insurance

11.1 Export credit insurance

The purpose of export credit insurance is to offer protection to exporters of goods or services who sell their products on credit terms. The exporter is insured against losses arising from a wide range of risks, which may be conveniently categorized into either *commercial risks* or *political risks*, although many private export credit insurers offer cover for commercial risks only. In order to protect the insurers in the private sector against adverse selection, an exporter is usually required to insure its entire book of export orders filled on credit terms, rather than being allowed to seek coverage in respect of countries where the peril is perceived to be the greatest.

11.1.1 Commercial risks

Commercial risks would generally include the following:

(1) The insolvency of the purchaser.
(2) The default on payment by a private purchaser at the end of the credit period or after some specified period following the expiry of the agreed term of credit.
(3) Non-acceptance of goods delivered to the purchaser, where such goods comply with any contracts in existence.

11.1.2 Political risks

The scope for losses arising from risks of a political nature is wider than that in respect of commercial risks and would generally encompass all political events which have an impact on any contractual relationships covered by civil law, including the following:

(1) Cancellation or non-renewal of an insured's export licence after a contract has been struck.
(2) War and other such disturbances in the purchaser's country of domicile which affect the fulfilment of the contract.

(3) Foreign currency conversion risks, i.e. difficulties and delays in remitting money from the purchaser's country, including losses arising as a result of a moratorium on external debt issued by that country's government.

(4) Transfer risks (also referred to as 'third country transfer risks') where one country can freeze the assets and bank accounts of another country held locally.

(5) Any action of a foreign government which in some way hinders the enactment of the contract, including import/export restrictions, the confiscation or expropriation of goods and the nationalization of corporations and industries.

(6) Transactions between private exporters and public purchasers, i.e. the default on payment by a public purchaser.

11.1.3 The rationale behind export credit insurance

In its purest form, export credit insurance provides exporters of goods and services with a significant degree of financial security, thus allowing companies to pursue a bolder export policy, by accepting new purchasers and entering into new overseas markets, but with a smaller impact from the risks of non-payment and political instability. Indirect effects of the purchase of such insurance might include the use of policies as security against bank loans and other financial arrangements. The insurance content of such policies is typically supplemented by the extensive support services which are generally provided by export credit insurers. In particular, such insurers usually have access to extensive information from credit rating agencies and foreign embassies, and are able to provide information to their policyholders regarding the creditworthiness and trading records of potential purchasers of their goods. Such services may be charged for either on a standing charge basis, a per usage fee, or may be built into the premium structure.

Extensions to the basic coverage offered can take many different forms, for example:

(1) A manufacturer of specialist goods (which would not necessarily be resaleable elsewhere) might seek additional insurance from the date that the contract is struck to the date of shipment, in order to protect against the risk of the purchaser being subsequently unable to fulfil its contractual obligations prior to completion of the manufacturing process.

(2) A policyholder with significant financial exposure arising from one-off products, for example, ship-building, would probably not be covered under the standard terms of its policies as a result of the high monetary values involved. Extensions to coverage in such circumstances might be granted on a discretionary case by case basis.

(3) An exporter may often need to offer credit terms which are longer than permitted under the policy's standard conditions, particularly where it is common practice within a specific manufacturing sector to do so.

11.1.4 Limits of indemnity

Generally, cover is provided up to some specified percentage of any loss, typically between 80 per cent and 95 per cent. An excess may also be payable by the insured in respect of certain predetermined types of loss, with the limits of coverage applying to the balance of the claim amount. The element of co-insurance acts, to some extent, as a deterrent to the abuse of the coverage purchased; for example, exporters might simply claim on their policies rather than seek to effect a bad debt collection programme, or find alternative purchasers for goods not taken up by the original buyer.

11.1.5 Recoveries and subrogation

In any event, the export credit insurer will generally seek to effect recoveries on claims paid, either through the courts, via factors; through pressure from British embassies in the purchaser's country of domicile; or via some other form of debt collection in order to offset individual losses. More typically, the goods concerned would be taken into the insurer's possession where possible, and an alternative buyer sought. If, however, the insurer does not have the necessary administrative or resale capabilities, an arrangement may be entered into with the policyholder such that a specified proportion of any resale revenue is remitted to the insurer. A claim can therefore be settled quickly irrespective of any subsequent recovery prospects, thereby maintaining the insured's cash flow position, but still leaving the insurer free to pursue the possibility of effecting recoveries at a later stage.

11.1.6 Who provides export credit insurance?

Schemes are often operated by the governments of individual countries, as the potential volatility of this form of insurance means that only very large private insurers could weather exceptionally poor claims experience. Furthermore, re-insurance of this form of business is difficult to place in the commercial market owing to the substantial levels of coverage required. State schemes were therefore started up with the original intention of both encouraging and facilitating the export of domestic goods and services abroad. In particular, state-backed schemes have the added attraction of generally being considered to be less likely than private insurance companies to withdraw cover for political risks in respect of specific countries (e.g. in the event of the outbreak of war) and are thus in a position to provide cover for risks which might not be insurable in the commercial market.

There exist, none the less, a number of private insurance companies which can continue to provide coverage in respect of commercial and political risks under such circumstances via the vehicle of re-insurance with the respective governments. Furthermore, whereas Lloyd's of London once represented the sole private market for the insurance of political risks, cover is now available from the American International Group, Chubb, LaReunion/UIC, PanFinancial, Professional Indemnity Agency, Citicorp and Exporters Insurance Company.

11.1.7 Policy conditions

Typically, private export credit insurers tend to provide short-term cover only, whilst state organizations additionally insure medium- and long-term risks, as well as offering cover in respect of risks for substantial sums insured and 'national interest' risks. The period over which the insurer is on risk in respect of any one underwriting year depends on the amalgamation of the following.

(1) The duration of any pre-shipment coverage, for example during the course of the manufacturing process.
(2) The length of the credit terms offered.
(3) The period over which the policy is in force.

Typical policy conditions for short-term cover might comprise the following:

(1) A policy is generally in effect for 12 months such that all contracts entered into and all goods shipments notified to the insurer within this period are covered.
(2) Credit terms from 90 days up to one year from the date of shipment or the date of receipt of goods.
(3) Any period between striking a contract and the eventual shipment of completed goods to be limited to 24 months.
(4) Premiums levied on the basis of the value of each shipment covered under the policy at terms fixed at the outset for the duration of the policy.
(5) Limits on the maximum value of any individual contract or shipment.

11.2 Short-term export credit insurance

As its name suggests, short-term export credit insurance exists to cover exporters against the risks inherent in trading on relatively short (usually up to six months) credit terms with buyers overseas. These types of exports account for the vast majority of exports from the UK and are generally not associated with the longer term 'project' activities looked after by the government's Export Credit Guarantees Department. However, they cannot be entirely divorced from those activities, as much of the project work will also subsequently lead to orders for parts, spares and further services which are then sold on a short-term basis.

The risks for exporters of non-payment by overseas customers can be divided into two separate areas: *commercial* risks and *political* risks. Commercial risk covers straightforward insolvency of the debtor; some credit insurers are also prepared to offer cover for protracted default which, broadly speaking, is where the buyer turns out to have insufficient funds for the goods, and the cost of winding him or her up might be more than the amount of the original debt. On political risk the cover is less straightforward, and can be subdivided into three different areas.

(1) *Inconvertibility.* This covers the failure of the buyer's country to transfer foreign exchange as a result of economic, financial or political difficulties. This is the most common cause of political risk claims.

(2) *Contract frustration/cancellation.* This covers the failure to pay, where this is due to war (except between the UK and the country of the buyer), any measure of the government of the buyer's country which directly prevents performance of the contract and the cancellation or non-renewal of valid import/export licences.

(3) *Public buyer default.* This covers the contractual default of a public buyer which can be the government, a government agency, a regional or local authority, a nationalized undertaking or a state trade organization.

Notwithstanding the Single European Market and the greater similarity between what have hitherto been divided into 'domestic' and 'export' trades, exporters will still need to consider both the creditworthiness of the buyer (hopefully *before* accepting the order) and the political risks inherent in trading with the country itself. Even for trade with some EU countries, political risk cover is still sought by exporters.

11.2.1 Companies offering credit insurance

Details of companies offering credit insurance are given below. It should be noted that the Export Credit Guarantee Department (ECGD) is a Government Agency under the Department of Trade and Industry.

The Export Credits Guarantee Department (ECGD)

The Export Credits Guarantee Department (ECGD) has four operating rules.

(1) ECGD underwrites export deals on credit terms longer than two years, both through credit lines and individual packages of cover for specific contracts.

(2) ECGD provides reinsurance – for certain high-risk markets, or larger and longer exposures – to private sector credit insurers, notably NCM, Trade Indemnity and Coface.

(3) ECGD underwrites short-term cover for a small number of national interest markets that are too risky for private sector insurers.

(4) ECGD underwrites long and large extended term deals beyond normal short-term insurance parameters.

NCM Credit Insurance

This subsidiary of the Netherlands-based NCM group formerly operated as the short-term arm of ECGD, but has now fully adapted to life in the private sector. It offers a rapid turn-round time for credit limit requests and has introduced policies tailored to the needs of small or novice exporters. It now also offers a global policy for multinationals.

Trade Indemnity

Now owned by the French-based Euler group, this leading underwriter is well established in the export field. It has widened the scope of its products to meet the needs of small but experienced exporters trading across a wide range of markets both within and outside OECD.

Euler ownership has given it added financial resources and strengthens its ability to cater for multinationals. Trade Indemnity has also introduced a banker's endorsement and monitoring arrangement that should allow banks and factors to increase lending to exporters against the security of credit insurance cover.

Lloyd's of London

Lloyd's of London syndicates have a long established niche as underwriters of political risks in difficult markets. They have adapted to the growing importance of private buyer risk by introducing cover against commercial credit risk – through a facility led by Hiscox Syndicate 33.

Gerling Namur

In 1994 Belgium-based Namur Insurances of Credit merged with the German group Gerling to create a new multinational credit insurance group. It has become an established player in Britain, and a number of other European companies, offering cover against political and commercial risks in around 100 markets.

AIG

This is one of the world's leading composite insurers and its main operation in London provides substantial credit and political risk cover.

Coface

France's leading credit insurer now actively provides both commercial and political risk cover for British companies. It has been upgrading its global cover package for multinationals and also now offers managed credit insurance for small firms through its offshoot CIMCO.

Other underwriters

Other credit or political risk insurers include Exporters' Insurance Company, Unistrat, Peoples Insurance, CITI, Trade Underwriters Agency, Hermes, and Foreign Credit Insurance Association (FCIA). The first two offer medium as well as short-term cover.

11.2.2 Types of policy available

The vast bulk of policies written are on the so-called 'whole turnover' principle, where the insurer will cover as much of the exporter's book of debts as possible, although this may be restricted to certain markets or the activities of certain divisions, commensurate with there being a suitable spread of risk to offer the insurer.

Percentage indemnities will vary with the trade covered, buyer countries and the quality of the customer book, but are generally between 80 per cent and 95 per cent. Premiums are usually expressed as a percentage of turnover, and there will also be a small administration charge. The exporter generally justifies covering him- or herself up to a certain level by reference to an agreed set of criteria, with the insurer agreeing specific credit limits for the larger customers thereafter. Actual amounts of indemnity and first loss will vary according to the level of risk the exporter is prepared to take for himself. However, as with all credit insurance, the value of the service lies just as much in the early warning of a deteriorating situation as it does in the ability to pay claims after the event.

Policies can also be written on a 'catastrophe' basis, where the exporter will accept a very high level of first loss, or excess, him- or herself, with the insurer taking losses thereafter, either to an agreed ceiling level, or to the value of the individual credit limits agreed on the buyers. Still other policies can be written on a 'specific account' basis, although both the exporter and the insurer need to make a careful assessment of the quality and spread of the risk in these cases, and the cost is naturally likely to be higher, given the element of selection against the insurer.

Political risk cover is offered by Trade Indemnity on the basis of the three different types described above and is, of course, contingent on the overall spread of risk being offered to it. Other insurers may insist on all the above types of risk being covered, but individual firms will, of course, vary.

Lastly, some insurers (including Trade Indemnity) are able to offer policies that combine both domestic and export cover. This can be done on the basis of OECD countries and commercial risk only (as with Trade Indemnity's Multi-Market policy), or else on the wider field of all potential markets, and a degree of political risk.

In the final analysis, the exporter must view all the risks inherent in overseas trade and weigh up the price/risk benefit of taking out an insurance policy to cover him- or herself. Whilst the European Single Market had been heralded almost as the start of a 'Golden Age', it is also true that it signifies the beginning of a period of greater instability both in the UK and the EU as companies start both to look for new markets and to find their own home markets threatened. The quick replacement of cash flow and balance sheet protection offered by credit insurance should be seriously considered. The emergence of the Euro may reduce the currency risk in the EU focused markets.

11.3 Berne Union

The International Union of Credit and Investment Insurers was established in 1934 with ECGD as a founder member. It now acts as a forum for international consultation on overseas investment insurance but its main objective is to work for the international acceptance of sound principles of export credits and investment insurance, and the establishment and maintenance of discipline in the terms of credit for international trade. This is achieved partly by *ad hoc* meetings between members and partly by regular meetings and, in the case of export credit insurance, the circulation through the secretariat of information about defaulting buyers and claims experience. Day-to-day contacts have been developed with the object of restraining competition on credit. To an appreciable degree, these arrangements act as a brake upon the tendency of export credit terms to lengthen. The exchange of information on contracts in negotiation helps to curb the worst excesses of international credit competition.

■ □ ■ ■ 12

Export finance

12.1 Introduction

Trade finance has become a strong bargaining point in the conduct of international trade. Both the seller and buyer are keen to adopt positions in the negotiating strategy which will reduce their financial risk and secure the best deal possible. It involves three areas: currency, credit terms and method of payment.

The seller may opt to use his own currency, thereby ensuring profit margins are maintained and any currency risk variation passes to the buyer. Conversely, the importer may decide only to accept quotations in his own currency such as the French franc and pass any currency risk to the overseas seller based in the United States. Also, the exporter keen to get business may quote in the buyer's currency and thereby enable the buyer to compare quotations with other suppliers based in other countries.

Further options exist with the seller and/or buyer opting for a third currency such as the US dollar, thereby sharing the currency fluctuation risk. More recently (from 1 January 1999) the Euro currency, acceptable in all fifteen European Union states, removes all such currency risk and enables comparisons to be made on Euro quotes from all the EU states (see pp. 437–41).

Whenever buying or selling goods in currencies other than their own, importers and exporters become exposed to currency risk from the fluctuations in the exchange rate in the period between prices being agreed and payment being received. Management of this exposure is essential to minimize the potential risks and to maximize the profit from the underlying transactions. The technique of protecting against future exchange rate movements is usually referred to as 'hedging'. It can be exercised by three methods: spot contracts, forward contracts and currency options (see pp. 266–8).

A further factor is the granting of credit. Whereas at one time the ability to sell goods abroad depended on quality, delivery and price, a new factor has now entered the equation which tends to play an increasingly important part – the ability and willingness to give credit. The granting of credit terms, which are growing longer as buyer pressure increases, means that the exporter is without his or her money for longer periods of time. This automatically reduces cash flow and creates a finance problem for the exporter who, sooner or later, has to seek assistance from his or her bank. The financial aspect of selling goods abroad, which at one time was just a normal step in the export procedure, has now assumed such importance that it has become a problem in its own right. The task of exporting overseas has therefore become a more complex operation, demanding higher professional standards – especially in the area of trade finance. Selling overseas requires a different financial strategy compared with selling in the domestic market. Delivery takes longer, contracts are more complex and payment arrangements more complex. The prime consideration is to ensure that payments are received on schedule and that the exporter safeguards his or her financial interest as much as possible.

The criteria of the method of payment is specified in the contract of sale and is reflected in the export/commercial invoice. Choice of method will involve the following considerations:

(1) the range of available financing options;
(2) the usual contract terms adopted in the exporters/manufacturer's country;
(3) how quickly payment is required (timescale);
(4) the political situation in the importer's/buyer's country;
(5) the availability and cost of foreign currency to the importer/buyer;
(6) the terms of the contract of sale;
(7) exchange control regulations, if any;
(8) the nature of the relationship between buyer and seller;
(9) whether the cost of any credit can be arranged by the supplier (exporter) or buyer (importer);
(10) the funding resources of the importer;
(11) importer risk – non-payment of invoices, delayed payment of invoices and insolvency of buyer;
(12) exporter risk – problems in producing the correct documentation and failure to supply goods in accordance with the sales contract;
(13) country risk – political and economic instability, transfer risk, war and import/export regulations;
(14) transportation risk – risk associated with the mode of transport, e.g. marine risks and storage facilities in ports;
(15) foreign exchange risk – fluctuating exchange rates affect pricing and profit.

Many of the risks can be insured against or mitigated through the payment mechanism. However, reducing the exporter's risk may result in the counter parties having to accept a greater degree of risk and may increase costs, both of which can impact on the exporter's competitiveness.

12.2 Financing the trade cycle

The growth in international trade has greatly increased both the demand for trade finance and the degree of sophistication with which it is delivered. There is now a much greater choice of financial solutions for importers and exporters to consider when developing an international trading strategy. Organizing finance is an important part of any strategy and a key contributor to success in international trade. Indeed, the availability of finance can be a major factor in securing new business as it provides the flexibility to offer competitive terms to overseas trading partners.

The criteria for the chosen payment mechanism has been explained on p. 245 and particularly focuses on customers requirements, your assessment of the risks, the terms of trade and cost. Every company's trade cycle is unique although there will be elements (e.g. purchasing, manufacturing, shipping, credit, etc.) which are common to them all. Each stage in a trade cycle places different demands on a company's finances, but a key component in determining the overall level of working capital required for any business is the time taken between the start of the cycle (i.e. ordering goods or raw materials) and receipt of payment for corresponding sales of finished products.

Many International Trade Banks provide advice to traders to ensure, at each stage of the particular trade cycle, that a structure can be put in place to provide working capital for the different stages in the cycle and in consequence directly relate to the needs of the client business. As the bulk of international trade is undertaken on terms of 180 days or less, these facilities are an important consideration for any company involved in importing or exporting.

12.3 Export and import prices

In the uncertain situation of today, price policy has become much more important but at the same time more difficult. When rates of exchange remained stable for many years prices found their own level. Such price policy as there was, was probably not the outcome of serious research and careful consideration but just 'happened'. Because price policy could be followed for a long while, few traders were equipped to deal with frequent changes. In November 1967, exporters were faced with stark reality; few had any contingency plans to deal with the UK devaluation and over a weekend had to decide what to do about export prices.

Some held their sterling prices level and passed on to their overseas dealers and customers the 'full benefit of devaluation'. In consequence, they were flooded with orders which they were unable to manufacture, finance, or deliver on time and so lost many orders and customers. Some in similar businesses held their overseas prices level by raising their sterling export prices and in consequence upset their customers who thought they were being cheated out of a lower price to which they were entitled.

International trade was first conducted by merchant adventurers who travelled with their goods from place to place. At each place they sold what they had bought and purchased what was available locally and, for this purpose, they used either barter or what passed for currency in that place. Then they moved on to another country and repeated the process. This is basically the principle on which many multinational companies operate.

As a matter of policy, the first decision to make as regards pricing is whether to charge in each market 'what it will bear', or whether to charge a price that covers costs and gives a reasonable return on the capital employed. If one does not charge what the market will bear, somebody in that market will add the difference and make an easy profit. The final consumer is not likely to be charged any less. If on the other hand, a price based on cost is more than the market will bear, then orders will be lost.

When considering what policy adjustments to make in the wake of devaluation, it should be borne in mind that a 10 per cent devaluation does not mean a 10 per cent change in the local price. The sterling price is only a part of the final cost to the consumer. Customs duty, import and distribution costs and local mark-ups are expressed in local currency and are not affected. Duty, if *ad valorem*, may vary with the price but the rest of the additions are more or less constant and, in many cases, double the export price by the time the goods are finally sold. So, a 10 per cent devaluation corresponds to about a 5 per cent change in local price.

The whole question of pricing then will revolve around the following factors.

(1) How far minimum costs and return on capital can be related to what the market will pay. This will involve a close study of the market, its extent and potential, the strength of competitors and the elasticity of demand for profit.
(2) To what extent the fluctuation in exchange rates can be used to advantage.
(3) What credit terms are usual in the market and whether the cost of the credit is borne by the buyer.
(4) Sources of raw material and possible price changes.

As a basic principle of price policy there is much to recommend selling in the customer's currency and using the forward exchange market. It is a good marketing ploy and a courtesy to the buyer. He or she knows exactly how much the goods will cost in his or her own currency and has no preoccupation with exchange rates. By selling in foreign currency, the exporter has assumed the exchange risk him- or herself but some protection against any exchange rate fluctuations is afforded by selling the currency in the forward exchange market. This is a simple operation through one's bank and means that one is now quoted a rate of exchange at which one's currency will be exchanged when received. Moreover, with currencies such as the deutschemark, which are at a premium forward, the forward rate of exchange will be more favourable and more sterling will be received in exchange for the currency received.

It is apparent then that export prices must be established in the market place always bearing in mind the cost. There are many instances of goods being sold abroad at prices far below that which the market would be prepared to pay and, on the other hand, many cases of markets lost because the calculation of cost was too high. Marginal selling is not a sound policy; every sale should show some return.

As far as import prices are concerned it is 'what the market will pay' which is all important. Consumer goods have to be retailed at a price which the customer will pay. Raw materials must be at a price which will enable the end product to sell at a profit. Many of the bulk raw materials are sold through specialized commodity markets. Goods purchased at prices expressed in foreign currency will, of course, be subject to exchange rate fluctuations but, as in the case of exports, the exchange risk can be covered in the forward exchange market by buying the currency forward.

12.4 Payments for imports and exports

Credit terms and the method by which payment will be effected are agreed at the time the sales contract is concluded. If the relationship between the buyer and seller is good, then it may have been agreed to trade on 'open account' terms. This means simply that the seller will despatch the goods directly to the buyer, send him or her an invoice and await the remittance of payment from the buyer, as in domestic trading.

There are several methods by which the debtor may remit payment to his supplier.

(1) *Debtor's own cheque*. This is not a very satisfactory method from the creditor's point of view. Apart from the usual risk that the cheque may be unpaid, it has to be sent back through banking channels to the buyer's country for collection, thus incurring additional expenses. Cheque clearance cycles vary enormously across the world. Negotiated cheques allow the exporter to obtain the immediate value of the cheque or for a pre-set forward value date in the currency of the cheque. Lock boxes provide a fast and secure method of receiving cheque payments from overseas. Cheques are not sent to the seller but are paid directly by the buyer into the seller's bank via a PO Box number reducing the clearance cycle.

(2) *Banker's draft*. This would be a draft drawn by the buyer's bank on its correspondent bank in the exporter's country. As such it is good payment but there is always the danger that the draft may be lost in the post and a bank draft cannot be 'stopped'. A new draft could only be issued against indemnity.

(3) *Mail transfer (MT)*. This is the most common method of payment. The debtor instructs his or her bank to request its correspondent bank in the exporter's country to pay the specific amount to the exporter. The whole procedure is done by entries over banking accounts; the buyer's bank debits his account and credits the account of the correspondent bank which, on receipt of the payment instructions, passes a reciprocal entry over its account with the remitting bank and pays the money over to the exporter. The instructions between the banks may be by ordinary mail, swift or air mail.

(4) *Telegraphic transfer (TT)*. The procedure is similar to that of MT except that the instructions are sent by tele-transmission. This means that the payment is effected more quickly.

Where 'open account' terms have not been agreed, then it is for the exporter to arrange for payment to be collected from the buyer. The usual way in which this is done is by the use of bills of exchange. This is the traditional method of claiming that which is due from the debtor, and has been used as a basis for international trade throughout its history.

Instead of merely sending the documents to the debtor with only the covering invoice, the exporter draws a bill of exchange on the debtor for the sum due and attaches the documents to the bill. This is then sent through banking channels for presentation to the buyer. There are several advantages in the employment of bills:

(1) The bill of exchange is an instrument long recognized by trade custom and by the law; there is in consequence an established code of practice in relation to bills.

(2) The bill is a specific demand on the debtor and, if it is drawn in proper form in respect of debt justly due, the debtor refuses it at his or her peril.

(3) The bill is a useful instrument of finance (Chapter 14).

(4) The bill provides a useful mechanism for the granting to an overseas buyer of a pre-arranged period of credit. Thus if an exporter has, for some reason, to offer his or her buyer a period of credit, say 90 days, then the bill can be drawn at 90 days sight. At the same time, the exporter can maintain a degree of control over the shipping documents by authorizing release of the documents on payment, or acceptance of the bill. The bill does provide an instrument on which action can be taken at law.

It should be noted that the drawing of a bill of exchange on the buyer does not guarantee payment and the seller has lost control of the goods to some extent as they are out of his or her country. Moreover, he or she may have to arrange for storage and insurance or even reshipment.

The procedure for the exporter, having obtained the shipping documents, is to draw the bill and lodge it with his or her bank, together with the documents for collection. When lodging the bill, the exporter must give to his or her bank very precise and complete instructions as to what action to take in certain circumstances: whether to forward the bill by air mail, etc., and ask for proceeds to be remitted by telex/fax or air mail; whether the documents are to be released against payment or acceptance of the bill; whether the bill is to be 'protested' if dishonoured; whether the goods should be stored and insured if not taken up by the buyer; whether rebate may be given for early payment; who is the Case of Need to whom the collecting bank may refer in case of dispute (usually the exporter's agent).

The exporter's bank will forward the bill and documents to its correspondent bank in the buyer's country passing on exactly the instructions received from the exporter. The correspondent bank (collecting bank) will present the bill and documents to the buyer, and release the documents to the buyer in accordance with the instructions received. If the arrangement was for payment to be made immediately then the bill of exchange will be drawn at 'sight' and the instructions will be to release documents against payment (D/P). If a period of credit has been agreed, then the bill will be drawn at say '90 days' sight' and the instructions will be for the documents to be released against acceptance by the buyer of the bill (D/A). In this case, the buyer signs his or her acceptance across the face of the bill, which now becomes due for payment in 90 days' time and the buyer obtains the documents of title to the goods. The collecting bank will advise the remitting bank of the date of acceptance, and hold the bill until maturity, when the collecting bank will present it to the buyer for payment. In case of dishonour, and if so instructed, the collecting bank will arrange 'protest' by a notary. This procedure provides legal proof that the bill was presented to the drawee and was dishonoured, and enables action to be taken in the courts without further preliminaries.

The procedures and responsibilities of the banks and other parties are laid down in the 'Uniform Rules for Collection' issued by the International Chamber of Commerce – Publication No 522 – 1995 Revision, in force as of 1 January 1996 and subscribed to by the major banks throughout the world.

The method of collecting payment described above is based on the documentary bill, but in certain circumstances use may be made of a 'clean' bill, that is, a bill to which no documents are attached. Such bills may be drawn for the collection of monies due for services, etc. or for any debt which is not a payment for goods. A 'clean' bill may also be used to obtain payment for goods sent on 'open account', especially where payment is overdue.

Because they are a traditional and accepted means of obtaining payment in international trade, bills of exchange can be used, with one or two exceptions, throughout the world. In the case of some markets, it would be unwise to operate without the protection a bill can provide.

12.5 Documentary credits and allied documents

Apart from 'cash with order', the documentary credit provides the most satisfactory method of obtaining payment. It provides security of payment to the exporter, and enables the buyer to ensure that he or she receives the goods as ordered and delivered in the way he or she requires. It is an arrangement whereby the buyer instructs his or her bank to establish a credit in favour of the seller. The buyer's bank (issuing bank) undertakes, or authorizes its correspondent bank in the exporter's country, to pay the exporter a sum of money (normally the invoice price of the goods) against presentation of shipping documents which are specified in the credit. It is a mandatory contract and completely independent of the sales contract. It is concerned only with documents and not the goods to which the documents refer. Liability for payment now rests with the issuing bank and not the buyer.

The usual form of these credits is the 'irrevocable' credit, which means that it cannot be cancelled or amended without the agreement of the beneficiary (the exporter) and all other parties. Such a credit, opened by a reputable bank in a sound country, means that the exporter can rely on payment being made as soon as he or she has shipped the goods and produced the documents called for in accordance with the terms of the credit. The security provided by an irrevocable credit may be further enhanced if the bank in the exporter's country (advising bank) is requested by the issuing bank to add its 'confirmation'. The exporter then has a 'confirmed irrevocable credit' and he or she need look no further than his or her own local bank for payment. With a credit which is not 'confirmed', however, the point of payment is the issuing bank (abroad), although the advising bank would usually be prepared to negotiate with recourse.

The credit will set out in detail a description of the goods: price per unit and packing; name and address of the beneficiary; the voyage, that is, port of shipment and port of destination; whether the price is FOB, CFR or CIF; and whether part shipments and transshipment are allowed. In some cases, the ship will be nominated.

Details of insurance (if CIF) and the risks to be covered will also be shown. The credit will specify a latest date for shipment and an expiry date which is the latest date for presentation of documents. The basic documents which are usually called for are as follows.

12.5.1 Invoice

The amount must not exceed the credit amount. If terms such as 'about' or *'circa'* are used, a tolerance of 10 per cent is allowed (in respect of quantity the tolerance is 3 per cent). The description of the goods on the invoice and the packing must be exact and agree with the credit. An essential part of the description includes the marks and numbers on the packages. These must appear on the invoice. The invoice should be in the name of the buyer.

12.5.2 Bills of lading

This is the document of title to the goods (see pp. 301–15), without which the buyer will not be able to obtain delivery from the shipping company. The credit will call for a full set (they are usually issued in a set of three). They must be clean, that is, bearing no superimposed clauses derogatory to the condition of the goods such as 'inadequate packing', 'used drums', 'on deck', etc. Unless the credit has specifically permitted the circumstances contained in the clause, the negotiating bank will call for an indemnity. The bills of lading must show the goods to be 'on board' – 'received for shipment' bills are not acceptable. They may, however, have a subsequent notation, dated and signed, which states the goods to be 'on board' and they are then acceptable. Under the regulations set out in the 'Uniform Customs and Practice for Documentary Credits' – ICC Publication No 500 – 1993 Revision in force as of 1 January 1994 – articles 23–26, the following bills of lading will be accepted:

(1) Through bills issued by shipping companies or their agents even though they cover several modes of transport.
(2) Short form bills of lading which indicate some or all of the conditions of carriage by reference to a source or document other than the bill of lading.
(3) Bills covering unitized cargoes such as those on pallets or in containers.

Charter party bills of lading which do not contain the full conditions of carriage but are detailed in a separate charter party agreement are not acceptable unless specifically allowed in the credit under article 25 of UCP500.

There are many variations for the signing of the Bill of Lading by the carrier, the ship's Master or a named agent signing on their behalf. Any agent issuing a bill of lading must name the carrier on whose behalf they are acting. To constitute naming the carrier, the shipping company name appearing on the bill of lading must be specifically identified 'as carrier'. An extensive list of acceptable variations was published by the ICC in their position paper No 4 dated 1 September 1994.

Unless specifically authorized in the credit, bills of the following type will not be accepted:

(1) Bills of lading issued by forwarding agents.
(2) Bills which are issued under and are subject to a charter party.
(3) Bills covering shipments by sailing vessels.

The bills must be made out 'to the order of the shipper' and endorsed in blank. If the sales contract is CIF or CFR, then the bills must be marked 'freight paid'. The general description of the goods including marks and numbers must match the invoice. The voyage and ship, if named, must be as stated in the credit. Unless transshipment is expressly prohibited in the credit, bills indicating transshipment will be accepted provided the entire voyage is covered by the same bill. Part shipments are permitted unless the credit states otherwise. Besides stating an expiry date for presentation of documents, credits should also stipulate a specified period of time after the issuance of the bills during which the documents must be presented for payment. If no such period is stipulated in the credit, banks will refuse documents presented to them later than 21 days after the issuance of the bills of lading.

12.5.3 Sea Waybill

This document (see p. 313) has been developed to reduce the problem inherent in short voyage where the documentation (bill of lading) is not available at the time of arrival of the vessel. It is also used increasingly by multinational industries and their subsidiaries (see p. 314). However, it is not a document of title. It is a receipt for goods and evidence of carriage and should be handled in a similar manner to an air waybill.

An original document is not required as delivery is made to the named consignee against proof of identity – usually a delivery order on the consignees headed stationery. The shipper can vary the consignee and delivery instructions at any time prior to delivery. To counteract this problem certain carriers will apply control or waiver clauses to the waybills to meet the requirements of buyers, insurers and financiers. Sea waybills cannot be issued 'to order' or to order of a named party. The non-negotiable sea waybill provisions are found in article 24 of UCP500.

12.5.4 Multi-modal transport document

When goods are carried by more than one mode of transport (usually in containers), a combined (multi-modal) transport document is recommended as the multi-modal transport operator accepts liability for carriage of the goods throughout the entire journey (see p. 308). Where part of the journey is undertaken by sea, some types of multi-modal transport document can convey title to the goods. The multi-modal transport document provisions are found in article 26 of UCP500.

12.5.5 Air waybill or air consignment note

Goods which are transported by air require a waybill to act as a receipt for despatch (see p. 297). It will usually show that the goods are consigned either to the buyer or to the issuing bank and may bear a notified party name and address. Unlike bills of lading, air waybills are not issued in sets and do not convey title to the goods. The copy marked – original[3] (for shipper) should normally be presented under a documentary credit.

The principal requirements for this document under a letter of credit include:

(1) the correct shipper and consignee;
(2) the airports of departure and destination;
(3) the goods description must be consistent with that shown on other documents;
(4) any weights, measures or shipping marks must agree with those shown on other documents;
(5) it must be signed and dated by the actual carrier or by the named agent of a named carrier – for example EFGH Forwarding Ltd as agents for the carrier Air India (if the credit states that a house air waybill is acceptable, the forwarder's signature alone will suffice);
(6) it must state whether freight has been paid or is payable at destination.

If required by the letter of credit, it must also carry a specific notation stating the actual flight date, otherwise the date of despatch will be taken to be the date of issuance of the air waybill. The provisions of the Air Transport document are found in article 27 of UCP 500.

12.5.6 Insurance

The document must be as stated in the credit (policy or certificate) and issued by an insurance company or its agent. Cover notes issued by brokers are not acceptable.

The details on the policy must match those on the bills of lading – voyage, ship, marks and numbers, etc. It must also be in the same currency as the credit and endorsed in blank. The amount covered should be at least the invoice amount; credits usually call for invoice value plus 10 per cent. The policy must be dated not later than the date of shipment as evidenced by the bill of lading. The risks covered should be those detailed in the credit. If cover against 'all risks' is called for (which is obtainable) a policy which states that it covers all insurable risks will be acceptable. The provisions for insurance are found in articles 34–36 of UCP500.

According to circumstances, the credit may call for other documents such as a consular certificate; a packing list; a certificate of origin; quality, analysis or health certificate (ensures to buyer that the goods are as ordered); an air waybill; railway (CIM) or road (CMR) consignment notes or Post Office receipt; and pre-shipment inspection documentation including Certificate of Inspection/clean report of findings (see pp. 328–30) and courier receipt (small parcels/packets).

The credit may stipulate a last shipment date and the bill of lading must show shipment by that date. Extension of the shipment date automatically extends the expiry date but not vice versa.

It is very important that exporters, when they receive advice of a credit established in their favour, check the details immediately to see that the goods and terms agree with the sales contract, and they can comply with all the terms and provide all the documents required. If any amendment is required, this can then be taken up with the advising bank in good time for action to be taken before expiry.

Besides the basic irrevocable credit (confirmed or not), there are revocable credits which, as the name implies, can be cancelled or amended at any time without notice to the beneficiary. They do not constitute a legally binding undertaking by the banks concerned. Once transmitted and made available at the advising bank, however, its cancellation or modification is only effective when that bank has received notice thereof and any payment made before the receipt of such notice is reimbursable by the issuing bank. The value of these credits as security for payment is plainly doubtful. They are used mainly for parent companies and subsidiaries, where a continuing series of shipments is concerned or as an indication of good intent.

Where a buyer wishes to provide his or her supplier with the security of payment by documentary credit, but at the same time requires a period of credit, he or she may instruct his or her bank to issue a credit calling for a bill of exchange drawn at so many days after sight instead of the usual sight draft; this would, of course, be an irrevocable credit. In this case, the beneficiary, when presenting the documents, would not receive immediate cash as under a sight credit but his or her term bill would be accepted by the bank. It could then be discounted in the money market at the finest rates. Thus the beneficiary would still receive payment, but the buyer would not be called upon to pay until the bill matured – see the documentary credit flow chart illustrated in Figure 12.1.

12.5.7 Methods of settlement and availability of documentary credits

According to UCP500 (article 10) documentary credit may be made available in one of four ways as detailed below.

(1) *Sight payment.* Payment is made to the seller locally upon presentation of conforming documents. A sight draft is usually called for although payment can be made against documents alone. If payment to the seller is made before the account is debited, interest will be charged from the date of payment to the date that the paying bank is reimbursed. If the buyer wishes, he or she can authorize the paying bank to claim payment by tele-transmission and have the seller's account debited upon receipt of the claim.

(2) *Deferred payment credit.* This type of credit does not require the presentation of a draft. The nominated bank is authorized to debit the issuing bank's account at a future date against presentation of conforming documents. The date for payment is defined in the documentary credit, usually as a specific number of days after the date of despatch of goods or after the date of presentation of the documents. It has become increasingly popular where the buyer does not wish the credit period to be represented by a bill of exchange as usually, under local law, it attracts stamp duty.

Consequently, when documents are presented 'in order' by the seller, the bank does not accept a bill of exchange but instead gives a letter of undertaking to the seller advising him or her when he or she will receive his or her money.

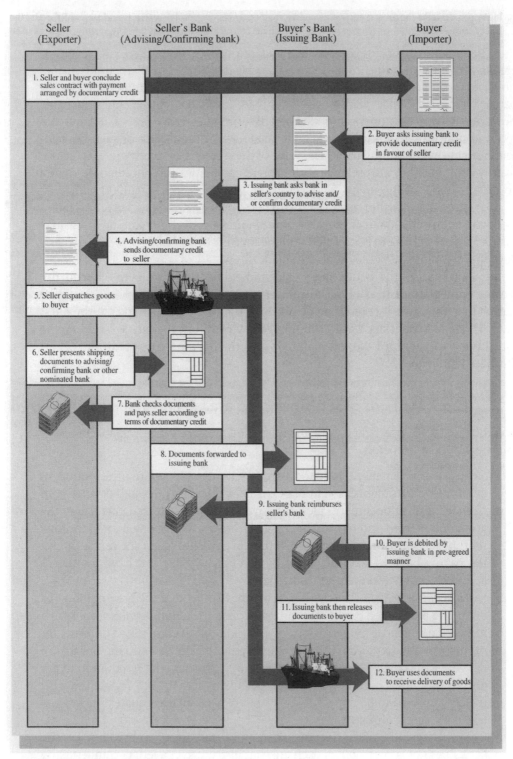

FIGURE 12.1 Documentary credit flowchart

Reproduced courtesy HBSC Midland Bank plc

The main disadvantage is that, should the exporter wish to receive his or her money immediately, he or she does not have a bill of exchange to have discounted. Hence, if the credit is unconfirmed, the undertaking to effect payment on the due date is that of the issuing bank. Payment will only be effected on the due date by the nominated bank after taking account of the same factors involving sight payments. However, if the credit is confirmed, the undertaking to pay is made by the confirming bank. Payment will then be made on the due date by the nominated bank (if any) or by the confirming bank.

(3) *Negotiation Sight or usance drafts* may be drawn and negotiated by a bank. The credit may be made freely negotiable with any bank or negotiation may be restricted to a bank nominated by the issuing bank. Under this type of credit, the seller is responsible for any negotiation interest unless the negotiating bank is specially authorized by the buyer to charge interest to his or her account.

(4) *Acceptance credits*. This type of credit requires a presentation of a usance draft drawn on the bank nominated as accepting bank. The draft is accepted by the bank, payable at a future date, usually fixed in the documentary credit as a specific number of days from the date of despatch of goods.

Originally this facility was provided by merchant banks. The bank establishes its own credit in favour of the exporter. The credit provides for bills to be drawn by the exporter on the bank which are accepted by the latter and can then be discounted in the money market at the finest rates. It is usual for such credits to run parallel with the bills drawn by the exporter on his or her overseas buyer and which he or she lodges with the bank for collection. The bills under the credit will be drawn on the same terms as those of the buyers and in due course the payment received for the commercial bills will meet the dues to the bank on its acceptances.

12.6 Transferable credits

Article 48 of UCP500 covers the provisions of transferable credits, which we will now examine. These arise where the exporter or seller is obtaining the goods from a third party, say the actual manufacturer, and as a middleman, does not have the resources to buy outright and await payment from his or her overseas buyer. Part or all of their rights and obligations under the credit are transferred to the actual supplier of the goods (transferee). The credit is established in favour of the middleman seller (prime beneficiary), and authorizes the advising bank to accept instructions from the prime beneficiary to make the credit available, in whole or in part, to one or more third parties (second beneficiaries). The credit is then advised to the second beneficiary in the terms and conditions of the original, except that the amount and unit price are reduced and the shipment and expiry dates shortened. The original credit is for the price the buyer is paying to the prime beneficiary, but the latter will be obtaining the goods at a lower price and so the credit is transferred for a smaller amount. When the second beneficiary presents shipping documents, he or she obtains payment for his or her invoice price, and the prime beneficiary is called upon to substitute his or her own invoice and receive the difference (i.e. profit). The negotiating bank then has documents in accordance with the original credit.

Where there is more than one second beneficiary, the credit must permit part shipments. If the prime beneficiary does not wish his or her buyer and supplier to be aware of each other, he or she may request that his or her name be substituted for that of the opener on the transfer credit, and that shipping documents be in the name of a third party, blank endorsed.

In the event that the name of the ultimate supplier is known, the buyer can restrict the transfer to that party. Otherwise the buyer could be faced with receiving goods from an unknown supplier without knowledge as to their integrity or ability to provide goods of the required quality. Any subsequent presentation of documents may be made by the transferee rather than the original beneficiary.

12.7 Back-to-back credits

Back-to-back credits arise in circumstances similar to those of the transferable credit and particularly where the supplier as well as the buyer is overseas. In this case, the middleman receives a credit in his or her favour from the buyer and asks his or her bank to establish a credit in favour of his or her supplier against the security of the credit in his or her own favour. There are two separate credits, not one as in the case of a transferable credit, and this can create problems in the matching of documents and credit terms.

Consider the example of a trader who identified that metals readily available in Eastern Europe were urgently required in India. However, in view of the sums involved, the seller insisted that payment by the trader be by means of a Letter of Credit. As the ultimate buyer in India was also willing to issue a Letter of Credit in favour of the trader, the two documents were matched and the deal was successfully concluded to the satisfaction of the East European supplier, Indian buyer and the traders. Back-to-back Letters of Credit are complicated and exporters are advised to contact their international bank for advice.

12.8 Revolving credits

Revolving credits are used where there are shipments in a series at intervals and the parties wish the programme to proceed without interruption. An example would be a structured work flow such as a production run or growth season. A credit is established for a certain sum and quantity of goods with a provision that, when a shipment has been made and documents presented and paid, the credit automatically becomes re-available in its original form and another shipment can be made, and so on.

Such credits can revolve either by time or by amount. In the case of a credit which revolves by time, a stated amount is available in a given period. The full amount is then automatically available when a new period is entered. A credit which revolves by amount is usually expressed as being available up to a fixed amount for anyone drawing.

If the credit revolves automatically the amount drawn immediately becomes available again on the conditions specified in the credit. For credits which do not revolve automatically, each instalment can only be reinstated by way of an amendment to the credit. This option gives the client more control over the operation of the credit.

A further variant is a cumulative revolving credit which, for credits which revolve by time, allows undrawn amounts in a particular time period to be carried forward to a subsequent period. A non-cumulative credit means that any undrawn portion cannot be carried forward in this way.

12.9 Red clause credits

Originally a feature of the Australian wool trade, red clause credits contain a clause (traditionally written in red ink) authorizing the nominated bank to advance a proportion of the value of the credit to the seller before shipping documents are presented. This enables the seller to purchase raw materials or to pay other costs (e.g. transportation) prior to receiving full payment once confirming documents have been presented.

Advances of this nature are entirely at the buyer's risk and are generally made against a simple statement from the seller that they will refund the amount if they do not ship the goods as required. Unless the buyer has made other arrangements, the buyer's account will be debited as soon as an advance has been made.

Advance payments under a credit are more common where they are payable to the seller upon production of a bank guarantee. In this case, the buyer would be able to claim from the guarantor bank if the seller did not repay the advance. If the buyer has any reason to doubt the standing of the guarantor bank, it would be advisable to have such guarantees issued (not simply advised) through the buyer's bank or another major bank well-known to the buyer.

12.10 Bank finance for exports factoring and forfaiting

Theoretically, a company should be able to finance all its operations from the resources available to it, that is, its capital plus whatever it is able to borrow from the bank. Its capital will depend on how much the members of the company are prepared to invest in the enterprise, and its borrowing from the bank will depend on such factors as the balance sheet figures, profit and loss, turnover, etc. or on the security it can offer by way of mortgages, life policies and stocks. Both these sources are subject to strict limitations and, for reasons already mentioned above, they are bound to prove inadequate for a company expanding its export trade. To meet the cash flow problems engendered by long credit terms, extra sources of finance must be tapped over and above the basic sources of capital and bank lending. This finance can best be found through channels relative to the export transactions themselves and, in particular, to the method of payment. Let us examine the various methods by which payment is made and what type of finance it is linked to.

(1) *Sales on open account.* Here the exporter is entirely dependent on the goodwill of the buyer to remit payment when due. Admittedly, the outstanding debts will increase the debtor item on the company's balance sheet and may, therefore, enable it to obtain additional overdraft facilities from the bank. The best answer to the problem of finance in this case would be by the use of the services of a factoring company or credit insurance resource (pp. 259–61).

(2) *Collection by means of bills of exchange drawn on the buyer.* Extra finance may be obtained by discounting the bills with the bank or obtaining loan accommodation against the bills outstanding for collection. The bank has some element of security in the documents, covering the goods, which are attached to the bills. The common short form bill of lading has replaced in some trades the traditional shipping company 'long form' bills. It is identical in legal and practical terms to the traditional bills but is simpler and can be used with any shipping line. The possibility of obtaining bank finance in this way is enhanced if the export sale is covered by a credit insurance policy, the rights under the policy being assigned to the bank.

(3) *Documentary credits.* Under a confirmed irrevocable letter of credit, the exporter is assured of payment immediately he or she has shipped the goods and presents correct documents to the bank and so his or her need for finance is reduced. With an unconfirmed letter of credit, however, payment is still subject to the risk of non-transfer by the issuing bank, but in these circumstances provision may be available under a basic credit insurance policy. In both cases the exporters may be able to obtain some extra help from his or her bank to produce and ship the goods on the strength of the payment assured under the credit.

As outlined above, export finance is also available from merchant banks by means of an acceptance credit facility.

The services of a confirming house, which acts for the buyer, will provide payment promptly on shipment as the confirming house arranges the credit terms required by the buyer. Exporting through an export merchant will also provide ready cash as the merchant will buy the goods (making it a home sale) and handle the sale to the overseas buyer him- or herself.

12.11 Standby letters of credit

This type of credit differs from other types, in that the buyer and seller hope it will never be drawn upon. Standby letters of credit are often used as security for open account trading where the seller requires some kind of 'back up' in the event of the buyer not paying for the goods. They normally require the issuing bank to make payment to the seller upon presentation of documents evidencing non-payment by the importer. They are also commonly used in some countries as a substitute for a bank guarantee which, due to the regulations in that country, are not generally acceptable; a prime example of this method is seen in the USA.

In such instances, standby letters of credit have the advantage of being subject to the Uniform Customs and Practice for Documentary Credits Brochure 400, whereas at the moment there are no internationally agreed regulations for bank guarantees.

12.12 Counter-trade

During the past ten years the volume of world trade conducted under counter-trade terms has much increased. Today it features in the trading techniques of over 100 countries and represents up to 10 per cent of world trade. Basically, counter-trade is an umbrella term for a whole range of commercial mechanisms for reciprocal trade. These mechanisms include barter, counter-purchase, offset, buyback, evidence accounts and switch trading. The common characteristic of counter-trade arrangements is that export sales to a particular market are made conditional upon undertakings to accept imports from that market. For example, an exporter may sell machinery to country X on condition that it accepts agricultural products from country X in payment. Simple barter deals like this are unusual, and most counter-trade deals are much more involved.

Exporters are aware of the potential demands for and the complexities of counter-trade, since it has over recent years become a common feature of trade with more than half the countries in the world. Counter-trade can be a complex, expensive and uncertain mode of trading. It has the potential to distort and disrupt the growth of trade, inasmuch as it replaces the pressures of competition and market forces with reciprocity, protection and price setting. It introduces an unfair bias against small and medium-sized firms who may be less able to handle the additional costs and staff effort entailed. It increases the risks that subsidized (often low-grade) goods will be dumped in the home market (although most of these in practice go to Third World markets).

Counter-trade is an inherently *ad hoc* activity. The mechanics vary according to local regulations and requirements, the nature of the goods to be exported and the current priorities of the parties involved.

12.12.1 Forms of counter-trade

Counter-purchase

Concurrently with, and as a condition of, securing a sales order, the exporter undertakes to purchase goods and services from the country concerned. There are two parallel but separate contracts, one for the principal order which is paid for on normal cash or credit terms, and another for the counter-purchase. The value of the counter-purchase undertaking may vary in value between 10 per cent and 100 per cent (or even more) of the original export order. The agreement can vary from a general declaration of intent to a binding contract specifying the goods and services to be supplied, the markets in which they may be sold, the penalties for non-performance and, perhaps, other matters. The goods offered may be quite unrelated to those exported, and the agreement may involve parties unrelated to the sales contract. Counter-purchase is the most common mode of counter-trade, particularly with Eastern Europe and with a number of developing countries, notably Indonesia.

Barter

The direct exchange of goods for goods. The principal exports are paid for with goods (or services) supplied from the importing market. A single contract covers both flows; in the simplest case no cash is involved. In practice, supply of the principal exports is often held up until sufficient revenue has been earned from selling the bartered goods. Though less common than counter-purchase, barter has been sought by some African and Latin American countries with extensive currency restrictions, and by some oil-dependent countries.

Buyback

A form of barter, in which suppliers of capital plant or equipment agree to repayment in the future output of the investment concerned. For example, exporters of equipment for a chemical works may be repaid with part of the resulting output from that work. Most common in connection with exports of process plant, mining equipment and similar orders, buyback arrangements tend to be much longer term and for much larger amounts than counter-purchase or simple barter deals. The CIS favours long-term buyback on policy grounds as a form of industrial cooperation.

Offset

A condition of exporting some products, especially those embodying advanced technology, to some markets is that the exporter incorporates into his final products specified materials, components or sub-assemblies, procured within the importing country. This has long been an established feature of trade in defence systems and aircraft, but it is becoming more common in other sectors, especially where the importing country is seeking to develop its own industrial capabilities. A variant of offset arises in some large contracts, for which the importing country often demands that successful bidders establish local production and other forms of long-term industrial cooperation.

Switch trading (or swap deals)

Imbalances in long-term bilateral trading agreements, usually between East European countries and developing nations, sometimes lead to the accumulation of uncleared credit surpluses in one or other country; for example, Brazil at one time had a large credit surplus with Poland. Such surpluses can sometimes be tapped by third parties, so that (for example) French exports to Brazil might be financed from the sale of

Polish goods to France or elsewhere. Such transactions are known as 'switch' or 'swap' deals, because they typically involve switching the documentation (and destination) of goods on the high seas. Switch deals can be very complex, involving a chain of buyers, sellers and brokers in different markets.

Evidence accounts

Companies or traders with a significant level of continuing business in certain markets may be required to arrange counter-purchased exports from those markets at least equivalent to their own imports with the country concerned. For example, a multinational firm with a local manufacturing subsidiary in a developing country may be required to ensure counter-purchased exports of equivalent value to their subsidiary's imports of materials and equipment. Since it is not practical to balance this kind of trade item by item, the firm may maintain an 'evidence account', debiting its own imports and crediting the exports it has arranged over a period. The evidence account must be maintained more or less in balance year by year.

There are many variants to these broad categories, depending on the market, the exports concerned, outside circumstances (e.g. trends in commodity prices) and the expertise of those involved. It is not unusual for a large export deal to involve several counter-trade arrangements (e.g. some long-term buyback, plus some counter-purchase or barter to finance initial down payments). In general terms, counter-trade is sought for one or more of four main reasons.

(1) To finance trade which, due to lack of commercial credit or convertible currency, would otherwise be precluded.
(2) To exploit a buyers' market to obtain better terms of trade or similar benefits.
(3) To protect or stimulate the output of domestic industries (including agriculture and minerals extraction).
(4) As a reflection of political and economic policies which seek to plan and balance overseas trade.

The particular consideration applying, and the national counter-trade requirements to which they give rise, vary in every market. An understanding of the particular issues in a given country can often enable an exporter to propose more flexible or cheaper alternatives to onerous counter-trade obligations which none the less satisfy the needs of the importer or his or her principals.

12.12.2 Counter-trade markets

Western industrial markets

Counter-trade remains unusual in trade between the industrialized countries, which transact 75 per cent of their trade between one another. The major exceptions have arisen in defence, aviation and large high technology deals, which often involve an element of direct offset or closely related counter-purchase. In recent years, some European countries (notably Portugal and Greece) have sought counter-purchase for other large export orders, but only on an *ad hoc* basis. Australia and New Zealand, which require offset for public sector purchases, are the only OECD countries with mandatory counter-trade requirements.

East European markets

Counter-trade has been an established feature of trade with the East European markets since 1945, and affects on average something over 25 per cent of their trade with the West.

Developing countries

The main growth in counter-trade demands in recent years has come from the less developed countries (LDCs) of Latin America, Africa and Asia, largely reflecting the effects on their external trade of the international recession. Common factors have been the LDCs' inability to secure or to service trade credit due to accumulated debt problems; loss of currency-earning capabilities because of depressed commodity markets; and a wish to improve their access to Western markets and industrial know-how. Although many LDCs have on occasion sought counter-trade arrangements – usually commodity counter-purchase or barter – the number of deals actually transacted has been constrained by the lack of effective organizational arrangements in the LDCs and by their inability to provide sufficient marketable goods for the counter-purchase. Indonesia was the first LDC to introduce mandatory counter-trade requirements and has since been followed by a number of others; a further group have more or less formal administrative rules with a similar effect. But even in Indonesia, less than 10 per cent of external trade has in practice involved counter-trade.

Oil exporters

In certain oil-producing countries – especially Libya and Iran – exporters bidding for public sector contracts may be asked to accept oil in exchange for goods. There may be several motives for this, the most likely being a desire on the part of the oil producers to secure an assured outlet for their oil at a high rate. By comparison with most other commodities, oil is a relatively serviceable means of exchange, since the size, sophistication and efficiency of the world oil market means that it can be converted into cash fairly easily. Oil barter deals are in essence straightforward transactions; goods are exchanged for oil rather than cash. All the normal considerations which apply to cash deals, notably the need to earn a profit, should be applied to oil barter. The addition, however, of two extra parties to the contract, the oil-producing company and the oil-distributing company, whose interest in the contract do not necessarily coincide with those of the principal participants (i.e. the exporter and the end-buyer), inevitably complicates the issue. The responsibility for overcoming those complications normally rests with the exporter, since he or she is the link between the other three parties.

Counter-trade is a growth market and one for the experienced professional. Approximately one in ten succeed and even the successful transactions can prove more expensive and more difficult than originally foreseen. Major risks include: loss of profits on the principal exports because the costs of counter-trade have not been anticipated; contractual commitments to purchase large quantities of unmarketable goods without any means of disposing of them; and cancellation of export orders because of other parties' failures to meet counter-trade obligations.

A few large exporting firms which regularly encounter counter-trade demands, for example, those regularly trading with East European markets, maintain an in-house capability to handle counter-traded goods on their own account. For the great majority of exporters, however, it is strongly advisable to obtain the assistance of outside specialists. Specialist services of different kinds are offered by trading houses, brokers, consultants and/or agents, bankers and suppliers of market intelligence, usually for a fixed fee or commission.

Additional costs, which exporters should anticipate, will arise from the discount or 'disagio' necessary to dispose of the goods taken in counter-trade. The disagio reflects the marketability of the goods concerned and varies between 2–3 per cent for certain high-grade minerals and commodities to as much as 25–30 per cent for low-quality manufactured goods and machinery. The exporter will be advised to include as far as possible sufficient margin in his or her selling price to cover these costs, but the scope for this can be constrained in competitive bidding.

The simplest method of handling counter-purchase undertakings is to assign the obligation – for a fee – to a third-party trading house or broker, whereafter the exporter need have no further involvement in the counter-trade transaction. Sometimes the third-party trader can be an open signatory to the counter-purchase contract, but often the 'demandeur' country will insist on dealing only with the exporter. Where local counter-trade requirements are not clear-cut or institutionalized, that is in most markets, extended and sensitive negotiations will be necessary, in parallel with those over the exports, before arrangements are settled. The retention of specialized advice during these negotiations will usually pay for itself, if only through the avoidance of costly mistakes. Often the exporter's bankers will be able to advise what support is appropriate and make the necessary arrangements.

12.13 Factoring

The practice of exporters using factoring companies is very much on the increase. Their prime function is to administer the sales ledgers and collect payments once the goods have been shipped. Such factoring companies provide a complete range of services which cover those aspects of exporting, so leaving the manufacturer free to concentrate on export production and sales. For a small service charge of between 0.75 and 3 per cent of turnover, they will provide multi-currency and multi-language sales accounting backed by credit management, which is exercised in the customer's country by the factor's own employees or agents. Also included in this service charge, embracing the administrative and credit cover service, is 100 per cent protection against losses due to the insolvency of the customer and, in some cases, protection against political risk and exchange rate fluctuations. For advances against invoices until they are paid, the factoring company usually charges 1.5 per cent over the base rate. Factoring cannot effectively meet the particular needs of every industry and the most suitable companies are likely to have an expanding turnover in excess of £200 000 and to be selling consumer goods, light industrial products or services on short-term open account credit to buyers in the developed countries of the world. Products include textiles, clothing, food distribution, consumer durables, engineering and electronic equipment.

Basically, factoring operates on the principle that an exporter has an agreement with a factoring company to buy all the exporter's receivables in agreed market(s). The factor becomes responsible for collecting customer payments and taking the credit risk, whilst the factor will pay the exporter 'on account' a proportion (usually up to 85 per cent) of the credit approved sales immediately upon delivery – if the exporter so wishes – with the balance being paid when the customer pays the factor or becomes insolvent. If the buyer does not pay, the factor effects payment of the balance after a set period (typically 120 days) from the date payment fell due, which allows time for any problems to be resolved between the commercial parties. Factoring has five key features: export credit assessment of one's customers; 100 per cent protection against customer failure; efficient collection of outstanding invoices; flexible finance geared to one's volume of sales; and cover against foreign exchange risks.

The advantages to the exporter of using a factoring service are; that it expands sales in overseas markets by offering prospective customers the same terms and conditions as local competitors; offers open account terms, merely invoicing the customer and granting credit terms typical in the customer's market; is fully covered against credit losses; improves cash flow by fast collection and remittance, as well as through savings in administration costs; and it provides a flexible source of working capital linked directly to the growth in export sales.

Export factoring is most suited for short-term debts (typically up to 90 days) involving the sale of products or services which are complete at the point of invoicing and for trade with those parts of the world in which an open account is the accepted method of transacting business. Most factors operate a 'two factor' system whereby a correspondent factor in the buyer's country is used to assess the credit standing of the buyer. Factoring can also provide finance where credit protection is already available to an exporter through a credit insurance policy.

Factoring will also help importers and buyers by expanding their purchasing power without using existing bank credit lines; enabling them to buy goods without incurring the delays and complications of opening lines of credit; generating new sources of product supply; and providing a local point for payment in their own country.

Many factoring companies are members of a worldwide organization called Factors Chain International (FCI), formed in 1968 with 80 member factoring companies located in 30 countries. Membership of such an organization provides expertise in each of the 30 countries in the business of managing trade credit and, for the exporter, lessens the problems which can arise through differences in language, law and trade practice thereby facilitating the exporter's development of overseas business.

12.14 Forfaiting

Forfaiting is a method of international trade finance involving the discounting of bank-guaranteed overseas trade bills or notes. It has no recourse to the exporter as he or she surrenders or relinquishes his or her right in return for cash payment from the forfaiter. In such circumstances, the exporter agrees to surrender his or her rights to claims for payment on goods or services which have been delivered to the buyer. Any type of trade debt can be forfaited (i.e. surrendered for cash) but the most common is trade payee; bill of exchange accepted by the buyer; or promissory notes from the buyer. A forfaiter can provide finance for any type and duration of trade transaction but usually credit is provided for the export of capital goods which require finance for periods of between three and ten years.

Forfaiting is a simple form of trade finance involving the purchase of trade receivables from the beneficiary on a totally without recourse basis. It was introduced into Europe during the late 1950s, primarily to finance the sale of capital goods to Eastern European and Third World countries. At that time an increasing number of foreign buyers in these countries were demanding medium-term finance from the suppliers as a condition of sale. Forfaiting was thus created to satisfy this increasing demand.

Today forfaiting has developed into an alternative method of financing trade and is used throughout the world. It can be applied in the sale of capital goods, small projects, commodities, service contracts and even lease contracts. Traditionally, it is a means of providing medium-term (three to five years) and fixed rate finance, but transactions are now also structured on a floating rate interest bearing basis and for shorter and longer periods of credit (90 days to ten years).

The financial instruments evidencing the obligations of the foreign buyer are predominantly promissory notes or bills of exchange. Such transactions can be structured using deferred payment letters of credit and by assigning the debt in the books of a supplier owed to him under the financial terms and conditions of a supply contract. In addition to such instruments, the 'aval' or irrevocable and unconditional guarantee of the foreign buyer's local bank is required, unless the buyer is of such financial standing and international repute that a guarantee is considered unnecessary.

Although the full sale price can be financed, in a typical forfaiting transaction the supplier receives 10–20 per cent of his or her sale price in cash as a down-payment shortly after signing the supply contract. After manufacture and at the time of delivery of the goods involved, the supplier then receives promissory notes or bills of exchange evidencing the remaining 80–90 per cent due. These promissory notes or bills of exchange usually have incorporated into their face value an element of interest mutually agreed between the supplier and the foreign buyer. A series of promissory notes or bills of exchange is issued evidencing the various repayments during the agreed period of credit (e.g. two-year period of credit – four promissory notes or bills of exchange maturing six, 12, 18 and 24 months after delivery of the goods).

The supplier sells the series of promissory notes or bills of exchange to a forfaiting bank on a without recourse basis. The forfaiting bank deducts interest in the form of a discount at a fixed rate for the entire period of credit involved. The discount rate can be fixed at the time of delivery of the promissory notes or bills of exchange for purchase or up to 12–18 months in advance, thus enabling the supplier to build the discount costs into their sale price. The bank forfaiting may hold the promissory notes or bills of exchange until maturity or may sell them, again on a non-recourse basis, to another forfaiter. The ultimate holder in due course presents them for payment at maturity to the bank at which they are domiciled.

The processing of a forfait transaction is as described below.

(1) Commitment letter including fixed discount rate given by forfaiting company to the supplier.
(2) Sales contract agreed between the supplier and the foreign buyer.
(3) Goods manufactured and delivered.
(4) In exchange for title to the goods, a series of promissory notes or bills of exchange is delivered to the supplier.
(5) Supplier endorses promissory notes or bills of exchange to the forfaiting company on a without recourse basis.
(6) Forfaiting deducts interest at the discount rate agreed at (1) from the face value of the promissory notes or bills of exchange and pays the discounted proceeds to the supplier.
(7) At maturity, the forfaiting company presents each promissory note or bill of exchange for payment.
(8) Forfaiting company receives payment.

The documentation used in forfaiting is given below.

(1) a note or bill purchase agreement executed between the forfaiting company and the supplier (two to three pages);
(2) promissory notes or bills of exchange;
(3) guarantee or aval;
(4) signature confirmations and authentications;
(5) copies of necessary governmental approvals;

An 'aval' is an unconditional and irrevocable guarantee written on the face of a promissory note or bill of exchange. As transfer of the guarantee is effected purely by endorsement of the promissory notes or bills of exchange, the aval is the preferred method of guarantee.

The wording of avals is as follows:

(i) Promissory note
Per aval
(name and signature of the guarantor)

(ii) Bill of exchange
Per aval for (name of the drawee/foreign buyer)
(name and signature of the guarantor)

12.15 Guarantee

In some countries the term 'aval' has no legal significance and, in these instances, the guarantee of the guarantor has to be incorporated into a separate document.

Guarantees (and bonds) are used extensively in international trade to secure performance or other obligations. They provide the beneficiary with access to a sum of money should the principal (applicant) fail to fulfil contractual or other obligations in respect of an underlying transaction, contract or order. Such guarantees usually promise payment on demand, i.e. upon presentation by the beneficiary of a simple written demand for payment, or against a written demand accompanied by documentary evidence that the sum is owing. A bank guarantee is, by its nature, a separate transaction from the commercial contract on which it may be based. The bank (the guarantor) is not in any way connected with or bound by this contract, even though it may be referred to in the guarantee.

Unlike documentary credits, guarantees do not, in general, follow any specific format or wording; they tend to be constructed case-by-case. In some countries, guarantees may be subject to local laws and jurisdiction irrespective of what the guarantee might state. For example, some legal systems do not recognize expiry dates on guarantees which can pose problems if release from liability is difficult to obtain from the beneficiary.

The following are the essential requirements of such letters of guarantee: they are irrevocable; unconditional; fully transferable; abstract (the guarantee must not be dependant on performance of the underlying supply contract); and divisible (each individual repayment amount and date must be specified). A summary of the most popular guarantee types is given below:

(1) Tender guarantee to support an initial bid or tender for a contract.
(2) Advance payment guarantee secures repayment of any monetary advance.
(3) Performance guarantee covers a failure to fulfil contractual obligations.
(4) VAT/duty deferment bond allows VAT/duty payable on imports to be deferred.
(5) Retention monies guarantee secures the release of any monies withheld pending completion of a contract.
(6) Carnet or customs guarantee removes the need to pay duty on goods or vehicles imported into countries on a temporary basis (see p. 198).

FIATA NVOCC Bond

A recent bond adopted by the freight forwarding industry is termed the FIATA NVOCC Bond. It was introduced by FIATA to help those forwarders operating to the USA who are required to post a US$50 000 bond with the Federal Maritime

Commission. It took two years to negotiate with Intercargo of the USA following the passage into law of the FIATA sponsored Bonding Amendment Act. The bond is only available to BIFA trading members.

12.16 Less common methods of trade

Consignment trade

Consignment trade describes the situation whereby goods sent are by an exporter to a nominal importer in another country, that nominal importer being, in fact, a nominee or agent of the exporter. The intention is that the merchandise shall come into the physical possession of the agent whose duty it is to sell the merchandise on the exporter's behalf and remit to his principal the proceeds of sale, less all expenses of handling, storing and transport, customs duties and fees and his commission.

Participation

Participation implies a joint venture where a British manufacturer takes a share with a local concern in either marketing the exporter's product, local assembly or local manufacture.

Licensing

Licensing is where a licence is granted to an overseas company to manufacture the products on a royalty basis using either the manufacturer's brand name or the name of the licensee.

12.17 International exchange rates

The subject of foreign exchange relates to the exchange of various currencies one for another. On the practical side it concerns the methods of settling foreign debts, the means of payment and the services of banks and brokers. Settlement of debts between parties in the same country is quite simply effected by the payment of money, which the creditor is prepared to accept as it is the legal tender of the country. Where the payer and recipient live in different countries and use different currencies, however, there arises the need for a system of conversion – the foreign exchange market. Unlike the markets in commodities or stocks and shares, the foreign exchange market has no centre but consists merely of telephonic communications between dealers (at the banks) and brokers.

12.17.1 Rate of exchange

The price of one currency in terms of another is called the rate of exchange; it is the number of units of one currency that will be exchanged for a given number of units of another currency. Hence rates against sterling are the number of foreign currency units to the pound. A glance at the financial press shows that two closing rates are quoted for each currency; the higher is the market's buying rate for that currency and the lower the market's selling rate. Transactions between dealers are conducted at approximately these rates. A banker who is asked to buy or sell foreign currency relies upon the market for cover, and the prices at which he or she can obtain this cover are market rates. Hence in quoting to his or her customer he or she bases his or her rates on those ruling in the market; adjusted to make provision for profit.

The market rates quoted in the press are 'spot' rates, i.e. those applied to transactions for completion immediately or at the latest within two working days from the date of the deal. If the exchange rate has moved in your favour between the signing of a contract and its settlement date, an exceptional benefit over and above that anticipated from the contract terms may be derived. Equally the exchange rate may have moved in the opposite direction, adversely affecting the profitability of the underlying contract. As currency is a commodity like any other, its price will be governed by the interaction of demand and supply and hence by short- and long-term factors influencing buyers and sellers. The short-term factors fall into two categories: commercial and financial.

Commercial operations

Commercial operations relate to trade in goods and services which make up the current account of the balance of payments and give rise to payments and receipts in various currencies, thereby determining supply and demand in the foreign exchange markets. Where a country's total purchases exceed its sales, there will be an excess supply of its currency, which will cause its price to decrease; in other words the rate of exchange will fall. Expectations of future movements in exchange rates give rise to 'leads and lags'; a debtor will pay a foreign currency debt before it is due if he or she expects that currency to appreciate in value (lead) or delay payment if he or she expects it to depreciate (lag).

Financial operations

Financial operations come under a variety of headings.

(1) *Stock exchange operations* – the purchase of securities on foreign stock exchanges (bourses) by private or corporate investors in order to yield a return, or in the expectation of a capital appreciation. These are portfolio investments as opposed to 'industrial' investments, which represent capital placed by manufacturers in subsidiary or associated enterprises abroad.

(2) *Banking operations* – the transfer of funds by bankers for investment or deposit in foreign centres.

(3) *Speculation* – transactions based on the expectation that the exchange rate of a particular currency will change in response to some political or natural event. Whether the operator buys or sells a currency depends on whether he or she anticipates a rise or fall in value.

(4) *Interest payments* – interest on loans and dividends from investment.

(5) *Loan payments* – the issue of a loan in one country on behalf of a borrower in another gives rise to a payment across the exchanges from the country of the lender to that of the borrower which will have an adverse impact on the exchange rate of the lending country's currency and cause that of the borrowing country to appreciate. This effect would be offset if the proceeds of the loan were used to purchase goods or services from the lending country. Upon repayment of the loan the reverse effect will occur.

(6) *Intergovernmental transfers* – governments borrow from, and lend to, each other in the same way as private individuals and trading companies; the payments resulting from such loans have the same effect as that outlined above.

(7) *Exchange stabilization* – these are official operations in the foreign exchange market in order to control exchange rate movements by varying the relation between supply and demand. These operations are usually directed at keeping fluctuations to a minimum, although sometimes a government may deliberately seek to raise or lower the exchange rate of its currency.

12.17.2 Forward exchange

In view of the increasing amount of business conducted on credit terms, it is quite likely that a merchant will be liable to pay his or her supplier in the latter's currency at a future date or to receive foreign currency at a future date from a buyer. With exchange rates floating at present, he or she is vulnerable to any changes in currency values that may occur in the interval between conclusion of the contract and the date on which payment is due. It is to provide cover against such exchange risks that the 'forward exchange' market came into existence. The merchant contracts with a bank to purchase or sell one currency in exchange for another at a predetermined rate on an agreed future date. He or she thus knows how much he or she will eventually pay or receive in his or her own currency, and any intervening fluctuations in the exchange rate will not affect him or her.

Forward contracts may be 'fixed' or 'option'. A fixed forward is a contract with a specific performance date. A forward option stipulates a period of time during which performance is to take place, the actual date then being chosen by the customer. It should be clearly understood that the 'option' is not whether the customer deals or not – he or she is fully committed to the transaction – it relates only to the date on which he or she takes or delivers the currency concerned. Basically, the forward contract is one of the simplest hedging techniques allowing the importer or exporter to fix the exchange rate for the sale or purchase of a specific quantity of a currency for delivery at an agreed future date.

As a forward contract is a legally binding contract between the bank and the customer, a bank credit line is required to cover the amount and period of all forward contracts outstanding at any one time. The period of a forward contract can range from one day after spot value up to five years depending on the currencies involved. Maturity of the contract can be arranged either for settlement on a specific date (fixed contract) or on or between two dates (option dated contract) where the precise delivery date is not known.

The key benefit from a forward contract is that the importer or exporter knows in advance the exact value of future transactions in domestic currency terms. As well as eliminating the exchange risk this can aid cash flow management and assist with budgeting, costing and pricing processes. However, one does not have the opportunity to gain from beneficial exchange rate movements during the life of the contract.

12.17.3 Forward rates

The forward exchange rate is linked to the prevailing spot rate and is derived from the interest rate differential between the two currencies over the term of the forward contract. It is not a view of the likely exchange rate movement during that term.

The rates for forward exchange deals are quoted as a premium or discount on the spot rate, i.e. an amount above or below spot; sometimes they are at 'par' with spot. For example, if the forward dollar/sterling rate is quoted at a discount on the spot rate (measured in the conventional way as the number of dollars to a pound) then, in terms of dollars, sterling is cheaper forward than spot. Conversely, if the forward rate is at a premium, sterling is dearer forward than spot. In calculating the rate for a forward deal, a premium is added to the spot rate, whereas a discount is deducted from it. Forward margins (discount or premium) are determined by interest rate differentials and by market expectations of future spot exchange rates. Currencies in which interest rates are relatively low tend to be dearer forward than spot in terms of currencies in which interest rates are relatively high. The press usually quotes forward margins for one, three and six months forward, but by arrangement with the bank it is possible to cover for longer periods, depending on the currency concerned.

A customer who has contracted to buy foreign currency but finds that he or she no longer requires it will still have to take delivery of the currency at the agreed forward rate; he or she can then sell it back to the bank at the ruling spot rate. Similarly, if the customer has not received the foreign currency he or she has contracted to sell, he or she will have to buy the amount required at the ruling spot rate for delivery to the bank. In practice, the bank may merely debit or credit the difference to the customer's account. Where circumstances cause a delay in fulfilment of a contract it may often be extended at an adjusted rate by arrangement with the bank (p. 266).

From the above it will be seen that the forward exchange market enables the ordinary merchant to protect him- or herself against fluctuations in exchange rates. Problems can still arise, however, where expenditure and receipts are expressed in a number of different currencies. One example of this is found in connection with freight charges. For the sake of convenience a shipowner's rates of freight are expressed in a single currency called the 'tariff currency', usually the US dollar. Nevertheless, freight can be paid in another currency, so that agreement has to be reached on the basis for conversion of the sum involved. Where adjustments in relevant currency values have resulted in a reduction in the rates of freight or increases in shipowners' operating costs, it has been the practice of shipowners to increase tariff rates of freight or to introduce or increase a 'currency adjustment factor' (CAF) (pp. 127–8).

A shipowner naturally calculates in terms of his or her own currency and if it depreciates against the tariff unit he or she seeks to impose a surcharge to protect the real value of his or her revenue in relation to his or her expenditure, which may be in a variety of other currencies.

There has been a tendency to regard the CAF as a means of keeping ratios of past rates of exchange fixed for all time. Changes in the terms of trade owing to the different rates of inflation in various countries have not been taken into account when calculating sea freights. Relationships between currencies have, however, changed considerably. When the value of sterling was falling, the system favoured the British exporter in terms of freight rates; when sterling began to appreciate, however, shipowners in other countries applied a currency adjustment. The situation became more complicated when rates of exchange were allowed to float and the dollar was effectively devalued.

12.17.4 Factors influencing level of exchange rates

The level of an exchange rate plays a crucial role in an exporter's strategy. It is a high risk area and exporters continuously study the exchange rate money markets to keep abreast of market trends and the best method available to counter such variations, as discussed earlier (pp. 264–5). Moreover, one must bear in mind that a currency devaluation cheapens exports but increases the cost of imports. This latter point is compounded when a proportion of the exported product contains imported components thereby yielding only a marginal benefit in the export price.

A wide range of factors determine the level of individual country exchange rates. The major ones are detailed below, but it is stressed that the significance of each factor will be determined by local market conditions.

(1) The yield on the money markets reflected on the Central Bank interest rate level. This is found in the forward exchange rate which is linked to the prevailing spot rate and is derived from the interest rate differential between the two currencies over the term of the forward contract
(2) The actual central bank interest rate.
(3) The Balance of Trade and Balance of Payments performance and constituents. For example, a continuing trade deficit with no evidence of improvement will put pressure on the exchange rate level causing it to decline in value unless remedial measures are taken such as raising interest rates or curbing imports. An

example is Japan, with no indigenous sources, relying on imported raw materials and energy for its export base.

(4) The indebtedness of the country, such as IMF loans. This applies particularly to LDCs.

(5) The short- and long-term market prospects in a country and particularly its composition of agricultural, industrial, commercial and service sectors. Recent trends in many countries have seen an increase in their service sector activities, particularly in tourism, banking and overseas investments. This may occur in a service and manufacturing economy as found in the USA or in primarily agricultural economies involving commodities such as those which exist in many less developed countries in Africa.

(6) The economic forecast and range of economic indicators – inflation, interest rates, money supply, employment and production.

(7) The government's mandate to manage the economy and the government's competence to actually devise and carry out effective policies to sustain and develop its economy in a competitive global market.

(8) Whether the currency is traded on the open market or relies on a third currency such as the US dollar or the euro. Many non-convertible currencies use the US dollar as found in the less developed countries.

(9) The general market mood of the currency and its expectation as interpreted by economists, bankers and traders.

(10) Any unforeseen situation emerging such as hostilities, earthquake or political developments.

(11) The shipping and international trade cycle predictions and trends.

(12) Policies adopted by international agencies such as the IMF, the World Bank, WTO and G8. In the recent Far East currency crisis, the World Bank granted conditional loans based on an agreed economical recovery programme to South Korea, Thailand and Malaysia. These loans will help to sustain their currencies and economic recovery.

(13) The level of international reserves.

(14) The gross and net external debt expressed as a percentage of the gross domestic product.

(15) The country's net foreign debt and debt service.

(16) The country's net debt service as a percentage of exports of goods and services. This identifies the ability of a country to fund its indebtedness and the impact it will have on its economy sustainment and growth.

(17) Any technological or infrastructure development providing improved prospects for a particular economy such as the provision of a hydro dam, installation of a coal, gas or oil fired energy plant.

(18) A country joining a trading bloc such as the European Union.

(19) Circumstances which create uncertainty.

(20) The monetary policies adopted by a country.

(21) The financial market mechanism in a particular country.

(22) An analysis of the currency performance and factors determining its variation. Currencies which move from a strong to a weak position usually fall due to a

variety of circumstances. The financial markets may decide to sell the weak currency and retain the stronger currency. Such turbulence of currency fluctuation is serious for any major trading currency.

(23) A rise in the price of a barrel of crude oil on the world market will undermine the trade balance of some LDCs reliant on oil as an energy resource and may account for more than 25 per cent of their import bill annually.

(24) Stock exchange operations, banking operations, interest payments, loan payments, intergovernmental transfers and exchange stabilization (see pages 265–6 inclusive).

12.17.5 Currency options

In our consideration of exchange rates it is appropriate to consider currency options. A currency option is the right to buy or sell a currency against delivery of a base currency at an agreed exchange rate. The buyer of the option has the right to exercise this option at any date up to and including an agreed date, but he or she has no obligation to do so. The buyer of the option pays a premium for the provision of this right.

Currency options are true options and are different in kind from option date forward contracts which provide an option only as to the date when exchange shall take place, but require exchange at some time within the option period. True options may be regarded as 'whether to exchange' options, as opposed to 'when to exchange' options.

A 'call' option provides the right to buy the currency and sell the base currency at the agreed rate; a 'put' option provides the right to sell the currency and buy the base currency at the agreed rate; Thus, for instance, a treasurer may transact:

Swiss franc call against US dollar (can buy Swiss francs)
Yen call against US dollar (can buy yen)
Canadian dollar put against Swiss Franc (can call Canadian dollar)
Swiss franc against euro (can sell euro)

A currency option is essentially a form of insurance against movements in exchange rates. In this respect, it may be seen as an alternative to forward cover in the foreign exchange market for import and export trade. However, since the holder is not obliged to exercise the option, it is particularly suitable for covering contingent cash flows such as those arising when tendering for a contract.

Advantages of currency options are detailed below:

(1) Where cash flow is hedged by a forward contract, the company achieves protection against adverse currency movements – the downside risk is eliminated. Unfortunately, this method also eliminates any upside potential that otherwise would have accrued to the company if exchange rates had moved in its favour.

By contrast, a principal advantage of an option is that it provides protection against downside risk in the same way as a forward contract, but since there is no obligation to exercise the option, the upside potential is retained.

(2) The option buyer knows at the outset what his 'worst case' will be; having paid the premium no further expense is payable. When the main objective is simply to limit downside risk, this is a powerful advantage. In many commercial applications, the option premium can be built in to the pricing process, thus fixing minimum margins.

(3) Since there is no obligation to exercise an option, options are ideal for hedging contingent cash flows (which may or may not materialize) such as in tenders.

(4) Options may be used as a 'ratchet' to lock up profit to date on a currency position whilst retaining any remaining upside potential.

The premia for currency options are dependent upon three principal factors:

(1) the difference between the exercise price and the current spot price;
(2) the time until expiry of the option;
(3) the volatility of the exchange rate concerned.

An option premium is normally thought of as consisting of two components, intrinsic value and time value. The intrinsic value is simply the profit difference, if any, between the existing spot price and the exercise price. That is, for a call option where the buyer has the right to buy sterling at a strike price of 1.50 and the current spot price is 1.5275, then the intrinsic value is 2.75 cents. All this means is that a call option at 1.50 exercised today would provide an instant profit of 2.75 cents by selling the option proceeds into today's spot market. So one way to think of intrinsic value is: 'the gain that would result if the option were exercised today'. It is useful when evaluating the relative attractiveness of options at different strike prices to strip out the intrinsic value so that the time value alone can be seen.

Time value is more complicated. It is a measure of the amount the exchange rate might be expected to move in the holder's favour during the balance of the time to run. It is therefore apparent that time value will depend not only on the time to expiry, but also the expected volatility of the exchange rate. The more volatile the exchange rate, the greater is the chance that a given level might be reached during the time left to run. It also follows from this reasoning that the greater the current loss at any time (i.e. the further the price will have to rise in order to profit from exercise of the option), the lower will be the likelihood of this happening so that the time premium will be correspondingly lower to reflect this.

A number of theoretical models have been used in the field of stock options which attempt, with varying degrees of success, to estimate time value depending on time to run and historical volatility. Meanwhile market operators – never people to be overawed by theoreticians of any kind – continue to base their pricing on the ancient and well-tested principle of simply seeing what they are able to sell the option for at the time. Nevertheless, from the above we can establish certain basic conclusions.

(1) The option premium may be thought of as the sum of the intrinsic value and the time value.

(2) Intrinsic value is the profit that would arise if the option were exercised today.

(3) Intrinsic value can never be negative, since at this level the option would not be exercised. (The buyer is under no obligation to exercise at a loss, and therefore presumably will not do so.)

(4) Time value can never be negative, although it will fall continuously towards zero as expiration date approaches.

(5) At any given time, there will be a choice of exercise prices and expiration dates in the market.

(a) The more distant maturity dates will have higher premia than the near ones, because the time value will be higher.

(b) For call options, the higher the exercise price, the lower the premium; intrinsic value will be lower.

(c) For put options, the lower the exercise price, the lower the premium; intrinsic value will be lower.

The above propositions provide an initial framework for option pricing, but we can take this a few steps further. We have seen how time value varies with time; now we take a look at how it varies with exercise price.

For ease of discussion let us consider a sterling call option. It is readily apparent that if the price is now 1.4980, then a strike price of 1.50 is more likely to be exceeded in the time left to run than is a price of 1.55. It is generally true that the further 'out of the money' the option is, then the less the time value will be, owing to the reducing chance of seeing a profit in the time left to run.

An option at a strike price of 1.50 is really a one-way bet; a downward movement costs little, but an upward movement is pure profit, hence the time value will be high. This is no longer the case for, say, an option at 1.45 because, as time goes by, some of the existing unrealized profit could be lost – there is now a downside risk as well as an upside potential. The time value for 'in the money' options will thus be lower. Deeply in the money options may even have time values very close to zero.

12.17.6 Average rate options

Where an exporter or importer has a series of regular payments or receipts and has budgeted for a particular exchange rate over the period, an average rate option will provide the same protection as a currency option, but because of the averaging process, will be achieved with lower premium cost. Although having the characteristics of a currency option, an average rate option does not involve the physical buying and selling of currency; the underlying transactions are settled independently.

The company selects the rate it wishes to protect – the strike price – and agrees a mechanism by which the bank can calculate the 'average' rate. Average rate options are available in all major currencies for periods up to two years and the basis for deriving the average rate can be daily, weekly, monthly or any other period relevant to the underlying cash flows.

At the end of the period the company is compensated by the bank if the average exchange is worse than the strike price. Compensation is not paid if the average rate is better than the strike price; the company will have benefited from the favourable rate movements when the underlying transactions were settled. However, unless the company deals at the same time as the bank fixes its reference rates, there is likely to be a variation between the bank's average rate and the company's actual dealing average.

12.17.7 Foreign currency accounts

Any importer or exporter who regularly undertakes business in a foreign currency could benefit from a foreign currency account. This is especially appropriate where a company is both paying and receiving funds in a currency as, by using a foreign currency account, the company can avoid the costs associated with converting the currency each time there is a transaction. Additionally, opportunity exists to earn interest on currency balances, together with the flexibility and convenience in all transactions. Moreover, the exporter can tender and invoice in the buyer's currencies.

Borrowing in a foreign currency, repayable from currency receipts, can eliminate exchange risk and may be less expensive than borrowing in the exporter's national currency. This can reduce costs and provide the ability to tender and invoice in the buyer's currency, both of which can be critical success factors in obtaining new business.

12.18 Euro currency

On 1 January 1999 a single European currency – the euro – was introduced in eleven European Union countries together with the formation of an economic and monetary union. The eleven countries in the euro-zone include Austria, Belgium, Finland, France, Germany, Ireland, Italy, Luxembourg, the Netherlands, Portugal and Spain. It has resulted in a real change to the business environment throughout Europe. The eleven countries also share a single interest rate set by the European Central Bank and a single foreign exchange rate policy. The European Central Bank is responsible for the monetary policy of these euro-zone countries involving a total population of 270 million.

The euro has produced the following benefits and features.

(1) Cheaper transaction costs – countries in the euro-zone do not have to change currencies when doing business.
(2) Stability of exchange rates resulting in countries in the euro-zone no longer being affected by currency fluctuations when trading with each other.
(3) Transparent price differences – it has become more obvious when different euro-zone countries charge different prices for the same goods and services.
(4) Companies operating in Europe have simplified their accounts and finances by trading in the euro not only in the euro-zone of eleven states, but also in other countries outside the euro-zone embracing the four other states in the European Union and also other European non-EU member countries. This extends to budgetary financial management and has resulted in much tighter and more

realistic financial controls and disciplines following the removal of cross-border currency risk fluctuations.

(5) Companies situated outside the euro-zone but part of the European Union (embracing the countries of Greece, the UK, Portugal and Sweden) trade in the euro both as importer and exporter. This produces a competitive advantage in securing business as product price comparisons will be in the euro, leading to intensified competition.

(6) Importers and exporters throughout Europe gain from using the euro as bank charges have fallen and payments have been speeded up.

(7) Businesses have experienced fewer legal problems with the euro in price agreement whereas hitherto this was more prevalent in the national currencies.

(8) Cross-border competition has increased, placing companies outside the euro-zone in a less favourable position against competitors within the zone who share the same currency.

(9) The euro has produced an impetus of cross-border mergers and other joint ventures. This is particularly evident with companies in the euro-zone who share the same currency thereby making the merger and joint ventures rather easier.

(10) Distribution and procurement within the euro-zone has become simpler and cheaper because companies do not undergo any exchange rate risk when trading.

(11) Raising finance has become easier and more attractive in the euro-bond and euro-equity share market. Hitherto, the national currencies embraced one country whereas the euro extends to 11 countries thereby spreading the risk under the management of an economic and monetary union through the European Central Bank which controls the interest rate level.

(12) Companies have found it necessary to re-focus their marketing and product sourcing strategies to combat opportunities and threats emerging from the transparency of euro pricing with no exchange risk implication and greater price stability compared with the national currency.

(13) Companies worldwide who export into the euro-zone tend to trade in the euro. This enables the buyer to draw price comparisons from other sources both within the euro-zone and outside it. Moreover, any currency risk fluctuation would arise with the seller based outside the euro-zone.

(14) The development of computerized technology will provide a further aid to stimulate the economic growth of the euro-zone, particularly trade within the zone. It will further reduce any culture or management cross-border barriers and provide market and business confidence, with the euro and the European Central Bank influenced by determining a common interest rate in a single market.

12.18.1 Special Drawing Right (SDR)

The increasing globalization of financial markets has created a vast pool of resources for investment, economic growth and social advancement. At the same time, as is evident in the financial turmoil that erupted in southeast Asia in mid-1997 and the crisis which affected Russia from 1998, it has brought increased risk – the risk that capital flows will dry up or reverse as market confidence falters. The international reverberations of the Asian crisis – characterized by plunging exchange rates and equity prices – were probably the most far-reaching of the postwar period. The crisis first broke out in July 1997 in Thailand when, following several episodes of exchange market pressure and reserve losses, the authorities abandoned the peg of the baht to the US dollar. This action, in turn, raised doubts about the viability of exchange rate arrangements elsewhere. Spillover effects were soon felt in other countries in the region, especially Indonesia, Korea, Malaysia, and the Philippines and exposed underlying structural weaknesses in these economies. Growth in Japan also turned negative in late 1997 and the first half of 1998, which intensified market pressures.

The SDR (special drawing right) is an international reserve asset created by the IMF in 1969 and allocated to its members to supplement existing reserve assets. The IMF has allocated a total of SDR 21.4 billion in two series of allocations since 1970. As of April 30 1998, holdings of SDRs by member countries amounted to 1.8 per cent of their total non-gold reserves.

Member countries of the IMF are eligible to receive allocations of SDRs and may use SDRs in transactions and operations among themselves, with 15 'prescribed institutional holders' and with the IMF itself. The SDR is the unit of account of the IMF and is used as a unit of account, or as a basis for a unit of account, by a number of other international and regional organizations and international conventions. The SDR can also be used to denominate private financial instruments. In addition, as of April 30 1998, the currencies of four member countries were pegged to the SDR. See Table 12.1 which gives the SDR valuation as at August 31 1998.

The value of the SDR is determined daily on the basis of a basket of five currencies; the US dollar, the Deutsche mark, the French franc, the Japanese yen, and

TABLE 12.1 SDR Valuation on 31 August 1998

Currency	Currency amount[1]	Exchange rate on 31 August[2]	US dollar equivalent[3]
Deutsche mark	0.4460	1.75820	0.253669
French franc	0.8130	5.91350	0.137482
Japanese yen	27.2000	140.89000	0.193058
UK sterling	0.1050	1.67630	0.176012
US dollar	0.5820	1.00000	0.582000
Total			1.342221

SDR 1 = US$1.342221
US$1 = SDR 0.745034[4]

[1] The currency components of the SDR basket.
[2] Exchange rates in terms of currency units per US dollar, except for the pound sterling, which is expressed in US dollars per pound.
[3] The US dollar equivalents of the currency amounts divided by the exchange rates.
[4] The official SDR value of the US dollar, which is the reciprocal of the total of the US dollar equivalent – that is, 1 ìç 1.342221, rounded to six significant digits.

Data IMF Treasurer's Department

the UK pound sterling. The value of the SDR tends to be more stable than that of any single currency in the basket; movements in the exchange rate of any one component currency will tend to be partly or fully offset by movements in the exchange rates of the other currencies.

The SDR valuation basket is revised every five years, most recently on 1 January 1996. The currencies included in the current basket, which are those of the five member countries with the largest exports of goods and services during 1990–94, remain unchanged from the previous basket. However, the initial weights of these currencies were modified to reflect changes in their relative importance in international trade and reserves.

The SDR interest rate, which is adjusted weekly, is a weighted average of the yields on specified short-term instruments in the domestic money markets of the five countries whose currencies are included in the SDR basket. The financial instruments used in this calculation were reviewed in 1995 and remain unchanged. These instruments are the market yield on three-month US treasury bills, the three-month German interbank deposit rate, the three-month rate on Japanese certificates of deposit, the three-month rate on French treasury bills, and the market yield on three-month UK treasury bills.

12.18.2 Use of SDRs

IMF members may use SDRs in a variety of voluntary transfers. These include transactions 'by agreement'; that is, spot exchanges of SDRs for other monetary assets and operations among themselves and with prescribed holders. In addition, SDRs may be used in operations under the Enhanced Structural Adjustment Facility. These operations require the involvement of prescribed holders because the IMF's Special Disbursement Account and accounts administered by the IMF may not hold SDRs directly.

The use of SDRs between members and the IMF consist of receipts of SDRs by the IMF's General Resources Account from members, and transfers of SDRs from the General Resources Account to members. IMF receipts mainly take the form of charges levied on members' use of IMF resources, repurchases (repayments) and quota subscriptions. Transfers from the IMF consist mainly of purchases (drawings); remuneration on members' creditor positions; and repayments of, and interest payments on, IMF borrowing.

Countries indebted to the IMF continued to acquire substantial amounts of SDRs in transactions by agreement during 1997/98 to discharge their financial obligations to the IMF and build up their holdings of SDRs. They also sold in transactions by agreement most of the SDRs they received in purchases and ESAF loan disbursements.

Transactions by agreement increased to SDR 8.6 billion during 1997/98 from SDR 7.4 billion in 1996/97. The IMF continued to help arrange transactions by agreement by bringing together participants and prescribed holders that are ready to buy or sell SDRs, either under standing arrangements or on an *ad hoc* basis. These transactions continued to be facilitated by the cooperation of 12 members that stand ready to buy or sell SDRs for freely usable currencies at any time, under 'two-way arrangements', provided that their SDR holdings remain within certain limits.

According to the Articles of Agreement, members with a balance of payments need may also use SDRs to acquire foreign exchange in a transaction 'with designation'; that is, one in which another member, designated by the IMF, provides a freely usable currency in exchange for the SDRs. The IMF may designate members to provide currencies in exchange for SDRs on the basis of the strength of their balance of payments and reserve positions within certain limits. However, since September 1987, no transactions with designation have taken place, because all exchanges of SDRs for currency have been accommodated through transactions by agreement.

12.18.3 SDR allocations

One of the IMF's principal goals is to facilitate the expansion and balanced growth of international trade, which requires adequate levels of reserves. If the IMF identifies a long-term global need for reserves, it can supplement existing assets through an allocation of SDRs. The timing and size of that allocation are determined by the Board of Governors of the IMF. The IMF has the authority to create unconditional liquidity by allocating SDRs to all member countries in proportion to their quotas. It cannot allocate SDRs to itself or to prescribed holders. The most recent allocation was on 1 January 1981, when SDR 4.1 billion was allocated to the IMF's (then) 141 member countries.

At present, more than one-fifth of IMF member countries have never received an SDR allocation, because these countries joined the IMF after the last SDR allocation. In addition, other members have not participated in every allocation. For some time, the Executive Board has been in broad agreement that the IMF should make a special one-time 'equity' allocation of SDRs to allow all members to participate in the SDR system. Following a broad review of the role and functions of the SDR in the light of changes in the world financial system and to ensure that all participants in the SDR Department receive an equitable share of cumulative SDR allocations, the Board of Governors adopted a resolution in September 1997 proposing a Fourth Amendment to the IMF's Articles of Agreement. If approved by the membership, the Amendment would provide for a special one-time allocation of SDR 21.4 billion, which would double the current level of cumulative SDR allocations and would raise all participants' ratios of cumulative SDR allocations to quota, under the Ninth General Review of Quotas, to a common benchmark ratio of 29.32 per cent. The proposed amendment, which will become effective when approved by three-fifths of the members having 85 per cent of the total voting power, also provides for future participants to receive a special allocation following the date of their participation or the effective date of the Fourth Amendment whichever is later. The proposed amendment would not affect the IMF's existing power to allocate SDRs based on a finding of a long-term global need to supplement reserves as and when that need arises.

The IMF aims for a target amount of net income each financial year to add to its reserves, after both covering its administrative expenses and remunerating its creditor positions. The rate of charge on the use of IMF resources is linked to the SDR interest rate, which changes weekly, while the rate of remuneration is equal to the SDR interest rate. At the beginning of each financial year, the IMF sets the rate of charge as a proportion of the SDR interest rate, so as to achieve a predetermined net income target. This mechanism ensures that the IMF's operational income is adjusted to reflect its main operational costs. Since December 1997, the IMF also levies a surcharge on the use of credit under the Supplemental Reserve Facility (SRF).

In April 1997, the proportion of the rate of charge to the SDR interest rate for 1997/98 was set at 109.6 per cent to achieve a net income target of SDR 99 million or 5 per cent of the IMF's reserves at the beginning of the financial year, with the proviso that any income in excess of the target should be used to reduce retroactively the proportion of the rate of charge for the year.

Following a review of the IMF's income position at mid-year, the proportion of the rate of charge to the SDR interest rate for 1997/98 was retroactively reduced to 107.0 per cent from the initial 109.6 per cent, and SDR 31 million was returned to the members which had paid charges through the third quarter of the financial year. Furthermore, it was decided that the net operational income derived from the SRF (after meeting the expense of administering the ESAF Trust) was to be excluded from other income and be placed in the IMF's General Reserve at the end of the financial year. After that exclusion, by the end of the financial year, actual income exceeded the target by SDR 22 million, which again was returned to members which paid charges during the year, thereby further retroactively reducing the rate of charge to 105.6 per cent of the SDR interest rate for 1997/98.

To strengthen its financial position against the consequences of overdue obligations, the IMF has adopted 'burden-sharing' measures to accumulate additional precautionary balances and to distribute the financial burden of overdue obligations between debtor and creditor members. As part of this mechanism, adjustments are made to the rate of charge and the rate of remuneration. The resources so generated are intended to protect the IMF against risks associated with arrears and to provide additional liquidity. For 1997/98, the adjustments under burden-sharing resulted in an average rate of charge of 4.65 per cent and an average rate of remuneration of 3.97 per cent. After the retroactive reductions of the rate of charge, SDR 164 million was added to the IMF's reserves, of which SDR 65 million was added to the General Reserve and the rest to the Special Reserve. Total reserves increased to SDR 2.13 billion as of 30 April 1998, from SDR 1.97 billion a year earlier. For 1998/99, the Executive Board set the rate of charge on the use of IMF credit at 107 per cent of the interest rate.

13

Transport distribution analysis

Transport distribution analysis is featuring increasingly in the exporter's or shipper's evaluation of the technique of processing an export order. Undoubtedly this is due to much increased competition in world markets and the desirability of attaining the best method of distribution considering all the circumstances. Moreover, an increasing number of export companies now have their own shipping department, which is building up an expertise of international distribution techniques designed to secure the best method of distribution for their company products. The result is that these shipping and logistics departments are doing more than earning their keep and are thereby helping to keep their companies' products competitive in very competitive overseas markets. Transport features very much in such an analysis and it is, therefore, appropriate that an examination be made first of the salient points that influence a transport service.

13.1 The relative importance of speed, frequency, reliability, service quality and cost of transport

Basically, there are five factors which influence the nature of a transport service: speed, frequency, reliability, cost and service quality.

Speed is important to the shipper who wants to market his or her goods by an accurate arrival date and to eliminate banking charges for opening credits. This can be achieved by selecting the fastest service available and thereby obtaining the minimum interval between the time the goods are ordered and the date of delivery at their destination. Speed is particularly important to manufacturers of fast-moving consumer goods (fmcg) as it avoids expense and the risk of obsolescence to the retailer carrying large stocks. This is particularly so in the case of ladies clothing which is influenced by fashion, and retails in a very sensitive market. Reduced stocks result in less warehouse accommodation needs, less working capital by which the company operates, and overall, a better cash flow situation as the turnover is quicker. These factors strongly favour air freight which features very prominently in the distribution of fashionable ladies clothing on certain routes, particularly the North Atlantic.

The development of the wide-body aircraft has enabled airlines to develop new markets through more competitive pricing. An example is the Boeing 747-200C which has a 29-pallet arrangement 96×125 in (2.45 m $\times$ 3.10 m), a maximum main deck volume of 536 m^3 and lower deck volume of 170 m^3. The maximum pallet height is 3.05 m with side door loading, and 2.42 m with nose loading. Maximum payload is 100 000 kg, subject to volume and routeing. Such aircraft have facilitated the development of the intermodal sea–air market (p. 93).

Perishable products, computer software, electrical products, livestock – such as day-old chicks, and a range of commodities found in the air freight consolidators' market, require a regular and fast service to ensure successful trading. Air freight is ideal for such products, especially for the longer-distance markets where transit times are critical.

The continuous expansion of the network of global deep-sea container services has been a major stimulant to world trade and has facilitated the development of new markets. It has bridged the gap, in distribution terms, between the wealthy markets of North America and Europe, with the lower GDP markets of the Orient, especially the newly industrialized countries. Speed, frequency, reliability and competitive pricing have been the key factors in such trade development.

An area of rapid expansion is the refrigerated cargo market. It may be a trailer, cargo wagon or swap-body, as found in the European and pan North American markets, or in the reefer containers worldwide. A major operator in this field is Sealand, who operate 13 000 all-electric refrigerated containers involving a trio of 12.20 m (40 ft) models. They range from a capacity of 57.20 m^3 to 66.80 m^3 and tare weight of 4320 kg to 5350 kg. Products carried range from the frozen hardy and sensitive chill to tropicals and flower bulbs.

The development of the reefer container has enabled a growing volume of tropical fruits, Mediterranean citrus fruits, European dairy products and Australian meat products to be distributed in a quality condition on a global basis; the reefer cargoes are shipped at controlled temperatures throughout the transit. Many such cargoes first entered the market using air freight services, for example tropical fruits, but as the volume built up the reefer container took over with a high volume base and lower distribution cost, which was fully integrated into a temperature-controlled network extending to computer-temperature-controlled warehouse distribution points. In drawing such a comparison one must bear in mind that the modern air freighter has a capacity of 100 tonnes compared with Evergreen's latest generation of vessels conveying 6600 TEUs. Another factor to be borne in mind is that airlines offer more frequent services compared with sea transport.

Improvements will continue to be sought in all areas of physical international distribution. This involves the continuing expansion of multi-modalism (Chapter 5), development of improved technology in the global distribution infrastructure and renewed efforts to improve transit times through dedicated services. Overall, this will yield greatly improved door-to-door services within the total physical distribution concept involving all its ingredients. It will develop further existing markets, identify new ones and expand the global network. The 'just-in-time' concept will be further expanded.

The foregoing demonstrates that regularity and frequency of service are factors in the development of the market, coupled with a competitive transit time at an acceptable freight rate. A balance must be sought between the cost of the service to the shipper, the value added benefit it brings to the goods conveyed, and the frequency and transit times. Modern ship management has substantially reduced voyage time through port rationalization, modern high tech transshipment methods and a growing reliance on feeder service under the one-stop port operation concept involving the hub and spoke container network (pp. 63–8). This has extended to the infrastructure resources at the ports which are continuously being modernized under multi-modalism. Moreover, the development of Electronic Data Interchange (EDI) has facilitated the unimpeded flow of goods thereby aiding the overall planning of the global distribution of goods from the factory to the warehouse.

Speed is not so important where generally low value cargoes are being carried as in the world tramp trades and where many trades are moving under programmed stockpiled arrangements. In this category are included coal, minerals, ores, etc. and other cargoes which normally move in ship loads and have a low value. These demand a low transport cost.

Frequency of service is most important when goods can only be sold in small quantities at frequent intervals. This is a very strong selling point in favour of the air freight operator, particularly in long-distance markets and is relevant as frequent schedules coupled with fast transits enable stocks to be quickly replenished thereby avoiding excessive stockpiling.

To the tramp charterer, frequency of sailings is not of paramount importance. He must not, of course, allow his stocks to run down too fast, but he will have a margin within which he can safely operate, and will come in to buy and ship when conditions suit him.

Reliability is an essential requirement to the shipper whose goods are sold against expiry dates on letters of credit and import licences. Furthermore, the shipper relies on the operator to deliver his traffic in good condition, which is now becoming an important factor in very competitive overseas markets. To the shipper, therefore, reliability infers that the ship, air freighter, TIR road haulage unit, etc. will depart and arrive at the advertised time; the ship or air freight operator will look after the cargo during pre-shipment, throughout the voyage or flight and after discharge; and finally, the operator can be relied upon to give adequate facilities at the docks or airport and at his offices to enable the appropriate documents and other formalities to be satisfactorily completed. In short, prestige in the liner cargo or air freight trades goes with the reliance that the shipper can place on any particular operator. Reliability infers service quality and, in recent years, this has been a very competitive area amongst both ship and air operators. The shipper has come to expect the merchandise to arrive in accord with a predetermined schedule and in a good mercantile condition, otherwise the product will be very vulnerable to competition.

Transport costing of individual services is fast becoming an important aspect in transport management today. Transport is a commodity that is difficult to cost, particularly when a multifarious service or joint supply is offered, for example, a vehicular ferry conveying passengers, motorists, cars, lorries and/or trailers, etc. The position is more complex when on one sailing the vessels conveys motorists with their cars, whilst on another it is simply lorries and trailers with their drivers. The same applies to an aircraft which may be exclusively used for passengers on one flight and for a mixture of passengers and cargo on another.

The operator endeavours to devise a tariff which will maximize revenue and optimize fleet use. This involves market pricing whereby the rate is pitched at the level which will attain high load factors on individual sailings or flights. (Such a philosophy is developed more extensively in Chapter 7.) Therefore, one sees the rate in one direction differing from the rate in the reverse direction, with the sole aim being to attain good capacity utilization. Such an example is found in the commodity air freight rates found on the North Atlantic services.

In very broad terms, the operator will formulate tariffs which will cover all his or her direct or variable costs and make a contribution to indirect or fixed costs. The direct cost represents expenses actually incurred in the service provision including fuel, day-to-day maintenance, dues or tolls, crew cost, etc. Indirect costs embrace administration, depreciation, sinking-fund asset-replacement provision, insurance, annual overhaul and survey costs, etc. The indirect costs are apportioned by flight or voyage relative to the transport user throughout the year. In situations where traffic flows are imbalanced, producing differing tariffs in each direction, an element of cross subsidization takes place to produce a long-term, overall profitable service. Tariffs on scheduled services tend to be rather more rigid compared with chartered vessels or aircraft which are influenced by the economic market forces of supply and demand. (It must be recognized that the foregoing analysis deals only with the freight cost assessment and excludes ancillary expenses, viz. customs clearance, handling costs, collection and delivery, etc.)

The shipper marketing goods of relatively low value must seek the lowest possible transport charge, as the freight percentage of the total value may have a direct bearing on the saleability of the commodity. This involves the tramp vessel which is ideal for this market. The shipper thus has a prime interest in the availability of tramp shipping space at any particular time by reason of the fact that freight and chartering rates will vary, reflecting the economic forces of supply and demand. In a market situation where there are plenty of vessels, the shipper will be able to charter at a rate which will be only marginally above the operating costs of the vessel. In the opposite situation, he or she will be forced to pay more, but there is a limiting factor on the price of the commodity at the point of sale to the rate which the shipowner may receive. In these conditions, the premium returns are earned by the operators of the most efficient ships. In weak market conditions their relative efficiency ensures a small profit while others just break even. Where the market is strong, the proven reliability shown before will ensure that the services of such vessels will be sought out before opportunities are taken up. To conclude, the tramp operator will endeavour to cover his direct costs, and contribute to indirect costs in the overall fixture rate concluded. A similar criterion applies to the chartering of an air freighter.

In the liner trade and scheduled air freight services, the tariffs are more stable and are controlled primarily under the aegis of the liner conference system or IATA. Both the ship and air operator are able to hold their rates at a fair level to show a very modest profit margin based on a fairly high load factor. They must be careful not to hold their rates so high that they price the goods out of the market. At this point, there is need for joint consultation between the shipper and carrier.

However in both the liner trade and air freight market, the freight forwarder or container operator, NVOCC (p. 94), are tending to play a greater role in rate-making due to the fact that they offer not only the trunk haul such as the maritime or flight element, but also the feeder service (collection and delivery) to and from the seaport, ICD CFS or airport in their tariff structure. This trend will continue as both the shipowner and airline prefer to concentrate on providing a quality service and rely on the freight forwarder or container operator to market it.

Moreover, the freight forwarder, container operator and TIR road haulier operator in the liner trades and scheduled air freight markets, offer facilities for consolidated consignments at very competitive rates and transit times. This market is fast expanding particularly in air freight and is ideal for the small exporter.

Quality of service is tied up in all the ingredients which make up the service to the shipper. This includes customer care, reliability, degree of technology, tracking of cargo, level of computerization, quality of equipment, flexibility, competitiveness of tariff and transit time, attitude of staff and, above all, professionalism. Carriers who operate a successful business must be adequately trained and professionally qualified to meet the challenges and opportunities of the market. The closer the carrier gets to the shipper, and empathy develops between them, the more successful the business will become to the mutual benefit of both parties.

To conclude, as we progress beyond the millennium, the pattern of world trade will change with further growth from North America and Europe and the recovery of the former tiger economies in the Far East. Growth will be stimulated as trade is facilitated by a much greater degree of integration between carriers, agents, customs, airport, seaports, railways, road hauliers and shippers to develop multi-modalism. It will feature more prominently the role of free trade zones, Distriparks and trade centres such as Rotterdam and Singapore; development of free trade areas such as the EU and NAFTA; expansion of sea–air networks, expansion of the sea-land bridge such as the trans-Pacific routes serving the west coast ports of Los Angeles, San Francisco and Seattle which are integrated with the double-stack container train transportation distribution to various points in the USA; Electronic Data Interchange in all its areas; and finally, the high-capacity container. The key factor will be flexibility to meet changing market needs and the total commitment to produce a quality service. This will be aided by market research on a continuous basis and good planning. Overall, it will become a global market logistically driven, relying on a very sophisticated and highly efficient shipping and air network.

13.2 Evaluating the suitability of transport modes of an international consignment

Transport distribution analysis to the exporter and shipper involves the process of deciding which is the most ideal mode(s) of transport and route for a particular consignment. Multi-modalism features strongly in this evaluation for fmcg. The ultimate selection can vary seasonally and by quantity. Some services vary considerably from summer to winter due to market demand and climate conditions. Moreover, the despatch of a small quantity, urgently required may be ideal for air freight, but a larger consignment, needed less urgently for later despatch may be suitable for a deep-sea container LCL schedule under consolidation arrangements.

In a world where countries are trying to improve continuously their overall trade balance, an increasing number are insisting on shipment by their own national airline or shipping service irrespective of the commercial or economic advantages there may be in using competitive services. This involves both tariff and non-tariff barriers which impede the free flow of goods and is fully explained in *Maritime Economics Management and Marketing*. This is a difficult situation to combat, but the UK exporter must strive to sell his or her goods under CIF or CIP and buy under EXW or FCA terms to maximize income to the UK balance-of-payments account and thereby exert his or her influence on the transport mode and routeing of the consignment.

Today more and more exporters are setting up their own shipping offices which should be more than self-financing. This means that the cost of running such a department should more than offset the savings realized through international distribution costs. In some companies, such a department has its own TIR road fleet and leases or hires containers. Alternatively, many multinational industries and large departmental stores are entrusting their international distribution arrangements and product outsourcing to a mega container operator such as P&O Nedlloyd, who have specialist logistical departments for such clients.

To conclude, the exporter must continuously review his or her international distribution arrangements and the following are the more important aspects to consider in the evaluation of transport mode and routeing suitability, etc.

(1) *The customer's choice* is the prime consideration and this is usually found in the export sales contract. It is interrelated with the delivery trade terms. Moreover, there is continuous evidence of the importer insisting on the goods being conveyed on his or her country's national shippingline or airline to save hard currency.

(2) *The nature of the commodity*, its dimensions, weight and whether any special facilities are required for it during transit (for example, livestock requires special facilities, gold requires special security or a strong room, and meat requires refrigerated accommodation). This is a major consideration, and one must establish through research and enquiry whether the actual dimensions are ideal to maximize the use of the available container capacity and lessen the risk of

broken stowage. Moreover, one must bear in mind broken stowage usually attracts additional freight payments. The enterprising exporter will constantly review the configuration of the consignment with the shipping department working closely with the production and design departments. In so doing the consignment may be able to be componentized, thereby enabling it to have a better loadability in the container with reduced freight cost. It may open up other options for distribution such as multi-modalism and the intermodal sea–air services.

(3) *The degree of packing and cost thereof.* Packing costs can form a very significant proportion of the overall distribution expense. For example, a consignment sent under 'tween deck tonnage usually requires very extensive packaging, possibly involving a wooden case, whereas cargo despatched by cargo wagon, containerization and air freight requires less – particularly so for the latter two. In the case of air freight, packing needs are very much reduced and numerous consignments are conveyed affixed to a pallet with the cargo enveloped in a plastic cover to protect it from scratching, dust, moisture, etc. Likewise, an examination of the type and quality of the packing used can often produce favourable results for the exporter or shipper. One must endeavour to ensure the packing needs are adequate and not over-generous thereby incurring increased packing costs without justification. Numerous specialized packing companies exist and the exporter new to the business is strongly advised to consult them.

(4) *The degree to which the consignment as presented aids handling.* For example, palletized cargo facilitates handling by fork lift truck employment, whilst cartons are ideal for containers, etc. Conversely, the awkwardly shaped cargo may require special facilities and handling arrangements and may be subject to a freight surcharge. Additionally, such consignments encourage broken stowage and tend to be more prone to damage which increases their premium level. In the ideal situation the consignment should be easy to handle from the time it leaves the factory premises until it reaches the retailer. Accordingly, much progress has been made to develop a code of internationally standardized package sizes which will aid distribution and optimize the use of containers and other forms of unit distribution, that is, stillages, pallets, etc. A point to bear in mind is the growing tendency to stack cargo to make the best use of warehouse cubic space and accordingly the consignment needs to be adequately robust to survive this situation. This is particularly significant with the growth of Distriparks and warehouse management.

(5) *Any statutory obligations imposed relative to the transit.* This is applicable to dangerous cargo and refrigerated foodstuffs. Certain products need special facilities both in the transport mode and terminal. This in itself restricts the choice of route, service and transport mode. For example, the movement of meat, offal, etc. requires special facilities both by the operator who ships it and in terms of inspection facilities at the import terminal. Additionally, most countries have weight and length restrictions on road vehicles. This is particularly relevant to the overall weight of containers. Likewise, there are restrictions on road haulage driver's hours and some EU countries restrict road

haulage movement at weekends. Statutory obligations also influence the type of packaging, for example, as found in the Australian trade in the use of straw and wood and the marking of cargo.

(6) *Dangerous cargo*. Again regulations are stringent regarding the packaging, stowage and mixture of dangerous cargo with other cargoes during transit. This can restrict service, routeing and schedules. The international distribution of dangerous cargo requires the most careful evaluation, as controls are tending to become more stringent (pp. 160–81).

(7) *Suitability of available transport services*. For example, air freighters have limited capacity, weight allowances and dimensions and the cargo may require extensive collection and delivery arrangements. Moreover, it may be necessary to componentize the cargo to enable it to be carried in an air freighter, container, swap-body or trailer within the prescribed weight and dimensions limitations imposed per consignment. Additionally, air freight offers fast transits and reduced packing needs. In contrast, the deep-sea multi-modal container service will have a much slower transit time, probably lower collection and delivery expenses (if it is a consolidated consignment), slightly more packing expense, less frequent service, but a lower freight rate. The Ro-Ro operator will have similar features as the containerized consolidated consignment except that in the UK–Continental trade the transit time is likely to be more competitive with air. Overall, this aspect requires very careful consideration and one must bear in mind that an increasing number of exporters are now using their own vehicles to distribute their products in the UK–Continental trade. In exceptional circumstances, the shipper may resort to chartering an aircraft or vessel if sufficient cargo is available. Remember that some services may be so popular as to have no cargo space available for the next few sailings or flights.

(8) *The transit time and related urgency of consignment*. To determine the transit time overall one must take into consideration the periods of collection and delivery of the cargo. The opening of the Channel Tunnel in 1995 has provided new physical distribution opportunities. The multi-modal or intermodal service tends to provide a quicker transit. Similarly a major infrastructure improvement was completed in 2000 and opened up the Scandinavian region for Denmark to become the main route between northern and central Europe. The project involved a suspension bridge – Europe's longest – providing a 14 km permanent road and rail link between Denmark's Jutland peninsula and the island of Sealand via Fünen. Additionally, the scheme involves a 16 km fixed road and rail link between the Danish capital Copenhagen and the Swedish city of Malmö, with three bridges, an immersed tunnel and an artificial island. The project will connect with a 1800 km multi-modal project in Sweden and Finland known as the Nordic triangle. It will link Malmö by road and rail with Stockholm and via two routes to the Norwegian frontier. It will also extend to Finland via the Stockholm–Turku ferry. From Turku the links – by road and rail – will proceed via Helsinki to the Russian frontier. Countries which have a poor infrastructure, usually those less developed countries, tend to have poor distribution resources

to and from airports and seaports. Moreover, customs clearance, especially at ports, is sluggish and the multi-modal services are still in the process of evaluation and development. Air freight services offer the fastest schedules and are particularly suited to the urgent consignment.

(9) *Quantity of cargo and period over which shipment is to be made.* In broad terms, the greater the quantity available for shipment, the lower the overall distribution cost per tonne or kilogram. For example, if the exporter can originate a full container, trailer or cargo wagon load, the overall freight charge will be much cheaper than despatching the cargo under consolidation arrangements. Furthermore, a guaranteed substantial quantity of cargo conveyed over a period of time could attract a concessionary tariff. This is particularly relevant to sea transport. Again, if the circumstances are favourable, it may be advantageous to charter an aircraft or ship.

(10) *Insurance of cargo.* The premium is determined by numerous factors but primarily by the nature of cargo and mode of transport plus type of packaging. Air freight cargo insurance with its quick transits and low risk of damage and pilferage tends to have the most favourable premium rates. Container shipments are also competitive, bearing in mind the longer transit time involved.

(11) *Incoterms 2000.* This requires careful evaluation to ensure the correct term is used for the mode of transport (pp. 333–54). Two divisions exist, one for all modes (i.e. combined transport) and one for the conventional port-to-port and sea carriage only. To the exporter wishing to maximize control of the multi-modal transit, CIP, DAF, DDU or DDP should be used. Conversely, for the buyer who wishes to bear the majority of the distribution cost and risk under multi-modal transit, there exist the options of EXW or FCA. The use of FOB and CIF are confined to the conventional seaport-to-seaport operation and remain widely used. Close liaison between the buyer and seller should be maintained to ensure each fully understands their responsibilities – risk and cost – under the Incoterms 2000 used.

(12) *Freight and documentation.* In broad terms, the actual cost of sea freight tends to be very much lower than air freight, but it is not practicable to consider such cost in isolation as one must bear in mind the total overall distribution cost to embrace all the elements, viz. packing, insurance, etc. to obtain a fair assessment. Air freight tariffs, compared with road and rail, likewise tend to be high, but the margin lessens significantly the longer the transit. Documentation costs between various transport modes do not vary a great deal but, with the development of the combined transport concept in recent years involving multi-modalism, it has tended to become simplified on the basis of through rates and consignments notes with no intermediate customs examination in transit countries. The development of the LEC and LIC (pp. 191 and 494) is on the increase for regular volume shipments. It yields maximum benefits both to the buyer and seller of localized customs control.

(13) *Overall distribution costs.* Emerging from the foregoing it is clear that it is necessary to produce an overall distribution cost and evaluation of realistic

alternatives in order to arrive at a firm conclusion. The four most decisive factors are terms of export sales contract, commodity specification, freight and overall transit time, including service quality – in short the overall value added benefit obtained by using the transport mode(s) selected. Other factors embrace the cost of packaging – very significant in air freight, the convenience and reliability of the service, charges for insurance, documentation and warehousing. For example a frequent service requires less storage in a warehouse, a reduced risk of product obsolescence, less working capital, the facilitation of smoother production flow and better customer relations that emerge through a regular, reliable service. Moreover, aspects such as a low risk of pilferage or damage and better marketable condition of goods on arrival – the latter becoming of greater importance as competition intensifies – need careful evaluation. A significant factor will be the cargo quantity and, in exceptional circumstances, it may be economic to charter an air freighter or vessel. Alternatively, for the small exporter the consolidated air freight container services, or Ro-Ro services are the more suitable. Overall a plan must be devised and ideally full use should be made of the multi-modal transit where available for fmcg.

(14) *Express service.* The development of the air freight express service in recent years has been outstanding. Examples include the Speedbird Courier Service offered by British Airways and the Post Office Packet services. They are ideal for samples, small parcels and documents.

(15) *Planning.* Planning is an essential ingredient in a successful physical international distribution strategy. All parties involved in the transit should feature in the plan which enables adequate coordination, effective use of resources, commitment and continuous monitoring and review to be achieved. Furthermore, coordinating one shipper's distribution strategy with another operating in identical regions or areas could yield substantial freight cost savings and improved service. For example, it may be more economical to despatch a full trailer load, or container once every ten days, rather than use the daily consolidated service.

(16) *Credit insurance.* This needs careful evaluation (pp. 231–7).

(17) *Free trade zones.* The development of free trade zones (p. 187) and Distriparks (pp. 90–3) provides the most favourable advantage for the international entrepreneur wishing to set up a distribution point overseas. Such a base would serve markets in the region while assembly and processing would be sourced by imported products from the most cost-effective and competitive countries.

(18) *Re-export.* A large volume of goods is re-exported material and shippers should minimize their customs tariffs duties by using IPR and OPR (p. 197).

(19) *Logistics.* To conclude, the shipper transport mode choice is one which is very much logistically driven (see Chapter 6) and which is influenced by the added value the service offers to both exporter and importer.

13.3 Transport distribution analysis

Transport distribution analysis is the technique by which alternative methods of distribution are analyzed and the optimum pattern of transportation selected. It is often called physical distribution management.

In the home market, it is possible to retain overall control of sales outlets and related distribution arrangements. However, where exports are involved, problems of greater complexity arise. Exporting is driven by a market-led approach on a value added basis; this involves a customerized approach. Overall, it involves the fusion of four contracts all of which operate within a disciplined timescale and require continuous monitoring to sustain cost control by all the interested parties. Today shippers are increasingly looking at the total production and value added chain within the just-in-time concept. The one-stop operator will look after all the arrangements regarding the execution of the export sales contract. Distribution involves not one manager, but several in one or more aspects of distribution efficiency. Production planning, components sourcing, effective deployment of company resources, type of documentation, channels of distribution, method of payment, cash flow, level of profitability, loadability of transport mode, cargo routeing, frequency of despatch, customs planning, inventory controls and level of sales, can be substantially improved if the most ideal pattern of physical distribution and Incoterm 2000 is selected.

We will now identify the various elements involved, as previously discussed on pp. 284–8, and examine case studies of actual international consignments.

(1) *Quantity, type of packages and their configuration.* This must specify the quantity of cargo available for despatch and the method of packaging (pp. 150–4).
(2) *Total weight of consignment.* This should be quoted on a net or gross weight basis usually in kilograms.
(3) *Total volume of shipment.* This should be given on a m^3 or ft^3 basis. Remember that different tariff structures apply to air, road and sea transport. Usually, for certain high-volume commodities, there is an advantage in despatching by air, whereas for sea transport weight and measurement rates (whichever produces the greatest revenue) will apply.
(4) *Value of goods ex-works.* This is the value of the goods at the factory awaiting collection for shipment.
(5) *Packing cost.* In sea transport, packing cost can represent a formidable percentage of the total distribution cost but, with air freight, it is much reduced and is a strong marketing point in persuading the shipper to use this mode of transport (pp. 146–50).
(6) *Inland charges at point of origin.* This incorporates all the costs incurred in transporting the consignments from, for example, the factory production site to the nominated airport or seaport for despatch overseas (p. 123).
(7) *Freight.* This embraces the air and sea freight comparisons. Usually, air freight rates are more expensive than sea transport, but each has a differing tariff structure (pp. 122–8).

The decision over the most profitable method of distribution, however, cannot be based on pure freight cost alone. The related costs and revenues must also be evaluated. Overall, this involves, when applicable, a transshipment cost either at the airport or seaport to another aircraft or vessel to the ultimate airport or seaport destination.

Basically, the most critical management decision in distribution is the selection of the transport mode. It determines three elements – transport costs, transit time and quality of service. In general, there is an inverse relationship between transit time and transport costs. The quicker the transit, the higher the transport cost. Conversely, the slower the transit, the cheaper the transport cost. With regard to quality of service, an unreliable cheap service is unlikely to obtain strong market support in a situation where arrival times are of paramount importance for the importer (buyer).

(8) *Inland charges at destination*. This includes cartage, handling charges, customs clearance, agency expenses and demurrage. Overall, it includes the transportation cost from airport or seaport to ultimate destination. Insofar as shipping is concerned, it could involve transshipment to lighterage.

(9) *Duty and taxes*. This includes VAT or its equivalent. Likewise it includes import duties. Advantages for air distribution may materialize if duties are based on FOB value (value at the place of exportation). This arises from reduced packing costs and reduced costs to the airport of departure. Duties, for example, are assessed on FOB value in USA, Canada and South Africa. Conversely, it may be a disadvantage to air freight if the duties are based on CIF value (value at place of importation or destination) as the pure air freight is likewise subject to duty. Similar advantages and disadvantages arise relative to sea transport. Some Customs duties are assessed on the gross weight which is particularly advantageous to air freight, with less packing producing a lower tare weight; Mexico and Switzerland are applying this policy.

(10) *Insurance*. Faster transits involving a reduced risk of damage and pilferage on air freight tend to produce more favourable insurance premiums compared with sea transport.

(11) *Unpacking/refurbishing*. The inherent advantages of air freight tend to favour such a shipper insofar as unpacking and refurbishing are concerned when compared with maritime transport. Reduced packing tends to make unpacking less expensive. Moreover, any special refurbishing process for the goods before use is not necessary, such as degreasing of machinery and apparatus, ironing of textiles, etc.

(12) *Cost of capital tied up with transit*. During the time of transportation from door to door either the exporter or importer has invested money into the merchandise without receiving an equivalent interest, or deriving a profit from it. The longer the transit and the higher the merchandisable value, the greater the capital investment involved. This factor may be of minor importance for a single shipment, but carry greater significance for all consignments during a specified period.

(13) *Inventory and storage costs*. The costs of keeping stocks at the place of production and consumption involves four basic elements as follows:

(a)   cost of capital tied up in inventories;
(b)   obsolescence, deterioration, insurance, taxes, etc.;
(c)   administration and handling;
(d)   warehousing and accommodation.

The cost percentage on the average stock value may be as high as 25 per cent per year, but much depends on warehouse location and size, plus type of commodity. The specific advantages of air freight, namely speed, safety, reliability and frequency may result in a reduced lead time for the importer and enable him or her to increase the shipping frequency for the fast-moving items. Instead of shipping quantities covering the demand for several months, it might be more favourable to air freight more frequently, covering only several weeks' demand. This produces a lower working stock, less warehouse accommodation and reduced risk of stock deterioration or obsolescence; it extols the concept of just-in-time. The consignment itself should be of optimum size to contain transportation cost.

Both the high quality of air freight and the shorter lead-time considerably lower the risk of stockpiling, commodity deterioration or obsolescence to the importer, thereby reducing his or her financial risk. A reduction of working and service stocks results in a reduced average stock level for the importer so that the turnover rate is increased, and the inventory and storage cost decreased.

(14) *Marketing*. With regard to marketing, many export-orientated companies find themselves having great difficulty achieving their marketing objectives because insufficient consideration is given to distribution. Sales and advertising combine to stimulate demand for a product but, unless – by planned distribution – the product is at a point-of-sale when the consumer decides to purchase, a sale is often lost. Even if the sale is not lost, customer service standards fall, in that the customer is forced to delay purchase and, while the demand may be so strong that the delay is suffered, the likelihood of a repeat purchase at a later date is reduced. A similar situation applies to 'after-sales service', a good example being a spare part. The speed with which the customer can obtain a replacement part for a machine strongly influences his opinion of the supplier, and therefore the likelihood of repeat purchase.

Quick delivery is often vital in providing a high level of customer service which would otherwise only be achieved by holding prohibitively high levels of stock. In fact, situations do exist where the setting-up of a stock-holding could be uneconomic, and dependence is totally upon rapid transit. A good example emerges from test marketing, where a company testing a new product whose success is uncertain will meet demand direct from production without expensive stockpiling.

(15) *Speed*. A high-speed transport mode reduces stock levels – both static and transit – and the financial implications are, therefore, apparent. In effect, the average lead time between manufacture and sale is shortened and this must mean a

saving in financial resources. In reality, it improves a company's cash flow or liquidity.

(16) *Other cost and revenue factors.* In addition to the transportation and distribution costs already mentioned, the specific performance criteria of a transport mode have an influence on other cost and revenue factors in ordering, production and administration. These 'hidden' advantages are often difficult to evaluate but they require consideration by both the exporter and importer to find the most profitable method of distribution.

We will now examine two case studies of transport distribution analysis, which appear in Tables 13.1 and 13.2.

The following points are relevant in the foregoing transport distribution analysis including the two examples given:

(1) With the growing development of maritime container services and Ro-Ro services in UK–Continental trade, the advantage differential, particularly in terms of packing cost, reduced transit times and service quality, is being moderately reduced in comparison with air shipment. Conversely, the air

TABLE 13.1 Distribution analysis – example A: textiles from London to Japan. Gross weight for surface transportation: 1024 kg (165.97 ft³)

	Air transportation cost in UK £s	Surface transportation cost in UK £s
Value ex-works	5500	5500
Transportation cost		
Packing	12	60
Transportation to air/sea port of departure, handling	15	50
Air/sea freight	725	130
Transportation from air/sea port of destination, handling	9	14
Import duties	1020	940
Insurance	14	46
Cost price	£7295	£6740
Cost of capital tied up in transit	7	67
Unpacking/refurbishing/storage	Not evaluated	Not evaluated
Total cost	£7302	£6807
Cost difference	+7%	
Time advantage	38 days	

Cost determinants
(a) Value per kg ex-works   UK £6.00
(b) Freight proportion air/sea   5.5:1
(c) Density   238 in³/kg

TABLE 13.2 Distribution analysis – example B: electrical appliances from London to South Africa. Gross weight for surface transportation: 173 kg (21.89 ft³)

	Air transportation cost in UK £s	Surface transportation cost in UK £s
Value ex-works	2600	2600
Transportation cost		
Packing	19	53
Transportation to air/sea port of departure, handling	5	20
Air/sea freight	117	12
Transportation from air/sea port of destination, handling	13	43
Import duties	130	134
Insurance	6	7
Cost price	£2890	£2869
Cost of capital tied up in transit	4	34
Unpacking/refurbishing/storage	Not evaluated	Not evaluated
Total cost	£2894	£2903
Cost difference	+ 0.3%	
Time advantage	41 days	

Cost determinants
(a) Value per kg ex-works   UK £15.00
(b) Freight proportion air/sea   9.9:1
(c) Density   219 in³/kg

freighter is becoming larger with bigger capacity containers thereby reducing unit costs.

(2) The differential between air and surface transit, particularly in terms of overall cost, freight rates and packing expenses, tends to be very narrow on relatively short distance transits, as experienced in the UK–Continental trade.

An example of rates strategy is found in a case study regarding the shipment of industrial products in Malaysia. It involved the Selangor Cement Company based in Rowang which had an annual production capacity of 6 million tonnes, but it was seriously under-utilized due to a recession in the late 1980s and the need to develop export markets became urgent in order to avoid closure. Suitable markets for bagged cement were found in Tahiti, Nepal, Sri Lanka, Vietnam, Taiwan and China. At this time, the bulk of Malaysian shipments of clinkers and cement in bags passed through Kampung Acheh in Lumut and Bumirel in Port Dickson. Such ports had low port charges but also poor facilities.

Port Klang, the major port of Malaysia, saw a market potential in such business and negotiated to secure the business. It was able to offer improved port facilities compared with the minor ports used. The shipper recognized such advantage but looked for a competitive price for a guaranteed annual shipment of 100 000–150 000 tonnes. Rowang was also conveniently situated close to Port Klang. A key factor was shipment which was made under F10 terms (p. 492). The cost from Rowang to Lumut or Port Dickson, inclusive of ports cost and inland transport, was $19.50 per tonne on shipper's account. In comparison the cost of inland transportation between Rowang and Port Klang was $8.00 per tonne and Selangor Cement Company would divert the bulk of the traffic if the total port costs did not exceed $11.50 per tonne, inclusive of port charges, wharfage and stevedorage.

To achieve the $11.50 per tonne objective it would be necessary to provide a dedicated transit shed at Port Klang to enable the shipper, at his expense, to undertake all the processing of the cargo. This would include: off-loading the bags from the lorry or wagon onto the shipper's pallets; palletizing cargo embracing the use of plastic sheets and strapping the cargo into unit loads or pallets; and finally, stacking the unit loads or pallets in the transit shed. Port Klang would not be involved in such activities. However, it would be necessary for industrial relations reasons to hire fork lift trucks and drivers from Port Klang. The transit shed rental was $8.07 per square metre for each 28-day period.

Overall, the deal yielded the following rates per tonne:

	Existing rates as in port authority tariff		Proposed negotiated rates with shipper	
	Palletized	Non-palletized	Palletized	Non-palletized
	$	$	$	$
Port charges	5.50	5.50	3.50	3.50
Wharfage	2.50	2.50	2.50	2.50
Stevedorage	3.50	5.60	3.40	5.60
Total	11.40	13.60	9.40	11.60

Accordingly, the $9.40 rate per tonne was achieved for direct shipment and loading of the palletized cargo. It produced the following financial results for Port Klang and enabled them to enter the cement market:

Proposed consolidated rate inclusive of port charges, wharfage and stevedorage (50 000 tonne at $9.40 and 50 000 tonne at $11.60)	1 050 000
Transit shed rental – 20 weeks	93 750
Hire of forklifts 50 000 tonne – 200 tonne per gang – 250 gangs and $66 per forklift	16 500
Hire of drivers 50 000 tonne – 200 tonne per gang – 250 gangs and $19 per driver	4 750
	$1 165 000

Additional income to the port would accrue from ancillary services such as pilotage, tugboats and berthing. The shippers disbursement costs were calculated as follows:

	Palletized cargo		Non-palletized cargo	
(A) *Fixed cost per tonne*				
Port charge	3.50		3.50	
Wharfage	2.50		2.50	
Stevedorage	3.40		5.60	
		$9.40		$11.60
(B) *Variable cost per tonne*				
Transit shed rental	1.12		0.47	
Hire of fork lift and drivers	0.46	$1.58	0.45	$0.92
		$10.98		$12.52
Less wharfage payable by shipowner		$2.50		$2.50
		$8.48		$10.02

Overall, this case study demonstrates that for guaranteed shipments a rebate can be granted, which in this case was $2.00 per tonne.

To conclude, transport distribution analysis forms an important evaluation today in helping the exporter or importer to decide on the best method of transportation. Airline operators, together with some maritime cargo operators, provide cargo consulting or distribution advisory services which the shipper is well advised to use. Alternatively, the freight forwarder can always help in this regard.

An example of a new development in transport distribution is emerging in Switzerland. It concerns Danzas, one of the top five European freight forwarders, which is increasingly moving away from its traditional forwarding, customs brokerage and transportation origins. Danzas sees its role as providing total logistics for large internationally active customers. According to the market, an exporter or importer with a production line in Korea needs not only a European distribution system, but also the pipelines and gateways which feed this distribution system from production sites within and outside Europe. One of Danzas' moves into total logistics was with the world-famous Swiss confectionery firm, Jacobs Suchard Tobler. From the initial negotiations in November 1988, Danzas devised and built an entire temperature-controlled warehousing and distribution system at Schaffhaussen in northern Switzerland. The warehouse was built and completed within nine months and, since the beginning of 1990, the Danzas Logistics Centre at Schaffhaussen has been handling the worldwide distribution of the entire finished goods output of Jacobs Suchard Tobler.

Jacobs Suchard Tobler's annual throughput of mostly branded chocolates and confectionery is around 26 000 tonnes and consists of over 100 000 individual consignments. These consignments have to be distributed throughout the world in carefully controlled conditions. The Danzas Logistics Centre in Schaffhaussen was built to Danzas' specifications with the support of the Technische Universität Berlin. It comprises over 6500 tonnes of steel and concrete and is located on the main road axis of northern Switzerland and is connected to the Swiss railway network (SBB). The maximum dimensions of the building are 100 m long × 17.6 m high × 61 m wide covering an area of 5826 m². It is staffed entirely by Danzas employees – 50 in total.

The Danzas Logistics Centre is divided into five main areas: goods reception; high-rack storage; order processing and consolidation zone; goods despatch; and offices. The goods reception area for Jacobs Suchard Tobler's production has a surface area of 736 m^2 and a storage capacity of 3311 m^3. Palletized goods are received either by road via four ramp height loading bays or by rail at the 48 m SBB-connected loading area. The pallet details are automatically recorded before the pallets move to the storage area. The fully automated high-rack storage area comprises 13 rows with a height of 15 m and three different pallet heights. The rows vary in length between 49 m and 63 m and provide nearly 57 000 m^3 of storage space. The storage area is served by three rail-mounted narrow-aisle lift trucks. The total capacity of the storage area is 12 507 pallets weighing up to 750 kg, each with a maximum size of 1300 mm × 900 mm × 2000 mm high.

The order processing zone consists of five order lanes, each 56 m long, which can hold a total of up to 1000 pallets at any time. Orders are individually processed and fed to the goods despatch area. The goods despatch area has six loading bays for trailers, containers and swap-bodies, four loading bays for vans for local deliveries and a 48 m long SBB rail-connected loading bay.

The Centre is controlled by interrelating computer systems with material flow simulations to optimize automatic warehousing operations. The heating (16°C + 1°C/–2°C) and relative humidity (30–60 per cent) in the east and west wings of the high-rack storage area are independently controlled. Heating in the goods reception, goods despatch, order processing and consolidation areas is independently controlled at 18°C (±2°C).

With this dedicated automatic warehouse, Danzas has not only constructed a new building, but has also installed a software package, developed in-house, for the management of all warehousing functions, including the computer link to Jacobs Suchard Tobler, Switzerland.

14

Export documentation

An important part of export practice and management is a good comprehension of the various documents involved in processing the export consignment. Moreover, the need to understand the role of such documents and their limitations together with likely problems which they may encounter is likewise important. If an exporter has any doubt over the role of, or query over, a particular document the best course to follow is to contact his or her bank or freight forwarder.

In processing an export consignment involving extensive documentation, one must bear in mind there can be up to four contracts to execute. These include: the export sales contract, the contract of carriage, the financial contract and, finally, the contract of cargo insurance. All these have to be reconciled with the processing of the export consignment. The need to have the relevant documentation correctly completed and the checklists found in this and Chapters 12 and 15 closely adhered to, cannot be stressed too strongly. Failure to do so results in delay in payment for goods, loss of goodwill between buyer and seller, late delivery of the merchandise, and so on. Successful international trade is only realized through complete professionalism in the use and execution of documentation with a zero error rate, otherwise delays are encountered when processing the goods through customs, making payments, etc. which are costly to the shipper. Documents presented to customs and banks are frequently incorrect, resulting in delays in customs clearance and extra charges having to be met by the shipper, payment delays occurring and extra bank charges arising.

This chapter, in the main, excludes documentation relating to customs and finance, which is covered in Chapters 9, 10 and 12. A study of the various documents now follows. The subject is comprehensively dealt with in the companion volume *Shipping and Air Freight Documentation for Importers and Exporters* (second edition) Witherby, 2000.

14.1 Air waybill

The air waybill is the consignment note used for the carriage of goods by air. It is often called an air consignment note and is not a document of title or a transferable or negotiable instrument. The document travels with the cargo and it is not possible to use it as a negotiable instrument for letter of credit purposes, as the cargo would arrive at the destination airport days or sometimes weeks before the air waybill's arrival via the banking system, thereby allowing the consignee to take delivery of the goods (p. 350). The air waybill is basically a receipt for the goods for despatch and is *prima facie* evidence of the conditions of carriage. Overall, there are usually twelve copies of each air waybill for the shipper, the sales agent, the issuing carrier (airline operator), the consignee, as a delivery receipt, for the airport of destination, the third carrier (if applicable), the second carrier (if applicable), the first carrier, as an extra copy for the carrier (when required), as an invoice and at the airport of departure. Copies 1, 2 and 3 are the originals. Not every copy is used for all consignments, but merely as circumstances demand. For example, the second carrier's copy would be used only if the consignment was conveyed on another airline to complete the transit – such as British Airways conveying it for the first leg of the journey and Air Canada for the remainder. The conditions of carriage are found on the reverse of the air waybill document and are subject to the Carriage by Air Act 1961. This is based on the Warsaw Rules and a number of other conventions (p. 133).

The standard IATA air waybill (AWB), used worldwide, is the most important feature of the simplified system of documentation for air freight moving internationally. It is the basic airline document covering the movement of shipments on international air freight services. A single air waybill covers carriage over any distance, by as many airlines as may be required to complete the transportation. When goods carried by one airline for part of the journey are transferred to another airline, the original air waybill is sent forward with the consignment from point of original departure to the final destination. When issued by the airline, the air waybill features a unique reference number which commences with the carrier prefix. The air waybill is the key to tracing the flight details of the consignment.

The new 'universal' air waybill (UAWB) was introduced from 1 January 1984 and its use is mandatory. It is compatible with the United Nations (UN) layout key and can be used for both domestic and international transits.

The Warsaw Convention stipulates that the air waybill is mandatory in use and must be completed in at least three parts embracing: (a) the carrier (signed by the consignor), (b) for the consignee (signed by the consignor and carrier) and (c) for the consignor (signed by the carrier). The air waybill must contain the following data:

(1) The place and date of its execution.
(2) The name and address of the shipper.
(3) The names and addresses of the consignor and consignee.
(4) Customs data – the AWB is regarded as the skeleton pre-entry document, containing the following information: first carrier (airline); departure and destination airports and any special route to be followed; agents' IATA code (when the shipper is using an agent); value of goods and currency; full technical description of cargo dimensions, commodity code, rate class chargeable weight and freight rate.
(5) Total freight amount prepaid and/or to pay at destination is precisely defined.

(6) Details of any ancillary charges payable.
(7) Signature of the shipper or agent.
(8) Signature of the issuing carrier (airline operator) or agent.
(9) Details of booked flight and actual flight.

Efficient service depends on the accuracy and completeness of the air waybill. Hence shippers themselves must give clear and complete forwarding instructions to the airline or agent. To facilitate this procedure they may use the 'Shipper's Letter of Instruction', a standardized form which may be obtained from any airline, approved IATA Cargo Agent or forwarder. The main functions of the standard air waybill are as follows.

At departure airports it is a contract of carriage, a receipt for goods, provides a unique reference for handling inventory control and documentation reference, includes a description of goods and full rating information, includes special handling requirements, and provides basic details for the aircraft manifest. Post-flight information includes a document source for revenue collection, interlining accounting and proration and cargo statistics. At destination airports the air waybill provides a basic document for notification to the consignee, customs clearance and delivery to the consignee. Additionally it is a source document for clearance and delivery charges accounting.

Where more than one package is involved, the carrier can require the consignor to make out separate air waybills. The air consignment note must be printed in one of the official languages of the country of departure, for example, French, German, etc. Erasures are not admissible, but alterations can be made provided they are authenticated by the consignor's signature or initials. If quantities, weights, or values are altered, they must appear in words as well as figures.

The air freight consolidation market continues to grow (p. 133). This involves the IATA-accredited Air Freight Agency providing a consolidation service and enters into an agency agreement with a forwarder in the country to be served. Usually it is the same company which has a global network. The agent markets the consolidation service and despatches the merchandise as one consignment with the airline. Consolidation usually takes place at the forwarders' premises, usually near or on the airport. Alternatively, it may be at the airline export shed and placed on a pallet or ULD. The documentation involved is the Master Air Waybill (MAWB), which is issued by the airline and identifies the forwarder as the shipper and the consignee as the forwarder in the destination country. Details of all the packages in the consolidation feature in the MAWB including weight, volume and cargo description. Such consignment details are often recorded on a cargo manifest which is attached to the MAWB. The IATA Air Freight Agency issues to each shipper a House Air Waybill (HAWB) which provides a cargo description and records the MAWB number as a cross-reference. The HAWB should contain the information set out under documentary requirements when this need arises.

Under a documentary letter of credit, certain specific information or instructions to be shown on the air waybill may be requested. This usually includes: names and addresses of the exporter, importer and the first carrier or airline, the names of the airports of departure and destination together with details of any special routes, the date of the flight, the declared value of the merchandise for customs purposes, the number of packages with marks, weights, quantity and dimensions, the freight charge per unit of weight or volume, the technical description of the goods and not the commercial description, whether the freight charge has been prepared or will be paid at the destination, the signature of the exporter (or his or her agent); the place and date of issue, and finally the signature of the issuing carrier (or his or her agent).

Today many major world airlines have a fully computerized air freight documentation system permitting online access by major shippers, agents, customs and handling companies. It also extends to the use of bar codes for automatic verifications. This enables cargo handling and sorting to be undertaken electronically. An example of an air waybill is found in *Shipping and Air Freight Documentation for Importers and Exporters*, and p. 482 of this book.

14.2 Bill of exchange

Under the terms of the Bills of Exchange Act 1882, a bill of exchange has been defined as an unconditional order in writing addressed by one person to another, signed by the person giving it, requiring the person to whom it is addressed to pay, on demand, or at a fixed or determinable future time, a certain sum in money to or to the order of a specified person or bearer. Drafts can be drawn either at sight – payment to be made on demand or on presentation – or at a particular 'tenor' ('usance') – payment to be made at a fixed or determinable future date, usually within 180 days of sight of the bill of exchange by the drawer – or within 180 days of the date of the draft. The general procedure for letters of credit is for drafts to be drawn on a bank, but some credits require them to be drawn on the importer. Drafts can be drawn in pairs called 'first' and 'second' bills of exchange.

The bill of exchange is a popular way of arranging payment. The most normal procedure is for the exporter (seller) to hand the bill of exchange together with the documents to the exporter's (seller's) bank who will send them to a bank overseas for 'collection'. The overseas bank will notify the buyer of the arrival of the documents and will release them to him or her subject to one of two conditions. First, if the bill is drawn at 'sight', the buyer pays the amount of the bill in full, or secondly, if the bill is drawn payable after a certain number of days, the buyer accepts the bill, i.e. he or she signs across the bill his or her agreement to pay the amount in full at the due date.

The salient benefit of this method of payment is that the exporter (seller) can maintain control of the goods until the importer (buyer) has agreed to pay for them. However, there is still no absolute guarantee the importer (buyer) will pay, but legal procedures exist in most countries to recover money owing against bills of exchange.

The bill of exchange contains the following data:

(1) the date;
(2) a specific sum, which should agree with the amount on the export invoice;

(3) the 'tenor', that is, whether payment is to be at sight or at a stated period after sight or at a fixed date;

(4) the name of the drawee;

(5) the name and signature of the drawer;

(6) the name of the payee or order or bearer;

(7) the endorsement of the payee where applicable.

Overall, the bill of exchange should be so worded to conform to what is laid down in the credit. The following discrepancies tend to arise in processing bills of exchange and should be avoided:

(1) document drawn incorrectly or for a sum different to the credit amount;

(2) designation of the signature on the document not specified if required, e.g. director or partner.

14.3 Bill of lading

A bill of lading is a receipt for goods shipped on board a vessel, signed by the person (or his or her agent) who contracts to carry them, and stating the conditions in which the goods were delivered to (and received by) the ship. It is not the actual contract, which is inferred from the action of the shipper or shipowner in delivering or receiving the cargo, but forms excellent evidence of the terms of the contract. It is a document of title to the goods which is the subject of the contract between the buyer (importer) and seller (exporter). It is the most important commercial document in international trade, and is used to control delivery of goods transported by sea (see specimen bills of lading pp. 475–7).

Before examining the salient points, function and types of bills of lading, we will first consider two acts which play an important role in the role and function of this document, namely the Carriage of Goods by Sea Act 1971 which succeeded the Carriage of Goods by Sea Act 1924, and the Carriage of Goods by Sea Act 1992 which repealed the Bills of Lading Act 1855.

The bill of lading starts its life (in almost all cases) containing or evidencing the contract of carriage between the carrier and the shipper, under which the carrier and the shipper promises that the goods will be carried from the port of loading and safely delivered at the port of discharge. During the voyage the ownership of the goods will be normally transferred from the original seller to the ultimate receiver who will take delivery of the goods from the ship. There may in exceptional cases be 100 or more buyers who (or whose banks) will pay for the goods and then receive payment from the next buyer in the chain. During this process the goods are, of course, not in the possession of any of the parties. They are, or should be, safely on board the ship, steadily crossing the ocean. Neither the buyer of an unascertained portion of a bulk nor an indorsee after discharge have rights against the carrier.

The defect at the heart of the Bill of Lading Act 1855 was considered to be the linkage between property in the goods and the right to sue on the bill of lading contract. Under the 1992 Act this is removed.

The 1992 Act provides that any lawful holder of the bill of lading has the right of suit but that *only* he or she has the right (thus preventing more than one claimant for the same breach of contract). If, as can arise, the actual loss has been sustained by someone other than the holder of the bill of lading, the holder must account for the damages to the person who has suffered the actual loss. The Act also recognizes the rights of suit of someone who became holder of the bill of lading after discharge of the cargo, provided that he or she did so under arrangements made before that date (thereby preventing trading in bills relating to goods known to be damaged – in effect, trading in causes of action). Finally, the Act recognizes the rights of parties interested in two forms of shipping documents which are commonly used today but do not appear within the 1855 Act. The consignee under a sea waybill and the holder of a ship's delivery order will both have the right to sue on the contract in question.

This will affect the P & I Clubs who can no longer take unmeritorious defences based on lack of title to sue. Those involved in the bulk commodity trades will gain rights they did not previously have, as will the consignees named in a waybill. Less obvious is the new feature in which the banks who finance international trade will now be able to enforce the bill of lading rights in their own name.

In examining other legislation relative to maritime transport, it is relevant to mention that international conventions set out minimum terms and conditions out of which carriers cannot contract to the detriment of merchants. Carriers can, of course, accept terms more favourable to merchants. Generally speaking, international conventions aim to regulate international carriage and, in most cases, national carriage is allowed freedom of contract, although in most countries there are standard trading conditions which are usually applied.

The Hague Rules were agreed at an international convention in Brussels in 1924 and govern liability for loss or damage to goods carried by sea under a bill of lading. They are officially known as the 'International Convention for the Unification of Certain Rules Relating to Bills of Lading' and were signed in Brussels on 25 August 1924 and given effect in the UK by the Carriage of Goods by Sea Act 1924. The Hague Rules apply to all exports from any nation which ratified the Rules. This is virtually universal wherever they have not been superseded by the Hague–Visby Rules or Hamburg Rules (p. 304), either by the application of law or by contractual incorporation into the terms and conditions of the relevant bill of lading.

The main features of the Hague Rules are as follows:

(1) Minimum terms under which a carrier may offer for the carriage of all goods other than live animals, non-commercial goods including personal and household effects, experimental shipments and goods carried on deck where the bill of lading is claused to indicate such carriage.

(2) The carrier has to exercise due diligence to provide a seaworthy vessel at the voyage commencement, and this cannot be delegated. Additionally, the goods must be cared for adequately during the transit. Provided the carrier complies with these requirements, if loss or damage still occurs, he or she can rely on a number of stated defences. The majority of these elaborate on the general principle that the carrier is only liable for loss or damage caused by his or her

own negligence, or that of his or her servants, agents or subcontractors. However, the carrier remains protected in three situations where the loss or damage has been caused by negligence as detailed below:

(a) negligence in navigation;
(b) negligence in the management of the vessel (as opposed to the care of the cargo);
(c) fire, unless the actual fault or privity of the carrier.

Liability in the UK was £100 per package before the Hague–Visby Rules superseded the Hague Rules. Other nations have set alternative limits: the USA, US$500; Japan ¥100000; and Greece DR8000. In 1968 at an international conference the Hague Rules were revised primarily in the area of limitation. The amended rules, the Brussels Protocol, were signed on 23 February 1968. They are more popularly known as the Hague–Visby Rules and are reflected in the UK Carriage of Goods by Sea Act 1971.

Limitation was amended to provide a weight or package alternative and originally the limits were set in Poincare Francs – a fictitious currency. This proved unacceptable and, accordingly, the 1979 Special Drawing Rights (SDR) Protocol was adopted in February 1984. Currently there are 27 member countries, primarily European and including the UK. Limitation in terms of SDRs is now the greater of SDR 666.67 per package or unit, or SDR 2 per kilo.

The Brussels Protocol, embracing the Hague–Visby Rules, became operative in 1977 and has 34 contracting member states and a further six countries who have enacted legislation broadly in line with the Rules. The Visby amendment applies to all bills of lading in the following situations:

(1) the port of shipment is in a ratifying nation, or
(2) the place of issue of the bill of lading is in a ratifying nation, or
(3) the bill of lading applies Hague–Visby Rules contractually.

At their June 1997 Centenary Conference, the CMI who drafted the original Hague Rules and the Visby Protocol, debated the possibility of creating greater uniformity in the law of the carriage of goods by sea. The outcome was inconclusive and the only course of action agreed upon was to cooperate with the UNCITRAL in its wide consideration of the carriage of goods issues. Hence, this eliminates any early action on carriers' liability issues as the problems inherent in overcoming the difficulties in changing from a paper based to an EDI based method of trading and overcoming the Document of Title conundrum seemed to have assumed priority.

In March 1978 an international conference in Hamburg adopted a new set of rules, termed the Hamburg Rules. These radically alter the liability which shipowners have to bear for loss or damage to goods in the courts of those nations where the Rules apply. The main differences between the new Rules and the old Hague–Visby Rules are given below.

(1) The carrier will be liable for loss, damage or delay to the goods occurring whilst in his or her charge unless he or she proves that he, his servants or agents took all measures that could reasonably be required to avoid the occurrence and its

consequences. The detailed list of exceptions set out in the Hague and Hague–Visby Rules is no longer available to the carrier. In particular, the carrier is no longer exonerated from liability arising from errors in navigation, management of the ship or fire.

(2) The carrier is liable for delay in delivery if 'the goods have not been delivered at the port of discharge provided for under the contract of carriage within the time expressly agreed upon or in the absence of such agreement within the time which it could be reasonable to require of a diligent carrier having regard to the circumstances of the case'.

(3) The dual system for calculating the limit of liability, either by reference to package or weight as found in the Hague–Visby Rules has been readopted, but the amounts have been increased by 25 per cent to SRS 835 per package and SDR 2.5 per kilo. The liability for delay is limited to an equivalent of two and a half times the freight payable for the goods delayed, but not exceeding the total freight payable for the whole contract under which the goods were shipped. In no situation would the aggregate liability for both loss and/or damage and delay exceed the limit for loss and/or damage.

(4) The Hamburg Rules cover all contracts for the carriage by sea other than charter parties, whereas the Hague/Hague–Visby Rules apply only where a bill of lading is issued. The Hamburg Rules are therefore applicable to waybills, consignment notes, etc.

(5) The Hamburg Rules cover the shipment of live animals and deck cargo, whereas the Hague/Hague–Visby Rules may not.

(6) The Hamburg Rules apply to both imports and exports to and from a signatory nation, whereas the Hague/Hague–Visby Rules apply only to exporters.

The Hamburg Rules became operative in November 1992, involving the requisite minimum 20 nations. In 1998 there were 25 signatory nations with a strong contingent of African nations but only two European states – the Czech Republic and Hungary. The adoption of the Hamburg Rules destroys the uniformity which currently obtains with the Hague and Hague–Visby Rules, thereby creating a third force in the market.

The liability of the carrier under any of the foregoing sea carriage conventions is subject to the overriding provisions of the relevant Merchant Shipping Acts relating, *inter alia*, to limitation of liability. In the UK this involves the Merchant Shipping Act 1979, which implemented the 1976 International Convention on Limitation of Liability for Maritime Claims (LLMC) which became operative from December 1986. A 1996 Protocol to the 1976 LLMC was agreed on 3 May 1996 as part of the Hazardous and Noxious Substances diplomatic conference in London to up-date the levels of liability introduced on 1 December 1986. The new limits are detailed below and are likely to be operative in 2000/2001.

(1) In respect of claims for loss of life or personal injury:
   (a) 2 million SDRs for a vessel with tonnage not exceeding 2000 tons.
   (b) For a vessel with tonnage in excess thereof, in addition to that mentioned in (i):

for each ton from 2001 to 30 000 tons 800 SDRs;
for each ton from 30 001 to 70 000 tons, 600 SDRs;
For each ton in excess of 70 000, 400 SDRs.

(2) In respect of any other claims:

(a) 1 million SDRs for a vessel with tonnage not exceeding 2000 tons.
(b) For a vessel with tonnage in excess thereof, in addition to that mentioned in (i):

for each ton from 2001 to 30 000 tons 400 SDRs;
for each ton from 30 001 to 70 000 tons 300 SDRs;
for each ton in excess of 70 000 tons, 200 SDRs.

The salient points incorporated in a bill of lading can be conveniently listed as follows:

(1) the name of the shipper (usually the exporter);
(2) the name of the carrying vessel;
(3) a full description of the cargo (provided it is not bulk cargo) including any shipping marks, individual package numbers in the consignment, contents, cubic measurement, gross weight, etc.;
(4) the marks and numbers identifying the goods;
(5) port of shipment or dry port/CFS;
(6) port of discharge or dry port/CFS;
(7) full details of freight, including when and where it is to be paid – whether freight paid or payable at destination;
(8) name of consignee or, if the shipper is anxious to withhold the consignee's name, shipper's order;
(9) the terms of the contract of carriage;
(10) the date the goods were received for shipment and/or loaded on the vessel;
(11) the name and address of the notified party (the person to be notified on arrival of the shipment, usually the buyer);
(12) number of bills of lading signed on behalf of the Master or his or her agent, acknowledging receipt of the goods;
(13) the signature of the ship's Master or his or her agent and the date.

There are several types and forms of bills of lading and these include the following.

(1) *Shipped bill of lading.* Under the Carriage of Goods by Sea Act 1971 (Hague–Visby Rules), the shipper can demand that the shipowner supplies bills of lading proving that the goods have been actually shipped. For this reason, most bill of lading forms are already printed as shipped bills and commence with the wording: 'Shipped in apparent good order and condition.' It confirms the goods are actually on board the vessel.

This is the most satisfactory type of receipt and the shipper prefers such a bill as there is no doubt about the goods being on board and, in consequence, dispute on this point will not arise with the bankers or consignee, thereby facilitating the earliest financial settlement of the export sale.

(2) *Received bill of lading.* This arises where the word 'shipped' does not appear on the bill of lading. It merely confirms that the goods have been handed over to the shipowner and are in his or her custody. The cargo may be in his or her dock, warehouse or transit shed, or even inland such as at a dry port/CFS/ICD, etc. This bill, therefore, does not have the same meaning as a 'shipped' bill and the buyer under a CIF or CFR contract need not accept such a bill for ultimate financial settlement through the bank unless provision has been made in the contract. Forwarding agents will invariably avoid handling 'received bills' for their clients unless special circumstances obtain.

(3) *Through bills of lading.* In many cases it is necessary to employ two or more carriers to get the goods to their final destination. The on-carriage may be either by a second vessel or by a different form of transport (for example, to destinations in the interior of Canada). In such cases it would be very complicated and more expensive if the shipper had to arrange on-carriage him- or herself by employing an agent at the point of transshipment. Shipping companies, therefore, issue bills of lading which cover the whole transit and the shipper deals only with the first carrier. This type of bill enables a through rate to be quoted and is growing in popularity with the development of containerization. Special bills of lading have to be prepared for such through-consigned cargo.

(4) *Stale bills of lading.* It is important that the bill of lading is available at the port of destination before the goods arrive or, failing this, at the same time. Bills presented to the consignee or his bank after the goods are due at the port are said to be stale. A cargo cannot normally be delivered by the ship owner without the bill of lading and the late arrival of this all-important document may have undesirable consequences such as warehouse rent, etc.

(5) *Groupage and house bills of lading.* A growth sector of the containerized market is the movement of compatible consignments from individual consignors to various consignees usually situated in the same destination (country or area) and forwarded as one overall consignment. The goods are consolidated into a full container load and the shipping line issues a groupage bill of lading to the forwarder. This is the ocean bill of lading and shows a number of consignments of groupage of a certain weight and cubic measurement in a cargo manifest form. The forwarder issues subsequent cross referencing to the ocean bill of lading, through the house bill of lading. It is merely a receipt for the cargo and does not have the same status as the bill of lading issued by the shipowner. Shippers choosing to use a house bill of lading should clarify with the bank whether it is acceptable for letter of credit purposes, and ideally ensure it is stipulated as acceptable before the credit is opened. Advantages of groupage include: less packing; lower insurance premiums; quicker transits (usually); less risk of damage and pilferage; and lower rates when compared with such cargo being dispatched as an individual parcel or consignment (p. 138).

(6) *Transshipment bill of lading.* This type is usually issued by shipping companies when there is no direct service between two ports, but when the shipowner is prepared to transship the cargo at an intermediate port at his or her expense.

(7) *Clean bills of lading.* Each bill of lading states: 'in apparent good order and condition', which of course refers to the cargo. If this statement is not modified by the shipowner, the bill of lading is regarded as 'clean' or 'unclaused'. By issuing clean bills of lading, the shipowner admits his or her full liability of the cargo described in the bill under the law and his or her contract. This type is much favoured by banks for financial settlement purposes.

(8) *Claused bills of lading.* If the shipowner does not agree with any of the statements made in the bill of lading he or she will add a clause to this effect, thereby causing the bill of lading to be termed as 'unclean', 'foul' or 'claused'. There are many recurring types of such clauses including: inadequate packaging; unprotected machinery; second-hand cases; wet or stained cartons; damaged crates; cartons missing, etc. The clause 'shipped on deck at owner's risk' may thus be considered to be claused under this heading. This type of bill of lading is usually unacceptable to a bank.

(9) *Negotiable bills of lading.* If the words 'or his or their assigns' are contained in the bill of lading, it is negotiable. There are, however, variations in this terminology, for example, the word 'bearer' may be inserted, or another party stated in the preamble to the phrase. Bills of lading may be negotiable by endorsement or transfer.

(10) *Non-negotiable bills of lading.* When the words 'or his or their assigns' are deleted from the bills of lading, the bill is regarded as non-negotiable. The effect of this deletion is that the consignee (or other named party) cannot transfer the property or goods by transfer of the bills. This particular type is seldom found and will normally apply when goods are shipped on a non-commercial basis, such as household effects.

(11) *Container bills of lading.* Containers are now playing a major role in international shipping and container bills of lading are becoming more common in use. They cover the goods from port to port or from inland point of departure to inland point of destination – which can be an inland clearance depot, dry port or container base. Undoubtedly, to the shipper, the most useful type of bill of lading is the clean, negotiable 'through bill', as it enables the goods to be forwarded to the point of destination under one document, although much international trade is based on free carrier (named place) FCA, free-on-board (FOB), cost, insurance, freight (CIF) and carriage and insurance paid to (named point of destination) CIP (pp. 350–1) contracts.

(12) *Combined transport bill of lading.* With the development of combined transport operations, an increasing volume of both liner cargo trade and bulk cargo shipments will be carried involving the bill of lading being issued in association with a selected Charter Party. An example is found in the Combined Transport Bill of Lading 1971 – codename 'Combiconbill' issued with selected Charter Parties. See also pp. 233 of *Elements of Shipping* 7th edition. The combined transport document rules are found in the ICC Rules for a Combined Transport Document (brochure no. 298). They are widely used by major container operators and reflect the earlier Tokyo–Rome Rules, the Tokyo Rules and TCM Convention.

(13) *Straight bill of lading.* A 'straight bill' is one where the consignee is clearly nominated by name without any qualification ('To the order of' or similar). It is the opposite of an 'order bill' which is one where the consignee is shown as being 'To Order' or with a named person qualified by the words 'To the order of' or similar. The straight bill is not negotiable and cannot be used to transfer title by endorsement (or passage of a blank endorsed bill) in the way that an order bill can. In the USA, the Pomerene Act provides that delivery of goods represented by a straight bill can be made to the nominated consignee without surrender of any documentation but merely upon production of proof of identity. Elsewhere in the world the position of the carrier delivering against a straight bill is unclear.

(14) *Negotiable FIATA Combined Transport Bill.* This document is becoming increasingly used in the trade and is a FIATA bill of lading (FBL), employed as a combined transport document with negotiable status. It has been developed by the International Federation of Forwarding Agents Associations and is acceptable under the ICC Rules Uniform Customs and Practice for Documentary Credits (ICC publication no. 500) – revision 1993. The FIATA bill of lading should be stipulated in letters of credit where the forwarders' container groupage service is to be utilized and a house bill of lading is to be issued (see also pp. 306–9). FIATA states that a forwarder issuing a FIATA bill of lading must comply with the following:

(a) the goods are in apparent good order and condition;
(b) the forwarder has received the consignment and has sole right of disposal;
(c) the details set out on the face of the FBL correspond with the instructions the forwarder has received;
(d) the insurance arrangements have been clarified – the FBL contains a specific delete option box which must be completed;
(e) the FBL clearly indicates whether one or more originals have been issued.

The FIATA, FBL terms create more shipper obligations in the areas of packing, general average, payment of charges and description of goods. Additional rights are also conferred on the forwarder in the areas of lien, routeing of cargo and storage handling and transport of consignments.

(15) *FIATA Multi-modal Transport Bill of Lading (MTBL).* The FIATA Multi-modal Transport Bill of Lading (MTBL) is recognized worldwide as a negotiable document of title in line with the International Chamber of Commerce Uniform Rules for such documents. It is widely stipulated in Letters of Credit and Shipping Instructions and is recognized by the ICC Banking Commission Group as a carrier's bill and by the British Bankers Association. The FIATA MTBL carries the logo of the ICC in addition to that of FIATA and BIFA. BIFA is the sole UK authority to approve and register applications to use the MTBL. Applicants must be trading members of the Association and must show evidence of sufficient liability insurance over 2 SDRs per kilo. Members are only authorized to issue BIFA supplied or licensed MTBLs in the UK. If overseas agents or branches wish to issue an MTBL they may do so after approval by their local forwarders' association, provided that the association is an Ordinary Member of FIATA.

Basically the bill of lading has four functions. Broadly, it is a receipt for the goods shipped, a transferable document to the goods thereby enabling the holder to demand the cargo, evidence of the terms of the contract of affreightment but not the actual contract, and a quasi-negotiable instrument.

Once the shipper or his or her agent becomes aware of the sailing schedules of a particular trade, through the medium of sailing cards or some form of advertisement, he or she communicates with the shipowner with a view to booking cargo space on the vessel or container. Provided satisfactory arrangements have been concluded, the shipper forwards the cargo. At this stage, it is important to note that the shipper always makes the offer by forwarding the consignment, while the shipowner either accepts or refuses it. Furthermore, it is the shipper's duty, or that of his or her agent, to supply details of the consignment. Normally, this is done by completing the shipping company's form of bill of lading and the shipping company then signs the number of copies requested.

When the goods have been received on board the ship, the bill of lading is dated and signed by or on behalf of the carrier, usually by the Master of the ship or his or her agent, and stamped 'freight paid' or 'freight payable at destination' as appropriate. If the cargo is in good condition and everything is in order, no endorsement will be made on the document and it can be termed a 'clean' bill of lading. Conversely, if the goods are damaged or a portion of the consignment is missing, the document will be suitably endorsed by the Master or his or her agent and the bill of lading will be considered 'claused' or 'unclean'. The complete set of bills of lading is then returned to the exporter (seller) for prompt despatch to the importer (buyer). The buyer must have a negotiable bill of lading with which to clear the goods at the port of destination.

Bills of lading are made out in sets and the number varies according to the trade. Generally, it is two or three – one of which will probably be forwarded immediately, and another by a later mail in case the first is lost or delayed, together with a number of non-negotiable copies for office and filing use. In some trades, coloured bills of lading are used, to distinguish the original (signed) bills from the copies which are purely for recording purposes. The reverse of the bill of lading bears the terms and conditions of the contract of carriage. The clauses on most bills of lading are similar in effect if not in wording.

Where the shipper has sold the goods on letter of credit terms established through a bank, or when he or she wishes to obtain payment of his or her invoice before the consignee obtains the goods, he or she will pass the full set of original bills to his or her bank, who will in due course arrange presentation to the consignee against payment. The financial role of the bill of lading is explained in Chapter 12.

The shipowner or his or her agent at the port of destination will require one original bill of lading to be presented to him or her before the goods are handed over. Furthermore, he or she will normally require payment of any freight due, should this not have been paid at the port of shipment. When one of a set of bills of lading has been presented to the shipping company, the other bills in the set lose their value.

In the event of the bill of lading being lost or delayed in transit, the shipping company will allow delivery of the goods to the person claiming to be the consignee, if he or she gives a letter of indemnity. This is normally countersigned by a bank and relieves the shipping company of any liability should another person eventually come along with the actual bill of lading.

Many bills of lading are consigned 'to order' and in such situations are endorsed, normally on the reverse, by the shipper. If the consignee is named, the goods will only be released to him or her, unless he or she transfers his or her right by endorsement subject to the bill of lading providing for this.

The following items are common discrepancies found in bills of lading when being processed and should be avoided.

(1) Document not presented in full sets when requested.
(2) Alterations not authenticated by an official of the shipping company or their agents.
(3) The bill of lading is not clean when presented, such as, when it is endorsed regarding damaged condition of the specified cargo or inadequate packing thereby making it unacceptable to a bank for financial settlement purposes.
(4) The document is not endorsed 'on board' when so required.
(5) The 'on board' endorsement is not signed or initialled by the carrier or agent and likewise not dated.
(6) The bill of lading is not 'blank' endorsed if drawn to order.
(7) The document fails to indicate whether 'freight paid' as stipulated in the credit arrangements, viz. CFR or CIF contracts.
(8) The bill of lading is not marked 'freight pre-paid' when freight charges are included in the invoice.
(9) The bill of lading is made out 'to order', when the letter of credit stipulates 'direct to consignee' or vice versa.
(10) The document is dated later than the latest shipping date specified in the credit.
(11) The document is not presented within 21 days after date of shipment or such lesser time as prescribed in the letter of credit.
(12) The bill of lading details merchandise other than that prescribed.
(13) The rate at which freight is calculated, and the total amount, is not shown when credit requires such data to be given.
(14) Cargo has been shipped 'on deck' and not placed in the ship's hold. Basically, 'on deck' claused bills of lading are not acceptable when clean onboard bills of lading are required.
(15) Shipment has been made from a port or to a destination contrary to that stipulated.
(16) Other types of bills of lading have been presented, although not specifically authorized. For example, bills of lading issued under a charter party, or forwarding agents' bills of lading are not accepted unless specially authorized in the letter of credit.
(17) The document has not been issued by a freight forwarder, unless it indicates that such a freight forwarder is acting as the actual carrier or as the agent for a named carrier.

(18) If the credit terms stipulate the bill of lading should evidence that the goods are available to the 'order of a named party', it does not evidence that the goods are 'Straight Consigned' to that party. In the case of the former transfer of title it is simply a matter of endorsement; in the latter case, the bill of lading cannot be endorsed in favour of third parties unless it specifically states otherwise.

(19) If the credit terms stipulate that the bill of lading is to be issued to your order, it is endorsed by you as required in the credit.

(20) The presentation comprises a full set of originals plus (if required in the credit terms) the specified number of non-negotiable copies.

(21) The bill of lading does not include any detrimental clauses relating to defective goods or packing.

(22) The document does not show shipment of goods other than or in addition to those required.

(23) The vessel name and/or port of loading and/or port of discharge are not prefaced with the word 'intended'.

(24) It does not bear a clause with reference to 'Part Container Load' which further stipulates that goods will not be released until all bills of lading issued for that container load are presented.

(25) The document includes 'Notify Parties' as defined in the credit.

(26) If the terms of the credit require the bill of lading to show the freight charges these are shown.

Our study of the bill of lading would not be complete without a consideration of the national standard shipping note (NSSN), the common short-form bill of lading, and the common short-form sea waybill.

(1) The NSSN has replaced the mate's receipt in most UK ports, and comprises a six-part set, copies of which are retained by these parties handling the goods until they are finally onboard, from which a 'shipped' bill of lading is issued. The document is compiled by the supplier of the goods, or the shipper or freight forwarder, giving full details of the goods similar to those found on the bill of lading, against which it is matched before issue. It accompanies the merchandise to the port or terminal. The document is unacceptable for use with shipments of goods classified as dangerous.

The document also harmonizes the information to be shown among shippers and encourages the provision of better-quality information. Furthermore, it provides a multi-port set of documents for use in different areas of the port and in shipping line offices as proof of delivery of goods in the form of a dock terminal receipt featuring haulier details and receiving authority remarks, loading information and is a means of cross-checking information provided for the issue of bills of lading. The NSSN is an approved document as a skeleton customs pre-entry presentation. It is used internationally for the delivery of non-hazardous conventional break-bulk cargo, full container loads (FCL) and less than container loads (LCL) to the ports, container bases and depots. It is also used sometimes in connection with shipments by air.

The document covers shipper and forwarder and provides bills from port to port and through-transport including container bills of lading. It does not cover combined transport bills of lading. A revised SITPRO standard shipping note was introduced on 1 July 1999 (see specimen p. 478) and it is fully aligned to the UN layout key and has 17 boxes.

The common short-form bill of lading is fully negotiable and the normal bill of lading lodgement and presentation procedures remain unchanged. However, instead of the mass of small print on the reverse, there is an approved 'short-form' clause on the face which incorporates carriers' standard conditions with full legal effect. It has the following salient features.

(1) The short-form bill of lading is widely used in the trade. It may be used by shippers and freight forwarders and presented for signature to the carrier or his or her authorized agents, after a perusal and acceptance of the carrier's standard terms and conditions to which the incorporation clause in the short-form bill of lading refers.

(2) The short-form is suitable for outward shipments from the UK involving 'through' transit, or 'port-to-port' carriage of cargo for both break-bulk and unit loads of all types traditionally covered by 'long-form' bills of lading.

(3) The short-form is based upon an internationally accepted layout adopted by the UN. Such widespread acceptance of its format facilitates fast and accurate recording, processing, transmission and receipt of data relating to the movement of cargo.

(4) As confirmed by the ICC, it is acceptable within the 'uniform customs and practice for documentary 'credits'. (ICC brochure no. 500 refers – see p. 246, Item 6.)

(5) The short-form bill of lading is a document recommended by the Chamber of Shipping for use with all outward shipments from the UK and particularly by all UK shippers and carriers and their conference associates.

(6) The short-form is a document of title under which the contracting carrier undertakes to deliver the subject goods against surrender of an original document.

(7) The short-form is a 'received-for-carriage' bill with provision for endorsement evidencing goods shipped onboard when so required.

(8) The short-form is suitable for conventional and through-liner services irrespective of whether the vessel is chartered or owned by the contracting carrier. (Use of the form is not currently permissible for goods carried by combined transport operators.)

(9) It is described as a 'short-form' document because of the use of an abridged standard clause on the face of the document which incorporates the conditions of carriage of the contracting carrier. The change eliminates the mass of small print on the reverse side of bills of lading without affecting the status of the document or rights and obligations of any interested party.

(10) It is a document fully aligned to the SITPRO 'master' document with the opportunity to complete the bill of lading from such a document without any additional typing.

(11) The short-form bill of lading is an aid to achieving lower stationary costs through (a) a reduced need to hold a variety of stocks of long-form bills of lading, with individual carriers' names and conditions, plus (b) the elimination of the risk of using obsolescent forms together with the attendant complications.

The use of the negotiable bill of lading which has to be surrendered to the carrier at the destination in order to obtain delivery of the goods is traditional, but not without disadvantages. The document has to follow the goods and often, for commercial or financial reasons, passes through a variety of hands, resulting in the goods being held up at their destination pending arrival of the document – and thus expenses and additional risks are incurred and customer goodwill is probably lost.

This can be resolved through the use of a non-negotiable type of transport document – a sea waybill – in place of the negotiable traditional bill of lading. The basic feature of the sea waybill is that it provides for delivery to the consignee named in it without surrender of the transport document (see specimen sea waybill p. 477). The sea waybill has the following salient features which are similar in many ways to the common short-form bill of lading.

(1) It is a common document upon which the shipper adds the name of the contracting carrier to be used.

(2) It is a non-negotiable document consigned to a named consignee and not requiring production to obtain possession of the goods at destination.

(3) It is a received-for-shipment document, with an option for use as a shipped document.

(4) It is an aid to achieve lower stationery costs through: (a) a reduced need to hold stocks of individual carriers' bills with individual carriers' names and conditions plus (b) it eliminates the risk of using obsolescent forms together with attendant complications.

(5) It is a document fully aligned to the SITPRO 'master' document with the opportunity to complete the waybill from such a document without any additional typing.

(6) It is described as a 'short-form' document because of the use of an abridged standard clause on the face of the document which incorporates the conditions of carriage of the contracting carrier. The change eliminates the need to reprint documents to accommodate changes and conditions.

(7) It facilitates the earlier release of the goods – if received for shipment – and thereby reduces delays associated with negotiability. Moreover, it helps the speedier flow of goods to the consignee. One must bear in mind the named consignee is not required to produce the sea waybill to obtain possession of the goods at destination.

(8) The sea waybill is widely used in the trade. It may be used by shippers and freight forwarders and presented for signature to the carrier or his or her authorized agents, after a perusal and acceptance of the carrier's standard terms and conditions to which the incorporation clause in the sea waybill refers.

(9) It is suitable for outward shipments from the UK involving 'through' transit, or 'port-to-port' carriage of cargo for both break-bulk and unit loads of all types. Moreover, it is suitable for conventional and through-liner services, irrespective of whether the vessel is chartered or owned by the carrier.

(10) It is based upon an internationally accepted layout adopted by the UN. Such widespread acceptance of its format facilitates fast and accurate recording, processing, transmission and receipt of data relating to the movement of cargo.

(11) A waybill is not a document of title. Accordingly, it is not mandatory subject to the relevant Carriage of Goods by Sea Act, or the Hague or Hague–Visby Rules as obtains for a bill of lading.

(12) The popularity of the waybill will intensify as EDI develops (Chapter 15). It is an ideal document for EDI transmission.

(13) The waybill is a personal contract between the carrier and shipper to which the consignee never becomes a party. This gives the shipper the right of stoppage in transit at any time. It also means that the consignee cannot sue the carrier in his or her own name and that the carrier must settle claims with the shipper rather than the consignee.

(14) The Carriage of Goods by Sea Act 1992 recognizes the rights of the consignee in the sea waybill and the rights to sue on the contract (see p. 301).

(15) The sea waybill cannot be used in documentary credits as it is not a document of title (see p. 247).

The commercial and financial feasibility of using the sea waybill clearly rests with the shipper and consignee and is dependent upon the type of trade transaction involved. The waybill is the natural choice for trading between multinational companies and associated companies, where no documentary transaction is involved and also for open account sales. It can also be used for transactions between companies where a documentary credit transaction is not required. However, it can additionally be used in many cases involving banking transactions.

The point at which waybills are released will depend upon whether the document is 'received for shipment' or 'shipped onboard'. In signing waybills, the carrier or his or her agent is required to insert the carrier's transmission address within the signature or date stamp.

If a received-for-shipment document were issued and the cargo was subsequently short-shipped or a carrier's clause required (for example, to indicate that damage was sustained whilst the goods were on the quay) then a qualification report should be issued to the shipper, consignee and those concerned within the carrier's organization; information concerning such reports should also be made available to insurers on request. Use of the 'shipped' option would, however, obviate the need for a qualification report, and, in such circumstances the normal bill of lading procedures would apply.

If a 'shipped onboard' document were issued, then the provision of the 'shipped' option should be in a manner which if the document were to be presented under a documentary credit, will satisfy 'Uniform Customs and Practice for Documentary Credits' 1993, No. 500. This refers to a procedure whereby waybills can be endorsed to specify that the goods mentioned have been loaded onboard a named vessel or shipped on a named vessel, the loading onboard date being specified.

As we enter the next century, the waybill will become more widely used, especially between established consignors and consignees who have been trading for many years and wish to take full advantage of EDI benefits.

To conclude our study of bills of lading, it is relevant to mention that the legislation is not identical in every country, as has been demonstrated in earlier pages (pp. 301–5), through various conventions.

14.4 Cargo insurance policy and certificate

It is most important to have insurance cover against loss or damage that may occur during shipment. The export sales contract with the buyer must clearly state who is responsible for arranging the insurance at all stages from the time the merchandise leaves the exporter's premises until the buyer takes possession. This embraces transportation of the goods to the seaport, airport, or inland clearance depot, the period during which the merchandise is stored awaiting shipment or loading, the periods whilst the goods are on board the ship, aircraft or other conveyance such as the through international road transport, the off-loading and storage on arrival, and finally transportation to the buyer. This involves primarily Incoterms 2000 (pp. 336–9).

The cargo insurance policy is fully explained in Chapter 10 (see specimen p. 483).

Overall, the insurance policy certificate must contain the following:

(1) the name and signature of the insurer;
(2) the name of the assured;
(3) the endorsement of the assured when applicable so that the rights to claim may be transferred;
(4) a description of the risk covered;
(5) a description of the consignment;
(6) the sum or sums to be insured;
(7) the place where claims are payable together with the name of the agent to whom claims may be directed.

Basically, the insurance policy certificate must embrace the following relative to the processing of the international consignment:

(1) cover the risk detailed in the credit arrangements;
(2) be in a completed form;
(3) be in a transferable form;
(4) be dated on or before the date of the document evidencing despatch, for example, bill of lading;
(5) be expressed in the same currency as that of the credit.

The insurance policy certificate must avoid containing the following discrepancies when presented under a letter of credit.

(1) The amount of cover is insufficient or does not include the risks mentioned in the credit.

(2) The insurance is not issued in the currency of the credit.

(3) The insurance policy certificate is not endorsed and/or signed.

(4) The certificate or policy bears a date later than date of shipment/despatch.

(5) The goods are not correctly described.

(6) The alterations on the insurance policy certificate are not authenticated.

(7) The insurance policy certificate is not in a transferable form when required.

(8) The carrying vessel's name is not recorded.

(9) The insurance policy certificate does not cover transshipment when bills of lading indicate it will take place.

When a policy is called for under a letter of credit, a certificate is not acceptable. However, a policy is acceptable when a certificate is requested. Broker's cover notes are not acceptable unless specifically permitted in the credit.

It is important to bear in mind when the shipper, exporter, or agent is preparing the insurance document for presentation to the bank, that it is in the currency of the documentary letter of credit; the insurance is for the value specified in the credit; it covers all risks specified in the credit; the insurance document is dated prior to the despatch of goods or indicates that cover is effective from the shipment date; and finally the insurance policy is presented when the credit so stipulates.

14.5 Certificate of origin

The certificate of origin specifies the nature, quantity and value of the goods, etc. together with their place of manufacture. Such a declaration, stating the country of origin of the goods shipped is required by some countries, often to simplify their customs duties. It is frequently incorporated in the customs invoice. In a minority of cases, the declaration has to be authenticated by a Chamber of Commerce. It could also incorporate the selling price of the goods termed the current domestic value (CDV), in which case it is likely to be embraced in the invoice.

Generally, certification of origin for non-preferential purposes is a trade policy issue with wider connotations than preferential origin. It may be required to identify favoured nation status goods, in order to reduce import duties or, from a negative perspective, to identify commodities originating from certain regions or countries the importation of which may be restricted or prohibited. The declaration may also be made on other commercial documents, such as the packing list or consignment note (*inter alia*). The documentation for each system varies, but comprises basically of one of the following.

Certificate of Origin

This is a standard document and is required in a number of countries. The certificate must conform to specific conditions, which govern the format and layout of the document as well as specifying the quality of the paper required, for example, it must be printed with a guilloche background. It must be endorsed by an authorized body in the issuing country before it is valid.

Arab Certificate of Origin

This is required for exports to Arab nations – with the exception of Iran, which accepts the EU Certificate. Some countries also require the EU Certificate of origin, but endorsed by the Arab Chambers. The form is in a prescribed format, with both the language of the issuing country and Arab box titles. Normally it has to be authenticated by both the local Chamber of Commerce and the Arab Chamber of Commerce before it is valid.

Combined Certificates of Value and Origin

The use of these documents has reduced over the past few years, however, they are still required in some highly regulated markets, such as Nigeria. Some other countries such as South Africa require certificates of origin only (e.g. the DA 59). The requirement for the layout of the document is often more relaxed than for other similar forms and the document tends to replace the commercial invoice for official purposes. The information supplied is the same as in the invoice with supplementary declarations.

14.6 Certificate of shipment

The FIATA Forwarder's Certificate of Receipt (FCR) and Forwarder's Certificate of Transport (FCT) are becoming increasingly accepted in the trade as the recognizable document confirming a receipt of the goods.

The FCR and FCT are usually issued under FCA Free Carrier Incoterms 2000, involving a multi-modal transport operation. Alternatively, they may be used when the supplier sells the goods ex-works or when the goods are being despatched via a forwarder's groupage service and a recognized document is needed to prove that the goods are no longer in the control of the seller. In such situations, the freight forwarder would be acting as principal or as road carrier.

14.7 Charter party

A charter party is a contract whereby a shipowner agrees to place his or her ship, or part of it, at the disposal of a merchant or other person (known as the charterer), for the carriage of goods from one port to another port on being paid freight, or to let his or her ship for a specified period, his or her remuneration being known as hire money. The terms, conditions and exceptions under which the goods are carried are set out in the charter party.

A very large proportion of the world's trade is carried in tramp vessels. It is quite common to find that one cargo will fill a whole ship and, in these circumstances, one cargo owner or one charterer will enter into a special contract with the shipowner for the hire of his or her ship. Such a contract is known as a charter party. It is not always a full ship, although this is usually the case. There are basically two types of charter parties: demise and non-demise.

A demise or 'bareboat' charter party arises when the charterer is responsible for providing the cargo and crew, whilst the shipowner merely provides the vessel. In consequence, the charterer appoints the crew, thus taking over full responsibility for the operation of the vessel, and pays all expenses incurred. A demise charter party is for a period of time which may vary from a few weeks to several years.

A non-demise charter arises when the shipowner provides the vessel and her crew, whilst the charterer merely supplies the cargo. It may be a voyage charter for a particular voyage, in which case the shipowner agrees to carry cargo between specified ports for a prearranged freight. The majority of tramp cargo shipments are made on a voyage charter basis. Alternatively, it may be a time charter for a stated period or voyage for a remuneration known as hire money. The shipowner continues to manage his or her own vessel, both under non-demise voyage or time charter parties under the charterer's instructions. With a time charter, it is usual for the charterer to pay port dues and fuel costs, and overtime payments incurred in an endeavour to obtain faster turn-rounds. It is quite common for liner companies to supplement their services by taking tramp ships on time charter, but this practice may lessen as containerization develops.

There are several types of non-demise voyage charter and these are given below. It will be seen that they all deal with the carriage of goods from a certain port or ports to another port or ports and the differences between them arise mainly out of payment for the cost of loading and discharging and port expenses.

(1) *Gross form of charter*. This is probably the most common form of charter used by tramp ships today. In this form, the shipowner – in return for a higher freight – meets the cost of employing the stevedores at either the loading port or the port of discharge or both.

(2) *Net terms*. Under those terms the cargo is loaded and discharged at no cost to the shipowner. The cost of stevedores at the loading port is borne by the shipper and, at the port of discharge, by the receiver. The term net terms is not in common use but is generally referred to as 'free-in-and-out' (FIO) with exactly the same meaning.

(3) *FIO charter*. Under this charter the cargo is loaded and discharged at no cost to the shipowner. The cost of stevedores at the loading port is borne by the shipper and at the port of discharge by the receiver.

(4) *Liner terms*. Under this charter, usually found in the short sea trade, the shipowner is responsible for loading, stowing and discharging the cargo. Usually the shipowner selects and appoints the stevedores, but this can be an area of discussion during the fixture negotiations.

(5) *Lump sum charter.* In this case, the charterer pays a lump sum of money for the use of the ship and the shipowner guarantees that a certain amount of space (that is, bale cubic metres) will be available for cargo, along with the maximum weight of cargo that the vessel will be able to carry. A lump sum charter may be on either a gross basis or an FIO basis. Such a charter is very useful when the charterer wishes to load a mixed cargo – the shipowner guarantees that a certain amount of space and weight will be available and it is up to the charterer to use that space to his or her best advantage.

The above forms of charter are all quite common today and, in each case, the ship owner pays the port charges.

There are, of course, numerous variations that may be made to the above broad divisions and this is a matter for negotiation when the vessel is being 'worked' for future business. For example, the gross and FIO charters may be modified to an FOB charter (free on board) meaning that the charterer pays for the cost of loading and the shipowner pays for the cost of discharge, or alternatively the charter may be arranged on the basis of free discharge, that is, the charterer pays for the cost of discharging. The same general terms of contract are found in all the above types of charter.

The Baltic Exchange based in London provides a unique professional market for cargo interests, shipowners, shipbrokers, port operators, agents and all those involved in international freight transport by sea. Overall, it is a market place which is self-regulated with strict business ethics. It deals with cargoes, buying and selling ships, commodities and aircraft chartering. The chartered tonnage may be for a voyage, period of time (time charter), trip time chartering, contract of affreightment, joint ventures, pooling, paralleling or bare-boating.

The shipowner may be a fleet mega-operator or a single operator (family business), or the vessels may be state-owned tonnage, privately owned national registered tonnage, offshore registered privately owned tonnage or bare-boat. The charterer may be a single commodity dealer, a trader, a state enterprise, a ship operator, a liner operator involving NVOCC or parallel tonnage.

The modern Baltic Exchange increasingly relies on electronic communications. Today, there are some 400 chartering and brokerage firms in the Baltic Exchange in London, together with about 150 sales and purchase operations of ships. The London based broking firms handle most of the world's sale and purchase deals. The Agents for the Greek shipowning community in London employ some 3000 brokers, though not all are Baltic Exchange members. Traditionally, the Baltic Exchange membership has been drawn from those based in the City of London, but since 1994 overseas members have been permitted. This latter category, subject to the same business ethics of the Baltic Exchange, is growing quickly.

The services provided by the shipbroker are wide ranging. Nowadays modern communications, – E-commerce and the Internet, relying on computers and VDUs – enable brokers to keep abreast of current developments and opportunities, but the tradition of meeting face to face continues. The Baltic Exchange brokerage clientele is in daily contact with the other major international dry cargo market centres based in Hamburg, Oslo, Piraeus, New York, Tokyo, Hong Kong and Singapore.

It will be appreciated that the terms and conditions of a charter party will vary according to the wishes of the parties to the contract. Nevertheless, the Chamber of Shipping together with the Baltic and International Maritime Conference have approved a number of charter parties (about 50) for certain commodities in specified trades. These include primarily the tramp trades, namely coal, wheat, timber, ore, etc. The parties to the contract are free to make any amendments to such charter parties to meet their needs and there is no obligation to use any particular charter party for a particular trade.

The subject of chartering is dealt with extensively in Chapter 15 of *Elements of Shipping*.

14.8 Convention on the Contract for the International Carriage of Goods by Road (CMR)

The international convention concerning the carriage of goods by road (CMR) came into force in the UK in October 1965, and is fully explained on pp. 53–5.

The contract of carriage, found in the CMR consignment note, is established when it is completed by the sender and carrier with the appropriate signatures or stamp being recorded thereon. The senders and the carrier are entitled respectively to the first and third copies of the consignment note, and the second copy must accompany the goods. If the goods have to be loaded in different vehicles, or are of different kinds, or are divided into different lots, either party has the right to require a separate consignment note to be made out in respect of each vehicle or each kind or lot of goods. The CMR consignment note is not a negotiable or transferable document or a document of title.

The consignment note must contain the following particulars: the date when and the place where it is made out; the names and addresses of the sender, the carrier and the consignee; the place and date of taking over the goods, and the place designated for delivery; the ordinary description of the nature of the goods and the method of packing and, in the case of dangerous goods, their generally recognized description; the number of packages and their special marks and numbers; the gross weight of the goods or their quantity otherwise expressed; charges relating to the carriage; the requisite instructions for customs and other formalities; and a statement that the carriage is subject, notwithstanding any clause to the contrary, to the provisions of the convention.

Furthermore, the consignment note must contain the following particulars where applicable: a statement that transshipment is not allowed; the charges which the sender undertakes to pay; the amount of 'cash on delivery' charges; a declaration of the value of the goods; a declaration of the amount representing any special interest in delivery; the sender's instructions to the carrier regarding insurance of the goods; the agreed time limit for the carriage; a list of the documents handed to the carrier. Where the carrier has no reasonable means of checking the accuracy of the statements in the consignment note as to the number of packages and their marks and numbers, or as to the apparent condition of the goods and their packaging, he must enter his reservations in the consignment note specifying the grounds on which they are based. Where the sender requires the carrier to check the gross weight of the goods or their quantity otherwise expressed or the contents of the packages, the carrier must enter the results of such checks; and any agreement that open unsheeted vehicles may be used for the carriage of the goods. The parties may enter any other useful particulars in the consignment note.

The sender is liable for all expenses, loss and damage sustained by the carrier by reason of the inaccuracy or inadequacy of certain specified particulars which the consignment note must contain, or by reason of the inaccuracy or inadequacy of any other particulars or instructions given by him or her.

The carrier is liable for all expenses, loss and damage sustained by the person entitled to dispose of the goods as a result of the omission of the statement that the contract is subject to the convention.

For the purposes of the convention, the carrier is responsible for the acts and omissions of his or her agents and servants and any other persons whose services he or she uses for the performance of the carriage as long as those agents, servants or other persons are acting within the scope of their employment.

There is a duty on the carrier to undertake the following:

(1) to check the accuracy of the statements in the consignment note as to the number of packages and their marks and numbers, and the apparent condition of the goods and their packaging;
(2) if the sender so requires him or her, to check the gross weight of the goods or their quantity otherwise expressed or the contents of the packages;
(3) to check that the statement that the contract is subject to the convention is properly included in the consignment note.

The sender is responsible for the accuracy and adequacy of documents and information which he or she must either attach to the consignment note or place at the carrier's disposal for the purposes of customs or other formalities which have to be completed before delivery of the goods.

There is a duty on the sender:

(1) to ensure that the goods are properly packed,
(2) in the case of dangerous goods, to inform the carrier of the exact nature of the danger and indicate, if necessary, the precautions to be taken (pp. 160–81),
(3) to ensure the accuracy and adequacy of certain specified particulars which the consignment note must contain and of any other particulars or instructions given by him to the carrier.

The great majority of international road transport European (EU) consignments are conducted under open account payment terms. A bank will normally only make an advance against goods conveyed by CMR International Consignment Note if the goods are consigned to a bank in the buyer's country and are only to be released under payment by the buyer. The CMR consignment note must be carried on all hire-and-reward journeys involving an international transit.

14.9 Courier receipt

This document is used where the goods are despatched by courier service, usually involving small parcels and packets. Under UCP500 the presentation of a receipt issued by any courier company is allowed unless one is specified in the letter of credit.

Customs forms CN22 and CN23 (Royal Mail International packages)

Exporters despatching packages by Royal Mail International Services (see p. 143) are required to complete customs declaration form CN22 for goods up to a value of £270 and form CN23 for goods above £270. It is attached to the mail item with an SP301 plastic wallet. It features details of consignor, consignee, senders reference (bar coded label), list of contents and number of articles, country of origin of goods, net and gross weights (each item to be shown separately), any supporting documents, whether the contents is a gift or sample and the sender's signature. Goods originating within the EU and being despatched to member states do not require a customs declaration.

14.10 Dock receipt

This may be issued by a Port Authority to confirm receipt of cargo on the quay or warehouse pending shipment. It has no legal role regarding processing financial settlement of international consignments.

14.11 Exchange permit

The exchange permit is found particularly in Middle East trades and is usually associated with the issue of an import licence. They are usually issued by government departments, Chambers of Commerce, or Chambers of Industry, thereby authorizing import of a specific commodity. It is a means of regulating the flow of specific commodity imports and the funds associated with them.

14.12 Export Cargo Shipping Instruction (ECSI)

At the time of booking a cargo for shipment, exporters or their agents complete the Export Cargo Shipping Instruction and forward it to the shipping company. It provides all the relevant data which the carrier needs to complete the bill of lading and specifies who is responsible for freight charges. This includes packing specifications. Additionally, the ECSI makes provision for supplementary services such as customs entries. It applies to both general, LCL and FCL cargo.

14.13 Export invoicing

Export documents are never static – there is a continual stream of new overseas import regulations along with new developments and a constant issue of new forms, etc. Accordingly, the requisite invoice for a particular market should be checked to ensure the correct one is used otherwise serious delays will be encountered in processing the export order through customs. Moreover, the exporter's invoice should be carefully and accurately completed. Details of the various types of invoices are now examined.

(1) *Commercial invoice.* The commercial invoice gives details of the goods and is issued by the seller (exporter). It forms the basis of the transaction between the seller and buyer, and is completed in accord with the number of prescribed copies required. Usually it bears the exporter's own headed invoice form stationery. The invoice gives a description of the goods, stating prices and the relevant Incoterm 2000 exactly as specified in the credit, as well as shipping marks. Overall, it contains the following information:

   (a) name and address of buyer (importer) and seller (exporter);
   (b) buyer's reference, that is, order number, indent number, etc.;
   (c) number and types of packages;
   (d) weights and measurements of the consignment;
   (e) place and date of issue;
   (f) details of actual cost of freight and insurance if so requested;
   (g) total amount payable, embracing price of goods, freight, insurance and so on;
   (h) the export and/or import licence number;
   (i) the contents of individual packages;
   (j) the method of despatch;
   (k) shipment terms;
   (l) letter of credit number and details – if so requested;
   (m) country of origin of goods;
   (n) signature of exporter.

Basically the invoice is a document rendered by one person to another in regard of goods which have been sold. Its primary function is a check for the purchaser against charges and delivery. With regard to insurance claims, and for packing purposes, it is useful evidence to verify the value and nature of the goods and, in certain circumstances, it is evidence of the contract between the two parties, for example, packing not being up to specification may give underwriters redress against the sellers. The invoice is not necessarily a contract of sale. It may form a contract of sale if it is in writing and contains all the material terms. On the other hand, it may not be a complete memorandum of the contract of sale and, therefore, evidence may be given to vary the contract which is inferred therefrom. In particular circumstances, the commercial invoice can be certified by Chambers of Commerce and/or legalized by the resident consul in the UK.

(2) *Consular invoice.* Consular invoices are mandatory when shipping goods to certain ports of the world particularly to those countries which enforce *ad valorem* import duties. This applies particularly in South America. The invoices are specially printed documents which must be completed exactly in accordance with requirements and certified by the consul of the country to which the goods are consigned. This is done at the nearest convenient consular office to the port, airport or ICD of departure. The invoices are issued at the consular office and a fee is payable on certification, often based on a percentage of the commercial invoice value of the goods. The consul of the importing country retains one copy, returns one copy to the shipper, and forwards further copies to the customs authorities in his or her own country. The consular invoice may be used in some circumstances as a certificate of origin. The forms are available from consuls or possibly through Chambers of Commerce and freight forwarders. In many countries both the consular invoice and the commercial invoice are required.

(3) *Customs invoices.* Customs invoices may be required by the authorities of the importing country. An adequate number should be provided for the use of the customs authorities overseas.

(4) *Pro-forma invoice.* This type of invoice is prepared by the exporter and may be required in advance for licence or letter of credit purposes. The document includes the date, name of the consignee, quantity and description of the goods, marks and measurements of packages, cost of the goods, packing, carriage, freight, postage, insurance premiums, terms of sale, terms of payment, etc. The pro-forma invoice is despatched to the buyer to facilitate obtaining from the bank the requisite currency to buy the goods and subsequently issue a letter of credit. Additionally, it may be needed for an import licence. In countries with serious hard debt problems delays can be experienced by the buyer when seeking the necessary funds, and exporters, when dealing with such territories, tend not to process the order until receipt of the letter of credit.

The following discrepancies relating to processing invoices under letters of credit do arise and should be avoided:

(1) value exceeds credit amount;
(2) amount differs from that of bill of exchange;
(3) prices of goods not as indicated in credit;
(4) omission of the price basis and shipment terms, for example, FCA, CFR, CIF, FOB, CPT, etc.;
(5) inclusion of charges not specified in the credit;
(6) invoice not certified, notarized or signed as required by credit;
(7) buyer's name differs from that mentioned in the credit;
(8) invoice not issued by the exporter;
(9) invoice does not contain declaration required under the credit;
(10) description of goods differs from that in the credit;
(11) extra charges and/or commissions are not levied unless authorized within the credit terms;

(12) when combined Certificates of Value and Origin (CVO) are required the Certificate of Origin should have been completed and signed.

(13) when the transport document (e.g. bill of lading, air waybill, etc.) is required to indicate the amount of freight paid, the invoice does not show an amount in excess of or less than this sum (similarly, when an insurance premium has to be stated, either separately or on the insurance document itself, check the invoice does not reflect an amount in excess of, or less than, this figure);

(14) Marks, weights, number of cases/packages, name of vessel, etc. agree with the bill of lading and all other documents.

The following items must be borne in mind when the shipper, exporter or agent prepares the invoice and presents them to the bank under a documentary letter of credit.

(1) The invoice description of the goods agrees exactly with the documentary letter of credit.

(2) The invoice is addressed to the importer.

(3) The invoice includes the exact licence and/or certificate numbers required by the credit.

(4) The invoice shows the terms of shipment mentioned in the credit.

14.14 Export licensing

The UK strategic export controls are imposed by an Export of Goods (Control) Order made under the Import, Export and Customs Powers (Defence) Act 1930. They are administered by the Export Control Organization of the Department of Trade and Industry. Three types of licence are provided: open general export licence (OGEL); the Open Individual Export Licence (OIEL); and the individual or bulk licence.

Such exchange controls on goods are imposed for a variety of reasons including; the collective security of the UK and its allies in NATO; foreign policy requirements; international treaty obligations and commitments; the UK non-proliferation policy; and concerns about terrorism or internal repression.

In 1993 the DTI introduced a code of practice on export licensing control compliance. Controlled goods include arms and military equipment; high-technology industrial goods for example chemical and petroleum equipment, electrical and electronic equipment (including computers), scientific apparatus and instruments, atomic energy materials, antiques and scarce materials.

14.15 Health certificate

A health certificate is issued when agricultural and animal products are being exported to certify they comply with the relevant legislation in the exporter's country. It is issued at the importer's request to comply with the country's health regulations and confirms the product was in a good condition at the time of inspection – prior to shipment – and fit for human consumption. A health certificate issued in the UK confirms that the Food Hygiene Regulations have been complied with.

14.16 International Convention concerning the Carriage of Goods by Rail (CIM)

The international Convention concerning the Carriage of Goods by Rail (CIM) has existed in some form since 1893 and is described on pp. 57–61. It permits the carriage of goods by rail under one document, a consignment note (not negotiable), under a common code of conditions applicable to 29 countries, mainly situated in Europe and the Mediterranean areas. It embraces the maritime portion of the transit subject to it being conveyed on shipping lines as listed under the Convention. Advantages of using CIM throughout a rail consignment involving a container or cargo wagon include through rates under a common code of conditions, simplified documentation and accountancy, flexibility of freight payment, no intermediate handling (usually), nor customs examination in transit countries, through transits, and minimum customs documentation.

The CIM consignment note is completed by the shipper, agent or originating rail carrier and has six copies. It embraces the original of the consignment note, the invoice, the arrival note, the duplicate of the consignment note, the duplicate of the invoice, and a supplementary copy.

The following information must be recorded in the CIM consignment note:

(1) The date and originating rail station of the consignment.
(2) The names and addresses of the sender and the consignee.
(3) The originating rail station accepting consignment and the station or place designated for delivery.
(4) The ordinary description of the nature of the goods and method of packing and, in the case of dangerous goods, their generally recognized description.
(5) The gross weight of the goods or their quantity.
(6) The charges relating to the carriage.
(7) The requisite instructions for customs and other formalities.

The foregoing may also be required under a letter of credit. Such a document is used for cargo wagon, containerized movement, and swap-body, passing through the Channel Tunnel or international rail transits. From 1 January 1993 a form known as Consignment Note CIM was introduced. It is also known as a truck waybill.

14.17 Instructions for despatch

International IATA scheduled airlines require shippers to complete an Instructions for Despatch form (IDG) to enable an air waybill to be raised detailing the carriage to be performed. Shipping documents and advices should be attached securely to the freight or posted to the airport of despatch. The IDG will feature all details of the consignment including consignor, consignee payment arrangements and departure and destination airports. Cargo airlines will also accept a letter of instruction as a substitute for the IDG.

14.18 Letters of hypothecation

This is a banker's document outlining conditions under which the international transaction will be executed on the exporter's behalf, the latter of whom will have given certain pledges to his or her banker. It may be by direct loan, acceptance, or negotiations of draft thereto.

14.19 Letters of indemnity

The role of the letter of indemnity is to permit cargo to be released to a consignee without production of the original endorsed bill of lading, or to permit the issue of a duplicate set of documents when the original bills of lading have been lost or mislaid in transit. It is a document of legal and commercial convenience, and should be used with care and caution. The need for this form arises from the risks involved in permitting delivery of cargo without an original bill of lading, or in issuing a duplicate set of bills of lading. It usually requires the counter signature of a reputable bank – but this is not necessary when it is submitted on behalf of a national government.

14.20 Mate's receipt

A Mate's receipt is sometimes issued in lieu of a bill of lading. It has no legal authority regarding the processing of the financial settlement of international consignments but merely confirms cargo is placed on board a ship pending issue of a bill of lading. In many countries the National Standard Shipping Note has replaced the Mate's receipt.

14.21 Packing list

In recent years the role of the packing list document has intensified and it is becoming a mandatory document required by customs and banks under documentary credit systems. It is very much in evidence in containerized shipments.

The document, sometimes called a packing note, is provided and completed by the shipper at the time the goods are despatched and accompanies the goods and the carrier's documents such as bill of lading, sea waybill, air waybill, CIM and CMR consignment notes throughout the transit. It is placed in the container, trailer, pallet, ULD, etc. The packing list gives details of the invoice, buyer, consignee, country of origin, vessel or flight date, port or airport of loading, port or airport of discharge, place of delivery, shipping marks, container number, weight and/or volume (cubic) of the merchandise and the fullest details of the goods, including packaging information.

14.22 Parcel post receipt

The parcel post receipt is issued by the Post Office for goods sent by parcel post. It is both a receipt and evidence of despatch. It is not a document of title and goods should be consigned to the party specified in the credit. An airmail label should be fixed to a postal receipt in respect of air parcel post despatch; alternatively the Post Office should stamp the receipt 'air parcel'. Goods sent by post should be consigned to the party specified in the documentary credit. See also p. 143, Customs Form CN22 and 23.

14.23 Phytosanitary (plant health) certificate

The importation of all plant material, forest trees and other trees and shrubs, and certain raw fruit and vegetables must be accompanied by a phytosanitary certificate in most countries. In some countries the importation of certain species of plants from certain areas of the world is prohibited. Application for such plant health certificates should be made to the agricultural department of the exporting country.

14.24 Pre-shipment inspection certificate

An increasing number of shippers and various organizations, authorities and governments in countries throughout the world are now insisting on inspection of goods. This embraces their quality, the quantity being exported and the price(s) proposed and market price(s) comparison at the time of shipment. An organization which undertakes such work – which can extend to transshipment *en route* – is the Société Générale de Surveillance (SGS) or ship classification societies such as Bureau Véritas. The SGS representative will examine the goods at the place of manufacture or assembly prior to despatch. This is to ensure they comply with the description found in the export sales contract, bill of lading or export invoice. Subsequently the goods will be examined and checked as they are loaded into the container or onto the ship. In situations where sellers are at variance with SGS opinion, they may present their position to the SGS principals, either directly or through the importer.

If everything is in order, a clean report of findings (CRF) will be issued by SGS to their principals. This is required together with other commercial documents such as the bill of lading, the letter of credit, the invoice in order to obtain payment via the commercial bank and/or customs clearance import. If a non-negotiable report of findings (NNRF) is issued by SGS, the seller (exporter) may opt to discuss the matter with the principal involved, who remains the final arbiter. Such a situation arises where goods are shipped before SGS inspection has taken place. In due course, SGS will issue the pre-shipment inspection certificate to confirm the goods have been supplied in accordance with the contract.

The SGS do not have the right to approve or prevent shipment of the goods. The opinion expressed by SGS is given after all the factors are provided to SGS by the seller. It is made in good faith but without any liability to the seller for any loss, damage or expense arising from the issuance of the report of findings. Currently some 35 countries require that both the letter of credit and contracts relevant to the import of goods contain a condition that a Clean Report of Findings covering quality, quantity and price must be presented together with other documents required to negotiate payment.

The International Federation of Inspection Agencies (IFIA), on behalf of the members administering government-mandated pre-shipment inspection programmes, is promoting the following Code of Practice to be observed by those members.

(1) Activities of pre-shipment inspection companies (hereinafter 'PIC') in the country of export may be undertaken on behalf of a foreign government, government agency, central bank or other appropriate governmental authority and may include:

(a) physical inspection for quantity and quality of goods;
(b) verification of export prices, including financial terms of the export transaction and currency exchange rates where appropriate;
(c) support services to the customs authorities of the country of importation.

(2) The general procedures for physical inspection of goods and the examination of the price of exports out of any particular country will be the same in all exporting countries and the specific requirements established by the importing country will be administered by the PIC in a consistent and objective manner.

(3) The PIC will provide assistance to exporters by furnishing the information and guidelines necessary to enable exporters to comply with the pre-shipment inspection regulations of the importing country. This assistance on the part of the PIC is not intended to relieve exporters from the responsibility of compliance with the import regulations of the importing country.

(4) Quantity and quality inspections will be performed in accordance with accepted national and international standards.

(5) The conduct of pre-shipment activities should facilitate legitimate foreign trade and assist bona fide exporters by providing independent evidence of compliance with the laws and regulations of the importing country.

(6) Pre-shipment activities will be conducted and the Clean Report of Findings, or notice of non-issuance thereof, will be sent to the exporter in a timely and convenient manner.

(7) Confidential business information will not be shared by the PICs with any third party other than the appropriate government authority for which the inspection in question is being performed.

(8) Adequate procedures to safeguard all information submitted by exporters will be maintained by the PIC, together with proper security for any information provided in confidence to them.

(9) The PIC will not request from exporters information regarding manufacturing data related to patents (issued or pending) or licensing agreements. Nor will the PIC attempt to identify the cost of manufacture, level of profit or, except in the case of exports made through a buying agent or a confirming house, the terms of contracts between exporters and their suppliers.

(10) The PIC will avoid conflicts of interest between the PIC, any related entities of the PIC or entities in which the PIC has a financial interest, and companies whose shipments the PIC is inspecting.

(11) The PIC will state in writing the reason for any decision declining issuance of a Clean Report of Findings.

(12) If a rejection occurs at the stage of physical inspection, the PIC will, if requested by the exporter, arrange the earliest date for re-inspection.

(13) Whenever so requested by the exporter, and provided no contrary instruction has been issued by the government authority, the PIC will undertake a preliminary price verification prior to receipt of the import licence on the basis of the binding contractual documents, pro-forma invoice and application for import approval. An invoice price and/or currency exchange rate that has been accepted by the PIC on the basis of such preliminary price verification will not be withdrawn, provided the goods and the previously submitted documentation conform with the information contained in the import licence. The CRF, however, will not be issued until appropriate final documents have been received by the PIC.

(14) Price verification will be undertaken on the basis of the terms of the sales contract and it will take into consideration any generally applicable and allowable adjusting factors pertaining to the transaction.

(15) Commissions due to an agent in the country of destination will be treated in confidence by the PIC and will be reported to the appropriate government authority only when so requested.

(16) Exporters or importers who are unable to resolve differences with the PIC may appeal in writing, stating facts of the specific transaction and the nature of the complaint, to a designated appeals official of the PIC. Exporters wishing to appeal the results of a pre-shipment inspection may also seek review of the decision of the PIC in the importing country.

In cases where a PIC is considered not to have observed any article of this Code of Practice, this may be reported to the Director-General of IFIA.

The World Trade Organisation's Uruguay round of talks in 1994 established an independent review procedure administered jointly by an organization representing PIC Agencies and an organization representing exporters – to resolve disputes between an exporter and PIC Agency. The obligations placed on PIC user governments include non-discrimination, transparency, protection of confidential business information, avoidance of unreasonable delay, the use of specific guidelines for conducting price verification and the avoidance of conflicts of interest by the PIC Agencies.

The Pre-shipment Inspection System (PIS) has been introduced for the following reasons.

(a) To minimize the loss of foreign exchange through over-invoicing; concealed commission payments and illegal money transfers.
(b) To minimize losses of revenue and duty payments through under-invoicing.
(c) To reduce evasion of import controls and help combat smuggling.
(d) To help control landed prices and therefore control local inflation.
(e) To avoid dumping of cargo through the incidence of shipping merchandise of substandard goods.
(f) To avoid the incidence of loss through shipment of underweight cargo or short shipments.

A specimen of the documents is found on pp. 104–15 of *Shipping and Air Freight Documentation for Importers and Exporters*

14.25 Quality certificate

A quality certificate is issued by the exporter and confirms for the importer that the quality/specification of a particular consignment of goods is in accord with the export sales contract at the time of shipment. It is usually required under letter of credit terms.

14.26 Shipper's letter of instruction

A shipper's letter of instruction is a standardized form prepared by the shipper and submitted to the airline or IATA agent giving clear and complete forwarding instructions. It has no legal content, but the exporter is responsible for the validity of the data relative to the cargo description on the air waybill. Misrepresentation of the facts by the exporter has serious legal implications. The document (in duplicate) is handed to the vehicle driver at the time the goods are collected. The duplicate copy should be signed upon receipt of goods by the airline or its IATA agent as proof of goods for shipment and returned to the shipper.

14.27 Ship's delivery order

A delivery order is written authority to deliver goods, etc. to a named party in exchange for the bill of lading, usually at the port of destination. It is issued at the port of destination and is subject to all the terms and conditions of the carrier's bill of lading. It must not contain any reservations or clauses other than those appearing in the bill of lading except where increased obligations or extra cost may be incurred in giving delivery beyond the bill of lading. The document is issued at the port of destination in exchange for an original bill of lading and is legally recognized as a token of an authority to receive possession.

The delivery order should be addressed to the ship's Master, and the need for it arises, for example, when the buyer may not wish to know the identity of the supplier abroad for trade reasons. Hence the delivery order issue may prove a useful document. It is important the document is endorsed by the party to whom it is made out. However, if it is issued in one port for delivery in another and the freight is payable at destination, the order would then be 'consigned' to the carrier's agent to ensure that it would have to be presented and released before collection of the goods is authorized.

14.28 Veterinary and health certificate

A veterinary or health certificate may be required when livestock, domestic animals or agricultural products are being exported. It should be signed by the appropriate health authority in the exporter's country.

14.29 Weight certificate

A weight certificate confirms that the goods accord with the weight specified on the bill of lading, invoice, certificate of insurance or other specified document. In so doing it confirms to the buyer, seller, insurance company or other specified party that the goods were at a specified weight at the time of shipment. It is requested by the importer to confirm the weight of the goods is in accord with the export sales contract at the time of shipment. It is usually required under a letter of credit involving a bulk cargo shipment.

■ □ ▨ ■ 15

Processing the export order

An important activity of export practice is the processing of the export consignment through all its numerous procedures. It is an area which must be fully understood by the exporter. However, before examining the procedures involved, we must first consider the contract of affreightment embraced in the terms of delivery.

15.1 Contract of affreightment: terms of delivery: Incoterms 2000

The basis of a price quotation depends on the correct interpretation of the delivery trade terms. The export marketing manager will, through experience, accumulate information which will enable him or her to quote accurately. It is important to bear in mind each delivery trade term quoted embraces three basic elements: the stage at which title to the merchandise passes from the exporter (seller) to the importer (buyer), a clear definition of the charges and expenses to be borne by the exporter and importer, and finally, the stage and location where the goods are to be passed over to the importer.

The international consignment delivery terms embrace many factors including, in particular, insurance, air or sea freight plus surface transport costs, customs duty, port of disbursements, product cost, packing costs, etc. Moreover, the importance of executing the cargo delivery in accordance with the prescribed terms cannot be overstressed and this involves a disciplined process of progressing the export sales contract order dealt with elsewhere in this chapter. In the ideal situation, the sales export contract order, also embracing the delivery terms, should be undertaken on a critical path analysis programme devised by the export marketing manager in consultation with department colleagues within the company, and relevant outside bodies, that is, booking shipping space, processing financial aspects, obtaining export licences, etc.

There must be no ambiguity in the interpretation by either party of the delivery terms quoted, particularly in the area of cost and liabilities. If such problems arise, much goodwill is lost and the exporter could lose the prospect of a repeat order in a competitive market. Moreover, costly litigation could arise. It is essential, therefore, that the exporter (seller) and the importer (buyer) agree on the terms of delivery and their interpretation. Such a situation could be overcome by quoting the provisions of Incoterms 2000 dealt with in the latter part of this section. It must be borne in mind that special provisions in individual export sales contracts will override anything provided in Incoterms 2000. In addition, it should be remembered that breaches of contract, and their consequences, together with the ownership of the goods are outside the influence of Incoterms 2000.

The need for every exporter to have a thorough knowledge of Incoterms 2000 cannot be over-stressed, and likewise the sales and marketing personnel who negotiate the export sales contract terms on behalf of the seller. The booklet Incoterms 2000, No 560 is available from local Chambers of Commerce.

An international trade deal can involve up to four contracts and the exporter (seller) must have a broad understanding of each of them. The four contracts are: the contract of carriage, the export sales contract (usually involving Incoterms 2000), the insurance contract, and the contract of finance. (See ICC booklet No. 500 on Uniform Customs and Practice for Documentary Credits, 1993.) There are three main areas of uncertainty in international trade contracts and their interpretation: the uncertainty as to which country's law will be applicable to their contracts; the difficulty emerging from inadequate and unreliable information; and the serious problem of the diversity of interpretation of the various trade terms. The latter point can involve costly litigation and loss of much goodwill when a dispute over the interpretation of such terms arises. Hence study ICC booklet No 5600.

The role of Incoterms 2000, adopted in 96 countries, is to give the business person a set of international rules for the interpretation of the more commonly used terms such as FOB, CIF and EXW in foreign trade contracts. Such a range of terms enables the business person to decide which is the most suitable for their needs, knowing that the interpretation of such terms will not vary by individual country.

It must be recognized, however, that it is not always possible to give a precise interpretation. In such situations, one must rely on the custom of the trade or port. Business persons are advised to use terms which are subject to varying interpretation as little as possible and to rely on the well-established internationally-accepted terms. To avoid any misunderstandings or disputes the parties to the contract are well advised to keep trading customs of individual countries in mind when negotiating their export sales contract. However, parties to the contract may use Incoterms as the general basis of their contract, but may specify variations of them or additions to them relevant to the particular trade or circumstances. An example is the CIF (cost insurance freight) plus war risk insurance. The seller would base his or her quotation accordingly. Special provisions in the individual contract between the parties will override anything in the Incoterm provisions.

An important point to bear in mind is the need for caution in the variation, for example, of CFR (cost and freight), CIF (cost insurance freight) or DDP (delivered duty paid): the addition of a word or letter could change the contract and its interpretation.

It is essential that any such variation be explicitly stated in the contract to ensure each party to the contract is aware of its obligations and acts accordingly.

The seller (exporter) and buyer (importer) parties to the contract must remember that Incoterms only define their relationship in contract terms, and has no bearing directly or indirectly on carriers' obligations to them as found in the contract of carriage. However, the law of carriage will determine how the seller should fulfil his or her obligation to deliver the goods to the carrier on board the vessel as found in FOB, CFR and CIF. A further point to be borne in mind by both seller and buyer is that there is no obligation for the seller to procure an insurance policy for the buyer's benefit. However, in practice many contracts request the buyer or seller to arrange insurance from the point of departure in the country of despatch, to the point of final destination chosen by the buyer. A summary of the 13 terms are given below (see also Figure 15.1, p. 337, Incoterm 2000 group analysis):

Incoterms 2000

Group E	EXW	Ex-works
Departure from factory – all carriage paid by buyer		
Group F	FCA	Free carrier
Main carriage unpaid by seller	FAS	Free alongside ship
	FOB	Free on board
Group C	CPT	Carriage paid to
Main carriage paid by seller	CIP	Carriage and insurance paid to
	CFR	Cost and freight
	CIF	Cost, insurance and freight
Group D	DAF	Delivered at frontier
Arrival – carriage to	DES	Delivered ex-ship
delivered paid by the seller	DEQ	Delivered ex-quay
	DDU	Delivered duty unpaid
	DDP	Delivered duty paid

Incoterms 2000 can be divided into recommended usages by modes of transport as under: all modes (i.e. combined transport), EXW, FCA, CPT, CIP, DAF, DDP, DDU; and conventional port-to-port or sea transport only FAS, FOB, CFR, CIF, DES, DEQ. The seller must ensure the correct terms are used. Consider a containerized contract applying FOB or CFR where the risk transfers from seller to buyer on loading onboard ship. On delivery damage is discovered. It is impossible to show where damage arose, before or after shipment. Under FOB/CFR a dispute would ensue; under FCA/CPT it would be clear that the risk would be with the buyer once the goods are in the hands of the combined transport operator for carriage. Incoterms 2000 reflect the changes and development of international distribution during the past decade, especially the development of combined transportation and associated documentation, together with electronic data interchange. In analysing each term the seller and buyer should identify the following aspects

Seller

    (1) supplying good(s) in conformity with the contract;
    (2) licences and authorizations;
    (3) place of delivery (not delivery of goods);
    (4) carriage of goods contract and insurance;
    (5) documentation and notice to buyer;
    (6) transfer of risks;
    (7) transfer and division of costs;
    (8) checking, packages, marking;
    (9) other obligations.

Buyer

    (1) licences and authorizations;
    (2) notices, receipt of documents;
    (3) taking delivery;
    (4) transfer of risks;
    (5) transfer and division of costs;
    (6) other obligations.

The use of bills of lading is now becoming less common in the liner trade and is being replaced by non-negotiable documents such as sea waybills, liner waybills, freight receipts and combined or multi-modal transport documents (p. 475). Ultimately the transmission of such information will be by automatic data processing techniques; SITPRO are very much involved in such developments. As we progress into the next millennium with the expectation of more competitive pricing, the buyer/importer will demand a delivered Incoterm 2000 price quotation. This will allow the buyer to compare the quotations on a like-for-like basis from different originating countries, and will enable them to avoid having to calculate the distribution cost as an add-on to the Incoterm 2000.

15.2 Factors determining choice of Incoterms 2000

Personnel involved in negotiating the sales contract have a wide choice in selecting the cargo delivery term most acceptable to the sale. The prime consideration is to ensure that each party to the contract is clearly aware of their obligation to ensure the consignment is despatched without impeding the transit arrangements. The following factors are relevant in the evaluation of the choice of the cargo delivery term.

    (1) Basically, the buyer is the stronger party in such negotiations, especially as he or she has to fund the carriage charges directly through his payment to the carrier under FCA/FOB or indirectly through CIP/CIF to the seller.

    (2) The seller has the opportunity of controlling the transit arrangements together with cost when concluding the arrangement, and funds them directly with the carrier. He or she may, through other contracts, be able to get a discount through the volume of business generated to the trade or route.

    (3) An increasing number of Third World and Eastern European countries now follow a policy of directing all cargoes on to their national shipping line or

Incoterms 2000 – Group Analysis

Group E

> EXW – Ex Works (... named place) – suitable for all modes of transport – buyer collects and responsible for all carriage

Group F

> FCA Free Carrier (... named place) – suitable for all modes of transport – main carriage unpaid

> FAS Free Alongside Ship (... named port of shipment) – suitable for maritime and inland waterway transport only – main carriage unpaid

> FOB Free On Board (... named port of shipment) – suitable for maritime and inland waterway transport only – main carriage unpaid

Group C

> CPT Carriage Paid to (... named place of destination) – suitable for all modes of transport – main carriage paid

> CIP Carriage and Insurance Paid to (... named place of destination) – suitable for all modes of transport – main carriage paid

> CFR Cost and Freight (... named port of destination) – suitable for maritime and inland waterway transport only – main carriage paid

> CIF Cost Insurance and Freight (... named port of destination) – suitable for maritime and inland waterway transport only – main carriage paid

Group D

> DAF Delivered at Frontier (... named place) – suitable for all modes of transport – delivered at frontier point

> DDU Delivered Duty Unpaid (... named place of destination) – suitable for all modes of transport – delivered at named place of destination

> DDP Delivered Duty Paid (... named place of destination) – suitable for all modes of transport – delivered at named place of destination

> DES Delivered Ex Ship (... named port of destination) – suitable for maritime and inland waterway transport only – delivered on board the vessel at the named port of destination

> DEQ Delivered Ex Quay (... named port of destination) – suitable for maritime and inland waterway transport only – delivered on the named quay (wharf) at the specified port of destination

E Term – is the term in which the seller's obligation is at its maximum.

F Term – requires the seller to deliver the goods for carriage as instructed by the buyer.

C Term – requires the seller to contract for carriage on usual terms at his own expense.

D Term – requires the seller to be responsible for the arrival of the goods at the agreed place or point of destination at the border and within the country of import. The seller must bear all the risk and cost in bringing the goods thereto.

FIGURE 15.1 Incoterm 2000 analysis

Salient Features Emerging From Incoterms 2000

(a) the Incoterms have tended to focus on the tangibles in the contract of sale and not intangibles as found in computer software;

(b) Incoterms embraces the contract of sale and relations between the buyer and seller. It only has an interface with the contracts of insurance, transport and finance and no *prima facie* legal specifications regarding the duties the parties may wish to include in the contract of sale;

(c) Incoterms remain primarily intended for use where goods are sold for delivery across national boundaries;

(d) revision needed to adapt to the terms of contemporary commercial practice;

(e) substantive changes have been made in two areas: customs clearance and payment of duty obligations under FAS and DEQ (see pp. 345–7) and loading and unloading obligations under FCA (see p. 350);

(f) the terms are, wherever possible, the same expressions as those in the 1980 UN Convention on the Contracts for the International Sales of Goods;

(g) the opportunity has been taken in the 'introduction' of ICC booklet No 560 to clarify a number of terms featured in the 13 Incoterms. These include shipper, delivery, usual, charges, ports, places, points, premises, ship, vessel, checking, inspection, no obligation, customs clearance, and packaging;

(h) a feature of the 1990 revision of Incoterms identified the clauses dealing with the seller's obligation to provide proof of delivery permitting a replacement of paper documentation by EDI messages provided the parties had agreed to communicate electronically. The 2000 revision has endeavoured to improve upon the drafting and presentation of the Incoterms in order to facilitate their practical implementation.

FIGURE 15.2 Incoterms 2000 – salient features

airline and buy under EXW/FCA/FOB/CIF terms. For example, a government may require all imports to be bought on a FOB basis and all exports sold on CIF. This saves hard currency and develops their shipping and airline companies. It also reflects, in many situations, cargo preference laws enforced by the buyer's government as part of their trading policy.

(4) The seller, under CIP/CIF terms, can maximize the national income from such a sale and thereby despatch the consignment on the seller's national shipping line or airline, and likewise obtain insurance cover through brokers.

(5) In some circumstances neither the buyer nor the seller has any choice to make. This applies to some commodity trades where there are standard international contracts of sale which relate to specific Incoterms 2000.

(6) Conversely, with regard to item (2) the buyer may wish to take charge of the transit arrangement and cost when concluding the arrangements and selects the carrier and funds them directly with the transport operator(s). This may include EXW/FCA/FOB terms.

Overall, the most decisive factors in determining the most acceptable Incoterm are experience of the trading market and the development of a good business relationship between seller and buyer on a long-term basis. Every effort should be made to sell under combined transport terms.

15.3 Description of Incoterms 2000

EXW (Ex-works)

This term means maximum involvement by the buyer in arrangements for the conveyance of the consignment to the specified destination. The exporter merely makes the goods available by an agreed date at his or her factory or warehouse. The seller minimizes his or her obligations whilst the buyer obtains the goods at the lowest possible price, by arranging to use his or her national shipping line or airline and by securing insurance cover in his or her own country. This eliminates the need to fund such provisions using hard currency and thereby improves the importer's trade balance. This practice is on the increase nowadays, particularly in Third World and Eastern European markets. The seller's obligations cease when the buyer accepts the goods at the factory or warehouse. It is usual for the buyer to appoint an agent in the seller's country to look after all the collection, transportation, insurance and documentation arrangements, possibly in consultation with the national shipping line or airline.

The term provides two options: 'Ex-works cleared for export', and 'Ex-works uncleared for export'. The following is based on 'uncleared for export'. The principal obligations of the seller include:

(1) supplying the goods in accord with the contract of sale;
(2) making available the goods to the buyer at the customary delivery point, or as specified in the contact of sale to enable the goods to be conveyed on the transport unit arranged by the buyer;
(3) providing at his or her expense the necessary packing (if any) to enable the buyer to convey the goods on the specified transport;
(4) giving the buyer prompt notice when the goods will be available for collection;
(5) bearing all risk and expense of the goods until they have been placed at the disposal of the buyer as specified in the contract of sale;
(6) rendering the buyer on request every assistance to provide, in the country of delivery or of cargo origin, all the relevant documentation required in the process of exportation.

Obviously the responsibilities of the buyer are more extensive. These include:

(1) taking delivery of the cargo and paying for the goods in accord with the contract of sale terms;
(2) funding any pre-shipment inspection expense;
(3) bearing all the cost and risk of the goods from the time they have been placed at his or her disposal by the seller in accord with sales contract terms;
(4) funding any customs duties and taxes arising through exportation;
(5) bearing additional costs incurred and related risks inherent through the failure of the buyer to give instructions about the place of delivery within the prescribed period;
(6) funding all costs in obtaining the documents required for the purpose of importation and exportation and for passing through the countries of transit.

The EXW term should not be used where, according to regulations of the country of export, the buyer cannot directly or indirectly obtain the export licence. In such a situation, the FCA term should be used.

FOB (free on board) (sea transport)

Under such terms the goods are placed in the ship by the seller at the specified port of shipment detailed in the sales contract. The risk of loss of, or damage to, the goods is transferred from the seller to the buyer when the goods pass over the ship's rail. Under such terms the seller bears all the cost and the risk of conveyance up to the ship's rail and the buyer accepts the residue of the transit cost, including sea freight and insurance. This term is used frequently in international trade and is to the advantage of the buyer because the cargo can be conveyed on his or her national shipping line, thereby ensuring it is funded by the national currency. Insurance provision can likewise be arranged in his or her own country with similar benefit. It is usual for the buyer to appoint an agent in the seller's country to look after the pre-shipment, documentation, insurance, etc. arrangements in consultation with the shipping company.

The principal seller's obligations found in a FOB sales contract include:

(1) supplying the goods in accord with the contract of sale;
(2) delivering the cargo on the named vessel at the specified port of shipment within the agreed period or on the agreed date and in so doing promptly informing the buyer;
(3) providing at his or her expense any export licence or other governmental authorization necessary for the export of goods;
(4) bearing all costs and risks of the goods until such time as the cargo has effectively passed over the ship's rail at the named port;
(5) providing at his or her expense the customary packing of the goods unless it is the custom of the trade to ship the cargo unpacked;
(6) paying the cost of any cargo scrutiny prior to delivery of the cargo;

(7) supplying at the seller's expense the requisite documentation as proof of delivery of the goods alongside the named vessel;

(8) providing the buyer on request and at the buyer's expense the Certificate of Origin;

(9) supplying the buyer on request and at the buyer's expense every assistance to obtain a bill of lading, sea waybill and other documentation issued in the country of shipment or origin necessary for the importation process both in transit countries and the destination country.

The buyer's responsibilities are extensive. These include:

(1) arranging at his or her own expense and risk the pre-shipment cargo inspection

(2) bearing all cost and risk of the cargo from the time it has passed the ship's rail at port of shipment and paying the price as specified in the sales contract;

(3) bearing all the cost and risk emerging from the failure of the shipowner to fulfil the contracted pre-shipment arrangements (such as the cargo being shut out) – this is subject to the seller making the cargo available at the loading berth in accord with the sales contract, and in the event of the buyer failing to give pre-shipment details to the seller within the prescribed period, all additional cost and risk to be borne by the buyer;

(4) paying all cost to the seller to obtain bills of lading, certificate of origin, consular documents and any other documentation required to process the cargo through importation both in transit countries and in the country of destination.

The FOB term may only be used for water transport. When the ship's rail serves no practical purpose, such as Ro-Ro or container traffic, the FCA term should be used.

CFR (cost and freight – named port of destination)

Under this term the seller must pay the costs necessary to bring the goods to the named port of shipment, the risk of loss or damage to the goods, as well as of any additional expenses, is transferred from the seller to the buyer when the goods pass over the ship's rail. This is identical to CIF except that the buyer is responsible for funding and arranging the cargo insurance.

The seller's obligations in CFR include:

(1) supplying the goods in accord with the contract of sale terms;

(2) arranging and paying for the conveyance of the goods to the specified port of destination by the customary route and funding any unloading charges at the destination port;

(3) providing and paying for any export licence or other governmental authorization necessary to export the cargo;

(4) arranging and paying for, on a specified date or in a specified period, the cargo loading at the agreed port (if no such loading date or period is quoted, such a task to be undertaken within a reasonable period);

(5) bearing all the cargo risk until such time as it passes over the ship's rail at the port of shipment;

(6) supplying promptly and paying for the clean shipped negotiable bill of lading for the agreed destination port, together with any invoice of the goods shipped;

(7) providing and paying for the customary packing of the goods unless it is the custom of the trade to ship the cargo unpacked;

(8) funding any cargo scrutiny prior to loading the cargo;

(9) paying any cost of dues and taxes incurred relative to the process of exportation in respect of the cargo prior to shipment;

(10) providing the buyer on request and at the buyer's expense a Certificate of Origin and consular invoice;

(11) rendering the buyer on request and at the buyer's expense and risk every assistance to obtain any documents required in the country of shipment and transit countries necessary for the conveyance of the cargo to its destination.

A point for the seller to note especially with the CFR term is the need to supply a full set of clean onboard or shipped bills of lading. If the bill of lading contains a reference to the Charter Party, the seller must also provide a copy of the latter. The buyer must ensure these provisions are complied with by the seller.

The factors relevant to the buyer include:

(1) acceptance of the documents as tendered by the seller (subject to their conformity with the terms of the contract) and payment of the goods, etc., as specified in the contract of sale;

(2) receiving the goods at the port of destination and, with the exception of the sea freight, all the costs and charges incurred during the voyage(s);

(3) funding all unloading expenses at the destination port including lighterage, wharfage, etc. unless such costs have been included in the freight or collected by the shipowner at the time freight was paid;

(4) funding any pre-shipment cargo inspection arrangements;

(5) undertaking all the risk when the cargo has passed the ship's rail at the departure port, in the event of the buyer failing to give instructions (by the specified date or within agreed period) relative to destination port, all additional cost and risk will be borne by the buyer subject to the goods being duly appropriated to the contract;

(6) paying all the costs to obtain the Certificate of Origin and consular documents;

(7) meeting all charges to provide any other documentation specified relative to processing the consignment in the country of shipment or transit countries;

(8) paying all customs duties and other taxes raised at the time of importation;

(9) obtaining and paying for any import licence or related documentation required at the time of importation.

In the CFR contract sale the buyer can arrange the cargo insurance in his or her own country thereby saving foreign currency. Many importers are tending to favour this arrangement. The CFR term should be used only for sea and inland water transport. When the ship's rail serves no practical purpose as in the case of Ro-Ro or container traffic, the CPT term should be used.

CIF (cost, insurance, freight)

This is a popular cargo delivery arrangement. The seller, in addition to CFR obligations, is obliged to procure marine insurance against the risk of loss of, or damage to, the goods in transit. In other words, the seller contracts with the insurer and pays the insurance premium.

The salient features of the contract as far as the seller is concerned include:

(1) supplying the goods in accordance with contract of the sale terms;
(2) arranging and paying for the carriage of the goods to the specified destination port by the customary route and funding any unloading charges at the destination port;
(3) providing and paying for any export licence or other governmental authorization necessary to export the cargo;
(4) arranging and paying for, on a specified date or within an agreed period, the cargo loading at the agreed port (if no such loading date or period is quoted such a task to be undertaken within a reasonable period);
(5) informing the buyer promptly when loading is completed;
(6) arranging and paying for insurance of the cargo in a transferable form against the risk of loss or damage during the transit – such cover shall be Institute Cargo Clauses (Institute of London Underwriter) and embrace the CIF price plus 10 per cent, and the insurance will be in the currency of the contract;
(7) bearing all the risk of goods until they have effectively passed the ship's rail at the port of shipment;
(8) supplying to the buyer promptly, at the seller's expense, a clean negotiable 'shipped onboard' bill of lading for the agreed port of destination and insurance policy or certificate of insurance;
(9) providing and paying for the customary packing of the goods unless it is the custom of the trade to ship the goods unpacked;
(10) paying the cost of any cargo scrutiny prior to loading the cargo;
(11) bearing any cost of dues and taxes incurred relative to the process of exportation in respect of the cargo prior to shipment;
(11) providing the buyer on request and at the buyer's expense a Certificate of Origin and consular invoice;
(12) rendering the buyer on request and at the buyer's expense every assistance to obtain any documents required in the country of shipment or transit countries necessary for the conveyance of the cargo throughout the transit.

A point to bear in mind concerning insurance cover is that the seller has to procure marine insurance against the buyer's risk of loss or damage against minimum coverage and duration to the goods during the carriage.

The responsibilities of the buyer include:

(1) acceptance of the documents as tendered by the seller (subject to their conformity with the terms of the contract) and payment of the goods, as specified in the contract of sale;
(2) funding any pre-shipment cargo inspection arrangements;
(3) receiving the goods at the agreed destination port and bearing, with the exception of the freight and marine insurance, all costs and charges incurred during the voyage(s);
(4) funding all unloading expenses at the port of destination, including lighterage and wharfage, unless such costs have been included in the freight or collected by the shipowner at the time freight was paid;
(5) undertaking all the risk when the cargo has passed the ship's rail at the departure port;
(6) in the event of the buyer failing to give instructions, by the specified date or within an agreed period, relative to the port of destination, all additional cost and risk will be borne by the buyer subject to the goods being duly appropriated to the contract;
(7) paying all the costs in obtaining a Certificate of Origin and consular documents;
(8) meeting all charges to provide any other documentation specified relative to processing the consignment in the country of shipment or transit countries;
(9) paying all customs duties and other taxes raised at the time of importation;
(10) obtaining at his or her own expense any import licence or related documentation required at time of importation.

The CIF terms enable the seller to obtain the maximum income from the sales contract with the insurance and freight charges contributing to the invisible exports if the goods are carried on the national shipping line and the insurance is effected in the country of origin. The CIF term should be used only for sea and inland water transport. When the ship's rail serves no practical purpose as in the case of Ro-Ro or container traffic, the CIP term should be used.

DES (delivered ex-ship – named port of destination)

This sales contract terms is not used extensively. It obliges the seller to make the goods available to the buyer on board the vessel at the destination port as specified in the sales contract. The seller has to bear the full cost and risk involved to bring the goods to the destination port.

The seller's main obligations include:

(1) supplying the goods in accord with contract of sale terms;
(2) making the goods available to the buyer on board the vessel at the agreed destination point to enable the cargo to be conveniently discharged;
(3) bearing all risk and expense of the cargo conveyance to the destination port until promptly collected by the buyer;

(4) providing and paying for the customary packing of the goods unless it is the custom of the trade to ship the goods unpacked;

(5) paying the cost of any cargo scrutiny prior to collection of the cargo by the buyer;

(6) promptly informing the buyer of the expected date of arrival of the vessel and providing the buyer with a bill of lading and any other documents necessary to enable the buyer to take delivery of the consignment;

(7) providing the buyer on request and at the buyer's expense the Certificate and consular invoice;

(8) rendering the buyer on request and at the buyer's expense every assistance to provide the requisite documentation issued in the country of shipment and/ or origin required for importation in the destination country or transit countries.

The obligations of the buyer include:

(1) bearing all the risk and expense from the time the cargo has been placed at the disposal of the buyer on board the vessel awaiting discharge at the destination port;

(2) bearing all the cost associated with the provision of documentation obtained by the seller necessary for the importation of the goods both in destination and transit countries;

(3) obtaining at the buyer's expense all licences or similar documents necessary for the importing process;

(4) bearing all customs charges and other duties and taxes incurred at the time of importation.

DEQ (delivered ex-quay – named port of destination)

Under this term the seller arranges for the goods to be made available to the buyer on the quay or wharf at the destination port detailed in the sales contract. The seller has to bear the full cost and risk involved to bring the goods to the quay. But the buyer has to clear the goods for import and to pay for all formalities, duties, taxes, and other charges upon import.

The seller's obligations include:

(1) supplying the goods in accord with the contract of sale terms;

(2) making the goods available to the buyer at the specified quay or wharf within the period given in the sales contract and bearing all the associated risk and cost: the buyer being responsible for clearing the goods for import and paying for all the formalities;

(3) providing and paying for the customary packing of the goods unless it is the custom of the trade to ship the cargo unpacked.

The buyer's task is twofold:

(1) to take delivery of the goods as specified in the contract;

(2) to bear all the expense and risk of the goods from the time the cargo has been effectively placed at the disposal of the buyer.

The cost of the pre-shipment cargo inspection is borne by the buyer unless when mandated by the authorities of the country of export.

The DEQ term should not be used if the seller is unable to obtain the import licence, either directly or indirectly.

FAS (free alongside ship – named port of shipment)

The obligations of the seller are realized when the goods have been placed alongside the ship in the quay or on lighterage at a specified port of shipment. At this stage and thereafter the buyer has to bear all the cost and risk of loss of or damage to the goods excluding export customs clearance.

The salient features of FAS for the seller include:

(1) supplying the goods in accord with the contract of sale terms;
(2) arranging delivery of the cargo by the date or within the agreed period alongside the specified vessel at the loading berth and port as named by the buyer;
(3) to obtain at the sellers expense any export licence and other official authorization and carry out all custom formalities necessary for the export of the goods;
(4) bearing all cost and risk of the goods until they have been effectively delivered alongside the specified vessel and cleared through customs;
(5) providing and paying for the customary packing of the goods unless it is the custom of the trade to ship the cargo unpacked;
(6) rendering to the buyer on request and at the buyer's expense the Certificate of Origin;
(7) assisting the buyer on request and at the buyer's expense to obtain any documents issued in the country of origin or shipment including bill of lading and/or consular documents required for importation of the goods into the destination country and their passage through transit countries.

The buyer's responsibilities include:

(1) giving the seller prompt notice of the name of the vessel, loading berth and delivery dates;
(2) bearing all the expense and risk of the goods from when they have been effectively delivered alongside the vessel as specified which includes the export clearance undertaken by the seller;
(3) funding any additional cost and accepting the risk in the event of the vessel not arriving on time or the shipowner being unable to accept the cargo;
(4) in the event of the buyer failing to notify the seller of the name of the vessel, and port of shipment within the prescribed period, the buyer would bear all consequential cost and risk from the expiry date of the notification period, subject to the goods being duly appropriated by the seller to the contract including export customs clearance;

(5)   meeting all cost of obtaining any documents necessary for the importation of the goods, including the bill of lading and consular documents.

The cost of the pre-shipment cargo inspection is borne by the buyer unless when mandated by the authorities of the country of export. This criterion applies to other Incoterms where applicable.

The FAS term should not be used where, according to regulations of the country of export, the buyer cannot obtain the export licence.

DAF (delivered at frontier – named port)

Under the 'delivered at frontier' term the seller's obligations are concluded when the goods have arrived at the named frontier point place or customs examination border. It is usual, to avoid ambiguity, to quote the two countries separated by the frontier. This term is used primarily for rail or road borne traffic but can be used for other transport modes in varying circumstances. Its use could become more common through the development of the combined transport operation for international consignments. The term requires the seller to clear for export.

The seller's main obligations include:

(1)   supplying the goods in accord with the contract of sale terms at the seller's risk and expense;

(2)   placing the goods at the disposal of the buyer at the specified frontier point within the stipulated period and in so doing providing him or her with the necessary customary documentation including consignment note, export licence, delivery order, warehouse warrant, etc., to enable the buyer to take delivery of the cargo;

(3)   funding any customs charges and other expenses incurred up to the time when the goods have been placed at the buyer's disposal, and bearing all the risk throughout this period;

(4)   obtaining and paying for all documentation necessary for the exportation of the cargo, including transit countries' needs and placing them at the disposal of the buyer as appropriate;

(5)   funding all transport costs (including incidental charges raised during the transit) up to the nominated frontier point, if no particular frontier point is quoted, the seller may choose the one which is most convenient to him or her provided he or she notifies the buyer promptly and it offers adequate customs and other facilities to enable the contract to be executed satisfactorily by both parties;

(6)   supplying the buyer on request the through consignment note embracing the origin and destination place in the importing country – such a request to be executed by the seller on the condition he or she incurs the risk, or expense other than it is customary to incur;

(7)   in the event of the goods being unloaded on arrival at the frontier point, such cost to be borne by the seller, including lighterage and handling charges (this would also apply if the seller used his or her own transport);

(8) promptly notifying the buyer that the goods have been despatched;

(9) providing and paying for the customary packing of the goods unless it is the custom of the trade to ship the cargo unpacked;

(10) funding any cargo scrutiny necessary to transport the goods to the specified frontier point;

(11) bearing any additional cost incurred to place the goods at the buyer's disposal;

(12) rendering to the buyer on request and at the buyer's expense all reasonable assistance to obtain documents inherent in the importing process in the destination country.

The buyer's obligations include:

(1) accepting delivery of the goods at the specified frontier point and to accept all transportation and handling costs therefrom;

(2) meeting the risk and customs duties and other costs incurred from the time the goods have been placed at the buyer's disposal relative to the process of importation of the cargo;

(3) funding incidental expenses incurred to unload the cargo at the specified frontier point, in the event of the buyer not taking delivery of the cargo duly put at his or her disposal in accord with the sales contract, the buyer will pay all additional cost and bear all the risk resulting therefrom;

(4) obtaining at his or her expense any import licence and other documentation required to process the cargo through importation;

(5) funding any additional expense incurred by the seller to obtain the consignment note for the buyer which could include documentation;

(6) supplying the seller on request with details of the ultimate destination of the goods;

(7) funding any expense incurred by the seller to provide the buyer with any third-party certificate of conformity of the goods stipulated in the contract of sale.

The cost of the pre-shipment cargo inspection is borne by the buyer unless when mandated by the authorities of the country of export.

In addition to the foregoing eight cargo delivery terms, which are the most popular, five other terms appear in Incoterms 2000. A brief commentary on them follows:

DDP (delivered duty paid – named point)

It will be recalled that under the term 'ex-works', the seller has the minimum obligation in terms of despatching the cargo. Conversely, the term 'delivered duty paid' places the maximum obligation on the seller regarding the cargo despatch arrangements. Under such terms the seller is responsible for the conveyance of the goods at his or her own risk and expense to the named destination located in the buyer's country in the country of sale. This includes the task of processing the cargo through both exportation and importation including duties and taxes plus customs clearance, loading and unloading, together with the related documentation which the buyer usually obtains as necessary on request but at the seller's expense. The seller may use his or her own transport throughout the conveyance.

The buyer's role is to accept the goods at the named place of destination, and the buyer is responsible for all subsequent movement costs of the goods including handling. Any form of transport can be used. The cost of the pre-shipment cargo inspection is borne by the buyer unless when mandated by the authorities of the country of export.

The DDP term should not be used if the seller is unable to obtain, directly or indirectly, the import licence. If the parties wish that the buyer should clear the goods for import and pay the duty, the DDU term should be used.

Hence the seller fulfils his or her obligation when he or she has delivered the goods, cleared for export, into the charge of the carrier named by the buyer at the named place or point. If no precise point is indicated by the buyer, the seller may choose, within the range stipulated, where the carrier shall take the goods into his or her charge. When, according to commercial practice, the seller's assistance is required in making the contract with the carrier (such as in rail or air transport with fixed freight rates), the seller will act at the buyer's risk and expense. This term may be used for any mode of transport.

DDU (delivered duty unpaid – named point)

The seller fulfils his or her obligations when the goods have arrived at the named point or place in the country of importation. The seller has to bear the full costs and risks involved in bringing the goods thereto, excluding duties, taxes and other official charges payable upon importation. If the parties wish to include in the seller's obligation some of the cost or official charges payable upon import of the goods (such as value added tax, VAT) this should be made clear by adding words to this effect (for example, 'delivered duty unpaid, VAT paid'). The term may be used irrespective of transport mode.

FCA (free carrier – named place)

This term is primarily for the combined transport operation such as a container or Ro-Ro operation involving a road trailer and sea ferry. The term is based on the FOB principle except that the seller fulfils his or her obligations when he or she delivers the goods into the custody of the carrier at the named place found in the sales contract or subsequently agreed by the parties. The chosen place of delivery has an impact on the obligation of loading and unloading the goods at that place. If delivery occurs at the sellers premises, the seller is responsible for loading. If the delivery occurs at any other place, the seller is not responsible for unloading. This term is likely to be used by a freight forwarder engaged in the international road haulage business. The risk of loss of or damage to the goods is transferred from the seller to the buyer at the time the nominated carrier accepts them at the prescribed place and not at the ship's rail as with FOB. When the seller has to render to the buyer, or other person prescribed, the bill of lading, waybill or carrier's receipt as evidence of the delivery acceptance of the goods, the seller's contractual obligations are fulfilled.

Hence the seller fulfils his or her obligation when he or she has delivered the goods, cleared for export, into the charge of the carrier named by the buyer at the named place or point. If no precise point is indicated by the buyer, the seller may choose within the range stipulated where the carrier shall take the goods into his or her charge. When, according to commercial practice, the seller's assistance is required in making the contract with the carrier (such as in rail or air transport with fixed freight rates), the seller will act at the buyer's risk and expense. The FCA term may be used for any mode of transport. The buyer must contract at his own expense for the carriage of goods from the named place, except when the contract of carriage is made by the seller at the buyers request, risk and expense.

CPT (carriage paid to – named point of destination)

Under the CPT term the seller pays the freight for the carriage of the goods to the named destination. The buyer's risk commences when the goods have been delivered into the custody of the first carrier. Moreover, at this point the buyer accepts full liability for any additional cost incurred in the conveyance of the goods. On request, the seller may have to provide a bill of lading, waybill or carrier's receipt to the buyer or other person prescribed, at which stage the seller's obligations are fulfilled. In common with the 'free carrier' term, CPT is ideal for the multi-modal transport operation which includes Ro-Ro and container movements.

CIP (Carriage and Insurance Paid to – named point of destination)

The CIP term is identical to the previous item except that the seller also funds the cargo insurance. Again it is ideal for the combined transport operation and the seller's liability ceases when the cargo has been accepted by the first carrier at the named place and any requested bill of lading, waybill or carrier's receipt has been handed over.

Exporters should fully comprehend the 13 Incoterms described. A major feature of Incoterms 2000 is that it recognizes the electronic message (EDI). Hence the seller and buyer may communicate the document electronically. The importance of all those involved in negotiating and executing sales contracts understanding the foregoing cargo delivery terms cannot be overstressed. The following checklist may prove helpful to the seller (exporter).

(1) Endeavour to do as much planning as possible for each exported consignment. Close liaison with the buyer's agent is essential.
(2) Ensure the personnel concluding the export sales contract are fully conversant with the Incoterm used, especially the impact it will have on the total price of the goods at the time of exportation and the workload and responsibility imposed on the seller regarding transportation and documentation. Substantial

income may be realizable if the transportation and insurance arrangements are undertaken by the exporter using his or her national airline or shipping line and effecting the insurance in the exporter's country.

(3) Exercise great care in selecting a suitable forwarding agent, both in the seller's and buyer's country (pp. 417–20).

(4) Monitor closely the stages of the product being exported. It will help to identify any problem areas and, through the adoption of remedial measures, lessen the risk in the future.

(5) If the distribution arrangements are unsatisfactory, endeavour to establish what the competitors offer – can any lessons be learned?

(6) Study closely the Uniform Customs and Practice for Documentary Credits 1993, ICC brochure No. 500, when dealing with commercial documentary credits.

(7) Review distribution arrangements and cargo delivery terms regularly to ensure that they are the most suitable in the situation obtaining.

(8) With the growth of multi-modalism globally, endeavour to use one of the terms outlined in Figures 15.1 – EXW, FCA, CPT, CIP, DAF, DDU and DDP.

The formulation of the export sales contract represents the conclusion of some possibly difficult negotiations and accordingly, particular care should be taken regarding the preparation of its terms. It must be borne in mind that an exporter's primary task is to sell his or her products at a profit and, therefore, the contract should fulfil this objective insofar as his or her obligations are concerned. Above all, they should be capable of being executed under reasonable circumstances and ultimately produce a modest profit. It is, of course, realized that in the initial stages of developing a new market overseas a loss may be incurred, but with a long-term marketing plan objective of increasing market share, the exporter should ultimately gain a favourable profit level. A further point to remember is that the export sales contract also has regard to the cargo delivery terms reflecting the contracts of carriage insurance and finance arrangements.

Details of the typical content of a UK export contract are given below, but it must be stressed that such contracts differ by individual country:

(1) The exporter's (seller's) registered name and address.

(2) The importer's (buyer's) registered name and address.

(3) A short title of each party quoted in items (1) and (2).

(4) The purpose of the contract. For example, it should confirm that the specified merchandise is sold by the party detailed in item (1) to the addressee quoted in item (2), and what the latter has bought according to the terms and conditions laid down in the contract.

(5) The number and quantity of goods, precisely and fully described to avoid any later misunderstanding or dispute. In particular, the contract must mention details of any batches and reconcile goods descriptions with custom tariff specifications.

(6) The price. This may be quoted in sterling depending on its general stability or some other currency which is not likely to vary in value significantly

throughout the life of the contract, such as American dollars or Deutchemarks. Goods sold in the seller's currency ensures the exporter maintains his or her profit margin and any currency exchange risk is experienced by the buyer who is compelled to convert sterling into his or her local currency, which may not be stable. Conversely, the seller quoting in the buyer's currency ensures the importer can compare the quotation with other suppliers and is assured there will be no currency risk. The seller runs the risk of the buyer's currency being unstable and consequently this may erode the seller's profit margin unless adequate provision can be made (pp. 241–3). The euro, currently the national currency in 11 countries within the European Union, eliminates any currency risk between the seller and buyer in export contracts undertaken within the euro-zone states (see p. 437). To counter inflation, particularly in a long-term contract, it is usual to incorporate an escalation clause, and to reduce the risk of sterling fluctuations implications, the tendency is to invoice in foreign currencies.

(7) Terms of delivery. It is important that the correct Incoterm 2000 is selected (pp. 336–9).

(8) Terms of payment, for example, open account, cash with order, letter of credit, open account or documents against payment or acceptance. Again this requires careful consideration (p. 254).

(9) Delivery date and shipment date or period. The exporter should check with his or her production department that the delivery date quoted is realistic and that the shipping or air freight space will be available on the date or period specified. The exporter's obligations regarding the latter will depend on the terms of delivery.

(10) Methods of shipment, for example, container, cargo wagon, Ro-Ro or air freight. An increasing volume of trade is now conveyed under combined transport operation arrangements.

(11) Method of packing. It is desirable that both parties be fully aware and agree on the packing specification to ensure no dispute arises later regarding packing or any variation to it.

(12) Cargo insurance policy or certificate terms (see pp. 206–25).

(13) Import or export licence details or other instructions. The period of their validity must be reconciled with the terms of payment and delivery date or shipment date or period.

(14) Shipping, freight and documentary requirements and/or instructions. This includes marking of cargo.

(15) Contract conditions, for example, sale, delivery, performance (quality) of goods, arbitration, etc. With regard to arbitration, this tends to speed the settlement of any disputes without costly litigation.

(16) Signature. Both parties must ensure the contract is signed by a responsible person at director or managerial level, and the date should be recorded.

Obviously the terms of the export sales contract will vary by circumstance but other areas which may feature include agency involvement, after-sales activities such as the availability and supply of spares, product servicing, training, advertising and promotion cost and so on. Additionally, it must be reconciled with any logistics-driven strategy (see pp. 120–1) and outsourcing of components and third country assembly as found in the NIKE case study (see p. 32). Moreover, any risk areas must be evaluated and minimized such as currency fluctuations, liquidation of the buyer and political developments.

A copy of the contract should be retained by each party. It must be recognized that an increasing volume of business is conducted on the basis of the export invoice containing the contractual terms. Again one must stress that such a document must be carefully compiled to reflect the terms of the original quotation to the buyer and the importer's acceptance.

15.4 Receipt of export order

A sound export management strategy is required when processing the export order. Full use should be made of computerization (p. 365) and the tactics adopted to execute the strategy require continuous review in the light of changing market conditions. Six areas need especial attention: cash flow; administration; payment; insurance; risk areas; and total cost.

The timescale for payment of the goods can impose a severe strain on the smaller company with limited cash resources. A range of options exist for earlier payment with much improved cash flow such as providing up to 80 per cent of the value of the export invoice on shipment through factoring (pp. 261–63).

An efficient sales ledger is desirable and companies which do not wish to handle much of the documentation work can entrust it to those companies who prepare all the export documentation and institute credit control on behalf of the exporter.

Payment for the goods needs an effective and professional system. This requires continuous monitoring.

Insurance is an area which is subject to premium variation in the light of market conditions and the risks encountered. Ensure the insurance cover is adequate and check such provision particularly whilst the goods are in the possession of the exporter including the leg from the seller's premises to the departure airport or seaport or ICD.

Finally, the total cost of the export credit processing must be continuously evaluated. This includes bank charges and the varying cost of the payment options including the timescale and resultant risk. It also should embrace the cost of running a shipping department to handle all the documents compared with entrusting the work to freight forwarders, banks or companies which take over the sales ledgers of their clients accounts.

Before dealing with the export order acceptance, it is essential that a number of check-points be processed as detailed below.

(1) *Terms of payment.* A full audit of the buyer's needs to be undertaken to establish creditworthiness. Usually a bank can help in this regard. Additionally, the following points require attention: payment timescale; relations with the buyer,

short- and long-term; the political situation regarding the buyer's currency; nature of the order; terms of payment; exchange control – import regulations; currency profile – whether it is a convertible currency and the exporter's ability to offer credit terms; and the cost and risk to the seller embracing timescale, bank charges and insurance. Exporters who have regular overseas clients would be able to monitor the buyer payment profile found in the customer's portfolio. The range of payment options are found on pp. 243–5.

(2) *Credit insurance* – arrange credit insurance to safeguard the transaction.
(3) *Orders* – retain the customer's official order in writing.
(4) *Contract* – advise your customers in writing of the agreed contract terms.
(5) *Delivery* – ideally ensure that Incoterms 2000 are used.
(6) *Currency* – decide in good time whether there is any exchange rate risk and if the exporter should forward sell.
(7) *Despatch* – ensure the seller has proof of despatch as such documentation is likely to be required for any subsequent claim.
(8) *Continuously monitor progress* of the goods throughout the transit duration.
(9) *Product liability.* Check any product liability implications as, for example, obtain in the USA.

The following points should be checked prior to the order of acceptance:

(1) An adequate and clear description of goods indicating tariff or trade code number. This area requires special attention to ensure the correct customs tariff classification is used. Options may exist to present the cargo in a different profile and thereby have a changed tariff which may be more favourable to the buyer in import duty terms (pp. 261–4).
(2) Specification – use metric units.
(3) Quantity to be supplied with delivery programme details.
(4) Price: (a) amount or per unit, (b) currency, (c) delivery terms which may involve part shipments over scheduled period and/or transshipments: ensure they are specific, e.g. CIF (New York).
(5) Terms of payment including provisions for currency rate variation.
(6) Terms of delivery, ex-stock, forward, etc. relevant estimate.
(7) Transportation mode(s), that is, container, air freight, sea freight or road haulier – check out the implications if a sea–air or sea–rail land-bridge is involved.
(8) Insurance.
(9) Packaging and packing.
(10) Offer by pro-forma invoice (pp. 324–5).
(11) Identity of country of origin of goods and country of shipment together with the requisite customs documentation – this may involve the buyer requesting certificates of origin or inwards or outwards processing relief (pp. 197–8).

Prior to receipt of the indent or order, a customer may need a pro-forma invoice, essential before a customer can open a bank credit in the supplier's favour. On receipt of the indent or order from the overseas client, the export marketing manager will check the specification and price in the order with the quotation, together with its period of validity. Care must be taken to ensure the client is not trying to take advantage of an out-of-date quotation. For example, where the quotation was CIF, the export marketing manager must note whether the customer wishes the supplier to arrange for freight and insurance on his or her behalf. The method of payment will be noted and checked with quotation terms. For example, where payment is to be made under a documentary credit, the documents required by the banks must be carefully noted. The required delivery date in particular must be noted. If the delivery date is given and the client has been obliged to obtain an import licence for the particular consignment, the date of expiry must be noted.

Given below is a receipt of order checklist.

(1) Goods:

   (a)   quality,
   (b)   quantity,
   (c)   description.

(2) Payment:

   (a)   price,
   (b)   method, i.e. letter of credit, open account, or documents against payment or acceptance,
   (c)   timescale,
   (d)   currency variation provision.

(3) Shipment:

   (a)   mode(s) of transport, route, transshipment,
   (b)   any constraints, i.e. packing, weight, dimensions, statutory restrictions,
   (c)   timescale,
   (d)   any marks, i.e. special marking on cases or cartons to identify them.

(4) Additional requirements:

   (a)   insurance,
   (b)   inspection requirements,
   (c)   documentation,
   (d)   specific packing – see item 3(b),
   (e)   commissions or discount.

(5) Comparison with quotation. A pro-forma invoice is a document similar to a sales invoice except that it is headed 'pro-forma'. It is not a record of sales effected, but a representation of a sales invoice issued prior to the sale. As the pro-forma invoice contains all relevant details, for example, full description of goods, packing specifications, price of goods with period of validity, cost of cases and, where relevant, cost of freight and insurance, it is used for quotations to customers and for submission to various authorities. Terms of payment are also always shown but it may not be possible to give shipping marks until a firm order is received. When used as quotation the pro-forma invoice constitutes a binding offer of the goods covered by its price and condition shown.

As soon as the exporter receives the letter of credit, he should check it against his pro-forma invoice to ensure both documents agree with each other. Usually, the contract will be in a more detailed form than the letter of credit, but it is important the exporter should be able to prepare his or her documents complying with both the contract and the credit. For general guidance the following checklist should be adopted by the exporter.

(1) The terms of the letter of credit which may be revocable or irrevocable.
(2) The name and address of the exporter (beneficiary).
(3) The amount of the credit which may be in sterling or a foreign currency.
(4) The name and address of the importer (accreditor).
(5) The name of the party on whom the bills of exchange are to be drawn, and whether they are to be at sight or of a particular tenor.
(6) The terms of the contract and shipment (i.e. whether EXW, CFR, CIF, FOB, CIP and so on).
(7) A brief description of the goods covered by the credit. Basically too much detail may give rise to errors which can cause delay.
(8) Precise instructions as to the documents against which payment is to be made.
(9) Details of shipment including whether any transshipments are allowed. Data on the latest shipment date and details of port of departure and destination should be recorded. Advantage is gained to permit shipment 'from any UK port' thereby permitting the shipper a choice in the event of strike action. Similar remarks apply to the port of discharge.
(10) Whether the credit is available for one or more shipments.
(11) The expiry date.

It is important to check the reverse side of the letter of credit and any attachments thereto, the credit as further terms, and any conditions which form an integral part of the credit. Ideally both the seller (exporter) and the buyer (importer) should endeavour to make the credit terms as simple as practical.

In situations where the seller (exporter) is uncertain of just how much of the credit he or she will draw, arrangements should be made with the buyer (importer) to have the value of the documentary letter of credit prefixed by the word 'about'. This will permit up to a 10 per cent margin over or under the amount specified. The word 'about' preceding the quantity of goods similarly allows a 10 per cent margin in the quantity to be shipped. Alternatively the documentary letter of credit may specify a 'tolerance' – such as '7.5% to 5% more or less' – by which the seller (exporter) should be guided.

Documentation will usually involve the clean onboard bill of lading or, for air freight, the air waybill. For international rail movement it is the CIM consignment note, and for the international road haulage transit the CMR consignment note. Particular attention should be given to pre-booking cargo space on the required sailing or flight, and for container traffic, booking a container suitable for the goods. With regard to items sent by parcel post or air freight, the credit and despatch arrangements may vary slightly insofar as the foregoing is concerned.

Today most exporters have a computer software package which progresses the export sales contract as for example Export Master Systems Ltd (see p. 367–71).

15.4.1 Functions and procedures of export documentation

We will now consider the processing of export documentation (pp. 358–60) and the various procedures involved. Details of the salient points follow:

10 March (extracts from original folder)	Order received for delivery end-April All wool tissues (Description of goods – wool and worsted piece goods) Order No. B 2 Market: Lebanon Port: Beirut Packing type: six cases wood, waterproof paper, paper lined cases Marketing: LAS Beirut 6

Time scale of deliveries

15 March	*Pro-forma*
1 April	Payment terms (L/C, etc.) received
2 April	Payment terms checked
5 April	Works store promise
18–22 April	Receiving/closing date of shipment
23 April	Insurance dealt with
25 April	Sailing date
28 April	Letter of credit – shipping date
4 May	Bill of lading required by this date
7 May	Completion of documentation to bank
12 May	Proceeds received
15 May	Letter of credit expiry date

It must be recognized that the number of documents and their type vary by individual consignment, mode of transport, commodity, contract of sale, importing country, customer's country, statutory obligations, financial arrangements, etc.

15.5 Processing the export consignment

The task of processing the export order from the time of the initial enquiry until payment for the goods is received is an important one. Basically, it involves the execution of four contracts each within a certain timescale: the contracts of sale, finance, insurance and carriage. All are interrelated and the order processing sequence of an export order is as follows:

(1) manufacturer receives, in export sales office, initial export enquiry;

(2) costing department calculates approximate total weight or volume of the finished packed goods;

(3) details of weight and measurement of goods are submitted to shipping department to obtain insurance and freight rates to destination delivery point (this involves obtaining quotations from freight forwarders and checking out documentation required such as export licence, certificate of origin, etc.);

(4) costing department completes non-transport calculations;

(5) credit controller obtains satisfactory status report on potential customer;

(6) insurance and freight quotation submitted to costing department to formulate overall quotation;

(7) formal quotation prepared including currency, terms of delivery (Incoterms 2000) and required terms of payment;

(8) quotation sent to prospective overseas buyer – it includes a validity clause;

(9) telex, fax or electronic mail sent asking buyer to expedite reply;

(10) purchase order (offer) received;

(11) export sales office checks out stock availability, manufacturing lead time and delivery schedules;

(12) export sales office re-checks credit status report and notes any change from item (5);

(13) agree to accept order only if customer will pay by confirmed letter of credit;

(14) export sales office raises order acknowledgement (acceptance) to establish sales contract;

(15) export sales office despatches acknowledgement to buyer (NB: if seller not being paid by letter of credit, pass to item (23));

(16) await receipt of letter of credit if item (13) applies;

(17) letter of credit received;

(18) export sales office checks out whether all the conditions can be met;

(19) export sales office requests amendment or extension to letter of credit;

(20) export sales office awaits amendment or extension to letter of credit;

(21) export sales office receives amendment or extension to letter of credit and checks out all the conditions have now been met;

(22) export sales office confirms all the conditions have now been met and despatches acknowledgment to the buyer;

(23) export sales office issues authority for the goods to be manufactured and packed. (The task of monitoring progress of manufacture of goods and packaging is handled by the Shipping Department who maintain close liaison with the Production Department to ensure the despatch date is maintained within the timescale as defined in the letter of credit, export or import licence, and that cargo space is booked on carrier's flight, sailing or trailer);

(24) Shipping Department establishes total weight and measurement of packed goods and has the completed order checked out;

(25) Shipping Department raises shipping documents and cargo shipping instructions noting any letter of credit conditions including any pre-shipment inspection obligations;

(26) Pre-shipment inspection completed (if applicable) and clean report of findings issued. Goods despatched to airport, seaport, inland clearance depot, etc. in accordance with the terms of sale Incoterms 2000 and freight forwarders or buyer's agent instructions (documents to be provided include BL/AWB/CMR consignment note, packing list, export licence, certificate of origin, certificate of insurance, commercial invoice, etc). The range and nature of the documents will vary by commodity, terms of sale or destination country. These will be provided by the seller. The task of processing cargo through customs is likely to be undertaken by the freight forwarder, unless the seller has the goods cleared under the local export control arrangement, in which case the seller handles all the export documentation and customs clearance arrangements);

(27) await shipping documents;

(28) shipping documents received confirming goods despatched on specified flight, sailing or trailer – buyer informed;

(29) documents checked by Shipping Department – errors found, and corrected documents requested;

(30) receive corrected documents;

(31) Shipping Department collates documents and letter of credit;

(32) seller raises bill of exchange signed by a director;

(33) Shipping Department checks all documents against letter of credit;

(34) Shipping Department presents all documents to the bank within agreed timescale;

(35) seller awaits payment or acceptance of the bill of exchange;

(36) seller receives funds from the bank (if the funds are not in the seller's currency (i.e. sterling), the exporter should sell at spot or place, against which finance should have been arranged under (15));

(37) legal requirements followed such as VAT.

It will be appreciated the foregoing arrangements will vary by circumstances and many companies computerize their export consignment processing. A critical area of variation is the terms of payment, the method of carriage and the customs arrangements. It is important to bear in mind the seller is responsible for providing the buyer with all the requisite documents to enable the goods to be processed and imported through customs in the destination country. These must be checked out by the seller. The overall factor to bear in mind is to adhere to the timescale to ensure the goods arrive on the agreed date, and all the documents are in order to support the consignment arriving in a quality condition.

15.6 Presentation of documents to the bank: checklist

When preparing his or her documents for presentation to the bank, the exporter should bear in mind the following points which can form a checklist.

(1) All the documents are presented within the expiry date.

TABLE 15.1 Export documents required

	Bank	Customer	Agent	Customs clearance	Consulate	Total
Commercial invoices	–	3	–	–		3
Certified invoices	3	1	2	1	3	10
Certificate of origin	–	–	–	–	–	
Bill of lading	2/2	2 copies	–	–	2	2/4
Certificate of shipment	–	–	–	–	–	
Insurance policy	–	–	–	–	–	
Insurance certificate	–	–	–	–	–	
Weight and contract note	1	1	–	–	1	3
Bank draft statement	1	–	–	–	–	1

(2) Goods are shipped within the stipulated period.

(3) Documents are presented to the bank within 21 days of the date of shipment or despatch or such shorter time as laid down in the letter of credit.

(4) The aggregate amount of the drawing is within the credit amount.

(5) All documents requiring endorsement are correctly endorsed, for example, bills of lading, bills of exchange, insurance documents.

(6) Invoices contain exact credit description.

(7) Invoices are addressed to the importer.

(8) Invoices contain exact licence numbers and/or certifications required by credit and such certifications are signed, and must be worded exactly as specified in the credit.

(9) Invoices show terms of shipment mentioned in the credit.

(10) Quantity, weight – both gross and nett – shipping marks, unit price, etc. agree with credit and with all the relative documents.

(11) Bills of lading show goods 'onboard' a specified named vessel.

(12) Bills of lading show correct name and address of party to notify.

(13) Bills of lading are in a full set of signed originals (that is, 2/2, or 3/3) or as called for by the credit.

(14) If FOB shipment, ensure bills of lading show freight payable at destination.

(15) If CFR or CIF shipment, ensure bills of lading are marked 'freight paid' or 'freight pre-paid'.

(16) Insurance document is in currency of credit.

(17) Insurance is for correct value (for example, as specified in the credit).

(18) Insurance covers all the risks as specified in the credit.

(19) Original letter of credit accompanies the presentation.

(20) The insurance document is dated prior to despatch of the goods or specifically states that cover is effective from shipment date.

(21) Insurance certificate is not presented where credit stipulates insurance policy.

The foregoing checklist must not be regarded as exhaustive, it merely deals with the salient points. To the exporter dealing with a documentary letter of credit, the following data must be contained on it relative to a consignment by sea.

(1) The name and address of the beneficiary.
(2) The type of credit (revocable or irrevocable).
(3) The amount of credit in sterling or a foreign currency.
(4) Whether the credit is available for one or several drawings or shipments.
(5) The expiry date.
(6) The name of the party on whom the drafts are to be drawn and whether they are at sight or of a particular tenor.
(7) Precise instructions as to the documents against which payment is to be made.
(8) A brief description of the goods covered by the credit (too much detail may give rise to errors which can cause delay).
(9) Shipping details including whether transshipments are allowed. The names of the ports of shipment and discharge should also be recorded, and the latest date for shipment.
(10) The terms of contract and shipment (that is, whether ex-works, FOB or CIF).

Credits should further state that they are subject to the Uniform Customs and Practice for Documentary Credits (1993 UCP) International Chamber of Commerce Publication No. 500.

The following checklist must be rigorously adopted by the exporter when handling the letter of credit.

(1) Is it confirmed by a British bank?
(2) Is the quantity described correct?
(3) Is partial shipment permitted or required?
(4) Is the letter of credit irrevocable?
(5) Is the name of the exporter and that of the customer complete and spelt correctly?
(6) Is shipment permitted from any place in the UK, or only one named point?
(7) Does the named destination quoted (port of discharge) agree with the letter of credit?
(8) Are the following needed?

    (a) export licence,
    (b) import licence,
    (c) exchange licences.

(9) Is the letter of credit amount sufficient to the quotation? The following aspects should be checked:
    (a) cost of goods plus profit element,
    (b) inland transport cost to ship, including wharfage and handling charges at port of loading, or similar charges relative to air freight or air freight charges,
    (c) shipping – sea freight or air freight charges,

(d) forwarding fees,

(e) consular fees,

(f) insurance cost,

(g) inspection and/or miscellaneous charges.

(10) If it is 'on-deck' cargo, does the letter of credit authorize 'on-deck' shipment?

(11) Compare the contract of sale with the letter of credit to ensure its compatibility.

(12) If a chartered vessel is involved, does the letter of credit state 'charter party/bill of lading acceptable'?

(13) Can the exporter comply with the insurance risk required in the letter of credit and does the credit request a policy or certificate?

(14) Does the expiration and shipping date give sufficient time to assure payment?

(15) Is the letter of credit irrevocable?

(16) Can the exporter obtain the following relevant executed documents to conform with the letter of credit?

(a) bill of lading,

(b) air waybill,

(c) parcel post receipt,

(d) invoice packing list,

(e) consular invoice,

(f) certificate of origin,

(g) insurance policy or certificate,

(h) certificate of inspection,

(i) certificate of quality,

(j) certificate of health,

(k) pre-shipment inspection – Clean Report of Findings.

Circumstances do arise which make it impossible for the exporter to present documents to the bank exactly as stipulated or within the prescribed time. Moreover, unforeseen circumstances can arise. In such situations, a number of options exist for the exporter after presenting the documents to the bank.

(1) Request the advising bank to fax, telex or e-mail the issuing bank for permission to effect payment despite discrepancies in the documents. The actual fax, telex or e-mail cost would be for the beneficiary's account.

(2) Ask the advising bank to accept a guarantee order that the exporter requests payment against an undertaking to hold the bank harmless for any loss or damage incurred through making payment against presentation of irregular documents.

(3) Instruct the advising bank to send draft and documents to the issuing bank on a collection basis, that is, documents to be delivered to the importer against authority to pay.

In circumstances where the documents can be corrected or amended, the exporter should arrange for this to be done ensuring that the documents are returned to the paying bank as soon as possible but within the expiry date of the credit. The exporter should remember to check the reverse of, and any attachment to, the credit; further terms and conditions may appear and form an integral part of the credit. Basically, the simpler the credit terms between the exporter and the importer, the easier it is for trade to take place and expand between the parties and countries concerned.

Although it is often desirable for the UK exporter to ensure that the credit is opened in sterling, that is, the currency of his or her country, this may not be possible and a foreign currency may be used. In the EU the euro is adopted for international trade transactions within the euro-zone (see p. 437). To protect him- or herself from any losses due to rate fluctuations in the period between the time he or she ships the goods and receives payment, he or she may wish to sell the foreign currency forward to his or her bank. The bank will quote him or her a special rate and, no matter what happens to the exchange rate in the meantime, the importer knows exactly how much he or she will receive. On the other hand, there may be distinct advantages in invoicing in foreign currencies.

In circumstances where extended credit is granted to the importer, the beneficiary should be contracted to pay interest and will receive an acceptance or usance credit providing for payment at a future date.

At the time of drawing up the contract, the period, rate and method of payment of interest should be agreed with the importer and can be incorporated in the price, or the importer could ask his or her bank to add a clause in the credit stating that the interest is for the importer's account and may be claimed accordingly. Alternatively, the term 'discount charges are for buyer's account' could be incorporated in the credit terms. Interest rates fluctuate, sometimes on a daily basis.

Following presentation of documents in order, the accepted bill can be discounted (that is, sold to a discount house) usually by the bank accepting the bill, or by the beneficiary's own bankers. An interest charge is levied by the discount house which, if for the buyer's account, will be paid by the importer. In effect, the beneficiary then receives settlement as if the bill had been drawn at sight.

If the credit makes no reference to settlement of the discount charge, the bill can still be discounted at any time, but the interest charge levied should be for the beneficiary's account. Unless the credit specifies that drafts are needed in duplicate, a single draft will be acceptable.

Many credits stipulate the name of the port from which shipment is to be made but in some circumstances it may be advantageous to the exporter for shipment to be allowed 'from any UK port', thereby providing a choice. This must be arranged in consultation with the importer and provides a degree of flexibility. It can be extended to include the port of discharge.

There are three features which are basic for export success in terms of documentation: namely quality of management, quality of staff, and effective communication. Exporters are not simply selling a product, they are also selling their – hopefully – efficient service. It is vitally important to examine each problem as it arises, to obtain correct information without delay, to use it effectively and to make correct decisions.

The overseas customer has the same attitude to business detail as the good businessman in the UK. Hence, he or she will be impressed by clarity and accuracy and will be suspicious of the exporter who fails to produce the correct documents in the correct sequence. Export documents must be precise and accurate. Documentation is required for the following reasons:

(1) To provide a complete and specific description of the goods including values and all relevant details so that goods can be correctly assessed for customs purposes.
(2) Documents may be needed for exchange control regulations – quantitative or quota restrictions and also for statistical purposes.
(3) The buyer requires the relevant documents for his or her own purposes, for example, in order to obtain the goods.

Delays in the delivery or despatch of shipping and other documents has reached serious proportions in recent years and has resulted in excessive delays in despatching goods. These delays have arisen for many reasons which can be summarized as follows.

(1) Non-availability at time of despatch of commercial invoices and packing lists.
(2) Late submission of bills of lading by manufacturers and/or shippers to shipping companies, etc.
(3) Delay in releasing bills of lading by shipping companies.
(4) Errors in compilation of bills of lading, insurance certificates, etc.
(5) Delays in communication between clerical staff in seaports, airports, ICDs, dry ports and CFS and shippers.
(6) Delay in obtaining necessary consular invoices.
(7) Inadequate scrutiny at time of receipt of letters of credit.
(8) Delay by banks in processing documents due to discrepancies found in them.
(9) Delay due to one or more of the following:

   (a) letter of credit expired or withdrawn,
   (b) partial shipment, i.e. only part of consignment sent,
   (c) stale or incorrectly completed bill of lading,
   (d) insurance certificate not enclosed, or dated after shipment, or cover incorrect in terms of value or currency,
   (e) incorrect invoices, consular documents or draft drawn incorrectly.

(10) Documents sent by surface post when they could be delivered by air.
(11) Documents sent to small local branches of banks when the main or foreign branches deal with shipping documents.
(12) Wrongly completed documents including customs invoices, delaying customs clearance. To overcome the foregoing problem, the exporter should do the following:

   (a) employ the professional services of a freight forwarder, and/or
   (b) provide an adequately trained staff of good calibre,

(c)   study the letter of credit carefully so there is time for amendments to be made if necessary and send copy to freight forwarder,

(d)   apply the aligned documentation system (This involves the use of the simplified method of documentation with standard-size forms. By engaging the aligned system and mechanization, and one-run series of production, the complete operation is speeded up. Discuss the matter with SITPRO),

(e)   maintain a record of documents flow and status reports in order to isolate consistent bottlenecks with a view to correction,

(f)   utilize fully electronic mail and other aids for the rapid transmission of information when appropriate,

(g)   develop a computerized documentation system (pp. 367–71).

Finally, it must be stressed that an increasing number of multinational industries entrust their international trade distribution and product sourcing arrangements to mega-container operators' logistic divisions. Two market leaders in this field are P&O Nedlloyd and Hapag-Lloyd – the latter involving Pracht Forwarding and Logistics. Such developments have arisen through more sophisticated production and distribution systems developed globally – materials sourcing from one country, production and assembly in two or more countries, followed by distribution worldwide.

15.7 Computerized export department

Our study of processing the export consignment would not be complete without examining the increasing role computers play in processing the export consignment. The subject is also examined in a wider context under Electronic Data Interchange – EDI, Chapter 16.

A successful export computerization project requires careful preparation and planning. It yields the following benefits and features.

(1)   Word processing eliminates routine administration export correspondence such as shipping instructions.

(2)   Exporters tend to have a long list of overseas customers. Electronic mail provides global access to world markets and overseas customers involving the Internet.

(3)   Exporters maintain complex and often multiple pricelists for many territories which can be created on a word processor and updated as required.

(4)   Computer systems can provide spreadsheets which are ideal for monitoring distribution costs, territory analysis and forecasting.

(5)   Similarly, the computer is ideal for maintaining accounts.

(6)   Modern computer networks have access through electronic data interchange to shipment information, customs and airline interfaces, tracking and tracing, document preparation, rating and routeing, sailing schedules, port information, accounting and invoicing, estimated time of arrival, cargo reservation and so on.

(7) Computers eliminate laborious and time-consuming aspects of export administration thereby improving staff morale and productivity.

(8) Computerized systems allow a firm to produce accurate delivered prices, and rapid quotations which benefits sales activities.

(9) Establishing an efficient computer system can improve order processing and administration, up-grade general performance and order costing control and thereby increase profitability.

(10) Valuable time can be saved by management personnel delegating to less senior staff costings and administrative tasks which hitherto were too complex.

(11) Following on from item (10) management and export staff can devote more time to business development and sales-oriented activities and less to administrative and clerical functions.

(12) Computerized systems permit high-speed assembly of export orders.

(13) Similarly quicker assembly, extension and printing of export quotations are facilitated.

(14) Automatic export order processing and production of commercial and internal export documentation can be carried out.

(15) Order and shipment progress chasing and status reporting becomes more straightforward.

(16) The computer can speed up the production of shipping and customs documentation.

(17) Consignment costings can be produced easily, including those for multiple product shipments.

(18) A computer allows for the provision of a general export database, including products with costs and packing specifications; customers; territories with commission agents; currency exchange rates; Incoterms 2000; and container and trailer specifications.

(19) A modern export department computer unit would need the ability to interface with other computer networks within the company via a specially designed module.

Overall, the installation of a sound computer export package will allow a company to develop a modern image of an export company participating at the global level, with a logistic and computer management culture.

Given below are the specifications for modules found in two areas of the computer network, namely export quotations and order processing.

The *export quotation module* creates a fully documented quotation on screen, rapidly and accurately, and prints the data on the exporter's stationery for despatch to the overseas client. The computer system:

(1) uses standard customer, territory and product details from file, or allows one-off entry;

(2) takes prices automatically from pricing and costing calculations or from list prices (with optional mark-up or discount) or allows manual entry;

(3) prepares quotations in any currency, automatically converting pre-set prices in the currency selected;

(4) prints quotations as pro-forma invoices, if required, showing customer and consignee details, shipping marks, sales and payment terms, origin, shipment method and delivery time;

(5) handles percentage surcharges or discounts for one item only or for the whole quotation;

(6) allows flat-rate surcharges or deductions;

(7) permits any rate of VAT on any item;

(8) calculates all extensions automatically;

(9) shows packing specifications per item or for the whole quotation only;

(10) permits the use of invoicing 'clauses';

(11) allows the insertion or deletion of items at any point;

(12) prints ready-to-use quotations on standard stationery;

(13) stores quotations on file for later use or modification, or for conversion into orders.

The *order processing module* comprises the following facilities and would be fully integrated with the pricing and costing quotations and consignment costing modules:

(1) high-speed order assembly from standard information on file or manual input;

(2) automatic conversion of quotations or pro-forma invoices into orders (with or without alteration);

(3) adaptation of past orders for creation of repeat or similar new orders;

(4) documentation as required: masters; confirmations; works, stores and purchase orders; marking instructions; credit control applications; shipping instructions; shipment advices; commercial invoices; packing lists; commission credit notes and all relevant shipping, customs, banking, insurance and origin documentation;

(5) order status reports;

(6) progress chasing;

(7) automatic preparation of documents triggered by appropriate status or order.

15.7.1 Export software – Exportmaster Systems Ltd.

Whilst most export software products have limited their functionality to the area of shipping documentation, the 'Exportmaster Systems Ltd.' package addresses the entire export transaction cycle (Figure 15.3). The exporter can work out delivered prices for different export destinations, incorporating selling expenses and distribution costs through from ex-works to be delivered duty paid. These prices can be used for quotations and pro-formas which are produced, along with personalized letters, during the processing and progress-chasing of sales enquiries. Before issuing a quotation, the exporter is able to check its profitability against known or estimated distribution and selling costs. Date-based deadline reporting ensures that offers are chased up or progressed when necessary.

The program can convert quotations into orders, and orders can also be prepared from scratch. A user-configurable processing system takes the order through

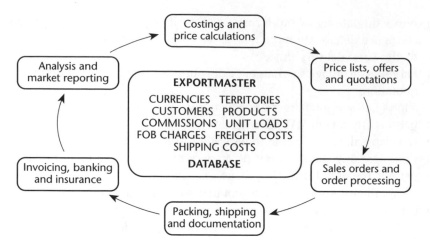

FIGURE 15.3 The Exportmaster Systems Ltd transaction cycle

all stages of preparation, producing company internal documents, as well as commercial paperwork such as confirmations, requests for shipping instructions and routine correspondence items. Additional facilities for the export trader permit the sourcing of required items from multiple potential suppliers with automatic production of purchase orders for the suppliers eventually selected.

If export packing is involved, the program holds details both of the outers and of their precise contents, from which packing lists and allocation sheets can be printed. Exportmaster Systems Ltd. can produce a full set of shipping documents for the consignment, printing them on to pre-printed stationery or on to plain paper using images stored in a laser printer's memory to reproduce the official documents. Customs documents are produced in a similar fashion but the program first sorts and totals the goods by their customs tariff classifications. Facilities exist to transmit documents direct to fax lines without intermediate printing or to have documents printed out at remote locations, for instance, at a despatch department in a factory elsewhere in the country.

After shipment, the program can produce final invoices, bank documents, insurance declarations and other similar items. In particular it can calculate a final shipment costing, showing the net profitability of the consignment once all final selling and distribution costs are known. The finished shipment details can be processed by the sales analysis module to provide management reports and budget monitoring, covering volumes, revenues, costs and profit margins. This information can be used as the basis for the marketing and market-pricing decisions with which the transaction cycle begins.

Additional modules cover items such as stock control, European Community VAT and INTRASTAT reporting requirements, part-shipments, shipment consolidations, commission agency management, links to accounts packages and many other functions. A multinational variant of the Exportmaster Systems Ltd. program permits exporters to run the software at their own or their dealers' offices in different countries and link them together inter-actively for quotation and order-processing purposes using the international telephone network.

Exportmaster has adopted a highly automated approach to the recent changes in European Union VAT and INTRASTAT reporting requirements. Exporters need only maintain certain EC VAT and INTRASTAT information against their standard products and regular customers. They then process their export orders in the normal way. The system automatically reports on all European Union orders during an accounting period and creates the necessary declarations. These are the ESL (EU Sales List), which is a declaration of values of transactions with EU customers for VAT purposes, and the SSD (Supplementary Statistical Declaration) which is a declaration of intra-Community movements of goods and which replaces the information previously supplied on C88 (SAD) forms which are no longer used within the EU.

The EU VAT and INTRASAT declarations may be printed on to the official pre-printed stationery or on to plain paper with the design of the official form being reproduced digitally by the use of laser software. As an alternative, the program allows the reports to be produced in the form of EDI (electronic data interchange) messages which can be submitted to HM Customs and Excise either on diskette or electronically via a Value Added Network such as Tradanet or IBM Info-Exchange. An Exportmaster Systems Ltd. operations flowchart is found in Figures 15.4(a)–(d).

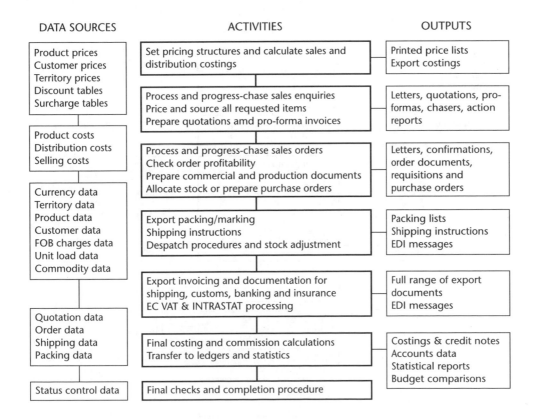

DATA SOURCES	ACTIVITIES	OUTPUTS
Product prices Customer prices Territory prices Discount tables Surcharge tables	Set pricing structures and calculate sales and distribution costings	Printed price lists Export costings
	Process and progress-chase sales enquiries Price and source all requested items Prepare quotations amd pro-forma invoices	Letters, quotations, pro-formas, chasers, action reports
Product costs Distribution costs Selling costs	Process and progress-chase sales orders Check order profitability Prepare commercial and production documents Allocate stock or prepare purchase orders	Letters, confirmations, order documents, requisitions and purchase orders
Currency data Territory data Product data Customer data FOB charges data Unit load data Commodity data	Export packing/marking Shipping instructions Despatch procedures and stock adjustment	Packing lists Shipping instructions EDI messages
	Export invoicing and documentation for shipping, customs, banking and insurance EC VAT & INTRASTAT processing	Full range of export documents EDI messages
Quotation data Order data Shipping data Packing data	Final costing and commission calculations Transfer to ledgers and statistics	Costings & credit notes Accounts data Statistical reports Budget comparisons
Status control data	Final checks and completion procedure	

FIGURE 15.4 (a) – (d) Exportmaster Systems Ltd. operations flow chart

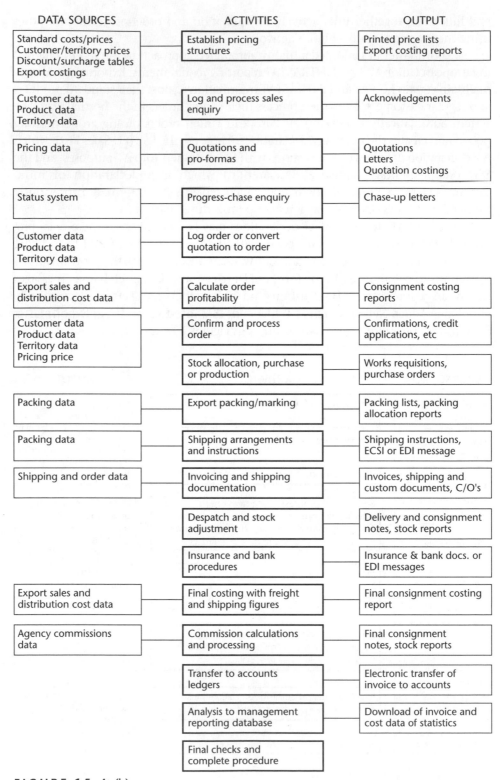

DATA SOURCES	ACTIVITIES	OUTPUT
Standard costs/prices Customer/territory prices Discount/surcharge tables Export costings	Establish pricing structures	Printed price lists Export costing reports
Customer data Product data Territory data	Log and process sales enquiry	Acknowledgements
Pricing data	Quotations and pro-formas	Quotations Letters Quotation costings
Status system	Progress-chase enquiry	Chase-up letters
Customer data Product data Territory data	Log order or convert quotation to order	
Export sales and distribution cost data	Calculate order profitability	Consignment costing reports
Customer data Product data Territory data Pricing price	Confirm and process order	Confirmations, credit applications, etc
	Stock allocation, purchase or production	Works requisitions, purchase orders
Packing data	Export packing/marking	Packing lists, packing allocation reports
Packing data	Shipping arrangements and instructions	Shipping instructions, ECSI or EDI message
Shipping and order data	Invoicing and shipping documentation	Invoices, shipping and custom documents, C/O's
	Despatch and stock adjustment	Delivery and consignment notes, stock reports
	Insurance and bank procedures	Insurance & bank docs. or EDI messages
Export sales and distribution cost data	Final costing with freight and shipping figures	Final consignment costing report
Agency commissions data	Commission calculations and processing	Final consignment notes, stock reports
	Transfer to accounts ledgers	Electronic transfer of invoice to accounts
	Analysis to management reporting database	Download of invoice and cost data of statistics
	Final checks and complete procedure	

FIGURE 15.4 (b)

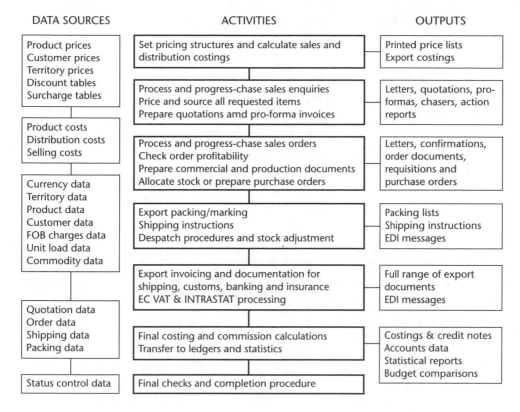

FIGURE 15.4 (c)

Recent developments in Exportmaster's 32-bit version for Windows 95, 98 and NT include on-screen preview and manipulation of documents, direct faxing and e-mailing of documents and the acquisition of sales enquiries and orders from the exporter's Internet Website.

Recommended reading

INCOTERMS 2000 – ICC publication No 560

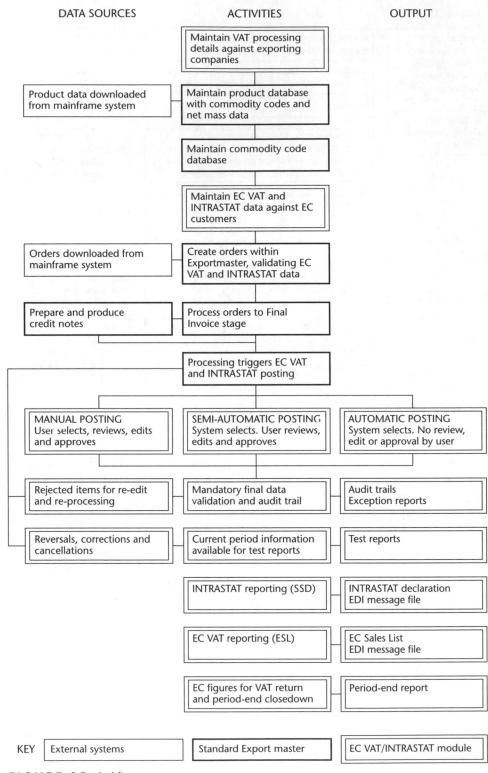

DATA SOURCES   ACTIVITIES   OUTPUT

Maintain VAT processing details against exporting companies

Product data downloaded from mainframe system

Maintain product database with commodity codes and net mass data

Maintain commodity code database

Maintain EC VAT and INTRASTAT data against EC customers

Orders downloaded from mainframe system

Create orders within Exportmaster, validating EC VAT and INTRASTAT data

Prepare and produce credit notes

Process orders to Final Invoice stage

Processing triggers EC VAT and INTRASTAT posting

MANUAL POSTING
User selects, reviews, edits and approves

SEMI-AUTOMATIC POSTING
System selects. User reviews, edits and approves

AUTOMATIC POSTING
System selects. No review, edit or approval by user

Rejected items for re-edit and re-processing

Mandatory final data validation and audit trail

Audit trails
Exception reports

Reversals, corrections and cancellations

Current period information available for test reports

Test reports

INTRASTAT reporting (SSD)

INTRASTAT declaration
EDI message file

EC VAT reporting (ESL)

EC Sales List
EDI message file

EC figures for VAT return and period-end closedown

Period-end report

KEY   External systems   Standard Export master   EC VAT/INTRASTAT module

FIGURE 15.4 (d)

16

Electronic data interchange

16.1 Introduction

Electronic Data Interchange (EDI) has been defined as 'the application to application exchange of computer held information in a structural format via a telecommunications network'. In reality, it means that the data pass from an application on one computer into an application on another computer without printing or manual manipulation. It requires structured data – normally in a neutral data standard – to allow further processing. Basically, it permits paperless trading with no boundaries or time zones.

As we progress through the millennium the pattern of world trade will change, with an increasingly global supply chain. It will become a global market and network (see pp. 119–20). Many companies will source components in one part of the world, assemble them in another and sell them in yet another. It is already starting to have a significant macro-economic impact on world trade patterns, a complex process.

16.2 Electronic commerce

Moreover, recent developments in electronic connectivity have dramatically reduced both the price and complexity of EDI system integration. Electronic commerce – the ability to conduct business electronically – is transforming the way business is carried out, improving the speed, accuracy and efficiency of business processes and fundamentally changing business relationships. The dramatic rise of the Internet and World Wide Web as business tools underlines the importance of these new ways of working. Organizations cannot afford to ignore the opportunities they present, and departments that develop a good business plan and implement electronic commerce can be in the vanguard for their organizations.

The form is the most important concept of EDI, in that it allows an EDI system to send and receive partially completed information, which it can pass through as well as add to the form without re-entering the original data. The elimination of data re-entry allows for greater efficiency and business process cost savings.

The heavy reliance on the Internet as a strategic information systems platform can pose future problems as currently it is not regulated. If a problem occurs with the Internet's ability to send and receive data, currently there is no organization responsible for immediately correcting the problem. Hence, an Internet platform that undergoes 'system down' problems can ultimately render the user unable to communicate or others to communicate with the user. In 1999 the World Trade Organisation decided to consider this situation.

EDI used to be all about big companies trading with other big companies – nearly always working via a third-party service provider or Value Added Network (VAN). Today, smaller users are being drawn inexorably into the frame, and the VANs are having to change tack in order to safeguard their position.

The main catalyst for change is the Internet. This has shifted the focus of the communications business away from proprietary networks and towards the cheaper, more open environment of the World Wide Web. Until lately, most mulinational organizations have held back from demanding EDI compliance from their smaller suppliers; but now the signs are that they want to extend the use of EDI throughout their supplier base. In recent years the VAN operators have recognized this need to extend the reach of EDI to smaller users. There have been a variety of solutions including postal- or fax-based services, in which conventional EDI messages are passed to suppliers in hard-copy form. The problem with such techniques is that they are bound to sacrifice some of the speed, accuracy and transparency of the real thing.

Enter the Internet, which has been undergoing massive expansion just as the need for more accessible EDI has emerged. All the leading VANs have grasped this nettle, and have been developing services which allow Internet links to their existing EDI networks.

Many business and government experts regard electronic commerce as driving wealth creation globally and by 2002 over 25 per cent of government transactions will be done electronically.

To put it simply, electronic commerce can be defined as 'doing business electronically . . . across the extended enterprise'. At a more detailed level the e-centre definition reads: 'Electronic commerce covers any form of business or administrative transaction or information exchange that is executed using any information and communications technology'. This embraces the three main areas of activity, namely: business to business; business to consumer; and government to nation (that includes both businesses and citizens). This definition has been used in the work with the EURIM (European Information Markets) working party on electronic commerce. The leading information exchange tools included in this definition are the Internet and the World Wide Web, intranets, extranets, e-mail and electronic data interchange (EDI). The short definition also embraces the important concept that by trading electronically you reach into your company to share information (via intranets) and reach out from your company to your suppliers and your customers and to the wider global market place by use of extranets or the open world of the Internet.

16.3 Trends and drivers in the development of electronic commerce

16.3.1 Web-based transactions

Use of the Internet as a business tool has increased dramatically since 1996, particularly with the development of the World Wide Web and its intuitive and user friendly graphical user interface. Worldwide business access to the web is predicted to grow from 1.3 million at the end of 1997 to 8 million by 2001, with much of this growth occurring in the Pacific Rim and Europe. Common applications of such information exchange tools include marketing and advertising, publishing, the exchange and dissemination of information on a global scale and, more recently, commercial transactions.

Among the most recent advances is the use of the World Wide Web for business-to-business and business-to-consumer transactions. Much of the recent research has signalled the huge potential of the online transactions market with a number of key developments making the World Wide Web a better place to conduct business-to-business and business-to-consumer transactions. The first of these is security. While the Internet's lack of security has been the most significant operational issue facing organizations considering using the Internet for business, recent surveys indicate a growing confidence that such problems are being overcome. (see p. 377). Two contributing developments are the SET credit card standard and the provision of secure merchant servers by many of the Internet Service Providers (ISPs). The Consumers' Association state that making credit card payments over the Internet is no less secure than using your credit card in a restaurant or over the telephone.

The Secure Electronic Transactions (SET) standard supports credit card transactions and provides integrity, authentication and confidentiality for Master-Card and Visa. SET uses digital certificates which verify that the actual card holder is making the purchase. Merchant servers allow a secure environment within which the complete procurement cycle can be carried out. Online catalogues and product information are displayed on the merchant's customerized and branded Website for customers to browse. Credit card details are entered to complete the purchase and the merchant server system relays the information to a bank or recognized financial organization to handle the credit card authorization or verification and the exchange of funds. A key feature of the system is the provision, at each stage, of transaction confirmation messages passing from the bank to the merchant server provider and on to the merchant and customer.

While there is no doubt that the provision of credit card security standards and secure merchant servers are creating the right technical environment to enable web transactions to increase, cultural factors will play an equally important role in how this market expands. Thus we are likely to see, for example, a change in the buying habits of both the individual and the corporate buyer in order to encourage uptake. To exploit the web, transaction market organizations need to consider how to encourage customers to change their shopping habits and start to go online. Incentives and a different range of services and information need to be provided to convince the customer that purchasing online really does offer significant advantages over the more traditional purchasing route. More imaginative, helpful, up-to-date and information-rich Websites would go a long way to making online transactions more attractive to the consumer and business community.

16.3.2 Internet and extranets bring electronic commerce to SMEs

The door to the benefits offered by electronic commerce will only stay open to small and medium sized enterprises (SMEs) if the Internet becomes more commonly accepted for virtual trading. SMEs must consider the Internet alongside the more traditional VAN-based services that have already developed extensive and sophisticated EDI communities and established the UKs larger businesses as Europe's leading electronic practitioners.

A critical area is the paramount need for any company seeking to synchronize and share data electronically to include Internet communications in its strategy if SMEs are not to be locked out at this stage of the development of electronic commerce. The potential for convergence between traditional electronic commerce and the Internet was under discussion at the Electronic Commerce Conference in London in 1998.

16.3.3 EDI and the Internet

EDI is not a new technique and, in some markets, it has become the way to exchange commercial information. EDI concerns the regular electronic exchange of commercial information, in a standard format, between established trading partners. In the past EDI has been seen, in particular by the SME community, as an expensive and technical solution mainly of benefit to large organizations. However, there is no doubt that over the last 15 years EDI has driven major improvements and changes in the retail, manufacturing and health care industry sectors, with, for example purchasing in these sectors a key area for implementation.

Among the most recent advances is the use of the World Wide Web for business-to-business and business-to-consumer transactions. Much of the recent research has signalled the huge potential of the online transactions market with a number of key developments making the World Wide Web a better place to conduct business-to-business and business-to-consumer transactions. The first of these is security. While the Internet's lack of security has been the most significant operational issue facing organizations considering using the Internet for business, recent surveys indicate a growing confidence that such problems are being overcome.

Interest in the potential of exchanging EDI messages over the Internet has been aroused largely because of the costs of traditional EDI via dedicated Value Added Networks (VANs). The Internet by comparison is easy to connect to, on a global basis, with relatively low charges, significantly undercutting some of the traditional VANs. The VANs respond to this argument by stressing the high performance levels and secure, controlled nature of their networks compared to the 'open' unregulated

Internet. Successful trials include the first successful exchange of digitally-signed EDI data over the Internet in a recent initiative by the US-based Commerce Net organization.

The development of 'simpler' EDI techniques such as web-based EDI forms or 'Lite EDI' is also likely to impact on the purchasing function. These initiatives involve the user accessing the Website of a particular trading partner, selecting products from a catalogue or product and part list and completing an online order form. The information on the completed form is then translated into an EDI standard format and sent to a trading partner who processes the EDI message in the normal way. The essence of this approach is to make EDI more accessible to the SME which may have found it easier, cheaper and less daunting to set up web access than to manage a fully integrated EDI implementation.

The development of extranets in providing a secure trading environment, with the benefits of common TCP/IP communication standards and web browser interfaces, offers great potential to expanding not only electronic commerce transactions over the web, but also the spread of information which is of benefit to customers, suppliers and other interested parties.

EDI is an effective solution for the automatic exchange of large volumes of commercial information on a regular basis between known trading partners and is ideal for some purchasing scenarios. It is clear that those organizations which have already made a significant investment in integrating EDI with their business applications and in the establishment of trading partner communities are unlikely to suddenly stop doing business electronically in this way. EDI, the Internet and web-based solutions each have different advantages over each other and a likely future scenario involves a merging of all three.

16.3.4 Intranets

Intranets – internal company (corporate) controlled networks using Internet communication protocols and web browser technology – have the potential to fundamentally change the way people in large organizations communicate with each other. At the same time, the corporation has full control over who uses the intranet and what information is accessed. Intranet development has shown major growth during the period 1997–99, largely because it is seen as a cost-effective and efficient mechanism for making information available to all parts of an organization.

Common applications range from making company-wide information, such as telephone directories, training and human resources information, available to all employees through the provision of sales, support and product data to a network of remote sales offices. Through the use of firewall security solutions, a corporate intranet can also have an external connection to the 'Open Internet'.

16.3.5 Extranets

An extranet can be defined as a private Internet technology-based business network used by a community of trading partners. Extranets are run on a 'community controlled' basis – that is, all the participants in this network know each other and have a common interest, which can even be the exchange of information or actual business transactions performed in a secure environment. An example is a 'hub' purchasing from its 'spoke' suppliers.

The development of extranets in providing a secure trading environment, with the benefits of common TCP/IP communication standards and web browser interfaces, offers great potential to expand not only electronic commerce transactions over the web, but also to spread the information which is of benefit to customers, suppliers and other interested parties.

16.4 Case studies

16.4.1 Wickes – an EDI-based supply chain

Wickes, the £500 million turnover UK DIY chain, applied for and obtained the e-centre UK's Award for Excellence in 1997. This award is endorsed by the DTI through its Information Society Initiative. Wickes brought all its suppliers into the award and is the first chain to gain approved status for all suppliers – 70 per cent of which are small companies (SMEs). This is part of Wickes' continuing drive for high standards.

During 1997/8 Wickes expects to process between four and six million electronic business documents. With a six figure investment over two years, Wickes has streamlined, automated and integrated procedures, from orders to remittance advice. EDI's inherent discipline and accuracy has reduced the order-to-delivery cycle from four or five days, to just 48 hours.

Future plans include the use of bar coding to enable pallets to be scanned on delivery, plus a new tranche of information sharing, including price and product exchange, shortage notes, returns notes, order confirmation and supplier inventory data. This moves the company into the realms of ECR (efficient consumer response) for more efficient replenishment, improved customer service and reduced costs. Goods are now brought to the consumer at a lower cost, and customer service is enhanced with the right products on the shelf at the right time and in the right quantities. EDI has allowed Wickes to massively re-engineer its business processes.

16.4.2 Trading on the Internet – AMP Connect

http://connect.amp.com

AMO Inc is a global supplier with a large European presence of connection systems and products for the electronics and telecommunications industries. Its 250 000 lines include the plastic seat for the microprocessor in your PC and many connectors used in the consumer electronics and white goods industries. One of AMP's key services is AMP Connect which gives customers the ability to browse, select and order connector products from an online catalogue which features product data specifications. A highlight of the site is its multi-lingual capability which supports AMP's global customer base. This huge electronic catalogue is up-to-date and avoids all the physical problems involved in the updating, production and distribution of large paper-based catalogues. The site is well designed and laid out to meet the needs of buyers, engineers and designers who are encouraged to download the connector specifications and design them into their products – an excellent way to lock in your customer to your products.

16.4.3 H&R Johnson Tiles Ltd

http://www.johnson-tiles.com

This Staffordshire-based wall and floor tile manufacturing company is discovering the benefits of external e-mail, EDI (electronic data interchange) and of using the web for ordering purposes. For example, Johnson's have developed a web-based system which allows their distributors to browse catalogues, check stock levels and then place orders. In addition, Johnson's are experienced EDI users and are now using this expertise to encourage their smaller trading partners to trade electronically. It is the ability to take orders via the web and via EDI which has demonstrated H&R Johnson's electronic commerce flexibility. The site is very customer friendly and features the ability to locate a tile distributor on a regional basis.

16.4.4 BAT – EDI and logistic case study focus

The fourth case study is found in British American Tobacco (BAT). The strategy intended to make BAT the world's biggest tobacco manufacturer in the next ten years involved folding four of its UK businesses into one. The result was to raise to over 170 the number of markets and territories that the company's UK logistics department has to serve.

The process of restructuring that BAT started in the early 1990s has been followed by a programme of selective expansion. This has been partly by acquisition, as with the recently purchased Mexican tobacco manufacturer; partly by the formation of joint ventures, notably in Russia, Eastern Europe and Central America; and partly by licensing agreements, such as its contracts with the state-owned Turkish and Indian tobacco monopolies. The agreement signed with the Turkish tobacco enterprise took 15 years to bring to fruition.

An underlying benefit has been to enable the company to use its global presence to optimize through the economies of scale, whether in the purchase of wrapping material, tobacco leaf – or transport services. This emerges from a 'best practice' structure that extends across the span of supply chain management, from materials acquisition to final product delivery.

The logistics department has been operating since mid-1993 from BAT's Southampton plant. Staff had previously been based at two sites. This structure has enabled the logistics team to operate as independent coordinators of supply and demand requirements, balancing the needs of production and marketing to optimum effect. Of the 68 members of the department, half are involved in customer service. Their responsibilities are divided along geographical lines in relation to the 450 customers that the UK company serves. Distributors, retailers and duty-free outlets in the Far East account for around 73 per cent of the UK company's exports, Europe for 8 per cent, Africa for 9 per cent and Saudi Arabia and the Gulf states for around 10 per cent. In some countries, supplies are also held in third-party warehouses, as well as in a company-owned UK warehouse, to service duty-free customers.

The Southampton factory's entire output is exported. It comprises such famous brands as Benson and Hedges, State Express 555 and John Player Gold Leaf. The output can exceed 50 billion cigarettes a year. Additionally, the logistics department purchases a further 60 billion cigarettes from other BAT companies and handles their distribution.

Annual departmental costs are put at £10 million, spend on freight at £18 million and warehousing worldwide at £7 million. The logistics department's involvement starts when one of the liner shipping companies with which it works is instructed to load containerized tobacco leaf in the country of origin. The harvested leaf is placed in boxes which are fork lifted into 40 feet containers, each capable of holding 96–99 bales. The containers are filled to optimum capacity. Brazil, the USA, Kenya, Zimbabwe, India, China and Turkey are among the countries from which the company sources tobacco leaf, placing orders two years ahead of the delivery date.

When the containers reach Britain, they are moved to BAT's 375 000 ft^2 tobacco store in Oxfordshire, where the leaf is held at an ambient temperature in strictly hygienic conditions. The leaf is released to the factory in blend sets for immediate introduction to the manufacturing process. Normally, the factory receives between eight and ten loads of leaf a day, amounting to between 800–950 cases. The production department will specify what blends it needs. The leaf is normally on site for no longer than 48 hours before being fed into an automated production process. The only manual involvement occurs when the palletized boxes of banded cigarettes are fork lifted into the 40 ft containers in which they are shipped. No cigarette stocks are held on site and wrapping material is held only to cover production requirements for four to five days.

The logistics department manages the interlocking processes of materials planning and delivery, production planning up to three years in advance, production scheduling, order processing delivery, invoicing and customer service. A commercial team provides back-up covering areas such as risk management and liaison with HM Customs and Excise, together with freight contract negotiations. An in-house insurance service department at its head office arranges cover, spreading risk by placing business with a number of underwriters. The company has experienced few losses from theft despite the spread of its customer base in the expanded European Union. BAT's team of freight buyers, comprising executives from Germany, Brazil, USA and Britain, meets formally four times a year when executives from liner shipping companies are invited to tender for contracts of 12 months' duration. As one of the world's biggest volume shippers, the company sets stringent service criteria while capitalizing on its immense purchasing power. The individual lines' performances are reviewed every quarter.

The outstanding feature of the logistics department has been its investment in EDI systems. Like all such exercises, this entailed an intensive management effort to build systems that would enable the company to communicate electronically with a growing number of its customers and suppliers. The investment was mainly in management time – buying into EDI in terms of hardware and software is small, and it has been a key factor in the ability to absorb the extra work that the department had to undertake as a result of the restructuring.

It estimates that, but for the EDI process, BAT would have been compelled to engage between five and seven additional staff. Self-billing has enabled suppliers to receive payment quickly while reducing documentary errors and queries to near zero. It has strengthened relations with both customers and suppliers with whom the company is now trading electronically. Customers are able to re-stock more quickly, buying smaller quantities and, as a result, tying up less capital in stock. EDI has improved 'visibility' during the supply chain process and enabled BAT to do more, and more complicated, work.

BAT makes one in eight of the cigarettes chosen by the world's one billion tobacco smokers.

16.4.5 Summary – salient points

It is clear that electronic commerce is a reality and in some markets it is already the only way to conduct business. With the rapid development of solutions aimed at making the World Wide Web a more secure business environment this trend can only continue. Electronic commerce techniques are fundamentally changing the way international business is done and traditional ways of working are constantly being re-appraised. International business managers need to understand very clearly that the winners will be those who embrace these new opportunities. You only need a very short checklist to guide you.

(1) Obtain a senior, budget holding business sponsor to champion your electronic commerce projects.
(2) Develop and agree a project plan.
(3) Start with a small, simple, realistic project and implement it quickly – thereby hopefully showing some clear business benefits. Set up a project team with your champion, the IT department and a business person who really has hands-on experience of the business process.
(4) Talk to your key trading partners and discuss the benefits of electronic commerce with them.
(5) Conduct awareness and training sessions. Wherever possible refer to real case studies, ideally from other companies in your sector.
(6) Join the e-centre in your country to obtain sane and sensible advice.

The development of an effective integrated global supply chain including all the processes involved in the trade and payment cycle has to be carefully planned, predicted and controlled. Traditional management thinking and past-based procedures are too slow, error prone and inflexible for a global supply chain to operate competitively. This is exemplified when one bears in mind that 11–14 participants are involved in any single export–import process. Overall, the process embraces: banks – exporter – forwarder – customs – port – carrier – port – customs – forwarder – importer.

Planning and coordinating the movement of goods and flow of payment through such a complex system to a predictable level of certainty is virtually impossible without the disciplines which only EDI provides. The use of EDI can provide important cash savings and also enables a company to provide better levels of customer service and gain a competitive edge over its rivals. Thinking further ahead, companies may look to EDI to provide new business opportunities.

The benefits of EDI can be divided into three areas: strategic; operational; and opportunity. They include the overall functioning of the business and affect the very business the company is undertaking. These can include a faster trading cycle, just-in-time manufacturing, terms of trade being dictated by bargaining power and the need to respond to highly competitive market entrants.

Operationally the benefits include reduced costs. These can be split down into paper and postage bills cut dramatically; a reduction in capital tied up in stock; and manual processing costs. There will be improved cash flow, security and error reduction, mainly from the elimination of rekeying or transcribing information from one medium to another and acknowledged receipt.

One benefit which is easier to quantify is that as companies insist on EDI trading, a company offering this service will increase its chances of obtaining a wider choice of trading partners. They may even lose them if they do not use EDI.

The cost of installing the EDI facility will vary by company and its scale of operations. At the top end of the scale the EDI facility can be integrated into a complex mainframe computer software system. Installation investment will be high, but will be suitable only for a large or multinational company. A small company can get into EDI by purchasing a PC and an EDI enabling package, or just by buying an EDI enabling package to run on its existing PC. As indicated earlier (pp. 375–8) the cost of EDI provisions has fallen sharply recently.

Companies should estimate how much of the information typed into their computers is being entered from another computer printed document. Industry estimates indicate that 70 per cent of the data entered comes from another printed document. The potential for errors to be made is high. Errors may simply waste time, but they could have very serious results, with orders made out and goods invoiced in the wrong quantities at the wrong prices and being sent to the wrong addresses. By using EDI, the costs of raising invoices and statements are dramatically reduced. As far as payments are concerned the major banks are already involved.

In 1992 the Port of Singapore indicated that EDI yielded the following benefits:

Paper reduction costs	25%
Error reduction costs	33%
Inventory reduction	23%
Improved customer relationships	23%
Improved supplier relationships	15%
Competitive advantages	19%
Improved trade facilitation	15%
Others	6%

Overall the benefits EDI brings to international trade can be summarized as follows.

(1) The standard messages that are being developed are for both national and international trade.
(2) Standard procedures being introduced between seller, buyer, trade-related services, customs, etc. to support the implementation of the messages.
(3) The hardware, software and network services required are not restricted to national boundaries and should not need to be altered for communication with parties abroad.
(4) Language independence is built in through the use of United Nations data elements and international code sets – e.g. terms of payments and deliveries, harmonized coding system for commodities and services, codes for identifying parties and locations, etc.
(5) The reduction of the paperwork required in cross-border trade and across the transport chain.

When using EDI, the company is making use of an electronic post office. A system where you send your information to a postbox, which collects its information and sends it on to your customer. So you send the information when you want to and there is no need for you to be directly connected to your customer's computer. This electronic mailbox is known as the 'network'.

There are numerous Value Added Network (VAN) providers worldwide. The information sent over an EDI system is structured, and the actual structure of the message will depend on which type of business you are in. All the network providers can supply information on specific industries. Once you take the first step towards getting involved, a suitable package can frequently be provided by your existing systems supplier often working with your current applications. The network providers all have a range of options (pp. 384–7).

EDI reduces the need for large stocks of goods, makes ordering quicker, payment quicker, generally speeds up the business cycle and engenders closer relationships between suppliers and their customers.

16.5 UN–Edifact standards: their development and maintenance

Recognizing the uncoordinated growth of EDI standards development in North America, Europe and further afield, the United Nations Economic Commission for Europe, in its working party on trade facilitation UN/ECE WP4, which has representatives and observers from some 60 countries and many international organizations (European Commission, IATA, International Chamber of Commerce, International Chamber of Shipping, ISO), appointed three rapporteurs for North America, East and Western Europe. With the support of international experts drawn from industry and national groups, these rapporteurs have the task of progressing the development of EDI standards under the guidance of the UN/ECE WP4.

The rapporteurs' teams groups are now operational in North America, Eastern and Western Europe and the Far East. Details of the Edifact Board for Western Europe is given below. The same structure and activities are reflected in the other rapporteurs' teams.

16.5.1 Edifact Board Western Europe

The Edifact Board, comprises its steering committee, secretariat, message development, technical assessment, maintenance, and promotion and documentation groups. The board, with representation from the European Commission, EFTA, trade associations, pan-European EDI user groups and the European standards body, CEN, will develop and direct policy, monitor and regulate the work of the steering committee and ensure that Edifact developments are adequately resourced and controlled.

The steering committee, on behalf of the Edifact Board, will coordinate the activities of the workgroups on Edifact standards for the EU and EFTA, as well as ensuring coordination and active cooperation with the other rapporteurs' groups following agreed procedures and timetables, ensuring integrated development and implementation of Edifact standards through the UN/ECE.

The message development groups have as their task the development of UN standard messages. The groups with representation from pertinent disciplines (trade, industry, transport, banking, insurance and customs) will be responsible for carrying out the work programme as approved by the steering committee. The messages, agreed with the message development groups in the other rapporteurs' group, are published at different status levels (draft, for trial use), prior to reaching full UN recommendations. Certain common trade messages may also be introduced as European CEN standards.

The maintenance group is responsible for the maintenance of the Edifact Board directories (data elements, segments, messages and code sets), to support and reflect the work of message development and technical assessment. These directories are available on a database maintained by the secretariat at the CEC, to which access will be provided to authorized bodies.

The technical assessment group is responsible for ensuring that messages developed by the message development groups, or other secretarial groups, conform to the guidelines laid down by Edifact.

The secretariat is responsible for the running of the support database and tracking the change requests which are passed, through technical assessment, to the appropriate message development group for processing.

16.5.2 Industry-specific EDI organizations

Over the past few years, several national and pan-European associations dealing with EDI have been formed, either specifically concerned with EDI – e.g. Edifice (European Electronic Industry EDI Association) – or as part of existing associations such as the CEFIC (European Council for the Chemical Industry) EDI project. These associations have been a major factor in progressing the development and implementation of EDI.

The ANA (UK Article Number Association) was one of the first major EDI projects in Europe, triggering similar projects in the retailing sector in several European countries. Odette, in the automotive sector, was the first pan-European EDI association, followed quickly by other pan-European groups.

Through direct participation in the Edifact Board, steering committee and message development groups, these industry-specific EDI associations are instrumental in the development of UN standard messages meeting their sector's requirements in the widest European and International sense.

The Tedis programme encourages the formation of 'EDI associations' and their active participation within the Edifact Board framework as a most effective means of consolidating user requirements for message development, progressing implementation and promotion and coordination of EDI, both within their specific industry and between the various sectors. Most industries are closely involved with transport companies and financial institutions, as well as administrative functions like customs. The need for close liaison between the different sectors is a result of these intimate relationships.

Although the structure and composition of an EDI association will reflect its industry's requirements and trading relations, the role and responsibility of the association with regard to EDI message development must be within the Edifact development framework in order to avoid further duplication of effort or confusion of standards. The same holds true during implementation and operation; user groups should not introduce operational procedures that may isolate the group from others, or oblige small or medium sized companies to implement a number of different operational procedures. Details of the industry-specific EDI associations are given below.

Odette: Organization for data exchange by tele-transmission in Europe

Odette was formed early in 1984 and is made up of national delegates, representing both the manufacturers and suppliers of the automotive industry in a particular country. The countries involved at present are: the UK, France, Belgium, Germany, Italy, Sweden, Spain and the Netherlands.

The activities of Odette are carried out through established workgroups and extend beyond EDI into barcoding label standards, standardized containers and the interchange of engineering data. Odette consists of:

(a) a plenary committee – a decision-making body, which meets some four times a year, with representatives from each country;
(b) an executive made up of one member from each country;
(c) a permanent secretariat office;
(d) some nine working groups covering message development, EDI syntax application, telecommunications recommendations, implementation, legal aspects, barcoding, engineering data and containers.

As international or European standard messages were not available in the initial phase of the project, Odette has placed high priority on the development of trade messages such as an invoice or purchase order between vehicle manufacturers and their suppliers. As the UN-Edifact message development activity produces definitive versions of these messages, Odette will consider migration towards support of the standard messages.

CEFIC-EDI: Council for the European Federation of the Chemical Industry

CEFIC represents the 15 national chemical federations of Western Europe. It has, as corporate members, most of the major chemical companies with headquarters in Europe. The CEFIC/EDI first phase (1987–88) involved 17 corporate members and five federations. After successfully concluding technical trials, the CEFIC/EDI set up was adapted for 1989.

CEFIC/EDI has a two-tier structure: on the one hand, the CEFIC/EDI forum, a platform for all CEFIC members interested in EDI; on the other hand, an operating structure with a coordination group and three working groups. A messages group deals with message development for the chemical industry in line with UN-Edifact, at present in the areas of trade, transport and administrative requirements: a technical integration of Edifact and X.400 as well as the operational requirements of EDI (translation software). Thirdly, a business group studies the innovative business opportunities of EDI. In addition, a committee takes account of national developments.

CEFIC has a permanent EDI information desk and coordinates representation to all Edifact Board groups. CEFIC also liaises with CIDX, the American counterpart of CEFIC/EDI, and with other European groups like Odette and Edifice.

Edifice: European Electronic Industry EDI Association

The Edifice group was formed in 1986, with participation from electronics industries from the UK, France, the Federal Republic of Germany, Sweden, the Netherlands, Switzerland and Italy. Several of the participating companies are subsidiaries of major US electronics companies. The group provides a forum for discussion and agreement of EDI practices within the electronics and electronics component industries. The group has regular plenary meetings reviewing UN-Edifact message development, results and progress of pilot trials and network problems, as well as future interchanges with customs and transport companies.

Edifice is participating at all levels on the Edifact Board and message development groups. Edifice will be developing messages required by participating companies and putting them forward as proposals for future UN standard messages.

EAN-COM: International Article Numbering Association, EDI project

The International Article Numbering Association, perhaps best known for the 'barcode' product numbering system, has been entrusted by its member companies with the development of a standard communication system including telecommunications facilities for trade messages. The association takes part in the UN ECE/WP4 proceedings and EAN-COM is an active member of the Edifact Board and message development groups dealing with trade, transport and finance. With some 100 000 companies associated to the national EAN groups, EAN-COM activities will reach a large number of small and medium sized enterprises in Europe and further afield.

Several EDI implementations at national level have been operational for some years now based on earlier UN syntax rules (TDI); for example, ANA Tradacom in UK and UAC Transcom in the Netherlands. Migration to UN-Edifact is under discussion for these projects. New national implementations and international transactions will be based on the UN-Edifact standards.

Rinet: Re-insurance and insurance network

Rinet was set up in 1987 in Brussels by eight insurance and re-insurance companies to provide EDI and network services. This featured both the insurance and re-insurance services in Europe. The services will be extended eventually to cover insurance and re-insurance companies from all over the world. The group participates at all levels of the Edifact Board and the message development group for insurance. Specific messages developed by Rinet will be proposed as UN standard messages.

EDIS: EDI association for transport and harbours

This group was formed in 1987 with participation from several national and harbour EDI projects, namely the UK (DISH-Data interchange shipping, Dedist (Sweden), Intis (Rotterdam harbour) and Segha (Antwerp harbour). The group takes part in the Edifact Board message development group for transport.

COST 306: EDI trial projects in the transport sector

COST 306 is a European Commission and EFTA initiative to promote EDI trials in the transport sector.

Tedis transport sector

The Tedis transport group was formed within the framework of the Tedis programme, to coordinate the various EDI transport and transport-related services in the member states and EFTA covering rail, road, air, sea and deep-sea transport. It is an extension or continuation of the COST 306 initiative on a broader basis.

The group will work on the coordination of several horizontal activities defined in the Tedis programme, concentrating initially on the telecommunications and legal aspects of EDI. The group will base its work on the results of existing projects and liaise whenever necessary with other sectorial groups in Europe. The message development activities will be carried out through the Edifact message development group for transport.

16.6 Global freight – EDI

An example of EDI is best exemplified by examining one of the Value Added Networks involved in global freight. The following discussion is based on the VAN Freight Network Ltd.

16.6.1 The exporter

Recent studies have shown that more than 50 per cent of documentary credits are incorrect on first presentation. This results in lost orders, costly delays and lower profits for exporters. EDI helps exporters to eliminate these frustrating and expensive errors. Standard documents for exporters and other shippers serving domestic markets can be created more accurately, amendments made more rapidly and the data transmitted quickly and reliably. Orders can be fulfilled faster and more cost-effectively.

16.6.2 The freight forwarder

Much of the information needed by the freight forwarder already exists on the customer's computer. Currently forwarders must re-input the information on to their own computer, print out the documents and then despatch them. The creation of additional documents involves re-inputting much of the data that already exists. In addition, errors often require documents to be re-created adding to the waste of time and money.

    EDI reduces paperwork, expensive telephone calls and wasteful communications costs. Forwarders can receive the essential data from their customers as an electronic message direct to their computers via Freight Network. They can also create their own databases using the Freight Network software. Either way costly inputting and re-inputting can be eliminated. Existing computerized forwarding systems can be connected to the service both simply and inexpensively.

16.6.3 The carrier

Many of the largest carriers have developed their own EDI systems for the transmission of data internally and for 'paperless trading' relationships with their customers (Figure 16.1). The problem with most customer-based systems is that they require the carrier's dedicated terminals to be installed in the offices of the shipper or freight forwarder. Many of the carriers have recognized the difficulties involved for all parties in this approach. Freight Network gives carriers the ability to send and receive messages to and from all their customers and suppliers of services rapidly and easily. It also enables the carriers to use the vital data without re-keying.

16.6.4 The importer

EDI has grown rapidly on a bilateral basis where buyer and seller agree to exchange standard data electronically between their respective computers. These developments

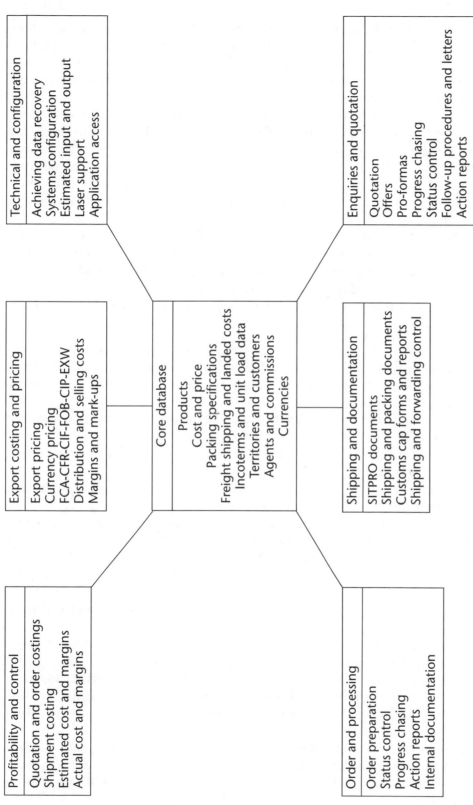

Technical and configuration

Achieving data recovery
Systems configuration
Estimated input and output
Laser support
Application access

Enquiries and quotation

Quotation
Offers
Pro-formas
Progress chasing
Status control
Follow-up procedures and letters
Action reports

Export costing and pricing

Export pricing
Currency pricing
FCA-CFR-CIF-FOB-CIP-EXW
Distribution and selling costs
Margins and mark-ups

Core database

Products
Cost and price
Packing specifications
Freight shipping and landed costs
Incoterms and unit load data
Territories and customers
Agents and commissions
Currencies

Shipping and documentation

SITPRO documents
Shipping and packing documents
Customs cap forms and reports
Shipping and forwarding control

Profitability and control

Quotation and order costings
Shipment costing
Estimated cost and margins
Actual cost and margins

Order and processing

Order preparation
Status control
Progress chasing
Action reports
Internal documentation

FIGURE 16.1 Export office computer unit embracing database and operational modules

have until now only benefited the largest companies. Freight Network makes these vital benefits available to all types of companies and organizations – without them having to invest in expensive computers and software development. It provides its software to forwarders and their customers and associates to enable them to take advantage of the benefits of EDI.

Electronic information and transfer provides a competitive edge for domestic and international trading partners. The messages can easily be created from data already stored on a company's existing computer system. Alternatively, the messages can be created on a modest personal computer using software supplied free of charge by Freight Network. When the message is ready for transmission, one dials up the Freight Network system via a telephone line and a modem to transmit the messages. The Freight Network computers convert the data in the messages into standard formats and automatically set up the communications according to the destinations provided. The message is sent to an electronic mailbox or directly to a computer. If the recipient has only a fax or telex machine, the Freight Network computers automatically make the necessary conversion.

Nineteen fully operational messages are available through the network as detailed below:

(1) *Customer/freight enquiry* – The exporter, importer or freight forwarder can enquire about any aspect of a future freight movement or service availability.
(2) *Acknowledgement of enquiry* – The forwarder or carrier sends or receives a customer or freight enquiry message.
(3) *Quotation request* – A message to enable the importer, exporter or forwarder to place a freight quotation request with suppliers of services.
(4) *Quotation response* – This enables the forwarder or carrier to respond to a quotation request.
(5) *Pre-booking advice* – Exporter or forwarder provides provisional details and timing for the cargo, to secure space.
(6) *Firm booking* – Exporter or forwarder provides firm booking of freight requirements including detailed instructions for placement of empty equipment and collection when loaded and asks for confirmation by return.
(7) *Confirmation of booking* – Forwarder or carrier provides confirmation that space has been booked, and that other arrangements are acceptable. Electronic transfer provides rapid and accurate confirmation to the customer that his booking is accepted.
(8) *Transport order* – This enables the exporter, forwarder or importer to send a standard message for any type of transport requirement.
(9) *Shipping instructions* – Exporter or forwarder provides final details of goods to be shipped, instructions for handling and documentary requirements. Accurate export cargo shipping instructions sent electronically greatly reduce the risks of error or misinterpretation.
(10) *Bill of lading, waybill, housebill* – Forwarder or carrier provides bill of lading, waybill or housebill details to the customer and other interested parties. Electronic transfer of information provides accurate details to the customer at

the earliest opportunity, replacing the paper document. Electronic transfer of the information prior to issue of the negotiable bills documents allows the customer to vet the content against other documentary requirements and make amendments if necessary.

(11) *Air waybill* – Forwarder or carrier provides air waybill details to the customer for air movement of goods to the destination.

(12) *Freight invoice* – Forwarder or carrier provides details of charges as a summary invoice. Electronic transfer of invoice details allows automation of the payment cycle and, dependent on the terms of trade, allows earlier confirmation by the exporters of charges to be incorporated into the commercial invoice to the buyer.

(13) *Groupage manifest* – Shipping companies, airlines, forwarders or hauliers can send the carrier manifest message, irrespective of mode of transport.

(14) *Confirmation of despatch* – This message confirms time and place of despatch to the destination.

(15) *Schedule of charges* – Forwarder or carrier provides the customer with a schedule of the charges to be made by third parties involved in the movement of the goods. Electronic notification of forthcoming charges gives early advice to the shipper.

(16) *SAD* – Exporter, forwarder or carrier, depending on responsibilities allocated in the shipping instructions, provides export and/or import details of the customs documentation to customs authorities and/or overseas partners. Electronic transfers of customs documentation provides faster and more accurate clearance to load or to import.

(17) *Changes in transport mode movement* – Forwarder or carrier provides details of any changes in sailing or flight schedules which affect a consignment to the customer. Electronic transfer provides accurate, automated identification of consignments effected as quickly as possible, allowing all parties to check potential implications such as letter of credit expiry.

(18) *Electronic mail* – Used by any party in the transport chain to relay any other information or instructions not specifically catered for by a structured message to any other party.

(19) *Status message* – The forwarder, exporter or importer can establish the status of a consignment at any given time from despatch to final destination.

The growth of EDI and the establishment of international data standards under the Edifact organization has led to a new shipping lines EDI initiative, Ediship. Ediship has been formed by ten major lines in order to create the cooperative business environment in which critical mass support for EDI can be achieved. Exporters can electronically interchange information on bookings and cargo shipping instructions, as well as receiving bill of lading and invoice data. The opportunity also arises to interchange key data with banks to speed the complete documentary process.

EDI facilities are also available to help importers with schedule information, consignment progress tracking and customs clearance routines. The major benefits accruing from Ediship initiatives include:

(1) Reduced paperwork bringing savings in administration costs through less handling of documents.
(2) Reduced overheads through the elimination of all double handling of information or re-keying of information into systems.
(3) Improved accuracy. The once-only data entry process eliminates the need for repeated checking of information, reducing error tracing and correction procedures.
(4) Faster receipt of information. This can result in savings in terms of lower stock levels in industry, quicker clearance by customs and the speedier production of statistics by government.
(5) Speedier invoice/payment cycle, thus presenting opportunities to the seller to reduce borrowings and interest payment on loans made to finance the movement of goods.
(6) Greater control of transportation through speedier communications with a reduction in possible delays and subsequent economies.
(7) A common type of data transfer based on internationally recognized standards.
(8) A more efficient service with faster updating and passing-on of shipping information.
(9) More stable relationships between organizations leading to more favourable mutual terms of trading.

Most documents in the documentary credit process are capable of being effectively transmitted by EDI, except for the bill of lading, as the document of title function requires an original document to operate effectively. As this function is the basis of security for payment and receipt of goods in the documentary credit process, it is clear that a solution must be found to this problem before total electronic trading is feasible. A possible solution is the sea waybill. Given below is an example of an EDI system based on the shipowner Sealand.

The EDI system is a computerized system using standardized electronic versions of common business documents. These include bills of lading, freight bills, purchase orders and so on. Shippers with a mainframe computer have online access to Seatrac thereby enabling shippers to book, trace and monitor shipments on a 24-hour basis. It provides an 'in house' capability to shippers to call up a vessel schedule and reserve booking space. Moreover, it will rapidly track any shipment. The system has built-in security and all transactions are confidential. Seatrac uses standard IBM or IBM compatible hardware and does not require a dedicated unit.

Shippers despatching shipping instructions are despatched in an EDI environment thereby reducing the risks of any errors, misbillings and delays in the documentation process. Likewise, Sealand are able to receive the bill of lading and export documents on a 24-hour basis. The booking system provides direct access to effect an immediate cargo reservation. In regard to cargo arrival notices, the shipper has adequate advance notice to enable the customs clearance arrangements to be adequately planned. Sealand's EDI system is also linked to the seaports served, and cargo tracing is available together with freight billing.

To conclude our review of EDI in management terms, we can simply say that it yields the following benefits:

(1) it creates a high management and business profile;
(2) it provides an easy-to-use system for management data analysis, and data access;
(3) it facilitates accuracy, speed and efficiency;
(4) it quickens the decision-making process;
(5) it raises an organization's international profile and access;
(6) it utilizes high technology;
(7) there is a value added benefit to the organization;
(8) it makes an organization more cost effective.

Failure to become involved in EDI will result in businesses or companies no longer being competitive in the market place.

Recommended reading

SITPRO News

■ □ ■ ■ 17

Export market entry options and strategies

17.1 Introduction – market selection criteria

When a company begins to think about marketing its goods or services overseas (see p. 29) the decision process involves four stages: (a) deciding which market to enter (see p. 6); (b) choosing the market entry option and strategies; (c) formulating a marketing plan; and (d) deciding on a marketing organization (see p. 38). In this chapter we will examine the second phase. A range of market entry options exist and the factors which influence the final selection are now briefly outlined.

(1) *The company objectives*. These will be found in the company business plan. They will be determined by company resources and the market forecast and profitability. The Multi-National Industry (MNI) has capital, experience and production capability, whilst the small to medium sized enterprise (SME) may have limited capital, production resources and experience. An MNI is usually better able to take risk and has more negotiating power than an SME.

(2) *Legal and political constraints*. This extends to agency agreements, channels of distribution, patent registration, licensing, joint ventures, tariff barriers, franchises, repatriation of funds, taxation employment law and exchange control.

(3) *Political and economic stability*. Stable markets favour more commitment by the exporter especially in investment terms. Some countries offer special tax concessions to generate inward investment.

(4) *Culture*. The skills, abilities and management culture of the company towards international portfolio development will affect the selection. A number of aspects of the company culture are influential here, including technical and design competences, international logistics capability and computer literacy.

(5) *The product*. The nature of the product or service and the degree of adaptation and competitiveness it will have in world markets. This will embrace the product life cycle evaluation.

(6) The company's experience in the market.

(7) Any long-term development in the market.

(8) The level of competition, both short- and long-term.
(9) Developed or underdeveloped; homogeneous or heterogeneous; near or distant markets.
(10) Open or closed markets featuring non-tariff and tariff barriers. (see p. 412)
(11) Market category classification – is it a key market or a cluster market complex?
(12) Member of any economic trading bloc or customs union and the accruing benefits.
(13) Urgency or speed of entry to the market available, such as a licence (see pp. 407–11) or a franchise (see p. 405).

17.2 Indirect and direct exporting

Basically, there are two methods of exporting – indirect and direct. *Indirect exporting* is the process of selling goods overseas through a third party, thereby relinquishing control of the selling process of the goods. This has the advantage to the exporter of obviating any need to have an extensive, internationally-focused organization as usually no contact is made with the overseas buyer. Examples of indirect exporting include a local buying office (p. 423), piggy back operations (p. 411), an export house (p. 404) and trading houses (p. 412). This is an attractive mode of entry for an SME as a first step to selling in the international trade market.

Conversely, *direct exporting* is the process whereby the exporter becomes fully involved in and totally committed to the process of exporting on a proactive basis. This generates a proactive situation compared with the indirect exporting which is reactive. Hence, the exporter becomes fully involved in the seven 'Ps' of the marketing mix – product; place; promotion; price; process; people; physical aspects – on an international basis. It does usually involve significant capital commitment and resource allocation of management and production coupled with any adaptation of the product to meet the overseas buyer's needs. Examples of direct exporting include agents (p. 396), distributors (p. 396), joint ventures (p. 406), licensing (pp. 407–11), consortia (p. 405), franchising (p. 405), strategic alliances (p. 412), mergers and acquisitions (p. 402), management contracts (p. 411) and wholly owned subsidiaries (p. 412).

17.3 Market entry strategy

Companies must have a strategic focus in their decision-making process of selecting and entering a market or a series of markets overseas. This also applies to first time exporters. The following strategic considerations are relevant.

(1) To have a customer portfolio which has an international base.
(2) To increase production, thereby lowering unit cost and permitting more competitive pricing.
(3) To spread the market risk, on the basis that the greater the number of markets served the greater the spread of opportunity and risk.

(4) To raise the company profile, thereby raising the capital value of the company and attracting fresh capital into the company to keep pace with new technology and provide funds for research and development, especially in high tech areas.

(5) To realize a more volume based and productive utilization of the company infrastructure.

(6) To increase market share and dominance.

(7) To focus on being a marketing led company rather than one which is product led.

(8) To increase the general competitiveness of the company and its product range in all areas of the company profile and on an international scale.

(9) To ensure the long-term future of the company.

(10) To develop a proactive rather than a reactive company which is globally focused and market research driven, with a continuous focus on the client base and market place environment.

(11) To develop an international brand image which permeates throughout the company with a particular focus on the product, personnel and overall commitment of the company to its customers and the overseas markets served.

(12) To use all available management techniques in the company operation and management, featuring budgets, marketing plans, logistics, computer literacy, control and audit techniques. It is also vital to have a workforce which is well-trained and well-qualified at all levels, with key personnel being multi-lingual, professionally qualified and capable of working in a high tech environment.

(13) To have the appropriate membership of a trade association and accreditation of management quality BS5750 (see pp. 417–20).

(14) To increase the profitability of the company and return on investment.

We will now consider in more detail the range of market entry options.

17.4 Market entry options

17.4.1 Agents and distributors

The narrow definition of 'agent' in export practice is that he is a party who acts for the exporter, the latter being the principal. The agent does not make a profit but is paid a commission on all orders secured, for which his or her principal obtains eventual payment. It is usual for agents to work for a number of principals, offering a cohesive group of products which are not in direct competition with each other.

There are variations in the type of agency which work on a 'commission only' basis according to what the parties consider suitable to the product and the market. Some examples are given below.

(1) *Fee or retainer.* When it is clear from the outset that it will take some time before the product gets established in the market, and thus before the agent can earn a worthwhile commission, it is up to the principal to offer some alternative financial inducement to motivate him or her until a straight commission

becomes a viable proposition. Where the agent is selling a range of products for one principal on a commission basis, the agent may be offered a fee to launch a new product which, though within the general range, is an untried newcomer to this market, or some entirely fresh range of products being launched by the principal.

(2) *Expenses incurred by the agent.* These may be paid by the principal or shared between the parties on an agreed basis. This introduces a variation from the 'commission only' type of agency. Such expenses may be a 'once only' arrangement such as setting up showroom facilities. Alternatively, they may be continuing, involving the agent being charged with scanning local technical journals and buying them for the principal when appropriate. Additionally there is the cost of E-comerce and fax transmittals. Some special variation of the commission only arrangement can be introduced to cover the agent's outlays or to share them in special circumstances, for example an exhibition where it is decided to take a stand, or some exceptional venture in local publicity.

(3) *Stockist agencies.* This situation arises where the agent sells on commission but undertakes to buy for his or her own account – or to share in the cost of – stocks of some of the items within the range. This could significantly improve sales turnover where the goods are such that the demand is always for prompt delivery, for example, components for automobile repair services in a foreign country.

(4) *After-sales service.* Many technical products are such that it is necessary to provide a manufacturer's guarantee. This may be undertaken by the agent who sells on commission and may include a repair service outside the maker's guarantee arrangements. Stocks or parts will have to be carried in the market by the agent and, usually, workshop facilities will have to be made available. This involves the provision of an operating manual and a period of training provided by the principal for the workshop personnel. The details of the arrangement between the parties vary widely according to individual circumstances. The principal may supply free spares or stocks, or they may be sent on a consignment basis. Alternatively, the agent may be required to equip a workshop and carry spares at his or her own expense.

(5) *Consignment stocks.* The market where sales are made must have goods available for immediate delivery as soon as the commission agent concludes the sale. Such stocks can be entrusted to the agent providing he or she owns or rents suitable warehousing space. Such an agent must be of outstanding integrity and sound financial standing. Moreover, one must ensure the law of the country involved recognizes the continuing legal ownership by the principal of goods physically held by the agent. The alternative is for the stock to be held by an independent warehouseman in the name of the principal, who then sends buyers' delivery orders to enable them to call on the warehouse for release of the goods for which the order was placed through the commission selling agent.

(6) *Salaried agent.* In this situation the agent is resident in the country of operation and is paid a salary, with or without expenses and fringe benefits, by his or her

principal. This may prove suitable where the products are capital goods or when the principal is a firm of consultants such as a consortium. Such an agent could keep the principal in touch with conditions in his territory and advise on local opportunities and official tenders over a period of years. For example, he or she could tender on behalf of his or her principal for medical equipment or harbour navigational facilities.

(7) *Distributor/agent.* In some markets, conditions are such that they are dominated by one large firm which dwarfs its competitors, but the market potential cannot be fully exploited unless the smaller concerns are enticed into the sale of the products. The large firm acting as a distributor can also secure orders for shipment direct to the small ones. Such transactions are remunerated on a commission basis. The contract of agency between the principal and such a firm must be drafted with special care, but even so it may prove in practice that the small firms are squeezed out of effective marketing because of the uplift in the price they pay to cover the agent's commission. At best they are somewhat restricted in their activities. This type of agency has proved effective where the big firm comprised members of ethnical or religious majority groups or ruling caste, particularly where the small firms belonged to the minority and monopolized sales to other people in the minority grouping.

(8) *Export management agency.* The function of the export management agent is to act as the manufacturer's export department, either for all markets abroad or for a selected number clearly agreed in advance. He is briefed in regard to the products, both technically and as to future production flows and possible changes in quality and quantity. Price is agreed and a rate of commission fixed, with or without some contribution to the agent's expenses (generally, or for specific purposes such as travel) or a fee plus commission payable on results. It is usual for the export management to be authorized to appoint agents in foreign territories within the agreed sphere of operation. On the other hand, the management does not usually incur any financial risk – he or she would not be expected to put through orders from parties of doubtful standing and would invariably advise the manufacturer about financing; thus the merchants who operate manufacturer's agency departments often take over the goods EXW, FCA or FOB.

Some care must be taken to differentiate between the form of agency explained above and the group sales concept detailed on p. 39. In the latter case, the manufacturers work together as an entity to market their products. However, in an export management agency situation, the agency takes over the export function and decides what shall comprise his or her group of products to be marketed overseas.

(9) Del credere *agent.* Where a commission selling agent, whatever his or her other terms of reference, undertakes that orders passed to the principal will be paid for in due course by the buyers, he or she is called a *del credere* agent, that is, he or she undertakes a credit risk. Great care is necessary in defining the responsibilities and rights of this special type of agent, and when and how he or she is paid his or her *del credere* commission. Thus, the principal must be

certain to instruct the collecting bank when a document is lodged with a *del credere* agent named as 'case of need', that is, if the buyer refuses the bill, the agent is empowered to take possession of the documents and/or the goods.

It must be stressed that there exists a wide variety of different types of agents and the foregoing are only the most common ones. Moreover, one must bear in mind that there are certain similarities in the role of the agents, confirming houses and export houses. The latter two are to be explained later in this chapter.

It is appropriate, however, when examining the role of the agent, to consider the distributor. For example, the manufacturer markets some of his or her products in some territories through commission selling agents, but in other areas through importers, stockists or distributors, who buy the goods for their own account and earn a profit (not a commission) as a basis of their remuneration. The role of the distributor in the overseas market has become increasingly significant and the following are the salient points of difference between the distributor and selling agent.

Selling agent	*Distributor*
(1) Not financially involved	Buys for own account
(2) Leaves importation to the buyers whose orders he passes to the principal	Imports the products
(3) Is paid a commission at an agreed percentage on orders secured	Marks up the supply price to cover his profit
(4) Any service necessary is rendered by the buyer	Where necessary undertakes responsibility for the service
(5) Carries no stock except for showroom purposes	Normally carries a stock
(6) Unlikely to be involved in publicity except where required to give advice or report on impact	Likely to be involved in local publicity
(7) May be authorized to engage sub-agents	Appoints sub-distributors
(8) No control of resale prices	Controls selling prices in countries where retail price maintenance is possible
(9) Leaves distribution to the buyers	Undertakes distribution in the market

To conclude our study of agents, we now detail the salient clauses usually found in an agency agreement. The clauses may be varied to meet individual circumstances and others may be added as required.

(1) Details of parties to the contract, i.e. names, registered address and short title of each party.
(2) Purpose of contract. For example, it must state in specific terms that A appoints B as an agent, and that B agrees to act in that capacity in accord with the terms of agreement.

(3) Details of the products involved. For example, A will supply and B will sell the merchandise prescribed including any brand names.

(4) Territory. The agreement must outline the geographical area over which the agent is given exclusive sales rights.

(5) Precise duties of the principal embracing any reference to sales outside the agency, handling direct enquiries, etc.

(6) Precise duties of the agent. This will incorporate situations such as dealing with other suppliers particularly of a competitive nature. It will provide a description of the goods, the manufacturer, any warranties, and the method of promoting such competitive products.

(7) Exceptions, reservations or restrictions imposed on either one or both parties to the agency agreement.

(8) Method of quoting prices. For example, whether FCA or otherwise.

(9) Agent's purchase and resale. This clause will reflect the type of agency agreement involved as described earlier. For example, if the agent is buying for his or her own account, such as when acting as a distributor, he or she may appoint sub-distributors subject to the manufacturer's approval; fix sale prices and retail list prices; and report back to the manufacturer. This clause requires adequate deliberation and consideration.

(10) Consignments – in particular terms of delivery. This will embrace under what terms merchandise will be delivered, who pays landing charges, duty, customs clearance, cartage, warehousing, stevedoring, insurance in warehouse or bond and accounting arrangements. Additionally, it should detail property in the goods, arrangements for release to the buyers and disposal of stock on termination of agreement.

(11) Spares for general maintenance and service. A clause on this item should also outline general arrangements and disposal of the items on termination of the agency agreement.

(12) Cost of airmail, e-mail, faxes and unusual expenses – not mentioned elsewhere in the agreement – and responsibility for their payment. Most exporters would insist on telex and fax facilities being available.

(13) *Force majeure*. This clause negates responsibility of the principal where *force majeure* prevents delivery from a factory or, in respect of goods ready to leave, prevents despatch or causes diversion of a cargo carrying ship or aircraft.

(14) Permissive clause. In situations where the products do not meet the competition in design, suitability to market or price, whether or not the agent can handle other goods of the same category. This clause is usually found in a commission agency rather than sole distributorship.

(15) Commission. The actual commission scale – fixed or sliding rate and how the agent will be credited or remitted. This requires careful deliberation, particularly in an area of floating currencies and devaluation implications.

(16) Accounting. The agent should keep proper books and render periodical statements including consignment stocks where applicable. Provision should be made for accounts to be audited or examined by the principal or his or her representative.

(17) Overprice. This usually arises in contracts between merchants and agents in raw materials and semi-finished product trades. It embraces general conditions and the authority of the agent to try to overprice. Moreover, it details the allocation between the two parties to the agreement of the overprice apportionment.

(18) Publicity. A general agreement regarding sales literature and catalogues, including responsibility for translations, policy in regard to exhibitions, local advertising and special propaganda. It should detail the apportionment of cost between the two parties to the agreement.

(19) Report. The agent to submit reports at prescribed times and likewise the principal, to keep the agent informed of product development and trade generally. It will extend to production and marketing policy.

(20) General conditions. Any general conditions not mentioned elsewhere in the agreement and which either party mutually wishes to introduce. For example, to pledge the principal credit or to start legal proceedings without his or her consent.

(21) The duration of the agreement and notice of termination of agreement by either party – the latter may be one or three months or any other prescribed period.

(22) Breach of contract clause. This involves a case of breach or default by either party or by the agent without mention of breach of any principle. It also embraces a summary of determination upon liquidation or compensation with conditions or attempts to assign benefits of contract.

(23) Laws and arbitration. This must indicate which country's law will apply and that disputes will be settled by arbitration in accordance with the terms prescribed in this clause. This will avoid costly litigation and speed up settlement.

(24) Assignment. Neither party has the right to assign the benefits of the contract without the prior consent of the other. This may be qualified by a merger sub-clause showing what would happen if the original legal entity of party is merged into another legal entity.

The contract document finishes with space for the signature of the parties and an indication of capacity of signatories and witnesses, including formal application of a company's seal where applicable.

The agent and distributor is employed by small, medium size and large companies. It constitutes the intermediary between the seller (exporter) and buyer (importer). Hence, the exporter does not have direct contact with the distributor to determine market research data such as buyer behaviour, buyer profile, product acceptance and selection criteria and size of buyer's account. Further data are not available on market trends and market profiles. Nevertheless, these shortcomings are usually overcome through continuous dialogue between the seller and the buyer involving visiting the market, distributors' or agents' monthly reports, and regular meetings. A similar analysis applies to the agent, but usually the exporter is closer to the buyer (importer) than is the case when a distributor is employed. Overall, there is a need to develop an empathetic strategy between the exporter and the agent or distributor to realize the best results and develop market research-led strategies.

Factors determining the selection of agent or distributor include the following.

(1) Membership of the appropriate Trade Association and BS5750 registration – 'Management of quality' accreditation if applicable.

(2) Profile of the agent or distributor and nature of business. Ideally one should appoint an exclusive agent – one who does not sell or promote goods or services competitive to the principal business.

(3) A value added benefit emerging from employing the agent or distributor.

(4) Volume of business the agent or distributor will generate and his or her business record and achievements.

(5) The agent's or distributor's resources, including financial, marketing and selling resources, equipment and computerization, nature of the accommodation and training of personnel.

(6) Professional qualifications of the Directors and overall quality of the management and resources.

(7) Evaluation of the business plan on how the agent or distributor will tackle the principal business.

(8) EDI access. (see pp. 373–93)

(9) Any association with a legal dispute or fraud.

It is usual to draw up a short list of agents and distributors to evaluate their skills and proposals and their degree of commitment to the task. This involves visiting the market and the agents' and distributors' premises and meeting their staff.

17.4.2 Company acquisition

A quick way of entering a market is to buy a locally-based company and develop a strategy of product specification in line with the overseas buyer brand image. This tactic is often termed merger and acquisition. The locally-based company is already established in the market and the foreign buyer may be able to provide much needed capital input, technical specification, management operation and marketing skills in a high tech computerized manufacturing or service environment. For example, the company's product lifecycle may be in decline and with no financial resources to invest in research and development and a foreign buyer may be able to provide a high tech state-of-the-art new replacement product to revitalize the company's future prospects.

There are other considerations to be taken into account in the merger and acquisition strategy. On the downside the disadvantages include encountering a culture hostile to foreign investment; the political implications; and the risk of funds being repatriated in the event of nationalization or severe exchange controls; However, the advantages include acquiring an additional market, gaining access to an established distribution network and having an immediate source of revenue in a new market. In addition, the company acquired may be treated as a wholly-owned subsidiary to gain maximum tax advantages.

17.4.3 Concessionaires

Concessionaires operate as distributors with a special authority granted by the manufacturer to work in a particular market area, usually on a basis of exclusivity.

They tend to be experts in their field and have good contacts in their particular trades. The advantage to a manufacturer or exporter is that regular business is assured, but there is no direct contact with the buyer, and the channels of distribution to that market will be restricted to the activities of the concessionaire.

Thus a manufacturer might make what, at first sight, appeared to be an opportunist sale to a merchant and then receive a repeat tender, coupled with a request for exclusivity for the particular territory in which the merchant is active. This could, in turn, develop into a regular relationship by which the merchant becomes the concessionaire for that market.

17.4.4 Confirming houses

The basic function of a confirming house is to assist the overseas buyer by confirming, as principal, orders already placed so that the exporter may receive payment from the confirming house as and when the goods are shipped. Any credit period the buyer may require is arranged and carried by the confirming house which takes over the credit risk from the supplier. A confirming house, as an export house, is used extensively by the small (or medium-sized) supplier involved in the export business.

17.4.5 Consortia

These are groups of organizations which work together as a unit in order to achieve a common purpose. The consortium may operate as a group seller or a group buyer and sometimes will use a nominee in order to preserve anonymity during negotiation of a contract. Consortia tend commonly to be engaged in bidding for large tenders, particularly where the size of the order is feasible only by employing the combined capacity of individual members.

Many consortia of this type have been set up on the initiative of the leading firms of consulting engineers, with the end-products in the foreign country ranging from civil projects such as large dams, irrigation, railway modernization and extension, hospitals, dredging undertakings and harbour installations, to construction works in the electrical field such as power generation, sub-stations and television transmitters.

Since each major undertaking of a consortium is likely to be so different in its nature from any other project put out to tender by foreign governments, municipalities or other principals, it follows that many of these consortia are set up specifically for only that one project and, when this is completed, the consortium is dissolved. Some of the parties may collaborate again on another contract, possibly bringing in new members, but it rarely happens that a second venture is so exactly like the first that the consortium can function unchanged.

From the very nature of these undertakings it follows that the negotiations between the members of the consortium are protracted, difficult and complicated, even before the nominee can submit the tender. This type of operation is always highly technical and, for every tender that is accepted, there will be more than one which is not secured. This involves having to write off the heavy expenses incurred. Such projects are usually associated with ('turn key') cargo delivery terms.

17.4.6 Export houses

Export houses have three main functions as detailed below.

(1) An export house can act as an export merchant buying goods outright and selling them on his or her own account. The merchant may buy goods from the exporter against the requirements of an overseas customer. Alternatively, the agent may buy the product and market it overseas. Finally, the agent, by virtue of his or her international trading activities, may indulge in compensation trading, switch deals, etc. (indeed, in any barter type transaction).

(2) An export house can act as an agent but retain the role of the principal throughout the transaction. In such circumstances, the export house will promote the exporter's products overseas; carry the credit risk on the overseas buyer; attend to the physical and clerical work involved; stock goods at home and overseas on the exporter's behalf; follow-up delivery dates or delays; deal with formalities overseas; and occasionally provide an after-sales service. Basically, the degree to which the foregoing work is undertaken by the export house will vary according to individual circumstances and is a matter for negotiation. In the main, the small (or medium-sized) export business usually finds it cheaper and more cost effective to engage an export house as their agent rather than employ their own export staff or overseas representative to undertake such work. The payment for these services may be in the form of commission, with the agent quoting the agreed export selling price to customers overseas. Alternatively, there may be some other form of remuneration to the export house negotiated by the exporter. For example, the export house may calculate the export price with the exporter on a 'cost plus profit margin' basis. The profit margin would be for the export house financial controller, who is responsible not only for sales of the product, but also its advertising, marketing, distribution, etc.

(3) An export house can act for an overseas buyer in return for which commission is earned. In such circumstances, the export house may find sources of supply or deal with suppliers (exporters) nominated by his or her principal. In either case, the export house will arrange shipment and insurance; progress and despatch of orders; and confirm and finance contracts on the buyer's behalf.

The export house may be a buying agent or merchant. The role of the export house varies: the large ones undertaking virtually all the roles outlined above, and the smaller ones offering a more specialized but less extensive service. Few, if any, export houses are prepared to deal with all goods for all destinations. Most specialize in particular markets, types of goods, or in certain types of products for particular markets. To the exporter who is interested in export house activity, it is suggested he or she contacts the British Export Association whose address is found in Appendix A.

17.4.7 Franchising

Franchising is a growth global market. It is focused on both the manufacturing and service sector. Overall, however, franchising has a high service element. It involves the legal right to use branding, products and methods of operation being transferred to a third party. The major examples of franchising found today are in the retailing sector.

Franchising has been defined as a contract between a manufacturer, wholesaler or service company (called the franchiser) and an independent entrepreneur (the franchisee) who purchases the right to own and operate the franchise. The franchiser will receive an initial fee, royalty on sales, lease fees for equipment, profit share or some combination of these four. The three main forms of franchising are manufacturer sponsored retailing, as found in the car industry where a dealer retails automobiles subject to certain conditions imposed by the manufacturer; manufacturer sponsored wholesaling, as found in the soft drinks industry; and, thirdly, service sponsored company retailing, as found in the fast food and car hire businesses. In short, franchising is a facility granted by a principal to a retailer to sell on the principal's behalf a particular product or service using the principal's name, for example McDonald's. In such a situation the retailer must conform precisely to the code of practice stipulated by the Principal.

There are two types of agreement between the franchiser and the franchisee: an area development agreement and a master franchise agreement. Basically, the agreement features identification of rights embracing territory location, extent of rights to use the franchiser's name, payment of fees, franchisee's obligations, sale of the business and termination of the agreement. Royalties may be based on a percentage of sales or a flat management service fee reviewed annually.

An area development agreement will feature the degree of transferability, whether exclusive or non-exclusive rights are to be granted; the number of outlets, exclusive or non-exclusive rights; provision of additional outlets in the event of favourable market conditions; and finally termination arrangements and disposal of outlets.

In contrast, a master franchise agreement includes a specified territory; exclusivity; performance schedule, embracing agreed sales targets; fees – initial and on-going; default clauses, with the arbitration and national law applicable; intellectual property safeguards; training provision; taxation aspects and the rights to be granted.

The franchising market is one of increasing market penetration and is very much in evidence in the global village. It provides to the franchiser speed of entry to an overseas market, and an outlet for the franchiser's goods or services over which he or she has virtually complete control. It does involve capital commitment in terms of premises/retail outlets and facilitating the franchise launch in terms of stock provision, marketing, training and control systems. Overall, it is very much involved in the brand management business on a global scale.

17.4.8 Joint venture

An increasing number of companies are now developing their overseas markets through joint ventures. As a form of market entry, it provides greater cover over sales and distribution; develops local manufacturing packing and assembly; permits technology transfer; provides control over cost and production quality; and enhances market penetration, growth and customer loyalty. A joint venture can bring a new dimension to the business of the new joint company.

Basically, a joint venture is the process of two trading companies from different countries – at least one of them being local – forming an agreement and a new company to market and/or manufacture or produce goods on a joint basis. Both companies must have the same management culture ideology and have jointly competitive features and advantages both wish to exploit. Each company contributes its complementary expertise or resources to the new joint company. Both parties have an investment obligation, the extent of which varies by circumstances. The scale of the shareholding may vary from 10 per cent to 90 per cent but generally is around 25–75 per cent. In many developing countries, governments stipulate a minimum national holding in a joint venture of 60 per cent which constitutes a majority local shareholding. In such circumstances the host country would have the majority of directors on the basis, for example, of four to three in favour of the host country.

The rationale for companies opting for a joint venture include the following.

(1) An exporting company can achieve quick access to a market, thereby gaining competitive advantage and an early return on investment.

(2) Host countries may impose severe import restrictions making it virtually impossible to enter that market; thereby the joint venture is seen as a profitable option, providing a local manufacturing base.

(3) Joint ventures share the risk between the two companies, in proportion to their investment portfolio.

(4) Costs are shared, particularly in the area of research and development which can be very substantial in, for example, the pharmaceutical industry. Similar remarks apply to new plant for car manufacturers.

(5) Manufacturing within an economic bloc or customs union provides free circulation of goods within the bloc without any trade barriers. This enhances the market share and, additionally, it may offer tax incentives and development grants.

(6) Global business today is becoming more competitive with the number of players in the market being reduced through joint ventures and merger acquisitions, a favourite strategy of the multinational industries. The factor driving such strategies is lower unit costs and greater competitiveness. This may be achieved through lower labour and materials cost and lower overheads.

Overall, the joint venture may provide a better capital investment return and facilitates better market research strategies through the new company management structure, and interface with the market and customer.

The procedure to follow prior to embarking on a joint venture would be similar to the points below.

(1) Thoroughly research the host company.
(2) Establish how the foreign partner is going to raise capital and under what terms.
(3) The degree of host government investment especially in the areas of:

(a) capital construction,
(b) land availability,
(c) labour force deployment, training and redundancy,
(d) timescale,
(e) product and plant specification constraints,
(f) technology,
(g) expatriate employment terms,
(h) procurement – raw materials and components sourcing and any constraints,
(i) marketing, both domestically and internationally,
(j) quality control,
(k) the legal environment,
(l) the attitude to competition domestically and internationally
(k) arbitration.

The joint venture is very much a growth market as we enter the new millennium.

17.4.9 Licensing

Licensing is a method of market entry offering a low level of investment and speed of market entry and is ideal for the licensee who is keen to manufacture his or her product in the licensor country. A licence is granted to an overseas company to manufacture products on a royalty basis in accordance with the licensing agreement terms agreed by the licensor and licensee. It confers the right on the licensee to use a combination of the following: technical know-how, patent rights, trade marks rights and copyrights. Both parties to the licence agreement benefit from increased profits. However, it is important to stress that usually it is far better to market products in overseas territories than to licence the patents and/or the production know-how.

The rationale of adopting a licensing strategy by an exporter/licensee incorporates the following features.

(1) Licensing involves a limited financial commitment and low level of management resources, together with speed of market entry.
(2) It overcomes any government controls such as import duty tariff and non-tariff barriers, and encourages more competitive pricing in distant markets subject to high freight charges by resorting to local manufacture.
(3) Licensing enables the licensor to market the product as a local manufacture thereby overcoming any national prejudicial effects not favouring imported goods.

(4) The licensee gains access to the licensor's market base and channels of distribution.

(5) Overall, it allows a better return on capital and avoids costly product entry and launch costs in an overseas market with the attendant risks. Moreover, the price is likely to be very competitive.

(6) Licensing allows for speedier entry and access to the market especially in comparison to a joint venture or industrial transplant. This is particularly relevant for fast moving consumer goods (fcmg) and for small and medium-sized enterprises (SMEs).

(7) Licensing enables the licensee to enter a market with an established customer in place.

Advantages to the importer or licensee include the following.

(1) The acquisition of an internationally recognized brand name thereby enhancing existing sales and reputation.

(2) The extension of the existing product range by acquiring new products which complement existing products.

(3) The development of 'know-how', particularly where high tech products are concerned, thereby avoiding costly research and development. Also new products give additional marketing strength and tangible product advantages over competitors.

(4) It is a low cost venture for the licensee with no research and development costs but simply the expense of setting up the plant to manufacture the goods.

A company may seek to license the production or use of a product; copyright work, process, business format or trade mark which a licensee might accept either has a use or value on its own, or would have if incorporated into another product. Technology, know-how, or a business format may be suitable for licensing, but whatever you wish to license needs to be exclusive to you and not in the public domain, otherwise the foreign party will see no need to buy a licence. If a product or process is protected by a patent, a potential licensee will only feel a need to enter a licensing agreement if he or she cannot readily circumvent the patent. For that reason, some companies prefer not to patent know-how and technology, where it is eligible for patent protection, in the belief that patent registration can aid competitors' research or that, in fact, the new process or product has a finite life span. Hence, the licensee must see a licence as giving him or her tangible benefits as earlier described.

A licensor can sell a licence for a fixed period and for a fixed once-only fee or, more usually, will seek a smaller initial 'disclosure' fee and an ongoing royalty directly related to production or sales value or volume. Alternatively, the rights may be sold without time limit, but this is more likely to be the case if the licensor believes his or her licensed product has only a limited life span before it becomes obsolescent.

Licences can also be granted on an inter-company basis between associated companies and parent corporations. This may be a way of clearly demonstrating ownership rights, or of increasing the level of funds that can be repatriated from foreign markets (although foreign royalties often attract a certain level of tax remittance). Where a product formulation is being licensed a manufacturer may be able to protect his or her formula further by agreeing, as part of the licensing agreement, that a base mix of ingredients will be supplied to the licensee. In such a case the licensor may choose to recover his or her royalties in the form of a mark-up on the price of the base mix, which will generally be used as a fixed proportion of the final product.

The licensor will need to establish that the product or process being licensed can or will comply with all applicable foreign market rules and regulations, such as those relating to labelling, packaging, health and safety, and ingredient usage or composition. All trademarks and patents should be clearly registered in the licensor's name, who can then grant the licences to associated companies or independent licensees.

Overseas licensing can pose many problems and the disadvantages are as detailed below.

(1) *Competition from the licensee* – when the licensing agreement finally expires, the licensor may find he or she has established a competitor in the former licensee.

(2) *Market exploitation* – the licensee – even if he or she reaches an agreed minimum turnover, may not fully exploit the market, leaving it open to the entry of competitors. He or she may inevitably lose control of the marketing operation.

(3) *Revenue* – licence fees are normally a small percentage of turnover and will often compare unfavourably with what might be obtained from the licensee's own manufacturing operation.

(4) *Product quality* – quality control of the product is difficult – and the product could be sold under the licensee's own brand name.

(5) *Government* – governments often impose conditions on remittances of royalties or on component supply.

(6) *Disagreements with licensee* – arguments will arise however carefully the licensing arrangement is drafted. A disaffected licensee can be a serious problem.

Larger companies might create a licensing team, incorporating marketing, legal, financial and technical personnel. Smaller companies with limited resources may only be able to develop through a single individual, but can take advantage of assistance from government departments concerned with promoting trade and investment and also use the services of outside specialist consultants in identifying and developing opportunities.

A licensing agreement is an important step for a company to take and one which should not be taken lightly. The first stage is to formulate a plan with an objective and adhere to it throughout. A competent legal adviser should be employed from the outset: he or she would have the help of the licensing adviser(s) who would be familiar with the legislation of both countries. Great care must be taken not to reveal any detailed information during the preliminary discussions. Details of the points to be covered are as follows.

(1) Legality in both countries.
(2) The parties and their responsibilities.
(3) To retain the products, trade marks, patents and know-how copyrights.
(4) Territories and exports to other countries.
(5) Finance: royalties, payments and methods of payment, currency.
(6) Transfer of information, methods, staff and training.
(7) Patents: usage, quality control, infringement, exclusion, patent laws.
(8) Cross licences and grant back.
(9) Audit and control.
(10) Performance based on minimum sales or royalties.
(11) Procedures for settling disputes such as an arbitration clause.
(12) Applicable laws by which an agreement will be enforced.
(13) Investment obligations to plant and machinery.
(14) Restriction clause limiting licensee to compete with similar products or markets.
(15) Secrecy clause.
(16) Product development.
(17) Product pricing and supply.
(18) Insurance cover.
(19) Training.
(20) Sub-licensing.
(21) Assignment clause.
(22) Duration of licence and provision for termination.

The selection of a licensee requires careful evaluation and the following points are relevant.

(1) With a specific process for treating a raw material ingredient or waste product, identify producers or users of the ingredient or raw material or generators of the waste item.
(2) If a raw material involved is only produced or sold through certain private or government agencies, then enter discussions with those agencies to establish which of their customers might have applications.
(3) For mass markets, seek to identify which companies presently produce similar products, or who distributes them to the end user.
(4) If production requires certain ingredients, seek out producers of those ingredients to establish if they have an interest in expanding to supply end-users of the ingredient or raw material.
(5) If a product is in a very specific market category, such as an automobile component, consider approaches to the producers of such items who might benefit from a product range extension.
(6) If the product must be a component or an integral part of another product, consider who might derive a technical or earnings benefit by incorporating your product.

The criteria for appointing the licensee should have regard to the following.

(1) Membership of a Trading Association.
(2) Qualifications, calibre and experience of Directors and Senior Managers.
(3) Last three years' annual published accounts.
(4) Experience of the type of business in which you are interested.
(5) Current product range and product volumes.
(6) Outcome and conclusions of any market research exercise undertaken to find suitable licensee.
(7) Production and distribution facilities.
(8) Market share and marketing capabilities.
(9) Any association with a legal dispute or fraud.
(10) Date the company was formed and experience and contacts in the market.
(11) Degree to which licensee projects a modern outlook and encourages staff training and adoption of modern techniques e.g. computers, e-mail.
(12) Legal constraints in licensee appointment – local conditions.
(13) Relationships with other organizations.
(14) General competitiveness.
(15) Any major shareholdings.
(16) Political stability of the licensee country.

To conclude, we can say that licensing, too, is a growth market.

17.4.10 Management contracts

Management contracts is another growth sector of the export business, primarily focusing on the service sector. It broadly involves the provision of management teams to operate a project following its completion. This may be a hospital, power station, railway electrification or signalling system, mass transit system or hydro scheme. An example can be seen in the company Alstom, who supply power turbines to China under a turn key contract and on completion provide management teams to run the plant and maintain it. These are high tech projects and the management contract provides for training and operation. Ultimately, the management of the plant is handed over to the Chinese.

17.4.11 Piggybacking

Piggybacking arises when two products are promoted one on the back of another, such as greenhouses and garden furniture. This involves two manufacturers: the first manufacturer (greenhouses) carries and promotes the products of the second manufacturer (garden furniture).

The first manufacturer, termed the carrier, is experienced in the market place and has a customer portfolio base. He or she earns commission by acting as an agent or distributor selling garden furniture. Accordingly the carrier adds value to his or her product range and thereby enhances market penetration and sales revenue by jointly offering greenhouses and garden furniture.

17.4.12 The strategic alliance

The strategic alliance – or, as it is called in the maritime industry, the operational alliance – is another growth area in the export market. The impetus to form a strategic alliance comes primarily from marketing, and from the financial, R&D and efficiency considerations of operating in a competitive global market. It involves two like-minded, similarly focused companies forming an alliance which results in the concentration and centralization of the companies' facilities.

An example is the Neptune Orient Line (NOL) and American President Lines (APL) whose global container alliance, formed in 1996, yielded annual savings of £80 million. This was realized by utilizing common resources such as berths, shipping agents, a computerized network, marketing resources and ship management. The alliance produced a unified fleet and exploited the economies of scale of its global container operation.

The automobile and pharmaceutical industries are globally very competitive. High costs are incurred in the research and development involved in new car models and new drugs. These can be only financed through the large market base and centralized R&D facilities as found in a strategic alliance.

Other examples of strategic alliances embrace cross licensing, the development of the manufacturer–supplier relationship, technology transfer swaps and sharing marketing and distribution arrangements.

17.4.13 Trading companies

Trading companies are long established and are widely used in the market place. They involve numerous contacts with overseas buyers seeking a range of products. The trading company is used especially by SMEs who are seeking markets for their goods. It is a low cost method of entering an overseas market and is unlikely to involve any direct contact between the exporter and buyer as the trading company undertakes all the negotiation and distribution arrangements. Trading companies are also involved in counter trade.

17.4.14 Trade barriers

Trade barriers generate a serious impediment to the free flow of trade between nations. There are two forms of trade barrier: tariff and non-tariff barriers. There are a number of reasons why trade barriers may be put in place.

(1) To protect a domestic industry or range of industries from imported goods.
(2) To restrict or control the level of imports, thereby managing the trade balance on a bilateral or multilateral country basis.
(3) To sustain a nation's currency exchange rate and to protect it from trade market speculators.
(4) To ensure imported goods are not priced more competitively than domestic manufacture.

(5) To preserve employment levels by restricting imported goods and so protecting home industries.

(6) To raise government revenue through import tariffs and higher taxation on overseas companies resident in the country.

(7) To maintain product standards and specifications or to develop more onerous measures for imported than for domestically produced goods.

(8) To provide an administrative customs entry examination system which is inadequate in terms of resources to cope with the import volume, thereby generating delays and complexity by having all the documentation in the domestic market language.

We now briefly consider examples of tariff barriers.

(1) *Import tariff.* An import duty raised on a range of goods. It may be 30 per cent and is often adopted by less developed nations to raise government revenue. It is relatively easy to administer and in some countries the import tariff is raised to protect the indigenous manufacturer in areas of agricultural, automobiles and/ or a range of consumer goods.

(2) *Ad valorem.* This is based on a percentage of the declared value of the goods.

(3) *Temporary import levies.* These are duties raised on a short-term basis to counter an economic crisis in a country. They may be imposed in the aftermath of a devaluation.

(4) *Anti-dumping tariff.* A tariff introduced to counter the dumping of specific goods. The effect of the tariff is to bring the goods imported into line with the indigenous manufactured products.

(5) *Specific duty.* This applies to a limited range of products selected for economic or political reasons.

(6) *Preferential duty.* This is an agreement, on a bilateral or multilateral basis, permitting imported goods to enter the market at a preferential import duty rate. It may be duty free and is practised by the European Union (see p. 199).

(7) *Countervailing duty.* Such duties are imposed on imports to counter the effects of export subsidies used by an exporting country.

(8) *Discriminatory duties.* This tariff is raised on goods originating from a specific country and is imposed to counter a trade imbalance or for political reasons.

(9) *Compensatory levy.* This links the goods the country wishes to import to the types of goods it wishes to export, thereby endeavouring to strike a balance between the level of imports and exports. Accordingly, a payment may be undertaken on exportation to qualify for a concessionary import duty in the destination country.

The range of non-tariff barriers are likewise extensive.

(1) *Import licence.* This controls and restricts the quantity and value of specific imported products.

(2) *Quota system of both imports and exports.* This again regulates the quantity and/or value of goods imported and/or exported. An example arises on a ceiling of 100 000 cars permitted to be imported to the UK from Japan.

(3) *Financial controls*. This includes exchange controls: prior import deposits based on import value; credit restrictions; repatriation of profits from foreign companies; multi-exchange rates involving discriminatory exchange rate policies favouring the indigenous manufacturer.

(4) *Restrictive customs procedures* resulting in onerous and lengthy import procedures. This includes product valuation, inspection, documentation, health and safety regulations, permits, licences, etc.

(5) *Discriminatory* government and private procurement strategies usually favouring the local national source of supply.

(6) *Restrictive* administrative and technical regulations which prolong the importing process.

(7) *Product requirements* featuring standards, packaging, labelling, marking, product testing, product specifications, etc.

(8) *Government participation*. This embraces subsidies, administrative instructions and government procurement and state trading favouring indigenous resources.

Finally, one of the largest impediments to trade can be the culture of the people, nation and government. A number of nations have a nationalistic culture strongly favouring their own products and services. Other nations particularly the USA and UK have a strong open market culture exhibited in the way the populace buys quality high tech products at competitive prices without recourse to the place of manufacture.

17.5 Visiting the overseas market

A critical aspect of conducting overseas business is the continuous need to visit that overseas market to keep in touch with existing clients and identify or develop new ones. Importantly, such visits display a company's total commitment to the market and the customer base, but they also provide an opportunity to keep in touch with market potential and risk, while evaluating the legal, political and competitive environment. In short visiting the overseas market is a form of market research and intelligence gathering. The rationale for the overseas visit may arise due to any of the following reasons.

(1) To see existing clients and identify or develop new ones.
(2) To attend or participate in a trade exhibition.
(3) To appoint an agent or distributor.
(4) To attend or run a sales conference or seminar.
(5) To evaluate market opportunities prior to entering a market.
(6) To negotiate a contract.
(7) To formulate or develop a licence agreement or joint venture.
(8) To visit the market prior to making a tender for the contract.
(9) To conduct a training session and/or briefing meeting with agents, distributors, importers or franchisers prior to the launch of a new product.
(10) To discuss export potential with representatives of governments or other agencies.

The key to any overseas visit is pre-planning and adequate research of the market, its culture and protocol. Ideally, personnel visiting the market for the first time should have a culture briefing. Additionally, the personnel should have a good appraisal of the market and the competitors together with the areas of opportunities and risk. Furthermore, the Executive must be multi-lingual and competent in the language of the buyer or clientele. Personnel able to converse freely in the buyer's language are in a strong position for conducting business. Speaking the local language presents a favourable image in negotiations as it displays a commitment to the country visited and smooths the way in opening business opportunities. It develops the culture and business synergy essential in competitive global business.

The following points are relevant to the planning of an overseas visit.

(1) Formulate an itinerary and involve the agents, distributors and clients in the schedule. Take advice on the timescale of the visit and allow time for flight delays and prolonged negotiations. Focus particularly on entertainment.

(2) Conduct in-house meetings prior to and following the overseas trip. Identify the objective of the visit and obtain data on customer portfolios, recent orders received and executed, problem areas, summaries of any previous visits, and details of company structure and senior management. It is very important that appointments are made with the decision makers in the company and not the influencers.

(3) At an early stage, book flights and other travel arrangements with some degree of flexibility. Also, check the passport, visa and medical requirements.

(4) Any samples, videos, brochures in the language of the buyer, training manuals, etc. should be up-to-date and should present the company in a favourable image. Check whether an ATA Carnet may be required (see p. 198).

(5) Ensure that details of next of kin and the itinerary plan are deposited with key personnel in the company.

(6) Hotels should be four or five star with adequate secretarial and conference facilities. Many exporters have contractual arrangements with International Hotel chains thereby obtaining discount rates and priority reservations.

(7) It is common practice to take a gift as a token of goodwill. Advice should be sought if in doubt what to take.

(8) Entertainment is a critical part of an overseas visit. Again advice should be sought. Local restaurants may be favoured in preference to the resident hotel.

(9) The dress code should be appropriate for both business engagements and entertainment and leisure. Leisure engagements should be free of any business dialogue.

(10) Business cards, which should be double sided reflecting both the exporter's and importer's language, should be presented.

(11) The travelling executive must be fully briefed on the visit. In particular, he or she should have details of product specifications, competitive advantages, the benefits of the product to the importer, value added concept, price details, terms of delivery and timescale, non-price areas warranty training, spares, manuals, etc.

(12) The executive must be in continuous contact with his or her parent office to resolve any local problems. Ideally, after each company or client visit, a report should be produced and any problem areas resolved, preferably before the executive returns home. The key to the success of any overseas visit is adaptability and endeavouring to meet the needs and specifications of the buyer. A spirit of empathy between the seller and buyer should be developed at all times.

(13) A provisional negotiating plan should be devised prior to each client visit.

(14) Market research, as indicated earlier, is a key aspect of a successful overseas trip. In particular, research the competition and the pros and cons of the exporter's product in relation to other products on the market. In addition, identify the product areas which most interest the buyer and how they can be improved on. Bear in mind the environment in which the product will be used or consumed.

(15) A company culture which embraces logistics and computer technology is vital to any negotiations.

(16) The executive must be fully aware of any local technical, health and safety, packaging or consumer liability legislation. Also, he or she should be conversant with the relevant export contract terms embracing Incoterms 2000, UCP500, transportation, exchange control, import tariffs, documentation and so on. Particular attention must be given to funding the export contract and any financial package with attendant currency risk.

The foregoing list must not be regarded as exhaustive as each visit will vary, but the key to a successful trip is adequate preparation before the visit and developing empathy with the client during the visit. On return to the parent company the executive must produce a report and circulate it to the relevant personnel and departments and conduct a debriefing meeting. An action plan should then be prepared – and controlled to ensure adequate execution.

17.6 Chartered shipbrokers

The basic function of the shipbroker is to bring together the two parties concerned: the shipowner and the cargo owner. In following negotiations between them, a charter party is ultimately concluded. The broker's income is derived from the commission payable by the shipowner on completion and fulfilment of the contract.

A further role of the shipbroker, other than fixing vessels, is acting as agent for the shipowner. As such, he or she is responsible for everything which may concern the vessel whilst she is in port. This includes customs formalities, matters concerning the crew, loading and discharging of vessels, bunkering and victualling, and so on. The duties of the shipbroker can be summarized as follows.

(1) As a chartering agent whereby he or she acts for the cargo merchant seeking a suitable vessel in which to carry the merchandise.

(2) As a sale and purchase broker acting on behalf of the buyer or seller of ships, and bringing the two parties together.

(3) As an owner's broker whereby he or she acts for the actual shipowner in finding cargo for the vessel.

(4) As a tanker broker dealing with oil tanker tonnage.

(5) As a coasting broker involving vessels operating around the British coast and/or in the short-sea trade, e.g. UK–Continent. Additionally, at the same time, he or she can act for the cargo merchant in this trade should circumstances so dictate. The deep-sea broker, however, will act for the shipowner or cargo merchant, but not both at the same time.

There is no doubt the shipbroker is a person of many parts. In reality, he or she fulfils an intermediary role.

17.7 Freight forwarder

Basically a freight forwarder is a person or company which is involved in the processing and/or movement of goods across international boundaries on behalf of another company or person. The freight forwarder provides services in two main fields: the movement of goods out of a country on behalf of exporters or shippers – in which case the forwarder would be termed an export freight agent; and bringing goods into the country on behalf of importers – in which case the forwarder is called an import freight agent, customs clearance agent or customs broker.

The freight forwarder has four prime activities:

(1) to provide a range of independent services such as packing, warehousing, port agency, customs clearance;

(2) to provide a range of advice on all the areas relative to the international consignment distribution as found in transport distribution analysis (pp. 279–89);

(3) to act as shipper agent processing transport and/or shipping space on behalf of his or her principal or shipper and executing his or her instructions;

(4) as a principal, usually as a multi-modal transport operator, conveying the goods from A to B, crossing international frontiers and usually involving several carriers, often as an NVOCC.

The freight forwarder provides some or all of the services considered below, depending on the trade in which the company operates and the resources available.

17.7.1 Export

(1) *Transport distribution analysis* – an examination of the options available to the shipper to distribute the goods (pp. 279–89).

(2) *Transportation arrangements* – a major function involving the booking and despatch of the goods between the consignor and consignee premises or other specified points.

(3) *Documentation* – provision of all the prescribed documentation for the goods having regard to all the statutory requirements and terms of the export sales contract.

(4) *Customs* – all the customs clearance arrangements including documentation and entry requirements at the time of exportation and importation.

(5) *Payment of freight and other charges* – payment of freight to the prescribed carrier including any handling charges raised by the airport, seaport or elsewhere during the transit.

(6) *Packing and warehousing* – packing of goods for transit and warehousing provision.

(7) *Cargo insurance* – insuring goods during transit.

(8) *Consolidation, groupage and special services* – many forwarders specialize in consolidation offering major benefits to the shipper (pp. 133–35).

17.7.2 Import

(1) *Notification of arrival* – the process of informing the importer of the date and location of the goods' arrival and the requisite documents required for customs clearance. It is likely the exporter and importer will have different agents and the two agents will liaise to ensure the smooth flow of the goods through customs, keeping their principals fully informed. Full use will be made of the EDI system.

(2) *Customs clearance* – presentation and clearance of the cargo through customs. This involves paying close attention to all the requisite documents. Many major seaports and airports now operate a computerized customs clearance system thereby speeding up the process and eliminating the risk of errors (pp. 190–2).

(3) *Payment of VAT duty freight and other charges* – the forwarder will co-ordinate and effect payment of all such payments on behalf of his principal at the time of importation. This avoids delay in the despatch of the goods to the importer.

(4) *Delivery to the importer* – the process of delivering the goods to the importer's premises following customs clearance.

(5) *Breaking bulk and distribution* – the agent may be an umbrella agent whereby he or she consolidates not only his or her own client's merchandise, but also those of other agents with whom he or she has a contractual arrangement. On arrival of the goods in the destination country, the cargo is handed over to the respective agents to process through customs and to distribute.

The freight forwarder will despatch cargo by air or surface transport modes. Air transportation will involve scheduled passenger aircraft; combi – the modern generation of jets permitting a flexible use of space combining freight and passengers according to market demands; chartered aircraft; and scheduled freighters. For surface distribution the forwarder will deal with containers, usually involving multi-modalism; international road transport and trucking, embracing the Ro-Ro ferry; international rail movement, involving the through train or wagon via the train ferry or the Channel Tunnel; and finally the specialized movement involving project forwarding, consolidators, bloodstock, 'out of gauge' loads, household effects, refrigerated goods or bulk liquids. An increasing number of freight forwarders provide services as an NVOCC or an NVOC (p. 94).

The freight forwarder is very closely involved in the customs clearance and processing arrangements, at the time of both exportation and importation. Today an increasing number of the major forwarders have the facility to undertake, on their own premises, the clearance of cargo at the time of exportation and/or importation. This speeds up the operation and avoids delays at sea- and airports. It is an important feature of multi-modalism. At the export stage, this process is known as Forwarders Local Export Control (FLEC), and at importation, Forwarders Local Import Control (FLIC). Under FLIC the examination of cargo takes place at the forwarder's premises, whilst the actual entry can be lodged at the seaport or other entry processing unit (EPU) convenient to the forwarder.

The British International Freight Association (BIFA) represents the freight forwarding industry and incorporates the Institute of Freight Forwarders. Both organizations are committed to developing the industry and the attainment of quality control through the application of the British Standards in Quality Systems, BS5750 (p. 420). BIFA has established a Quality Assurance Manual, and also lays down trading conditions, and companies engaged in the business of moving freight for a period of not less than three years can apply for Registered Trading Membership, provided they meet the criteria laid down by the Association. Affiliated Trading Membership is also available to other firms not directly involved in the freight moving industry yet having a working relationship with the forwarder.

Circumstances giving rise to the employment of a freight forwarder by an exporter or importer include:

(1) firms dealing in an unfamiliar overseas market;
(2) companies endeavouring to sell under DDP terms;
(3) complex shipping or customs arrangements;
(4) the workload of the exporter being subject to significant peaks and troughs;
(5) the exporter being a small firm which needs to concentrate on the core activity of marketing the product overseas;
(6) a freight forwarder can obtain more favourable freight rates especially for groupage shipments;
(7) a freight forwarder can access priority booking of cargo space on transport modes, and can provide specialist services or resources including groupage, antiques handling, perishable cargo, livestock, 'out of gauge' consignments, etc.

The exporter examining the merits of having an in-house shipping department in preference to employing a freight forwarder must consider the capital and revenue expenditure in office space and equipment; the volume of overseas business; the number of markets and their degree of similarity; the availability of suitably qualified staff; the pattern of the business and degree of seasonal variation; and the nature of the business including the degree of specialism. A detailed financial appraisal is required to make this decision.

Monitoring the performance of a freight forwarder enables the exporter to ensure the situation remains competitive. The exporter should monitor the budget against actual results in terms of price, transit time, etc.; seeking buyer and consignee opinion; undertaking test transits; and assessing the overall quality and reliability of the service and the competence and calibre of the management. Shippers, in their freight forwarder choice evaluation, should check out the viability of the forwarding company; any legal disputes; the trading conditions; the calibre of the management and their qualifications; experience of other customers; degree of technology utilized; quality of overall service; competitiveness of the tariffs; nature of the business and suitability of the equipment and resources; the company position in the market; the liability insurance maintained by the firm; and so on.

Project forwarding is a growth area of freight forwarding. It is often allied to 'turn key' projects. Project forwarding involves the despatch and conveyance arrangements which stem from a contract award. For example, a company in country A has a contract with a consortia in country B to build a factory which involves the importation of substantial quantities of merchandise, especially technical equipment. Thus a great deal of coordination, involving buyers and sellers in terms of despatch arrangements and the site construction programme, is required. These tasks can be undertaken by a forwarder who is contracted specifically for the freight movements associated with this project.

To conclude, shippers wishing to use a freight forwarder must consider in their selection and economic criteria the following:

(1) membership of BIFA is highly desirable as is a BS5750 registration;
(2) profile of the freight forwarder and nature of his or her business;
(3) value added benefit emerging from employing the freight forwarder operations;
(4) alternative cost of the shipper doing the work and the requisite organization structure;
(5) volume of business and any seasonal variation;
(6) terms of export sales contract.

An increasing number of shippers entrust part of their business to the freight forwarder, especially spasmodic shipments to new markets, whilst the core of the business is undertaken in-house through their own shipping department directly with a carrier. Smaller companies with limited experience and resources tend to use a freight forwarder. Finally, the role and image of the freight forwarder is changing. An increasing number operate as an NVOCC and thereby form part of the multi-modal network, especially through the European trucking system and global container network.

17.8 Management of quality: BS5750

As we progress through the millennium the dominance of 'Management of Quality' will become paramount and companies which do not have the appropriate achievement of registration, as found in BS5750, are unlikely to survive in a competitive environment. Moreover, such companies are unlikely to be successful in competitive tendering as a prerequisite will be that the successful tender has BS5750 registration.

Basically, BS5750 is a set of guidelines for the professional management of any commercial venture. It is particularly geared towards manufacturing industries; but it does encompass service industries including transport and freight forwarding; the BIFA fully endorses BS5750. Overall, BS5750 focuses attention on aspects of the organization, and its management systems and procedures, rather than the specific technicalities of the product or service. The strategy is simple: reliable and consistent assurance of quality emerging from a well-structured, professionally run company.

BS5750 is in three parts, and Part II is given below because of its relevance to the freight forwarding industry.

(1) Clear policies and strategies for quality with well-defined operational and service standards.

(2) Structured and effective management organization with specific allocation of responsibility for all aspects of quality management.

(3) A documented quality system and operational procedures.

(4) Specified methods of understanding and recording customers' service requirements and verification that the needs have been met.

(5) Timely and precise control of all documentation including procedures, standard forms, paperwork systems and software. This to include the relevant communication of all revisions and amendments.

(6) Knowledge of the quality abilities of suppliers and evidence that this is taken into account in purchasing decisions.

(7) Establishing routines for work planning and the execution of the basic administrative and legislative systems of the business.

(8) Management controls and performance measurement and corrective action.

(9) Clear plans and procedures for identification and rectification of mistakes, deficiencies and causes of customer complaints.

(10) A code of conduct to cover product handling, packaging, transportation and storage whenever these activities are performed within the company.

(11) Pre-planned and structured senior management reviews of the major aspects of the quality system supported by formal routine auditing of all operational practices and procedures.

(12) Appropriately experienced and trained personnel.

(13) Records to demonstrate consistent compliance with all the foregoing issues.

Organizations in the UK which conduct the assessment and registration include the British Standards Institution (BSI), Lloyd's Register Quality Assurance Ltd (LRQA) and Bureau Veritas Quality International (BVQI). Companies, on achievement of registration, will be subject to routine annual surveillance and periodic re-assessment to confirm the continued effective operation of the quality system. BS5750 also complies with International Standard ISO9000 and European Standard EN29000.

17.9 Institute of Export

The Institute of Export is a professional body founded in 1924 as the British Export Society and incorporated as the Institute of Export in 1935. The Institute's principal objective is to maintain a continuous supply of export executive staff to British industry and commerce by means of its educational activities.

Membership consists mainly of professional exporters employed in manufacturing companies, export merchant houses and other export organizations. It also extends to certain categories of brokers, civil servants, insurance officials, lawyers, shipowners, and other occupations concerned with export trade.

The objects of the Institute are detailed below:

(1) To promote industry and commerce and particularly international trade in goods and services of all kinds.
(2) To examine, research and analyse problems connected with industry and commerce, particularly international trade in goods and services of all kinds; to publish the results of such work together with recommendations and advice; and to make the same available to all persons, firms or companies whether or not members of the Institute.
(3) To further public education with regard to commerce and industry, and particularly the need for exports and the methods of realizing the same; and further, to educate those who are or may become involved or interested in international trade in all aspects of the same.

The Institute of Export assists both its individual and company members through the medium of its employment bureau, which is officially licensed. It aims to provide candidates for job specifications in the export field.

The Institute issues an educational handbook and interested readers are advised to obtain a copy. The Institute of Export address is found in Appendix A.

17.10 International credit clubs

A number of finance houses can arrange finance through associated companies in other countries, for imports and exports between their respective countries. Credit can be arranged for all classes of durable goods for periods normally of up to two years, but for longer in special cases. Credit can also be provided to enable foreign buyers to take into stock goods imported from the UK and to hold them pending their sale.

International credit clubs, which are reciprocal agreements between leading finance houses in Europe, have also been formed to help exporters of substantial items of capital equipment so that foreign customers can obtain instalment credit finance quickly and cheaply. Similar facilities also exist in both customer and industrial hire purchase. Most of these organizations offer a number of ancillary services such as market research, shipping and forwarding advice on all matters relating to export credit.

17.11 Local buying offices

Many marketing organizations in foreign countries buy so much from UK sources that they find it financially advantageous to maintain buying offices in the UK, particularly in London. In some instances, this office may be part of a chain of buying offices covering Europe. It is usual for the buying office to look after affreightment, insurance and finance.

The advantages of a UK manufacturer dealing with a local buying office is that he or she gets a prompt acceptance of orders; saves time and costs in visiting the markets; avoids outlay on publicity; and avoids excessive correspondence with foreign markets. Against all this must be reconciled the fact that buyers 'shop around' so keenly that their prices are highly competitive, leaving little or no margin of profit for the manufacturer, whilst there is seldom much prospect of repeat orders. The Export Buying Offices Association address is found in Appendix A.

17.12 Case study on developing customer relations

It is appropriate that we conclude this chapter with a case study courtesy of Alstom, the leading Anglo-French global manufacturer in engineering, on how the manufacturer is adapting to the changing needs of their customers in a global environment. This case study emphasizes the reduced product lifecycle cost, improved efficiency and greater equipment availability. Above all, it extols professionalism in the conduct and development of international trade together with the need to adapt to customer needs in the spirit of empathism.

With the growing level of privatization in power and rail utilities and the increasing level of private investment in infrastructure projects, the role of the manufacturer is changing. In addition to supplying equipment, the manufacturer must also be able to provide sophisticated services that enable customers to concentrate on their core activities. There has been an enormous change in the customer–supplier relationship. The traditional concept of carrying out corrective maintenance and unscheduled repairs has been expanded to include preventive inspections, maintenance partnerships, plant upgrading, training and joint product development.

The scale of the change is demonstrated by the fact that customer services accounted for more than 20 per cent of Alstom's turnover in 1996 and this is set to increase in the years to come. That 'entrepreneurial' customers are drawing on the full range of the Company's abilities is proving to be mutually beneficial to all concerned. By making available advances in technology and experience of the operation of similar equipment worldwide, Alstom is able to reduce the customer's operating costs.

17.12.1 Improving performance

Work carried out for Tractebel, in Belgium, at the Tihange and Doel nuclear power stations, which entered service in 1975 and 1982 respectively, was undertaken to improve the plant's competitiveness. The project involved replacing the turbine rotors with rotors built using the latest technology – not only are they more efficient but the modern rotors require maintenance at less frequent intervals. The work was carried out in just 33 days. The success of the project led to similar retrofit orders in the USA and France.

In the rail transport sector, Alstom refurbished 350 passenger cars operated by the Kowloon Canton Railway Corporation. The work included fitting extra doors to enable passengers to enter and leave more quickly. As a result, the trains will need to spend less time in each station and the service will be able to carry more passengers.

In Canada, a number of freight locomotives have been refurbished to enable them to haul passenger trains. The locomotives are being extended and auxiliary electrical generators fitted.

Environmental issues are also driving the demand for plant upgrading. At EdF's 250 MW Blénod coal-fired power plant in France, work carried out by Alstom Stein Industrie on the boiler-firing system reduced NOx emissions and increased operating efficiency.

17.12.2 Sharing experience

That operators may benefit from the experience of others is the philosophy behind the setting up of user groups such as that in China for the operators of Alstom supplied power stations and those set up by European Gas Turbines (EGT) for gas turbine operators. EGT's customers are also able to participate in product development. User group member Alex Fraser, CHP engineer at Arjo Wiggins Buckland Paper Mill in the UK says: 'I am impressed with EGT's desire to involve customers. We would like to play whatever part we can to improve and sustain the service from EGT and get our machines running to the 99 per cent target envisaged. With this in mind, I would like to encourage the trialling of mutually beneficial ideas and modifications'.

Another initiative, ECCLIDE, was developed to improve the operation of hydrogenerators but is equally applicable to other types of electrical machines. By collecting and analysing operational data, advice is provided to operators on preventive maintenance, spare parts management and technical issues.

17.12.3 Reducing costs

In the North Sea, EGT has underwritten the operation of gas turbines on five of BP's production platforms. Their 'risk and reward' contract for the Andrew platform places a percentage of the contract value at risk against agreed performance targets. The reward element is a share in the platform's profits.

Cost reduction is also one of the aims of EGT's three-year maintenance contract for the four Frame 9FA gas turbines at PowerGen's Connah's Quay power plant in the UK, one of the world's largest combined-cycle power plants.

To meet the need for a local presence, EGT set up service centres in Singapore, Argentina, Australia and the UK. Together with the use of remote diagnostics systems, the centres are able to provide the level of service customers need. Condition monitoring through the use of datalinks and remote sensing equipment is becoming commonplace and helps to reduce the risks involved with plant operation by providing an early warning should things start to go wrong and the planning of a 'fast track' for service or repair work.

It is probably in rail transport that the outsourcing of maintenance is most commonplace. According to Michel Olivier, deputy managing director of Alstom Transport Division: 'The Division's success has been brought about by its ability to carry out work at a lower cost than train service operators.' When Alstom received the order from RENFE (Spanish National Railways) for the AVE high-speed train, a maintenance unit was set up in Madrid. Alstom is paid a royalty on the basis of the number of kilometres the trains cover in service. The royalty is subject to strict reliability and availability commitments which Alstom has always met. The Madrid unit uses a computer-based system to assess the status of any vehicle or component and to provide lifecycle cost evaluations. The data obtained also contributes to product development.

Since the Madrid unit was set up, its activities have been extended to suburban trainsets and rolling stock rehabilitation. According to Juan Gasol, head of the unit: 'It is essential to work with our customers, be close to them, possess a profound knowledge of their needs and even be capable of putting ourselves in their shoes. We use the same language and have the same objectives: availability, reliability and quality. We must anticipate our customers' needs as well as those of our customers' customers.'

The need to reduce lifecycle costs has led to the development of some novel types of contracts. In the UK, the outsourcing of maintenance has largely been brought about by the privatization of British Rail and the Government's Private Finance Initiative. The demand covers both routine maintenance and overhaul and refurbishment to bring rolling stock up to standard every 10–15 years. The contract to supply London Underground with 106 trainsets for the Northern Line includes a 20-year guarantee that trains will be available for service. Alstom is also responsible for much of the trackside equipment and has taken over the line's maintenance depots. The depots have since become the most efficient on the London Underground network and this has helped Alstom to win a maintenance contract for the Jubilee Line rolling stock. But it is not only for its own products that Alstom is able to provide such services. In 1994, for example, a 10-year maintenance contract was won in Mexico for 300 diesel locomotives and 24 electric locomotives built by other manufacturers.

17.12.4 Fast response

To offer an efficient service, a supplier must be close to the customer and be able to respond quickly. Alstom New Zealand maintains a major share of the high-voltage transmission grid operated by Trans Power New Zealand. Their three-year contract is designed to encourage innovation and continuous improvement and to minimize supply disruption. The grid comprises 13 000 km of HVAC and HVDC lines, 183 substations, two control centres and a telecommunications network.

Through more than 120 operating units in 40 countries, Alstom's T&D Division provides a local service based on products designed to local standards. Typical of these units is Jakarta-based PT Alstom T&D Indonesia, which specializes in the maintenance of high-voltage gas-insulated sub-stations. By keeping a safety stock of replacement parts, the Division is able to complete repairs in the shortest possible time. Customer visits play a key part in this service and provide a check on how equipment is being used, its condition and the maintenance already carried out. They enable customer satisfaction to be assessed and future maintenance needs to be defined.

The Division also offers comprehensive assistance contracts, such as that with SEP in the Netherlands covering a 400 kV sub-station. The contract not only guarantees the availability of replacement parts but, in the event of a serious fault, the despatch of a senior engineer.

Similarly, in the rail transport sector, through its GT Railway Maintenance subsidiary, Alstom maintains the signalling and electrification equipment in the Midlands, eastern England, mid-Wales and on the West Coast main line between London and Carlisle.

17.12.5 Long-standing relationship

The development of customer–supplier partnerships is not a new idea. The involvement of Alstom Engineering Systems (ESL) with the Joint European Torus (JET) project dates back to the 1970s. The project aims to prove the feasibility of nuclear fusion as a power source. Initially engaged to study and develop construction methods and procedures for the Torus and its ancillary systems, ESL now carries out routine maintenance and systems installation. The company has also provided services and equipment for most of the UK's nuclear power stations going back over the past 30 years. At Sizewell B, the UK's first PWR nuclear power station, ESL is carrying out maintenance work on the nuclear and turbine fluid systems equipment.

An illustration of the breadth of the Company's expertise is its contract with British Airport Authorities at Terminal 1 of London's busy Heathrow Airport. This covers the operation and maintenance of the airside baggage handling system and involves being on call round the clock, allocating and re-allocating flight make-up chutes, identifying baggage, monitoring the system and liaising with airlines, Heathrow's duty management and Customs and Excise.

17.12.6 Meeting objectives

The commissioning of equipment in very short timescales, either to enable production to start ahead of schedule or for emergency needs, is another aspect of customer service. Installation of three Tornado gas turbines on BP's Andrew platform in the North Sea helped production to start six months ahead of schedule and below budget. 'The way in which EGT met the challenge to provide products at minimum cost, without compromising safety or quality, in a spirit of trust and co-operation, has been quite remarkable,' says John Martin, BP's project manager. 'Andrew stands as a tribute to what can be achieved by the sheer enthusiasm and commitment of the whole team.'

In Chile, the speedy installation of four 150 MW Frame 6B gas turbines within three months of the letter of intent enabled the customer to meet 'emergency' power requirements. There are many other similar examples worldwide.

17.12.7 Training needs

Training is also an essential part of customer service. The philosophy is that well-trained engineers are able to respond to faults much faster and much better. At the T&D Division's Villeurbanne training centre in France, for example, over 70 different courses provide customers with the technological expertise needed to design sub-stations, install, operate and maintain equipment and to diagnose faults. The courses ensure that the latest technical and operational experience is readily available. More and more trainees are using the centre each year, demonstrating the confidence placed in Alstom by some of the world's largest utilities.

The evidence is clear, Alstom is no longer just an equipment supplier; it is a company dedicated to serving the customer, providing services across the full range of its activities. In the words of Juan Gasol of the Company's Transport Division: 'without our spirit of collaboration, we would be unable to achieve the success we are currently reaping.'

■ □ ■ ■ 18

The Single Market entity and European Economic Area

18.1 Physical distribution, considerations and strategy

The objective of creating a single 'common' market in the European Community dates back to the European Economic Community (EEC) Treaty (the Treaty of Rome) which established the Community in 1957. In 1985, European Community (EC) Heads of Government committed themselves to completing the Single Market progressively by 31 December 1992. It incorporates the Netherlands, Belgium, Luxembourg, the Federal Republic of Germany, France, Italy, Denmark, the Irish Republic, the UK, Greece, Spain and Portugal. In total, the 12 states have a population of 360 million people.

The Single European Act came into operation on 1 July 1987 and committed the EC to the aim of progressively establishing a Single Market over a period expiring on 31 December 1992. It defines the Single Market as 'an area' without internal frontiers in which the free movement of goods, persons, services and capital is ensured in accordance with this 'Treaty'. Progress towards completing the Single Market has taken as its starting point the Commission's White Paper, submitted to EC Heads of Government at the Milan European Council in June 1985. This outlined the Commission's programme for action to remove the remaining obstacles and distortions in trade between member states by the end of 1992. The Single Market means a process of liberalization which allows market forces to work.

18.1.1 Organization of the European Community

There are four main Community institutions: the Commission, the Council, the Parliament and Court of Justice.

The Commission has its headquarters in Brussels and Luxembourg, and has the following functions:

(1) It proposes Community policy and legislation. It is then for the Council to discuss and, if appropriate, adopt or amend the proposals.
(2) It executes the decisions taken by the Council of Ministers, and supervises the day-to-day running of Community policies.

(3) It is the guardian of the Treaties, and can initiate action against any member states which do not comply with EC rules.

The Commission has 20 members chosen by agreement of the Community governments. Each Commissioner is in charge of an area of Community policy, which embrace: external relations; internal market and industrial affairs; competition; agriculture; transport; science; research and development; financial institutions and company law; energy; and customs union and indirect taxation. Each Commissioner formulates proposals within his or her area of responsibility, aimed at implementing the Treaties.

The Council is the Community's decision-making body. It agrees and adopts legislation on the basis of proposals from the Commission, and has its headquarters in Brussels. The term Council not only embraces Ministerial Meetings (the Council of Ministers), but also working groups (Council Working Groups) of officials from the member states and the Committee of Permanent Representatives of the Member States in Brussels.

The European Parliament is a directly elected body of 518 members. Under the EC Treaties, its formal opinion is required on many proposals before they can be adopted by the Council. Members are elected for a period of five years. The secretariat of the Parliament is in Luxembourg.

The European Court of Justice rules on the interpretation and application of Community laws. It has 13 judges and judgments of the Court are binding on each member country.

18.1.2 Single Market constituents

The creation of the Single Market involved radical changes in nine areas summarized below:

(1) European standards involving the development of the 'Euro-brand' product acceptable in all 12 states (currently, in 2000, there are 15 states).
(2) Liberalization of public purchasing, with contracts being awarded on merit and not on nationalistic prejudice.
(3) Liberalization of open markets in information technology and telecommunications.
(4) Liberalization of financial services embracing insurance, banking and investment, securities, etc., thereby permitting freedom of capital transfer through the Community.
(5) Liberalization of transport services, involving deregulation of shipping, air transport and road haulage.
(6) Acceptance of professional qualifications gained in one state and recognized in the remaining states, thereby permitting freedom of labour mobility amongst the professions.
(7) Abolition of state subsidies, unfair competition and restrictive agreements and abuses amongst companies within the market.

(8) Adoption of one trade patent throughout the Community, and one patent law, instead of ten pieces of legislation as previously, leading to greater access to intellectual property.

(9) Elimination of physical barriers to trade, thereby permitting freedom of movement of goods and people across frontier points for inter-Community transits.

A commentary on each of the areas now follows.

18.1.3 European standards

The provision of a Euro-brand product specification acceptable in all twelve states (currently, in 2000, there are 15 States).

Previously member states had their own standards and laws which are important in setting quality and safety requirements for goods sold in their national home market. The standards were drawn up by national standards bodies such as the BSI. National standards have been a serious barrier to trade when different standards apply in member states, or a bigger obstacle when member states do not recognize each other's arrangements for testing and certifying products to ensure that they meet national or European standards. These 'technical' barriers fragmented the market, and they add to costs by forcing producers to modify their products, or by subjecting them to different national testing and certification procedures if they wish to sell them in other member states.

The Single Market entity permits any product which can be sold in the member state in which it is produced to be freely marketable in all other parts of the EC, unimpeded by different national standards and testing and certification practices. It incorporates the following guidelines relative to individual products:

(1) Adopt a unified level of quality and safety which products must meet within the EC.
(2) Adopt common standards and specifications.
(3) Accept other member states' tests and certificates relative to products manufactured within the EC.

The Euro-brand product particularly affects the following range:

(1) Machinery, personal protective equipment, construction products and toys.
(2) High technology products.
(3) Medicinal products.
(4) Food, covering labelling, additives, foods for special dietary uses and materials, and articles in contact with food.

The implication of the Euro-brand product can be summarized as follows:

(1) It enables the manufacturer to produce a product in one state and sell it throughout the remaining states without any mandatory modification. It is likely that some products will be modified to meet consumer needs or to reflect cultural tastes and territorial or climatic needs.

(2) The opportunity to manufacture a product of one specification for a market of 370 million people enables the entrepreneur to exploit the economies of scale in production, distribution and servicing the market.

(3) Economies of scale realized through high production and sales volume lowers unit costs, which allows flexibility in pricing strategy to aid market penetration. Companies which fail to extend their product sales to other states are likely to be less competitive in their home market than imported goods from other states at lower prices.

(4) It facilitates efficiency in loadability through improved stowage conveying standardized Euro-brand products.

18.1.4 Public purchasing

The second area is the liberalization of public purchasing by governments and other public bodies.

In 1992 purchases by governments and other public bodies accounted for some 15 per cent of the Community's gross domestic product. The single market has resulted in public bodies buying on the basis of fair competition, not national identity, and will have particular regard to the following:

(1) Procedures are now more open: for example, through clear requirements to give information on future contracts, to stop using specifications which keep out foreign suppliers and to publish details of contracts awarded.

(2) Enforcement of procedures have been strengthened so that complaints about discrimination can be pursued effectively and action taken against those who violate the rules.

Exporters, both large and small, have good opportunities to enter such markets. It is likely that the competition will be keen but the market profile benefit will be high. Moreover, the financial risks are low and successful tenders or executed contracts can lead to offers of contracts in other states and markets outside the EC. A close monitoring service should be devised to ensure the potential exporter is able to tender. Details of such contracts are available in the trade journals and international press. Further details are available from the trade associations, Chambers of Commerce and Department of Trade and Industry, British Overseas Trade Board.

18.1.5 Open markets in information technology telecommunications

The next area is the liberalization of the information technology and telecommunication markets.

The markets for many information technology products and services are global. The absence of a European Single Market has resulted in manufacturers having a small home base in a fragmented European market. Achieving a single competitive information and technology market in the EC gives users a wider choice, and manufacturers a large home base from which to tackle world markets.

Hitherto, each major information technology manufacturer makes equipment which operates in a particular way. No two systems are alike. The result is that users are locked into the system of a particular manufacturer from whom they must buy extra equipment to ensure that it is compatible with existing equipment and software. Moreover, in the past, member states have tended to favour a particular national information technology supplier. This has perpetuated a multiplicity of standards in the public sector so that, in practice, most national public sector markets are far from open. Additionally, users need to know that the equipment which they are buying conforms to agreed standards. This requires recognized testing and certification procedures.

Likewise, information technology is of increasing importance in the modern economy, and the EC market for information services is one of the fastest-growing sectors. An example is the EDI system (p. 373) and its application in International Physical Distribution systems. Crucial to this is the technology which allows information to be stored in electronic form, enabling it to be accessed easily and speedily, and the existence of a modern telecommunications network which allows information to be transmitted swiftly and accurately, thus doing away with traditional paper-based systems. These new services will enable suppliers and customers to exchange orders and process documentation directly and automatically via their computers; it will allow businesses to provide new services direct to consumers through telephone links in areas such as information services, cargo reservations, cargo tracking and schedules.

The foregoing areas are subject to a liberalization of attitudes and criteria, with a view to creating a Single Market in services and equipment. It will strive to adopt common equipment standards developed in a competitive environment. Users of information technology need to choose the most efficient system. Systems must be able to work properly and be compatible with other equipment. These two targets will be met through the development of open systems and interconnection standards for computers and communication, and open purchasing with public sector purchases conforming to BSI standards.

The objectives of the Single Market entity are contained in the Commission Green Paper on telecommunications services and equipment, which includes: full liberalization of the market for terminal equipment; accelerated work on common standards; complete separation of PTT's regulatory and operational functions; full application of the competition provisions of the EC treaty to telecommunications; a greater emphasis on the development of Europe-wide services; and a liberalized environment for point-to-point satellite telecommunications. It will bring a new era through EDI for international distribution in the EC.

18.1.6 Financial services

The liberalization of financial services is an important area in the realization of a single market concept.

The creation of a Single Market, however, goes beyond rights or establishment and assumes the right to do business throughout the Community across national frontiers, without the necessity of physically locating in all member states. Developments in new technology and systems of electronic transfer has increased the opportunities of doing business in this way, and the concern is that national restrictions should not prevent companies from taking advantage of them. This involves the liberalization of capital movements and the creation of a European financial area as follows.

(1) The liberalization of all capital movements, subject to a safeguard clause permitting temporary controls to be reimposed in certain specified circumstances.
(2) A requirement that monetary authorities in member states be permitted to put certain controls into operation immediately, without enabling measures.
(3) The establishment of a single facility providing medium-term financial support for any member state's balance of payments.

In the area of securities, common requirements have been established for the authorization of collective investment schemes such as unit trusts. With regard to insurance, EC insurers are able to cover the risk of potential policyholders in any member state irrespective of where the insurer is established. It provides a more liberal regime for large commercial and industrial risk, including all marine, aviation and transport business.

To conclude, freedom to transfer capital throughout the Community is essential for a Single Market in financial services. The objective was to remove restrictions on the movement of capital. It will result in no restrictions on raising finance in other countries or on the cross-border transfer of funds.

18.1.7 Transport services

The deregulation of shipping, road and air transport has much potential to improve transport utilization and, in so doing, reduce cost to the user.

Hitherto some member states required hauliers to have permits which limited the total number of journeys they could operate in a year; moreover, the number of permits issued was limited. Such restrictions have been lifted, thereby permitting a freedom of movement amongst road hauliers on journeys within the 15 states and relaxation of cabotage involving the collection and deposit of goods within a state.

In the area of shipping, liberalization operates on competition and unfair pricing practices, phasing out unilateral cargo reservation and deregulates coastal services.

The completion of the Channel Tunnel provides opportunities, through quicker travel by rail, to open up extensive tourist and trade markets. Overland rail freight services will provide quick, cheap and reliable services between the UK and major industrial and commercial centres in Europe.

Civil aviation also benefits from liberalization, which in this instance embraces the following:

(1) The potential for a cheaper and less restrictive fares structure in off-peak periods.
(2) Potential of a more competitive economy and business fares which may run counter to other airlines on the route.
(3) Permission for airlines to offer increased route capacity to meet market needs.
(4) All major air routes have been opened up to direct competition between airlines.
(5) Traffic rights have been made available on as many as 60 new routes out of the UK.
(6) The opportunity to have a more economic operation by combining two or more routes into a single multi-stop service.
(7) To establish a mechanism for scrutinizing potentially inter-competitive inter-line agreements.

The liberalization of the EC transport system will facilitate a cheaper and more extensive transport infrastructure to meet consumer demand. This is essential to wealth creation. Exporters, as they develop their business throughout the EC, must review: their distribution systems; location of warehouse and distribution centres; the ideal location for manufacturing centres; and plan for the most effective distribution system compatible with market needs in a very competitive environment. It will encourage the Districentre concept (pp. 90–3) and permit a shorter and quicker supply chain concept, also involving just-in-time (JIT) working. Also the direct supplier/buyer relationship development eliminates the intermediaries.

18.1.8 The professions

The freedom of establishment for the professions is established in the EEC Treaty. It recognizes the freedom of movement for people to work throughout the EC.

The adoption is intended of a system of mutual recognition of 'higher education diplomas' – i.e. professional qualifications so that everyone is able to practise their profession throughout the Community.

The outcome of such recognition of professional qualification throughout the EC will stimulate labour mobility, especially amongst people in the 20–35 age bracket and with good linguistic ability. Moreover, it will facilitate the development of multinational workforces throughout the community in all the professions.

18.1.9 Competition and state subsidies

The abolition of state subsidies, unfair competition and restrictive practices and abuses.

The EC competition policy has been designed to ensure that trade between member states takes place on the basis of free and fair competition. It is one of the basic principles in the EC Treaty that the EC provides a system ensuring that competition in the common market is not distorted. Powers and procedures enabling the Commission to enforce these rules in all areas except transport were laid down in 1962. These were extended to cover inland transport in 1968, to maritime transport in 1986, and to intra-EC air services in 1987.

18.1.10 Intellectual property

The laws governing intellectual property (patents, industrial designs, trademarks and copyright) are in one sense a derogation from the operation of the free market, intended to stimulate innovation. Firms can recoup their investment in technical or design improvements by having the right, for a limited time, to prevent imitation by others who have made no such investment. Firms can also protect the reputation and goodwill which they have built up by registering their trade or service marks, so obtaining the right to prevent others from using them.

While the EEC Treaty prohibits restrictions on imports and exports between member states, restrictions are allowable where they are justified 'for the protection of industrial or commercial property'. For example, the proprietor of a UK patent can use the rights which it gives him to prevent goods produced elsewhere in the EC from being imported or sold in the UK.

None of this, however, allows the owners of intellectual property rights to use them to divide up the market. Once the goods have been put on the market in the EC by the owner, or with his consent, he cannot prevent them from being reimported or resold. In other words, intellectual property rights cannot be used to reinforce a policy of differential pricing within the EC.

18.1.11 Physical barriers to trade

Physical barriers to trade involve the imposition of cross-frontier controls relative to persons and goods undertaken by immigration and customs.

Many steps have been taken to make trade easier across EC frontiers. The elimination of customs duties between member states has been one of the foundations of the Common Market. Less obvious, but nevertheless important, has been the continuing process of administrative harmonization and simplification which is bringing member states' arrangements gradually into line. SITPRO have played a major role in this area.

Many of these steps are technical in nature and deal with matters of detail. Individually their effect can therefore be small, but over time their cumulative impact has been substantial.

An EC Customs Code is another important step in providing a comprehensive framework for EC customs law, and promoting procedural harmonization (p. 201). This area is fully dealt with in Chapter 9.

18.1.12 Conclusion

To conclude our review of the Single Market entity the exporter must consider the following aspects:

(1) Examine current physical distribution, channels of distribution and market strategy and develop policies which will increase volume sales and thereby lower unit costs, improve market dominance and aid profitability.

(2) Analyse closely the market throughout the member states, identify major competitors and endeavour to determine their overall strategy in the Single Market.

(3) Undertake a SWOT (strengths, weaknesses, opportunities and threats) analysis of the exporter's company (product(s), physical distribution and service(s)).

(4) Review the option of a merger and acquisition policy. Enter negotiations with a merchant bank who can give guidance in this area. Merger and acquisition will increase a company's size and market dominance, increase cash flow and competitiveness, lower unit cost, develop market penetration, enlarge customer portfolio, increase skills, develop volume-oriented physical distribution networks and so on. The option may exist to merge with, or acquire a company with, an identical product or service, or something complementary, and of the same market profile. This may be, for example, a greenhouse manufacturer merging with a garden furniture company, or developing a working collaborative relationship.

(5) Critically review personnel resources, logistics, EDI and their adequacy. This may involve retraining, recruitment, etc.

(6) Review the distribution arrangements. This should be geared to a five-year marketing plan.

(7) Critically review the product mix and its adequacy in the market. Ensure it features modern technology and adequately research the market to ensure the product is consumer-led.

(8) Formulate an action plan and identify one person at least in the company to coordinate and develop the Single Market strategy. Such a position should be at senior level.

Additional impacts of the 1992 Single Market entity include increased competition (with lower unit cost), higher standards, greater labour mobility, greater job opportunities, new markets through previously closed procurement areas, more technology and cheaper distribution.

The foregoing analysis of the EC embraces EC/EFTA countries – translated into the European Economic Area (EEA) – and therefore involves 19 countries and a combined population of 375 million – with enormous wealth, good buying power and a favourable infrastructure.

A key area for the future will be physical distribution and devising strategies to achieve improved cost-effectiveness per product/tonne distributed. It will also be important to improve the supply chain timescale and set up distribution centres in key industrial areas. The concepts of just-in-time (pp. 101–15), EDI technology (pp. 373–93), multi-modalism (pp. 94–9) and Districentres (pp. 90–3) will all play a very decisive part.

To the great majority of companies the change will be very radical and profound. Personnel entrusted to lead, develop and execute such changes must be of high calibre and professionally qualified with good linguistic skills and an understanding, and experience, of the differing cultures of each of the 19 countries. Infrastructure will play a major role in the development of the Single Market and the residue countries emerging from the EEA. It will require an ongoing analysis and good market research and control skills to ensure the distribution networks are further improved and developed.

To conclude, the combined EC/EFTA reflected in the EEA will present a new era of opportunity both for its member states and the global markets. It will provide new opportunities for the company and entrepreneur, both within the EEA and outside it, to develop their exporting skills and take advantage of the Single Market with enormous wealth and the Euro-brand single specification supported by a good infrastructure.

18.2 The route to Monetary Union – the euro

The signing of the Single European Act in 1986 heralded the establishment of an economic union within the European Union (EU) with no barriers to trade and payment, or to the movement of capital and labour. This Single Market programme became effective from 1 January 1993.

To be fully effective an economic union such as the Single Market requires a complementary monetary union – incorporating a centrally managed monetary policy and a single currency. The move towards full monetary union is one of the most complex and controversial developments in the short history of European integration. However, economic and monetary union (EMU) has been a recurring ambition of the EEC/EC/EU since the creation of the original EEC in 1957. This is because it is seen as promising currency stability – thus fostering economic prosperity – and making possible a deepening of the links between member states over a wide range of matters: the so-called convergence process. The switch to economic and monetary union means replacing the currencies of those states joining EMU with a single currency the 'euro'.

On 3 May 1998 the European Union agreed to the establishment of a European currency (the 'euro'), the formulation of the European Central Bank and European Monetary Union (EMU). In 1998 the European Union had fifteen member states and eleven of them opted to adopt the euro currency: Germany, France, Italy, Spain, Holland, Belgium, Austria, Finland, Portugal, Luxembourg and Ireland. The countries which did not at that time opt to join the euro currency were: Britain, Denmark, Sweden and Greece. Countries endeavouring to join the EU in 2000 included the Czech Republic, Hungary, Poland and Slovakia.

The euro became a floating currency in its own right against the world currencies as from 1 January 1999, but before that could happen, two technical steps needed to be taken:

(1)   the bilateral exchange rates between the currencies of EMU member countries needed to be announced.
(2)   the all-important exchange rates into the euro for each State currency needed to be fixed simultaneously. This was undertaken almost immediately prior to the euro launch on 1 January 1999. January 1999 to January 2002 has been

designated as a transitional period to allow businesses, local authorities and other organizations directly concerned to adapt to the use of the euro as a currency, and to allow time for the actual production of the huge volume of new notes and coins required.

The existing national currencies of member countries will continue to be used – and these national bank notes and coins will remain in use until 2002 for cash transactions – since no euro notes or coins will initially be in circulation. The actual wording of the relationship of each EMU national currency to the euro after 1 January 1999 is that it will form a 'non-decimal denomination of the euro'. This reflects the fact that it is unlikely conversion will lead to round numbers.

The European Central Bank (ECB) will be the focus 'for co-ordinating the monetary' policy of the European Monetary Union grouping of EU countries. However, it is important to emphasize that it does so with the collaboration of all countries within EMU – and by operating in conjunction with the central banks of each state. Nevertheless, it is the ECB which is in overall control of the final monetary policy of each country, because the ECB will set each country's individual interest rate. (This is foreseen as a particularly challenging task, since there is bound to be conflict between the wishes of different countries as to the best rate for their economies at any particular time.)

The key decision-making body will be the ECB's Governing Council – consisting of members of the ECB's Executive Board plus the central bank governors of each participating state. The ECB's smaller Executive Board (around six members) will be responsible for the day-to-day running of this new and influential organization and for implementing the decisions of the Governing Council.

Detailed below are some unresolved issues relating to the European Monetary Union.

18.2.1 Fiscal policy problems

Many critics argue that the Achilles heel of EMU is fiscal policy, and one major area of concern is whether larger internal transfers will be required to deal with the impact of country-specific shocks. The problem is that in a monetary union, key policy decisions are made at the centre, and these decisions have important implications for fiscal policy which will continue to be conducted at the national level. Inside the union, a country gives up the right to implement independent monetary and exchange rate policies. This severely impairs the ability of a country to respond to country-specific shocks, and attention therefore focuses on fiscal policy which, in the absence of constraints, could be applied more actively to stabilize the economy. However, increasing the national budget deficit has implications for monetary growth and interest rates within the union.

It was to avoid the possibility of expansionary fiscal policy by one or two profligate nations jeopardizing the monetary policy of the ECB that the Maastricht convergence criteria included fiscal limits. In particular, there are limits on the size of the budget deficit (3 per cent of GDP) and on the size of the national debt (60 per cent of GDP). The problem is that when one country is adversely affected by a shock, and is unable to unbalance its budget sufficiently to accommodate that shock, it is taxpayers in other countries who must subsidize recovery. The extent to which countries will be prepared to do this remains uncertain, though it seems likely that such cross-border subsidization will be fiercely resisted.

The problem has been made worse in recent years by sluggish growth in many European countries, coupled with high and rising unemployment and adverse demographic trends such as state pensions which will make increasing demands on the public purse for many years to come. Countries will therefore find it increasingly difficult to resist upward pressure on their debt and deficit ratios, which will considerably restrict their ability to implement contra-cyclical stabilization policies.

The European Commission is well aware of this problem, and in a report it published in 1993 entitled 'Stable Money – Sound Finances', the suggestion was made that a central European budget might include taxes, such as a carbon tax levied on countries in proportion to overspills across national borders, and expenditures aimed at promoting stabilization. However, for a variety of reasons individual national states have given no support to this idea. At present (2000) the issue is unresolved: EMU will limit the fiscal powers of individual nations without offering any compensating fiscal influence from the centre.

Many economists have become increasingly concerned that a single monetary policy might not work as smoothly in different countries as anticipated. The problem is the so-called transmission mechanisms of monetary policy, that is, the speed and route through which changes in monetary policy work their way through to the economy. The most widely used instrument of monetary policy in EU countries is variations in the rate of interest. It is well known that a rise in interest rates will ultimately slow the economy down, with the result that unemployment rises and economic growth falls. However, the speed with which interest rates take effect differs substantially between different countries. In this context the IMF has suggested that countries can be divided into two groups: a slow response group (Germany, the UK, the Netherlands, Austria, Belgium and Finland) and fast response group (Denmark, France, Italy, Portugal, Spain and Sweden). The argument is that in the first group output bottoms out in about 11–12 quarters after a tightening of monetary policy, whereas it takes only 5–6 quarters to bottom out in the second group. However, the economic impact is almost twice as strong in the first group as in the second. The implication is that in EMU a tightening of monetary policy would take more time to affect some countries – and would exert a stronger impact on some than it would on others.

There are other problems – and it is by no means clear that a rise in interest rates exerts its influence in all countries in the same way. The usual argument is that a rise in interest rates increases the cost of capital and discourages investment both inwards and domestic/state investment. However, a different transmission mechanism is through changes in asset prices, which alter after a change in interest rates, or through the credit channel, since bank lending is discouraged after a rise in interest rates. This is a serious problem and the European Commission has acknowledged that different transmission mechanisms might pose a threat to EMU. Different transmission mechanisms result from differences in the degree of competition between banks, the share of bank credit in total financing, the extent to which the banking system is internationalized, the extent of property ownership in the economy and so on.

18.2.2 What options for the ECB?

Given these differences between nation states the question naturally arises about how the ECB will conduct its monetary policy. In recent years different European countries have adopted different strategies towards the common goal of price stability over the medium term. Nevertheless these strategies fall broadly into one of three categories: focusing on the exchange rate as the anchor for monetary policy, pursuing a monetary target or pursuing an inflation target. The optimal target depends on the particular circumstances in each country; and it is not clear which target the ECB will adopt. Whichever approach is adopted, monetary policy strategy must satisfy the following criteria:

(1) The strategy must be geared to the ultimate objective of price stability, and must be determined in a way that allows price stability to be safeguarded given the different financial structures and transmission mechanisms that exist in different countries.

(2) The monetary policy strategy must be transparent and comprehensible to all economic agents. This suggests a rule-based approach rather than pragmatism, since pragmatism implies that policy would be liable to change in response to different indicators. This would make policy less clear and less comprehensible.

(3) The monetary policy strategy must have long-term viability so that changing economic circumstances do not call the strategy into question and weaken the credibility of policy statements by the ECB.

Basically, the exchange rate is not a suitable anchor for monetary policy in a European monetary union. So what of the alternatives? In Germany, which has a long and enviable history of controlling inflation, the Bundesbank has pursued a policy of broad money targeting since 1974. This is clearly the option the Bundesbank would prefer the ECB to adopt, and their argument is strengthened by the recent experience of France, Italy and Greece which have all adopted targets for broad money in recent years and have all succeeded in bringing inflation down – most notably in Greece where inflation has fallen from over 20 per cent in 1991 to 5 per cent in 1997. However, other countries, including the UK, have adopted an inflation target and have succeeded in controlling inflation. But for all these countries, with the exception of Germany, important questions remain and it is unclear to what extent inflation has fallen because of the adoption of targets by the authorities. The 1990s has been a favourable period for monetary policy generally and there has been a widespread reduction in inflation rates throughout Europe irrespective of the way in which monetary policy has been conducted. By contrast Germany's strategy has a proven track record over a long period of time and this is likely to be the approach adopted by the ECB. It seems equally likely that the ECB will supplement its monetary policy strategy with elements of inflation targeting such as a comprehensive inflation forecast to give information to individuals, companies and markets.

Many economists compare the economy structure of the USA with the European Union. They regard the EU as a highly regulated market particularly in the labour and social sectors and increasingly so in the monetary sector with the emergence of the euro and the ECB with a stringent convergence criteria and common interest rates. This generates inflexibility and rigid economic strategies thereby inhibiting member states, particularly in the Euro-zone, the opportunity to initiate economic measures to counter periods of depression or generate an economic climate of opportunity and growth as it is democratically centrally controlled. Conversely, in the USA it is largely a deregulated market of 51 states with its own labour laws and flexible business environment. The Federal Reserve Bank, however, controls the national interest rate. Many economists believe this liberalization generates growth and enables companies and entrepreneurs to be flexible and adapt to economic opportunities as has been demonstrated during the past eight years.

18.3 Strategic analysis of the Single Market

Today (2000) the Single Market has fifteen members and came into effect from 1 January 1993. The fifteen members have a total population of 370 million. Moreover, in the foreseeable future the membership could rise to nineteen with the Czech Republic, Hungary, Poland and Slovakia all applying to join.

The successful international entrepreneur today is very conscious of targeting and sourcing markets which are competitively focused with low risk, ease of access and which are logistically and computer literate. This is particularly relevant in fast moving consumer goods (fmcg) with a limited product lifecycle and high development cost, which must be recouped in high volume sales with realistic profit margins to meet the return on the investment.

The single market has a range of features in its trade structure: these include common core product specification and limited local customized needs in terms of packaging, size of product to meet social and technical requirements, advertising reflecting the local protocol and value added benefit of the product or service to the user and consumer and the environment in which the product or service will be used.

It will be recalled that to achieve the maximum benefits of the Single Market the goods must be manufactured and produced in the member states to enable the goods to be transported in free circulation without any customs import duty. However, many Multi-National Enterprises (MNEs) set up assembly or distribution centres in the EU and conduct their EU business from this focal point through online computer access. The goods may be raw materials or products in a partially or completely finished condition enabling the MNE or SME to add value to it, thereby customizing the product. This focal point is called a Free Trade Zone which is free of any custom duty until the goods leave the zone to the retailer or consumer.

Such an area is found in the Distriparks of Rotterdam (see pp. 90–3) whereby, for example, the warehouses accommodate various spices from countries in the Far East such as Thailand. The spice is received in bulk in containers and stored in the warehouses. Each warehouse has online computer access to major distributors and clients throughout the single market. Orders are received daily and executed in accordance with the clients needs, involving packaging and quantity and quality control in accordance with retailers' and consumers' language regulations, the relevant mix of the spices and all relevant documentation. Such Far East Trading Houses and Companies are able to import the goods in bulk and on payment of the import duty are permitted to distribute the goods in free circulation throughout the fifteen states of the EU, thereby exploiting economies of scale in the production and supply chain analysis.

Some companies have more than one free trade zone independently operated and strategically geographically located, for example one in the Iberian Peninsula, one in the Dunkerque/Lille region, another one in northern Italy and one in northern Germany serving the North East European and Scandinavian region. A similar strategy exists with component parts where strategically located assembly points are focused on local market needs. Overall, the strategy is logistically focused and companies formulate their plans based on market demand and conditions, cost, infrastructure resources and the company business plan. Indeed, as more and more companies develop joint ventures (see p. 406), operating alliances (see p. 412) or undertake mergers and acquisitions (see p. 402), the distribution logistics plan changes and responds to maximize profitability, increase market share, develop market penetration and generate higher profits to facilitate greater investment in research, new technology and company expansion.

We now offer a broad strategic analysis of exporting within the 15 member states of the European Union.

(1) It is the wealthiest single market in the world with 370 million people of high literacy standards with a good standard of living. Overall, it has a Westernised–Mediterranean–Scandinavian market profile with high expectation of long-term growth in a stable environment of low inflation.

(2) The market has strong buying power with a rising living standard. Overall, it is highly consumer focused with the populace of the 15 states primarily exercising a non-nationalistic prejudice in consumer choice, based on the value added concept and personal taste and preference. The younger age segment especially favours a wide product source range based on their particular needs.

(3) One patent office exists to serve the fifteen states. Hence, once a product is patented, goods can be sold throughout the market with no market entry impediment.

(4) Emerging from item (3), speed of entry into the market is vitally important to gaining maximum market share, volume sales, competitive advantage and profitability. This is particularly advantageous for products with a short product lifecycle which would not be as profitable in a market where entry can be delayed by bureaucratic complexities including patent registration and acceptance certificates to confirm compliance with health and safety requirements. Such time delays enable existing players in the market place to capitalize on the situation by generating further promotion and product awareness strategies.

(5) There exists ease of access to the market for companies producing and manufacturing within the market. Hence, products produced in France – cheese, wine, cars and perfume – have free access to all the other 14 states with no trade barriers or customs duties. Hence, a new perfume or brand of cheese can be retailed, on launch, in all the 15 states.

(7) A unified integrated transport system exists with no impediment to freedom of movement at frontier points. Moreover, carriers' documentation and liability are common throughout the market. An increasing number of rail freight services are now operating Trans European services on dedicated schedules. Professional standards are high and the major European seaports are advanced in computer technology, logistics and multi-modalism, offering competitive rates and transits to inland industrial and commercial centres and to industrial and free trade zones. An increasing number of MNEs and SMEs are operating the LEC and LIC systems (see p. 194) for goods originating from or destined for outside the EU territories.

(7) The EU is a very low risk market generally. Financial risks are minimal with many companies conducting business on the open account basis. The provision of the euro, which operates in some 11 states (see pp. 473–9), eliminates currency risk fluctuations throughout businesses trading in the Euro-zone and generates price stability. The euro is further evidence of an integrated financial European Union.

(8) The market encourages businesses to expand as competition drives down prices and, to reduce costs in all sectors of their business, companies adopt a policy of reviewing their position in the market place in sourcing, production, distribution and profitability, adopting strategies such as merger and acquisition to improve their financial performance and market position. This involves rationalizing production, outsourcing components and centralizing R&D and control and administration. Moreover, freedom of capital movement is permitted throughout the EU which encourages such strategies.

(9) The market is high tech in all areas including production and communication, embracing the latest computer technology, EDI – paperless trading (see pp. 373–93). This encourages supply chain management with hub centres performing the assembly and distribution, and spoke centres supplying the componetized units.

(10) The single market is well served with market research data which the discerning exporter may use to evolve strategies of market entry and development. Much of the data is on Internet and, in addition, the EU and major trading associations produce a wide range of market reports and analysis. Specialist agencies also exist in all the member states.

(11) Mobility of labour is a key factor of the EU where personnel are able to take up employment in any of the 15 states. However, tax systems and the social structure do vary by state and it is unlikely that these areas will be unified in the short term.

(12) The Single European Market is essentially an open market permitting freedom of access with no exchange controls. It is a member of the WTO (see pp. 22–8) and champions their ideology and strategies.

(13) Low inflation is one of the key factors aligned to the convergence of EU economies. Such economic stability encourages investment, particularly inwards investment which generates growth.

(14) A common product specification exists with unified standards especially in health and safety areas. Having one specification reduces overall design and production costs, thereby allowing lower prices to be charged and hence stimulating market growth. Goods can, nevertheless, be customized to respond to individual EU states' needs in language, packaging, size, local operating needs, colour and capacity.

(15) The market is easy to serve and visit with a common ideology of doing business in an environment of stability, high standards, growth and increasing use of technology.

Overall, the single market is one of opportunity and exporters must focus on it seriously if they are to develop their business. Companies must feature the EU in their business plans, which in turn must be integrated into an international marketing plan. Personnel must be encouraged to be 'Europe focused' in order to identify and develop opportunities within the Single Market. Adaptability, total commitment, complete professionalism and, above all, determination, operating within the buyer's culture are some of the essential ingredients required to succeed. Creative thinking, empathy and well thought out strategies and planning all contribute to becoming a successful European entrepreneur, but, above all, his or her approach must be market research driven. Full use should be made of E-commerce and the Internet.

Recommended reading

The European – EU paper, published quarterly.

19

International physical distribution strategy and management

19.1 Introduction

Exporting is all about professionalism, logistics and profit motivation and closely involves international distribution strategy and management. This embraces the decision-making process of evolving the most suitable and acceptable method of distributing goods to international markets. It is market driven as the international distribution network continues to expand and develop into a high tech operation involving multi-modalism. Moreover, distribution is a fast-moving area, subject to continuous change, and it is market led. Hence the shipper needs to monitor continuously such changes, and feature in them, to remain competitive.

Distribution is also an area which is attracting senior management's attention on an increasing scale as world markets become more competitive and increasing emphasis is being placed on the 'total product concept': the value added benefit the importer obtains from the purchase of the goods. This benefit embraces not only the product and the related benefits associated with trading with the supplier in terms of product specification and non-price areas – after-sales, brand image, position of the company in the market place – but also the method of distribution adopted to enable the goods to reach the buyer. Factors which feature prominently in the choices made include efficiency and quality of service, together with total cost. Close liaison must be maintained between the exporter and the importer to ensure the correct decision is taken. An increasing number of carriers and distributors are obtaining BS5750 or ISO9000 quality standard registration to enhance their market profile (p. 417).

Today the exporter must be computer and logistically focused. Full use must be made of Electronic Data Interchange (EDI) resources and all the ingredients of the logistic elements including supply chain management, computerized warehouse operation and management, customer asset management, barcode systems for inventory control and just-in-time technology. Planning, tracking and adequate control systems with the ability to be flexible to meet changing market needs are essential in the logistic environment.

To devise the correct strategy the company must examine a number of factors which are detailed below.

(1) *Company objectives.* These will be found in the company's business plan spanning three to five years. The business plan will be reviewed regularly in the light of changing market conditions. Moreover, it will be market driven and feature company resource use and profitability annually. International distribution will feature in channels of distribution which will vary by overseas territory and product.

(2) *Company resources.* Large companies have substantial cash flow and human resources to develop specialism within the company, including the area of logistics (pp. 101–15). Moreover, the high volume of overseas business enables economies of scale to be achieved through lower unit cost. For example, discounted freight rates can be negotiated with carriers on volume-guaranteed contracts. Furthermore, larger companies tend to rely less on intermediaries in the management and execution of the distribution network, thereby realizing significant cost savings and exercising closer and more direct control over the total logistics operation. Also large companies tend to have experienced and high-calibre personnel, although the decision-making process can be slower compared with the smaller company.

In contrast, the smaller company has limited financial, production and personnel resources. Such companies do not have the high market profile of the larger company and financial resources to accept prolonged payment terms. Many rely on consolidated distribution networks, with its lower unit cost, rather than on full-load volume movements.

The extent to which both large and small companies have specialist personnel engaged in shipping and warehouse distribution activities depends on the markets, products, international distribution networks they serve, complexity of the operation and the volume of business involved. Companies which have dedicated personnel engaged in the distribution process have complete control over cost and complete performance monitoring of the services they use. Moreover, such companies can obtain competitive rates through volume and loyalty contracts and in so doing can introduce a mark-up on their quotation when trading in CFR, CIF, CPT and CIP terms. This mark-up contributes to the distribution management team cost.

(3) *The company's position in the market place.* The higher the company's profile, the more likely is the company to be a market leader and to play a dominant role in the distribution arrangements.

(4) *Legal and political constraints.* A number of governments insist that imported goods are conveyed on their national airlines or shipping services and buy FCA or EXW.

(5) *The sales forecast and market stability.* Companies may be reluctant to set up an extensive shipping and logistics department to cater for irregular shipments to an unstable market.

(6) *Level and nature of competition.* As overseas markets develop, the volume of trade and range of commodities and products sold increases. This stimulates the expansion of the infrastructure, which improves the quality of service provided by the carrier and the degree of high technology. Overall, the distribution

network becomes more integrated, quickening transit times, and thereby intensifying competition amongst carriers and suppliers or shippers to the market. Accordingly, the method by which the goods reach the buyer becomes extremely competitive as the options increase and the value added benefit becomes more closely analysed by the buyer in the selection process of the supplier. Hence the need for the exporter to choose the most advantageous and competitive distribution network to obtain and retain overseas business.

(7) *Cost.* In total, there are 30 cost elements in an international distribution network. These include: handling, freight, packing, customs clearance, insurance, import duty, exchange rates, agent's commission, interest on capital in transit, warehouse and so on (p. 353). Exporters should constantly monitor these costs and ensure they remain competitive in the market in which they operate and especially in terms of value added benefit.

(8) *Value added benefit.* The choice of distribution network should be evaluated on the perceived benefits it brings to the buyer and the resulting value added benefit. It may be integrated into a just-in-time system or Distripark involving processing, packaging and distribution or transit times which enable the goods to be commissioned on arrival, such as computers or foodstuffs distributed to retail outlets in a quality condition at an attractive price. Shippers are constantly looking for improved efficiency in the distribution network which they can transform into improved profitability and competitiveness derived from the imported product.

(9) *Flexibility of service.* A flexible distribution network enables the shipper to exploit market opportunities. Flexibility arises in the range of facilities offered by the carrier and route options such as can be offered by a truck operator in the European market.

(10) *Frequency of service,* transit time and services reliability are all major factors. Low frequency services involve a longer lead time to despatch the goods and generates higher stockpiling which does not favour a just-in-time strategy. Low-cost services port-to-port often result in sluggish transits and transshipments. Moreover, the cargo receives a low priority in the handling process. Sluggish transit times are usually unacceptable for consumer cargoes as it deprives the importer of the earlier arrival of the goods which may be disadvantageous to the buyer in a variety of ways. Basically competitive transit times and frequent, reliable services at a competitive rate are the best ingredients to facilitate overseas market development and enable the buyer to maximize his or her profits from the imported products. Moreover, in such situations, stocks can remain at an optimum low level and can be replenished as they are consumed.

(11) *Logistics.* As stressed earlier, the company must be computer and logistic literate and focused on these elements. This requires substantial investment in resources, including a trained workforce committed to this ideology. Many smaller companies find it difficult to fund such investment but there is the alternative of having an operating alliance with another company, thereby sharing the cost and adding value to the company services, leading to enhanced competitiveness.

(12) *Maximization.* The company business must strive to maximize business volume through flexible pricing strategies. This places particular emphasis on the need to generate high business volume to support the company infrastructure and the resources available to the shipper.

To conclude our analysis, it is important to view the exporter's international distribution strategy through the eyes of the buyer. The imported product is part of the buyer's business and it is essential that both work closely together to the mutual and profitable benefit of both parties. A constant dialogue must be maintained with the carriers and all parties involved in the distribution network. Moreover, shipping managers should regularly visit the markets they serve, attend management courses and keep up to date on infrastructure developments.

In our examination of the tactics of applying the strategy, one must remember that the options are numerous and international distribution operates in an extremely fast-moving market. Hence the partnership and dialogue between the exporter and importer must be vigorous and decisive, to ensure the distribution network chosen is the most competitive for the products conveyed in that market. Market research techniques must be used.

International companies today tend to focus on a global outlook. They constantly search for new sustainable markets. Moreover, they choose to manufacture in low labour-cost markets with technical skills responsive to adequate technical training and with sustainable neighbouring markets to buy their products. This involves transfer pricing and technology; inwards and indigenous capital investment; an indigenous labour force and transfer of management skills. In some situations, an industrial transplant takes place with the importer providing some 51 per cent of the inwards investment. Such strategies and the terms of the industrial transplant depend on the buyer's government regulations.

We will now examine the options available for applying the international distribution strategy, but stress that the international company would use a mixture of these options, depending on company resources, infrastructure, products, markets, competition and cost efficiency factors.

(1) Near and distant markets. Near markets are easier to serve, manage and control than distant markets. In addition, regular business and control systems are easier to set up; the freight cost is lower and transit time quicker. The distant market may be Malaysia despatching goods to the USA or the EU compared with the near market of Singapore or Hong Kong. Generally exporters tend to have a better comprehension of the near market, especially in the areas of its infrastructure, culture, risk and 'ongoing' developments. Many small companies target the near market in preference, as the distant market may prove costly to serve and will absorb a high proportion of their resources, including slower payments. The distant market is more difficult to control and manage without placing a permanent representative in the overseas territory.

(2) Destination seaports play an important part in the decision-making process, reflecting especially the buyer's needs. Countries which are not on the international container network, with modern container berth ports offering

a good infrastructure, and served by rail, are seriously disadvantaged. There is no doubt that shippers using the multi-modal container service providing a door-to-door or warehouse-to-warehouse service involving dedicated road or rail services from the port to the inland clearance depot, dry port, etc., are well placed competitively. Many such services involve a feeder service from a hub port. Alternatively, the route may be by combi carrier or Ro-Ro ferry – the latter being particularly popular in Mediterranean and cross-channel UK–Continental markets. International trucking is a competitive method of distribution providing a door-to-door or warehouse-to-warehouse service.

Factors influencing the choice of destination or feeder seaports include: overall efficiency, infrastructure, level of tariffs, overall transit time, degree of technology, general competitiveness, quality of management, range of facilities, proximity of port to the buyer's address, the number of shipping lines using the port and the range of ports served.

(3) The criteria for the selection of a destination airport are similar to those for the seaport. Airports are usually located closer to the buyer's premises than the seaport. Moreover, the flight frequency is much higher compared with the sailing programme and offers much quicker transits.

(4) Sea–land bridge and sea–air bridge. As we progress through the next millennium the development of the sea–land and sea–air bridge concepts will continue. Examples of sea–air bridges exist in Singapore and Dubai (p. 93). Such competitively priced services offer quick transit times and provide numerous benefits to the shipper. This transport mode opens up new markets, especially for perishable goods and products selling in fast-moving territories. It also enables limited local stockpiling, invaluable for production which relys on just-in-time and needs stocks to be replenished by quick transits. Exporters in the Far East have benefited enormously from such developments, especially products exported to the wealth-targeted markets of the EU and the USA.

(5) Distriparks, found in the major ports of the world such as Rotterdam and Singapore (pp. 90–3), provide a new dimension to international physical distribution. The supplier, shipper or exporter can lease warehouse accommo-dation in the port environs and assemble, process and label his or her products there with substantial cost savings. The componentized items involved in the assembly process can be sourced from the cheapest markets, and only attract import duty when they enter their market of sale. This is a growth market, especially for consumer goods and foodstuffs.

(6) Free trade zones. Similar to the Distriparks, the FTZ (p. 18) enables the user to lease land and accommodation from the port authority and undertake the manufacture and/or componentized assembly process. Again favourable cost savings are realized, including reduced local taxes and rates in the earlier years. Many are called 'industrial zones' and operate in countries which are keen to develop an industrial base. Alternatively, as practised by the Japanese, these zones can be used as an industrial transplant or assembly plant to vitiate the high freight costs, obtain more favourable import tariffs through componen-tized assembly, overcome the high Japanese labour cost and, finally, as a means

to enter markets which are restrictive by using local labour in the manufacturing and assembly process.

(7) Customs planning (pp. 461–3). This involves a wide variety of customs activities, including tariff costing outwards, duty preference and origin, freight procurement, VAT, outward processing relief, standard exchange relief, temporarily imported goods, customs warehousing, free zones, carnets, export licensing, export valuation and local export control. Too few exporters or importers examine closely the customs implications of international distribution and fail to check out whether any alternative exists in the customs import tariff payment and the relief options. Outward processing relief and inward processing relief are two examples. Moreover, many shippers do not comprehend the reduced import tariff yield when goods are shipped in a componentized or CKD condition rather than as the finished product. Furthermore, the level of import tariff varies by country and such concessions are often inherent in the adoption of Distriparks as assembly or processing plants or FTZs. Overall, customs planning is a complex area. Study Figure 19.2 on p. 453 on computerized customs clearance system.

(8) Districentre. An increasing number of the high-profile internationally based transport operators are offering the Districentre concept with an associated range of services. An example is P&O Nedlloyd who operate a complete logistic system as illustrated in Figures 19.1.

The P&O Nedlloyd Flowmaster system provides a total transportation service package geared to individual manufacturers and their customers' needs. It involves the manufacturer despatching all his products to a strategically located Districentre which is virtually a warehouse. At this stage, P&O Nedlloyd take over all the multiple contacts and customer's orders direct from and supplied by P&O Nedlloyd. The benefits include customerized services designed and delivered for each client's individual needs; fully integrated services capable of co-ordinating distribution logistics with procurement and production logistics; one-stop shopping for logistic services with most or all services coordinated at one Districentre; improved reliability to enhance clients' ability to keep promises made to their customers; broader market research for clients using an established distribution system; shorter lead times for clients seeking to streamline their reaction times in the market place; increased flexibility so clients' market opportunities are not limited by distribution constraints; lower logistic cost with economies of scale; higher satisfaction profile for both manufacturer and their clients; and finally, the value added benefits derived from such services. Overall, it is the process of the manufacturer, supplier and exporter contracting out of distribution and transport: P&O Nedlloyd undertake the complete management of the flow of goods and information and the provision of additional services such as invoicing, packing, sorting and stock control on their behalf. The concept emerges from four major trends which can be distinguished worldwide. In the first place, manufacturers are increasingly concentrating on their core activities: production and sales. Secondly, there is a tendency for manufacturers

HOW IT USUALLY IS

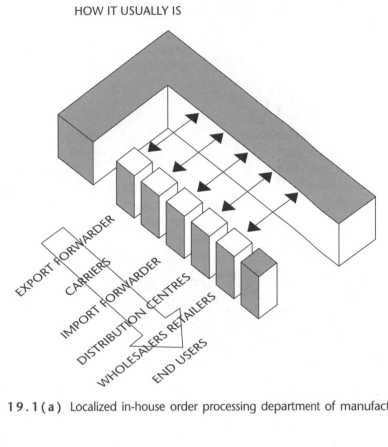

FIGURE 19.1(a) Localized in-house order processing department of manufacturing company

to organize their production decentrally and internationally. Thirdly, the lifecycles of products are becoming shorter so that fast, flexible distribution is increasingly essential. Finally, logistics and EDI are becoming essential in international distribution. Study Figure 19.3 on p. 454 on real time data systems at the Port of Felixstowe.

(9) The benefits of serving a Single Market as found in the EU are outstanding (see pp. 428–31). It offers a high volume of business, potentially good profitability, good infrastructure, very low risk, single product specification, good distribution logistically and computer focused, ease of market entry, free circulation within the market, single currency – the euro, labour mobility within the market and free capital movement. Moreover, there are no exchange controls involving repatriation of funds and generally a very stable and low inflation market. It provides opportunities to have regional distribution centres.

(10) Companies situated in economic blocs and customs unions should strive to export within the bloc or union. This offers the potential to develop volume business and take full advantage of the liberalization of trade within the bloc and the union. It provides an opportunity to develop logistically driven systems with its competitive advantages.

HOW IT COULD BE

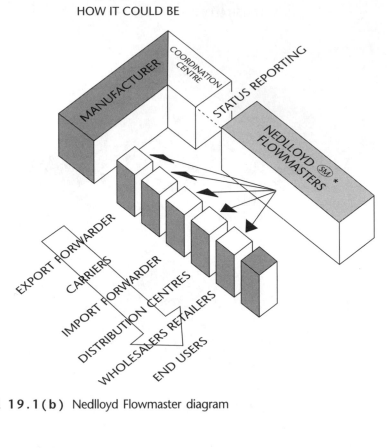

FIGURE 19.1(b) Nedlloyd Flowmaster diagram

(11) Routeing. The routeing of the consignment requires critical examination. The ultimate choice will influence transit time, transshipment resources, handling and any constraints on weight, length, etc., customs examination resources, total overall cost, reliability, frequency, mode of transport, value added benefit and insurance.

(12) Consolidation. The consolidation of cargo is a growth market by air, truck and container. It is economical and a network of services exists worldwide (p. 133).

(13) Packaging. Basically, packing is a form of protection and an aid to handling, identity and stowage. Excessive packing increases the volumetric size of the goods and can thereby increase freight cost on high volume products.

(14) Loadability and stowage. Aligned to packing is the general loadability and stowage of the cargo. Shippers with full-load truck and FCL containers should devise a stowage plan to ensure they make the best use of the cubic and weight capacity of the truck or container. Close consultation should take place with the production department to ensure the optimum size packing is devised to maximize loadability. Professional help should be enlisted from the road haulier or container operator and the situation should be continuously reviewed. A 10 per cent improvement in loadability will lower the distribution cost of the product and result in more competitive pricing.

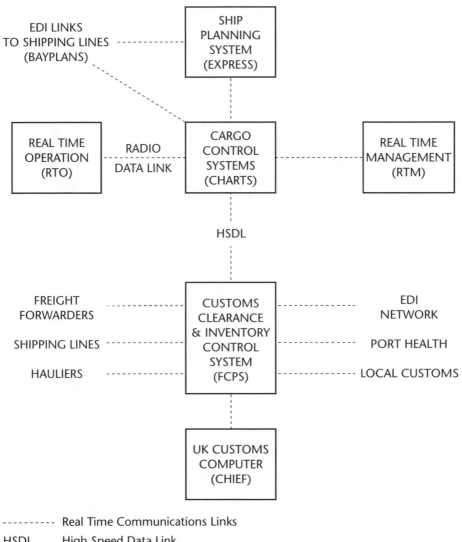

CARGO SYSTEMS INTEGRATION

EDI LINKS TO SHIPPING LINES (BAYPLANS)

SHIP PLANNING SYSTEM (EXPRESS)

REAL TIME OPERATION (RTO)

RADIO DATA LINK

CARGO CONTROL SYSTEMS (CHARTS)

REAL TIME MANAGEMENT (RTM)

HSDL

FREIGHT FORWARDERS

SHIPPING LINES

HAULIERS

CUSTOMS CLEARANCE & INVENTORY CONTROL SYSTEM (FCPS)

EDI NETWORK

PORT HEALTH

LOCAL CUSTOMS

UK CUSTOMS COMPUTER (CHIEF)

---------- Real Time Communications Links

HSDL   High Speed Data Link

EDI   Electronic Data Interchange

FIGURE 19.2 Computerized Customs Clearance system
Courtesy Felixstowe Dock and Railway Company

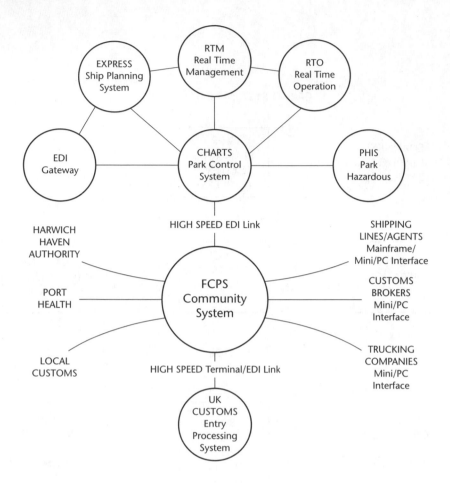

Key systems components include:

CHARTS A management control and planning system for container and Ro-Ro terminals, providing information relating to location, status and availability of cargo.

EXPRESS A twin screen colour graphics shipplanning system with EDI links to shipping lines.

FCPS The community system which processes customs entries and provides inventory control for all imports, exports and hazardous cargoes.

PHIS A park hazardous information system which holds an inventory of all hazardous cargo stores in the terminal.

RTM A real time graphical management system which constantly monitors cargo operations and updates system parameters to meet demands.

RTO A real time operational system, which schedules work to cargo handling equipment using radio data transmission and records the physical location of containers placed in the park.

Felixstowe operates an integrated set of computer systems 24 hours per day, 7 days per week, to support the physical operation and ensure cargo moves through the port in the shortest possible timescale.

Through extensive use of EDI and a dedicated network, shipping lines, agents, customs brokers and trucking companies carry out the majority of their business transactions electronically in real-time. This results in information becoming immediately available to those who need it and eliminates unnecessary, and time consuming, paperwork.

FIGURE 19.3 Real time data systems at the Port of Felixstowe
Courtesy of Felixstowe Dock and Railway Company

Good loadability and economical distribution can be achieved through the correct use of the mode of transport and type of transport unit. It arises in containerization where the range of container types continues to increase and the shipper must take full advantage of the situation to remain competitive. An example is the high-capacity covered or reefer container of 49 ft or 51 ft long. It may result in the shipper changing the existing distribution pattern and adopting transshipment arrangements to feed into this high-capacity container network.

(15) Distribution centres. Associated with the Distriparks, Districentres and free trade zones is the distribution centre. This concept exists whereby the exporter will centralize all his products on one distribution centre which will feed into the neighbouring market. Overall, it could be described as the cluster market distribution centre concept, and instead of the exporter sending goods under consolidated arrangements by truck or container, the merchandise can be despatched as a full truck or FCL container. This provides lower distribution cost and improves the service to the importer. In reality, it is very similar to the just-in-time or Districentre concept.

(16) Piggyback and trade associations. A number of exporters selling in common overseas territories have joined forces and operate common distribution channels apportioning the cost. In some situations, the product may be complimentary in the selling process such as two companies working together marketing furniture and furnishings. Such fusing of distribution arrangements lowers the cost significantly as the FCL is used rather than the LCL container movement. Potential exporters often join up with existing exporters in selling their merchandise such as the established overseas exporter selling garden furniture linking up with the company manufacturing greenhouses fresh to the export scene. Such a system is called a 'piggyback' where the inexperienced exporter works on the back of the established overseas exporter. The companies may be situated in neighbouring countries. Another example is a trade association working on behalf of its members through a marketing board promoting and distributing its products overseas; this is particularly evident in foodstuffs.

(17) Third countries. An increasing volume of business is now conducted on a third-country basis. For example, an order placed with a Japanese company can be supplied to the EU from a manufacturing plant in Taiwan. This may involve a different distribution network.

(18) Buyer's or importer's portfolio and empathy. The wishes of the buyer must be carefully considered and respected. Good relationships and lasting business developments emerge from the strategy of empathy whereby the exporter and importer share each other's views and objectives in the conduct of international trade. Special attention should be given to the infrastructure obtaining in the buyer's country and the most acceptable, efficient method of distribution.

(19) Currency. The freight rate may involve the exporter's or importer's currency or a third currency. Overall, the currency used requires careful evaluation and unstable and non-convertible currencies should be eliminated.

(20) Incoterms 2000. Some 13 Incoterms 2000 exist and the one selected should favour both the exporter and importer. An increasing use is now made of multi-modalism and combined transport operation and the appropriate terms used.

(21) Audit of carrier or freight forwarder. The selection of the most suitable freight forwarder and carrier requires careful evaluation (pp. 417–20). To test the feasibility of both, test transits should be undertaken. Moreover, a system should be devised to monitor transits to ensure quality is maintained and areas of weakness identified with a view to an early remedy.

(22) Direct or indirect marketing. Companies may sell directly to the end-user and thereby follow a strategy of direct marketing. In such situations, the exporter usually has complete influence over the distribution in consultation with the importer. Alternatively, the exporter may sell through an intermediary and have less influence over the distribution arrangements.

(23) Transport distribution analysis. This is fully explained on pp. 279–89 and shippers are well advised to use these criteria when the opportunity arises.

(24) EDI – Electronic Data Interchange is fully explained in Chapter 16. It is likely that the range of management information relative to international distribution will increase and also the efficiency of processing the cargo internationally.

(25) International distribution can be developed more efficiently when operating in an economic bloc or customs union, especially when free circulation obtains with no customs barriers at frontier points.

(26) The accelerating development of the LEC/LIC (see p. 191) as predicted by the WCO (see p. 183) will facilitate greater efficiency in international distribution. It removes customs barriers at the port, seaport or frontier point of entry or departure and speeds up transit times.

The foregoing list is comprehensive and requires careful evaluation. It points to the fact that international distribution has become highly sophisticated in the past decade and involves many elements each with cost, marketing and efficiency implications. Different products and different markets require different distribution networks. Overall, it is a fast-moving market and a strategy of creating empathy between the buyer and seller is paramount to ensure successful market development. A key factor is the channel of distribution chosen and related distribution network.

19.2 Decision-making process

The process of making the decision relative to the selection of the most acceptable channel of distribution will vary by circumstances. It will involve in particular cost, efficiency ratios, volume of business, transport mode options, nature of cargo, transit times, timescale of cargo shipments, value of cargo, loadability, infrastructure in the seller's and buyer's markets, level of competition and the long-term future of the market. It requires continuous market research and planning to coordinate resources to achieve objectives. Regular visits to the market enable the shipper to evaluate the best distribution network and encourages dialogue with the carrier.

The following checklist has been compiled as a guide to the relevant evaluation criteria.

(1) An evaluation of the international physical distribution of an export market in the following areas:

(a) Potential for sales and growth in the short and medium term.

(b) Market stability reflecting economic, political and social considerations.

(c) Short- and medium-term profitability.

(d) Whether it is a near or distant market.

(e) The infrastructure, both existing and planned, and its compatibility with the home market (focus especially on the sea and airports and road, rail and canal networks on which they rely).

(f) The routeing and distribution from the seaport or airport to the buyer's premises (including sea- and airport handling charges).

(g) The import regulations extending to licensing, tariffs and import duty documentation. This can include legislation confirming all insurance cover taken out in the buyer's country.

(h) The airlines, shipping companies serving the market and their schedules, rates, frequency, transit times, reliability and overall quality of service – consider whether the buyer's government practises flag discrimination, routeing cargoes on their national airline or shipping company.

(i) Availability and experience of company resources in terms of personnel, finance and overall logistics identifying cost factors both in the short and medium term. Companies today focus on logistics and EDI to develop efficient supply chains. Many rely on the logistical resources of a mega-container operator such as P&O Nedlloyd (see pp. 101–4).

(j) Availability or development of information technology, especially in the areas of management information control and monitoring systems, market feedback, data documentation processing and analysis of the various channels of distribution options.

(k) The risk areas in terms of exchange risk, political risk and restrictions in the market. For example, is it an open market with no tariff barriers to encourage imports and free trade?

(l) A profile of the importer and the airlines and shipping companies serving the country, both directly and through transshipment hub routes.

The exporter should produce a grid or comprehensive tabulation relative to the foregoing points as a first stage in the evaluation. The market forecast under item 1(a) will enable the volume of business to be identified on a monthly, weekly or daily basis and thereby reconcile it with the appropriate transport mode options and their loadability. This can be reconciled with the importer's access to any large storage capacity which can receive higher-capacity shipments such as the FCL rather than the LCL container which, in turn, lowers unit distribution costs. Modern warehouses are now computer controlled.

(2) The next stage is to summarize the data of (1) with a view to reconciling them with the export company's international physical distribution strategy. In so doing, carriers which look feasible may require further evaluation and discussions initiated between the shipping manager and carrier.

At this stage, the shipping or international logistics manager will probably have up to three options in response to earlier enquiries. A major factor is the total product cost of each option and the value added benefit each brings, both to the exporter and importer. Many shippers use transport distribution analysis (p. 279) to aid their decision-making. It is possible that shippers will tend to patronize carriers with whom they have existing contracts on other routes, or earlier favourable experience; but when serving new markets, a fresh approach may be desirable to retain competitiveness.

(3) The next stage is to carry out some test transits. In so doing each stage of the transit should be monitored in order to identify any problem areas. Full liaison must be maintained with all parties involved in the transit. A significant factor in the distribution network adopted is the loadability of the transport unit. This is determined by the configuration of the packing and its stowage effectiveness, with broken stowage at a minimum. This involves close liaison between the shipping manager, the production department and the carrier to ensure, for example, that the most suitable truck or container is provided. Loadability can be improved by breaking down the consignment.

(4) The next stage is to evaluate the test transit(s), and following consultation with interested parties including the importer, decide on the most appropriate distribution network and firm up the total cost of the product.

(5) The final stage is to devise an action plan to execute the decision. Overall, it must be controlled by the shipping manager and be monitored through the budgetary control methods. Good planning is the essential ingredient to an efficient international distribution network, plus total commitment from all parties – production manager, importer, carrier, agent, port, etc.

19.3 Problem areas and possible solutions

International physical distribution is becoming a high tech and extremely competitive operation. Innovation and the striving for greater efficiency are very much in evidence as we move through the millennium. Generally, it is becoming more logistically and EDI driven. Areas of particular significance are the swap-body, the sea–land bridge, the sea–air bridge, high-capacity containers of 49 ft or 51 ft long and 9 ft 6 in high integrators (p. 133) and finally, the Channel Tunnel. Seaports are playing an increasingly decisive role in the development of trade and are market driven in their strategies and investment. However, one must acknowledge that problem areas do arise in the distribution network which the shipper must resolve. Given below are a number of problems together with possible solutions.

(1) Industrial disputes, or a build-up of traffic at a seaport, can seriously disrupt a service and result in the goods arriving late and beyond the expiry date of the import licence and letter of credit. Alternative routes should be explored at the earliest possible time to include transferring to air freight. Such situations usually build up over a period of a few days and a contingency plan should be devised at this stage and put in place.

(2) The range of truck and container types tends to increase, but it does generate an imbalance of their use. This is especially true in the container business. An example can also be seen in a market where liquid imports predominate and perishable foodstuffs and machinery are exported thereby requiring two different types of containers. It is primarily a problem for the carriers, but it can result in shortages of specific container types at peak times.

(3) Dangerous goods and indivisible loads, such as transformers or engineering plant with a weight of up to 250 tonnes, require special arrangements. Dangerous goods are described on pp. 160–74, but a key factor is to initiate the pre-shipment booking arrangements as early as possible. As for indivisible loads, these products require special arrangements and the freight forwarder specializing in such work usually has a project forwarding department to handle such transits. The following points are relevant in the international movement of indivisible loads.

    (a) The ports of departure, destination and any transshipment areas need to be checked out to ensure they can handle such a shipment, checking especially for the availability of heavy lifting equipment.

    (b) The shipowner will have to have a plan and specification of the shipment to evaluate the stowage and handling arrangements; and also to identify the weight distribution.

    (c) The transportation of an indivisible load to and from the ports requires pre-planning particularly regarding route and timescale. Usually such goods may only move at night under police escort and subject to the police and/or transport department's permission.

    (d) The rates for transporting indivisible loads are usually assessed on a cost plus profit basis. The cost can be very extensive as it incorporates any heavy lifting equipment and special arrangements to transport the goods overland to and from the ports. Freight forwarders tend to work closely with the correspondent agent in the destination country. Transshipment costs can be much reduced if a 'Mafi'-type six-axle trailer is used as in the Ro-Ro tonnage.

The advantages of the indivisible load shipment to the shipper, buyer or importer include lower overall transportation cost; quicker transit; much reduced site assembly cost; less risk of damage in transit; lower insurance premium; less technical aid and staff resources required by the buyer as there is no extensive site assembly work; equipment is tested and fully operational in the factory before despatch; no costly site assembly work; less risk of malfunctioning equipment; and earlier commissioning of the equipment which, in turn, results in the quicker productive use of the equipment with profitable benefits to the buyer overall.

(4) Companies need to monitor closely all transits and any irregularities, initiating early remedial measures with the parties concerned. If it is difficult to establish the cause of the problems, such as late arrival, damaged cargo, missing merchandise, etc., test transits should be undertaken. Computerization of the shipping office enables much of the routine work to be done much quicker and more accurately, especially documentation processing, thereby releasing staff for more managerial activities within the department (pp. 365–71).

(5) International physical distribution tends in some companies to have a low profile in the management structure, especially at the more senior level. This is now changing as companies become more globally focused in their market and acknowledge that to remain competitive they must have a professionally qualified team managing their international physical distribution as it is a budget driven element of the business.

(6) Exchange risk still remains evident in many markets. Advice should be sought from professional sources, especially the national bank of the importer's country.

(7) Cargo insurance features in Incoterms 2000. Exporters should check that the importer has insured the goods as specified in its contract and take contingency measures when in doubt.

(8) Documentary credits should be thoroughly checked on arrival to ensure they represent the terms already agreed and the exporter can comply with the distribution arrangements.

(9) Faulty documents are a frequent cause of late payment and late delivery of goods (pp. 241–51). Professionally qualified personnel handling such documents can reduce the risk, and attendance at training courses and seminars enables staff to keep up-to-date.

(10) Full use should be made of EDI resources and techniques.

(11) Finally, a logistics distribution plan should be devised and monitored using EDI resources.

19.4 Logistics strategy

Shippers are today increasingly looking at the total production and value added chain; in consequence, shippers are looking more closely at the logistics part of their business. Basically, the art of logistics is the ability to get the right product to the right place at the right time. As a result, the shipper is no longer interested in the point-to-point operator, such as airport-to-airport or seaport-to-seaport, but the total product involving the value added chain. This new approach is linked to the just-in-time concept in management techniques. In consequence, this has stimulated the expansion of express air services (p. 133) and integrated operators such as UPS, TNT, DHL and so on.

Integrated operators offer a complete package for the air cargo shipper, embracing not only collection and airport-to-airport flight, but delivery to the importer's address with a guaranteed arrival time. The integrator undertakes all the customs documentation and clearance. Products ideally suited to this market are the high tech and pharmaceutical industries, but it is less appropriate in the traditional engineering and manufacturing sectors. However, it is likely to grow quickly in the EU. Many of the integrators have logistics departments whose tasks are to identify customers' needs, tailor solutions to their specific problems and provide them with a value added service. Other areas covered by the integrators include provision of waybills, invoices and management reports, availability of a bonded warehouse, stock control and so on. Overall, the aim is to combine production, warehousing distribution and transport for shippers on a global basis.

Undoubtedly, the mega-container operators such as P&O Nedlloyd are driving the logistic global expansion (see Chapter 6). Many mega-container operators have their own logistics divisions thereby encouraging shippers to place their international distribution arrangements with the shipowners. This embraces all elements of the distribution network including warehousing, supplier selection, packaging, customs clearance and associated documentation.

With an increasingly competitive market, logistics operations are under close scrutiny to minimize the cost whilst maximizing the customer service. This involves supply chain modelling; warehouse and plant location; warehouse and transport operational modelling; stock optimization; warehouse design and equipment; systems and operations specification; and the implementation of change. Logistics strategies are particularly relevant in trading blocs, and this applies especially to the EU, ASEAN and LAFTA. Also, it is especially relevant to fast-moving products where competition is fierce and service quality is paramount to the customer. Costs must be kept at a minimum if the integrator is to remain competitive.

To conclude our brief analysis, it is likely the logistics strategy will feature more strongly in manufacturers' and suppliers' globalization of their markets and carriers will respond more to the challenge of change and opportunity as we move on through the millennium. Again planning features strongly in the formulation and execution of this strategy. It is market led, and market research plays an essential and continuous role.

19.5 Customs planning

For many years a large number of companies engaged in international trade regarded payment of customs duties and the cost of compliance with customs law and regulations as unavoidable expenses with little or no scope for planning. Today with ever-increasing competition in the market place, companies have to be more competitive in the product they sell. Moreover, with the EU Single Market entity, customs law has become more complex.

Customs planning produces savings not only to the exporter and importer, but also to the ordinary business. If a company uses imported components or manufacturers for export, savings can be realized by the judicious use of the reliefs and facilities available. Most manufacturers' products contain items 'bought in', many of them from sources outside the EU. Hence many of the customs planning considerations apply both to goods sourced from outside the EU and to the sale and export of finished and semi-finished products.

Customs planning involves arranging a company's affairs to ensure that it suffers minimum possible exposure to taxation within the law. The taxes involved are import duties, Common Agricultural Policy levies, excise duties and VAT. Savings can be realized in the cost of complying with customs requirements. Customs and Excise offer a variety of simplified procedures to ease both their own administrative burden and traders' costs of compliance. Effective customs planning offers the following benefits:

(1) minimizes the trader's exposure to customs duties;
(2) maximizes the trader's use of facilities and reliefs;
(3) minimizes the trader's cost of compliance;
(4) improves the trader's profitability and cash flow;
(5) avoids the risk of seizure and penalties.

Given below are the main areas of customs planning.

(1) The tariff is the centre of customs planning. It determines the rate of duty on imported goods according to their description and specification listed against a numerical commodity code. Situations can arise when the goods are wrongly described and attract a higher rate of duty than necessary.

Customs planning is desirable at the design stage of a new product, whether it is to be imported as a finished article for onward sale or to be used by the importer in a further manufacturing process. Furthermore, if imported items are to be used in the manufacturing process, one must evaluate the financial merits of importing components rather than sub-assembly from individual components. For the business operating in more than one country, there is a further aspect to be considered. Over 50 countries now use the Harmonized System of Tariff Classification and Commodity Coding (HS). Hence the same item will be appropriate to the same commodity code in each of these states, although of course there are likely to be considerable differences in the rates of duty. Thus entrepreneurs must consider the impact in all countries into which they import to ensure that the advantage gained in one is not more than offset by advantages lost in others. Ideally it is worthwhile agreeing the appropriate commodity codes with suppliers when importing and with customers when exporting, well in advance of the consignment crossing international frontiers.

(2) More than two-thirds of the world trade governing customs valuation falls within an international code negotiated under WTO. Countries which are signatories to the code have the option of using cost, insurance and freight (CIF) or free on board (FOB). They can also choose whether to convert foreign to national currencies using the rate of exchange at the time of importation or exportation. Some countries, such as the EU member states, use a CIF value, whilst others, such as the USA, accept FOB. An exporter should be aware of

which of these variations his customer needs to apply to ensure that both gain maximum results.

(3) The customs value of the vast majority of the consignments is based on the price actually paid or payable for the goods by the importer. Adjustments upwards or downwards frequently need to be made to invoiced prices. These include commission, discounts, transport, insurance and price review clauses. These aspects are of a particular concern when applied to transactions between related parties such as trading between companies in a multinational group.

(4) Customs warehousing is amongst the most useful of the various reliefs available. It permits goods liable to import duty to be stored in Customs and Excise warehouses without duty or VAT being accounted for until the goods are removed from the warehouse. A limited range of minor handling operations may be carried out on the goods whilst they are in the warehouse, where they remain for up to five years. When required to be moved, they must be entered for export or removed to another similar warehouse or transferred to another regime such as Inward Processing Relief.

(5) The origin of imported goods and the route they follow to the EU has considerable influence on their liability to duty. If they are imported from a country with a preference agreement with the EU, then the rate is reduced or even zero. If not, inevitably the question arises as to whether the source can be changed or whether the specification can be varied to include less offshore elements of value.

Suspension of the full rate of duty may be available from specified countries at certain times in particular goods. Similarly, a quota may be in force which allows predetermined quantities of goods meeting certain tariff descriptions to be imported at a lower than full rate of duty. Hence the benefits of preferential rates of duty can be used to reduce manufacturing cost. They are also available to buyers of UK goods, provided that they are imported into a country that has entered into a trading agreement with the EU. Similar rules of origin and consignment apply albeit in reverse. The exporter who plans to ensure that his or her goods originate in the EU and can therefore provide a certificate of origin should find that his or her prices to many overseas customers are more competitive.

(6) Outward processing relief arises when the goods are exported for a manufacturing process and then returned to the EU. Prior authorization by customs is required before the relief is allowed. The duty payable on the goods returned is reduced by the nominal duty that would have been charged on the exported elements.

(7) The Open General Export licence has liberalized controls on exports to East European destinations. These are issued by the DTI and exporters need to ensure they comply with all the provisions of export control. Transgressions can prove to be costly to the company's finances and to its reputation. Hence careful planning and continued monitoring are essential.

(8) Inward processing relief is available to traders who are importing goods from countries that are not members of the EU. The imported goods may be used for

virtually any manufacturing process and are relieved from import duty, provided that the products are re-exported beyond the frontiers of the EU. The trader has to seek prior authorization from customs to suspend the import duty (the 'suspension' method) or to recover it once the products have been exported ('draw back' method).

This should not be regarded as an exhaustive list and other items would include free trade zones, processing for free circulation and anti-dumping duties. Customs planning forms an important element in the physical distribution strategy and requires continuous monitoring of the customs duties and regulations. Arthur Andersen is a market leader in this field.

19.6 Liner conferences

The liner conference is a collaborative form of organization whereby a number of shipowners offer their services on a given sea route on conditions agreed by their members. Conferences are semi-monopolistic associations of shipping lines formed for the purpose of restricting competition between their members and protecting them from outside competition. Conference agreements may also regulate sailings and ports of call and in some cases arrangements are made for the pooling of net earnings. Conferences achieve their object by controlling prices and by limiting entry to the trade. Their chief policy is to establish a common tariff of freight rates and passenger fares for the trade involved, members being left free to compete for traffic by the quality and efficiency of their service.

As we progress through the millennium the liner conference system is very much in decline. This is due to a variety of reasons including the development of multi-modalism; the inflexibility of the rates system and the recent US Shipping Act which came into force on 1 May 1999, termed the Ocean Shipping Reform Act 1998. Under the new legislation conferences cannot prevent a member from entering into an individual service contract nor can the conference require disclosure of negotiation of such contracts.

Carriers, conferences and other groups of carriers (assuming they have the requisite authority) will publish privately and make available to the public essential terms of the service contract which will be limited to commodities, minimum volume commitment, port ranges in the USA and overseas, and contract term. Service contract rates and charges will not be required to be published or made public nor will specific points or ports or service commitments. NVOCC may enter into service contracts as shippers, but they are not permitted to offer service contracts as carriers to their customers. Contracts may be for a specific percentage of a shipper's cargo. Conferences may agree on non-binding voluntary guidelines for individual service contracts.

In recent years the mega-container operator or shipowner has opted out of the liner conference system on many of their trades to follow a strategy of liberalization of freight rates and development of multi-modalism and operating alliances. The US development and further expansion of the liberalized mega-container rate strategy will accelerate the decline of the liner conference system in many liner cargo trades.

19.7 The future

As we progress through the millennium it is likely that the pace of change in the conduct and execution of international trade will accelerate. Such change will place more emphasis on management techniques and strategy in the computer literate, logistically focused globalization of international trade.

An increasing number of companies will have the majority of their business overseas with the home domestic market accounting for a diminishing proportion of their sales. MNEs and SMEs will engage in mergers and acquisitions, joint ventures and operating alliances in their endeavours to reduce cost, become more competitive, increase international business market share and rationalize production, research and development. Overall, this will result in such companies being able to expand their business further internationally, generating adequate profit to invest in high tech and logistic systems which will be so important in the future.

To match company expansion and the growth of world trade, physical distribution will play a larger part. For example, we can already see the development of the hub and spoke system in container networks, the continuing merger and operating alliances of the mega-containers, the increasing importance of ports and their infrastructure, the growing development of customs clearance at the trader's premises and the continuing expansion of multi-modalism. Air freight will continue to expand particularly on the long haul flights with larger capacity aircraft. More airports will be open in the Far East and globally existing ones modernized, especially their air freight facilities. The concept of sea–air bridges will expand further.

The political influence on trade will gain momentum. Governments will stimulate the enlargement of economic blocs and customs unions. This will result in such economies becoming more economic, productive and competitive, resulting in more investment and trade expansion. The WTO will facilitate such expansion.

This title is now 21 years old and the fourth edition has a complete focus on present and future practices and strategies. This latest edition reflects many changes and has been enriched by more case studies and an increased input from a larger number of organizations and companies. It is hoped the latest edition will help both students and undergraduates and international entrepreneurs in their endeavours to develop and execute a successful international trade strategy.

■ □ ■ ■ Appendix A

Addresses of national and international organizations involved in facilitating international trade development

Name and address of organization	Role of organization
Advertising Association 15 Wilton Road LONDON SW1V 1NJ	The professional body representing advertising focused companies
Association of British Chambers of Commerce 9 Tufton Street ·London SW1P 3QB	An Association of British Chambers of Commerce representing and coordinating their activities
Association of International Courier and Express Services PO Box 10 Leatherhead Surrey KT22 0HT	The professional body representing Couriers and Express Services Companies
Baltic and International Maritime Council (BIMCO) 161 Bagsvaerdvej 2880 Bagsvaerd Denmark	An international organization of shipowners, shipbrokers, ship agents and associations of shipowners
Baltic Exchange St Mary Axe London EC3A 8BH	An international shipping market/place where ship chartering is conducted involving both the shipowner and merchant through a shipbroker
British Exporters Association 16 Dartmouth Street London SW1H 9BL	A UK organization of some 200 companies which are specialists in all aspects of international trade.

Name and address of organization	*Role of organization*
British Food Export Council 301–304 Market Towers New Covent Garden London SW8 5NQ	Responsible for developing and facilitating UK food products overseas
British Importers Association Suite 8 Castle House 25 Castlereagh Street London W1H 5YR	A UK organization whose aim is to facilitate the importation of goods into the UK
British International Freight Association Redfern House Browells Lane Feltham, Middlesex DW13 7EP	The professional body representing Freight Forwarding Companies
British Maritime Equipment Council 4th Floor 30 Great Guildford Street London SE1 0HS	Marine standards, marketing, and marketing intelligence, finding an agent and exporting
British Shippers Council (BSC) Hermes House 157 St Johns Road Tunbridge Wells Kent TN4 9UZ	Organization representing British Shippers at both National and International level in all matters concerning the overseas transport of their goods whether by sea or air embracing the interest of both importers and exporters in Great Britain. Part of the FTA
British Standards Institution (BSI) Linford Wood Milton Keynes MK14 6LE	UK organization involved in formulation and management of British Standards for UK products
Chamber of Shipping (UK) Carthusian Court 12 Carthusian Street London EC1M 6EB	Trade organization representing UK shipowners
Chartered Institute of Logistics and Transport 80 Portland Place London WC1N 4DP	The professional institute for those personnel involved in logistics and transport
Chartered Institute of Marketing Moor Hall Cookham Maidenhead Berkshire	The professional institute for those personnel involved in marketing

Name and address of organization	*Role of organization*
Confederation of British Industries (CBI) Centre Point 103 New Oxford Street London WC1A 1DU	Organization which represents British industry
Cotecna International Ltd Hounslow House 730 London Road Hounslow, Middlesex	Organization responsible globally for processing pre-shipment inspection arrangements
Department of Trade and Industry Export Licensing Branch Kingsgate House 66–74 Victoria Street London SW1E 6SW	UK government department organization responsible for controlling/issuing export licences
Department of Trade and Industry Import Licensing Branch Queensway House West Precinct Billingham Cleveland TS23 2NF	UK government department organization responsible for controlling/issuing export licences
Department of Trade and Industry Market Desk Kingsgate House 66–74 Victoria Street London SW1H 6SW	UK Government department providing market research data/country profile in countries globally
European Union (EU) European Parliament 97–113 Rue Belliard 1047 Brussels Belgium	Headquarters of EU involving 15 countries
Exportmaster Systems Ltd 33 St Peter's Street South Croydon CR2 7DG	Company specializing in export software
Freight Transport Association (FTA) Hermes House 157 St Johns Road Tunbridge Wells Kent TN4 9UZ	Organization representing British shippers at both national and international level in all matters concerning the overseas transport of their goods whether by sea or air embracing the interest of both importers and exporters in Great Britain

Name and address of organization	*Role of organization*
Fruit Importers Association (FIA) D 114-115 Fruit and Vegetable Market New Covent Garden London	A national organization specializing in the facilitation of fruit importation into the UK
HM Customs and Excise UK Deferment Section Statistical Office Room 1204 Portcullis House 27 Victoria Avenue Southend on Sea Essex SS2 6AL	Customs organization dealing with VAT
Institute of Chartered Shipbrokers 3 St Helens Place London EC3A 6EJ	The professional institute for all those personnel involved in shipbrokerage
Institute of Export Export House 64 Clifton Street London EC2A 4HB	The professional institute for all those personnel involved in exporting and importing
Institute of Translation and Interpreting 377 City Road London EC1B 1NA	The professional institute for those personnel involved in translation and interpreting work
International Air Transport Association (IATA) Route de l'Aeroport 33 BP 672, 1215 Geneva Switzerland	A non-governmental organization of 55 member airlines responsible for international rates and fare levels. It also deals with documentation, cargo handling, legal matters, financial and technical aspects with a view to the facilitating and developing of international airline traffic by scheduled IATA services globally
International Association of Ports and Harbours (IAPH) Kotohira Kaikan Building 1–2–8 Taranomon Minato – Ku Tokyo 105 Japan	A non-governmental organization representing seaports internationally

Name and address of organization	*Role of organization*
International Chamber of Commerce (ICC) 38 Cours Albert 1 75008 Paris France	A federation of National Chambers of Commerce – embracing some 101 member countries – whose aim is to promote an expansion in international trade and investment by encouraging national economic growth
International Chamber of Commerce United Kingdom 14/15 Belgrave Square London WS1X 8PS	UK organization which is affiliated to the International Chamber of Commerce
International Maritime Organisation (IMO) 4 Albert Embankment London SE1 7SR	Global organization responsible for developing ship safety, maritime pollution, maritime dangerous cargo and ship construction and survey
International Maritime Satellite Organisation (INMARSAT) 99 City Road London EC1	Internationally owned cooperative which provides mobile satellite communication worldwide in the areas of commercial, distress and safety applications at sea, in the air and on land
International Monetary Fund (IMF) Washington DC 20431 USA	An international organization – embracing some141 member countries – which encourages monetary co-operation, exchange policy, promotes stable exchange rates among member nations and makes short term advances and 'standby credits' to members in temporary payment difficulties
London Chamber of Commerce 33 Queen Street London EC4R 1AP	Organization which represents the industrial and service sectors in London UK
Organisation for Economic Co-operation and Development (OECD) 2 Rue Andre Pascal 75775 Paris Cedex 16 France	International organization of 25 member countries whose aim is to promote economic and social welfare throughout the OECD area by assisting member countries in the formulation and coordination of policies designed to this end and to stimulate and harmonize members' efforts in favour of developing countries

Name and address of organization	*Role of organization*
P&O Nedlloyd Ltd Beagle House Braham Street London E1 8EP	A mega-container operator and shipowner
Pira International Rawdalls Road Leatherhead Surrey KT27 7RU	UK research association for paper and board, printing, publishing and packaging industries
SGS United Kingdom Ltd SGS House 217–221 London Road Camberley Surrey GU15 3EY	Organization responsible globally for processing pre-shipment inspection arrangements
Simpler Trade Procedures Board (SITPRO) 151 Buckingham Palace Road London SW1W 9SS	UK organization whose aim is to encourage the rationalization of international trade procedures and information flows associated with them
Technical Help for Exporters (THE) British Standards Institution 389 Chiswick High Road London W4 4AL	UK organization providing a versatile service identifying and supplying documents with translations where applicable with a view to giving assistance to UK manufacturers on foreign technical requirements
Trade Indemnity plc 12-34 Great Eastern Street London EC2A 3AX	UK organization involved in marine and cargo insurance
United Nations Commission International Trade Law (UNCITRAL) Vienna International Centre PO Box 500 A–1400 Vienna Austria	An international organization whose aim is to further the progressive harmonization and unification of the law of international trade
United Nations Conference on Trade and Development (UNCTAD) Palais des Nations CH–1211 Geneve 10 Switzerland	An international organization with 157 member countries whose aim is to help modify the traditional patterns of international trade so that developing countries would be able to play their part in world commerce

Name and address of organization	*Role of organization*
World Trade Organisation (WTO) Centre William Rappard Rue de Lausanne 154 CH–1211 Geneve 21 Switzerland	United Nations organization providing the legal and institutional foundation of the multilateral trading system. It provides the principal contractual obligations determining how governments frame and implement domestic trade legislation and regulations

■ ☐ ■ ■ Appendix B

Publications for the international entrepreneur

ABC – Air Cargo Guide
Business Monitor International
Container Journal International
The Economist
Economic Intelligence Unit (EIU) country reports
Exporting Today
Export Times
Freight Management (International)
Freight News
Handy Shipping Guide
Incoterms 2000 – ICC publication
Importing Today
International Chamber of Commerce (reports/publications)
International Freighting Weekly
Kellys Export Services
Lloyd's List and Shipping Gazette
Merchant's Guide (P&O Nedlloyd)
Overseas Trade (DTI)
SITPRO Annual Report
UCP500 – ICC publication

Various publications and handbooks on export and import practice and trade finance are available (usually free) from the major international banks, situated worldwide. Also leading national and international newspapers and journals frequently publish, as a supplement, a country report analysis or overview of a particular industry with a global focus.

■ □ ■ ■ Appendix C
Export documents

Readers may wish to study documentation in greater depth, in which case they are recommended to read the companion volume *Shipping and Air Freight Documentation for Importers and Exporters and Associate Terms* – published by Witherby & Co., London (2nd Edition 2000).

Bill of Lading for Combined Transport shipment or Port to Port shipment

| Shipper | B/L No.: |
| | Reference: |

P&O Nedlloyd

Consignee or Order (for U.S. Trade only: Not Negotiable unless consigned 'To Order')

Notify Party/Address (It is agreed that no responsibility shall attach to the Carrier or his Agents for failure to notify (see clause 20 on reverse))

Place of Receipt (Applicable only when this document is used as a Combined Transport Bill of Lading)

Vessel and Voy. No.

Place of Delivery (Applicable only when this document is used as a Combined Transport Bill of Lading)

| Port of Loading | Port of Discharge |

Undermentioned particulars as declared by Shipper, but not acknowledged by the Carrier (see clause 11)

| Marks and Nos; Container Nos; | Number and kind of Packages; Description of Goods | Gross Weight (kg) | Measurement (cbm) |

| * Total No. of Containers/Packages received by the Carrier | Movement | Freight payable at |

EXCESS VALUATION: REFER TO CLAUSE 7 (3) ON REVERSE SIDE (U.S. TRADE ONLY).

Received by the Carrier from the Shipper in apparent good order and condition (unless otherwise noted herein) the total number or quantity of Containers or other packages or units indicated in the box above entitled "Total No. of Containers/Packages received by the Carrier" for Carriage subject to all the terms and conditions hereof (INCLUDING THE TERMS AND CONDITIONS ON THE REVERSE HEREOF AND THE TERMS AND CONDITIONS OF THE CARRIER'S APPLICABLE TARIFF) from the Place of Receipt or the Port of Loading, whichever is applicable, to the Port of Discharge or the Place of Delivery, whichever is applicable. If the Carrier so requires, before he arranges delivery of the Goods one original Bill of Lading, duly endorsed, must be surrendered by the Merchant to the Carrier at the Port of Discharge or at some other location acceptable to the Carrier. In accepting this Bill of Lading the Merchant expressly accepts and agrees to all its terms and conditions whether printed, stamped or written, or otherwise incorporated, notwithstanding the non-signing of this Bill of Lading by the Merchant.

| Number of Original Bills of Lading | Place and Date of Issue | IN WITNESS of the contract herein contained the number of originals stated opposite has been issued, one of which being accomplished the other(s) to be void |

ORIGINAL

FOR P&O NEDLLOYD LTD, AS CARRIER:*

CANCELLED - SPECIMEN COPY

378007

2/DRS B/L3 10/97 (S)

*OPERATING IN PARTNERSHIP WITH P&O NEDLLOYD BV

FIGURE C1 Bill of lading combined transport shipment or port to port shipment
Courtesy of P&O Nedlloyd

F I G U R E   C 1 *continued* Bill of Lading Multi-modal Transport or Port to Port Shipment
Courtesy of Hapag-Lloyd

Non-Negotiable Waybill for Combined Transport shipment or Port to Port shipment

Shipper		Waybill No.:
		Reference:

P&O Nedlloyd

Consignee (If the name shown in this space is a Bank, the Bank named is specifically excluded from the list of parties coming within the definition of Merchant in the Carrier's contract of carriage and incurs no liability to the Carrier under said contract unless applying for delivery in its own name.)

Notify Party/Address (It is agreed that no responsibility shall attach to the Carrier or his Agents for failure to notify)	Place of Receipt (Applicable only when this document is used as a Combined Transport Waybill)

Vessel and Voy. No.	Place of Delivery (Applicable only when this document is used as a Combined Transport Waybill)

Port of Loading	Port of Discharge	

Undermentioned particulars as declared by Shipper, but not acknowledged by the Carrier

Marks and Nos; Container Nos;	Number and kind of Packages; description of Goods	Gross Weight (kg)	Measurement (cbm)

WAYBILL

* Total No. of Containers/Packages received by the Carrier	Movement	Freight payable at

Received by the Carrier from the Shipper in apparent good order and condition (unless otherwise noted herein) the total number or quantity of Containers or other packages or units indicated in the box above entitled "Total No. of Containers/Packages received by the Carrier" for Carriage from the Place of Receipt or the Port of Loading, whichever applicable, to the Port of Discharge or the Place of Delivery, whichever applicable, SUBJECT TO THE TERMS OF THE CARRIER'S STANDARD BILL OF LADING TERMS AND CONDITIONS AND TARIFF FOR THE RELEVANT TRADE, WHICH ARE MUTATIS MUTANDIS APPLICABLE TO THIS WAYBILL (copies of which may be obtained from the Carrier or his agents). Except for live animals and Goods which are stated herein to be carried on deck and are so carried, these terms and conditions are warranted by the Carrier in respect of the sea portion of the Carriage to apply the Hague Rules or Hague Visby Rules, whichever would have been applicable if this Waybill were a Bill of Lading. In either case the provisions of Article III Rule 6 of the Hague Visby Rules are deemed to be incorporated herein.
The contract evidenced by this Waybill is deemed to be a contract of carriage as defined in Article 1 (b) of the Hague Rules and Hague Visby Rules. However this Waybill is not a document of title to the Goods.
Delivery will be made to the Consignee named, or his authorized agents, on production of proof of identity at the Port of Discharge or the Place of Delivery, whichever applicable. Should the Consignee require delivery to a party and/or premises other than as shown above in the "Consignee" box, then written instructions must be given by the Consignee to the Carrier or his agent. Unless the Shipper expressly waives his right to control the Goods until delivery by means of a clause on the face hereof, such instructions from the Consignee will be subject to any instruction to the contrary by the Shipper.
Unless instructed to the contrary by the Shipper prior to the commencement of Carriage and noted accordingly on the face hereof, the Carrier will, subject to the aforesaid terms and conditions, process cargo claims with the Consignee. Claims settlement, if any, shall be a complete discharge of the Carrier's liability to the Shipper. The Shipper accepts the said standard terms and conditions on his own behalf, on behalf of the Consignee and the Owner of the Goods, and authorizes the Consignee to bring suit against the Carrier in his own name but as agent of the Shipper, and warrants that he has authority so to accept and authorize. The Shipper further undertakes that no claim or allegation in respect of the Goods shall be made against the Carrier by any person other than in accordance with the terms and conditions of this Waybill.

This Waybill is issued subject to the CMI Uniform Rules For Sea Waybills	Place and Date of Issue	IN WITNESS whereof this Waybill is signed.

CANCELLED - SPECIMEN COPY

P&O Nedlloyd

112002

P&O Nedlloyd Ltd, Beagle House, Braham Street, London E1 8EP   19/DRS W/B2 5/97 (S)

FIGURE C2 Non-negotiable waybill for combined transport shipment or port to port shipment
Courtesy of P&O Nedlloyd

FIGURE C3 Standard shipping note – for non dangerous goods only
Courtesy of SITPRO

DG

DANGEROUS GOODS DECLARATION, SHIPPING NOTE
& CONTAINER/VEHICLE PACKING CERTIFICATE
© SITPRO 1987

DANGEROUS GOODS NOTE

Special information is required for (a) dangerous goods in limited quantities (b) radioactive substances (class 7) (c) tank containers and road tankers (d) in certain circumstances a weathering certificate is required

SHADED AREAS NEED NOT BE SHIPPER COMPLETED FOR SHORT SEA RO. RO./RAIL

1 Exporter	2 Customs reference/status
	3 Booking number	4 Exporter's reference
	5 Port charges payable by * exporter / freight forwarder	6 Forwarder's reference
7A Consignee	other (name & address)
7 Freight forwarder	8 International carrier
	For use of receiving authority only
9 Other UK transport details (e.g. ICD, terminal, vehicle bkg. ref., receiving dates)	
	10A Consecutive no. or DG reference allocated by international carrier (if any)
10 Vessel Port of loading	
11 Port of discharge Destination	TO THE RECEIVING AUTHORITY Please receive for shipment the goods described below subject to your published regulations and conditions (including those as to liability)

SYSTEMFORMS LTD 01-505 6125
SITPRO APPROVED LICENSEE No. 09
(2.88)

MUST BE COMPLETED FOR FULL CONTAINER/VEHICLE LOADS:-

| Shipping marks SPECIFY: HAZARD CLASS, UN/ADR/RID/IMDG CODE (AS APPROPRIATE), FLASHPOINT °C. Number and kind of packages; description of goods † | 12 Receiving authority use | 13 Gross wt (kg) Net wt (kg) | 14 Cube (m³) of goods |

† PROPER SHIPPING NAME—PROPRIETARY NAMES ALONE ARE NOT SUFFICIENT.

CONTAINER/VEHICLE PACKING CERTIFICATE 15
It is declared that the packing of the container has been carried out in accordance with the provisions shown overleaf:-

Name of company

Signature   Date
of person responsible for packing container

DANGEROUS GOODS DECLARATION
I hereby declare that the contents of this consignment are fully and accurately described above by the correct technical name(s) (proper shipping name(s)), that the shipment is packaged in such a manner as to withstand the ordinary risks of handling and transport by sea, having regard to the properties of the goods to be carried, and that the goods are classified, packaged, marked and labelled in accordance with the requirements of the Merchant Shipping (Dangerous Goods) Regulations 1981 as currently amended. I further declare that if appropriate the goods are classified, packaged and marked to comply with the requirement of the European Agreement concerning the International Carriage of Dangerous Goods by Road (ADR) and of Annex 1 (RID) to the International Convention concerning the Carriage of Goods by Rail (CIM) or special arrangements made between the contracting parties to these Agreements.
The shipper must complete and sign box 17.

Total gross weight of goods   Total cube of goods

| 16 Prefix and container/vehicle number   Seal number(s) | 16A Container/vehicle size & type | 16B | 16C Tare wt (kg) as marked on CSC plate | 16D Total of boxes 13 and 16C |

DOCK/TERMINAL RECEIPT
Received the above number of packages/containers/trailers in apparent good order and condition unless stated hereon.
RECEIVING AUTHORITY REMARKS

Haulier's Name
Vehicle reg. no.

DRIVER'S SIGNATURE   SIGNATURE AND DATE

17 Name and telephone no. of shipper preparing this note

NAME/STATUS OF DECLARANT

DATE

Signature of declarant

890   *Mark X as appropriate. If box 5 is not completed the company preparing this note may be held liable for payment of port charges.
Non-completion of any boxes is a subject for resolution by the contracting parties.

SYSTEMFORMS LTD 01-505 6125
SITPRO APPROVED LICENSEE No. 09

FIGURE C4 Dangerous Goods Note
Courtesy of SITPRO

LEMBAGA PELABUHAN KELANG INTEGRATED EXPORT DOCUMENT   L.P.K. 333

Consignor (Name and Address of Shipper)

Integrated Export Document No.   Date:

A - 119419 - E

Integrated Shipping Document No.   Date:

Mode of Payment
☐ Cash ☐ Cheque ☐ Ledger A/c No. ....

To: The Traffic Manager, Lembaga Pelabuhan Kelang. In respect of the cargo mentioned below I/We request your approval for:-
☐ storage in your warehouse   ☐ direct shipment   ☐ re-export of overlanded cargo   ☐ export ex-private godown ....
☐ re-export of Transhipment cargo   ☐ waival of lifting charges   ☐ removal of shut-out/rejected cargo

I/We hereby declare that the weights and measurements
mentioned hereunder are correct. I/We undertake to pay all
charges to L.P.K.

Date: ....

....
Shipper/Agent

Class of Cargo (L.P.K. Classification)
☐ General ☐ Special ☐ Valuable ☐ Transhipment
Dangerous goods ☐ 1 ☐ 2 ☐ 3 ☐ 4
☐ others (specify) ....

Approved for:
☐ storage at ....
☐ direct shipment at ....
☐ re-export of overlanded cargo
☐ re-export of Transhipment cargo
☐ waival of lifting charges
☐ removal of shut-out/rejected cargo

Mode of Conveyance to Port
☐ Lorries ☐ Wagons ☐ Lighters

Loading Point

Vessel/Voyage No.

Vessel Id. No.

Date of Arrival | Date of Departure | Port of Discharge

Date: ....
Traffic Manager, L.P.K.

Marks and Nos. or Container Nos.	Nos. and kind of packages	Description of goods	Chargeable Weight	Grossweight (Tonne)	Measurement (M³)

CONTOH

MALAYSIA

FOR OFFICIAL USE

Cost Centre / Ship Code / Commodity Code	Handling Code / Destination Code	Chargeable Weight	Rate			Charges Payable	
			Code	$	¢	$	¢
Port Charges (Item 1)							
(Item 2)							
(Item 3)							
Additional Handling							
Lifting							
Valuable							
Storage	Days						
					TOTAL		

CONTOH

Date: ....
Signature & Staff No., L.P.K.

1st. Copy - Shipper

FIGURE C5 Integrate Export Document-Customs Document
Courtesy of Port Klang

1. Company name/logo (print or stamp)	THE BALTIC AND INTERNATIONAL MARITIME CONFERENCE UNIFORM TIME CHARTER PARTY FOR VESSELS CARRYING CHEMICALS IN BULK CODE NAME: "BIMCHEMTIME" PART I
	2. Place and date
3. Owners/full style and address	4. Charterers/full style and address
5. Vessel's name 6. Vessel's flag	7. Warranted average speed in knots on a daily bunker consumption of (also state grade(s) of bunker oil) (Cl. 4(b))
8. Vessel's d.w. all told on summer freeboard	
Vessel's tank capacity (state number of stainless steel tanks and coated tanks and total capacity of each category of tanks (100%) in cubic metres) (Cl. 4(a))	9. Vessel's cargo pumps (state number of pumps and designed capacity (cbm./w./h.)) (Cl. 4(a))
10. Status of cargo tanks on delivery (Cl. 4(c))	11. Status of cargo tanks on re-delivery (Cl. 13(b))
12. Maximum heating temperature (state if max. heating temperature is the same for centre- and wing tanks) (Cl.14)	13. Maximum number of types of cargo with complete segregation (Cl. 25)
14. Details of products to be carried (Cl. 4(a))	
15. Period of hire (Cl. 1)	16. Port or place of delivery (if applicable, also state time for declaration of port of delivery) (Cl.2)
	17. Earliest time for delivery (Cl. 2) 18. Cancelling date (Cl. 3)
19. Port or place of re-delivery (Cl. 12)	20. Number of days' notice of port and place of re-delivery (Cl. 12)
21. Trading limits and exclusions (Cl. 5)	
22. Bunkers on delivery (Cl. 9)	23. Bunkers on re-delivery (Cl. 9)
24. Charter hire (also state lump sum for overtime and extras) (Cl. 10 & Cl. 16)	25. Hire payment (state currency, mode and place of payment; also beneficiary and bank account) (Cl. 10)
per	
Lump sum for overtime and extras specified in Cl. 16	
26. Drydocking (state period between periodical drydockings and also when vessel last drydocked) (Cl. 20)	27. Overhaul and maintenance (indicate no. of hours agreed) (Cl. 21)
28. Compliance with regulations (Cl. 22)	29. War (state value of vessel acc. to sub-cl.(b) and names of countries acc. to sub-cl. (e)) (Cl. 32)
Indicate whether sub-clause (c) agreed or not (state "yes" or "no")	30. General average to be settled in (only to be filled in if place other than London agreed) (Cl. 34)
31. Applicable law (if not filled in, English law shall apply) (Cl. 42)	32. Place of arbitration/arbitration court (if not filled in, arbitration in London shall apply) (Cl. 43)
33. Numbers of additional clauses covering special provisions, if agreed	

It is mutually agreed that this Contract shall be performed subject to the conditions contained in the Charter Party consisting of Part I including additional clauses, if any agreed and stated in Box 33, and Part II including the specification as per the TECHNICAL FORM as well as the Tank Coating and/or Stainless Steel Resistance List referred to in Part II, Clause 4(a) and Clause 7, respectively. In the event of a conflict of conditions, the provisions of Part I shall prevail over those of Part II to the extent of such conflict but no further.

Signature (Owners)	Signature (Charterers)

FIGURE C6 Charter Party
Courtesy of the Baltic International Maritime Council

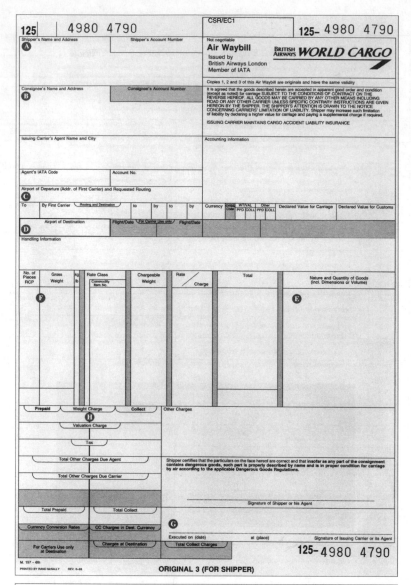

FIGURE C7 Air waybill
Courtesy of British Airways

Cert No. SYKX49554XX
Policy No.   SPECIMEN

Exporter's Reference

CERTIFICATE OF INSURANCE

Guardian Insurance Limited
A member of the Guardian Royal Exchange Group
Marine Department Civic Drive Ipswich IP1 2AN
Registered office: Royal Exchange London EC3V 3LS Registered in England No. 141885
A member Company of the Association of British Insurers

TELEPHONE - (01473) 202690
FACSIMILE - (0870) 9040119

This is to certify that   MACH ONE LIMITED

have effected with this Company a marine policy under which has been declared the interest specified and valued as below.

In case of any lawful claim hereon it is agreed that the same shall be settled by the COMPANY or the Claims Settling Agents named herein upon surrender of the original Certificate duly endorsed. This insurance shall be subject to the exclusive jurisdiction of the English Courts.

| Conveyance | Approved Vessel | From | United Kingdom | | |
| Via/To | | To | Australia | Insured Value/Currency | SPECIMEN |

Marks and Numbers	Interest
	200 Cases of Machinery and Spare Parts
	Invoice Number - 67/97/PX
	Packed in one Full Container Load
Container No. XXL/935/C	
Traction Products Sydney	

The above interest is insured subject to the terms of the Company's Standard Form of Marine Policy and to the conditions stated below.

Institute Cargo Clauses (A)
Institute Replacement Clause
Institute War Clauses (Cargo)   SPECIMEN
Institute Strikes Clauses (Cargo)
Institute Classification Clause
Institute Radioactive Contamination Exclusion Clause
Institute English Jurisdiction Clause

(The Institute Clauses referred to are those current at the date of this Certificate)

Claims payable in   Australia
                       ABC Claims
by   Sydney, Australia

In the event of damage which may involve a claim under this Certificate, immediate notice of such damage should be given to and a survey report obtained from   As Above

*This Certificate is not valid unless countersigned by an authorised signatory of the Assured.

S456 (5/1998)

For and on behalf of the Company

Manager & Underwriter

Ipswich, U.K.
Dated at   25 June 1998

*Countersigned

FIGURE C8 Certificate of Insurance
Courtesy of Guardian Insurance

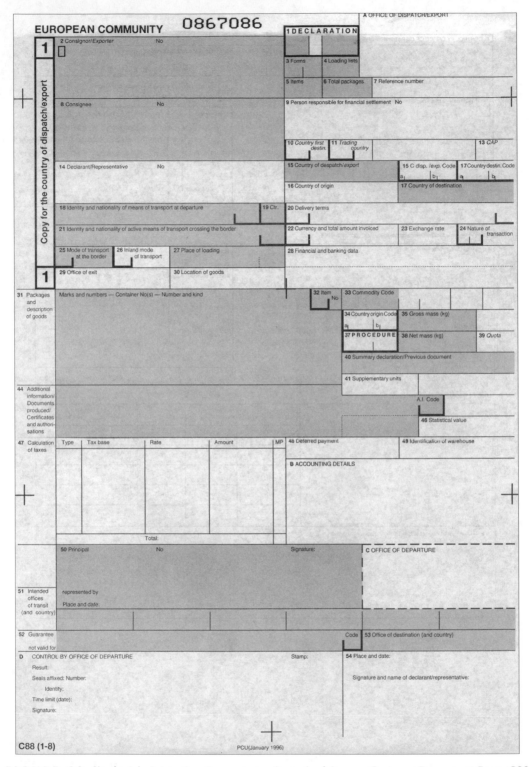

FIGURE C9 Single Administrative Document – Page 1 of 8-page Customs Document-Form C88
Courtesy of H.M. Customs and Excise

■ □ ■ ■ Appendix D

Glossary of shipping and international trade terms and abbreviations

AAA	Association of Average Adjusters
About	When referring to the amount or the quantity of items or the unit price of the goods, 'about' means plus or minus 10%. See Article 39 of UCP500.
A/C	Account current.
Acceptance	A written undertaking on the face of a bill of exchange to pay the bill amount on the due date. An alternative name for an accepted bill of exchange.
Accepting Bank	The bank which accepts a draft drawn under a documentary credit.
Accepting house	Financial house, often a merchant banker, specializing in financing foreign trade.
Act of God	Any fortuitous act which could not have been prevented by any amount of human care and forethought.
Action plan	A plan to identify each participant in a coordinated activity.
ADR	European agreement on the international carriage of dangerous goods by road.
Ad valorem freight	Freight rate based on percentage value of goods shipped.
Affreightment	A contract for the carriage of goods by sea for shipment expressed in charter party or bill of lading.
Agent	One who represents a principal, or buys or sells for another.
Air waybill	Air freight consignment note.
Aligned Export Documentation System	Method whereby as much information as possible is entered in a 'master document' so that all or part of this information can be reproduced mechanically into individual forms of a similar design.

Amendment	An alternation to the terms and conditions of the credit, issued at the request of the applicant.
AMT	Air mail transfer – a remittance purchased by the debtor from his banker in international trade.
ANF	Arrival notification form – advice to consignee of goods coming forward.
Arbitration	Methods of settling disputes which is usually binding on the parties concerned.
ATA carnet	Admission temporaire. International Customs document to cover the temporary export of certain goods (commercial samples and exhibits for international trade fairs abroad and professional equipment) to countries which are parties to the ATA Convention. Also covers the reimportation of such goods.
Athens Convention	International convention governing carrier's liability for passengers and their baggage by air.
Average bond	Bond in which cargo owners agree to pay their share in the general average losses, each contribution being determined by the average adjuster.
Average deposit	Cash security deposited by the consignee pending assessment of general average contribution.
Back freight	Freight (additional) incurred through cargo being returned from destination port, usually because its acceptance was refused.
BAF	Bunker adjustment factor. Freight adjustment factor to reflect current cost of bunkers.
Balance of trade	Financial statement of balance of a country's visible trade export and imports.
BIFA	British International Freight Association.
Bilateralism	Trade between two countries.
Bill of exchange	Written request from a creditor to a debtor ordering the debtor to pay a specified sum to a specified person or bearer at a certain date. It is usually referred to as a draft.
Bill of lading	Receipt for goods shipped on board a ship signed by the person (or his agent) who contracts to carry them, and stating the terms on which the goods are carried.
Bill of sight	Customs import form, used when importer cannot make customs entry complete owing to insufficient information from the shipper.
BIMCO	Baltic and International Maritime Council. A Danish based organization to which many shipowners belong that represents their interests and assists by preparing standard charter parties and other shipping documents and providing other advisory services including data on seaport and market reports.

B/L ton	Bill of lading ton. The greater weight or measurement of goods where 1 ton is either 1000 kilos or 1 cubic metre. Also called Freight ton.
Bond	Guarantee to customs of specified amount of duty to be paid.
Box	Colloquial name for a container.
B/P	Bills payable.
Break-bulk cargo	Goods shipped loose in the vessel's hold and not in a container.
Broken stowage	Space wasted in a ship's hold or container by stowage of uneven cargo, that is, irregularly shaped consignments.
Bulk licence	Licence issued to manufacturers and exporters to cover their requirements for certain bulk quantity or period.
Bulk unitization	Means to consolidate multiple packages or items into a single-load-device.
CABAF	Currency and bunker adjustment factor – a combination of CAF and BAF.
CAD	Cash against documents.
CAF	Currency adjustment factor – freight adjustment factor to reflect currency exchange fluctuations.
CAP	Common Agricultural Policy.
Cargo manifest	Inventory of cargo shipped.
Carr fwd	Carriage forward.
CB	Container base.
CCC	Customs clearance certificate.
CCLN	Consignment note control label number.
C & D	Collected and delivered.
CFR	Cost and freight (at named port of destination). Incoterm 2000.
CFS	Container freight station. Place for packing and unpacking LCL consignments.
CHIEF	Customs Handling of Import and Export Freight.
CI	Consular invoice.
CIF	Cost, insurance and freight (at named port of destination) Incoterm 2000. This term applies to sea or inland waterway transport only.
CIM	Convention international concernant le transport des marchandise par chemin de fer. International Convention on carriage of goods by rail.
CIP	Carriage and insurance paid to (to named place of destination). Incoterm 2000. This term applies to all modes of transport.
Clean bill of lading	A bill of lading which has no superimposed clause(s) expressly declaring a defective condition of the packaging or goods.

Closing date	Latest date cargo accepted for shipment by (liner) shipowner for specified sailing.
CMI	Comité Maritime International – an international committee of maritime lawyers.
CMR	Convention relative au contrat de transport international des marchandise par route. International Convention on carriage of goods by road.
C/N	Consignment note.
C/O	Certificate of origin or cash with order.
COGSA	Carriage of Goods by Sea Act. In the UK the 1924 version (Hague Rules) now superseded by 1971 version of the Hague–Visby Rules.
COI	Central Office of Information.
Collector's office	Customs accommodation where declaration(s)(entries) are scrutinized and amounts payable collected.
Conference	Organization whereby number of shipowners often of different nationality offer their services on a given sea route on conditions agreed by members.
Confirming Bank	A bank which adds it own undertaking to that of the issuing bank. The confirming bank is usually the advising bank.
Consignee	Name of agent, company or person receiving consignment.
Consignor	Name of agent, company or person sending consignment (the shipper).
Consul	Commercial representative of one country residing officially in another whose duties are to facilitate business and represent the merchants of his or her nation.
Convergence criteria	Established under the Treaty and relates both to performance with regard to price stability, government financial positions, exchange rates and long-term interest rates, and to the compatibility of national legislation, including the statutes of national central banks, with the Treaty and the Statute of the ESCB.
COT	Customer's own transport. Customer collects from or delivers to CFS/CY or other specified point.
COU	Clip on unit portable refrigeration units, or Central operating unit – body set up to coordinate consortium operations in a trade.
C/P	Charter party.
CPT	Carriage paid to (to a named place of destination). Incoterm 2000.
CRN	Customs registered number. A number allocated by Customs and Excise to an exporter or agent (freight forwarder) for use when exports are to be entered under SCP.

CSC	Container Safety Convention.
CT	Combined transport. Carriage by more than one mode of transport against one contract of carriage.
CTD	Combined transport document.
CTL	Constructive total loss.
CTO	Combined transport operator. A carrier who contracts as a principal to perform a CT operation.
Culture	The social economic and artistic resources in a country embodied in its institutions and other hybrid factions such as a museum. Overall culture is the environment and/or manner in which people live together in a society influenced by religion, education, family and reference groups, together with the forces of legal, economic, political and technological aspects. Basically it influences behavioural patterns.
Customs clearance	Process of clearing import/export cargo through customs examination.
CWE	Cleared without examination. Cleared customs without inspection
D/A	Deposit account.
DAF	Delivery at frontier. (At named place). Incoterm 2000. This term applies to all transport modes but primarily road and rail.
DDA	Duty (customs) deferment account.
DDP	Delivered duty paid (at named place of destination). Incoterm 2000. This term applies to all modes of transport.
DDU	Delivered duty unpaid (at named place of destination). Incoterm 2000. This term applies to all modes of transport.
Dead freight	Space booked by shipper or charterer on a vessel but not used.
Deferred rebate	System whereby shippers are granted a rebate on freight for consistent exclusive patronage over a given period.
Del credere	Agent/broker guarantee to principal for solvency of person to whom he sells goods.
Delivery order	A document authorizing delivery to a nominated party of goods in the care of a third party. It can be issued by a carrier on surrender of a bill of lading and then used by merchant to transfer title by endorsement.
Demurrage	Charge raised for detaining cargo, FCL container, trailer or ship for a longer period than prescribed.
DEQ	Delivered ex-quay (duty paid at named port of destination). Incoterm 2000. This term applies to sea or inland waterway transport only.

DES	Delivered ex-ship (at named port of destination). Incoterm 2000. This term applies to sea or inland waterway transport only.
Detention	Charge raised for detaining container/trailer at customer's premises for longer period than prescribed in the tariff.
DGN	Dangerous goods note.
Dis	Discount.
Discount market	Process of selling and buying bills of exchange and Treasury bills and providing a market for short-bonds.
D/N	Debit note.
D/O	Delivery order.
Doc credit	Documentary credit. The basis of international trade by means of which payment is made against surrender of specified documents.
D/P	Documents against payment.
Drawee	The party to whom a draft is addressed and who is expected to accept and/or pay it upon presentation.
Drawer	The party who issues a draft. Usually the beneficiary of the credit.
Drawing	A presentation of documents under a credit.
Due date	The date on which a usance draft or a deferred payment becomes due for payment.
Dunnage	Wood, mats, etc. used to facilitate stowage of cargo.
Dutiable cargo	Cargo which attracts some form of duty, that is, Customs and Excise, or VAT
DWT	Dead-weight tonnage.
ECB	European Central Bank. It has legal personality and ensures that the tasks conferred upon the Euro system and the ESCB are implemented either by its own activities pursuant to its statute or through the national central banks.
ECSI	Export Cargo Shipping Instruction – shipping instructions from shipper to carrier.
EDI	Electronic data interchange. The transfer of structured data from one computer system to another.
EDIFACT	EDI for Administration, Commerce and Transport. Organization responsible to UNECE for the development of standard EDI messages for administration, commerce and transport.
EDISHIP	An organization for exchanging data between carriers and merchants by electronic means.
Endorsement	Signing of a document, (e.g. draft, insurance document or bill of lading) usually on the reverse to transfer title to another party. Documents are often endorsed in blank to permit any future holder to gain title.
EDP	Electronic data processing.

EEA	European Economic Area. Combination of EC/EFTA.
EFTA	European Free Trade Area.
EHA	Equipment handover agreement. Agreement acknowledging condition signed when taking over carriers' equipment and returning it, which incorporates terms of contract under which equipment is taken over.
EPU	Entry Processing Unit. Customs office that processes customs entries.
ESCB	European System of Central Banks. It is governed by the Governing Council and Executive Board of the ECB
ETA	Estimated time of arrival.
ETD	Estimated time of departure.
Euro area	The area encompassing those Member States in which the euro has been adopted as a single currency in accordance with the Treaty and in which a single monetary policy is conducted under the responsibility of the relevant decision-making bodies of the ECB. The euro area or euro-zone or euroland comprises Belgium, Germany, Spain, France, Ireland, Italy, Luxembourg, Holland, Austria, Portugal and Finland.
European Commission	The institution of the European Community which ensures the application of the Treaty, takes initiatives for Community policies, proposes Community legislation and exercises powers in specific areas. In the area of economic policy the Commission recommends broad guidelines for economic policies in the Community and reports to the EU Council on economic developments and policies. It monitors public finances in the framework of multilateral surveillance and submits reports to the Council. It consists of 20 members.
European Council	Provides the European Union with the necessary impetus for its development and defines the general political guidelines thereof. It brings together the Head of State or Government of the Member States and the President of the European Commission.
European Parliament	It consists of 626 representatives of the citizens of the Member States.
Exchange rate	Price of one currency in terms of another.
Export house	An export merchant responsible for buying goods outright and selling them on their own account; acting as an export department or agent on behalf of a client; or acting for an overseas buyer.
Export licence	Government-issued document authorizing export of restricted goods.
Exporter's acceptance	Credit opened by an exporter with his own bank credit which entitles the exporter to draw bills on his own banker.

EXW	Ex Works (at named place). Incoterm 2000. This term applies to all transport modes.
Factoring	Company which administers the sales ledger and collects payments on behalf of an exporter once the goods have been shipped.
FAK	Freight all kinds. Term used to show that the freight rate charged is not based on the individual commodity, but freight all kinds.
FAS	Free alongside ship (at named port of shipment). Incoterm 2000. This applies to sea or inland transport only.
FCA	Free carrier (at named place). Incoterm 2000. This term applies to all modes of transport.
FCL	Full container load.
Feeder vessel	A short sea vessel used to fetch and carry goods and containers to and from deep-sea vessels operating on basis of hub and spoke concept.
FFI	For further instructions.
FIO	Free in and out. Cargo is loaded and discharged at no cost to the shipowner.
FIO & stowed	Free in and out. Cargo is loaded as a charge to the shipper including stowage, and discharging expense borne by the receiver.
Fixture	Conclusion of shipbroker's negotiations to charter a ship.
Floating exchange rates	Currency rate which varies according to world trade distortions and not subject to exchange control.
Floating policy	Cargo policy which underwrites series of consignments declared.
FOB	Free on board (at named port of shipment). Incoterm 2000. This term applies to sea or inland waterway transport only.
Forwarder's bill of lading	A bill of lading issued by a freight forwarder.
Forwarder's certificate of shipment	A document issued by a freight forwarder certifying that the goods have been shipped on a named vessel or service.
Forwarder's delivery order	A document issued by a freight forwarder authorizing the entitled party to deliver the goods to a party other than the consignee shown on the consignment note.
Forwarder's receipt	A document issued by a freight forwarder which provides evidence of receipt of the goods.
FPA	Free of particular average – insurers not responsible for partial loss claims with certain exceptions.
Freight	Amount payable for the carriage of goods or a description of the goods conveyed.
Freight ton	Tonnage on which freight is charged.
G/A	General average.

Groupage	Consolidation of several consignments into one overall consignment by air, road or sea usually under freight forwarder's sponsorship.
Groupage agent	One who consolidates, for example, LCL consignments to offer a carrier as an FCL. Also applicable to air and road transport.
GV	Grande vitesse – fast rail merchandise service.
Heterogeneous cargo	Variety of cargoes.
High stowage factor	Cargo which has a high bulk to low weight relationship, e.g. hay.
H/L	Heavy lift.
Hague Rules	1924 International Convention of Carriage of Goods by Sea.
Hague–Visby Rules	1968 Revision of Hague Rules.
Hamburg Rules	1978 UNCTAD Revision of Hague Rules.
HMC	Her Majesty's Customs.
HMC&E	Her Majesty's Customs and Excise.
IATA	International Air Transport Association.
IBAP	Intervention Board Agricultural Produce.
ICAO	International Civil Aviation Organisation.
ICB	International Container Bureau.
ICD	Inland clearance depot.
IMDG	Code International Maritime Dangerous Goods Code. The IMO recommendation for the carriage of dangerous goods by sea.
IMO	International Maritime Organisation.
Incoterms 2000	International Rules for the interpretation of trade terms and applicable from 2000. A list of 13 standard trade terms for foreign trade contracts compiled by ICC.
Indemnity	Compensation for loss/damage or injury.
Individual licence	Licence issued for one particular import or export consignment.
Inherent vice	A defect or inherent quality of the goods or their packing which of itself may contribute to their deterioration, injury, wastage and final destruction, without any negligence or other contributing causes.
Inland clearance depot	Customs cargo clearance depot situated inland which may be in close proximity to a seaport, airport or inland depot serving an industrial/commercial area.
Invisible exports	Income from exports embracing tourism, net shipping and air receipts, foreign investments, banking and insurance.
IRU	International Road Transport Union. Based in Geneva, its role is to develop national and international transport.
ISO	International Standards Organisation. International organization of national standards bodies responsible, *inter alia*, for setting standards for container construction.

Jus disponendi	(Latin) Law of disposal.
L/C	Letter of credit – document in which the terms of a documentary credit transaction is set out.
LCL	Less than container load – a parcel of goods too small to fill a container which is grouped by the carrier at the CFS with other compatible goods for the same destination.
LEC	Local export control – a system of clearing goods, containers and trucks at an exporter's premises.
Letter of hypothecation	Banker's document outlining conditions under which international transactions will be executed on an exporter's behalf, the latter having given certain pledges to his or her banker.
Letter of indemnity	A document indemnifying the shipowner or agent from any consequences, risk or claims which may arise through 'clean' bills of lading being irregularly issued.
LIC	Local import control – a system of clearing goods, containers and trucks at an importer's premises.
Liner	Vessel plying a regular trade/defined route against a published sailing schedule.
Liner terms	Freight includes the cost of loading into and discharging from the vessel.
LLMC	International Convention on Limitation of Liability for Maritime Claims – a 1976 limitation convention enacted in the UK by the Merchant Shipping Act 1979.
LNG	Liquefied natural gas - type of vessel.
LO-LO	Lift on-lift off. A container ship onto which and from which containers are lifted by crane.
Loading broker	Person who acts on behalf of liner company at a port.
Low stowage factor	Cargo which has low bulk to high weight relationship, e.g. steel rails.
Lump sum freight	Remuneration paid to shipowner for charter of a ship, or portion of it, irrespective of quantity of cargo loaded.
Manifest	List of goods/passengers on a vessel/aircraft/truck.
Market rate	Rate charged by brokers, discount houses, joint stock banks and other market members for discounting first-class bills.
Mate's receipt	Document issued to the shipper for ship's cargo loaded from lighterage and later exchanged for bill of lading.
MCD	Miscellaneous cash deposit.
M'dise	Merchandise.
Measurement ton	A cubic metre.
MMO	Multi-modal operator.
MT	Mail transfer – a remittance purchased by the debtor from his banker in international trade.
Negotiable bill of lading	One capable of being negotiated by transfer or endorsement.

Negotiation	The giving of value for a draft or documents which, under the credit terms, the issuing bank has undertaken to pay.
Negotiating Bank	The (nominated) bank which negotiates a presentation under a documentary credit. Usually located in the country of the seller.
Nominated Bank	The bank nominated in the documentary credit to pay, accept, negotiate or incur a deferred payment undertaking.
Notify Party	Party to whom arrival notification form is sent.
NSSN	National Standard Shipping Note.
NVOC	Non-vessel-owning/operator carrier.
NVOCC	Non-vessel-owning/operating common carrier. A carrier issuing bills of lading for carriage of goods on vessels which he neither owns nor operates.
OBO	Oil bulk ore carriers – multi-purpose bulk carriers.
O/C	Overcharge.
OECD	Organisation for European Co-operation and Development.
O/H	Overheight. A container or trailer with goods protruding above the unit profile.
Open cover	A cargo insurance agreement covering all shipments of the assured for a period of time, subject to a cancellation clause and a limit to the amount insured in any one ship. Other conditions include a classification clause.
OOG	Out of gauge. Goods whose dimensions exceed those of the truck or container in which they are stowed.
Overvalued currency	Currency whose rate of exchange is persistently below the parity rate.
O/W	Overwidth. A container or truck with goods protruding beyond the sides of truck, container or flat rack onto which they are stowed.
Paying bank	The bank which is to effect payment under the documentary credit. It can be the issuing bank itself or a nominated bank, usually the advising or confirming bank.
P & I Club	Protection and Indemnity Association. Carrier's mutual liability insurer.
Per pro	On behalf of.
PIRA (International)	Research Association for the Paper and Board, Printing and Packaging Industries.
P/L	Partial loss.
POA	Place of acceptance – where the goods are received for transit and carrier's liability commences.
POD	Place of delivery where the goods are delivered and carrier's liability ceases, or proof of delivery – a signed receipt acknowledging delivery.
POR	Place of receipt – where the goods are received for transit and carrier's liability commences.

Pre-entered	Process of lodging with customs appropriate documentation for scrutiny prior to cargo customs clearance and shipment.
Principal carrier	The carrier issuing a combined transport document regardless of whether or not goods are carried on his or her own, a third party's or a consortium member's vessel.
P to P	Port to port.
Rebate	An allowance made as discount on an account/rate.
Receiving date	Date from which cargo is accepted for shipment for specified sailing.
Reefer	Refrigerated.
Reimbursing bank	Normally a third party bank chosen by the issuing bank to honour claims made by the paying/negotiating bank under a letter of credit.
Removal note	Confirms goods clear of customs.
RN	Release note – receipt signed by customer acknowledging delivery of goods.
Ro-Ro	Roll-on/roll-off – a vehicular ferry service.
SAD	Single administrative document.
SCP	Simplified clearance procedure, under which exporters of goods not requiring special control may submit an abbreviated customs pre-entry or an approved commercial document at the time of export and provide the full statistical information after the goods are exported.
Settlement	Payment, deferred payment, acceptance or negotiation under a documentary credit.
Shipper	The person tendering the goods for carriage.
Shipping invoice	Document giving details of merchandise shipped.
Shut out	Cargo refused shipment because it arrived after closing date.
Sight 'On demand'	If a credit provides for payment or negotiation 'at sight', the issuing or confirming bank is obliged to pay or negotiate upon presentation of conforming documents.
Sine die	(Latin) Indefinitely – without a day being appointed.
SITC	Standard International Trade Classification – method of classifying all types of goods used in tariff.
SITPRO	Simpler Trade Procedures Board.
Slot	Space on board a vessel occupied by a container.
SOB	Shipped on board – endorsement on bill of lading confirming loading of goods on vessel.
SR & CC	Risks of wars, strikes, riots and civil commotions. A clause found in marine insurance.
SSN	Standard Shipping Note.
Stale bill of lading	In banking practice, a bill of lading presented so late that consignee could be involved in difficulties.

Straight bill of lading	An American term for a non-negotiable bill of lading, i.e waybill governed by the US Pomerene Act.
Stuffing/stripping	The action of packing or unpacking a container.
Subrogation	Process of substituting one person for another in marine insurance matters in which the latter inherits the former's rights and liabilities.
SWIFT	Society for Worldwide Inter-bank Financial Telecommunications – the secure computer network used to transmit documentary credits and other forms of international messages between banks.
TAN	Transit advice note.
Tariff terms	Conditions and scale of charges.
TCM	Draft convention on combined transport.
Tenor	The period of times for which a draft is drawn. The tenor may be at sight or usance.
TEU	Twenty ft equivalent unit – container measurement, i.e. 1×40 ft = 2 TEU; 1×20 ft = 1 TEU.
THE	Technical Help to Exporters – service of the British Standards Institution.
TIR	Transport International Routier. Bond conditions under which containerized and vehicular merchandise is conveyed internationally under the Convention.
T/L	Total loss.
Tramp	Vessel engaged in bulk cargo or time chartering business, i.e. not a liner vessel.
Transferable credit	One which may be transferred by the first beneficiary.
Transshipment entry	Customs entry for cargo imported for immediate re-exportation.
Trucking	Movement of containers, trucks between terminals and CFSs/CYs.
TT	Telegraphic transfer. A remittance purchased by the debtor from his banker in international trade.
TTO	Through transport operator. A carrier who contracts to carry goods (only part of which carriage he undertakes himself) on the basis that he is a principal whilst the goods are in his or her personal care, and as agent only whilst they are not.
UCP500	The Uniform Customs and Practice for Documentary Credits, ICC Publication No.500.
ULCC	Ultra large crude carrier.
ULD	Unit load device.
UN	United Nations.
UNCITRAL	United Nations Commission on International Trade and Law.

UNCON	Uncontainerable goods. Cargo which because of their dimensions cannot be containerized and which are therefore carried other than in a container.
UNCTAD	United Nations Conference on Trade and Development.
UNCTAD MMO	UNCTAD Multi-modal Transport Convention.
Undervalued currency	Currency whose rate of exchange is persistently above the parity.
Unit loads	Containerized or palletized traffic.
Usance	The credit period granted by the exporter to the importer and reflected in the documentary credit terms, e.g. 30 days after bill of lading date, 60 days sight, 90 days after shipment date.
Validity	The period, from the date of issue until the date of expiry, for which the credit is valid.
Vienna Convention	A 1980 United Nations Convention on contracts for the International Sale of Goods which came into force on 1 January 1988.
VLCC	Very large crude carrier.
WA	With average.
Warranty	An implied condition, express guarantee or negotiation contained in marine insurance policy.
Waybill	A receipt for the goods and evidence of the contract of carriage but not a document of title.
WPA	With particular average.
York Antwerp	Rules relating to the adjustment of general average.

NB: Readers are also recommended to study the *Dictionary of Shipping: International Trade Terms and Abbreviations* (4th edn), 1992 (14000 entries) (see further reading).

■ □ ■ ■ Further reading

Dictionary of English-Arabic Shipping/International Trade/Commercial Terms and Abbreviations, 1st edition (1988) A.E. Branch, Witherby & Co Ltd.

Dictionary of Shipping International Business Trade Terms and Abbreviations, 4th edition (1995) A.E. Branch, Witherby & Co Ltd (14,000 entries).

Elements of Port Operation and Management, 1st edition (1986) A.E. Branch, Chapman & Hall/Kluwer Academic Publishers.

Elements of Shipping, 7th edition (1997) A.E. Branch, Stanley Thornes Ltd.

Global Business Strategy, 1st edition (1997) R. John, G Letto-Gillies, H. Cox and N. Grimwade, Thomson Learning Business Press.

International Marketing Strategy, 2nd edition (1999) I. Doole and R. Lowe, Thomson Learning Business Press.

International Purchasing, 1st edition (2001) A.E. Branch, Thomson Learning Business Press.

Introduction to Marine Insurance, 2nd edition (1994) R.H. Brown, Witherby & Co Ltd.

Maritime Economics Management Marketing, 3rd edition (1998) A.E. Branch, Stanley Thornes Ltd.

Multi-lingual Dictionary of Commercial International Trade and Shipping Terms: English-French-Spanish-German, 1st edition (1990) A.E. Branch, Witherby & Co Ltd.

Schmitthoff's Export Trade, 9th edition (1990) C.M. Schmitthoff, Sweet and Maxwell.

Shipping and Air Freight Documentation for Importers and Exporters and Associated Terms, 2nd edition (2000) A.E. Branch, Witherby & Co Ltd.

■ □ ■ ■ Index